OLAP Solutions

Building Multidimensional Information Systems

Second Edition

OLAP Solutions

Building Multidimensional Information Systems

Second Edition

Erik Thomsen

Wiley Computer Publishing

John Wiley & Sons, Inc.

NEW YORK · CHICHESTER · WEINHEIM · BRISBANE · SINGAPORE · TORONTO

Publisher: Robert Ipsen
Editor: Robert Elliott
Developmental Editor: Emilie Herman
Managing Editor: John Atkins
New Media Editor: Brian Snapp
Text Design & Composition: MacAllister Publishing Services, LLC

Designations used by companies to distinguish their products are often claimed as trademarks. In all instances where John Wiley & Sons, Inc., is aware of a claim, the product names appear in initial capital or all capital letters. Readers, however, should contact the appropriate companies for more complete information regarding trademarks and registration.

This book is printed on acid-free paper. ∞

Published by John Wiley & Sons, Inc.

Published simultaneously in Canada.

This publication is designed to provide accurate and authoritative information in regard to the subject matter covered. It is sold with the understanding that the publisher is not engaged in professional services. If professional advice or other expert assistance is required, the services of a competent professional person should be sought.

Library of Congress Cataloging-in-Publication Data:

ISBN: 0-471-40030-0

Printed in the United States of America.

10 9 8 7 6 5 4 3 2 1

Advanced Praise for *OLAP Solutions, Second Edition*

"Erik Thomsen's book goes in depth where other books have not. In terms of completeness, readability, and merging theory and practice, I strongly recommend this book. If you buy only one book on OLAP this year, it should be *OLAP Solutions, Second Edition*."

W.H. Inmon
Partner, www.billinmon.com

"Erik Thomsen's first edition of *OLAP Solutions* is widely acknowledged as the standard desk reference for all serious practitioners in the areas of OLAP systems, decision support, data warehousing, and business analysis. All of us have benefited immeasurably from its clear, concise, and comprehensive treatment of multidimensional information systems.

The second edition of *OLAP Solutions* not only continues this great tradition, but also contains many new and profound contributions. In particular, by introducing the LC Model for OLAP and providing thorough examples of its application, this book offers a logically grounded, multidimensional framework and language that overcomes the conceptual difficulties generally encountered in the specification and use of OLAP models. *OLAP Solutions, Second Edition*, will revolutionize how we think about, build, and use OLAP technologies."

John Poole
Distinguished Software Engineer, Hyperion Solutions Corporation

"Erik has done it again! I found his latest work updated to reflect valuable new information regarding the fast-paced changes in OLAP tools and methods. I would recommend this book to those who already have the first edition on their bookshelves for the valuable, updated content that it provides and to those who need to move beyond the beginners' stage of working with OLAP products."

Alan P. Alborn
Vice President, Science Applications International Corporation

"This book is a 'must read' for everyone that purports to be a player in the field, as well as for developers that are building today's leading edge analytical applications. Readers who take advantage of this material will form a much greater understanding of how to structure their analytical applications."

Frank McGuff
Independent consultant

"This should be required reading for students and practitioners who plan to or are working in the OLAP arena. In addition to having quite a bit of practical advice, it is well suited to be used as a reference for a senior-level undergraduate or graduate-level data mining course. A 'relational algebra' for OLAP was sorely needed, and the real-world examples make you think about how to apply OLAP technology to actually help a business."

David Grossman
Assistant Professor, Illinois Institute of Technology

"This book is a comprehensive introduction to OLAP analysis. It explains this complex subject and demonstrates the power of OLAP in assisting decision makers."

Mehdi Akhlaghi
Information Officer, Development Data Group of the World Bank

*To Hannah and Max and the hopefully joyous lives
in which you'll be fully immersed by the time
you can understand this book.*

Contents

Preface

You should read this book if you are interested in technologies such as:

- OLAP
- Multidimensional information systems
- Data warehousing
- Databases
- Decision support systems (DSS)
- Executive information systems (EIS)
- Business intelligence (BI)
- Business analytics
- Data mining
- Data visualization
- Knowledge management (KM)

Or if you have goals such as:

- Synthesizing knowledge from data
- Modeling and analyzing large data sets
- Using information systems for real competitive advantage
- Implementing activity-based management (ABM)
- Tracking key performance indicators (KPI)
- Thriving on (rather than being burdened by), lots of fast-changing data and information
- Thinking clearly about business, economic, and social issues

This book is principally written for business and scientific analysts, IT workers, and computer science and technically oriented business students. The book's multi-level style (wherein technical points are kept in parentheses, sidebars, endnotes, appendices, or specifically technical chapters) also makes it valuable and accessible to IT managers and executives. It teaches you everything you need to know about the principles of designing and the skills for using multidimensional information systems. The application section of the book contains a computational model of a company and a full set of exercises through which you can improve your model- and formula-building skills. The book was written to be understood by any intelligent person who likes to think, though it helps if you have some understanding of spreadsheets and/or business analysis. If your background includes relational databases, logic, linear algebra, statistics, cognitive science, and/or data visualization, you will more easily appreciate the advanced material.

Preface to the Second Edition

In the last five years since I wrote the first edition of *OLAP Solutions*, OLAP (where the term OLAP stands for On-Line Analytical Processing, but really means multidimensional modeling and analysis) has evolved from a niche capability to a mainstream and extremely vital corporate technology. The number of business analysts and IT workers who are familiar with at least some of the basic concepts and who need to effectively use the technology has grown enormously. In addition, the way that OLAP functionality is being deployed has also changed during this time. The current trend is for OLAP functionality to be increasingly deployed within or as a layer on relational databases (which does not mean that R/OLAP beat M/OLAP), and for OLAP capabilities to be provided as extensions to general, relationally based data warehousing infrastructures.

Thus, I felt that it was necessary to write a new edition to *OLAP Solutions* that was totally focused on the underlying technology independent of how it is instantiated, and that provided a vendor-neutral set of tools, and formula creation skill-building exercises geared for OLAP application developers and business analysts (as well as university students).

How the Book Is Organized

The book is grouped into four parts plus appendices. Part 1 begins by defining OLAP (or multidimensional information systems), and explaining where it comes from, what its basic requirements are, and how it fits into an overall enterprise information architecture. Treating OLAP as a category of functionality, the section proceeds to show where traditional spreadsheets and databases run aground when trying to provide OLAP style functionality. The section ends by taking you, in a clear step-by-step fashion, from the world of ordinary rows and columns to a world of multidimensional data structures and flows. By teaching you how to think clearly in N dimensions, you will be prepared to learn how to design and/or use multidimensional information systems.

Part 2 describes the features and underlying concepts that constitute multidimensional technology. Chapter 4 provides an introduction to the language and teaching method used in the rest of the book. Chapter 5 describes the internals of a dimension, including ragged and leveled hierarchies and ordering. Chapter 6 describes multidimensional schemas or models and tackles the problems of logical sparsity and how to combine information from multiple distinct schemas. Chapter 7 teaches you how to write multidimensional formulas and provides you with a set of reusable formula building blocks. Chapter 8 describes the variety of ways that source data gets linked to a multidimensional model. Chapter 9 explains when data visualization is useful, how it works, and shows a variety of techniques for visualizing multidimensional data sets. Finally, Chapter 10 describes the different ways that multidimensional models and the tools that support them can be physically optimized, exploring optimization within machines, across applications, across network tiers, and across time.

Part 3 opens with a practical set of steps for designing and using multidimensional information systems. The subsequent chapters provide product-neutral application descriptions in an engaging dialog format, which will hone your application-building skills *if you think along with the dialog*. Chapter 12 is an introduction to the enterprise-wide OLAP solution for a vertically integrated international producer of foodcakes that serves as the context for Chapters 13 through 16. Each of Chapters 13 through 16 represents the working-through of the dimension and cube design and the key formula creation for a particular business process (specifically sales and marketing, purchasing, materials inventory, and activity-based management). Each of the application chapters begins with basic issues and moves on to more advanced topics. Chapter 17 is a single fully integrated cross-enterprise calculation example. The chapter takes you on a cross-enterprise journey from an activity-based management perspective, beginning with product sales and ending with materials purchasing, in order to calculate the earnings or losses incurred by a company during the sale of a particular product.

Part 4 extends and summarizes what you have learned from the first three parts. Chapter 18 provides a set of comprehensive criteria for evaluating OLAP products. Chapter 19 provides a comparison between OLAP languages for some of the major commercially available products. Chapter 20 looks ahead and describes the need for and attributes of unified decision support systems.

The appendices provide an index into the formulas defined in the book (Appendix A), descriptions of some industry activities in benchmarking and APIs (Appendix B), a quick summary of the product-neutral language used in the book (Appendix C), a glossary of key terms (Appendix D), some remarks on the distinction between dimensions and measures (Appendix E), some remarks on the logical grounding of multidimensional information systems and how those grounding needs compare with what is offered by canonical logic (Appendix F), Codd's original 12 Features (Appendix G), and a Bibliography.

Major Differences between the First and Second Edition

Although the second edition is divided into the same set of four parts as the first edition (where they were called sections), and although the overall goals of the two editions are the same, the differences between the two books are large enough that this edition could be considered a separate book. For those of you who are familiar with the first edition, the major differences between the second and first editions are as follows. In Part 1, the main differences are an expanded treatment of the relationship between OLAP and other decision-support technologies and an updated treatment of the challenges of SQL-99 (OLAP extensions) as opposed to the SQL-89 of the first edition. Part 2 introduces a product-neutral OLAP language and devotes entire chapters to each of the major logical components of OLAP technology: the internal structure of a dimension, cubes, formulas, and links. More complete treatment of hierarchies, formulas, visualization, and physical optimization are given. With the exception of Chapter 11 on practical steps, which was expanded, the rest of the chapters in Part 3, which represent a computational model of an enterprise within the context of activity-based management, are entirely new. In Part 4, the chapters on language comparisons and unified decision-support systems are also new.

The Style of the Book

Although the tone of the book is informal, its content is well grounded. (Chapter 5, with its description of the basis for dimensional hierarchies and the distinction between valid and invalid hierarchies and levels is perhaps the least informal chapter.) Throughout the book, the emphasis is on explanation and demonstration rather than formal proof or ungrounded assertion. Summaries are presented at the end of most chapters. Also, and especially in Parts 1 and 2, I make liberal use of illustrations. If you are learning these concepts (some of which are quite abstract) for the first time, you will benefit from working through the diagrams. Qualifying and additional points are enclosed in the form of sidebars, endnotes, and appendices.

Tools You Will Need

With the exception of Chapter 17 and Appendix F, you do not need any software or hardware to read this book or to perform the exercises contained herein. For Chapter 17, you will probably want to use a calculator to compute the derived values. And for Appendix F, which describes how to build an OLAP solution from a collection of worksheets, should you decide to avail yourself of the electronic worksheets on my companion Web site, you will need to have a copy of Microsoft Excel.

What's on the Companion Web Site

The companion Web site contains the worksheet data for Appendix F, in the form of Microsoft Excel 98 files. And it contains the answers to all exercises in Chapter 17, also in the form of Microsoft Excel 98 files. The Web site also contains the document "Building an OLAP Solution from Spreadhseets."

Acknowledgments

Although there are far too many people to name, it is with heartfelt gratitude that I extend thanks to John Silvestri, Joe Bergman, Steve Shavel, Will Martin, George Spofford, David McGoveran, Mike Sutherland, and Stephen Toulmin, for the quality and longevity of their dialog. I also wish to thank Phil de la Zerda of Inter Corporation, who provided me the opportunity to make many improvements to what had been a section on visualization in the first edition (and which became Chapter 9 in this edition); Vectorspace Inc., who provided me some time to finish parts of the manuscript; and to David Friedlander, whose creation of a fishcake manufacturing story as a part of a project on which we collaborated was the inspiration behind the Foodcakes International application presented in Part 3.

Special thanks go to Deanna Young for her work on the book's many graphic images, for her diligent editing, for managing all the formatting, and for her extraordinary patience in dealing with the myriad changes that occurred throughout the process. I am also grateful for the assistance rendered by the interns Sam Klein and Jorge Panduro with the cube calculation exercise in Chapter 17 and the application views in Part 3 (and Sam also for the syntax and other consistency checks), and for their consistently positive attitudes during the last couple of months. And I am grateful to the hard work and helpful suggestions of Bob Elliot, Emilie Herman, and the production staff at John Wiley & Sons.

This book is also a finer product thanks to the quality and candor of the efforts of the formal reviewers Frank McGuff, John Poole, Pat Bates, David McGoveran, George Spofford, John O'Connor, David Grossman, and Earle Burris.

Many extra special thanks go to George Spofford for his contributions as main author of Chapter 8 and co-author of Chapter 19. Sincere thanks are also extended to

Nigel Pendse for those contributions to the first edition (as the main author of Chapters 8 and 9), that continue to live on in Chapter 10 of this edition. And exceedingly special thanks are also extended to Steve Shavel for his contribution as main author of the Tractarian Approach section in Appendix F. The responsibility for any errors or omissions in those sections remains mine.

Loving thanks also go to my parents, who raised me to be observant and to think for myself.

This book was delayed for almost two years due to work pressures. Then, shortly after I committed to and embarked upon writing, I learned that my wife Marjorie was pregnant with twins, and so was forced to concentrate on this book during the same time that I would have preferred to focus on her extremely special needs and the preparatory needs of our children-to-be. Thus I am enormously grateful to her for the supporting and selfless (need I say saint-like) attitude she exhibited during the past nine months.

Finally, I would like to thank the unborn presences of our children that kept me inspired, especially during the writing of Part 3, where the characters Lulu and Thor were, no surprise, proxy for our known twins of unknown gender. As it turns out, they were born during the copyedit phase, and so I am delighted to announce that Lulu and Thor have become Hannah and Max.

The Need for Multidimensional Technology

A basket trap is for holding fish; but when one has got the fish, one need think no more about the basket. Words are for holding ideas; but when one has got the idea, one need think no more about the words.

CHUANG TSU

The Functional Requirements of OLAP Systems

Before you can appreciate or attempt to measure the value of a new technology, you need to understand the full context within which the technology is used. There's no point in trying to convince someone that he needs to adopt a revolutionary new mousetrap technology if that person doesn't know what mice are, or what it means to catch something. And so it is with On-Line Analytical Processing (OLAP) or multi-dimensional information systems.

The primary purpose of this chapter is to provide a supporting context for the rest of this book by answering the most common questions of someone who is either coming across the term OLAP for the first time or has had experience with OLAP, but isn't comfortable explaining its origins or essential attributes. Those questions include the following:

- What does the term OLAP mean or refer to: an activity, a set of constraints on an activity, a product, a collection of features, a database, a language, or what?
- What kinds of problems can OLAP help me solve? Can it help me figure out which products or customers are profitable? Can it help me pick better stocks?
  - If so, why? If not, why not?
- For the class of problems that OLAP helps solve, what are OLAP's nearest competitors?
- What makes OLAP better? (This is addressed in Chapter 2.)
- Is there anything that all OLAP has in common?
- What kinds of OLAP are there?

A secondary purpose for this chapter is to deflate as many as possible of the pseudo-technical buzzwords floating around the industry so that the reader is free to concentrate on the essential topics in this book.

Towards that end, this chapter will describe the following:

- The different meanings of OLAP[1]

- The type of activity for which OLAP is extremely useful

- The functional requirements for OLAP

Since there are many related topics that I wish to address in this opening chapter, I have made liberal use of sidebars and endnotes. Unfortunately, the quantity of related topics is more a reflection of the volume of marketing noise in the industry than it is a reflection of any underlying scientific complexity. Figure 1.1 represents a diagram-

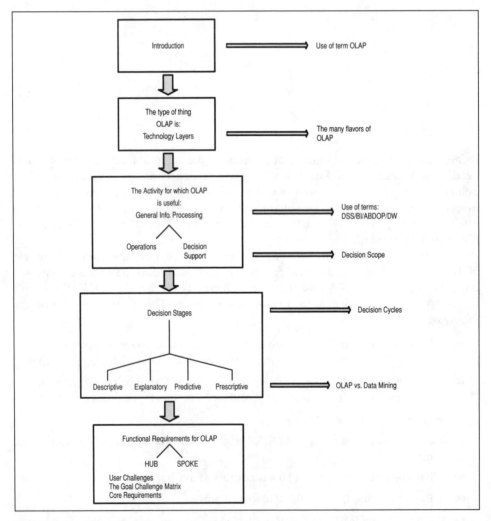

Figure 1.1   Diagrammatic summary of Chapter 1.

matic summary of Chapter 1 with the links identifying the place in the main argument to which each sidebar or endnote is linked.

In short, the functional requirements for OLAP are as follows:

- Rich dimensional structuring with hierarchical referencing
- Efficient specification of dimensions and dimensional calculations
- Separation of structure and representation
- Flexibility
- Sufficient speed to support ad hoc analysis
- Multi-user support

These requirements derive from the timeless goals of information processing, the distinct optimization requirements for decision support versus transaction processing, the distinct functional requirements for descriptive modeling versus other recursive stages of decision-oriented information processing, the application range distinction between different layers of computing architectures, and the challenges frequently found within the boundaries of Global 2000 corporations.

The Different Meanings of OLAP

As illustrated in Figure 1.2, the term OLAP has several meanings. The reason for this is that the essential elements in OLAP are expressible across several technology layers from storage and access to language layers.

Roughly, one can speak of OLAP concepts, OLAP languages, OLAP product layers, and full OLAP products.

OLAP concepts include the notion or idea of multiple hierarchical dimensions and can be used by anyone to think more clearly about the world, whether it be the material world from the atomic scale to the galactic scale, the economics world from micro agents to macro economies, or the social world from interpersonal to international relationships. In other words, even without any kind of formal language, just being able to think in terms of a multi-dimensional, multi-level world is useful regardless of your position in life.

OLAP formal languages, including Data Definition Language (DDL), Data Manipulation Language (DML), Data Representation Language (DRL), and associated parsers (and optional compilers), could be used for any descriptive modeling, be it transactional or decision support. In other words, the association of OLAP with decision support is more a function of the physical optimization characteristics of OLAP products than any inherent characteristics of OLAP language constructs.

OLAP product layers typically reside on top of relational databases and generate SQL as the output of compilation. Data storage and access is handled by the database.

Full OLAP products that need to include a compiler and storage and access methods are optimized for fast data access and calculations and are used for Decision Support System(s) (DSS) derived data descriptive modeling.

The boundary between OLAP languages and products is not sharp.

Technology Layer	OLAP Thinking	OLAP Languages	OLAP Product Layers	Fully Optimized OLAP Products
Concepts				
Language/Parsers				
Compilers				
Storage/Access				
File System				
System Topology (I/O, memory, CPU, cache)				
Hardware Components (Type of memory, bus, network connection)				
Hardware Material (silicon, copper, electric/optical)				

Figure 1.2   The different meanings of OLAP.

Where OLAP Is Useful

Desired Attributes of General Information Processing

The cornerstone of all business activities (and any other intentional activities for that matter) is information processing. This includes data collection, storage, transportation, manipulation, and retrieval (with or without the aid of computers). From the first sheep herders who needed to tell when sheep were missing, to the Roman empire that required status reports on its subjugates, to the industrial barons of the 19th century who needed to keep track of their rail lines and oil fields, to modern day enterprises of every variety, good information processing has always been essential to the survival of the organization.

The importance of good information can be thought of as the difference in value between right decisions and wrong decisions, where decisions are based on that information. The larger the difference between right and wrong decisions, the greater the importance of having good information. For example, poor information about con-

THE MANY FLAVORS OF OLAP

As if the marketing term OLAP wasn't enough, many vendors and a few industry pundits felt compelled—especially between 1995 and 1998—to create variants, typically in the form of a single consonant added to the front of the term OLAP to distinguish their letter flavor of OLAP from the others.

The original users of OLAP letter flavors were the vendors, such as MicroStrategy, who were selling OLAP product layers that sat on top of relational database systems and issued SQL to the database in response to user input. They offered only minor OLAP calculation capabilities and were generally read-only systems. Nevertheless, once relational databases beat OLAP systems as the repository of choice for data-warehousing data (a non-contest from the beginning), it was only natural for them to push the argument and claim that Relational OLAP (ROLAP) was better than OLAP.[2] That claim motivated the press to rebrand the non-ROLAP vendors as MOLAP to mean, of all things, multidimensional OLAP. Of course, once the cat was out of the bag, everybody needed a letter. I encountered DOLAP for database OLAP and DOLAP for desktop OLAP, HOLAP for hybrid OLAP, WOLAP for web OLAP, as well as M and R for mobile and remote OLAP. In April 1997, I chaired what was called the "MOLAP versus ROLAP debate."[3, 4]

Unfortunately, asking the question "Which is better, MOLAP or ROLAP?" makes as little sense as asking "Which is better, a car or a boat?" Obviously it depends what you're trying to do—cross town or cross a lake—and it depends on your constraints.

The existence of the ROLAP versus MOLAP debate is based on the false premise that the choice is binary. In fact the integration of multidimensional capabilities and relational capabilities is better described by a spectrum of possibilities where the notions of *pure* ROLAP and *pure* MOLAP are unattainable, theoretical limits.

In short, relational database products are far better equipped to handle the large amounts of data typically associated with corporate data-warehousing initiatives. Multi-dimensional databases are far better equipped to provide fast, dimensional-style calculations (although as you'll learn in Chapter 2 SQL databases are evolving to more efficiently support OLAP-style calculations). Thus, most organizations need some blend of capabilities, which, if it needed a letter flavor, would be HOLAP. But, as any proper understanding of OLAP would distinguish between the language or logical aspects of OLAP and its physical implementation, such a proper understanding of OLAP reveals that physically it can have any flavor. Thus the concept of H is subsumed in the physical characteristics of OLAP and no additional letter flavoring is required.

sumer retail trends results in poor buying and allocation decisions for a retailer, which results in costly markdowns for what was overstocked and lost profit-making opportunity for what was understocked. Retailers thus tend to value accurate product-demand forecasts highly. Good information about world events helps financial traders make better trading decisions, directly resulting in better profits for the trading firm. This is very valuable. Major trading firms invest heavily in information technologies. Good traders are handsomely rewarded.

Regardless of what information is being processed or how it is being processed, the goals or desired attribute values are essentially the same. Good information needs to be existent, accurate, timely, and understandable. All of the requirements are important. Imagine, for example, that you possessed the world's only program that could accurately predict tomorrow's stock prices given today's. Would you suddenly become fabulously wealthy? It also depends on the existence, timeliness, and understandability of the information. The program would be worthless if it could never get access to today's stock prices, or if it took so long to calculate the predictions that by the time you had independently calculated them they were already in the paper, or if you could access them with sufficient time to act, but received the information in some unintelligible form (like a typical phone bill).

Thus, OLAP, like any other form of information processing, needs to provide existent, timely, accurate, and understandable information.

The Distinction between Transaction and Decision Support Processing

Purchasing, sales, production, and distribution are common examples of day-to-day operational business activities. Resource planning, capital budgeting, strategic alliances, and marketing initiatives are common examples of business activities that generate and use analysis-based decision-oriented information.

The information produced through these higher-level activities is analysis-based because some data analysis, such as the calculation of a trend or a ratio or an aggregation, needs to occur as a part of the activity. The information is also decision-oriented because it is in a form that makes it immediately useful for decision making. Knowing which products or customers are most profitable, which pastures have the most lush grass, or which outlets have slipped the most this year is the kind of information that needs to be known in order to make decisions such as which products should have their production increased and which customers should be targeted for special promotions, which fields should carry more sheep, or which outlets should be closed. The

---

DW/DSS/BI/OLAP/ABDOP

In 1996, when I wrote the first edition, there was no term that adequately covered the whole of what we called analysis-based decision-oriented process (ABDOP). The focus of data warehousing was still very supply sided. The term decision support was end-user centric. I referred to OLAP and data warehousing as complementary terms within ABDOP. Since that time, the scope of the terms data warehousing and decision support have expanded to the point that they can, but do not typically, refer to the whole of what I called ABDOP. The term business intelligence also gained popularity and could also claim to cover equal ground, though it typically focuses on more end-user access issues. As of the time that I am writing this, May 2001, I most frequently see the term data warehousing used in conjunction with either the term decision support or business intelligence to refer to the whole of what I call the ABDOP space, without actually giving a name to that whole.[5]

decision orientation of the analysis is essential. It serves to direct analysis towards useful purposes.

In contrast, many operational activities are decision oriented without being based on analysis. For example, if a credit card customer asks to have her or his bill sent to an address other than her or his principal residence, a decision needs to be made. If the company policy states that bills must be sent to the customer's place of residence, then the decision is no. The policy information was decision oriented, but there was no analysis involved in the decision (at least not apparently).

Together, operations and decision-oriented analysis are at the core of all business activities, independent of their size, industry, legal form, or historical setting. This is illustrated in Figure 1.3, which highlights a number of diverse businesses in terms of their operational and analysis activities. Figure 1.4 shows the relationship between operations and analysis-based decisions for a merchant in 15th century Venice. Analysis-based decision-oriented activities take normal operating events (such as how much fabric is purchased on a weekly basis, or weekly changes in the internal inventory of fabrics, or sales of spices as inputs) and return changes to operating events (such as changes in how much fabric is bought on a weekly basis, or changes in what clothes are produced, or changes in the selling price for spices) as decision outputs.

For small businesses, it is common for the same inputs, including software, to be used in multiple ways. For a small book shop, a software consultant, or a donut stand, all operating and analysis aspects of the company may be effectively run by one person with a single program. Such a program might be a spreadsheet, a desktop database, or a prepackaged solution. For medium- to large-sized businesses and organizations, however, the world is significantly more complex. This creates a natural tendency for specialization.

Business	Operation	Decision-oriented Analysis
-Sheep farming 5000 B.C.	-Raise sheep for milk, wool, meat	-Grow/shrink herd, stay, or move on
-Trader in Venice 15th century	-Buy/sell fabrics and spices	-Pricing, suppliers, product line
-Railroad 19th Century	-Transport goods and people	-Track location, labor source
-Bank 20th Century	-Lending/borrowing money	-Interest rates -Target industries -Target customers -Portfolio analysis
-Retail clothing 20th Century	-Buy/sell consumer goods -Stocking, transporting	-How much shelf space/product -When to mark down -How much to buy

Figure 1.3 Operations and analysis activities for a variety of businesses.

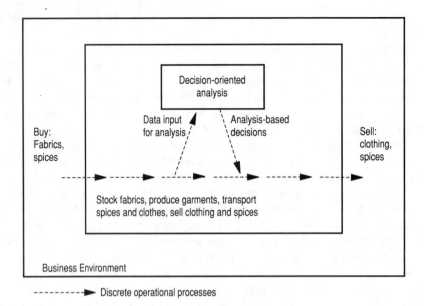

Figure 1.4   Operations and analysis activities for a merchant in Venice.

In a typical flow of daily operating events for an even moderately complex company, potential customers may ask sales staff questions about available products and make product purchase decisions that are actualized in sales transactions. In parallel with sales events, products are produced, their inputs are purchased, and all stages of finished goods are transported and stocked. The sales, production, and cost information that is constantly being generated would be recorded and managed in one or more database(s) used for operational purposes. To answer customer questions, perform sales transactions, and for other operational tasks, employees query these databases for operational information.

Operational software activities tend to happen with a relatively constant rate (during periods of normal operations and excepting certain peaks). Data is updated as frequently as it is read. The data represents a current snapshot of the way things are, and each query goes against a small amount of information. Operational queries tend to go against data that was directly input. And the nature of the queries is generally understood in advance (or else you'll be talking to a supervisor). For example, when a customer tells you her account number and you've pulled up her record from the database, you might ask that customer to tell you her name and address, which you would then verify against your record. Verifying a name and address involves retrieving and comparing nonderived data in the sense that the address information was not calculated from other inputs. The address was more likely furnished by the customer, perhaps in a previous order. The set of operations queries that are likely to be performed, such as retrieving the customer's record and verifying the name and address, is knowable in advance. It frequently follows a company procedure.

DECISION SCOPE

It is popular and convenient to think of operations and decision-oriented analysis as two distinct categories, especially because they correspond to the two major emphases in physical optimization—update speed and access speed. That is why I use the distinction in this book. The distinction, however, is more appropriately thought of in terms of a spectrum, much like hot and cold are more accurately described in terms of temperature differences. The common denominator is decision-making for both forms of information processing; the difference is the scope of inputs and outputs.

You can look at everyone in an organization from the part-time mail sorter to the chief executive as engaged in a continual process of decision-making. When you call a catalog company and the call center representative takes your name down after you've said it on the phone, he is making a decision (that he knows how to spell your name), so is the CEO when she decides to sell the company. Both persons are making decisions. The difference is scope. And scope is not binary.

Figure 1.5 shows a collection of decisions made by persons within an organization arranged by the scope of the inputs to the decision and the outcome of the decision. The bottom of the triangle shows the scope of the inputs and outputs. The top of the triangle represents the decision.

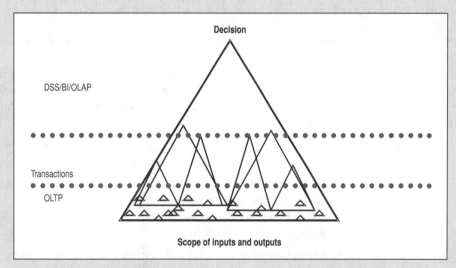

Figure 1.5   Decision scope.

In contrast to operations-oriented information activities and on a less frequent basis, managers and analysts may ask higher-level analytical questions such as

- What products have been most profitable for the company this year?
- Is it the same group of products that were most profitable last year?

- How is the company doing this quarter versus this same quarter last year?
- What kinds of customers exhibit the greatest loyalty?

The answers to these types of questions represent information that is both analysis based and decision oriented.

The volume of analysis-based decision-oriented software activities may fluctuate dramatically during the course of a typical day. On average, data is read more frequently than written and, when written, it tends to be in batch updates. Data represents current, past, and projected future states, and single operations frequently involve many pieces of information at once. Analysis queries tend to go against derived data, and the nature of the queries is frequently not understood in advance. For example, a brand manager may begin an analytical session by querying for brand profitability by region. Each profitability number refers to the average of all products in the brand for all places in the region where the products are sold for the entire time period in question. There may be literally hundreds of thousands or millions of pieces of data that were funneled into each profitability number. In this sense, the profitability numbers are high level and derived. If they had been planned numbers, they might have still been high level, but directly entered instead of derived, so the level of atomicity for a datum is not synonymous with whether it is derived. If the profitability numbers look unusual, the manager might then begin searching for why they were unusual. This process of unstructured exploration could take the manager to any corner of the database.

The differences between operational and analysis-based decision-oriented software activities are summarized in Table 1.1.

As a result of these differences between operational and analysis-based decision-oriented software activities, most companies of medium or greater size use different software products on different hardware systems for operations and for analysis. This is essentially because of three reasons:

1. Typical Global 2000 companies need software that is maximally efficient at operations processing and at analysis-oriented processing.

2. Fast updating, necessary for maximally efficient operations processing, and fast calculating (and the associated need for fast access to calculation inputs), necessary for maximally efficient analysis-oriented processing, require mutually exclusive approaches to indexing.

3. Analysis-based decision-oriented activities should have no impact on the performance of operational systems.

In a nutshell, whereas a typical family can get by with a station wagon for cruising around country roads and transporting loads, large corporations need racecars and trucks.

Software products devoted to the operations of a business, built principally on top of large-scale database systems, have come to be known as On-Line Transaction Processing systems or OLTP. The development path for OLTP software has followed a pretty straight line for the past 35 years. The goal has been to make systems handle larger amounts of data, process more transactions per unit time, and support larger numbers of concurrent users with ever-greater robustness. Large-scale systems process

Table 1.1 A Comparison of Operational and Analysis-Based Decision-Oriented Information-Processing Activities

OPERATIONAL ACTIVITIES	ANALYSIS-BASED DECISION-ORIENTED ACTIVITIES
More frequent	Less frequent
More predictable	Less predictable
Smaller amounts of data accessed per query	Larger amounts of data accessed per query
Query mostly raw data	Query mostly derived data
Require mostly current data	Require past, present, and projected data
Few, if any complex derivations	Many complex derivations

upwards of 1,000 transactions per second. Some, like the airline reservation system SABRE, can accommodate peak loads of over 20,000 transactions per second.

In contrast, software products devoted to supporting ABDOP have gone under a variety of market category names. This reflects the fact that the market for these products has been more fragmented, having followed what may seem like a variety of paths during the past 35 years. In addition to the power analyst-aimed DSS products of the 1970s and the executive-aimed EIS products of the 1980s, spreadsheets and statistical or data-mining packages, and inverted file databases (such as M204 from CCA, and Sybase IQ), not to mention what are now called OLAP packages have all been geared at various segments of the ABDOP market. This market has been called at various times data warehousing, business intelligence, decision support, and even OLAP. For reasons stated in endnote 1, I use the acronym ABDOP.

Figure 1.6 represents the ABDOP category. It shows the chain of processing from source data to end-user consumption. (Of course that chain is just a link within a larger and iterative cycle of decision making.) In between sources and uses, there may be multiple tiers of data storage and processing. Let's look at this more closely.

At one end there are links (possibly many) to data sources. These sources may include transaction systems and/or external data feeds such as the Internet or other subscription services. Note that the actual data sources, including the Internet, straddle the boundaries of the category. This is because boundary-straddling data also participates in some other functional category. For example, the transaction data also belongs to an OLTP system. Since the source data is generally copied into the ABDOP category, data and meta data (or data about the data) from the source(s) need(s) to be kept in sync with data in the ABDOP data store(s).

Since there are potentially multiple data sources, it may be necessary to integrate and standardize the information coming from the different sources into a common format. For large corporations there are frequently several stages of integration. Common types of integration include subject dimension integration (creating a single customer or supplier dimension from multiple source files) and metric integration (ensuring that derived measures are either calculated the same way or that their different methods of

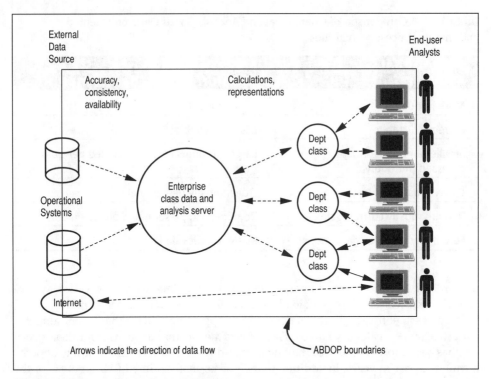

Figure 1.6   The ABDOP category in context.

calculation are well documented). Common types of standardization include standardizing the way a male/female binary response variable is encoded (such as mandating the use of Booleans) or standardizing the way a numeric value is encoded (such as mandating the use of eight-byte floating pointing numbers).

The raw data for analysis may be real or virtual. If it is real, this means there is an actual data store. If it is virtual, there may only exist links to the real source data that get invoked at request time, so the requester may not know whether the data requested is actually present in a single data store. (Of course, the time it takes to process a query may be an indication.) If the data store is real, there needs to be at least one data server.

Assuming that the organization in question is of moderate to large size, it is reasonable to assume that there exist two or more tiers of servers. An enterprise class data and analysis server is one that is in the relative category of most powerful server in the organization. (The term relative is used because one company's enterprise class server may be another company's PC.) There may be one enterprise class data server; or there may be many. Regardless of whether the organization is using a single processor-based server with 512MB of RAM and a 32-GB hard drive or a cluster of eight 16-way SMP boxes each with 32GB of main memory and each connected to an eight-TB disk array, the servers are more than just data servers. ABDOP servers need to perform analytical calculations. Some of the calculations may be associated with loads and performed in bulk. Others may be initiated by end-users.

Again, assuming the organization is of moderate to large size, a single enterprise class data and analysis server will connect to a number of department-level data and analysis servers. Network wires, if not WANs, may be used here and bandwidth may pose a problem (as you will see in Chapter 10).

At each stage in the ABDOP chain, from the original sources to final uses, the data is refined like any other raw material destined for producthood. When it finally reaches the user, the information has been cleansed, integrated, aggregated, extended, and otherwise enhanced to the point where it is immediately useful for decision making.

ABDOP is a natural, or software-independent, category of information processing that serves as the grounded framework for defining OLAP, data mining, decision optimization, data transformation tools, and relational databases as used for creating warehouse-like decision-support schemata. OLAP products, which are optimized for data access over data updates, focus on ABDOP rather than operational activities.

Decision Stages

So how does all this analysis-based information actually connect to decision making? Or, looking the other way, how do decisions connect to information sources? What's a decision anyway? See the "Decision Cycles" sidebar at the end of this chapter.

A good way to see all the information required for a decision is to examine how a challenged decision may be justified. Let's examine a decision to lower retail prices 25 percent in the eastern stores.

Any decision that can be justified needs to be based on at least one goal and one prediction. Try refuting that. Imagine you were trying to justify the decision to drop prices 25 percent, and when asked by your boss "Why are you dropping prices 25 percent? What are you trying to accomplish?" you responded that you had no goal; you weren't trying to accomplish anything in particular; you just felt like dropping prices. Aside from being a good candidate for being let go, if you don't have a goal, any decision is as good as any other. How could you defend the decision to drop prices 25 percent in the eastern stores as opposed to dropping them 50 percent in the west if there weren't a goal you were trying to accomplish through the decision? The kinds of algorithms you might use to find an optimal decision include linear programming and Monte Carlo Simulation. Tools that help you think through the options, exogenous variables, and contingent events associated with decisions are called decision-analysis tools.[6]

So having a goal is a necessary, but not sufficient grounding for a decision (as we're about to show). In addition to having a goal, you need to have at least one prediction. Say again you're talking to your boss about this price drop you're advocating and the boss buys into your goal of clearing inventory to make room for the fall line. However, the boss doesn't think that the sales discount should be 25 percent and wants to know how you can justify that discount amount as opposed to any other amount. The only way you could justify your decision to drop prices 25 percent is by sharing some prediction to which you have access that shows 25 percent as the discount amount most likely to just clear inventory. The kinds of algorithms you might use to make a prediction range from basic extrapolation to sophisticated model merging. Tools that help you make predictions fall under the category of either statistical packages or data mining.[7]

Where did that prediction come from? What if your boss isn't content knowing that you have a prediction, but wants you to justify that prediction. Upon what is a prediction based? To justify to your boss the need to drop prices 25 percent, you would need to show some analysis of past sales data that highlighted a pattern between changes in sales amounts and changes in price such that by assuming that the sales/price relationship holds constant over time, you can determine the price discount required to increase sales by the amount necessary to just clear inventory. Thus, predictions are extensions of patterns, relationships, or explanations. They require at least one assumption in order to be extended. All predictions require at least two sets of descriptions and at least one assumption. The kinds of algorithms you might use to discover patterns include regressions, decision trees, clustering, association rules, and neural nets. The tools that help you discover patterns are the same statistical and data-mining tools you would use to make predictions.

What if your boss is astute and buys into your predictive reasoning, but still wants to challenge your prediction? Where would he look? There's only one place. That's the descriptions upon which the patterns were based. If your descriptions are inaccurate, your predictions will be bogus regardless of your predictive reasoning—garbage in; garbage out. How would you defend your descriptions? Your first thought might be to defend your data collections practice. So you say to your boss that you use the finest quality control for data collection and are willing to risk your job defending the accuracy of your data inputs.

What if your boss responds that he believes your data inputs are accurate, but he still claims that your predictions are wrong, even though he grants you the logic is correct? What is he criticizing? How would you defend your actions, or your job? Well, if your source descriptions are accurate, it has got to be a problem with your derived descriptions. Derived descriptions include any kind of aggregation, allocation, difference, ratio, ordering, or product. Nearly all the information we reason with and look for patterns in are derived descriptions. This includes weekly product sales, daily register totals, total product costs, division earnings, overhead, cost of goods sold, market share, productivity, and profits. OLAP tools focus on creating derived descriptions. And, as you'll read about in this book, there are many ways to make mistakes. The right OLAP tools and techniques are your best way to ensure descriptive accuracy.

Thus, as illustrated in Figure 1.7 the type of activity for which OLAP products are useful is descriptive modeling, as opposed to explanatory, predictive, or prescriptive modeling, for decision-oriented derived representations (as opposed to source-oriented or nonderived representations) for larger-scope or decision-support applications.

Descriptive	Explanatory	Predictive	Decision making
aggregation allocation ratios scaling weighting type transforms	regressions clustering associations split finding probabilistic networks	Pattern extension Model management Model result merging	Goal seeking Simulations

Figure 1.7 Decision functions.

OLAP VERSUS DATA MINING

Another casualty of technology marketing was the publicly perceived relationship between OLAP and data mining. When OLAP technology took off in 1994 and 1995, it was only natural for vendors to try and repeat the same success with related technologies. Many attempts were made in the 1995–1997 time period to productize data mining and sell it in the same way that OLAP tools were sold. These attempts were of dubious merit from the beginning because the proper use of a data-mining tool requires basic knowledge of statistics and thus one can't sell data-mining tools to the same collection of casual business users to whom one can sell OLAP-style query tools. But beyond that, as a part of the sales and marketing process, multiple data-mining vendors felt the need to promote data mining by criticizing, or at least pigeonholing, OLAP. As a result, numerous ads appeared in journals that positioned OLAP as a technology that worked with aggregate or summary data whereas data mining worked with detail data. That distinction has stuck in the minds of enough people and is sufficiently incorrect that I routinely spend time dismantling it.

The distinction between OLAP and data mining has nothing to do with the distinction between summary and detail data. As I described earlier in this chapter, there is a valid distinction to be made between descriptive and explanatory modeling. The functions or algorithms typically found in OLAP tools (such as aggregation [in its many forms], allocations, ratios, products, etc.) are descriptive modeling functions whereas the functions found in any so-called data-mining package (such as regressions, neural nets, decision trees, and clustering) are pattern discovery or explanatory modeling functions.

In addition to the fact that OLAP provides descriptive modeling functions while data mining provides explanatory modeling functions, OLAP also provides a sophisticated structuring consisting of dimensions with hierarchies and cross-dimensional referencing that is nowhere provided in a data-mining environment. A typical data-mining or statistics tool looks at the world in terms of variables and cases.

While it is true that a good data-mining environment needs to connect to detail data, so too does a good OLAP environment (as you will have ample time to discover for yourself in Part Three of this book). Aggregation begins with detail data. Furthermore, most patterns actually discovered through the process of data mining are found within and between partially aggregated derived variables. Very few sales forecasters will create forecasts for stock keeping units (SKUs). Most product forecasts are done at the product, brand, category, or department level.

The fact that many data miners do their work without using OLAP tools doesn't mean they aren't using OLAP functions. On the contrary, all data miners do some OLAP work as part of their data exploration and preparation prior to running particular pattern detection algorithms. Simply, many data miners rely on basic calculation capabilities provided for either in the data-mining tool or the backend database.

I look forward to the day when the true complementary nature of OLAP and data-mining tools will be more widely appreciated and vendors will better support their dynamic integration. Examples of OLAP and data-mining integration are shown in Chapter 20.

At least I am not alone in this regard. Jiawei Han, the director of the intelligent database lab at the University of Illinois at Urbana-Champaign, co-author of the book *Data Mining: Concepts and Techniques*[8] and a leading researcher in the field of data mining, has long been a strong proponent of integrating data mining and OLAP.

The Functional Requirements for OLAP

The functional requirements for OLAP have a hub and spoke form. The hub, root, necessary, or minimal requirements on the logical side include support for multiple dimensions, hierarchies, dimensional formulas, and the separation of data structure and representation. Physically, the major requirement is sufficient speed to support ad hoc analysis. Any language or product that doesn't at least support these requirements can't with any seriousness be classified as OLAP supporting.

Of course the detailed requirements that end-user organizations have for OLAP solutions typically extend far beyond these minimal or core requirements. I considered arranging these additional requirements and corresponding capabilities in a weak-to-strong OLAP support axis, but after much reflection felt that beyond the minimal requirements, all others were inherently optional, contingent, or spokish in nature. One could, perhaps, argue that multiuser support is a necessary requirement for an OLAP product, but I would disagree. As useful and perhaps client-mandated as such a feature might be, it is certainly possible to build and analyze arbitrarily complex data sets in a multidimensional fashion without resorting to a multiuser environment. If multiuser support were a necessary requirement for a product to be called OLAP, then we would need yet another category to apply to any single-user multidimensional product; and languages that are user-quantity invariant would therefore lack an essential attribute of OLAP. Thus, I treated multiuser support as a contingent, albeit practical, necessity for any server-style OLAP product.

The one area where I do advocate distinguishing degrees of support is in dimensional structuring and the specification of calculations. However, to fully appreciate the choices available and thus the relative strengths and weaknesses of particular products, you will need to have read a good part of this book; so for now I leave the hub requirements undifferentiated. Between Chapters 5 and 7, these hub requirements will become differentiated.

User Challenges

Global 2000 organizations share many of the same information problems. For example, it may take too long to answer particular queries because every time a manager asks a question about a class of customers defined in terms of a set of attributes, a whole SQL routine needs to be written by a database programmer. Or it may take too much disk space to store all the relevant analytical data. Or it may just be impossible to allocate certain costs below the department level. Or it may be dangerous for more than a handful of users to be on the system at once. Or it may be impossible for end-users to edit the data. Or the company might want to perform nightly incremental computes, which means that all changes from operations need to be reflected in the analytical data within something as small as a four-hour window. Or reports, once generated, may be hard to reconfigure. Or the network may get jammed every time a client makes a request for data from a server.

The typical challenges for Global 2000 corporations are summarized as follows:

- Core challenges:
  - Many levels of detail from SKU codes to individual products, groups of products, product lines, brands, and more
  - Many data analysis factors including products, location, company organization, market, and time
  - Many derived calculations to specify and execute

- Contingent challenges:
  - Lots of data—very large data stores measured in the hundreds and thousands or even millions of gigabytes
  - Lots of users of the same data—hundreds and thousands
  - Lots of sites—hundreds, thousands, and more
  - Decentralized decision making—user-analysts aren't following predefined procedures; they are making autonomous decisions as to what data to access, and how to analyze it

One way to look at the functional requirements for OLAP is as an attempt to provide descriptive modeling with the desired attributes or goals of coverage, timeliness, accuracy, and understandability given the typically occurring challenges mentioned previously (see Figure 1.8).

To the degree that Global 2000 organizations share many of the same challenges, and they all share the same goals, they can be said to share a variety of common, though contingent, requirements. These include the ability to efficiently store, access, and perform calculations on large data sets; the ability to partition data sets across multiple logical drives; the ability to distribute calculations in time; and the ability to distribute calculations between an OLAP server and an underlying relational database. These spoke requirements are common to most Global 2000 organizations implementing OLAP solutions within the context of an enterprise decision-support framework and will be discussed later in this book, mostly in Chapter 10.

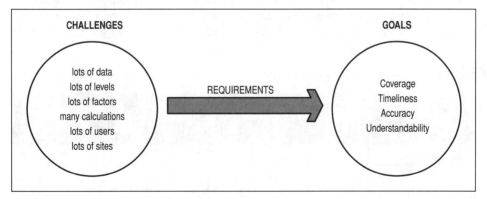

Figure 1.8 Requirements map challenges to goals.

The Goal-Challenge Matrix

Most OLAP challenges affect multiple goals. For example, in addition to speed, which is obvious, large amounts of data can affect accuracy and understandability as well as coverage or existence. On the input side, the presence of lots of source data means there will be an increased likelihood that some data is anomalous. And calculating with large amounts of data has its own complications that may introduce errors. There are likely to be missing and meaningless data that need to be properly dealt with, and there are likely to be differences in the way existent data need to be treated. For example, sales tax rates may need to be differentially applied to stores as a function of the cities and states they are located in because of differences in tax rates. Different cities in an economic analysis may need to be weighted as a function of their population. All of these data-quantity-derived challenges can affect the accuracy of source and derived data. The abundance of data can also affect the understandability of that data.

Getting a feeling for the whole of the data set requires more compression than with smaller data sets. There is thus more chance for compressing the data to the point where its essential features are no longer understood. The more source data there is, the more likely some physical optimization is applied, such as partitioning across multiple physical devices and storing the data in a source format (such as relational) that may, in turn, affect the ability of the system to create needed derivations. So the challenge of large amounts of data affects all OLAP goals.

Since most of the challenges affect multiple goals, a useful (and, I might add, multidimensional) way to think about the source of the functional requirements for OLAP (or the functional requirements for your particular OLAP-based project) is as a matrix of goal challenges as illustrated in Table 1.2.

For every intersection of a goal and a challenge, you should be able to identify the impact strength of the challenge on the goal. All intersections with high impact should connect to one or more functional requirements. For example, a product manager in an organization that has very deep product hierarchies and that uses multilevel marketing may find that the presence of lots of data levels has an especially strong impact on the accuracy and timeliness of calculated total product costs. Thus, the intersection of lots of levels with timeliness might be addressed by the functional requirement for strong aggregate management (a feature of some OLAP and now many relational products). The intersection of lots of levels with accuracy might be addressed by the

Table 1.2 The Goal Challenges for OLAP

GOALS/ CHALLENGES	LOTS OF DATA AND DERIVED DESCRIPTIONS	LOTS OF LEVELS	LOTS OF FACTORS	LOTS OF USERS	COMPLEX TOPOLOGY
Existence					
Timeliness					
Accuracy					
Understandability					

functional requirements for rich dimensional structuring, including the ability to input data at any level and a powerful calculation language that enables the manual override of otherwise calculated values (features present in several OLAP products).

Core Logical Requirements

Having seen that each of the challenges of descriptive modeling can affect multiple goals, and that the requirements for OLAP are the vehicle that maps challenges to goals or that accomplishes the goals given the challenges, it is time to look at the requirements.

1. Rich Dimensional Structuring with Hierarchical Referencing

As stated previously, rich dimensional structuring with hierarchical referencing is a necessary requirement for OLAP. The recognition that we live in a world characterized by highly multidimensional sets of interacting subsystems, each with many levels of data, detail, reality, or abstractions, is a fundamental insight. The ability of OLAP tools to efficiently model that complexity is one of their fundamental contributions.

2. Efficient Specification of Dimensions and Calculations

As stated in the Foreword, there is more to analysis than simply aggregating numbers. Sure, it is important to be able to correctly sum and average large quantities of data, but most of the important information to be gleaned results from the intelligent comparison of ratios and inferred trends over time and other dimensions. In other words, a good part of the querying that takes place in analytical processing contains embedded analysis. As you will see in Chapter 7 when we look at dimensional formulas, the combination of aggregating and comparison analysis can get pretty tricky.

For example, imagine you are the sales director for an electronic products company that just finished its first year of international operations. You might want to know which product categories experienced profit levels abroad that were the most different from their profit levels in the United States. You might want to see the results ordered from most positive to most negative. To answer this query, the system needs to perform a variety of calculations. Profits need to be calculated per product. As profits are derived values and can be calculated in many different ways, this task alone can be nontrivial. Profit values then need to be normalized so that they can be compared across products. Normalized profit levels then need to be aggregated to the product category level. This needs to be done across time for the United States and for the new foreign market. Time aggregations may need to be adjusted for differences in reporting periods and/or number of days per period. The profit level for each product group then needs to be compared between the two markets, and finally the differences in profit level need to be ordered from most positive to most negative. In an OLAP system, these types of calculations should be as straightforward to define as they are to say. To provide true OLAP functionality, a software tool needs to contain a sophisticated calculation language.

3. Flexibility

Flexibility is another crucial component of OLAP functionality. It carries a variety of meanings. There is flexible viewing, flexible definition, flexible analysis, and flexible interface. Systems need to be flexible in all these ways.

There are many ways to present or look at information. View flexibility means the user can easily choose to see information in the form of graphs, matrices, or charts, and within any form, such as matrices. The user can select how the information is mapped to the view form.

In terms of definitions, whoever has the relevant authority should be able to change the names of descriptors, the formatting of numbers, the definitions of formulas, the triggers for automatic processes, or the location of source data without incurring any undue penalty.

In contrast, the DSS systems of the 1970s and the EIS systems of the 1980s were often fast and powerful, but at the cost of being rigid. Usually a team of developers needed to write custom decision-support or aggregation routines. Thereafter, these routines were simply called. While they performed well, they were hard coded and thus inflexible. If an end-user wanted to change the way some aggregation routine was performed, it required programmatically editing the application. Generally speaking, the categories of data to be processed—such as the names of departments or the names of countries—were hard coded as well.

Interface flexibility is a more general form of what is sometimes called an intuitive interface. Intuitiveness or friendliness is so important that it almost deserves its own category. I have elected to keep it under the more general heading of flexibility because not everybody has the same concept of what's intuitive. Thus, to allow everyone the ability to interact with a system in the way that makes the most sense for them, what is needed is a flexible or friendly interface.

It is no good having a fast, powerful system if you cannot figure out how to use it and you don't understand what it is telling you. On the input side, interface flexibility or friendliness affects the user's ability to quickly define what the user wants to do. Like other types of flexibility, interface flexibility applies to a variety of areas such as model definition, model browsing, formula specification, direct data input, and external data source links. The friendlier the software, the less time you spend thinking about how to do something and the more time you spend actually doing it.

This is especially important in today's world. In earlier times, analysis tended to be performed by small groups of individuals within the organization who devoted most of their time to analysis. These people could afford the steep learning curves associated with DSS-style analytical systems. Today, however, analysis is increasingly performed by a wider scope of people, each of whom devotes only a small percentage of her or his time to analysis. They need an analytical environment that enables them to maximally leverage what they already know, so they can be up and running quickly. The standard paradigm for friendliness these days, on the input side, is a graphical user interface. Of course, friendly is whatever appeals to the end-user. There are many people who still prefer a command line supporting a well-documented 4GL for its greater speed and power of expression.

4. Separation of Structure and Representation

The degree to which grid-like data views (or any other kind of external representation) are flexible is in great part a function of the degree of separation between data structure and representation. Having this separation means that views can be reorganized by an end-user without making any structural changes to the data. If data needs to be restructured to support a new view, chances are the new view won't be created—certainly not in an ad hoc fashion. The lack of separation between structure and representation is one of the weak links for spreadsheets, as you will see in Chapter 2.

Core Physical Requirements

1. Fast Access

Speed is a crucial component of OLAP. It's more than just the thrill. It's about maintaining your train of thought. OLAP needs to support ad hoc analytical queries, some of which may require computations performed on-the-fly. For example, someone might start a session by querying how overall product profitability was in Europe last quarter. Seeing profitability was lower than expected, he might navigate down into individual countries while still looking at overall product profitability. Here, he might see that some countries were significantly below the others and so he would naturally navigate further down into product groups for these countries, always looking for some data that could help explain the higher-level anomalies. A first glance might not reveal anything unusual. Sales were where they were supposed to be, as were returns and manufacturing costs. Ah, but wait. Indirect costs were substantially higher for the errant countries. Further navigating into indirect costs might reveal that significant taxes were recently levied on those products (possibly the result of some trade dispute), which served to sharply reduce their profitability because prices remained stable due to market competition from domestic players.

Each step in this train of thought constituted a query. Each query was iterative in the sense that it followed the result of the previous one. Anyone engaged in this sort of querying wants to maintain the momentum. It would be difficult to follow this type of analytical thread if the mean response time per query were measured in days, hours, or even minutes. A commonly stated goal of OLAP systems is to provide a mean response time of five seconds or less regardless of the type of query or the size of the database.

In the past, analysts who needed quick response time placed data extracts in local, single-user applications that were fully dedicated to a single user/analyst. Today's challenge is for systems to provide blazing response time to access and computation requests while working with large data sets in a multiuser environment distributed across a network. Some tools provide for this by precomputing all aggregates. This can, however, lead to database explosion (as described in Chapter 10). Even if one could store all the precomputed results, the increase in the size of the database can actually offset any gains made to query response time by precomputing. For maximally efficient access, tools need to provide the right combination of precomputed and query-time computed results.

2. Multiuser Support

Even though multiuser support is not a necessary requirement, given the preponderance of OLAP servers and the practical requirement of multiuser support, it is discussed briefly in this section. Corporations are collaborative work environments. As a result of downsizing and decentralizing, the relative number of employees who need read/write access to decision-empowering analytical data is on the rise. Problems discovered by a regional sales manager, for example, may need to be communicated to a distribution or manufacturing manager for prompt resolution. Forecasts examined by senior executives may reflect data that was generated from a dozen or more separate departments. For global corporations, some of those departments may not even share the same country or language.

As with any complex issue, multiuser support is not a binary function. It is a question of degrees. There can be multiuser read based on separate caches for each user with no write-back capabilities. This may satisfy some applications like sales reporting where the source of the data came from operational systems. There can be multiuser read/write with all the processing done on the server. This may satisfy budgeting applications where the budget is centrally controlled on the server. And there can be multiuser read/write where the processing and data are distributed between client and server, where the server is intelligent enough to know when data should be processed on the server and when on the client, and where the server offers a multiuser cache. The goal for most OLAP vendors is this last form of multiuser support because it is the most flexible and makes the most efficient use of enterprise computing resources.

Summary

Information processing is a part of all organizations regardless of whether they use computers. The major subdivisions in information processing reflect the major subdivisions of organizational activity: operations and decision-oriented analysis. The term OLAP, when used to refer to a collection of products, denotes descriptive modeling for analysis-based decision-oriented information processing (ABDOP). These days, popular terms such as data warehousing, decision support, and business intelligence could all be used more or less synonymously with the term ABDOP. However, because the meaning of those terms are at the mercy of many marketing departments, I use the term ABDOP for its stability of meaning. The requirements for OLAP are derived from a combination of the goals of information processing in general and the challenges of descriptive modeling for ABDOP. The challenges have a hub and spoke form. The major hub requirements for OLAP are rich dimensional structuring with hierarchical referencing, efficient specification of dimensions and calculations, flexibility, separation of structure and representation, sufficient speed to support ad hoc analysis, and multiuser support.

In the next chapter we will look at why the two main traditional technologies for providing OLAP functionality—SQL and spreadsheets—are inadequate for the job.

DECISION CYCLES

Information is used for decision making within a framework of intentional activity. As illustrated in Figure 1.9, all intentional activity, whether performed by individual persons, corporations, or governments, can be represented in terms of collections of Decision-Execution-Environment-Representation (DEER) cycles.

The cyclically related action stages, roles, or functions, which I've labeled with descriptions that highlight the cyclical relationships are

- The decision, based on some previous representation

- The execution of the decision, based on some previous representation

- The environment in which the execution and consequences of the decision, based on some previous representation, take place

- The future decision-supporting representation of the environment in which the execution and consequences of the decision, based on some previous representation, take place

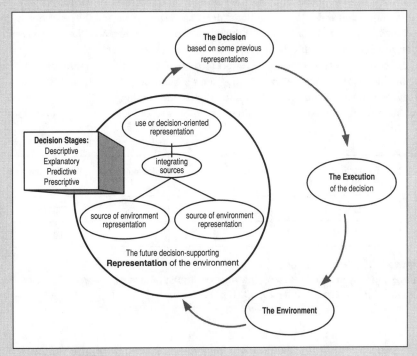

Figure 1.9   DEER cycle.   (*continues*)

DECISION CYCLES *(continued)*

Figure 1.9 shows a typical ABDOP system in a representation role used for making decisions that, when executed, produce results in an environment that can then be measured and represented within the ABDOP system.

It is important to keep in mind that value may be gained or lost at any phase in the cycle. Thus value may be gained or lost due to good or bad decisions, good or bad execution, lucky or unlucky environmental factors, and good or bad representations (information).

The main reason for looking at organizations and their information systems in terms of DEER cycles is to link together all the actions/events that co-exist in a naturally occurring implicit causal framework within the context of any intentional behavior.

For example, let's use the DEER cycle approach to reconstruct the causal events surrounding the promotional sales data shown in Figure 1.10. The promotional sales data itself is functioning as a representation. So what was the event that the sales data is a measurement of? Are there any distinguishing characteristics? Maybe it was a beautiful spring day and the high sales were more a function of the weather than the promotional pricing or advertising. If you think a little more about it, you can see there are at least two different DEER cycles sharing the same event space that need to be reconstructed to show the full causal links surrounding the sales data, the seller's and the buyer's, as illustrated in Figure 1.11.

So, if you want to be able to impact future promotions, you need to know the success of the event represented by the sales data for both the seller and for the buyer. This means you need to understand first (for the seller) the promotional decisions made, the information upon which the promotional decisions were made, and the execution of the decisions and, second (for the buyer) the purchasing decisions made, the information upon which the purchasing decisions were made, and their execution.

Using the DEER cycle approach to direct information collection is a form of methodology for decision value archeology. In the same way that a Hominid archaeologist would know to look for tool, shelter, and clothing remnants near food that was already found in an attempt to draw a picture of what life was like 500,000 years

Transaction ID	Item	Quantity	Price	Promotion	Total Amount
23917	412	4	25	30%	$70.00
23917	509	2	75	0%	$150.00

Figure 1.10   Promotional sales.
Image courtesy of Erik Thomsen, "Information Impact: Business Analytics Revealed Part 2," *Intelligent Enterprise,* June 29, 2001, p. 52.

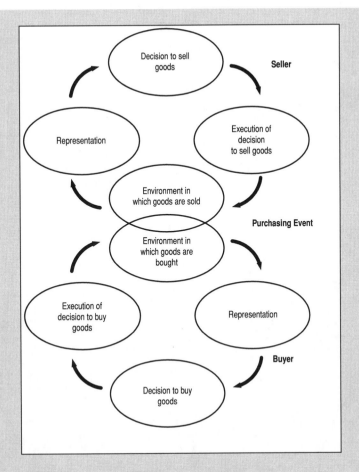

Figure 1.11 Promotional sales with causal link data.
Image courtesy of Erik Thomsen, "Information Impact: Business Analytics Revealed Part 2," *Intelligent Enterprise,* June 29, 2001, p. 52.

ago, a decision archaeologist would know to look for past and future related decisions, executions, and events surrounding a piece of found information in an attempt to draw a picture of the events causally connected to the information.

Decisions are thus made within a cycle of intentional activity. So what are the types of information that go into making a decision? Is there any built-in structure to it?

The Limitations of Spreadsheets and SQL

During the past 15 years, the two most commonly used product technologies for delivering analysis-based decision-oriented information to end-users have been databases and spreadsheets. Spreadsheets are typically used directly by end-users, while databases are usually set up and administered by IT professionals. With databases, end-users are normally given access either to canned query templates or to easy-to-use query tools existing within a managed query environment.

This chapter explores why traditional spreadsheet and database approaches to organizing, managing, and querying data are inadequate for meeting the core logical requirements of Online Analytical Processing (OLAP) applications. Those requirements are support for multiple dimensions, hierarchies, dimensional calculations, and the separation of structure and representation. We will start with a quick review of the last 15 years, during which time both spreadsheet and database vendors have added significant amounts of OLAP functionality to their products. You will see that technology producers have been aware for quite some time that the traditional tools in their original form did not satisfy end-users' analytical requirements. Then we will get into specific examples of where spreadsheet and database technologies break down. Since this is a written chapter, it will not be possible to provide direct evidence of any shortcomings in physical requirements such as calculation speed. (Issues of physical design are treated in Chapter 10. Also, there is a discussion of OLAP benchmarks in Appendix B.)

For those readers uninterested in the historical evidence that spreadsheets and SQL/relational databases have evolved toward supporting increasing amounts of OLAP functionality, you may safely skip the first section in this chapter.

The Evolution of OLAP Functionality in Spreadsheets and SQL Databases

Spreadsheets and OLAP

Spreadsheets were originally positioned against the calculator by promoting their capability to perform what-if calculations. Instead of having to rewrite a series of interdependent numbers (such as a total of line items in a budget) just to see what would happen if one or more inputs were changed and then manually reperform the computation, the spreadsheet enabled users to define the result in terms of a formula. In this way, users could simply change the value of an input and the spreadsheet would automatically recalculate the total. The need for spreadsheets was a no-brainer.

In the 1980s, as personal computers became more powerful and an increasing number of people were performing analyses on their desktops, the demand increased for higher-level functionality, to which the spreadsheet market responded in a variety of ways.

First came the spreadsheet add-ins such as Panaview, Look 'n' Link, and Budget Express. These add-in tools were designed to compensate for the difficulties that spreadsheets had with aggregating data and combining worksheets. For example, Budget Express enabled users to create a multilevel spreadsheet outline that they could then collapse and expand. This helped with aggregations. Look 'n' Link enabled users to link aggregations from one worksheet into a cell of another worksheet. This also helped users working with larger amounts of data.

The functionality embraced by the market in the form of add-ins eventually became incorporated into the spreadsheets themselves.[1] Packages like Lucid 3D offered linked worksheets. Version 3 of Lotus 1-2-3 added addressable pages to the rows and columns. In this way, if rows represented *products* and columns represented *stores*, pages could represent *weeks* and the total yearly sales of all products for all stores could be defined as *the sum across weekly pages for the all product by all store cell*.

Even with increased functionality, creating near-OLAP style functionality in a spreadsheet is still cumbersome. In the early 1990s I worked at Power Thinking Tools, which had developed a desktop multidimensional analysis tool. We were frequently asked the following question: Why can't I create a multidimensional model with a spreadsheet? We intuitively felt that spreadsheets weren't suited for multidimensional modeling, but we did some direct testing to better understand the obstacles.

We defined a small, yet typical multidimensional model for comparison testing. It consisted of *stores, time periods, products*, and *measures. Stores, time periods*, and *products* each contained several hierarchical levels. The test actions consisted of defining and performing simple aggregations, more complex aggregations that contained weighting and inferencing schemes, and a variety of views. Ad hoc queries were conducted as well. No serious analysis was performed.

It took an experienced spreadsheet macro programmer eight hours to define the macros and lookup tables necessary to create all the aggregation levels, calculations, and views. (The test was performed using Lotus 1-2-3, Quattro Pro, and Microsoft Excel.) Using our product, FreeThink, the entire model could be defined and calculated in less than 15 minutes.

By 1993, products such as Excel offered pivot tables. Pivot tables, or *n*-way cross-tabs, are multidimensional, and any survey of the OLAP market space would have to include a product like Excel because it offers some OLAP functionality. However, even today, Excel's pivot table functionality is not integrated into its core spreadsheet structures. Because you have to import data from your Excel worksheet into the Excel pivot tables, functionally speaking, the pivot table is not a spreadsheet.

These days, every copy of Microsoft Office 2000 comes with a version of something called *pivot table services* (not to be confused with pivot tables), which are part of Microsoft's client-resident OLAP technology. Vendors of client-tier OLAP applications, from Business Objects to Proclarity, that leverage Microsoft's client-server OLAP technology write to pivot table services.

OLAP, the Relational Model, and SQL Databases

SQL databases are the commercial implementations of the relational data model, which was initially defined by Edgar Codd in his 1970 paper, "A Relational Model of Data for Large Shared Databanks."[2] The conceptual schema of the relational data model is largely derived from set theory (and theory of relations) and the predicate calculus. The relational model defines, among other things, a declaratively oriented relational calculus and a procedurally oriented relational algebra. The combination of the calculus and the algebra defines a complete data definition language (DDL) and data manipulation language (DML). While the relational model freed the database designer/user from having to think about the physical storage and access of data, the relational model turned out to be overly focused on low-level detail for the higher-level work of developers and end-user analysts. It was particularly difficult to define decision support applications (or any other kind of application) that depended on complex data aggregation. As a result, soon after Codd published his original paper, work began on building higher-level abstractions into the relational model.

All through the 1970s and into the 1980s, many academic papers were written on adding abstraction capabilities to the relational model. Abstract data types are one approach to looking at the problem of aggregation. In many approaches, such as ADABPTL[3] and DAPLEX,[4] notions of hierarchy were added to relational concepts. In one groundbreaking article, Smith and Smith[5] wrote about adding two new abstraction types—aggregates and generalizations. Aggregate objects were complex data types or what today would be called *objects* (though interobject messaging was not a part of the aggregate type). For example, "Hotel Reservation" might be an aggregate consisting of the fields *date, time, reservation taker, confirmation number, name of reserving party, date of reservation, number of days of stay, number of persons in party, type of room requested* (including *bed types, smoking* or *nonsmoking, floor,* and so forth), and *price per night.* Another aggregate could be "Airline Reservation," consisting of the fields *date, time, reservation taker, confirmation number, date of flight, time of flight, flight number, number of seats, position of seats, fare class, method of payment,* and *special requests.* A generalization of hotel and airline reservations might be "Reservation." The fields associated with "Reservation" might be *date, time, reservation taker, reservation number, date of reservation, name of reserving party,* and *number of persons in party.* The fields associated with the generalization "Reservation" would be passed onto or inherited by any aggregate that was a child/specialization of the generalization "Reservation."

Even Dr. Codd wrote academically on the topic when in 1978 he published "Extending the Database Relational Model to Capture More Meaning."[6] His focus in that paper was on defining hierarchical data types and a variety of hierarchical relationships, such as subtypes and supertypes as extensions to the basic structures of the relational model. The work on database semantics led to the development of object-oriented(OO) programming methods, OO databases, entity-relationship data modeling, and knowledge bases.

By the early 1980s, with the release of SQL database products from Oracle and IBM, relational databases were becoming a commercial reality. As a part of that reality, SQL, which had evolved from experiments with database languages that attempted to implement the relational model, became the de facto standard commercial relational database language. By the early 1990s, more than 100 commercial database products supported some dialect of SQL.

Although SQL's original goal may have been to be an end-user query language (hence the original name SEQUEL from "Structured English Query Language"), the language proved too abstruse for typical end-users. In the same way that products were built to extend the capabilities of spreadsheets, products were built to extend the capabilities (or at least hide the syntax) of SQL. Query by example, graphical queries, natural language queries, and arranged end-user queries were all attempts to hide the complexity of SQL generation from the end-user. This occurred because analyzing data and exploring relationships were not part of the original SQL vocabulary. For example, classic texts such as *A Guide to the SQL Standard* by Chris Date and Hugh Darwin and *Instant SQL Programming* by Joe Celko do not even treat the most basic operations of analysis such as comparisons.[7] As you will see in the next section of this chapter, there is a good reason for this. Most types of comparisons are difficult to specify in SQL. That said, SQL-99 (the newest version of SQL as of December 2001) has recently incorporated a number of analytically oriented features as well as some OLAP extensions. These changes represent a redistribution of OLAP functionality from outside the SQL database engine to largely within it.

Plenty of circumstantial evidence suggests that neither spreadsheets nor traditional or even current SQL databases adequately meet users' needs for OLAP functionality.

Proving the Point: Some Examples

Indirect evidence is fine to whet your appetite. But now let's follow with some specific examples so you can see firsthand why it is so difficult to provide OLAP-style functionality with spreadsheets and SQL databases. The best way to judge the performance of SQL and spreadsheets is to put them to work on the same problem.

One metaphor for looking at the problem of generating analysis-based decision-oriented views from base data is to think of the entire process as an information economy, as illustrated in Figure 2.1. We have a common supply function; this refers to our base data and the rate at which it is refreshed. We also have a common demand func-

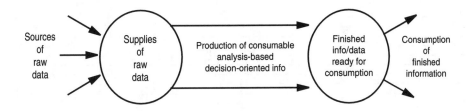

Figure 2.1   The information economy.

tion; this refers to analytical reports and views and the rate at which end-users consume/view them. In between we have a manufacturing logistics or production problem. The key production question may be phrased as follows: What is the most efficient method to define and produce the consumer information goods demanded by our end-users in an accurate, timely, and understandable fashion?

A Common Starting Point

Let's start with the desired outputs or finished consumable information. Imagine that you are the sales director for a retail organization and that you are responsible for the ongoing analysis of sales for all the products sold in all your stores. As a part of your normal analysis process, you want to see monthly sales totals by product and product category. You also want to see monthly total product sales broken down by region and store. In addition to cumulative totals, you want to see how the actuals vary from plans. These views or reports are illustrated in Figures 2.2 and 2.3.

Figures 2.2 and 2.3 represent typical decision-oriented information. For example, knowing that the sale of desks has been falling for the last 4 weeks relative to plan may help you decide that there should be a midwinter sale on desks. On the other hand, even if sales are slow this month relative to last month, if sales have been consistently slower this month for the past 3 years, it might indicate that it's some sort of

	Jan		Feb		Mar		Quarter 1	
	actuals	variance	actuals	variance	actuals	variance	actuals	variance
skin care	4,156	1.01	4,572	1.01	5,034	1.01	3,846	1.01
soap	2,517	1.00	2,769	1.00	3,051	1.00	8,391	1.00
rose water soap	1,342	0.99	1,476	0.99	1,629	0.99	4,472	0.99
olive oil soap	1,175	1.02	1,293	1.02	1,427	1.02	3,919	1.02
lotion	1,639	1.03	1,803	1.03	1,988	1.03	5,455	1.03
hypoallerg. lotion	1,639	1.03	1,803	1.03	1,988	1.03	5,455	1.03
furniture	4,953	1.06	5,448	1.06	5,998	1.06	16,484	1.06
office	3,796	1.09	4,176	1.09	4,598	1.09	12,625	1.09
bookshelves	1,501	0.99	1,651	0.99	1,821	0.99	4,998	0.99
dividers	2,295	1.16	2,525	1.16	2,782	1.16	7,626	1.16
home	1,157	0.99	1,273	0.99	1,405	0.99	3,860	0.99
mattresses	1,157	0.99	1,273	0.99	1,405	0.99	3,860	0.99
All products	9,109	1.04	10,020	1.04	11,027	1.04	30,331	1.04

Figure 2.2   Product manager's quarterly sales report.

Sales All products	Jan actuals	variance	Feb actuals	variance	Mar actuals	variance	Quarter 1 actuals	variance
Northeast	4,369	1.02	4,806	1.02	5,291	1.02	14,551	1.02
Ridgewood	1,995	1.04	2,184	1.04	2,407	1.04	6,600	1.04
Newbury	1,824	1.01	2,006	1.01	2,212	1.01	6,067	1.01
Avon	560	0.97	616	0.97	683	0.97	1,884	0.97
Midwest	4,740	1.06	5,214	1.06	5,740	1.06	15,779	1.06
Francis	2,643	1.11	2,907	1.11	3,203	1.11	8,778	1.11
Nikki's	1,390	1.00	1,529	1.00	1,687	1.00	4,631	1.00
Roger's	707	1.00	778	1.00	860	1.00	2,370	1.00
All companies	9,109	1.04	10,020	1.04	11,027	1.04	30,331	1.04

Figure 2.3   Regional manager's quarterly sales report.

as-yet-unaccounted-for seasonal variation, not indicative of a longer-term slowdown, and thus not cause for a sale. Regardless of how these views were generated, they are common to any decision-oriented analysis process.

Now let's consider the raw data from which these views were constructed. It is not as easy to define a common starting point as it is a common endpoint (unless we go all the way back to the original data-generating events). Different production techniques, notably SQL and spreadsheets, have such radically different logic that the source data will tend to be structured differently between them.

Imagine that all the data has been collected, refined, and now resides in a large base table. In addition, there may be some adjunct lookup tables. A star schema for this base data is shown in Figure 2.4.

This table schema is called a star schema because the central fact table is usually depicted as surrounded by each of the dimension tables that describe each dimension. In this example, the base sales data table is the fact table and each lookup table is a dimension table.

THE DIFFICULTY OF DEFINING A COMMON SOURCE DATA SET FOR SPREADSHEETS AND SQL

SQL, if thought of as a language for defining and manipulating relational tables, is supposedly application-neutral when it comes to structuring base data. Base data, in a relational sense, is supposed to be structured or normalized on the basis of its own internal relationships. This facilitates the database update operations that characterize transaction processing. But for many decision-oriented applications, SQL tables are intentionally denormalized (or physically optimized) to speed up queries.

When thinking through a problem with spreadsheets, the way that base data is structured (that is, the form of the data) has a great impact on what can be done with it. This will become even clearer as we get into the specific examples. It is important to bring this up now because it isn't possible to define a realistic starting point where the data has the same form for both spreadsheets and SQL. Rather, our common starting point will be defined in terms of the content of the data.

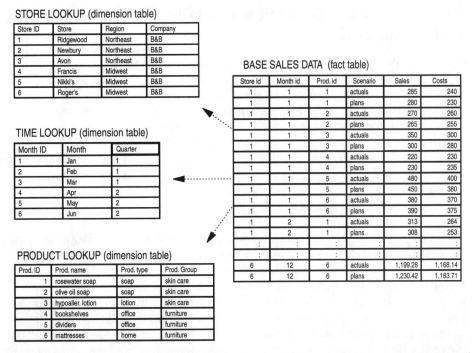

STORE LOOKUP (dimension table)

Store ID	Store	Region	Company
1	Ridgewood	Northeast	B&B
2	Newbury	Northeast	B&B
3	Avon	Northeast	B&B
4	Francis	Midwest	B&B
5	Nikki's	Midwest	B&B
6	Roger's	Midwest	B&B

TIME LOOKUP (dimension table)

Month ID	Month	Quarter
1	Jan	1
2	Feb	1
3	Mar	1
4	Apr	2
5	May	2
6	Jun	2

PRODUCT LOOKUP (dimension table)

Prod. ID	Prod. name	Prod. type	Prod. Group
1	rosewater soap	soap	skin care
2	olive oil soap	soap	skin care
3	hypoaller. lotion	lotion	skin care
4	bookshelves	office	furniture
5	dividers	office	furniture
6	mattresses	home	furniture

BASE SALES DATA (fact table)

Store id	Month id	Prod. id	Scenario	Sales	Costs
1	1	1	actuals	285	240
1	1	1	plans	280	230
1	1	2	actuals	270	260
1	1	2	plans	265	255
1	1	3	actuals	350	300
1	1	3	plans	300	280
1	1	4	actuals	220	230
1	1	4	plans	230	235
1	1	5	actuals	480	400
1	1	5	plans	450	380
1	1	6	actuals	380	370
1	1	6	plans	390	375
1	2	1	actuals	313	264
1	2	1	plans	308	253
:	:	:	:	:	:
:	:	:	:	:	:
6	12	6	actuals	1,199.28	1,168.14
6	12	6	plans	1,230.42	1,183.71

Figure 2.4 Common base table for sales data and lookup tables for stores, times, and products.

Notice how the stores, weeks, and products columns in the fact table in Figure 2.4 contain numeric values. Fact tables can grow to a huge number of rows. Because each value of the store, weeks, and product column is repeated many times, using a simple value in the base table and storing the full name only once in the dimension's lookup table saves space.

The lookup tables also contain hierarchy information relating each store, week, and product with its higher-level aggregations. For example, *store 1* in the base table of Figure 2.4 connects with the "Store Lookup" table where it has the name *Ridgewood* and rolls up to the *Northeast* region. *Product 2* in the base table connects with the "Product Lookup" table where it has the name *olive oil soap* and rolls up into the product type *soap* in the *skin care* products group. In practice, the lookup tables may also contain additional attribute information about the individual stores, times, and products (such as the square footage per store).

This base data content (that is, the collection of propositions or statements about the world), though not necessarily the base data form, would be the same regardless of whether you were going to build your analytical model with a spreadsheet, with an SQL database, or, as we will see later on, with a multidimensional tool. Consider it a common starting point.

Trying to Provide OLAP Functionality with a Spreadsheet

Now let's explore how we satisfy end-user information demands using spreadsheets.

The first problem you face with spreadsheets is deciding the form of the base data. Would you build one gigantic worksheet? And if so, how would you organize it? Would you nest weeks within stores within scenarios along the rows and then nest measures within products along the columns? Or, perhaps, would you nest measures within stores within products along the rows and nest weeks within scenarios along the columns? The possibilities are numerous. Also, the method you choose affects the ease of defining subsequent structures. For example, the auto-sum function in a spreadsheet will only work with contiguous cells, so cells that you want to sum need to occupy such contiguous ranges. You definitely have to think about how you are structuring your base data.

Probably, for manageability reasons, you would distribute the base data across a variety of worksheets. Here again, there are many options. You could create a separate worksheet for each product and/or each store and/or each week. Theoretically, any method will work. Of course, you will be faced with the unpleasant task of integrating data from many worksheets—perhaps hundreds or even thousands. For example, if you decide to break up the base data into groups of simple worksheets so that each worksheet can be managed more easily, and toward that end you decide that all base data worksheets will be organized with stores along the rows and measures along the columns, with a separate worksheet for each product, scenario, and week, and if you assume there are 100 products, 3 scenarios, and 13 measures (not an overly complex model), then you will have 3,900 separate base data worksheets. This is not a feasible solution. Spreadsheets are not geared for working with multidimensional data, OLAP's first logical requirement.

The next major problem you face is trying to aggregate the base data. Each of the worksheets will need to have the rollup information embedded for the purposes of defining aggregates, or you could define even more worksheets. In either event, there will be massive amounts of structural redundancy. For example, you will need to define city and regional aggregates for stores. Given that there are 3,900 worksheets, all organized by store, you will have to make 3,900 copies of a store-city-region hierarchy, one for each worksheet. Thus, spreadsheets do not provide support for hierarchies, OLAP's second logical requirement.

Hierarchies are not the only structures that are massively duplicated—so too are formulas. After all, spreadsheets work with cell-based formulas. Every aggregate cell needs to be defined with a formula. Not only do you have to repeat the store hierarchy information 3,900 times, but for each of those 3,900 times you would have to repeat, for example, the formula that sums *stores 1* through *3* into the Northeast region for each of 13 measures. So the formula that says "compute the value for the Northeast region as the sum of stores 1 through 3," which in a multidimensional model is defined once, would be defined 3,900 × 13 or 50,700 times across all your worksheets! Clearly, spreadsheets do not support dimensional calculations, OLAP's third logical requirement.

Defining hierarchies for the nonrepeated dimension values—in this example, *products, scenarios,* and *weeks*—is no less complicated. Creating product aggregates requires linking each underlying product worksheet to the appropriate aggregate worksheet on a cell-by-cell basis. With 100 stores and 13 measures per worksheet, this means creating 1,300 links for each aggregate worksheet. Can you think of anyone who really wants to do this?

Assuming that through some combination of perseverance and luck you have managed to create all the necessary aggregations, the question remains: How are you going to view the aggregates? As long as you are viewing information in the form in which you defined it for the purposes of aggregation, there is no problem. For example, if you defined your low-level spreadsheets with products nested within stores along the rows and variables nested within time along the columns, your aggregate view would look like that shown in Figure 2.5.

What if you wanted to compare how different regions performed for the same products? In other words, what if you wanted to see how toys sold in the Northeast as opposed to the Southeast? You would want to see a view, such as the one shown in Figure 2.6, where regions were nested inside of products along the rows. The view shows the same information as the one in Figure 2.5, but the arrangement is different.

Unfortunately, the spreadsheet offers no simple way to rearrange views. As any spreadsheet user knows all too well, you need to build the view from scratch. The fastest way (and the word "fast" is definitely misleading here) to build the new view is to create a new view template with just the margins filled in and then bring in the data through intersheet references. Because the organization of the two sheets is different, you will need one formulaic link per cell. Spreadsheets also have a problem with view reorganization. This is because spreadsheets cannot separate the structure of a model from the views of that model. This is OLAP's fourth logical requirement. For example, there is no way in a spreadsheet to capture the model's dimensional hierarchy information apart from creating worksheets that embody the dimensions in views.[8] As a

Sales
Actuals

		Quarter 1	Quarter 2	Quarter 3	Quarter 4
Northeast	skin care	7,191	9,556	12,857	17,889
	furniture	7,360	9,780	13,157	18,305
Midwest	skin care	6,655	8,843	11,905	16,565
	furniture	9,124	12,126	16,291	22,662

Figure 2.5 Aggregated spreadsheet view.

Sales
Actuals

		Quarter 1	Quarter 2	Quarter 3	Quarter 4
skin care	Northeast	7,191	9,556	12,857	17,889
	Midwest	6,655	8,843	11,905	16,565
furniture	Northeast	7,360	9,780	13,157	18,305
	Midwest	9,124	12,126	16,291	22,662

Figure 2.6 View reorganization.

USING SPREADSHEETS AS DISPLAY VEHICLES FOR MULTIDIMENSIONAL SYSTEMS

Before closing the book on spreadsheets, it is fair to say that spreadsheet and multidimensional products share the same display grid or matrix metaphor. This is why, as you will see in the next chapter, spreadsheets make such a fine vehicle for displaying views or slices of a multidimensional model. Because almost everybody is familiar with how to perform analysis with a spreadsheet, many vendors of multidimensional tools have intentionally used spreadsheet products as interfaces.

result, the same worksheets that represent your base data limit the aggregate views that can be created. And each view, such as the ones shown in Figures 2.5 and 2.6, represents a separate grid of numbers.

Although it is theoretically possible to create hierarchical multidimensional views with a traditional spreadsheet, it is practically infeasible. Add to this the fact that today's challenge is enterprise-wide and requires server and client resources combined across a network, and you can see why RAM-based spreadsheets can't create multi-user, multidimensional information systems.

Trying to Provide OLAP Functionality with SQL

As we have seen, it is not so easy to deliver OLAP-style functionality with a spreadsheet. Let's take a look at doing it with SQL. After all, SQL is a database language based on structured English. It is supposed to be powerful and intuitive. Look again at Figure 2.4. These are the base tables for our example model. Since it is straightforward in SQL to create dimension tables and star schemas, SQL—unlike spreadsheets—does support multiple dimensions.

If SQL were being used to perform the aggregations, it would create one aggregate table for each unique combination of aggregation levels. With four levels for time, three for stores, and three for products, there are 36 unique aggregation levels (including the base level), requiring 36 unique aggregate tables. The combinations are enumerated in Figure 2.7.

Each of the tables would have to be created with a separate CREATE TABLE statement. For example, the following SQL fragment would create the table for the quarter by region by product type aggregation level:

```
CREATE TABLE quarter-region-prodtype
( quarter (CHAR 16),
  region (CHAR 16),
  prodtype (CHAR 16),
  scenario (CHAR 16),
  sales (DOUBLE FLOAT),
  costs (DOUBLE FLOAT) )
```

	Time		Stores		Products
	Year		All		All
					Type
	Quarter		Region		Group
	Month		Store		Prod.

1	month.store.product	13	qtr.store.product	25	year.store.product
2	month.store.pr group	14	qtr.store.pr group	26	year.store.pr group
3	month.store.pr type	15	qtr.store.pr type	27	year.store.pr type
4	month.store.all prod	16	qtr.store.all prod	28	year.store.all prod
5	month.region.product	17	qtr.region.product	29	year.region.product
6	month.region.pr group	18	qtr.region.pr group	30	year.region.pr group
7	month.region.pr type	19	qtr.region.pr type	31	year.region.pr type
8	month.region.all prod	20	qtr.region.all prod	32	year.region.all prod
9	month.all strs.product	21	qtr.all strs.product	33	year.all strs.product
10	month.all strs.pr group	22	qtr.all strs.pr group	34	year.all strs.pr group
11	month.all strs.pr type	23	qtr.all strs.pr type	35	year.all strs.pr type
12	month.all strs.all prod	24	qtr.all strs.all prod	36	year.all strs.all prod

Figure 2.7 Thirty-six unique aggregation levels.

Then, to set up for populating the *quarter-region-prodtype* table, views that contain only the relevant aggregation levels would be created for each of the three lookup tables in Figure 2.4. For example, in order to create the *quarter-region-prodtype* table shown in the preceding SQL fragment, a view of the product lookup table would first be created that contained only product IDs and product types. Otherwise there would be a lot of unnecessary data replication because the columns of the original lookup tables that contained information about the columns that were not going to be used in the *quarter-city-prodtype* table, such as the product names and product groups columns in the *product-lookup* table, would needlessly be expanded upon joining with the base table. The SQL used to create these three lookup views is as follows:

```
CREATE VIEW quarter-name (quarter, month-id) AS
SELECT quarter, month-id
FROM time-lookup

CREATE VIEW region-level (region, store-id) AS
SELECT region, store-id
FROM store-lookup

CREATE VIEW product-type (prodtype, prod-id) AS
SELECT prodtype, prod-id
FROM product-lookup
```

Then each of the three lookup table views would be joined with the base table to create a modified view of the base table containing the aggregate identifier columns *month-id, region-id,* and *prodtype_id,* in addition to the base-level columns *region, month,* and *product.*

The modified base table view would be defined by the following SQL statement:

```
CREATE VIEW qrp-modified-base-table (month-id, quarter, store-id,
region, prod-id, prodtype, scenario, sales, costs)
AS
SELECT base-table.month-id, quarter, base-table.store-id, region, base-
table.prod-id, prodtype, scenario, sales, costs
FROM base-table JOIN time-lookup JOIN store-lookup JOIN prod-lookup
```

The actual aggregate table is then populated by the following SQL statement:

```
INSERT INTO quarter-region-prodtype
SELECT quarter, region, prodtype, scenario, SUM (sales),
SUM (costs)
FROM qrp-modified-base-table
GROUP BY quarter, region, prodtype, scenario
```

The aggregation functions for the variables would have to be defined within each of the aggregate tables. Repeating this process a total of 35 times will generate all the basic aggregate values, such as the sum of products across all stores. (We started off with the *month-store-product* level table, so 1 of the 36 was already there.) So, although SQL does support multiple dimensions, OLAP's first logical requirement, it does not offer strong support for hierarchies, OLAP's second logical requirement. SQL is flexible enough to define them, but there is no built-in support. The process as a whole is cumbersome. But how about generating some of the comparisons that were shown in Figures 2.2 and 2.3? Alas, this is not a trivial exercise.

Let's calculate the ratio between actuals and plans that is shown in the rightmost column of Figures 2.2 and 2.3. The problem is that the difference between actuals and plans for any measure is defined across the rows of the base table. For example, refer-ring back to the base table in Figure 2.4, to calculate the ratio of actuals to plan for the sale of *rose water soap* for the *Ridgewood* store in the first quarter (*store 1, time 1, prod-uct 1*), you would need to calculate the ratio between the sales figure in row 1 (the actu-als value) and the sales figure in row 2 (the planned value). SQL has no good way for defining interrow comparisons or inserting new rows that are defined in terms of arith-metic operations performed on other rows. SQL processing is column-oriented; there-fore, you need to somehow put plans and actuals in separate columns. SQL's lack of support for interrow calculations is a result of SQL's lack of support for dimensional calculations, OLAP's third functional requirement.

The way to place actuals and plans in separate columns is to create two views for each of the 36 already existing aggregate tables. One of the views will hold just the actual values, and the other will hold just the planned values. This is shown in the fol-lowing SQL statements. (For simplicity, the remaining examples pretend that the base data is joined with the appropriate names found in the lookup tables.)

```
/* create view of actuals */
CREATE VIEW actual-quarter-region-prodtype (quarter, region, prodtype,
act_sales, act_costs)
```

```
AS
SELECT quarter, region, prodtype, sales AS act_sales, costs AS act_costs
FROM quarter-region-prodtype
WHERE scenario = 'actuals'
/* create view of plans */
CREATE VIEW plan-quarter-region-prodtype (quarter, region, prodtype,
plan_sales, plan_costs)
AS
SELECT quarter, region, prodtype, sales AS plan_sales, costs AS
plan_costs
FROM quarter-region-prodtype
WHERE scenario = 'plans'
```

Figure 2.8 shows the view returned by selecting rows from the *actual-quarter-region-product type* view.

Notice that we haven't done anything useful yet in terms of calculating variances. All we've done is reorganize the data in order to get around SQL's limited interrow math by converting what had been row differences into column differences. To begin to use these columns, you now need to join them together in a query. The following SQL code will perform that join:

```
SELECT quarter, region, prodtype, act_sales, plan_sales
FROM actual-quarter-region-prodtype JOIN plan-quarter-region-prodtype
```

The join creates a table view that contains the *shared store, quarter,* and *product type* columns, and separate columns for actual sales and planned sales, as shown in Figure 2.9. This table is suited for the intercolumn arithmetic required for SQL computations.

Quarter	Region	Prod. Type	act_sales	act_costs
1	Northeast	soap	4,217	4,019
1	Northeast	lotion	2,974	2,474
1	Northeast	office	5,313	4,839
1	Northeast	home	2,047	1,918
2	Northeast	soap	5,603	5,339
2	Northeast	lotion	3,952	3,288
2	Northeast	office	7,060	6,431
2	Northeast	home	2,720	2,549
1	Midwest	soap	4,174	3,883
1	Midwest	lotion	2,481	2,266
1	Midwest	office	7,312	6,667
1	Midwest	home	1,812	1,342
2	Midwest	soap	5,546	5,159
2	Midwest	lotion	3,297	3,011
2	Midwest	office	9,718	8,860
2	Midwest	home	2,408	1,783

Figure 2.8 Table of actual values.

Quarter	Region	Prod. Type	act_sales	act_costs	plan_sales	plan_costs
1	Northeast	soap	4,217	4,019	4,316	3,995
1	Northeast	lotion	2,974	2,474	2,779	2,349
1	Northeast	office	5,313	4,839	5,081	4,634
1	Northeast	home	2,047	1,918	2,117	1,961
2	Northeast	soap	5,603	5,339	5,735	5,308
2	Northeast	lotion	3,952	3,288	3,693	3,121
2	Northeast	office	7,060	6,431	6,752	6,158
2	Northeast	home	2,720	2,549	2,813	2,606
1	Midwest	soap	4,174	3,883	4,068	3,777
1	Midwest	lotion	2,481	2,266	2,498	2,266
1	Midwest	office	7,312	6,667	6,551	5,948
1	Midwest	home	1,812	1,342	1,769	1,322
2	Midwest	soap	5,546	5,159	5,405	5,018
2	Midwest	lotion	3,297	3,011	3,319	3,011
2	Midwest	office	9,718	8,860	8,706	7,905
2	Midwest	home	2,408	1,783	2,351	1,756

Figure 2.9   View of the joined tables containing a column for actual and planned sales and costs.

Quarter	Region	Prod. Type	act_sales	plan_sales	variance
1	Northeast	soap	4,217	4,316	0.98
1	Northeast	lotion	2,974	2,779	1.07
1	Northeast	office	5,313	5,081	1.05
1	Northeast	home	2,047	2,117	0.97
2	Northeast	soap	5,603	5,735	0.98
2	Northeast	lotion	3,952	3,693	1.07
2	Northeast	office	7,060	6,752	1.05
2	Northeast	home	2,720	2,813	0.97
1	Midwest	soap	4,174	4,068	1.03
1	Midwest	lotion	2,481	2,498	0.99
1	Midwest	office	7,312	6,551	1.12
1	Midwest	home	1,812	1,769	1.02
2	Midwest	soap	5,546	5,405	1.03
2	Midwest	lotion	3,297	3,319	0.99
2	Midwest	office	9,718	8,706	1.12
2	Midwest	home	2,408	2,351	1.02

Figure 2.10   End-user view of variance data.

Now that the columns are suitably arranged, we can divide values across columns in a straightforward way. For example, the following SQL view will generate the table shown in Figure 2.10.

```
CREATE VIEW var-quarter-region-prodtype (quarter, region, prodtype,
act_sales, plan_sales, variance)
AS
SELECT quarter, region, prodtype, act_sales, plan_sales, act_sales/plan_sales
AS variance
FROM actual-quarter-region-prodtype JOIN plan-quarter-region-prodtype
```

Repeating this process a total of 35 times will generate all the correct views from which to compute variances for all the aggregate levels in the model. To generate the data values for our reports, using only summary tables, we will need to join up to 8 or 12 of them together, as the reports contain quarters and months combined with products, product types, product groups, and all products, or stores, regions, and the entire chain of stores.

Note how the months, products, and stores are all displayed along the rows. This is not how the information was displayed in Figures 2.2 and 2.3. In those figures, the months were displayed in a natural way across columns. It is common and useful to be able to organize data across rows and columns. It is done all the time with spreadsheets and in presentations. What about with SQL? How would you rearrange the view to show months along the columns? Basically, *SQL has no way to transpose rows and columns.* You can write a special-purpose view to transpose a particular column on a table whose values for that row are known to you, but it will be tricky to code, and it will require recoding if the values in the column change. Thus, SQL is also weak in its separation of data structure and representation, OLAP's fourth logical requirement.

You can see that SQL has no natural way to define comparative functions or provide flexible view reorganizations that involve the transposing of rows and columns. Something as simple as the ratio of planned sales to actual sales, which can be defined in a minute or two with a typical spreadsheet by copying a formula across a new variance column or, as you'll see in the next chapter, even more quickly with a multidimensional tool, is undefinable without going through a whole sequence of complicated maneuvers like the ones we just went through in this section. Ralph Kimball put this well when he said that a freshman in business needs a Ph.D. in SQL.[9]

SQL has other analytical limitations as well. Common analytical functions such as cumulative averages and totals, subtotals as found in typical spreadsheets, and rankings of data are not supported in standard SQL, though vendors have implemented extensions to support them. The topic has received some interest from notable relational experts.[10] Convenient expression of multidimensional aggregation, including partial aggregations across multiple dimensions at once, has also received attention.[11] The latest enhancements to SQL have taken steps to provide these capabilities.

One fundamental source of complication for SQL in performing analytical operations is its weakness at interrow computations, as shown previously. The SQL-99 standard, as implemented by vendors, supports user-defined (DBA-defined) stored functions that can be coded in procedural logic, thereby overcoming many of the current shortcomings. However, while any application can be created in a simple procedural language, the point is not *if* something can be done, but *how difficult* it is to do it. To code an interrow ratio function in a SQL-99 stored function would be akin to programming it in COBOL. Adding intrinsic row functions to SQL would make it extremely different from the SQL of today.

The organization of definitions in a SQL database is another limitation of SQL that affects even the proposed extensions for handling analytical functions and user-defined functions. All views (stored queries) and stored functions (in the SQL-3 standard)[12] would be organized by database schema, just as tables and indexes are. They are placed in a flat list structure, just like any one table. The structures that they would be called on to define and compute, however, would be hierarchical and multidimensional. The disparity of structure between the analytical elements and the operations that define them will cause them to be difficult to manage. (Even though a spreadsheet function does not have the general expressive power of a SQL query, you at least know where to go in a spreadsheet to view or modify a formula for a particular cell.) If you altered the definitional structure of a SQL database to give its catalog the same hierarchical and dimensional structure as the analytical information stored in its data tables, you would have gone a long way to metamorphose SQL into a multidimensional language.

Instead of using complicated procedures to contort SQL into providing analysis-based decision-oriented information, it is also possible to issue multiple simple SQL commands and perform the analytical functions on the client. The problem with this strategy is that the amount of data that gets returned is frequently too large for the client and overloads either the client or the network or both. For example, what if you worked for a large retail organization and you wanted to see your top 20 products in terms of cumulative sales? If you had 500 stores and weekly sales totals for 50,000 products, and you were 20 weeks into the year, you would have to send 500 million numbers across the network (dubious) to your desktop (highly dubious) to calculate 20 numbers. Rankings are an important class of comparative function. When large amounts of data are involved, it is not the kind of operation to be performed on the desktop.

Summary

Table 2.1 roughly summarizes the degree of support provided by spreadsheets and SQL databases as suggested by the examples in this chapter and from structured comparisons between spreadsheets and OLAP tools and from the publicly documented efforts to provide even basic OLAP functionality through extensions to SQL. This table also shows what one would like to see in an OLAP-supporting product for the four core logical requirements for OLAP. The numbers range from 1 to 5 with 5 being the highest. As you've seen in this chapter and can see here in summary, neither spreadsheets nor SQL databases provide enough support for OLAP's core logical requirements.

It is normal to want to be able to phrase analytical queries in a natural or near-natural way. If you want to see product totals and subtotals, this year/last year

Table 2.1   Comparison of Support for Core Logical OLAP Requirements

	SPREADSHEETS	SQL DATABASES	OLAP REQUIREMENTS
Multiple dimensions	1	5	4/5
Hierarchies	1	3	4/5
Dimensional calculations	1	2	4/5
Separation of structure and representation	1	3	4/5

comparisons, moving 52-week averages, top-selling products, changes in market share between this year and last year, or percent changes in margins, that's all you should have to ask for. Spreadsheets let you phrase analytical queries in a near-natural way but only for small amounts of data that can be organized in a two-dimensional grid. SQL lets you phrase simple queries based on columns of data in a near-natural way as long as they do not involve any analysis or interrow comparisons. Neither approach lets you easily phrase analytical queries against large amounts of complexly organized data.

Regardless of whether horizontally specialized OLAP vendors continue to find markets beyond the reaches of expanding relational database vendors, OLAP will continue to thrive as a data definition and manipulation technology independent of how and where it is physically instantiated.

Thinking Clearly
in *N* Dimensions

The notion of a *hypercube*, or a cube with more than three dimensions, is fundamental to an understanding of multidimensional software that uses hypercubes in the same way spreadsheets use worksheets and databases use tables. All browsing, reporting, and analysis are done in terms of hypercubes.

Hypercubes are typically introduced following a description of lower-dimensional surfaces such as lines, planes, and cubes. The reader is then left to visualize, by analogy, a higher-dimensional cube.[1] However, this is not the best approach because the path to understanding hypercubes does not pass through the length, width, and height of a physical cube.

This chapter shows you how to think clearly about *N*-dimensional data sets or things in the world by incrementally building on something understood by everyone: a two-dimensional row-by-column arrangement of data. By the end of this chapter, you will have a solid understanding of what hypercubes are and what they are not, and you will be ready to assimilate the information found in this book on OLAP solutions or multidimensional information systems.

Lower-Dimensional Data Sets

Let us start with a typical example of two-dimensional data. Anything that you track, whether it is hours per employee, costs per department, balance per customer, or complaints per store, can be arranged in a two-dimensional format.

Month	Sales	Direct Costs	Indirect Costs	Total Costs	Margin
January	790	480	110	590	200
February	850	520	130	650	200
March	900	530	140	670	230
April	910	590	150	740	170
May	860	600	120	720	140
June	830	490	100	590	240
July	880	500	110	610	270
August	900	620	130	750	150
September	790	300	90	390	400
October	820	540	100	640	180
November	840	570	150	720	120
December	810	600	120	720	90
Total	10,180	6,340	1,450	7,790	2,390

Figure 3.1 Sales, costs, and margin by month.

Figure 3.1 shows five columns of sales and cost data organized by month in a two-dimensional grid. This grid could easily be created in any spreadsheet program and displayed on any computer screen. Months are arranged down the rows. The total for all months is displayed on the bottom row. The grid has five columns: one for each sales or cost variable. The data set may be said to have two dimensions: a row-arranged month dimension and a column-arranged variables dimension. (In fact, there are a variety of ways of characterizing the dimensionality of a data set, which will be treated in depth beginning in Chapter 4. For now, it is sufficient to think in terms of 1-N locator or identifier or key dimensions with 1-N variables collected in a single variables dimension.)

Individually, sales, costs, and margins represent variables. Variables are the items we are tracking. If someone was to ask you the question, "What are you measuring or tracking?" you would respond, "Sales, costs, and margins." Each member or element of the variables dimension is a variable.

In contrast, the months represent how we are organizing the data. We are not tracking months. We are using months to individuate sales and cost values. If someone was to ask you the question, "From where are you getting your data?" or "How often are you making measurements?" you would respond, "We are tracking sales on a monthly basis." Months are a type of key, identifier, or locator dimension. Our simple data example has two dimensions: one locator dimension and one variables dimension.

What happens when we add a third dimension called products? It seems easy enough to visualize. After all, it is just a cube. Figure 3.2 shows a three-dimensional cube that represents products, months, and variables. But where is this cube that we are showing? Is it on the computer screen? Is it out there in the world? Is it in your mind? Where is it?

As Magritte might have said, the cube cannot be a part of the computer screen any more than an apple can be a part of a piece of paper (see Figure 3.3). The computer screen, like a sheet of paper, has only two (usable) physical dimensions. We can create

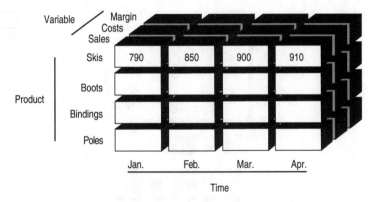

Figure 3.2 Three-dimensional cube: products, months, and variables.

Figure 3.3 This is not an apple.

a two-dimensional representation of a three-dimensional cube on a computer screen. It is done all the time. But we cannot create a three-dimensional representation of anything as part of a two-dimensional surface.

This raises the first of our dimension hurdles: *The actual two-dimensional screen display of data is separate from the metaphors we use to visualize that data.* The cube we visualized in Figure 3.2 is just that, a visual metaphor. It could have even been a real cube. But it is not the same as the two-dimensional display shown in Figure 3.4. Now why is this an important point? It is important because there are natural limits to what can be done with a two-dimensional computer screen. This limitation made software developers think long and hard about the optimal way of representing information with more than two dimensions on a flat computer screen for the purposes of viewing and manipulation.

Figure 3.5 shows a spreadsheet-like display of the three-dimensional data set visualized in Figure 3.2. Most of the display looks the same as for the two-dimensional

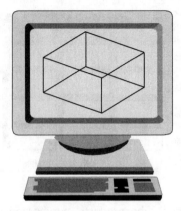

Figure 3.4   Flat-screen display of a cube.

page

| Product: shoes |

columns

| Variables: all |

	Sales	Direct Costs	Indirect Costs	Total Costs	Margin
January	520	320	110	430	90
February	400	250	130	380	20
March	430	300	120	420	10
April	490	320	150	470	20
May	520	310	180	490	30
June	390	230	150	380	10
July	470	290	160	450	20
August	500	360	150	510	-10
September	450	290	140	430	20
October	480	290	140	430	50
November	510	310	150	460	50
December	550	330	160	490	60

rows

| Time: months |

Figure 3.5   Typical three-dimensional display.

display shown in Figure 3.1. It is essentially a two-dimensional grid except, in the upper-left portion of the display, there is an icon called *page* with the label *Product: Shoes*. The *page* icon stands for a third, so-called page dimension.

The three-dimensional data set consisting of variables, time, and products is displayed on a computer screen in terms of the three display dimensions: *row, column,* and *page*. The row and column display dimensions correspond to the row and column

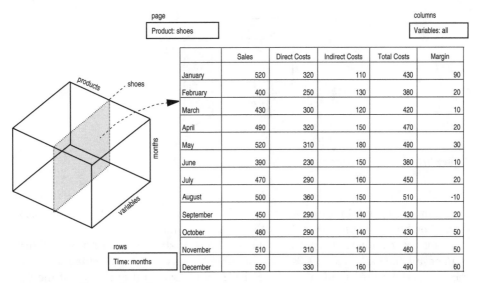

	Sales	Direct Costs	Indirect Costs	Total Costs	Margin
January	520	320	110	430	90
February	400	250	130	380	20
March	430	300	120	420	10
April	490	320	150	470	20
May	520	310	180	490	30
June	390	230	150	380	10
July	470	290	160	450	20
August	500	360	150	510	-10
September	450	290	140	430	20
October	480	290	140	430	50
November	510	310	150	460	50
December	550	330	160	490	60

Figure 3.6   Slice of the cube.

screen dimensions. We can see as many rows and columns of data as the screen's rows and columns permit. Given a large enough screen, we could see the whole of any two-dimensional data set. In contrast, the page dimension doesn't correspond to anything that is actually on the screen. No matter how big the screen, all that is seen is an indicator saying which page is currently visible: shoes, socks, shirts, and so on. Still, it is easy to visualize the relationship between the data shown on the screen and the whole of the data set stored in the computer. All you have to do is imagine a three-dimensional data cube and a screen display showing one slice of that cube, as illustrated in Figure 3.6.

Beyond Three Dimensions

Suppose that you are tracking different measures of different products by month for a chain of stores. You've now got a four-dimensional data set. What kind of visual metaphor should you use to represent the whole? How should the relevant information be organized on the screen? Trying to use a cube as the basis for a four- or higher-dimensional visualization can get very messy quickly. Figure 3.7 shows a picture of a *tesseract*, the technical name for a four-dimensional cube. It looks way too complicated —an indication that something is wrong. The cube metaphor shown in Figure 3.2 was easy to understand. Likewise, adding the notion of stores to the data set in Figure 3.1 didn't seem to add that much more additional complexity. So why, when we add just one more factor to the data set, does the complexity of its visualization skyrocket? And what would we do to represent a five- or six-dimensional data set? Another way of asking the question is, Why does the cube metaphor work so well for data of up to

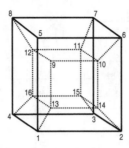

Figure 3.7 View of a tesseract.

three dimensions but break down as we add a fourth? This brings us to the second dimension hurdle: *the difference between logical and physical dimensions.*

To answer that question, consider what the great Austrian thinker Ludwig Wittgenstein postulated back in the 1920s.[2] For something to serve as a representation of something else, the representation needs to share some structural attributes of the thing represented. Thus, there needs to be some aspect of the cube representation that mirrors some aspect the data-generating events that explains why the cube metaphor works for lower dimensional data sets. There also has to be some structural aspect of the cube that is not mirrored by the data-generating events that explains why the cube metaphor breaks down for data sets of more than three dimensions.

Figure 3.8 is a simple sketch of an event that could have generated the data shown in Figure 3.6. It is a picture of a retailer selling a product to a customer in exchange for money and buying supplies from a supplier. It certainly doesn't look like a cube. Figure 3.9 displays a series of these pictures: one for each month and their correspondence with a cube arrangement of data. Yet there is something about the cube that makes it an intuitive representation of the event. Let's explore this further.

One attribute of any cube is that all its dimensions are coexistent at every point. This is illustrated in Figure 3.10, which shows how any point (x_n, y_n, z_n) in three-dimensional space is identified by its x, y, and z value. In terms of data representation, this means, for example, that one point in the cube might represent the fact that $1,000 worth of shoes was sold in February. Each fact in the cube is identified by one value from each

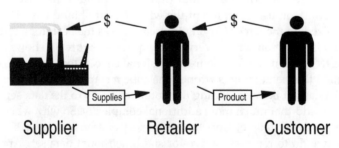

Figure 3.8 Retailer-centric view of the world.

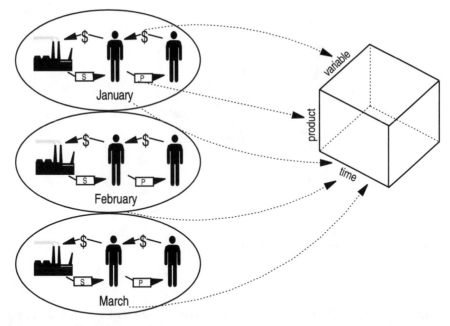

Figure 3.9 Events that could generate the data in Figure 3.6.

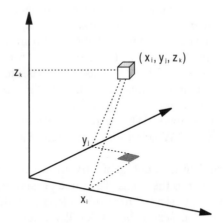

Figure 3.10 Points are identified by their *x, y,* and *z* values.

dimension. Going back to the event image in Figure 3.8, you can see that every business dimension of the event is also coexistent. For each sales transaction, one can always identify a product sold, a dollar amount, and a time. Thus, the attribute "coexistent dimensions" is shared by the cube and the data-generating events.

Another attribute of any cube is that each of its coexistent dimensions is independent of all the others. As illustrated in Figure 3.11, change can occur independently in

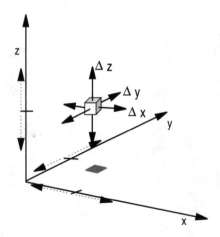

Figure 3.11 Change can occur by any value of any dimension.

any dimension. From the point 111, one can travel to the point 112, 121, 211, and so forth. In terms of the data generating event, this means, for example, that any product could be sold at any time. And at any time, any product could be sold. (Actually, the condition of independence may or may not hold for the variables, but it is safe to ignore that now. For a full treatment of variables and formulas, see Chapter 7 and for a discussion of interdependent dimensions, please see Chapter 20.) Going back to the event image in Figure 3.8, you can imagine that every business dimension is independent of every other. From shoe sales in February, you can navigate to shoe sales in March or sock sales in February. That's because products, stores, time, and variables are independent of one another. Thus, the attribute "independent dimensions" is shared by the cube and the data-generating events.

So where do things break down? What structural attribute of the cube is not shared by the data-generating events? What's another attribute of all cubes? Think about it for a minute.

What about angularity? In textbook geometry, the x axis is perpendicular to the y axis, which is perpendicular to the z axis. The three perpendicular angle-related axes translate perfectly into the physical dimensions of length, width, and height. Physical geometry is practical and has served humankind well for over two millennia. (Incidentally, the Greeks inherited their geometry from the Egyptians, who used it for surveying.)

Now, what does angle have to do with the relationship between variables, stores, time, and products? *Does it make any sense to say that stores are perpendicular to products or that customers are perpendicular to time?* It makes no sense at all. (It does make sense to say that the display of stores on the computer screen is perpendicular to the display of products, but that is a totally different topic.) Although there is nothing wrong with using an angle-based cube for representing events, the angle-based cube cannot represent more than three dimensions because there are only three angle-based independent dimensions to our physical space.

The angle-based definition of cube dimension relationships is not necessary for a useful representation of the event. A useful representation requires coexistent and independent dimensions regardless of how that coexistence and independence are defined. These two properties are logical properties, not physical properties. Any metaphor that provides a consistent definition of independent and coexistent dimensions will work.

Multidimensional Type Structures (MTSs)

Here we introduce a new metaphor for representing data, data-generating events, and, ultimately, OLAP meta data that is not based on angle-defined dimensions and that is capable of representing any number of event dimensions. If you want to give it a name you may call it a multidimensional type structure (MTS). An example of a simple representation in the new metaphor is shown in Figure 3.12 along the path between data-generating events and data cubes shown in Figure 3.9. Each dimension is represented by a line segment. Every member within a dimension is represented by a unit interval within the segment. As we are starting with a three-dimensional example, there are three line segments: one for time, one for products, and one for variables. Any union of one interval from each of the three line segments is connected to an element in the event and in the cube. For example, in Figure 3.12, the MTS highlights March shoe sales as does the cube. In the same way that one can move independently in each cube dimension, one can move independently in each MTS dimension, as shown in Figure 3.13.

In Figure 3.13, where there are 12 time periods, 10 products, and 5 variables, there are $12 \times 10 \times 5 = 600$ hypercube intersections, or potential data points. In this sense, an MTS is more descriptive than a physical cube. However, an MTS doesn't show actual data points, just possible combinations of dimension members. So here it is marginally less descriptive than a cube that can at least allude to (though it cannot actually

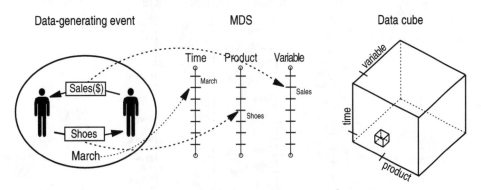

Figure 3.12   MTSs are a way of representing events.

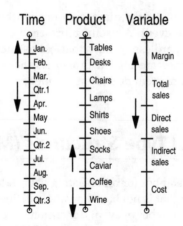

Figure 3.13 You can move independently in each MTS dimension.

show) all data points. Then again, the purpose of a visual metaphor is to give a useful representation of the structure of a model. It is the job of the display to show the data.

Adding a Fourth Dimension

Using an MTS, it is easy to add a fourth dimension to the model. Remember when we tried to add a store dimension to the cube? That's when things started to break down. But not with an MTS. It's a cinch. Just add a fourth line segment called *stores*, as shown in Figure 3.14. The MTS is not a pictorial representation of the data-generating event, but then neither was the cube. The MTS shows the number of data points extracted from the event and their logical organization. It shows all the dimensions one can browse in and how far one can go in any dimension. As you will see later in this book, an MTS can also show information about hierarchies and data flows within and

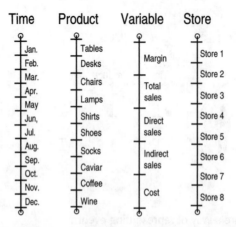

Figure 3.14 The fourth dimension may be represented by a fourth line segment.

between hypercubes. It shows more structural information than a cube, and it can show it for an arbitrary number of dimensions. If you want a more realistic picture of the event, you should consider using some enhanced version of the simple images I used in Figure 3.12 or perhaps using a camera. If you want a useful computer screen representation of the data in numeric form, you need to use some grid-like display form like the three-dimensional spreadsheet metaphor shown in Figure 3.6.

Representing Hypercubes on a Computer Screen

We've figured out why the physical cube metaphor breaks down, and we've introduced a logical visualization principle for representing the structure of *N*-dimensional data sets. We still need to see them on the computer screen. This brings us to our final dimension hurdle: *mapping multiple logical dimensions onto two physical (screen) dimensions*. Look again at the image of a three-dimensional grid-style interface, as shown in Figure 3.5. How are we going to represent four or more logical dimensions given our three display dimensions of row, column, and page? The answer is we combine multiple logical dimensions within the same display dimension. Let's examine this more closely.

Look at Figure 3.15. It shows a two-dimensional arrangement of products by variables with the name of each intersection explicitly written. Notice how each point or intersection in the two-dimensional grid is formed from one member of each dimension. Also notice how each member of each dimension combines with each member of the other dimension. In this simple example two products and three variables make a total of six product variable combinations.

Mapping the two dimensions into one dimension means creating a one-dimensional version of the two-dimensionally arranged intersections. Although any one-dimensional arrangement will work, the typical method is to nest one dimension within the other. For example, Figure 3.16 shows how to create a one-dimensional list of variables nested within products from the two-dimensional grid originally shown in Figure 3.15. Notice how the list scrolls through every member of the variables dimension for each product as it is scrolling through products. You can think of it as a generic loop:

```
For products = 1 to N

    For variables = 1 to N
```

	sales	cost	margin
shoes	shoe sales	shoe cost	shoe margin
socks	sock sales	sock cost	sock margin

Figure 3.15 Two-dimensional arrangement.

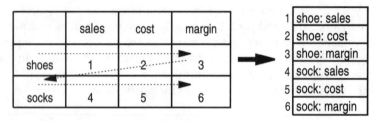

Figure 3.16   Nesting variables within products.

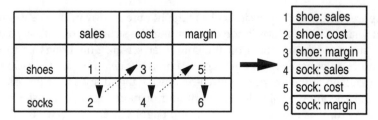

Figure 3.17   Nesting products within variables.

```
        End variables

    End products
```

This is what it means for variables to be nested within products. In contrast, Figure 3.17 shows how to create a one-dimensional list of products nested within variables

THE EFFECTS OF COMBINING DIMENSIONS

Two main things change as a result of combining dimensions: axis lengths and neighborhoods. One main thing does not change: truth criteria.

The first thing that changes is the shape of the viewable data. As you can see from Figures 3.16 and 3.17, the length of the one-dimensional list is equal to the product of the lengths of each of the two dimensions in the two-dimensional arrangement. When the lengths are as small as they are in these examples, the impact is negligible, but when the axis lengths are in the hundreds or thousands, it can make a real difference. For example, browsing through a two-dimensional grid of 100 by 100, which may fit all at once on your screen, is considerably easier than browsing through a list of 10,000 rows, which most certainly will require substantial scrolling. This doesn't mean you shouldn't combine dimensions, but you should be aware of how you are changing the shape of the data by combining them.

The second thing that changes as a result of combining dimensions is the set of neighbors surrounding any point. In two dimensions, each two-dimensional point has four immediate neighbors, when the two dimensions are combined; each point in a one-dimensional list has just two immediate neighbors. This is shown in Figure 3.18. Notice how in the top panel, where the data is arranged in two dimensions, the sales value for Newbury in February has four neighboring cells. Compare this with the lower panel, which shows the exact same data, only in one dimension. Here, the sales value for Newbury in February has only two neighbors. The changing of neighbors can affect analyses and graphical visualizations because they make use of information about neighbors. (For a discussion of multidimensional visualization, see Chapter 9.)

One important thing does not change during the process. No matter how dimensions are combined, and no matter how the data grids are arranged, they make the same statements, claims, or propositions about the world whose truth or falsehood are a function of the same criteria. (For a discussion of truth conditions, see Chapter 6.)

(Note the difference in adjacency)

	Jan	Feb	Mar
Ridgewood	555	611	677
Newbury	490	539	598
Avon	220	242	271

Jan	Ridgewood	555
	Newbury	490
	Avon	220
Feb	Ridgewood	611
	Newbury	539
	Avon	242
Mar	Ridgewood	677
	Newbury	598
	Avon	271

Note:

A [ ] highlights the adjacent cells

Figure 3.18   Two different dimensional structurings of the same data set.

from the same two-dimensional grid. Notice how in both figures, the number of elements is the same for the one- as for the two-dimensional arrangement. No data is lost by combining dimensions. (Actually, some information is lost as you will see later.) Any number of dimensions can be combined.

Now that you have learned how to combine dimensions, let us more fully demonstrate the process by adding two dimensions to our previous four-dimensional example. Figure 3.19 shows a six-dimensional data set consisting of products, times, stores, customers, variables, and scenarios. Figure 3.20 shows each dimension of Figure 3.19

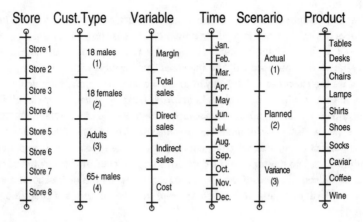

Figure 3.19   Six-dimensional MTS.

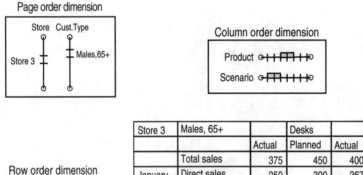

Store 3	Males, 65+		Desks		Lamps	
		Actual	Planned	Actual	Planned
	Total sales	375	450	400	480
January	Direct sales	250	300	267	320
	Indirect sales	125	150	133	160
	Total sales	500	600	425	510
February	Direct sales	333	400	283	540
	Indirect sales	167	200	142	170
	Total sales	525	630	375	450
March	Direct sales	350	420	250	300
	Indirect sales	175	210	125	150

▯ = highlights the values of the dimensions displayed.

Figure 3.20   Six-dimensional data display.

connected to a row, column, or page role of a three-dimensional grid display. Notice how multiple dimensions are combined in the row, column, and page dimensions of the grid display. The same visual display that works for three dimensions can easily be extended to work with *N* dimensions. From here on, we will call this type of display a

Page order dimension

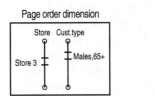

Column order dimension

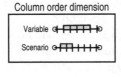

Row order dimension

Store 3	Males,65+	Direct sales		Indirect sales		Total sales	
		Actual	Planned	Actual	Planned	Actual	Planned
January	Desks	250	300	125	150	375	450
	Lamps	267	320	133	160	400	480
February	Desks	333	400	167	200	500	600
	Lamps	283	340	142	170	425	510
March	Desks	350	420	175	210	525	630
	Lamps	250	300	125	150	375	450

▯ = highlights the values of the dimensions displayed.

Figure 3.21   Different six-dimensional data display of the same MTS.

Page order dimension

Column order dimension

Row order dimension

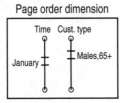

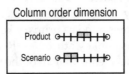

January	Males, 65+	Desks		Lamps	
		Actual	Planned	Actual	Planned
	Total sales	400	550	430	500
Store 1	Direct sales	250	315	242	290
	Indirect sales	180	200	150	180
	Total sales	500	600	425	500
Store 2	Direct sales	340	390	273	335
	Indirect sales	167	200	145	165
	Total sales	375	450	400	480
Store 3	Direct sales	250	300	267	320
	Indirect sales	125	150	133	160

▯ = highlights the values of the dimensions displayed.

Figure 3.22   Yet a third six-dimensional data display of the same MTS.

multidimensional grid display. Figures 3.21 and 3.22 show two different ways that the same six model dimensions can be mapped onto row, column, and page axes.

If you look at Figures 3.20 through 3.22, you will notice that there is always exactly one member represented from each model dimension shown on pages of the screen. There is no way around this fact. Try getting around it. You will see that if you attempt to show more than one member from a dimension represented as a page, you will need to choose how to arrange the two or more members, and the only choices you have (in a flat static screen display) are across the rows or across the columns. Of course, once the members of a dimension are displayed across the rows or columns, they are no longer being displayed on a page.

Multidimensional grids are so flexible that they can mimic any kind of regular table. After all, a table is just a special case of a grid where all or most of the dimensions are represented as columns. The table shown in Figure 3.23 can be thought of as a spreadsheet-like grid where five dimensions are represented as column headings whose members are the column values, and one dimension—in this case, the variables dimension—has its members represented as column headings. Tables, such as the one shown in Figure 3.23, where one of the dimensions has its members represented as column headings and where the rest of the dimensions have their members represented as row values, are frequently (and in this book will be) called *type one tables*.[3] Using this same nomenclature, Figure 3.24, which is discussed next, would be called a *type zero table* because it has zero dimensions whose members are represented as column headings.

Notice how every instance of a sales variable in the type one table is associated with an instance from every dimensional attribute. The key, locator, or identifier dimensions of the situation are represented as primary keys in the table. The variables of the situation are represented as nonkey attributes. Relationally speaking, this grid is a table in third normal form. This means that all of the nonkey attributes—in this case, sales and the number of units sold—apply to or are uniquely identified by all of the primary or dimension keys. There are no sales variables that are not associated with a product,

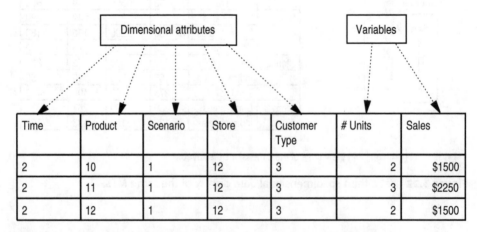

Time	Product	Scenario	Store	Customer Type	# Units	Sales
2	10	1	12	3	2	$1500
2	11	1	12	3	3	$2250
2	12	1	12	3	2	$1500

Figure 3.23   Electronic capture of point-of-sale data in a type one table.

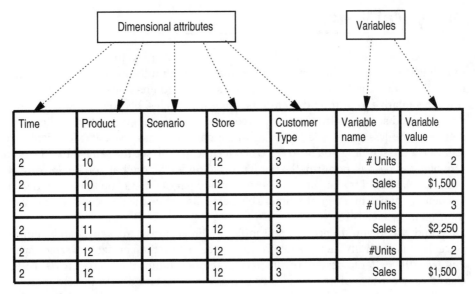

Time	Product	Scenario	Store	Customer Type	Variable name	Variable value
2	10	1	12	3	# Units	2
2	10	1	12	3	Sales	$1,500
2	11	1	12	3	# Units	3
2	11	1	12	3	Sales	$2,250
2	12	1	12	3	#Units	2
2	12	1	12	3	Sales	$1,500

Figure 3.24　Type zero table.

store, scenario, customer type, and time. For every unique dimensional combination, one and only one instance of a variable exists.

Finally, look at Figure 3.24, which shows a different table-like representation of the same data found in Figure 3.23. Although both table forms allocate one column per dimension, notice how in Figure 3.24 the individual variable names, sales and units, are treated as the values of a column called *variables.* Also notice the addition of a *value* column whose row entries are the data values that, in the preceding table, were situated in each of the variables columns. (For an in-depth discussion of the value dimension and how it relates to the dimensionality of a multidimensional model, see Chapter 4.)

As a practical matter, the table in Figure 3.23 will be shorter in rows and wider in columns than the table in Figure 3.24. The long and narrow table in Figure 3.24 will use more space for storing keys because it has an extra key column. It will also use less space storing missing data values.

The ability to easily change views of the same data by reconfiguring how dimensions are displayed is one of the great end-user navigational benefits of multidimensional systems. It is due to the separation of data structure, as represented in the MTS, from data display, as represented in the multidimensional grid. The actual method will be different from tool to tool, but the essence is the same. For example, the commands or actions to create Figure 3.20 are as follows:

1. Show variables nested within months along the rows of the screen.

2. Show scenarios nested within products along the columns of the screen.

3. Show stores and customer type along the pages of the screen.

Analytical Views

While there is no such thing as a right or wrong grid display, there are some rules of thumb that you should keep in mind when analyzing multidimensional data in grid form. First, nesting dimensions across rows and columns consumes many screen resources relative to putting dimensions into screen pages. Because we still live in an age of limited screen realty, the more screen space is consumed displaying dimension members, the less space is left for displaying data. The less space left for displaying data, the more scrolling you need to do between screens to see the same data. The more scrolling you need to perform, the harder it is to understand what you are looking at.

First, you should try keeping dimensions along pages unless you know you need to see more than one member at a time. This helps maximize the degree to which everything on the screen is relevant.

Second, when you do need to nest multiple dimensions across rows and columns, since there is generally more usable vertical screen space than horizontal screen space, it is generally better to nest more dimensions across columns than across rows. Thus, a classic view consists of one dimension across the rows and one to three dimensions nested in the columns with all other dimensions kept as pages, as shown in Figure 3.25. Compare this with the view in Figure 3.26, where four dimensions are nested in the rows, one dimension is shown along the rows, and no dimensions are left in the pages.

Third, before you decide how to display information on the screen, ask yourself "What do I want to look at?" or "What am I trying to compare?" For example, you may want to look at and compare actual costs across stores and time for some product and

Store.Paris

| | Actual | | | | Plan | | | |
| | Toys | | Clothes | | Toys | | Clothes | |
	Sales	Costs	Sales	Costs	Sales	Costs	Sales	Costs
Q1	320	200	825	750	525	603	750	629
Q2	225	220	390	250	554	600	365	400
Q3	700	600	425	630	653	725	720	530
Q4	880	850	875	700	893	875	890	889

Figure 3.25   Classic OLAP view.

				Q1	Q2	Q3
Actual	**Paris**	Toys	Sales	320	225	700
			Costs	200	220	600
		Clothes	Sales	825	390	425
			Costs	750	250	630
	NYC	Toys	Sales	500	310	880
			Costs	450	500	850
		Clothes	Sales	210	625	875
			Costs	225	600	700
Plan	**Paris**	Toys	Sales	525	554	653
			Costs	603	600	725
		Clothes	Sales	750	365	320
			Costs	629	400	530
	NYC	Toys	Sales	460	520	810
			Costs	325	610	875
		Clothes	Sales	655	725	890
			Costs	780	650	889

Figure 3.26   Inefficient OLAP view.

customer type. If this is the case, you should set your page dimensions to that product and customer type you are analyzing and organize your display to show stores and times for actual costs, as shown in Figure 3.27.

Now, what would you do if you were trying to compare the ratio between sales and advertising costs for low- and high-priced products across stores and times? You could try to see whether the returns on advertising for low- and high-priced products varied across stores or times. Perhaps it costs less to sell expensive products in high-income area stores, or perhaps there were better returns on advertising cheaper products during holiday time periods. How would you want to set up the screen to look at this? The complicating factor here is that what you are looking at—variables by product category—is itself a two-dimensional structure.

Page:

| product: shoes |
| variable: cost |
| scenario: actual |
| customer type: 2 |

	January	February	March	April
Store 1	1250	1700	1570	1140
Store 2	2000	1950	1290	1570
Store 3	1360	1580	1320	1440

Figure 3.27   Arranging data to compare costs across stores and time.

		December		January	
		High Price	Low Price	High Price	Low Price
Store 1	Sales (000)	450	200	340	280
	Costs	267	160	265	200
Store 2	Sales	402	400	350	450
	Costs	283	315	310	325
Store 3	Sales	250	460	200	500
	Costs	225	300	165	356

Figure 3.28   Two-dimensional comparison.

The way to show this type of information on the screen is to put one of the looked-at dimensions in the most nested position along one visible row or column axis and to put the other looked-at dimension across the other visible column or row axis, as shown in Figure 3.28. The more you think in terms of complicated multidimensional structures, such as the one shown in Figure 3.28, the more you may want to use graphical visualization techniques for displaying the information. (These techniques are discussed in Chapter 9.)

Although any combination of dimensions may be mapped to any combination of rows, columns, and pages, you will be most productive when you think about what you are trying to understand or learn before defining screen representations for your data.

Summary

In this chapter, you have seen why the cube is such a popular metaphor for representing multidimensional data and why the cube breaks down as a metaphor for data sets of more than three dimensions. Multidimensional type structures (MTS), which are based on logical rather than physical attributes, were introduced as a method of representing N-dimensional data sets and their associated properties. MTS can represent data of any dimensionality.

You also learned that the most common display for data in numeric form leverages a row-column-page metaphor. As the number of dimensions in an analytical data set typically exceeds three, multiple dimensions of information need to be combined onto each row, column, and page axis of a display device, thus making it possible to visualize and understand a multidimensional data set in terms of information presented on a flat computer screen.

Now that you have learned how to think clearly about *N*-dimensional data sets and how to display them on a two dimensional computer screen, it is time to start drilling into dimensional structures.

Core Technology

*Laws like the principle of sufficient reason, etc., are about
the net [of language] and not about what the net describes.*

LUDWIG WITTGENSTEIN

Introduction to the LC Model

The first edition of *OLAP Solutions* (Wiley 1997) included a software product called TM1. I used it in the application section of the book so that the reader could gain an understanding of both the conceptual and practical aspects of building Online Analytical Processing (OLAP) solutions. Even though the book was about OLAP—the fundamental technology—and not about the particular product TM1, the book did, all too often, get labeled a product book. Furthermore, one of the problems in the OLAP world with trying to provide a solid foundation for OLAP in general is that there hasn't been a generally accepted OLAP model. Every OLAP product has its own implicit model. So by using any product in this book, the book is invariably skewed to some degree in its application section toward that particular product. (Even the discussion of core technology may become skewed as that discussion needs to be consistent with the applications that follow.)

If you're going to include a product in a book to illustrate concepts, you should probably rely on either an easy-to-use, though obscure, product so as not to prejudice the market (which is what I did in the first edition), or an extremely popular one. I did consider using Microsoft's Analysis Services product with its MDX language for this book. However, with George Spofford we already wrote *Microsoft OLAP Solutions* (Wiley 1999), which details Microsoft's first version of its OLAP product, plus there are many more. George Spofford has also written an extremely thorough book on the MDX language, *MDX Solutions* (Wiley 2001). Additionally, as popular as Microsoft's product and language may become, owing in no small part to Microsoft's general market dominance, neither their product nor their language is ideal.

Thus, after much deliberation I decided for pedagogical purposes to use my own OLAP language and model called *Located Contents* (LC), in this book. Although I haven't done much to publicize it, most of the major vendors are aware of the LC model and a number of them are gradually incorporating its features. The LC model is a proper superset of every public OLAP product/model, which is to say that it can mimic any OLAP product/model simply by restricting itself. It is also fully grounded in math and logic, meaning, as described in the following sections, that the model provides for closure and a defensible definition of a well-formed formula. The LC model contains a complete language and through it you, the reader, will learn about hierarchies, multicubes, dimensional calculations, and all the fun stuff associated with solid OLAP analyses. Perhaps most important of all, you can reason in and with the LC language so when we get to the application chapters, you can think through the issues in LC and learn how to efficiently solve multidimensional modeling and analysis problems. The techniques you learn in LC will be applicable to any tool you may ultimately deploy and will enable you to understand the strengths and limitations of any tool(s) you use against a more general and vendor-neutral background.

The LC model will be presented throughout this section of the book as a vehicle for explaining the core aspects of OLAP technology. For example, the language for describing hierarchies is presented in Chapter 5 when I discuss hierarchies, the language for distinguishing different types of sparsity is introduced in Chapter 6 when I discuss hypercubes, and the language for defining different types of formulas is introduced in Chapter 7 when I discuss formulas. Although the LC model is used throughout the book, this book is not about the LC model. Parts of the model that go beyond traditional OLAP technology (as in the area of inheritance or multimedia pattern representation) have been left out of the book. Similarly, analyses that are straightforward in LC but nigh impossible with traditional OLAP tools have been left out as well. I have done my best to keep focused on topics and areas of application for which commercially available OLAP technology may be successfully used.

For now, the main thing you need to understand about the LC model, which is described at the end of this chapter, is symmetry. Assuming you have some prior exposure to OLAP or datawarehousing, and regardless of the product(s) you may have used or the literature you may have read, you have undoubtedly encountered the terms/concepts or features of dimensions, measures/facts, and attributes in such a way as to think that they were three fundamentally different types of primitive structures. In other words, somewhere in your system's meta data there is a place for dimensions, a place for measures, and a place for attributes.

As it turns out, anything that looks like a dimension[1] can also be used as a measure or attribute, and anything that looks like a measure can be used as a dimension or attribute. Anything that looks like an attribute can also be used as a dimension or a measure. I mentioned this in a few places in the first edition of *OLAP Solutions*, especially in Chapter 15, but stopped short of forcing the reader to think in terms of a single underlying structure. If it were just a matter of conceptual preference, I would not have taken the time to introduce a deeper and more unifying view in this chapter and use it throughout the book, but hardcoding the distinction between dimensions, measures, and attributes leads to many problems, including unnecessary difficulties from trying to support multiple schemata sharing the same data set, from trying to create even reasonably sophisticated models such as customer value models, from trying to have models refer to or derive from other models (recursion), and from trying to cleanly support data mining and statistics, not to mention lots of unnecessary administrative overhead.

Even though OLAP products do not currently support full symmetry, you will have an easier time designing applications if you think symmetrically, as the application chapters will show you later in the book. Who knows—maybe by the time you are reading this, some OLAP products will already be fully symmetrical.

Since symmetry is only one of several key attributes of the LC model, since every OLAP product comes with its own implicit model, since the OLAP models implicit in today's products are unnecessarily restrictive in a variety of different ways, and since I want you to be able to judge for yourself the disparity between different implicit models and the appropriateness of the LC model or any other multidimensional model you might come across or develop, this chapter will accomplish the following:

- Identify fundamental OLAP issues where the diversity between products is greatest
- Critique the product-based OLAP models that implicitly exist
- Describe the ideal features of an OLAP model
- Give an overview of the LC model for OLAP

A description of why neither the relational model nor canonical logic provides an adequate foundation for OLAP functionality is provided in Appendix F.

Disarray in the OLAP Space

There are many substantial differences between OLAP tools that reflect their different approaches, assumptions, and implicit models. However, before exploring these open issues, we need to corral the variety of terms used to describe similar things so as to minimize the potential for confusion. As the definitions of these term clusters are a part of what articulating a model is all about, I go no further at this point than identifying the clusters.

Terms Frequently Used to Refer to the Same Thing

- Dimension, factor, variable
- Element, position, instance, member
- Measure, fact, metric, variable, formula
- Attribute, property, characteristic
- Level, generation, ancestors, descendents, parent/child, hierarchy

Open Issues

The open issues that follow reflect important logical differences in the way products work. They represent what any inquisitive mind might pose after working with a variety of products and noticing that they differ not just in trivial ways but in seemingly fundamental ways as well. We are not looking at physical differences between products at this time. Those differences are real and will be discussed in Chapter 10, but they do not affect what we are calling a logical OLAP model.

The main logical issues are:

- Whether meta data is generic or nongeneric
- Whether hierarchies are an intrinsic part of a dimension
- What constitutes a cube
- How to interpret sparse cells
- Where formulas belong

Whether Meta Data Is Generic or Nongeneric

Is all structural meta data definable in terms of generic dimensions, or is there a justifiable basis for distinguishing between measures/variables and dimensions? There is not an obvious answer to this question. If you look to matrix algebra for guidance, you might think that all structural meta data could be defined in terms of generic dimensions. On the other hand, if you look to the relational model or the predicate calculus, you might be inclined to support the dimension/variable distinction. Some products, such as Microsoft Analysis Services, Oracle Express, and IBM's Metacube, distinguish variables (possibly called measures, facts, or metrics) as separate from dimensions. Other products, such as Essbase, Holos, and TM1, purport to treat all dimensions as generically equivalent. These latter products treat variables as members of a variables dimension.

Whether Hierarchies Are an Intrinsic Part of a Dimension

Are hierarchies (single or multiple) an intrinsic or necessary part of a dimension, or should hierarchies simply be specified by relating members from different dimensions? Although most products support the existence of one or more hierarchies within a dimension, a number of products such as Express from Oracle and Cross Target from Dimensional Insight do not have a built-in notion of intradimensional hierarchy. Do products that do not support intradimensional hierarchies suffer from any loss of functionality? If dimensions should support hierarchies, what constrains such hierarchies? Could any collection of linked nodes in an N-1 relation constitute a hierarchy or are there certain assumptions that need to be true about the relationship between the nodes?

What Constitutes a Cube

What defines a cube? Can all data fit into a single cube, or are there natural chunking principles by which data gets divided between different cubes? Some products such as

Express, TM1, and Analysis Services take a multicube approach to modeling data. Others, most notably Essbase (though the product has moved away from a pure hypercube approach since the release of its version 5), take a more hypercube—where everything can fit into a single cube—approach to modeling data.

How to Interpret Sparse Cells

What should empty cells (or sparse regions of cells) mean for an OLAP model? Is there any way or set of ways they should be treated? For example, should an empty cell mean that data is missing but potentially forthcoming as in a late sales report? Or should an empty cell mean that data could never apply to the cell, as would be the case in a two-dimensional model where one dimension was defined by employee names, the other dimension was defined by employee attributes, and you were looking at the cell defined by the intersection of an unmarried employee and the attribute spouse's name? Or should an empty cell simply mean that all zeros were suppressed, as is typically the case with retail transaction tables where only those products that were sold are reported?

Many products automatically treat empty cells as being equal to zero. Most products cannot distinguish between an empty cell that refers to a missing data value and an empty cell that refers to no meaningful value. Is this a problem? Given (as described in Chapter 6) that confusing missing, meaningless, and zero-valued data can produce calculation errors, you would think that an OLAP model should clearly distinguish between the various types of sparse data.

Where Formulas Belong

Where should calculations be defined in an OLAP model? Most tools provide for some dimension-based calculations as well as some additional rules or calculation scripts. Some products even support cell-specific calculations. Furthermore, the tools vary considerably in terms of the amount of calculations they support on the dimensions. Some tools support only intrasibling addition, subtraction, and division; others support a full range of functions with sophisticated referencing. Why is this? Is the distinction between dimension-based and script-based calculations logically grounded, in which case what is the logical basis for making this distinction, or is this a matter of convenience? If it is a matter of convenience, is this the end-user's convenience or the product developer's convenience? Is there an ideal distribution of calculations, or should all calculations be available from either a dimension or a scripting perspective?

Critique of Implicit Issue-Specific Approaches to OLAP Modeling

As shown previously, many products take different approaches to what are seemingly fundamental aspects of multidimensional modeling technology. If all approaches are equally justifiable, then the issues can't be fundamental. If the issues are fundamental, then some approaches need to be demonstrably better or worse. Or different approaches need to somehow correspond to different applications. What follows is a critique of the issue-specific approaches to OLAP modeling that are implicit in the main products.[2]

Treating All Dimensions Generically

The biggest problem with generic dimension approaches is their lack of explicit meta data support for the actual data.[3] Generic dimension approaches invariably use a measures or variables dimension whose members are the names of variables. The result of treating measures as members of a measures dimension is the implicit creation of a data dimension. By implicit I mean that the user may not perform any explicit action to define the data dimension, in which case, the data dimension is typically defined in terms of standard numeric machine types such as double-precision floating-point numbers or integers.

Expression 4-1 represents a prototype generic dimensional expression and illustrates how the data is not accounted for by any dimension values:

```
4-1   data = dim₁.valₙ, dim₂.valₙ, dim₃.valₙ
```

Expression 4-1 reads, "The intersection of one value from every dimension identifies or is associated with an element of data." For instance, expression 4-2 fits this framework:

```
4-2    500 = Measure.Unit_sales , Time.January , Store.Cambridge
```

It reads, "The intersection of the unit_sales member of the Measure dimension and the January member of the Time dimension and the Cambridge member of the Store dimension is associated with the data element 500."

The relationship between the data and meta data that this model implies is illustrated in Figure 4.1. Note that there are many ways to represent the data. The fact that I used a classic table does not imply that the differences between multidimensional models are defined in terms of tables. Tables are simply a well-understood data source metaphor.

You can see from Figure 4.1 that there is no model-contained dimensional meta data that accounts for the data values. Obviously, OLAP products need to deal with the data values. As was stated previously, current products associate the values of the implicit data dimension with the values of some standard machine types, at the very least; but those machine types are extrasystemic as far as the OLAP model is concerned.

Even when the data dimension is implicit, if there are different types of source data, such as strings, integers, currencies, or fractions, it is awkward to think in terms of a single data dimension, because that single data dimension really represents multiple types or domains—one for each kind of data. This is because the potential values of the data dimension, in the presence of heterogeneous data, become a function of the specific values of other dimensions. For example, the potential values for sales are different than the potential values for color or address where sales, color, and address are row values in a measures dimension. Since the value range for the data dimension is bound to specific collections of values (as variable names) from other dimensions, it

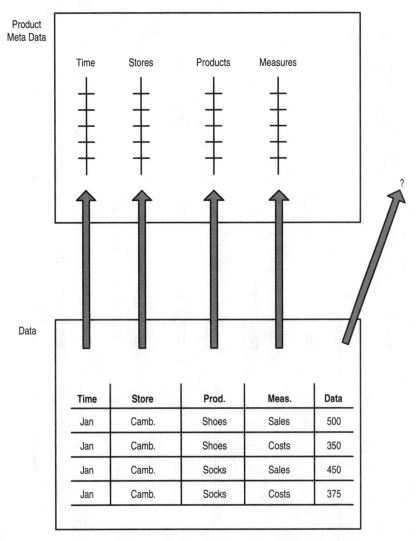

Figure 4.1 The generic dimensional approach doesn't account for the data.

can't be reused with different data sets independently of the variables' dimensions with which it is associated.

OLAP products that appear to take a generic dimensions approach and that enable multiple kinds of data, such as Essbase, may enable the user to assign a data type to members of the measures dimension. But if a tool provides for member-specific data types on the measures dimension, the tool is not really following a generic dimensional model.

Figure 4.2 illustrates the practical reality to which most so-called generic dimensional products subscribe.

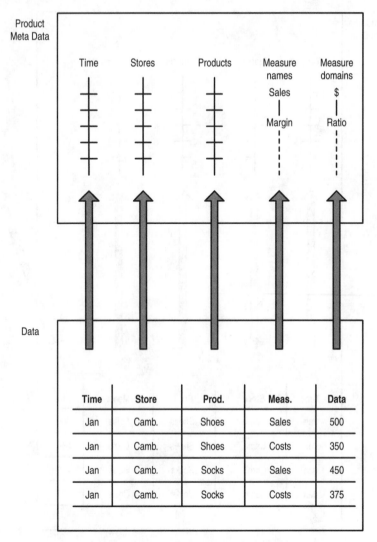

Product
Meta Data

Data

Figure 4.2   Practical reality for so-called generic dimensional products.

Another problem with generic dimensions is their inability to identify meaningful assertions or well-formed formulas in a data set (unless one interprets a so-called generic dimensional approach as treating the data dimension as what is asserted of the union of the nondata dimensions—again violating the so-called generic principle). Assertions are what are capable of being true or false. Data sets, whether considered to be relational or multidimensional, should consist of meaningful facts, which is to say facts capable of being true or false. If for some reason meaningless facts or nonsense enters the data set, the system should be able to detect a pseudofact as an invalid assertion and ignore it.

For example, given a row in a third normal form relation, every nonkey attribute field in the row is an assertion about the union of the key fields in the row. If the keys were store and time and the attributes were sales and costs, each sales field and each cost field would be an assertion about a particular store-time combination. In contrast, the store and time fields would not be assertions. They define the *that* (the logical subject) about which the attribute fields (the logical predicates) constitute assertions. Related to this, the so-called facts in a fact table are not, in isolation, facts at all. The value $500 in a sales column does not constitute a fact. It has no meaning in isolation and is incapable of being true or false. The fact is the predication of the term $500 of the subject composed of the terms Shoes-Boston-January. If all the dimensions are equivalent, then there is no way to tell what is being asserted of what and there is no way to know how to process empty cells.

Finally, by leaving out the dimension/variable distinction, an important means of describing data sets is needlessly lost. It's akin to describing a wine without making reference to color. For example, there is a huge qualitative difference between data sets that have a large number of data points and a small number of variables, such as a census study, and data sets that have a large number of interrelated variables but only a small number of data points per variable, such as a typical econometric model.

These last two issues represent problems with the generic dimensional approach if actually followed, but in practice, it isn't followed to this extreme. Distinctions are made between dimensions and measures through attributes assigned to members of the measures dimension. (Think of a dimensional version of *Animal Farm*—all dimensions are created equal, but some dimensions are more equal than others.)

Referentially Distinguishing Dimensions and Variables: Series Cubes

Although approaches that hardcode the distinction between dimensions and measures would appear to overcome the problems with the generic approach as illustrated in the example and Figure 4.3, they introduce new problems in their stead.

Expression 4-3 represents models that explicitly account for data as values of some measure. The superscript on the dimension term indicates which dimension is referred to by the term. The superscript on the member term indicates what dimension the member term belongs to, and the subscript on the member term indicates which member it is:

$$4\text{-}3 \quad \text{Meas.val} = \text{dim}^1.\text{mem}_n^1 \,, \; \text{dim}^2.\text{mem}_n^2 \,, \; \text{dim}^3.\text{mem}_n^3$$

In contrast with the generic dimension example given previously, this one reads, "Each unique intersection of a member from every dimension on the right-hand side of the equation identifies or is associated with some value of a measure (Meas.val) on the left-hand side of the equation."

For instance, expression 4-4 would fit this framework:

$$4\text{-}4 \quad \text{Units\_Sold. } 500 = \text{Time.January, Store.Cambridge}$$

It reads, "The value 500 of the measure Units_Sold is associated with the intersection of the January member of the Time dimension and the Cambridge member of the Store dimension."

The relationship between data and meta data that this model implies is illustrated in Figure 4.3.

This approach would seem to be better than the generic dimension approach because assertions are as easy to define as in the relational model and because all of the data is represented in the meta data; thus, nothing is extrasystemic. However, there is still a big problem. Approaches that hardcode the distinction between dimensions and measures embed that distinction in the meta data as illustrated in Figure 4.4.

This means that at the meta data level, there are two kinds of primitive structures—dimensions and measures—and each primitive structure has its own set of properties. For example, dimensions may have hierarchies, while measures may represent the left-hand side of an equation. A set of data elements (such as a column of sales figures or a column of store names) needs to connect either to a dimension or to a variable. This static or referential notion of meta data reduces the flexibility of any model because once a set of elements is defined as a dimension, it can't be used as a measure and vice versa. The only way to use a dimension as a measure is to replicate it in the meta data and to

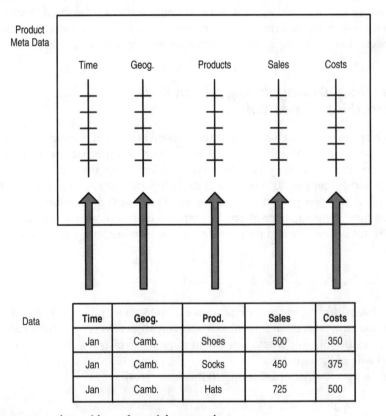

Figure 4.3 Meta data with a referential approach.

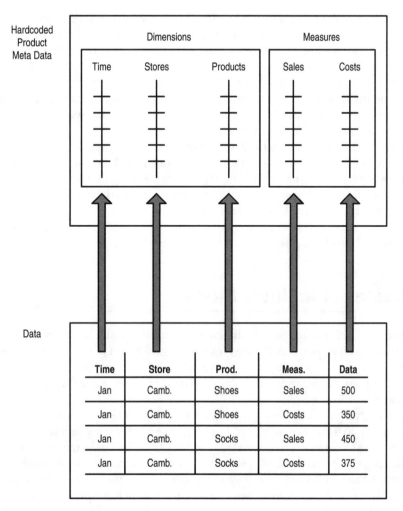

Figure 4.4 Hardcoded meta data.

create a separate model for each distinct pattern of meta data usage. Beyond the obvious problem of redundancy and the created challenge of maintaining consistency across meta data updates, this approach also makes it awkward—if not practically impossible—for multiple analytical views to collaboratively work on the same data, as each view would constitute a separate model.

Stuffing Everything into a Single Cube: Hypercubes

The biggest problem with single hypercube approaches is their lack of any natural chunking or segmentation principle. This surfaces when attempting to use hypercubes for modeling complex multidomain data sets.

From a hypercube perspective, two variables that share no dimensions in common and which have no way to be compared could still fit as adjacent members of a variables dimension in a hypercube that contains the union of the two sets of dimensions. An admittedly extreme example would be product sales dimensioned by product, channel, and time, and atmospheric pressure dimensioned by distance from planet surface and planet mass. The two variables would have no dimensions in common; the hypercube as a whole would be extremely sparse. One consequence of treating the world as a single hypercube is that the greater the variety of variables, the greater the amount of sparsity and the harder the cube is to understand.

Hypercubes would seem to violate what is intuitively the most natural criteria for defining a cube: intercomparability or interactivity, meaning that a logical cube defines a contiguous analytical space where the values of any variables (or data associated with the members of a variables dimension) may be meaningfully compared. If being in the same cube doesn't guarantee comparability, and anything can fit in a hypercube, then the term hypercube loses any practical meaning.

Attributes of an Ideal Model

The problems with pseudogeneric dimensions and with static hardcoded dimension-measure distinctions point to the need for a more general set of primitives for defining and manipulating or working within multidimensional models. The problem with hypercubes points to the need for defining an objective basis for delimiting the content of a cube.

Beyond solving these specific problems, are there any objective criteria for identifying an ideal model that can be agreed to in advance of proposing any model? I believe there are. What follows are a set of criteria for any OLAP model capable of supporting the full range of current OLAP products and of pointing to useful future product development not embodied in any product currently on the market. Please note that this is not a feature list. A comprehensive feature list for OLAP products can be found in Chapter 18.

WHAT'S A MODEL

The term *model* refers to at least a combination of a data definition language (DDL), a data manipulation language (DML), and possibly a data representation language (DRL). Leaving aside for the moment whether it makes sense to distinguish between these languages and, if so, under what conditions, a model needs to provide some method of defining an internal representation of an external data set, some method of connecting to such external data sets, some method of creating derived values, and some method of representing values.

Theoretic Groundedness

Theoretic groundedness is the degree to which a model is based on (or grounded in) logic and mathematics. It is one of the most important attributes of the relational model. A model that is inconsistent with either logical or mathematical principles is of limited value for decision support. Key model features, such as support for hierarchies and criteria for well-formed facts, need to be explicitly connected to their underlying theoretic support.

Logical Grounding

A logic-grounded OLAP model needs to define valid assertions or facts (that is, have some notion of a well-formed formula), correctly process invalid (missing and meaningless) assertions in addition to valid assertions, and provide for correct rules of inference. Yet the different implicit models for OLAP as described previously imply different definitions of a well-formed formula or valid assertion, different methods of working with sparse data, and different rules of inference. For example, generic dimensional approaches imply that any combination of dimension members defines a valid assertion. On the other hand, first-order predicate logic requires at least one subject (argument) and one predicate (function). So, it would seem that the ubiquitous data dimension needs to play the role of predicate, but this complicates the generic dimensional model. Approaches that stuff everything into a single cube would also seem to have logical difficulties. At the very least, they would need to distinguish valid from invalid intersections. Approaches that distinguish variables and dimensions would seem to have a cleaner interpretation in first-order logic—namely, that the union of the dimension elements at an intersection defines the subject, and each variable defines a predicate.

Mathematical Grounding

A mathematically grounded OLAP model needs to provide for rules of comparability and closure as well as preserve the determinism of inherently deterministic calculations such as summation. This is easier said than done. Queries for the dimensions in generic dimensional models can produce result sets whose elements, namely dimension members, were not a part of the original dimensional data set.

Worse than that, as shown previously with generic dimensional models, the model may not describe even the given data. (Using a relational analogy, all the data needs to fall within some domain.) If the model does not describe all the data, then some of the data is extrasystemic, or is unaccounted for by any domain and closure is violated off the bat. As extrasystemic, there would be no way to use that data as a dimension or create queries conditional upon the values of that data. For example, if time, store product, and variable were the dimensions, then value would be extrasystemic. If value is extrasystemic, then there would be no way to use, say, cost values as the basis for a dimension without creating a new model.

Furthermore, no current OLAP product supports the equivalent of what in the object database world are called user-defined types that specify a collection of instances and valid operators within a closed system of operations. OLAP products that support the notion of levels defined on ragged hierarchies may enable the user to define aggregation operations that produce inconsistent results (discussed in Chapter 5). Finally, OLAP products should be able to leverage the wide amount of existent mathematics. Explanatory and predictive modeling may rely on sophisticated mathematics such as neural nets, sets, matrix algebra, calculus, groups, and chaos. They may also rely on the ability to define data types with specified cardinality or specific operators. For example, in a simulation model one might need to define a large number of state variables where each state variable has a (possibly different) number of potential states. Although the calculation language provided by an OLAP model should be rich enough to support a wide variety of mathematical constructs, at the very least it would seem necessary to provide data structures such as composite data types that are suited to store the results of value-added mathematical calculations.

Completeness

An OLAP model needs to provide a DDL, DML, and a query language (though they may all be aspects of the same thing) capable of specifying multivariate, multilevel, multidimensional relationships. This covers all possible formula references, including hierarchical and positional offsets, conditional overrides, measured and derived values, and even sorting. If an OLAP model can't express these relationships, then its language is semantically incomplete.

Additional aspects of completeness include being able to recursively define models, associate multiple models with the same data set, and associate multiple data sets with the same model. For example, if a single data set can only be modeled in one way per model, then the same model cannot account for multiple users' schemata, and each user's schema needs to be represented as a separate model. This is inefficient since it means there will be duplicated meta data. It also means that it would require an additional meta data layer (meta meta data?) in order to translate between different schemata changes made within each schema. For example, if one analyst were looking at changes in sales across time and another analyst were looking at changes in the count of times per unique sales, and the first analyst made some projections that added new sales values, these, in a collaborative environment, should be passed through to the second analyst as additional times per sales tuple. But if the model does not support multiple schemata, then it would require a separate translation to update the second meta data schema given changes to the first.

Since, as was shown in Chapter 1, descriptive modeling is the backbone of decision support, an OLAP model needs to support (though not necessarily incorporate) all decision support systems (DSS) functions. This includes structural operations (operations that function on dimensional structures such as concatenate), statistical operations, nonparametric data-mining operations, mapping data types and operations, text operations (including text searches and summarizations), and visualization.

Efficiency

Efficiency has two meanings: irreducibility of operators and simplicity of expression. Following the first meaning, primitive OLAP structures and operators need to be irreducible. Given the previous discussion, this would seem to indicate the need to subsume dimensions and measures within a single underlying structure. This definition also points to subsuming structural operators and numeric operators within a single notion of operation.

Following the second meaning, OLAP models need to express complex relationships efficiently. For example, if a model has no notion of hierarchy, then it may inefficiently require the referencing of declared dimensional relationships for aggregation expressions. If a model has no notion of multiple hierarchies within a single dimension, then it may inefficiently require multiple dimension declarations to model multiple hierarchies.

Analytical Awareness

An OLAP model should offer subtle analytical help. This is because any OLAP model formalizes, to some degree, what might be called the analytical process. For example, unless you are testing the degree to which stores are independent from time, you do not want to analyze the correlation between store and time. In a model that distinguishes dimensions and variables, you would not analyze the correlation between dimensions as a part of any routine analysis. In contrast you would routinely analyze the correlation between variables. In a model that does not distinguish dimensions and variables, any analysis is as equally useful as any other. For example, in a hypercube model, it makes as much sense to ask for the variance in sales across stores and time as to ask for the variance in March across measures and stores. By formalizing the analytical process, an OLAP model would open the way for more intelligent automation.

Overview of the Located Content Model

As I stated at the beginning of this chapter, the LC model will be introduced over the next several chapters as each OLAP topic arises. The purpose of this overview is to give you an appreciation of the scope and degree of integration provided by types—the underlying structure in the LC model—by presenting you a mile-high look at a type-based approach to dimensional modeling, as well as to drill down in one spot, namely, that of symmetry, as it is the first thing you need to understand.

In addition, I want to reassure those readers who simply want to know how to build useful, maintainable, performable, and potentially complex OLAP solutions within some product's environment that *the use of the LC model as a pedagogical tool will simplify your path to OLAP enlightenment*. Although I have included some of the more clearly theoretical or abstract aspects of the LC model in this book, those snippets are tucked away in appendices, endnotes, or technical asides.

A Functional Approach

The LC model is a software data model grounded in functionally[4] based logic and mathematics that resulted from research conducted over the past 20 years by a number of individuals, including myself. (See Appendix F for a brief description of how the LC model's underlying logic relates to canonical logic.) Within the LC model, the term *locator* is roughly analogous to the term dimension for those products that distinguish dimensions and measures. The term *location* is roughly analogous to the concept of the intersection of one or more members from each of the nonmeasure dimensions. The term *content* is roughly analogous to the terms variable, fact, formula, measure, or attribute. The major difference is that the two LC terms (ignoring here the distinction between a unidimensional locator and a potentially multidimensional location) refer to functional or use distinctions for a single set of underlying types and not for any primitive difference between data structures.

Super Symmetry

Dimension and Measure

At a high level, the LC model is composed of types, methods of structuring types into schemas that have an LC form, and methods of connecting structured types to data sets through one or more models (or populated schemas). What are called dimensions and what are called variables in any OLAP product/model from, for example, Oracle's Express, Accrue's Lightship, Microsoft's Analysis Services, or IBM's Metacube would be treated as individual types in an LC model. Thus, in a typical situation, the classic dimensions Time and Store would be represented as types in an LC model as well as the classic measures Sales and Cost. Types define the limits of what can be defined, queried, and/or calculated. Since the distinction between a type used as a locator or dimension and a type used as a content or variable is based on how the type is used within an expression, there is no strict need for a user/analyst to declare types as locators or contents; the distinction is apparent from the form of the query, definition, or calculation.

In general, by parsing input tokens (and assuming here an expression in a textual language) into type names T^x (read "the type named x") and type instances i^x_N (read "the nth instance of the type named x), the contents are those types with unspecified instances.

Thus, the query:

```
select sales where store = Cambridge and year = 1996
```

parses into T^1: sales, T^2: store, i^2_N: Cambridge, T^3: year, i^3_N: 1996. This reads, "*Sales* is the name of type one; *store* is the name of type two; *Cambridge* is the name of the Nth (or some) instance of type two; *year* is the name of type three; and *1996* is the name of the Nth (or some) instance of type three."

The result set is the collection of instances for the type sales that correspond to Cambridge 1996. So for this query, sales is the content and store and time are the locators.

In contrast, for the query:

```
select store where sales > 300
```

the term *store* serves as the content since we are only given the name, and *sales* is the location as we are given the name and instance.

Figures 4.5 and 4.6 illustrate this symmetry provided by a functional approach.

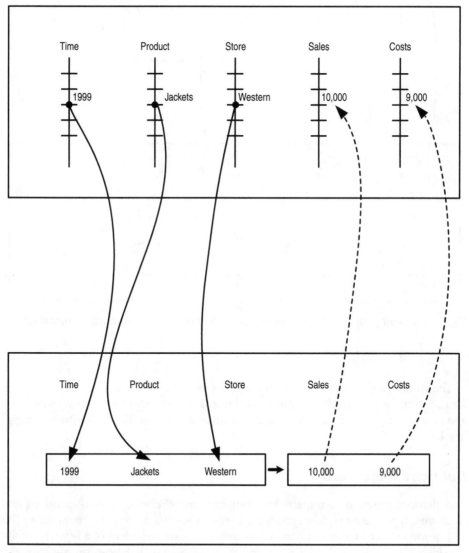

Sales.costs, Time.1999, Prod.jackets, Store.Western

Figure 4.5 Using time, product, store as dimensions, and sales and costs as measures.

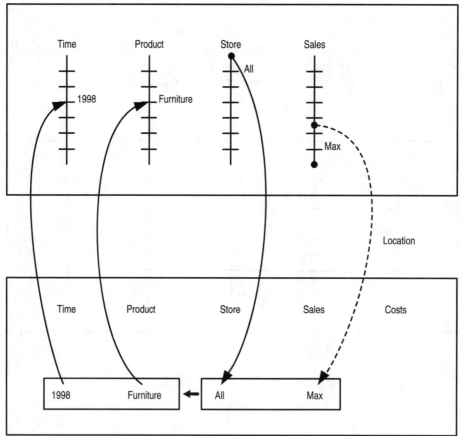

Figure 4.6 Using sales and stores as dimensions and time and products as measures.

The dimension/measure symmetry applies to all operations, not just querying. Thus, continuing this example, you could build a dimensional model using sales bins and store as dimensions, and using count of times as content. This is illustrated in Figure 4.7.

Data and Meta Data

In addition to providing symmetry between what are otherwise called dimensions and measures, types also provide symmetry between so-called data and meta data. The distinction between them is functional as well. Thus, the instances of a type (typically considered to be meta data) can be inputs to an equation whose outputs are the instances of another type. For example, one large store may have a list of carried products that is defined to be twice as numerous as the number of distinct products offered

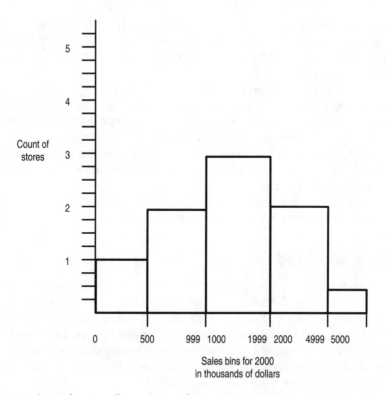

Figure 4.7   Using Sales as a dimension and Stores as a measure.

by a competitor. A large franchise company with a single slowly changing store dimension may want to analyze changes in the number of individual stores by time and country. Again, this is treating the so-called store dimension meta data as data.

Recursion

Not only are the distinctions between dimension and measure and between data and meta data functional, but in addition, the distinctions are better thought of as defining one stage, query, or calculation in an *N*-stage recursive process. Classic dimension/measure queries can be iteratively defined. So too can operations that analyze meta data or that use data to condition the instance ranges of types (in other words, using data as meta data).

Type Structures

Types can have any form of single or multiple hierarchy. Hierarchies can be leveled, ragged, or mixed. As you will learn in Chapter 5, there are natural rules for distinguishing well-formed hierarchies from illegitimate ones. Types, in this sense, provide for rich dimension structuring.

Types can be combined through structural operators such as Cartesian product, insert, concatenate, and 1-*N* and 1-1 correspondence. In this sense, types behave like sets and can support the set-like operators used in relational algebra. You will see this introduced in Chapter 6.

Types can also enter into equations with either the whole type serving as independent variable (right-hand side of the equation), dependent variable (left-hand side of the equation), or with an instance of a type serving, again, on either side of the equals sign. In other words, formulas may be associated with the instances of a type and/or between types. There are no restrictions to the calculations that can be defined in an LC model.[5] Data may be input from outside a particular LC model and/or derived. These features are described in Chapter 7.

Thus, types support a rich formula language and they integrate structural (more set-like) operations and numeric operations within a single DML.

Schemas and Models

A schema is defined by combining or structuring types in an LC form. Being structured in an LC form means (as illustrated later) that at least one type in the structure (the one used as a locator or classic dimension) has some instances already specified, and at least one type in the structure (the one used as a content or classic measure) does not have its instances specified. As you will learn in Chapter 6, the schema serves as a backdrop for parsing expressions, be they queries, definitions, or calculations.

A populated schema (or what is frequently called a model) is defined by connecting a schema with data. This is what the term cube (and its derivatives such as multicube) really mean.

For example, as illustrated in Figure 4.8, assume you have the types time, store, product, sales, and a data set comprised of a table whose columns have the same headings as the type names (and ignoring, until Chapter 7, the way in which the table-contained data is linked to the schema).

Using time, store, and product as locators, and using sales as contents would be represented by the following schema:

4-5   (Time. $\otimes$ Store. $\otimes$ Product.) ~ Sales

- Where the dot token "." means every unique instance of the type that precedes it and the operator "$\otimes$" means cross product so that the expression in parentheses refers to the cross product of the unique instances of Time, Store, and Product

- Where the operator "~" means the sets denoted by the expressions on either side of it are in one-to-one correlation with each other

- Where the existence of a type name without the dot token "." means some instance of that type

In words, you take the cross product of the distinct instances of time, store, and product and for every intersection associate some value of sales. This is the functional

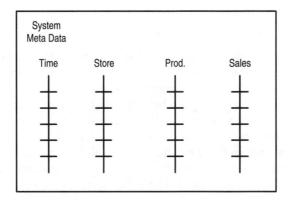

Source Data

Time	Store	Prod.	Sales
Jan	Camb.	Shoes	$10,000
Jan	Camb.	Shirts	$25,000
Jan	Paris	Shoes	$30,000
Jan	Paris	Shirts	$20,000
Feb	Camb.	Shoes	$12,000

Figure 4.8 A simple model.

definition of a cube that captures the sales measurement event. It implies that, when measuring sales you know in advance for which stores, times, and products you are doing the measuring. However, you don't know what the sales were. That's why they're being measured!

What if instead of measuring the sales values for particular store time product combinations, you want to measure the distribution of stores as a function of how much they sold of all products in the year 2000? Recall what the result set could look like. It was shown in Figure 4.7. But how would you express the schema using the same combinatorial operators that were just introduced? How about the following:

```
(Sales.bin. ⊗ Product.all ⊗ Time.2000) ~ Count(Store)
```

In words, it says to take the cross product of every sales bin with the *all* member of the product dimension and the year *2000* member of the time dimension and for every defined intersection associate some value for the count of stores.

Summary

In this chapter you have seen how beneath the single term OLAP there lies a sea of genuine product-based differences in approach to what constitutes an OLAP model. Furthermore, you've seen the variety of problems associated with common approaches such as generic dimension approaches, approaches that referentially distinguish between dimensions and measures, and approaches that try to stuff everything into a single cube. You saw the attributes of an ideal model and were introduced to the LC model that will be described in detail throughout this book as a pedagogical vehicle for explaining the many features of OLAP systems. I also drilled into one area, symmetry, because you need to understand that so-called dimensions and measures are really aspects of the same underlying structure (which I call a type) before getting into the next chapter on the internal structure of a type or what you might feel more comfortable thinking of as dimensional hierarchies (though all of that internal structuring can apply equally well to variables or formulas).

I want to stress that what follows is the most efficient way to give you a detailed knowledge of what multidimensional modeling and analysis or OLAP is, how OLAP works, and how you can take advantage of it to solve your business or other computational problems. For example, if you ever want to get beyond OLAP 101 and solve more challenging business problems, you need to know that many such problems require inverting so-called dimensions and measures in order to be solved. Anytime you want to understand how many stores, products, or customers met some sales, earnings, visit, lead, or cost criteria, you're inverting dimensions and measures. The fact that the current crop of OLAP products does not support this kind of symmetry should not deter you from using symmetry in your analyses. In the same way you would use a data-mining tool for pattern detection work (even though data mining may not be directly supported by your OLAP environment), you can use an underlying relational database (or even your OLAP environment) to create alternative, analytical star schemas (that is, ones where the dimensions and measures are inverted) for your more advanced OLAP work.

## CHAPTER 5

The Internal Structure
of a Dimension

Strong support for hierarchies is the second logical requirement for Online Analytical Processing (OLAP) and a principal one that distinguishes it from traditional SQL databases and spreadsheets. The two main approaches to defining hierarchies, as illustrated in Figure 5.1, are typically called ragged and leveled. You can think of them as different lenses for viewing the world. In the same way that if you wear blue-tinted glasses the world looks blue, if you wear leveled-hierarchy glasses the world looks leveled, and if you wear ragged-hierarchy glasses the world looks ragged. Is the difference between these approaches significant? If so, is one of these approaches better or more general than the other? (Is the world really leveled or ragged?) Or are the two approaches complimentary, each being better suited for some situations over others? Is it possible to combine both approaches within a single and more general notion of hierarchy or resolution?

By the end of this chapter, you will have learned why OLAP-enabled tools need to support both leveled and ragged forms of hierarchy and language in order to provide for complete hierarchical representations. In other words if a tool supports only ragged or only leveled hierarchies, there will be relationships that the tool cannot efficiently model or calculate. By understanding how products ought to behave, you will have an easier time working with whatever product you have inhouse because you will understand its limitations, and if you are looking for a tool you will know what questions to ask.

As was shown in Chapter 4, dimensions, variables or measures, and attributes or characteristics are aspects of a single underlying structure called types. Hierarchies are thus an aspect of types and not dimensions. (Rational numbers, for example, which one might be inclined to treat as variables, also have a hierarchical form.) However, if as a reader you are familiar with and feel comfortable thinking in terms of dimensional

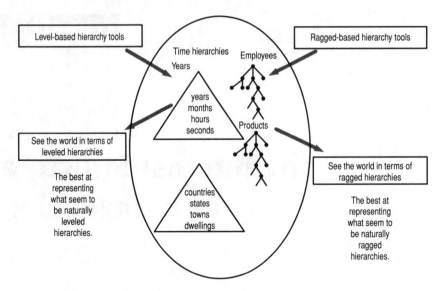

Figure 5.1 A tale of two hierarchies.

hierarchies as opposed to type hierarchies, then you may mentally substitute the term dimension for the term type while reading this chapter. As a matter of style, I will use the terms type and dimension interchangeably in this chapter.

This chapter is a combination of a minimally formal demonstration of the source of and types of hierarchies as well as an introduction to the dimensional language needed to define them for the purposes of model definition, formula creation, or simply data navigation. If you are new to OLAP and simply want to learn some of the common ways that data can be hierarchically referenced, you may wish to skip to the section titled *Dimensional Hierarchies* and focus on the referencing syntax subsections. If you are already familiar with OLAP tools and want to understand why different hierarchies arise and what their properties are, I encourage you to read the whole chapter.

The reasons I begin this chapter with a discussion of metrics and ordering include the following points:

- Hierarchies are a fundamental part of OLAP systems.

- There are substantial differences between the hierarchical approaches of different products.

- The choice of which hierarchical approach to use in an application has significant implications for the efficiency and possibly the correctness of that application.

- The source of the distinction between, and properties of, different kinds of hierarchies can only be explained by an appeal to ordering and metrics.

Since the issues surrounding dimensional hierarchies touch on many neighboring topics from object-oriented design to the foundations of mathematics, I made liberal use of endnotes and sidebars in this chapter.

Nonhierarchical Structuring

Ordering, metrics, and method of definition are the three nonhierarchical aspects of a type or dimension that provide a basis for the hierarchical structuring that follows.

Method of Definition

The two basic methods for the members, elements, or instances of a dimension to be defined are explicit (or list-based) and formulaic (or generative rule, or process-based). Most business dimensions, such as products, customers, employees, stores, channels, accounts, scenarios, and suppliers, are explicitly defined. This means that the instances of the dimension, such as the names of particular products or stores, originated from a list or collection of instances declared to be or simply treated as valid. This can be accomplished by reading in the distinct instances from an external table (as is typically done when OLAP cubes define their dimension instances based on dimension instances defined in the organization's data warehouse), or by someone manually entering values.[1]

Verification of the instances of an explicitly defined dimension can only be based on matching the dimension's instances with the instances of some master list. Absent some list of defined-as-true instances (regardless of whether that list is considered to be external or internal to the dimension), no instance verification is possible.

Some business dimensions such as time are or can be formulaically defined. Using a date data type, one can set a time range such as "this year by week" and fill in the appropriate week instances without appeal to any table of explicit instances. Any attempt to verify the instances of a formulaically defined dimension needs to use some instance-generating rule rather than a master list of explicitly defined instances. (To verify the instances of a time dimension by appeal to some list of valid instances would be to treat time as an explicitly defined dimension.)

Cardinality

The term cardinality is a fancy word for number of or count. (Although hierarchies are not a function of cardinality, it makes sense to mention it here with other non-hierarchical aspects of types.) The cardinality of a dimension is thus the number of instances in the dimension. (Unfortunately, the root term cardinal is also used to refer to a type of ordering.) Some business dimensions, like scenario or channel, may only have three to five instances; others, like customer or transaction, may have millions or billions of instances. Although the cardinality of a dimension does not directly affect its hierarchical structure,[2] it does affect a number of physical issues such as partitioning and indexing, which will be discussed in Chapter 10. Applications that access OLAP-stored data frequently need to know the cardinality of each of the data dimensions and so rely on API or other function calls of the form

```
Count (dimension)
```

Ordering

Some readers may remember from statistics class the difference between nominal, ordinal, and cardinal series. A list of political parties or a list of runners is a classic example of a nominal series. The placement of those same runners at a road race represents an ordinal series. The integers are an example of a cardinal series.

Since some of the differences between dimensional hierarchies are based on ordering, since ordering plays a major role in determining the permissible operations for a type, and since ordering is also an important concept for dimensional analysis (discussed in Chapter 20), a detailed definition of ordering differences is provided next. The matrices used here should be read as a compact representation of the possible relationships between any left-hand-side I instance and any right-hand-side I instance i_n^r. Each equality sign in each cell of each matrix represents the relationship between the i on the row as a left-hand-side term and the i on the column as a right-hand-side term.

Nominally Ordered Instances

If instances are nominally ordered, then all one can say is that two instances are equal ($=$) or not equal ($\neq$). Table 5.1 illustrates a dimension composed of four instances, the definable relationships between its nominally ordered instances. The instances arranged along the rows have the letter L as a superscript to indicate they represent the left-hand side of the relationship. The instances arranged along the columns have the letter r as a superscript to indicate they represent the right-hand side of the relationship.

$$i_n^L \circledD i_n^r : i_1^L = i_1^r ; i_1^L < i_2^r \ldots$$

Types composed of nominally ordered instances can be manipulated with set-like operators such as concatenate, intersect, and union. The only comparison operator they support is the test for equality or identity.[3] Nominal dimensions cannot support operations that compare differences or refer to instances via any directional means such as previous, next, first, or last. Most OLAP dimensions, such as stores, products, customers, and channels, are nominally ordered to the user (although an OLAP tool may automatically associate an ordinal value such as load time order or array offset in storage with a user-defined nominal dimension).

Table 5.1 Matrix of Nominally Ordered Instance Relationships

	i_1^r	i_2^r	i_3^r	i_4^r
i_1^L	$=$	$\neq$	$\neq$	$\neq$
i_2^L	$\neq$	$=$	$\neq$	$\neq$
i_3^L	$\neq$	$\neq$	$=$	$\neq$
i_4^L	$\neq$	$\neq$	$\neq$	$=$

Ordinally Ordered Instances

If one can rank instances but not assign any specific magnitude to the differences between them, the instances are ordinally ordered. Table 5.2 illustrates a dimension composed of four instances, the definable relationships between the ordinally ordered instances.

Note how in addition to distinguishing between sameness and difference, an ordinal series supports transitive comparisons of the form; i_2 is greater than i_1 and less than i_3. This forms the basis for operations such as next, previous, first, and last that are frequently used in dimensional referencing. These operations can be generalized to starting point, offset, and direction. The starting point is most often the current cursor position, or the first or last instances of the series.

Typically, dimensions are either defined to be ordinal as with a rank dimension, or the cardinal attributes of a nominal dimension are used to ordinalize the dimension. For example, a Store dimension, a typical nominal dimension, may be ordered by the attributes size and age, or by the measures sales or profitability, and so forth.

When attributes and measures are used to ordinalize a dimension, many different useful orderings can typically be applied. Furthermore, the relative position functions such as previous and next or up3 return a different instance or set of instances for each distinct ordering of the dimension. Thus, it is useful to be able to name each ordering and to refer to any ordering within the context of a relative position function. For example, expressions such as

```
Store.(size_order, this-1)
```

would refer to the previous position in the stores dimension ordered according to size, and expressions such as

```
Store.(age_order, first+3)
```

would refer to the fourth position in the Store dimension ordered by age.

Several products, such as Microsoft's OLAP product, support named orderings. My first product, FreeThink, supported the creation of libraries of named orderings that could be scrolled by the variables.

Table 5.2 Matrix of Ordinally Ordered Instance Relationships

	i_1^r	i_2^r	i_3^r	i_4^r
i_1^l	=	<	<	<
i_2^l	>	=	<	<
i_3^l	>	>	=	<
i_4^l	>	>	>	=

When creating an ordinal ordering of the instances of a nominal dimension in terms of the instances of a cardinal dimension, it is necessary to resolve the potential multiplicity of the ordered instances that may be associated with each unique value of the ordering instances. Thus, if ordering stores by square footage, and if several stores have the same square footage, you must decide how to resolve the multiplicity of same-ranked stores. Either stores with the same square footage can be randomly listed as shown in Figure 5.2, or there is a secondary ordering used, say rent per square foot, to assign each store a unique position—though this approach cannot guarantee there won't be a tie among two or more stores, or the multiplicity of stores that share the same square footage are treated as a single instance of Store.size_order. Any values that are subsequently dimensioned by Store.size_order need to be aggregated in some way as shown in Figure 5.3.

Cardinally Ordered Instances

If one can assign distances to and compare unit differences between the instances, then the relationship between the instances is cardinal. Table 5.3 illustrates a dimension composed of four instances, the definable relationships between the cardinally ordered instances. Another and more popular term for cardinally ordered instances is integers.

Store ID	Store Size	Sales
A	1,000	$12,500.00
B	1,500	$14,000.00
C	2,000	$30,000.00
D	2,000	$38,000.00
E	2,500	$40,000.00
F	3,000	$55,000.00

Figure 5.2   (Storeid.size_order.) ~ Store_size, Sales.

Store Size	Cnt (stores)	Avg. (sales)
1,000	1	$12,500.00
1,500	1	$14,000.00
2,000	2	$34,000.00
2,500	1	$40,000.00
3,000	1	$55,000.00

Figure 5.3   (Store.size_order.) ~ Sales.

Notice that the integers, as shown in Table 5.3, are codefined with their operations, and that the relationship between the integers is a part of their definition. In other words, the integers represent formulaically defined instances, and the meaning of an integer instance is its position in the series. The dimensions that most naturally possess cardinal properties are numeric, temporal, and spatial. As with numeric dimensions, the instances of temporal and spatial dimensions can be (though they are not necessarily) formulaically defined.

Although there may be many ways to cardinally order the instances of an otherwise nominal dimension, it is more typical for cardinality to enter with the definition of the dimension in standard OLAP applications, and much less common for a nominal dimension to be cardinalized. Cardinally ordering dimensions is more common, however, in advanced OLAP applications as shown in Chapter 20.

Stores, an otherwise a nominal dimension, for example, may be cardinally ordered by size, age, sales, profitability, and so forth in the same way they might be ordinalized. The difference between ordinalizing and cardinalizing can be seen with the following example. Table 5.4 shows a set of sales figures representing total transaction amounts for some store at some time, and the count of the number of times each transaction amount occurred.

Table 5.3 Matrix of Cardinally Ordered Instance Relationships

	i_1^r	i_2^r	i_3^r	i_4^r
i_1^L	$+/- 0$	$+1$	$+2$	$+3$
i_2^L	-1	$+/- 0$	$+1$	$+2$
i_3^L	-2	-1	$+/- 0$	$+1$
i_4^L	-3	-2	$+1$	$+/-0$

Table 5.4 Raw Sales Histogram

SALES AMOUNT ($)	COUNT OF TIMES
50	1
100	2
125	4
150	4
300	5
325	4
375	2
400	2

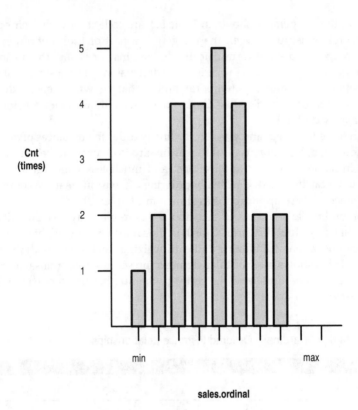

Figure 5.4   Ordinalized sales.

Figure 5.4 shows a histogram of the count of sales by an ordinalized version of sales amount. The X-axis in the graph shows each sales rank ordered from least to most. The graph appears to have a normal distribution with a maximum frequency around the middle four ordinal sales values.

In contrast, Figure 5.5 shows a histogram of the count of sales by a cardinalized version of sales amount. The X-axis in the graph is denominated in dollars and runs from $0 on the leftmost edge to $500 at the rightmost edge. Notice how in the cardinalized version all of the dollar amounts for which there were no sales are kept as information and shown as zero amounts. When the zeros are shown, it is clear that there is a bimodal distribution with frequent sales of around $125 and around $325.

In addition, you can perform arithmetic on cardinal dimensions, such as calculate the ratio of time spent courting a customer to time spent deriving revenue from that same customer as with the following expression:

```
First_sale {date} - First_contact {date} / Last_sale {date} - First_sale
{date}
```

Or you can define intervals and growth functions as with the following expression that might serve to define a unit of time based on two events, such as the first contact

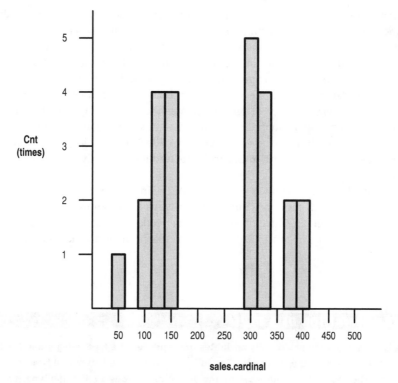

Figure 5.5   Cardinalized sales.

and first sale, and then as a function of some other condition modifying that time amount by a growth factor, possibly based on economic conditions or product price.

```
Time.(First_sale{date} - First_contact{date}) * Growth_Factor per day
{Integers}
```

Metrics

All Instances Are Associated with Metrics

At first glance, it might appear that a dimension is simply a collection of instances, with or without some hierarchical structure. After all, you can define hierarchies in a gazillion different OLAP products and none of them prods you to define units or metrics (except for those products that use the term metric to mean variable or measure). So how does the notion of unit or metric enter the picture? The quick answer is every time you use the terms parent, child, or level you are implicitly referring to a metric.

The name of a type or dimension (much like the name of a set) connotes the range of its possible instances. For example, a dimension named City implies that tokens that refer to cities such as Chicago or New York are valid instances of the dimension, while tokens that refer to colors such as red and blue are invalid instances. Even though OLAP tools don't force you to maintain homogeneous collections of instances as the elements of a dimension, best practices would dictate that you do. Consider the following example. If you were the equivalent of a data warehouse administrator on your first day at a new job, and you were familiarizing yourself with one of the company's dimensional models and you came across a dimension or type labeled "Products" and you saw mixed in with a bunch of product names the names of managers and towns, you would probably flag the manager and town names as anomalous, especially if you wanted to keep your job. Thus, types are, at least, collections of things, items, instances, members, positions, or elements that can be treated equivalently for the purposes of the model.

Think of the dimension name as shorthand for the inclusion condition or metric that all the instances have in common. But if there always exists some inclusion criteria or metric that every single instance of a dimension needs to meet, then a more accurate way of representing the instances would be as a collection of instance-metric pairs.

ON THE DEFINITION OF A TYPE[4]

There is no way to define necessary attributes or properties of a type independently of some set of voluntarily chosen criteria. The following general definition of a type is no exception. The criteria that is imposed on the definition of types are that the types so defined are rich enough to support a classical truth functional logic. At the very least (and we are looking for minimal criteria), this translates into the ability to define assertions and negations. This means it must be possible to assert or negate that some instance of some type is true or false. Thus, for example, given two types, Store names and Sales, if the set of valid store names includes Geneva, Paris, and Madrid and sales is defined on decimal integers, the following expressions represent assertions and negations of some sales value of some store:

> Assert: Madrid sales = $250
> Assert: Paris sales = $300
> Negate: Geneva sales = $350

Given the truth functional constraint mentioned, let's narrow down what we mean by the terms type and instance. The relationship between these terms is roughly analogous to the relationship between the terms set and member. That is to say, the identification of a type places a limit on what may be considered an instance of that type.

For example,

> A type called State might have valid instances such as MA, NY, CT, and VT.
> A type called Dollars ($) might have valid instances such as $1, $2, $3, and $4 .
> A type called Person_Name might have valid instances such as B. Smith, L. Jones, and K. Hardy.

CONSTRAINTS ON THE INSTANCES OF A TYPE

1. Multiplicity

A type needs to have at least two potential instances.

If some type, T^n (read the type named n), had only one potential instance, i_x^n (read some instance named x of the type named n), there would be no possibility of creating propositions where T^n serves as a predicate capable of assertion and negation. The general case is shown here:

$$i_y^n = (T^n, T^m.i_x^m)$$
$$<==>$$
$$!(i_y^n) \neq (T^n, T^m.i_x^m)$$

In words, some instance y of some type n is true of some instance x of some type m if and only if the negation of instance y of that same type n is false of that same instance x of that same type m.

For example, given a type called color with two color instances green and red, the condition states that green can be true of the instance of some other type such as the instance sea of the type "parts of earth" if and only if red is false of the color of the sea. Thus, if the type color could only assume the one color green, there would be no way to say that something had a color other than green or that if green is the true color then some color other than green is false. As a result, Booleans or binary types are the simplest possible types. (See the sidebar on "Types" at the end of this chapter.)

2. Uniqueness

The instances of a type need to be unique and mutually exclusive.

Given, for example, a type T^n with instances i_1^n, i_2^n, i_3^n, i_4^n. This means that all i's are different from each other (uniqueness) and that if any i_x^n is true within the context of a proposition, all other i's are false (and that no two i's can be true at the same time).

To see why this is necessary let's examine the converse. Assume that two instances in an explicitly defined dimension are the same or that $T^n. = i_1^n (1), i_2^n, i_3^n, i_4^n (2)$. Now consider the statement that $i_y^n(i_1^n (1)) = (T^n, T^m.i_x^m.)$ is true.

We can't say that the negation of $i_y^n(i_1^n (1))$ is false because there is another instance of i_y^n, namely $i_y^n(i_1^n (2))$ that would also be true. This violates the rules of logic.

What about mutual exclusivity? An example of a collection of nonmutually exclusive instances would be red, blue, green, small, or large. Something could be red and large. So red and large, though unique, are not mutually exclusive. The notion of mutual exclusivity is tied to the notion that a type denotes a single measurement or evaluation method or strategy. Clearly, we would need two different tools and/or procedures to measure color and size. For a single evaluation method we can say the output of evaluation strategy x is i_1 or i_2 or i_3 or i_4 or . . .

We typically represent a dimension and its instances as in the following expression:

```
City: Chicago, New York, Boston
```

But a more accurate description would resemble expression 5-2:

```
5-2    City.any:  City.Chicago, City.New York, City.Boston
```

Expression 5-2 reinforces the idea that every single instance in the dimension must adhere to the inclusion rule connoted by the dimension name. Now consider the simple month and year, and meter and kilometer dimensions that follow:

```
Time.metric. ∃ Month, Year
```

Read "the set of metrics for time are month and year."

```
Time.Month. ∃ Month.January, Month.February, ..Month.December
```

Read "the set of instances for months are January through December."

```
Time.Year. ∃ Year.1998,  Year.1999, Year.2000
```

Read "the set of instances for years are 1998 through 2000."

```
Distance.metric ∃ Meter, Kilometer
```

Read "the set of metrics for distance are meter and kilometer."

```
Distance.Meter. ∃ Meter.1, Meter.2,... Meter.1000
```

Read "the set of meter instances are 1 through 1000 meters."

```
Distance.Kilometer. ∃ Kilometer.1, Kilometer.2
```

Read "the set of kilometer instances are 1 and 2."

Everyone knows that 12 months are equivalent to one year and that 1,000 meters are equivalent to one kilometer. The ratios of 12 to 1 and 1,000 to 1 represent the scaling factor between the units or metrics of the time and spatial distance dimensions respectively. Thus, if we have some value denominated in terms of one year, we know to divide it by 12 to calculate the average value per month, and if we have 3 months' values we know to multiply them by 4 to estimate a value for the year. It is normal to treat meters, kilometers, months, and years as units or metrics.

Consider what you get for knowing the units of a measurement or value. In addition to being able to figure out scaling factors between levels of granularity, you also get a set of permissible operations. Meters can be added or subtracted and multiplied or divided. They can be divided by units of time. A glacier might move at a speed of three meters per year; a bureaucracy may move even slower. Consider what you lose if you don't know the units. How would you add five unknown-length units and three unknown-length units? There is no operation you can perform with the two different measures of length if you don't know the units with which they are measured. *Thus, you can't separate the translation aspect of metrics from the permissible operations aspect of metrics from the inclusion rule aspect of metrics.*

Although we typically associate the concept of metrics with dimensions whose instances are cardinally ordered as with the month-year and meter-kilometer examples previously, the role of defining instance membership rules, providing for quantitative comparability between scaling factors, and defining valid operations applies equally well to nominally ordered dimensions, as shown in the following section.

Consider again the city dimension example, but this time as part of a multilevel geography dimension with an added country level:

```
Geography.levels ∃  Country, City
Geography.City. ∃  Chicago, New York, Boston, Paris, Nice
Geography.Country. ∃  USA, France
```

In the same way that we talked about the scaling factor between months and years, we can talk about the scaling factor between cities and countries. The only difference is that the scaling factor may not be constant across the whole of the two dimension levels. For example, the scaling factor between cities in the USA and the country USA is 3 to 1, while the scaling factor between cities in France and the country France is 2 to 1. Although the collection of cities is nominally ordered and the collection of countries is nominally ordered, each city and each country is associated with a level or metric that provides inclusion rules, scaling factors, and permissible operations in the same way as with the month-year and meter-kilometer examples. Thus, the concept of metrics, which is being generalized here, is not restricted to cardinally ordered dimensions, but rather applies to all dimensions regardless of how they're ordered.

Since a dimension denotes a series of metric-specific instances and since there may be more than one metric associated with the instances of a dimension, as with the city/country or meter/kilometer examples previously, it is necessary to associate a metric (or ancestor/descendent rank or level value) with each instance of a type or dimension as follows:

```
Geography. _ Country.France, Country.USA, City.Boston, City.NY,
City.Northampton, City.Paris, City.Nice
```

The general form of a type is thus:

$$T^n \equiv m_0^n \ni i_1^n m_1^n, i_2^n m_2^n, i_3^n m_3^n, i_4^n m_4^n, \ldots$$

The type named n or T^n denotes the root metric m_0^n, and where the subscript n refers to the metric's serving as a root and the superscript n refers to the metric belonging to the type named n is composed of the set of m instance metric pairs denoted by the subscripts 1 through m, belonging to the type n as denoted by their superscripts.[5]

The Metric Basis for Hierarchies

When a dimension is composed of instances that do not all belong to the same metric, the metrics for the different instances need to be quantitatively comparable. This should be obvious if you reflect on any multilevel dimension with which you are familiar. For example, days, months, and years are quantitatively comparable and belong in one hierarchical dimension. Any information collected in units of days can be translated into units of months or years. On the other hand, the collection of instance.metric pairs red.color, blue.color, green.color, small.size, medium.size, and large.size have quantitatively noncomparable metrics as there is no quantitative way to compare colors and sizes. So the two sets of instances belong in different dimensions.

Figure 5.6 sums up the previous discussion on metrics with a classification tree for types. Recalling the conditions for a well-formed type that were presented in the preceding sidebar, a type needs to have two or more unique and mutually exclusive instances. Every instance is associated with a metric. If all the metrics are the same, the type is nonhierarchical. If there are two or more metrics and the metrics are quantitatively comparable, the type is hierarchical. If there are two or more metrics and they are not all quantitatively comparable, the type is invalid.

Thus, hierarchies are grounded in the notion of metric relationships and there is no way to define a hierarchy without making reference to metrics. Absent the notion of metrics, dimensions or types would lack any inclusion, scaling, or operational rules and would reduce to arbitrary collections of tokens incapable of internally supporting any mathematics or propositional logic.

So what does this mean for you if you're using an OLAP product that doesn't seem to provide for metrics? First off you should realize that any OLAP product you might be using definitely provides for some metrics. At the very least, your product will support one, and probably more, data types to be associated with what it may call measures or variables. These are your cardinal types. In addition, the instances of any other dimensions you might define are probably predefined as eight-byte strings.

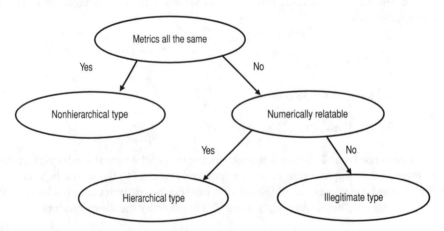

Figure 5.6   Classification tree for types.

Beyond the basics that your tool supports, you should manually keep track of the ordering and metrics (or units) you're associating with the dimensions you've defined. Though you may not be forced to define the ordering applicable to a set of products, stores, or customers, you should declare someplace in your manually maintained meta data the kind of ordering that applies to each of your dimensions, such as products, stores, time, channels, or customers. Many of them will be nominal, but some of them, like time or scenario or channel location, may be ordinal or cardinal. When it comes to the measures, variables, or contents (as you will experience first hand if you work through the calculation model on my companion Web site), you will have a much easier time building, communicating, and debugging your applications if you systematically track the units of your variables.

In the following section, you will learn how hierarchies may be differentiated as a function of the degree to which they are more efficiently described using a named level or ragged hierarchy language.

Dimensional Hierarchies

Overview

Most business and scientific dimensions have a hierarchical structure. Similar concepts include abstraction, grouping, multilevel relationships, aggregation, and consolidation. In an informal way, everybody is familiar with some hierarchical dimensions. Time, which we think of, for example, in hours, days, weeks, months, quarters, and years, forms a hierarchical dimension. Geography, which we may think of in terms of neighborhoods, cities, states, and countries, forms another hierarchical dimension. Corporate reporting structures, which frequently include a task, project, department, business unit, and company level, form a hierarchical dimension as well.

In contrast, a scenario dimension, which is common to most business models, typically has a small number of members such as an actual member, a planned or perhaps several planned members, and a variance member for each combination of planned and actual members. It would almost never be portrayed hierarchically.

In business, as in other types of human activity, hierarchies are a necessity of life. It would be impossible to run a company effectively if all the company's data were confined to the transaction level. Whether it is done in the computer or in your head, you need to track the performance of different types of product aggregations. Even if you ran a small company with a small number of products working out of a single storefront, you would still need to aggregate product sales over time and view your business in terms of larger time scales than that of your sales transactions in order to have the information required to decide which products are selling well and which are selling poorly. Here again, the benefit of multidimensional information systems is that they are geared for directly handling hierarchical dimensions.

The categories by which data are aggregated for analysis and reporting should be the same as the categories in terms of which you act or make decisions. If you make product-pricing decisions to maximize sales, then you need to look at product sales data aggregated by product price or price changes. As your analytical and decision-making criteria change, so too must your aggregation routines. Aggregation routines need to be flexible to support unplanned analysis.

Managers and analysts spend most of their time thinking about groups of things: groups of products, groups of customers, groups of accounts, and so on. Even when we think we are thinking about particulars such as particular sizes, colors, and widths of a specific men's shoe, we are usually considering a tight grouping such as the group of all individual shoes of the same size, style, color, and width. Where data is concerned, groups of things, such as all men's shoes, frequently mean derived things, such as the sum of men's dress and casual shoe sales (unless the data flow is top down, as discussed later in this book). In this regard, OLAP-style derived data queries are different from transaction queries as the latter generally return the same data that was input, such as the address of a customer, because data was originally supplied by the customer. Furthermore, groups are frequently changing. It is especially important for analysis-based decision-making to have strong support for flexible as well as deep and wide-fanning hierarchies.

The capability of multidimensional software to reference things according to their position along a hierarchy is incredibly useful for managing real-world applications. Hierarchical referencing may be more common than you think. In corporate organizations, for example, security and privileges are often defined along a hierarchy. Persons below a certain level may not be allowed to see certain data, or they may need authorization to make certain purchases. Sales and other corporate activities are aggregated along hierarchies. Budgeted resources are frequently allocated along a hierarchy. Some amount for total overhead that applies to a whole division may be allocated down the corporate hierarchy as a function of headcount or sales. In fact, a typical term for a corporate reporting organization is a reporting hierarchy!

As you will learn in the remainder of this chapter, there are different types of hierarchies. These hierarchical differences apply to the world in the sense that there are different kinds of naturally occurring hierarchies such as time and space, which are typically called leveled, and corporate reporting structures and product lists which are typically called ragged. It should be no surprise to the astute reader that these same hierarchical differences also apply to OLAP products, as these products were built to model the world. Thus, some products are built to most easily support leveled hierarchies and some products are built to most easily support ragged hierarchies. (Ideally, products should be able to support both.) Furthermore, these hierarchical types are not easily interdefinable. In other words, it is awkward to try to represent a leveled hierarchy in the world with a tool built to model ragged hierarchies, and it is awkward to try to represent a ragged hierarchy in the world with a tool built to model leveled hierarchies. So, you should be aware of the type of hierarchies you need to model in your world to solve your problems and make sure that your OLAP tools of choice can cleanly support those types of hierarchies.

Hierarchies in General

As stated at the beginning of this chapter, I want to present a semiformal or reasonably solid definition of hierarchies that you can use for modeling and tool analysis, while avoiding any arbitrary, if formal, definitions. (Many rigorous and formal definitions are arbitrary.) As a result I am trying to keep as much of the text as concrete as possible. That said, I believe you will benefit from spending at least a little time on what all hierarchies share to some degree because the referencing methods that apply to hierarchies in general apply to any combination of ragged or level hierarchies you may encounter. This is most clearly illustrated with a simple hierarchy.

Recall that a hierarchical type is composed of a collection of instance-metric pairs where not all the metrics are the same, but they are all quantitatively comparable. *There are thus two different ways that the instance-metric pairs are differentiated: by changes in a metric for a given instance, and by changes in instance for a given metric.* All notions of parent-child, ancestor-descendent, level, granularity, scaling factor, or resolution are forms of Δ m per i or m/i. This is illustrated in Figure 5.7.

All hierarchies have some Δm/i, parent-child, or many-to-one or scaling factor relationships. Within a hierarchical type, the metric of maximum scale or root has no parent metric. The metric of minimum scale or leaves has no children. The act of decrementing the m of any $i_n m_n$, such as $i_1 m_1$, is typically called *taking the child, taking the first descendent*, or *lowering the level of m* of $i_1 m_1$. Likewise the act of incrementing the m of either $i_2 m_2$ or $i_3 m_2$ is typically called taking the parent, taking the first ancestor, or increasing the level of m of either i_2 or i_3.

The inverse of Δm/i relationships are Δ i/m relationships. All notions of sibling and series (think time series) are forms of Δi/m. In Figure 5.7, there is only one Δ i/m relationship. The act of navigating or referring from $i_1 m_1$ to $i_2 m_1$ is typically called taking the sibling of or moving across the level from $i_1 m_1$. Any further refinements in Δ i/m relationships (such as cousin or distance or first/last functions) depend on additional attributes such as ordering. All type structure or dimensional referencing whether in OLAP, relational databases, or statistics grows out of combinations of Δm/i and Δi/m relationships. In other words, a series or relationships of the form Δm/i define the concept of, or are definitionally equivalent to "resolution," while a series or relationships of the form Δi/m define the concept of or are definitionally equivalent to "position."

All the standard terms for hierarchical relationships that I've mentioned before, namely parent/child, ancestor/descendent, resolution, level, and granularity, implicitly connote either a leveled or ragged hierarchy. Specifically, parent/child and

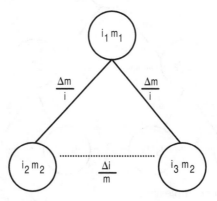

Figure 5.7 Delta M per I relationships.

ancestor/descendent connote a ragged hierarchy (and notice how the terms refer to Δm, not any absolute value for m, and thus the terms come in pairs) while resolution, level, and granularity connote a leveled hierarchy (and notice how these terms refer to absolute values for m and thus appear singly). Therefore, to avoid confusion, when I am referring to hierarchies in general, and trying to make the point that some feature or attribute is general to any kind of hierarchy, I will use the Δm terminology. This consists of referring to the m values of an instance or set of instances, the m distance between two instances, and the set of instances that share the same m value.

If you prefer anthropomorphic terms, you can certainly substitute the terms parent and child for up1 m and down1 m respectively. It is the implicit one-stepness to the terms parent and child that I find most limiting. (In fact, several products that implemented parent and child functions implemented them in this one-step fashion, thus making it necessary for the user to nest multiple parent or child calls to refer farther than one step from an instance.) Also, and this is not insignificant, real parent-child relationships are substantially more complex (and I'm not even referring to the human element here), in that every person as an instance has two biological parents. There is thus not a single parent much less a single grandparent for a person. That said, I will periodically use the terms *parent* and *child* in the book when I specifically mean up1 m or down1 m. It should make things a little less dry and besides, you should feel comfortable with these terms as they are frequently used by vendors and analysts.

Now let's add a few more elements to the simple type of Figure 5.7 as illustrated in Figure 5.8.

Look at the leaves of the hierarchy. Notice how there is still a clean sibling or $\Delta i/m$ relationship between $i_4 m_3$ and $i_5 m_3$ and between $i_6 m_4$ and $i_7 m_4$. But is there still necessarily a sibling relationship between any of the children of $i_2 m_2$ and $i_3 m_2$? It depends on whether m_3 is equivalent to m_4. Does m_2 represent weeks while m_3 and m_4 represent days as shown in Figure 5.9?

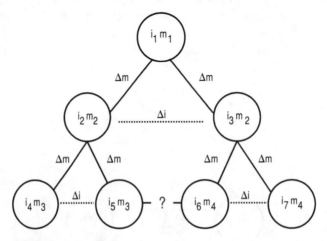

Figure 5.8 Some further complexity.

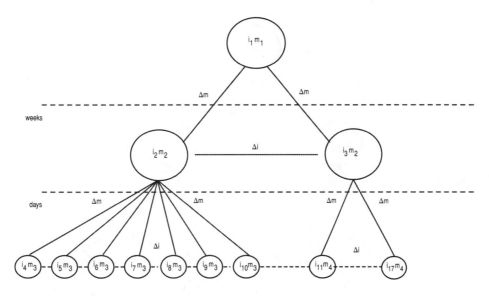

Figure 5.9 Time hierarchy for days and weeks.

Or does m_1 represent managers while m_2 and m_3 represent their direct reports as shown in Figure 5.10? Congratulations, you've made it to the junction of ragged and leveled hierarchies.

Ragged Hierarchies

One of the key distinctions between hierarchies is whether a group of instances that share the same m distance from either the root(s) or the leaves of the hierarchy also share the same m distance from either the leaves or the root(s). Consider Figures 5.11, 5.12, and 5.13. Given the hierarchy in Figure 5.11, let us say we wanted to reference all the elements that were the same distance from the root as home appliances, as shown in Figure 5.12. The collection includes the elements desks, chairs, beds, home appliances, and office equipment. All the elements in this collection are two m decrements from the root.

However, the members of the hierarchical dimension that are two m decrements down from the root are not all the same distance from the leaves. This is shown in Figure 5.13, which is composed of the same product hierarchy as Figure 5.12, but the collection of members the same distance from the bottom of the hierarchy as home appliances is highlighted. Home appliances is two m decrements from the root and two m increments from the leaves. However, when counting up from the leaves, no other member of the original top-down defined group is the same number of m increments from the leaves as home appliances. Hierarchies of the type just shown are called asymmetric or ragged. In practice, product, organizational, and territory reporting hierarchies are frequently ragged.

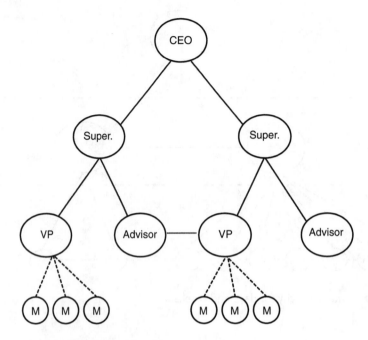

Figure 5.10   A ragged reporting hierarchy.

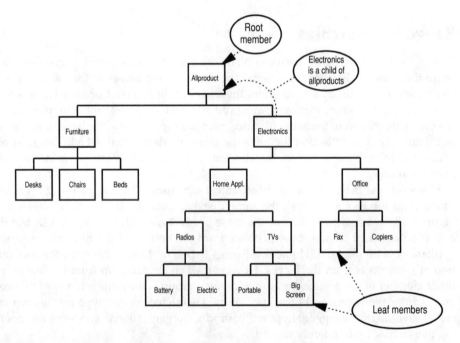

Figure 5.11   Product hierarchy for a manufacturer.

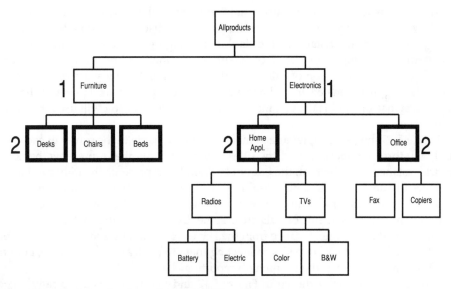

Figure 5.12   Referencing from the root within a hierarchy.

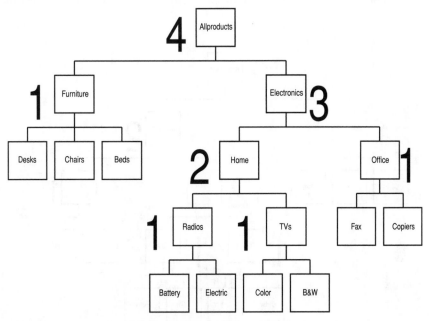

Figure 5.13   Referencing from the leaves in a hierarchy via the maximum distance.

The astute reader will have noticed that there is more than one way to count up from the leaves. Essentially, you can count the maximum distance, as was done in Figure 5.13, or the minimum distance, which is shown in Figure 5.14. Both counting methods are useful. For example, the notion of maximum distance is a better measure of hierarchy depth while the notion of minimum distance is a better measure of aggregation step when aggregations begin at the leaves and proceed upwards. However, the maximum distance method is the one more commonly used, and so I will use it by default in this book.

Figure 5.15 shows a simple ragged hierarchy with a name in the center of each node and with three numbers around the sides. The top left number represents the node's metric distance from the root, the bottom left number represents the minimum metric distance to a leaf, and the bottom right number represents the maximum metric distance to a leaf. This type of diagram enables you to see the degree of correspondence between the sets of elements calculated as some distance from the root and sets of elements calculated as some distance from the leaves. You can also see exactly which elements have different-length paths connecting them to the leaves. In this case, both the CEO and the COO have different-length reporting chains.

Whereas the hierarchy shown in Figure 5.12 and Figure 5.13 is a typically ragged hierarchy, the hierarchy shown in Figure 5.15 is a simple example of an extremely ragged hierarchy. While it may be more ragged than even a typical corporate reporting hierarchy, it is an accurate representation of a decision tree. Consider the binary decision process, as shown in Figure 5.16. Beginning at the root, and at each node, the process takes one of two paths so that a history of the process looks like the hierarchy

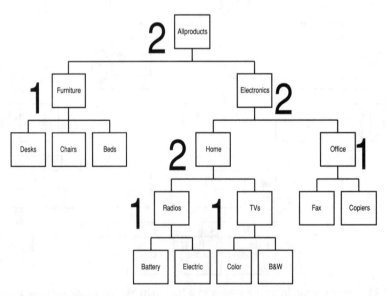

Figure 5.14 Referencing from the leaves in a hierarchy via the minimum distance.

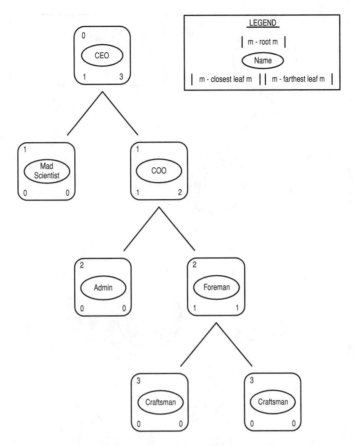

Figure 5.15 A simplified ragged corporate hierarchy.

shown in the figure. The decision tree could have just as easily had a nonbinary branching principle as shown in Figure 5.17.

Referencing Syntax

Here are summarized the main referencing relationships and the Located Contents (LC) syntax that works for ragged dimensions. Most products use one of two intratype referencing styles: dot notation or function argument notation. Using dot notation, you typically refer to the name of the type followed by a dot, then by the name of some instance followed by a dot, and finally by a referencing token as shown in this example:

```
Products.electronics.down1

Read ' move down one from the node labeled "electronics" in the
dimension labelled "products" '
```

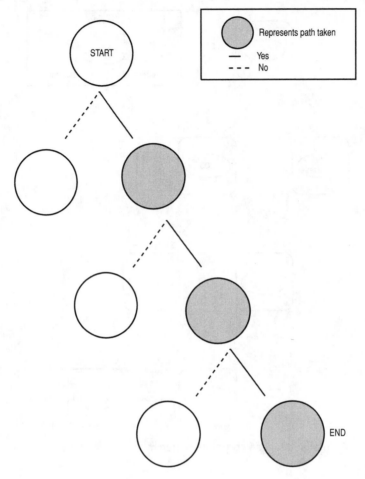

Figure 5.16   A binary decision tree.

Using function argument notation that same reference might have looked as follows:

```
Children(electronics , Products)

Read 'invoke the children function on the electronics member of the
Products dimension'
```

As I find the dot notation simpler to work with, especially for more complex relationships, it is the style that will be used in this book. That said, what follows are the main ragged referencing functions or syntax. The referencing examples work against the hierarchy shown in Figure 5.10.

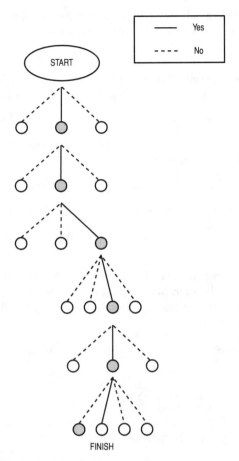

Figure 5.17   A nonbinary decision tree.

Given a type name and an instance in dot notation

`Type.instance.`

add any of

■ **under**, which refers to all elements that result from decrementing the metric of the given instance and not counting the given instance.

`Products.homeappliances.under yields (radios , battery , . . . )`

■ **atunder**, which refers to all elements that result from decrementing the metric of the given instance and counting the given instance.

`Products.homeappliances.atunder yields the same set as above plus the member 'home applicances'`

- **over**, which refers to all elements that result from incrementing the metric of the given instance and not counting the given instance.

```
Products.office.over >>  electronics , allproducts
```

- **atover** refers to all elements that result from incrementing the metric of the given instance and counting the given instance.

```
Products.office.atover >> same as above plus products.office
```

- **down***n* which refers to all elements that result from decrementing the metric of the given instance *n* decrements.

```
Products.electronics.down2 >> radios , TVs , Fax , Copiers
```

- **up***n* refers to all elements that result from incrementing the metric of the given instance *n* increments.

```
Products.fax.up2 >> electronics
```

Given these basic relationships, it is straightforward to define the slightly more complex relationships commonly referred to as sibling and cousin.

The siblings of any instance, including oneself, are simply the children of its parent, as with the following expression:

```
Type.instance.up1.down1
```

An example would be

```
Products.TV.up1.down1 >> Radios, TVs
```

The cousins of an instance are the grandchildren of the grandparent (note here the breakdown of the anthropomorphic metaphor).

```
Type.instance.up2.down2
```

An example would be

```
Products.TVs.up2.down2 >> Radios, TVs, Fax, Copiers
```

Now that you've seen classic ragged hierarchies, let's turn to classic leveled hierarchies.

Leveled or Symmetric Hierarchies

Although asymmetric hierarchies are common, not all hierarchies are asymmetric. Hierarchies, like the time hierarchy shown in Figure 5.18, where the collection of members some distance from the top or bottom of the dimension is the same regardless of which end you are counting from, are called symmetric hierarchies. With symmetric hierarchies, you can refer to members by their level. Thus, in Figure 5.18, the set of instances with the metric quarter is the set of all members two metric increments from the bottom and one metric decrement from the top; it can simply be referred to as the quarter level.

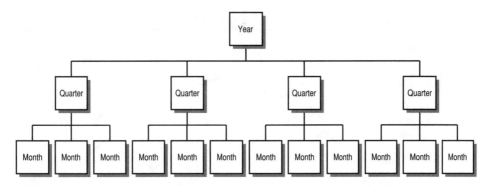

Figure 5.18   A symmetric hierarchy.

Whereas ragged hierarchies excel as a vehicle for aggregating irregularly clumped data, they provide no native support for cross-sibling analysis (although they sometimes support methods for doing some cross-sibling referencing, as shown later in this chapter under the heading *Orderings* in the section on deviate hierarchies. However, it needs to be qualified by saying that the function's semantics are not clearly defined for an arbitrary ragged hierarchy. Leveled hierarchies, by contrast, provide a notion of level that is the basis for performing any type of series analysis. The attributes and uses for level-based hierarchies are intertwined with the concept of ordering and thus I will successively describe dimension levels with nominal, ordinal, and cardinal properties.

Leveled Dimensions with Nominally Ordered Instances

The classic example of a business dimension that is represented with nominal levels is that of geography in the sense of named geographical locations, as illustrated in Figure 5.19. Note the named levels store, city, region, country, and all. One of the conditions that the instances need to meet is that levels are fully connected to each other. Every store connects to some city; every city connects to one or more stores. When collections of instances with the same metric are fully connected to the instances of an adjacent metric, all aggregate operations have deterministic results.

For example, aggregations of data between levels are equivalent. The sum of sales across all cities must equal the sum of sales across all stores. Counts and averages as well must produce identical results across levels. If they do not then the collections of instances are not fully connected and should be called named groups (described later in this chapter) instead of levels.

The general hierarchy referencing of Δ m/i that was used for the ragged referencing functions up/down applies just as well to levels. The issue is one of starting point. If you begin with an instance and move up or down, what returns is an instance or set of instances. If you begin, however, with a level and move up or down, what returns is a level. The astute reader may well have realized by this point that he or she will also

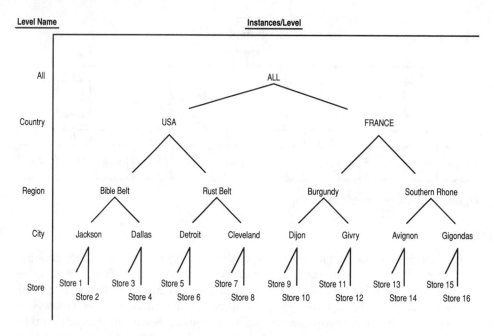

Figure 5.19   A business dimension represented with nominal levels.

need some method of requesting the level of some instance and the instances at some level. Thus, the following syntax is used:

- **under**   When applied to a level, it returns all the levels below the given level, not counting the given level.

```
Geog.Country.under >> Region, City, Store
```

When applied to an instance, it still returns all the instances below the given instance, not counting the given instance; in other words it behaves the same way it did with general and ragged hierarchies.

```
Geog.Avignon.under >> Store.(13, 14)
```

- **atunder**   When applied to a level, it returns all the levels below the given level counting the given level.

```
Geog.Country.atunder >> Country, Region, City, Store
```

- **over**   When applied to a level, it returns all the levels above the given level, not counting the given level.

```
Geog.City.over >> Region, Country, All
```

- **atover** When applied to a level, it returns all the levels above the given level counting the given level.

  ```
  Geog.City.over >> City, Region, Country, All
  ```

- **down*n*** Refers to the level that results from decrementing the given level *n* decrements.

  ```
  Geog.Country.down2 >> City
  ```

- **up*n*** refers to the level that results from incrementing the given level *n* increments.

  ```
  Geog.City.up2 >> Country
  ```

In addition to moving up and down levels, there is also a need to return the level of an instance or the instances at a level, as follows:

- Type.instance.level returns the name of the level of the instance:

  ```
  Geog.USA.level >> Country
  ```

- Type.instance.level.up/down 'x' returns the name of the level x units up or down from the level of the given instance:

  ```
  Geog.USA.level.down1 >> Region
  ```

- Type.instance.specifically named level atover the level of the given instance returns the name of the instance that is the ancestor of the given instance at the specified level:

  ```
  Geog.store.12.Country  >> France
  ```

- Type.level.instance. returns all the instances at the given level:

  ```
  Geog.USA.level.down1.i.>>  Bible belt , Rust belt
  ```

To simplify things, Type.level. also returns all the instances at a level as it makes no sense to ask for all the levels at a level. This notation will be used in the book.

In addition to directional referencing, levels can be used for explicit referencing, such as asking for the tax rate at the state level for a given store, as with the following formula:

```
Taxes owed = sales x (Tax rate, Geog.city)
```

This formula naturally applies to any element of the Geog dimension that is at or under the city level. It says to take the city tax rate for the city that is over the element whose sales is under consideration.

When using named levels, referencing data at particular levels in formulas can become much easier. For example, a formula can divide sales by the year level or the country-level sales without having to know how far away in the hierarchy the year-level value is from the current time member or how far away the country-level value is from the current geography member. Named levels help the person writing the formula concentrate on the meaning of the formula as opposed to the structure of the hierarchy.

Leveled Dimensions with Ordinally Ordered Instances

It is common for dimensions with nominal levels to get ordered according to some ordinal principle such as ordering the stores of a geography dimension by sales or the countries of a geography dimension by population. Given a leveled dimension where the instances of some level are ordinally arranged, it is possible to apply ordinal operations such as logistic functions to data sets dimensioned by the ordinalized level. The standard form for these data sets is as follows:

```
(Type.level.ordinal_ordering.)~ [Content1 , Content2 ,  . . . ]
```

In words, this reads that for every instance of the ordinally ordered level of the type on the left-hand side of the "~" operator there is a one-to-one association between each element on the left-hand side and some value of each of the contents on the right-hand side. Examples include the age of each runner (C) dimensioned by that runner's finish place (L), the median income of voters (C) dimensioned by political parties ordered by how they placed in the most recent election (L), or the return on investment (ROI) for new stores (C) dimensioned by the size rank of the store (L).

These types of analyses will be discussed in Chapter 20. It is also possible to use location-sensitive visualization techniques on ordinalized level dimensions. This will be discussed in Chapter 9. Recall from the earlier discussion of hierarchies that there are two basic types of relationships: $\Delta M/I$ and $\Delta M/I$. One of the weaknesses of ragged hierarchies is their lack of native support for $\Delta M/I$ functions. This is because, beyond the immediate siblings for an instance, there are no natural, nonhierarchy, traversing referencing functions. Even sibling traversal assumes that it makes sense to treat all the children of a common parent as belonging to the same metric. This assumption may or may not be true as it is quite easy for some children to be leaves while others contain deep subhierarchies. In these latter cases, it is not at all clear that it makes sense to treat all the siblings as equal.

What this means is that $\Delta i/M$ functions are sufficiently general for a ragged hierarchy that they can produce nonsense unless the designer manually verifies their semantics. This, of course, is one of the strengths of leveled hierarchies. You can always refer to the other instances of a metric, and metrics, in this sense behave like (and actually are) a series: nominal, ordinal, and/or cardinal.

Given that the instances can be ordered on a level-by-level basis, it is possible to use different sorting techniques for different levels. Consider again the geography dimension in Figure 5.19. Note the element connections in the figure such as the Dijon store connecting to the Burgundy region. Now what happens to the interlevel connections if you ordinalize the cities by size as shown in Figure 5.20?

Basically, the $\Delta M/I$ relationships have not altered. You can still navigate from Dijon to the Burgundy region. However, you can no longer take a vertical slice by requesting

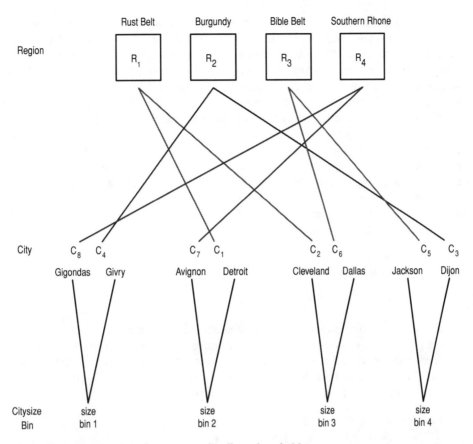

Figure 5.20   Connections between ordinally ordered cities.

Region.Burgundy.under and get back instances from the city level that are ordered by size.

Leveled Dimensions with Cardinally Ordered Instances: Time and Space

Time and space are the most pervasive examples of leveled dimensions or types whose instances are naturally cardinally ordered and that are typically used to represent business dimensions as opposed to measures (otherwise, I would have added mass as a pervasive leveled type as a variable). Their levels might be called seconds, minutes, hours, days, weeks, months, and years, or centimeters, meters and kilometers. In addition to all the type's instances belonging to one or another metric and for all the metrics being quantitatively comparable, all instances within a level are cardinally related. So you can add and subtract quantities along levels such as subtracting two months from a given month as you might do in a lag function where the future is related to the past.

A common function that you will encounter over and over again is relative referencing along the instances within a level based on the current cursor position. This is used to support all kinds of range queries from lags and leads to moving and cumulative aggregates. In other words, when an OLAP system is evaluating an expression, it is doing so relative to a dimensional context such as a set of stores and times.

For example, let's say that the time dimension is composed of months, quarters, and years and what's needed is to define a projected sales function based on historical growth rates over the last three months. In LC, you would refer to specific distances back and forth along the time dimension using the following syntax.

Time.month.this$+/-$"x" means from whatever is the current month (month.this) add to or subtract "x" units. Thus, in June, Time.month.this.-2 yields April and Time.month.this+2 yields August.

```
Projected sales,
        Time.Month.(this+3) =
        (Sales, Time.Month.this) x
        (Avg growth, Time.Month.((this-3) to this))
```

This reads the projected sales three months out equals the sales this month times the average growth in sales over the past three months. Levels whose instances are cardinally ordered support all the series-based formulas that were shown in the previous section. Thus, you may wish to compute a running average of the last three months' values for some variable as with the following expression:

```
Moving three month average sales =
Avg(Sales, Time.Month.((this-3) to this))
```

Even though today's OLAP tools do not model space very well, if at all, so that by far the greatest amount of relative cardinal referencing occurs, in an OLAP context, in the Time dimension, it is worth mentioning at least one relative range referencing example in space.

```
'Changes_in_economic_activity' ,
        Latitude.this.(+ or - "x") ,
        Longitude.this.(+ or - "x") ,
        Time.this =
         'Some_growth_factor' x
         ('Changes_in_economic_activity' , Latitude.this
,Longitude.this. , Time.(this -"x"))
```

In words, and assuming that the tuples defined by latitude.this and longitude.this denoted important economic spots, the expression says that changes in economic activity in some regions are driven by changes in neighboring economic hot spots at some earlier time.

Of course, there are many other occasions when one would want to leverage relative referencing in space, including gas dispersal, population movements, cultural fads, consumer tastes, and technology transfers.

Even though time and space are the dimensions that are most frequently associated with levels whose instances are cardinally ordered for the purpose of analysis, cardinal levels can apply to any dimension.

The fact that the instances of a level may be cardinally ordered doesn't mean the scaling factor between instances across two different levels is the same across the entire level. For example, although days and months are each cardinally ordered, there is not a constant scaling factor between days and months. Practically speaking, this means that in representing the dimension, explicit lineage links will still be needed as shown in Figure 5.21.

Space

Although space is naturally cardinally ordered, unlike time, space requires the combination of three dimensions to be modeled. The variety of geometries used to define space from basic rectangular to spherical typically lies either in mathematics or in geographic information systems modeling, but in any event are beyond the scope of today's OLAP tools.

In addition to working with time and space, most of the mathematics you learned can be rephrased in terms of levels with cardinally ordered instances. Any function defined on the integers or rationals is an example. We will look at examples of this kind of dimensional analysis in Chapter 20.

Constant Scaling Factors

So far, all of the leveled dimensions we've seen, even the ones with cardinally ordered instances, have had variable scaling factors. Now we look at leveled dimensions with constant scaling factors. Although it is logically possible for constant scaling factors to apply to a leveled dimension with nominally ordered instances, in practice, one sees

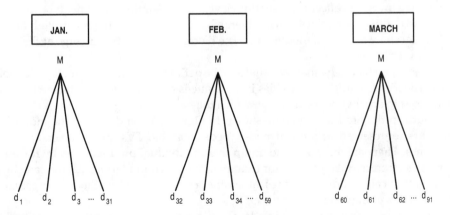

Figure 5.21 A time dimension with explicit lineage links.

constant scaling only in levels with cardinally ordered instances. As such I will look only at the latter.

Since the difference between instances is the same for cardinally ordered instances (that is, the total distance along any series of 60 seconds is the same), given the known relationship between levels such as the conversion between seconds and minutes, and the ordinal position of an instance, one can figure out the exact lineage connections for that instance. For example, second number 73 is a child of minute number 2 and hour number 1. Day number 40 is a child of month number 2.

With constant scaling factor dimensions, the dimension can be specified by defining the scaling factor between the levels. For example, one might define Time.levels. = Second, Minute, Hour where all three are expressed in integers. Then it suffices to state that Level.Hour = 60 x Level.Minute and Level.Minute = 60 x Level.Second. From that point on, one can determine an entire lineage from any given second, minute, or hour.

Of course, little except perhaps the pure numerics is constant. We've been known to add seconds every century or so and certainly hours get added and subtracted at least twice a year in most places. Space would appear to be a little more constant than time since all the hierarchies are derived, but even then, things like gravity can alter our space metrics. So the point here isn't to artificially define some idealized set of relationships that never hold, but rather to identify the main patterns of hierarchical structure that do exist and to show how two basic types of complimentary hierarchical vocabulary as reflected in commercial products can capture all the hierarchical relationships you will ever need to describe.

Multiple Hierarchies per Type

A single type may have more than one hierarchy. Stores, for example, in a Geography dimension may roll up by region and by store type. Products may roll up by category and by brand. Each hierarchy in a type is composed of a unique set of levels or hierarchically related instances. Although levels are unique within a single hierarchy, hierarchies may overlap, effectively sharing levels. For example, a time type may be composed of two hierarchies: a fiscal hierarchy and a calendar hierarchy. Both hierarchies may share a day and month level. The hierarchies may then diverge at the quarter and year levels.

For a ragged hierarchy that can otherwise be defined in terms of a parent-child table, the existence of multiple hierarchies in the dimension means that up hierarchy functions need to specify the hierarchy on which they are operating.

Return to the product hierarchy shown in Figure 5.11, and look at the individual products represented at the leaf nodes: beds, portable TVs, photocopiers, and fax machines. There are other ways to group these individual products than by furniture versus electronics. Take pricing, for example. As shown in Figure 5.22, the categories bargain, typical, and deluxe represent another equally useful method for organizing the members of the product dimension.

Choosing the appropriate middle levels of grouping or aggregation are critical to our understanding and our ability to make decisions because data have only one detail

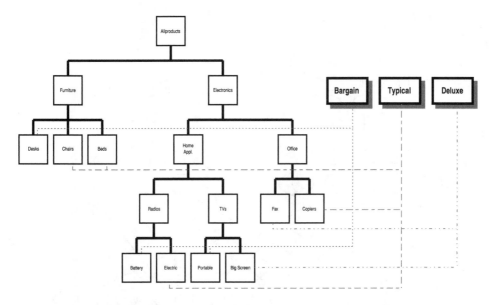

Figure 5.22   Dimensions can have multiple hierarchies.

level and one fully aggregated level but many intermediate levels. As shown in Figure 5.23, there are many paths to nirvana. Each path highlights some factors and hides others. For example, aggregating store-level product sales into cities, states, and countries highlights factors that are differentiated by region, such as economic zone-based differences in sales. The same aggregation path hides other factors, such as store size-based differences in sales. The nearly limitless number of intermediate levels, such as product price groups, product margin groups, product type groups, and product producer groups, enables us to experiment with different ways of looking at and understanding our data. This is one of the areas of convergence between dimensional structures and statistics. For example, techniques such as cluster analysis can help to identify the natural groupings in the data that then serve as useful intermediate levels of aggregation. (More on the relationship between OLAP and statistics in Chapter 20.)

Alternate methods of grouping do more than just rearrange the members; they create entirely different aggregate numbers Figure 5.24 shows two spreadsheets in two panels. Both spreadsheets are two-dimensional and are composed of a variables dimension and a product dimension. The variables dimension is identical between the two spreadsheets. The product dimensions share the same leaf nodes between the two spreadsheets; however, in Figure 5.24, A rolls up into furniture, home, and office products, whereas B rolls up into bargain and deluxe products. Not only are the numbers different, the number of numbers is different. Price and customer are two equally valid ways of grouping individual products. For most multidimensional products, the two rollups would be treated as separate hierarchies within the same dimension.

In this sense, a dimension may be thought of as a collection of leaf members and the set of hierarchy or group members created from that collection. In other words, all the members of a dimension—leaf members, intermediate level members, and root

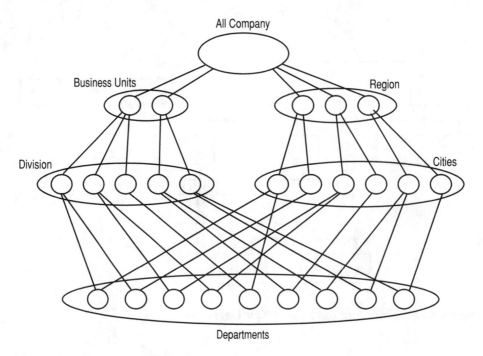

Figure 5.23 The many paths to nirvana.

	A				B	
	Sales	Costs			Sales	Costs
Beds	500	450		Tables	350	200
Tables	350	200		Fax	275	275
Furniture	850	650		Radios	150	125
Radios	150	125		Bargains	775	600
TVs	550	400		Beds	500	450
Home	700	525		Photocopiers	600	500
Fax	275	275		TVs	550	400
Photocopier	600	500		Deluxe	1650	1350
Office	875	775				

Figure 5.24 Different rollup paths produce different aggregate numbers.

members—form a single collection of members of the same type, which, as a whole, constitutes one factor/dimension in a multifactor/dimensional situation. Keep in mind that all members of a dimension, from leaf to root, can vary from analysis to analysis.

Looking again at Figure 5.22, if a dimension has multiple hierarchies, when traversing up the hierarchy from any node (child) that has two or more parents, see how it is necessary to specify the parent or root toward which you are navigating. For example, if from the member fax machines, you wanted to navigate up to office equipment, it would be necessary to indicate that you wanted to move in the direction of allproduct rather than in the direction of deluxe products. OLAP tools differ in how and if they provide this functionality. Many define a main hierarchy that is the default and force you, sometimes through less than intuitive steps, to specify an alternate that you may want to follow. Others offer a great deal of flexibility and provide for custom hierarchies that can be defined within the context of a report.

The following examples illustrate hierarchical referencing along a dimension that contains multiple hierarchies.

```
Time.fiscal_hierarchy.yearend
```

Read "the yearend member of the fiscal hierarchy of the time dimension."

```
Geography.store_type_hierarchy.department_stores
```

Read "the department stores level of the store_type hierarchy of the Geography dimension."

```
Myfavoritedimension.alernativehierarchy.most popular member.up1
```

Read "the parent of the most popular member of the alternative hierarchy of my favorite dimension."

Deviant Hierarchies

You ideally want a tool that supports both leveled and ragged hierarchies within a single syntax because it is awkward to try to represent ragged hierarchies with a level-based tool and to represent a leveled hierarchy with a ragged-based tool. So what are the awkward or deviant options?

Pseudolevels

A named level can be simulated with a tool that is based on ragged hierarchies, so long as it supports multiple hierarchies by introducing a member into the dimension that serves as a root for the level, and by making all members intended to belong to a common level as immediate children of that root. To represent the concept of a city level as shown in the ragged geography hierarchy in panel B of Figure 5.25, a root member named City needs to be added to the dimension and be made a parent of Chicago, Milwaukee, and Columbus, and so on. I call this technique pseudolevels, as it creates the named grouping of members, though without any of the semantic attributes possessed by levels. Figure 5.25 illustrates the pseudolevels in panel B contrasted against named levels in panel A.

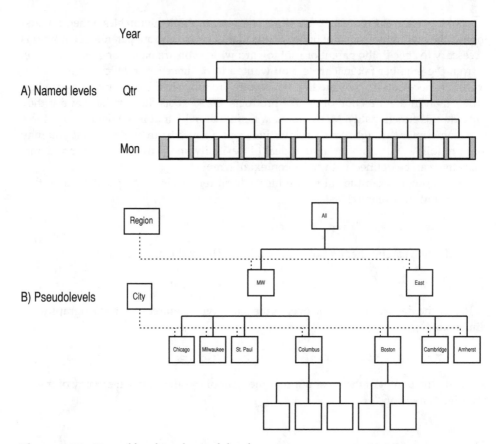

Figure 5.25   Named levels and pseudolevels.

When using pseudolevels, it is awkward to find out how the level for a member relates to other levels, or even to find the next level above or below, because the tool does not directly support this notion of level. (The adjacent-level information might be coded as an attribute of the level's root member.) Accessing members from one level to the next can be a little difficult as well. Say that a geography dimension is modeling countries, provinces/states, and cities using a level's root members of country, province, and city. To get the cities for the country France, you will have to obtain "all children of the member city that are also children of the member France." A tool may or may not be able to express this easily.

Ideally, a tool provides clean support for both irregular hierarchies and named levels that are semantically understood to be like levels of scale.

Ordering

By incorporating the notion of ordering into siblings so that there is a first, second, and so on up to last sibling, several OLAP products make it possible to refer to the same relative sibling in a ragged dimension within a relative or cousin function. The classic uses for these types of functions are relative time-based comparisons where someone wants to compare the first week of some quarter with the first week of the previous quarter or the first week of the same quarter for the previous year. As a note of caution, these types of ordering-based referencing functions do not have clearly defined semantics in an arbitrary ragged hierarchy.

For example, and referring to Figure 5.26 with a starting point of $Y_3.Q_2.M_2.W_2$, you might want to refer to the same relative week, previous month, and same absolute quarter and year

```
Y₃.Q₂.M₂.W₂.up1.prev1.W₂
```

or the same relative week and month for the previous quarter for the same absolute year

```
Y₃.Q₂.M₂.W₂.up2.prev1.M₂.W₂
```

or the same relative week, month, and quarter for the previous year

```
Y₃.Q₂.M₂.W₂.up₃.prev1.Q₂.M₂.W₂
```

Referring to the sample syntax, note that in order to make these references work, it is necessary to identify a previous member from within the ancestry. Again, this notion of previous sibling is a leveled notion for it assumes that the metrics of each sibling are identical, an assumption that cannot be made in a ragged hierarchy without adding level-like conditions. For products that support this type of referencing, either they make you specify the nearest root whose value does not change (this is quarter in the first example and year in the second) or they enable you to refer to a previous element

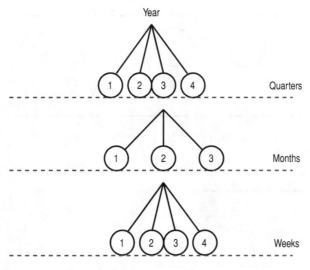

Figure 5.26 View of the time dimension hierarchy.

at some level in the hierarchy as described previously. Either way, the dimension against which the function is evaluated has elements of a leveled dimension and cannot be said to be purely ragged.

Dummy Members

In the same way that ragged hierarchy-based tools can provide some of the capabilities of levels by using pseudolevels, pure level-based tools can provide for some ragged modeling by making use of dummy members. How would you model with a ragged geography hierarchy with a level-based tool? Basically you need to associate each node with a level. Of course, the problem is that many nodes would need to associate with more than one level. For example, the stores report directly to the region level without passing through a city member. The way to get around this is by introducing dummy cities to represent the stores at the city level where there otherwise isn't any city. This is illustrated in Figure 5.27.

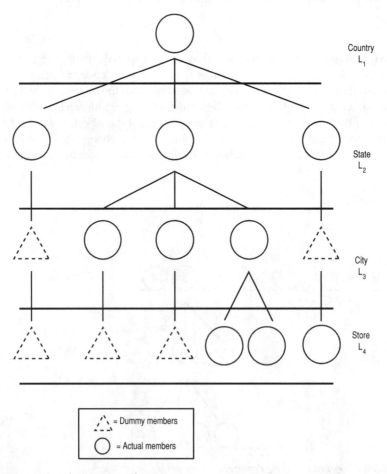

Figure 5.27   Using dummy members.

The thing to keep in mind when using dummy members is whether the dummy member figures in the meta data for its level and is counted as a member, capable of being seen as a member and whether it has any data associated with it. If the answer is no, then the use of a dummy member has turned the level into a named group because the level aggregates no longer correspond. This isn't necessarily bad, but you need to know what you're doing.

For example, if you used a level-based tool to define a ragged geography dimension composed of stores, cities, and states where some stores fed directly into states, you might create dummy city members to represent those stores that had no corresponding city. However, since the dummy members are otherwise invisible, if you were to query for the total sales across cities, that total would not include the values associated with the dummy members and city totals would be less than store totals. This is a clear violation of level properties. You should no longer think of the dimension as leveled. However, just because the dimension isn't leveled doesn't mean it's wrong. It could be that the city instances represent some specific city infrastructure that isn't present in those cities where stores feed directly to states.

Mixed Hierarchies

Finally, it should be clear by now that the world is pretty well mixed in terms of hierarchies. For most applications that you may ever undertake there are likely to be some types best modeled as ragged, some types that are best modeled as leveled, and some types that would benefit from a combination of leveled and ragged structuring. Real-world product hierarchies are frequently leveled near the root and become ragged towards the leaves. Therefore, from a tool perspective, an ideal dimension structure supports levels and raggedness equally well and within the same hierarchy.

When a hierarchy is defined with both ragged and level characteristics, the instances of any level must not contain any parent child relations, and for any two levels A and B (and assuming those levels to be adjacent to each other in the hierarchy[6]), where the instances of level A are considered up from the instances of level B, the levels must be related so that every instance of level A has one or more children instances in level B and no children that are not within level B; every instance of level B must have one and only one parent instance in level A and no parent that is not within level A. In other words, the levels must be fully connected. Figures 5.28 and 5.29 show examples of valid and invalid mixed hierarchies.

For mixed hierarchies (unlike extreme forms of either ragged or leveled hierarchies), the level descriptors and the lineage descriptors are independent. So it is important to be able to use both sets of descriptors for intratype referencing within the same type.

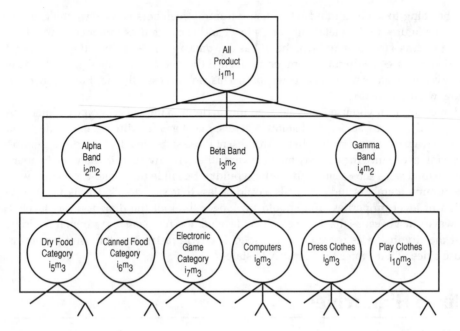

Figure 5.28 A valid mixed hierarchy.

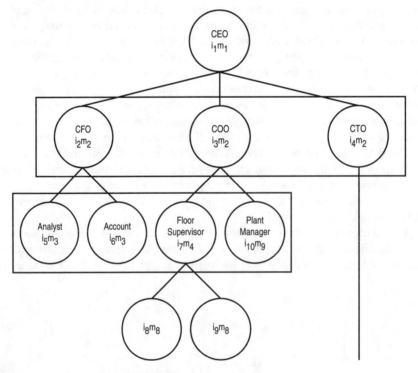

Figure 5.29 An invalid mixed hierarchy.

Summary

In this chapter you have seen why and how dimensional hierarchies are defined in terms of several nonhierarchical characteristics, including methods of definition, metrics, and ordering. You learned the difference between a valid and an invalid dimension or type; you saw how hierarchies originate from dimensions with multiple quantitatively comparable metrics; and you saw that while ragged and leveled hierarchies are reasonably independent and require distinct referencing syntaxes, they stem from a common and more general form of hierarchy. You were exposed to examples of referencing syntax for ragged and leveled hierarchies. You learned about multiple hierarchies, mixed hierarchies, and ways of using leveled hierarchy-based tools to mimic ragged hierarchies, and ways of using ragged hierarchy-based tools to mimic leveled hierarchies.

TYPES

The fact that types need to have at least two possible instances doesn't mean that you can't create seemingly monolithic types to represent the "universe" or the "world" or "everything possibly imaginable." For example, say you were to define a type to represent "anything imaginable" and give it just one *possible* instance, namely anything imaginable, so that it might seem that any expression could take this instance as a true assertion. Could you really create assertions and negations from this mono-instanced type? Or is something missing? Let's explore this more closely. Assume two types as shown in the following table:

TYPE NAME	THE IMAGINABLE	ANY COLOR
Type instance	Anything imaginable	Red
		Blue
		Green

Assuming each type is predictable of the other, we can create the following expressions: Red is anything imaginable; blue is anything imaginable; green is anything imaginable. Anything imaginable is red; anything imaginable is blue; anything imaginable is green. If we were now to imagine that anything imaginable were true as a content predicated of red, then according to the rules of logic, there must exist some other possible instance or value of the imaginable, whose value would be false of the same location, namely red. It is logically impossible to assert that anything imaginable is a true instance of the type the imaginable when predicated of the color red without being able to express what a false instance of the type the imaginable would look like.

Not only is it impossible to engage in truth function or assertion/negation expressions without types of two or more potential instances, but types bearing a single potential instance have no power to make any differentiations. If anything imaginable is supposedly true of anything, and anything is true of anything imaginable, then the type anything imaginable, with its single potential instance, is incapable of being used to differentiate anything, nor is anything differentiated by it. Thus, the mono-instanced type not only violates the basic tenets of logic, but it is furthermore void of any information-carrying capability.

## CHAPTER 6

Hypercubes or Semantic Spaces

Cubes or hypercubes, in the sense of working Online Analytical Processing (OLAP) models, are live or active or populated schemas, which is to say any schema whose data links are in use so that data are connected to the schema and being manipulated in accordance with the rules or formulas defined in that schema. Links need not replicate data. The data can reside in whatever form is dictated by the data source so long as it can be manipulated via a multidimensional schema. Although not typically the case, data can be entirely entered by hand directly into a model; in that case the data links are what connects the keyboard (or other input devise) to the schema. (Please refer to Chapter 10 for a discussion of different approaches to storing multidimensional data.)

What happens when source data that could exist or are thought to exist don't actually exist? What happens when there are more data in the source than can be accounted for in the type definitions? How is one supposed to connect multiple data sources of clearly different dimensionalities such as production and sales data to a single schema for some integrated analytical purpose? Are there natural segmentation principles for defining schemas?

In this chapter you will learn why a populated schema or model constitutes what I call a *semantic space* or a contiguous collection of facts or propositions that can be true or false. You will learn the steps you need to take to ensure your schemas are well defined. You will learn how to identify and treat separately the naturally distinct domains in your data or models, and you will learn how to bring them together when necessary into a multidomain model.

Meaning and Sparsity

One of the key attributes of a schema is its enforcement of meaningfulness. Consider the familiar schema

```
(Store. ⊗ Time. ⊗ Product.) ~ Sales, Cost
```

connected through a set of data links with some table T1 (illustrated in Figure 6.1), such as the following:

- Store. << Select distinct T1 Column (Col)1
- Time. << Select distinct T1Col2
- Product. << Select distinct T1Col3
- Sales. << Select T1Col4
- Cost. << Select T1Col5

where the << symbol acts like an assignment operator, and distinct means that the unique instances of each of the types Store, Time, and Product are set equal to the unique instances found in the columns to which they're connected.

The schema defines a semantic space or contiguous collection of facts consisting of statements or assertions about sales and costs for every store-time-product combination. If there are 10 stores, 10 times, and 10 products, there are 1,000 assertions about sales and 1,000 assertions about costs. Each assertion is a four-tuple with a three-tuple location and a one-tuple content.

```
Sales (Store.x , Time.x , Product.x) = Y
```

The above can be read as "The sales-as-content value for the location defined by Store x, Time x, and Product x is the Sales value Y."

If a formula is defined for margins based on sales and costs, without further specification, it will be applied 1,000 times, once for each instance of sales and costs. Integrity constraints, as set up when all the component types were initially defined, are maintained here. Thus, if you were to try to enter a string or other out-of-bounds value for sales, the schema would catch it.

	Col1	Col2	Col3	Col4	Col5
Row1	Store1	Time1	Product1	$500	$400
...					
...					
Row1000	Store 10	Time 10	Product 10	$400	$600

Figure 6.1 Table T1 (with only a few values filled in).

Additionally, *and unless otherwise restricted*, the schema defines the contents *sales* and *costs* to be applicable to the entire collection of locations defined by the intersections of stores, times, and products. This is why there are a thousand assertions. Thus, if connected to a data source, there are locations for which no sales or costs data are present, the schema (without further specification) should interpret the lack or sparsity of data to mean that the data are missing but otherwise forthcoming.

Another possible interpretation for sparse or nonpresent rows could be that rows only exist for items that were sold; therefore, nonpresent rows mean that zero amount of product was sold. Another interpretation could be that the nonpresent rows mean that a certain product is by definition not sold at a certain store and/or time and thus the contents sales and costs are not applicable to certain combinations of stores times and products. As you will learn in the following sections, the way in which these non-present rows or sparse or empty cells are interpreted is critical to the integrity of the application as a whole. Many OLAP tools are unfortunately lacking in methods to make the appropriate distinctions, which can lead to incorrect data derivations. For a technology whose claim to fame is creating derived data, that's a pretty serious flaw. A well-designed schema should correctly process (or allow an application to process) all types of invalid source data by either rejecting certain data, overriding certain data, substituting certain data, or inferring certain data.

Types of Sparsity

The terms "sparse" and "sparsity" are frequently associated with multidimensional data sets. Figure 6.2 is a view of a sparse four-dimensional matrix. The four dimensions are stores, time, product, and variables. The view shows variables and products along the columns, stores, and times along the rows. Notice all the sparse or blank cells.

Why are the sparse cells sparse? Does a sparse cell mean that data for the cell are missing but potentially forthcoming, like a late sales report? Does a sparse cell mean that data could never apply to the cell, such as the name of an unmarried employee's spouse? Or does a sparse cell simply mean that all zeros are being suppressed like the zeros associated with individual product sales in a store that carries many products but that only sells 5 percent of its items on any one day?

The term sparse has been indiscriminately used within the OLAP community to mean missing, inapplicable, and zero. The first two cases fall under the heading of what in the database world is thought of as invalid data. It is an important topic. E. F. Codd, in his expanded 18 features for OLAP, suggested that OLAP models follow the

		Indirect Sales			Direct Sales			Total Sales		
		Chairs	Tables	Total	Chairs	Tables	Total	Chairs	Tables	Total
Avon	January	150		150	250		250	400	0	400
	February	120	220	340	300	150	450	790	370	790
	March		300	300				300	300	300
Milwaukee	January	600	800	1400				1400	800	1400
	February	760			200	1350	2550	2550	1350	2550
	March	300		300				300	0	300

Figure 6.2 Viewing a sparse four-dimensional model.

relational model version 2 rules for handling missing data.[1] These entail what is called four-valued logic. This will be treated in depth later in this section.

The third case, where the term sparsity has been used to mean the existence of many zeros, is a special case of how to handle large numbers of repeating values where the repeated value happens to be a zero. Zero is just as valid a number as any other number. Technically, it is an integer. It is a perfectly well-formed statement to say that store x sold zero units of product y or that the difference in units sold between store x and store y is zero. It carries as much value as to say that store x sold 15 units of product y. You can add subtract and multiply with zeros (though, of course, you can't divide by them). You can compare them to other quantities and so on.

The confusion has arisen because OLAP applications frequently encounter large numbers of repeating zeros and large amounts of missing and meaningless data. The techniques for physically optimizing the storage of large numbers of repeating values are similar to, and sometimes the same as, the techniques for physically optimizing the storage of large amounts of missing data and meaningless locations or intersections.

Past Treatment of Invalid Data

Missing and meaningless values are not valid data. They cannot be treated in the same way as any other value. You cannot take the sum of three integers plus two missing values. You cannot compare the value of an integer with that of an inapplicable token. Special logical techniques are required to handle these cases. Improper treatment of nulls can cause inaccurate calculations. Mistaking a missing value for a zero, or mistaking a zero for a missing value, or assigning a proxy value where none is applicable all create incorrect results. For example, if a missing value is treated like a zero, then the sum of $3 + 6 +$ "missing" will be called 9, which is wrong. The right answer, in the absence of a proxy value, is "missing," or "9 + missing."

The accuracy of calculations is of crucial importance to the analysis of any data sets, whether or not they are multidimensional. The issue of how formulas should work with sparse data is an important one and is frequently debated in the database world. As it relates to the accuracy of calculations, especially in the sense of database queries and computations, it is a question of logic.

For most of its history, logicians have believed there were two logical values: true and false. Logical rules that apply to databases are expressed in terms of these two values. For example, querying a database to list all salespersons who sold more than $50,000 of product in March may be thought of as posing, to each salesperson's record for March, the question "Is it true that this salesperson sold more than $50,000 of product?" and listing all the records where the answer is "yes, the statement is true." This is illustrated in Figure 6.3.

Problems arise, however, when invalid data enter a logical system or database. Look again at Figure 6.3. Notice the blank entry for the commission field in row five. Now imagine the query, "Is it true that the value of the commission field in this row is greater than $50,000?" What would the answer be?

You could be a wise guy like Aristotle and say the statement is false; that is, it is false that the value of the commission field is greater than $50,000 simply because there is no value. But there is a problem with this answer. The problem is that the truth of the

List of employees, job titles and number of years with firm
(sorted alphabetically by employee name)

Employee name	Job Title	Commission	
Anderson	Sales	75,000	
Awklin	Sales	65,000	
Bundy	Sales	82,500	
Benson	Sales	58,000	
Burnett	Sales		Missing
Caloway	Marketing		N/A
Johnson	Sales	62,500	
Kreiger	Sales	55,000	

Late report·····►

Caloway not·····► a salesperson

Figure 6.3 Record sparsity.

answer is a function of how the question was phrased. In other words, if the query had had the form "Is it true that the value of the commission field is less than or equal to $50,000?" the answer would still, according to the same logic, be false. But according to logic, a proposition and its inverse cannot both be true or have the same truth value.

More likely you would say, "I don't know whether it is true or false because the data are missing." This is tacit acceptance of your inability to process the missing data as if it were existent. In the same vein, and answering the same query, if an employee did not draw a commission because that person was salaried, then the commission field would be inapplicable, as shown in row 6 of Figure 6.3. That is, commission does not apply because the employee draws a salary. "Not applicable" is similar to "missing" in that you cannot process it like a valid data value, but it is different from "missing" in that it would be wrong to assign it a proxy.

Logic has no rules for handling invalid data, yet such things as missing and inapplicable data regularly enter all kinds of databases—including multidimensional ones. Logicians are divided over the best way to deal with invalid data. Some prefer to use logical systems that work with three or more logical values. Terms such as "unknown" and "not applicable" are frequently given to these beyond-two-valued values. The extra values then enter into the formal calculus.

The main problem with the three- and higher-valued logics is that the meaning of the logical constants or operators, such as the negation term, which have been built up and used successfully over the last 2,000 years, depend on there being just two values. It is inconsistent to add a third or fourth term to the pool of logical values while continuing to use operators that assume there are only two values.[2, 3]

In the relational model, version 2, Codd advocates the use of four-valued logic. Like others who have gone before, he changes the meaning of the negation term, giving it two different meanings, as illustrated in Figure 6.4.[4]

For true and false propositions, the negation of a term yields a different term with a different truth value. The negation of true is false, and the negation of false is true. For

P	not (P)
T	F
A	A
I	I
F	T

T = true   F = false   A = missing   I = meaningless

Figure 6.4   The four-valued logic of the relational model, version 2.

missing and inapplicable propositions, the negation of a term is itself. So the negation of missing is missing and the negation of inapplicable is inapplicable. This inconsistency in the definition of negation produces several problems that have been described elsewhere.[5]

Some prefer to retain two-valued logic because of its desirable inferencing properties and exclude invalid data from entering the system.[6] They generally characterize invalid data as either the result of poor database design or as data about the data (sometimes called meta data). For example, rather than entering the null value for "spouse's name" into an employee database when an employee has no spouse, it would be better to enter the valid data value "no" into a field called "is married." A separate spouse table would contain the relevant spouse information. The improved database design would eliminate the invalid data.

The problem with this two-values-plus-meta-data approach is that it conflates two general classes of invalid data: missing and meaningless.[7] The two classes need to be individually treated because they affect computations in different ways. They just don't need to be treated as logical values on a par with true and false. Consider the following example.

Need to Distinguish Missing and Meaningless

Imagine you are the general sales manager for a chain of 100 department stores, and imagine you need to calculate the average monthly shoe sales per store for all 100 stores. In the simple case, all 100 stores sell shoes and all 100 stores reported their sales of shoes. The arithmetic is clear.

If all 100 stores sell shoes, but only 80 out of the 100 stores reported their sales, and the average for those 80 stores was $20,000, the arithmetic is no longer straightforward. It would not be accurate to state without qualification that the average shoe sales per store was $20,000. Any statement about shoe sales that applies to all stores in the chain must, implicitly or explicitly, assign a default value to the nonreporting stores. Saying that the average sales per store is $20,000 assumes that the average per nonreporting store is $20,000 as well. This default value for the nonreporting stores need not equal the average value of the reporting stores, however. For example, it may make more sense to assume that nonreporting stores sell a dollar value equal to what they sold the last period modified by some function of their previous growth rate.

If the reason why 20 stores did not report shoe sales is because they recently stopped selling shoes, then no statement should be created about shoe sales that applies to all 100 stores. In other words, no default value for shoe sales should ever be assigned to stores for whom the value is meaningless. In this situation, it would be accurate to state that the average sales for the 80 stores that sell shoes is $20,000.

However, in the same way that a proxy value may be substituted for a missing data point, there are times when an applicable measure or variable, such as slippers, may be substituted for the inapplicable variable, shoe sales. For example, it may be that shoes are thought of as footwear and, although most stores sell shoes, some specialty stores do not sell shoes, but do sell slippers. In this instance, it would make sense to report on the sale of slippers (modified by some appropriate function relating the average sales of shoes to slippers) where a store does not sell shoes.

Thus, when a measure or variable, such as shoe sales, is applicable but data values are missing, regardless of the reason, the missing values need to be assigned some type of default if they enter into operations with other data. (It is always possible to stipulate that missing data values be eliminated from a calculation as, for example, when a manager's bonus is tied to his or her store's sales figures and the bonus cannot be assigned until the actual sales figures are known.)

When a measure or variable (such as shoe sales) is not applicable to a location for whatever reason (such as a particular store that stopped selling shoes) and substitute variables are not being used, no default data value should ever be assigned to it for that location.

In general, the existence/nonexistence of data (such as sales reports) and the applicability/inapplicability of measures (such as the dollar value of shoe sales) may vary from location to location, or cell to cell, in a model. For example, if sales reports are late, then applicable data is missing for those stores. If a store changes its product lines, then certain variables may become inapplicable and/or applicable between time periods.

From my experience, and as described in the remainder of this section, the ideal approach is to combine two-valued logic with procedures for detecting missing and inapplicable data on an instance-by-instance basis.[8] This approach lets the user freely incorporate user-defined rules for substituting measures and data whenever invalid cases are found. For those situations where the system is left with missing and/or inapplicable data, formal rules are used to convert the mixed expressions containing missing and/or inapplicable data into a two-valued form where they can be processed via the use of traditional and consistent propositional logic.

Defining Application Ranges

Unless your data sets are perfectly dense (which is unlikely) or unless all sparsity means zero (again unlikely), it is essential that you maintain the distinction between missing and inapplicable data in your applications. The most unambiguous way to do this is by explicitly defining application ranges for those types used as contents within a schema. (You can do this through your own application documentation since application ranges are not typically supported by OLAP products.)

Recall any basic schema such as

```
(Store. ⊗ Time. ⊗ Product.) ~ Sales
```

This schema is expecting a sales value for every single store, time, and product intersection. Now in fact, stores rarely sell every product every day. A typical sales summary table that would feed this type of schema would have one row of information for every product sold on a store-by-time basis. So already there is an implicit interpretation rule—namely that the schema interprets the lack of a row for any particular product for any time by store as meaning that zero amount of that product was sold at that store that day.

Now what happens if some products, say winter garments, are inapplicable to (that is, by definition not sold in) certain stores, such as those in southern Florida, either in general or at certain times? In this case, the schema is not really correct as it stands. Sales are not applicable to every intersection of store time and product. Queries for average sales per store of winter garments, as shown in the previous section, will be incorrect. There needs to be some way to specify the inapplicability of winter garments to southern Florida stores or the application will incorrectly parse the absent rows for winter garments in southern Florida as meaning zeros instead of not applicable. This specification is the definition of an application range and requires some syntactic device for specifying applicability and inapplicability.

In Located Contents (LC), applicability and inapplicability are specified when the type as variable or content is defined as shown next in a continuation of the previous example.

```
Sales, (Time. ⊗ Store.Southern Florida.atunder ⊗ Product.Winter
garments.atunder) = n/a
```

The expression in parentheses specifies that portion of the total location—namely all intersections of southern Florida stores and winter garments—for which sales is inapplicable (n/a). You may be harboring several questions at this point such as why didn't I define the location range for which sales was applicable, or is *n/a* a value and if so to what type does it belong, or could one also have declared the same location range to be missing?

I didn't define the location range for applicability because the initial schema specification defines the content, sales, as applicable across the entire range of times, stores, and products. So the definition of this inapplicability may be thought of as an exception or qualification relative to the general schema that preceded it. *n/a* is a logical value and as such applies to any type and can be represented in dot notation as Type.n/a. Thus, one could pose a query for the ratio of sales growth increase for those stores that sell winter garments versus those that don't with the following expression:

```
Sales_Growth, Store.(Sales.n/a , Product.WinterGarments.atunder). /
Sales_Growth, Store.(Sales.a , Product.WinterGarments.atunder).
```

Finally, in the same way that n/a is a logical value and can be used to qualify any type, so too can the logical values applicable *a* (used in the expression above), missing *m*, and present *p*. Thus, the previous query could be restated to ask for the sales growth ratio of stores with present versus missing sales as shown here:

```
Sales_Growth, Store.(Sales.m , Product.WinterGarments.atunder). /
Sales_Growth, Store.(Sales.p , Product.WinterGarments.atunder).
```

Application Ranges in Use

The example shown in Figure 6.5 involves monthly sales reports sent from stores to the home office. At the end of March 2002, the home office wanted to calculate how many shoes were sold across all stores for the first quarter of 2002 in order to refine plans for the second quarter. Where actual figures were not available, an estimate had to be used to facilitate the planning process.

On February 1, 2000, as part of a specialization program, the Buckley store stopped selling shoes. The Ashmont and Painesville stores had not, as of March 31, 2000, reported their sales for March. The available data types per store and month, as highlighted in Figure 6.5(a), indicate that the Buckley store needed to be eliminated from any calculations involving February and March. By maintaining applicability information, this is easily done.

The available data per store and month, as highlighted in Figure 6.5(b), required that March figures for the Ashmont and Painesville stores be estimated since the measurements were applicable but were as yet unavailable.

Consider the following formula to calculate the average monthly shoe sales applied across all stores in the company for the first three months of 2000:

```
Shoe_Sales, L.leaf.above. = Avg(Shoe_Sales.a, L.leaf.)

If Shoe_Sales, L.leaf. = m
Shoe_Sales, L.leaf. = (Shoe_Sales, (Time.year.(this - 1))) *
Shoe_Sales_Growth_Factor
```

In words, the top line says the average value for shoe sales will be calculated at non-leaf levels of the location structure by averaging the shoe sales values wherever they are applicable at the leaf level. Without further specification this formula would return a value of missing if there were any missing values because no instructions are given for how to process missing values. The second section gives instructions for processing missing values and says to look at the value for shoe sales for each leaf level location. If it is applicable but missing, then substitute an approximation determined by taking last year's value and multiplying that by an expected growth factor. Then calculate the average shoe sales from all the valid values plus all the projected values.

Wherever the shoe sales variable is inapplicable, such as in the Buckley store in February and March, no substitution will be made for those locations. Where the shoe sales variable is applicable but data is missing, such as Painesville in March, the formula will create an estimate based on sales for the same period in the prior year. If there were no approximation clauses in the formula to deal with missing data, or they in turn were missing, then the formula as a whole would be unevaluable and would return a result of missing.

a) Shoes no longer sold, need to exclude these store–months from computations involving shoe sales

	Jan	Feb	Mar
Buckley	Items Sold / $ Sales Shoes 150 Coats 100 Shirts 250 Hats 45 Scarves 15	Items Sold / $ Sales Coats 85 Shirts 300 Hats 65 Scarves 15	Items Sold / $ Sales Coats 50 Shirts 400 Hats 90 Scarves 20
Middletown	Items Sold / $ Sales Shoes 100 Coats 85 Shirts 200 Hats 30 Scarves 30	Items Sold / $ Sales Shoes 120 Coats 75 Shirts 210 Hats 45 Scarves 25	Items Sold / $ Sales Shoes 150 Coats 100 Shirts 300 Hats 20 Scarves 20
Ashmont	Items Sold / $ Sales Shoes 150 Coats 350 Shirts 65 Hats 25 Scarves 15	Items Sold / $ Sales Shoes 105 Coats 110 Shirts 110 Hats 35 Scarves 10	Items Sold / $ Sales Shoe Coat Shir Hats Scar
Painesville	Items Sold / $ Sales Shoes 85 Coats 65 Shirts 15 Hats 25 Scarves 10	Items Sold / $ Sales Shoes 65 Coats 45 Shirts 10 Hats 10 Scarves 15	Items Sold / $ Sales Shoes Coats Shirts Hats Scarves

In order to compute a value involving these unreported figures, some implicit or explicit assumption must be made about them, or else the fact that they are not available must make the result unavailable as well.

b) Sample result

Shoe sales

	Jan	Feb	Mar
Buckley	150	...	....
Middletown	100	120	150
Ashmont	150	105	130
Painesville	85	65	75

Average sales	Quarter	
All Stores	103	2/12 N/A 2/12 est. 8/12 actual

Figure 6.5 Handling inapplicable versus missing data.

EVALUATING EXPRESSIONS WITH VALID AND INVALID DATA

The LC model offers a general method for evaluating formulas that contain a mixture of valid and invalid data. These procedures are outlined and illustrated in Figure 6.6.

The following procedure is repeated for each variable in the expression or formula. The application and the formula together determine the strategy for deciding what to do when you encounter an inapplicable variable or missing data. The procedure takes place per location, and per variable reference within the expression.

Phase One: Test for Applicability

Determine whether the variable is applicable to this location. If not, then refer to the evaluation strategy for what to do: Substitute another variable or value, drop the variable, or consider this computation to be invalid and stop. Substituted terms follow the same rules as do other expressions, so, if substituting a variable, bring it in and re-start phase one with it. If not, proceed to phase two.

Phase Two: Test for Missing Data

Determine whether the variable has a known value for this location. If not, then refer to the evaluation strategy for what to do: Substitute in another expression, drop the variable, or consider this computation to be invalid and stop. Substituted terms follow

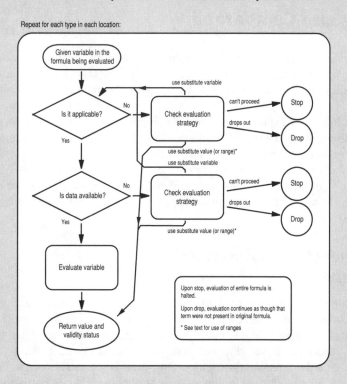

Figure 6.6   Procedure for handling invalid/missing information.

(continues)

EVALUATING EXPRESSIONS WITH VALID AND INVALID DATA *(continued)*

the same rules as other expressions, so, if substituting a term involving variables, bring the substitute term in and restart it at phase one.

Phase Three: Evaluate

At this stage, values are presented for computation.

Note that ranges of values as well as individual values may be substituted for invalid data. When logical data (truth values) are missing, the result may be, for the purposes of logic, true or false—essentially a range of values from false to true. Computing a result from this, at a logical level, would be equivalent to creating two scenarios: computing one result as though the value were true, computing a second result as though the value were false, and then comparing the results. If both outcomes are the same, then it didn't matter that the data was missing, and that result can be used. If the outcomes are different, then the missing data is significant, and the result is still unknown (pending further substitutions, of course). Simplifications can be made to the process so as to avoid the requirement that a computer actually processes all possible outcomes, but the logic remains the same.

Meaning and Comparability

In the previous section we explored how to deal with all types of logically sparse data within the context of a single, logical hypercube created by taking the Cartesian product of a set of dimensions and associating them in 1-to-1 correlation with a collection of variables.

Can or should everything be represented in a single hypercube? What happens if we need to add dimensions to a model? Is there a limit to the number of dimensions in a hypercube? Are there any natural cube structurings? If there are, how do you decide whether a new dimension belongs in an existing cube or in some new cube? If it turns out that you've got multiple cubes worth of data, how do you make comparisons between them? What are the limits of comparison? Is it possible to have two totally incomparable hypercubes?

When a New Dimension Needs a New Cube

Consider Figure 6.7, which shows a grid of implicitly actual values. Let's imagine that we now need to track actuals against plans and variances. The best way to do this is by adding a scenario dimension and explicitly reclassifying prior data as actuals. Because the new dimension reflects new data and connects to the old data, it works well as an addition to the initial dimensional structure. The modified cube is shown in Figure 6.8.

Now imagine we started tracking employees and the number of hours they spend on each type of task: customer help, stocking, and cash register. In addition to an employee dimension and a set of variables denoting hours worked per task, the data

	Jan	Feb	Mar	Apr
Store 1 Shoe Sales	200	250	150	270
Store 1 Shoe Costs	180	200	200	270
Store 1 Shirt Sales	320	350	400	300
Store 1 Shirt Costs	300	300	350	270

Figure 6.7 A grid of implicitly actual values.

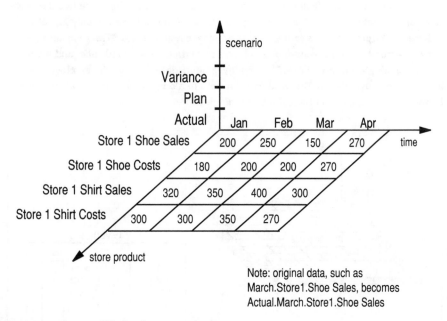

Figure 6.8 The modified cube.

would also contain the dimensions' store and time. Should these dimensions and associated data be added to the original cube in the same way that planned data with its associated scenario dimension was added, or should the data go into a separate cube? Does it make a difference? Let's try adding this new information to the original cube and see what happens.

In the modified model, sales measures continue to be identified by their store, time, and product, in addition to which they are further identified by an employee and task variable. On the face of it, this doesn't seem to make a lot of sense. According to the modified cube, sales are now a function of store, time, product, employee, and task. But measured sales values are not differentiated by employee or task per employee.

It would seem that employee task data describes a fundamentally different situation from the product sales data (even though the two situations share some dimensions) and thus ought to be defined as a separate data cube. This contrasts with the planned and variance data, which, though generated by a separate situation from that of the actual sales data, fit cleanly into the original model.

What is the difference between these two modifications? Why does one modification seem to fit and another seem not to fit?

VISUALIZING MEANINGLESS INTERSECTIONS

Figure 6.9 shows how for all but the allemployee and alltask members the regions defined by employee and task are empty. Look at the bottom right panel of the figure. You see two tables composed of one column each. We are starting with 22 data points. In the upper left part of the figure is the cube that results from combining the two data sets. The resulting cube is 11 by 11 by 2, giving it 242 intersections. There are only 22 data points in it: 11 product sales values and 11 employee hours values. Figure 6.8 shows where the numbers from the two original tables fit into the combined cube, and it shows all the meaningless intersections. The employee hours data fit along the employee by allproduct by hours region. The product sales data fit along the products by all employee by sales region. The rest of the cube is meaningless.

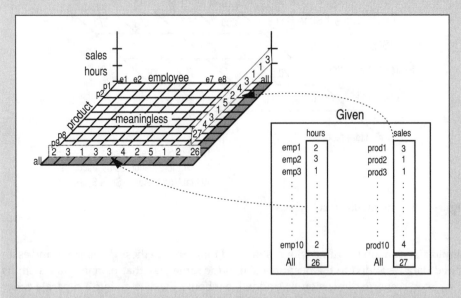

Figure 6.9 Except for allemployees and alltasks, regions defined by employee and task are meaningless.

The plan and variance data have the same dimensional structure as the original data. The original (actual) data and the new plan data are both dimensioned by store, time, and product. In addition, you can reclassify the sales variables (units sold, dollar value sold) as actual variables. Thus, the original data could have been dimensioned by store, time, product, and scenario where scenario had only a single member, the actuals member. In this way, the addition of plan and variance can be seen as the addition of new members to the scenario dimension. In contrast, the employee and hours data do not share the same dimensional structure as the original data. The original data are not dimensioned by either employee or hours per task, and the new data are not dimensioned by product or sales variables.

A Single Domain Schema

A logical hypercube or *single domain schema* is composed of a set of types in LC form, which is to say that some types are acting as locators and some as contents, and all the contents or variables apply to all the same locators or dimensions. According to this definition, the act of adding a scenario's dimension does not violate the definition of a logical hypercube because the new variables share the same identifier dimensions as the old variables. In contrast, the addition of an hour's variable and employee's identifier dimension does violate the definition of a logical hypercube because the new variables do not share the same identifier dimensions as the old sales variables.

In addition to the type-based definition of a single domain schema, there are two additional and complimentary ways to gauge the degree to which your data represents multiple domains' worth of information. The first way, described in the following section, is more data-oriented; the second way, described in the section on multidomain schemas, is more source semantics-oriented.

Data-Oriented Domain Testing

If two data sets belong in the same logical hypercube, the density of their combination will equal the weighted average of their densities prior to being combined, where the weighting is a function of the number of data points per data set. For example, if a perfectly dense cube is defined in terms of 100 stores, 10 time periods, 100 products, and 5 sales measures, it will contain 500,000 data points. If a second cube is defined in terms of 100 stores, 10 time periods, 100 products, 5 measures, and 3 scenarios where the 3 scenarios are plan, actual, and variance, and data exist only for plan, it will also contain 500,000 data points, but be only 33 percent dense. The combination of the two cubes would contain 1,000,000 data points and be 67 percent dense.

If two data sets do not belong in the same logical hypercube, the density of their combination will be less than that of either of the two original data sets. For example, if a perfectly dense cube is defined in terms of 100 stores, 10 time periods, 5 sales measures, and 100 products, it will contain 500,000 data points. If a second perfectly dense cube is defined in terms of 100 stores, 10 time periods, 200 employees, and 5 task measures, it will contain 1,000,000 data points. As separate cubes, they are each perfectly dense.

The density plummets, however, if the two cubes are combined. The combined cube would have 100 stores, 10 times, 100 products, 5 sales measures, 200 employees, and 5 task measures. This defines 500 million intersections, but we have only 1.5 million data points. By combining two perfectly dense cubes, we created one cube that was 98.5 percent empty!

Multidomain Schemas

The fact that data doesn't all belong in a single cube doesn't mean you don't want to bring it together for analytical purposes. Many analytical applications depend on data from more than one type of situation or domain, such as financial and marketing, or manufacturing and distribution, or demographic and sales. Consider all the analytical queries that depend on multidomain information, such as correlations of changes in production costs with changes in sales volumes, or correlations in time-lagged changes in free cash flow with changes in marketing campaigns. In the previous section, the query that broke the single hypercube's back required data from sales and from employees, but what exactly is a situation or domain? We've seen a type-based method and a data-based method for identifying a single domain schema. But how do they come about? What is the source of a domain? By what method can you count the number of domains in a data set? How does one construct a multidomain model?

Data sets are like packaged food. By the time you reach for that 16-ounce squashy, plastic-wrapped package on a supermarket shelf, many of the original differences between the food now packaged (such as whether it is of animal or vegetable origin) have been eliminated or occluded. Likewise, data sets with their rows and columns can look pretty much the same until you reconstruct the events for which the data are a representation. By looking at, or at least imagining, the data-generating events, and specifically the measurement process whose output is the data, you can understand the source(s) or cause(s) of the domain(s) represented by the data.

Thus, in the previous section where we looked at sales and employee data, it is not hard to see that there had to be two distinct measurement processes in place to capture the information. To capture the sales information, some device needs to be placed at each cash register or point of sale that records each sales transaction and the quantity and price of each item purchased and the dollar amount for the transaction as a whole. That device needs to have an internal list of known products and their associated prices, a clock to record the transaction time, and a location tag that identifies it with a particular cash register. To capture the employee information, a collection of devices needs to be in place that recognizes each employee, that recognizes different tasks, and that can record the times when an employee changes tasks. Although it is likely that the employees would simply fill out a time sheet to collect this information, there are several ways this could be accomplished using cameras. For example, each employee could have a small camera on her or his person recording actual movements from which subsequent pattern analysis is used to determine when the employee was performing which tasks. Cameras could be mounted so that they scan the locations associated with different tasks such as stocking, check out, and so forth, and where subsequent analysis is used to figure out who has entered what task's space at what time.

Regardless of whether one is relying on the employees' own internal recordings or on external cameras, the recording processes required for measuring the time each employee spends on each type of task is distinct from the recording processes required for measuring what items were bought for how much money. The two recording processes are not interchangeable. The events they are tracking are not interchangeable and the data sets that are produced by each of the recording processes, as defined by the types used to represent each data set, are not interchangeable. Thus, one would say that the sales data and the employee task data represent two different domains. Any initial representation of the data could be spoken of in terms of two distinct hypercubes or single domain schemas.

Now that it has been established that the sales and employee data belong to different domains of information and are represented as two separate schemas, the question remains, can we and, if so, how do we meaningfully compare them? Consider now the two following schemas:

```
(Store. ⊗ Time. ⊗ Product.) ~ Sales
(Store. ⊗ Time. ⊗ Employee.(Store.this). ⊗ Task.)~ Hours
```

Note the subexpression Employee.(Store.this). It says to take all the employees for each store as each store in the store dimension is scrolled. Otherwise, the cross product of stores and employees would be very sparse as most if not all employees work in only one store.

Clearly, any queries about how much of what product was sold when can be fully answered by looking only at the sales cube. Any queries about which employees spent how much time doing what tasks can be fully answered by looking only at the employee tasks cube. But what if you wanted to analyze whether certain employees or types of employees were better or worse at helping to sell certain products? Any analyses of this type would need a combination of information from each of the cubes.

As you will have already guessed, the basic method of comparing or analyzing information between different domains starts with joining the cubes along their common dimensions as I describe a little later. Additional complexity factors, such as joining cubes when the join dimensions are not equivalent (or conformed, to use a popular datawarehousing term), joining cubes when all that appears similar are the measures, or joining cubes when there do not appear to be any similar dimensions, are addressed at the end of this chapter.

Look again at the two cubes we defined previously: the sales data cube and the employee tasks cube. The two cubes share two dimensions: stores and time. In addition, the sales cube has a product, scenario, and measures dimension; none of them is shared by the employee cube. The employee cube has an employee and a task variable dimension that it does not share with the sales cube.

Practically speaking,[9] there are three main ways that OLAP products join dimensions: by creating single hypercubes, by creating virtual join cubes, and by referencing data between cubes. Each method presumes the join dimensions are either identical or have identical subsets (such as a geography dimension having a state level that might join with a state dimension).

I've already mentioned the single hypercube approach earlier in this chapter and in Chapter 4. Suffice it to say that given the huge amount of sparsity it creates, it is not an ideal approach for working with multidomain data. The second approach, which at the time of this writing is popular with products such as Microsoft's OLAP product, begins with single domain cubes and then joins them to create a virtual hypercube whose dimensions are the union of all the dimensions and whose measures, as identified along a measures dimension in each cube, are concatenated in the virtual join cube. The third approach leaves each cube separate, but allows the analyst to reference data in any cube from any cube.

Imagine you are trying to analyze whether there is any relationship between the amount of time that employees are spending at various tasks and the amount of products sold. How would you go about this? To compare the values of measures originating in two separate cubes, we first need to define a common denominator or analytical framework. By analogy, if you want to compare 2/3 with 3/4, you need to define both fractions in terms of a common denominator such as twelfths, that is, $2/3 = 8/12$ and $3/4 = 9/12$. Once both fractions share the same common denominator, their numerators may be compared directly; that is, you can directly compare the 9 in 9/12 with the 8 in 8/12. Because 9 is greater than 8, so 3/4 is greater than 2/3.

The common denominator between the two cubes is the union of their shared dimensions: store and time. Conversely, the union of the nonshared dimensions in each cube form the numerators. This holds true for the comparison of single values, one-dimensional series, or any dimensional volume. Figure 6.10 shows a schema for this multidomain model. Think of each of the subcubes defined by the union of the nonshared dimensions as a collection or array of contents and each intersection of the

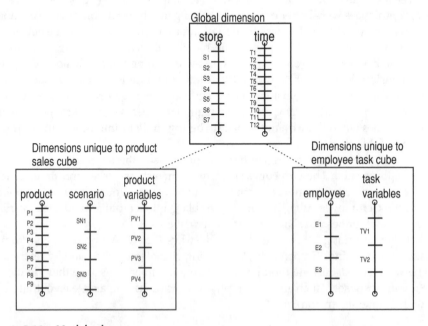

Figure 6.10   Model schema.

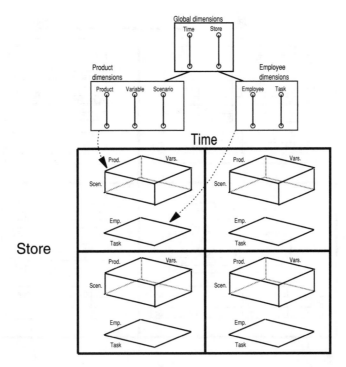

Figure 6.11 View schema.

sub-cube, such as young men stocking hours as a variable. Figure 6.11 shows a view schema and Figure 6.12 displays a sample view.

For example, to compare the sales of all products made at the Cambridge store for the month of March with the amount of hours that young men spent working the aisles, you define and compute a ratio like the following. Note the references to the specific cubes in the bold square brackets.

```
[Sales cube]: ('sales', Time.month.march , Product.all) ÷
[Employee hours cube]:('Hours' , Employees.young men, Task.
Working_the_aisles)
```

Then you look to the cell for the Cambridge store in the month of March for the value. The result is a single data point. Note the bolded terms in the expression. They identify the cube from where each of the variables comes and show what the comparison formula would look like in a tool that kept each cube's data separate. Alternatively, if you had created a single join cube called, let's say, "Sales & Employees" the same formula would have looked as follows:

```
[Sales & Employees cube]:
("sales", Time.month.march , Employee.all , Task.all , Product.all)4 ÷
("Hours" , Employees.youngmen , Task.workingtheaisles ,
Time.month.March , Product.all.)
```

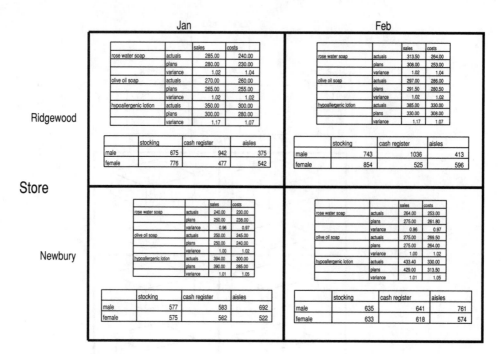

Figure 6.12   Sample view.

Note that in this expression, I repeated the qualifiers Time.month.march. and Product.all. I did this purely for expository purposes. In most tools, context is set on a variable-by-variable basis from left to right. Thus, once it was stated for the sales variable that it applied to the month of March for all time, that context wouldn't normally need to be repeated when parsing the Hours variable.

To analyze the relationship between changes in product sales and changes in young men's hours working the aisles, and doing it within a single join cube, you could define and compute a day-level series like the following (note the joining of the cubes):

```
[Sales & Employees cube]:
("sales", Time.month. , Employee.all , Task.all , Product.all) 4 ÷
("Hours" , Employees.youngmen , Task.working_the_aisles , Time.month. ,
Product.all.)
```

You could further compare young men's task-specific hours with the sales of electronic products by creating the following set of queries, superposing the three result sets as three separate line graphs as shown in Figure 6.13.

```
[Sales & Employees cube]:
Line A
("sales", Time.month. , Employee.all , Task.all , Product.electronics),
```

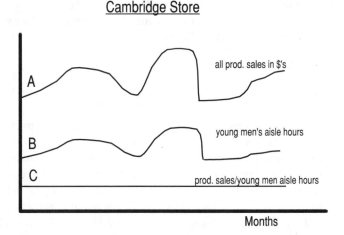

Figure 6.13 Comparison of data from three different cubes.

```
Line B
("Hours" , Employees.youngmen , Task.workingtheaisles , Time.month. ,
Product.all) ,

Line C
("sales", Time.month. , Employee.all , Task.all , Product.electronics) ÷
("Hours" , Employees.youngmen , Task.working_the_aisles , Time.month. ,
Product.all)
```

What this expression is testing for is whether there is any visible correlation between the company's sales of electronic products and the number of hours young men spend working the aisles. The implicit theory is that guys are more familiar with electronic products than women and their appearance in the aisles where they can provide customer support helps sales of those products. When the company tracks employee hours, it is relative to all products; therefore, the best that can be done here is to note a temporal and spatial correlation between the presence of guys on the floor and increases in sales of certain products.

Clearly, young men make good aisle workers with electronic products.

Not Applicable versus Nonvarying

Sometimes you will encounter variables that appear to be dimensioned differently, but which upon closer examination are revealed to be of the same dimensionality. It is common practice in the OLAP world to treat a variable that does not appear to vary in a dimension as if it were not applicable to that dimension. However, if a variable is constant along a dimension rather than not applicable to it, there are operations an analyst can perform on the former that can't be performed on the latter Thus, it is necessary, when trying to integrate data from multiple cubes, to test whether a variable is constant along or not applicable to the nonshared dimensions from the other cube(s). For example, consider the two schemas that follow:

```
(Store. ⊗ Time. ⊗ Product.) ~ Sales

(Time. ⊗ Product.) ~ Price
```

Notice how price is not dimensioned by store. This is a common representation for price. Now if we took this schema to mean that price is not applicable to stores, then in comparing prices and sales and following the methods outlined previously, we would define the common denominator between the two schemas as Time and Product. We would also be able to compare Store sales with prices per time and product. However, unlike the multidomain example, price isn't inapplicable to store; rather price doesn't vary by store. Price is applicable but contingently constant across stores. Therefore, the true schema for price includes Store as a locator dimension and allows for comparisons across stores as well as products and time.

Using Multidomain Schemas to Integrate Irregular Spreadsheets

Multidomain schemas are especially useful when trying to combine any kind of irregular spreadsheet or record-based data from across multiple departments.

Consider, for example, spreadsheet data belonging to two departments, such as sales and finance, where each department maintains its own data. Figure 6.14 shows a multidomain view of an integrated sales and financial reporting model for a retail corporation composed of two types of stores: low-cost consumer goods (Five 'n' Dime) and furniture (Furniture Land). Store and month compose the base level of the shared dimensions, with stores aggregating into chains of stores and months aggregating into quarters. The sales and financial reporting information coexists within each store-month cell. The financial information consists of a two-dimensional grid of financial indicators by planned/actual/variance. The sales information consists of a three-dimensional grid of product type by sales/cost information by planned/actual/variance. Computationally, the sales and cost figures from the sales spreadsheets are ready to be brought into the financial indicators spreadsheet where they drive the calculation of the financial indicators. Visually, the two hypercubes may be integrated as shown in Figure 6.13. Note how the two types of stores share the same financial subcube while the members of their product subcubes are different.

Multidomain Schemas for Organizing Irregular Records

Consider the irregularity of detailed operational information. Figure 6.15 shows a multidomain view of individual transactions and aggregate data records for the same stores discussed in the previous example. A furniture store may sell 5 units of furniture in 5 transactions one day and 60 units in 15 transactions the next. Different business

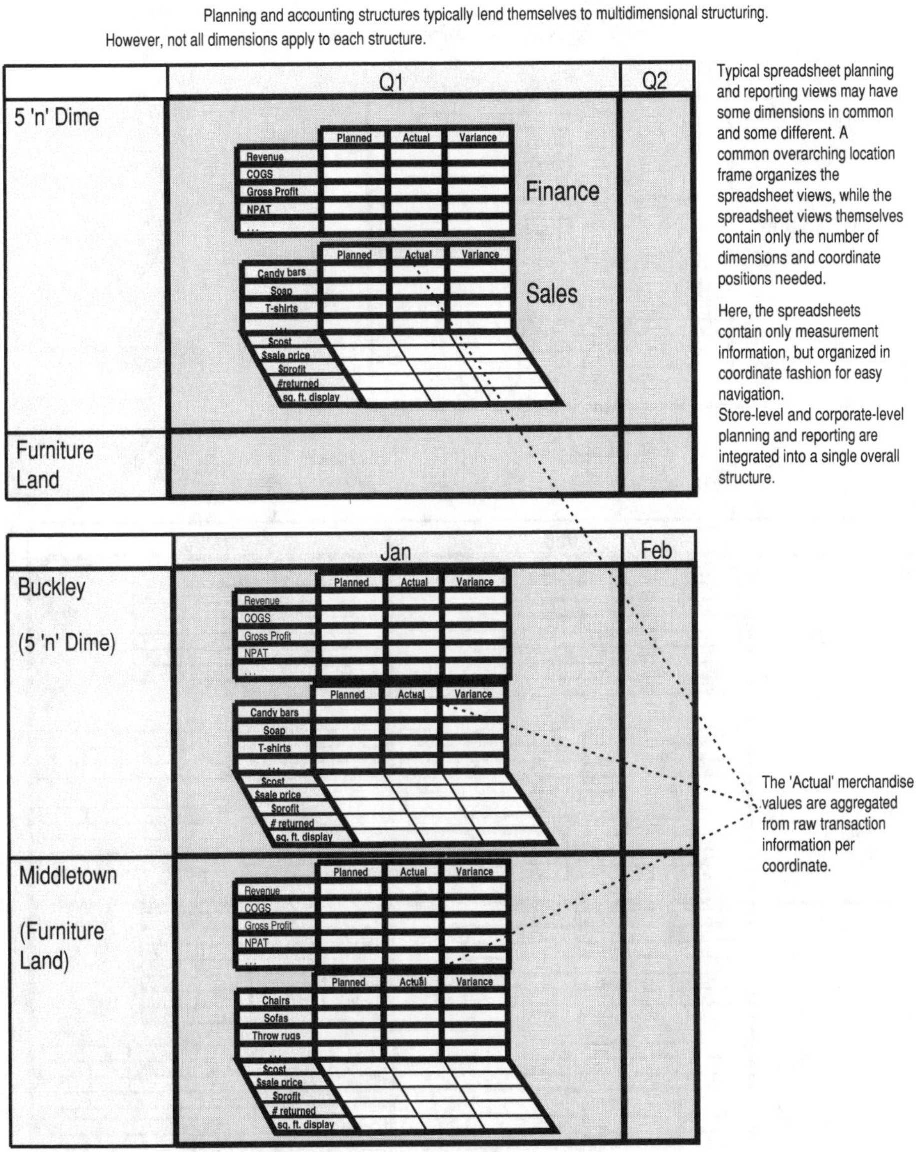
Planning and accounting structures typically lend themselves to multidimensional structuring.
However, not all dimensions apply to each structure.
Q1
Q2
5 'n' Dime
Planned
Actual
Variance
Revenue
COGS
Gross Profit
NPAT
...
Finance
Candy bars
Soap
T-shirts
...
$cost
$sale price
$profit
#returned
sq. ft. display
Sales
Furniture Land
Typical spreadsheet planning and reporting views may have some dimensions in common and some different. A common overarching location frame organizes the spreadsheet views, while the spreadsheet views themselves contain only the number of dimensions and coordinate positions needed.
Here, the spreadsheets contain only measurement information, but organized in coordinate fashion for easy navigation.
Store-level and corporate-level planning and reporting are integrated into a single overall structure.
Jan
Feb
Buckley
(5 'n' Dime)
Middletown
(Furniture Land)
Chairs
Sofas
Throw rugs
returned
The 'Actual' merchandise values are aggregated from raw transaction information per coordinate.

Figure 6.14 Multicube framework for organizing irregular spreadsheets.

A five-and-dime chain and a furniture store chain will have some data types in common, and others different to suit the business rules (e.g. no customer charge accounts at the five-and-dimes).

	Jan	
5 'n' Dime		

Total sales	8,500.00
# of sales	750
Year-to-date Sales	8,500.00
Head count	30

Furniture Land	

Total sales	7,250.00
# of sales	10
Year-to-date Sales	7,250.00
Head count	12

Acct #	Balance	Monthly
0277	895.00	37.30
0278	0.00	0.00
0279	247.30	24.50

Aggregate stores by chain · Tables appropriate to business rules per store · Transaction info per store, account info global to chain

	1/3/96	1/4/96
Buckley (5 'n' Dime)		

trans #	item	taxable	amt
101	curlers	y	2.50
101	shampoo	y	3.25
101	barettes	y	1.50
102	soap	y	1.00
102	toothpaste	y	3.50
103	newspaper	n	.50
103	t-shirt	y	4.50

trans #	item	taxable	amt
201	sunglasses	y	10.00
201	cigarettes	y	2.00
202	cap gun	y	5.50
202	caps	y	2.00
202	yo-yo	y	2.00
202	candy bar	5	.50

trans #	clerk	register	time	subtotal	tax	total
101	Jane	1	10:04	7.25	.37	7.62
102	John	2	10:07	4.50	.23	4.73
103	Jane	1	10:12	5.00	.23	5.23

trans #	clerk	register	time	subtotal	tax	total
201	Jane	1	10:04	12.00	.60	12.60
202	Mark	2	10:07	10.00	.50	10.50

Clerk	hrs worked
Jane	180
John	110

Total sales	16.75
# of sales	3
Year-to-date Sales	16.75
Head count	2

Clerk	hrs worked
Jane	160
Mark	120

Total sales	22.00
# of sales	2
Year-to-date Sales	38.75
Head count	2

Middletown (Furniture Land)		

trans #	item	taxable	amt
1141	sofa bed	y	500.00
1141	love seat	y	350.00
1142	4-post bed	y	1500.00
1142	body pillow	y	75.00
1142	sheet set	y	125.00

trans #	item	taxable	amt
1189	nightstand	y	85.00
1189	table	y	150.00
1190	table	y	450.00
1190	chairs	y	800.00
1191	foot stool	y	65.00
1191	recliner	y	350.00

trans #	clerk	total	terms	acct	acct #
1141	Janson	895.00	Charge - 24	Y	0277
1142	Becker	1785.00	Cash	N	

trans #	clerk	total	terms	acct	acct #
1189	Becker	235.00	Charge MC	N	
1190	Janson	1250.00	Charge -12	Y	0277
1191	Becker	415.00	Cash	N	

Clerk	hrs worked
Becker	180
Harris	60
Janson	110

Total sales	2550.00
# of sales	2
Year-to-date Sales	2550.00
Head count	3

Clerk	hrs worked
Becker	180
Harris	105
Janson	110

Total sales	1900.00
# of sales	3
Year-to-date Sales	4450.00
Head count	3

. . .

Figure 6.15 Multicube framework for organizing irregular records.

rules and thus fields apply to the two chains: The furniture stores allow credit accounts for customers, whereas the five 'n' dimes are strictly cash-and-carry. Several types of records are being organized. At the store-by-month level there is employee payroll information, line-item sales information, and overall sales information. At the chain-by-month level, the furniture chain tracks account balances. All stores track aggregate sales data. The multidomain model provides a general method for relating different sets of measurement complexes with each other.

Joining Cubes with Nonconformant Dimensions

So far, every time we have joined cubes, regardless of the method, the dimensions through which the cubes were to be joined were identical. What happens when the join dimensions are not identical? How do you compare product sales across time when the products offered are not the same? How do you compare employee productivity across time when the employees are not the same? How do you compare the potential return on investment across dramatically different business opportunities? Regardless of the dimensionality of the source cubes whose information you wish to compare, you still need to find a common denominator as described previously. The tricky part is creating that commonality.

The most straightforward and most common cases are those where some instances of some dimension, most typically product and employee, are known to change over time and the organization, most likely a datawarehousing group, has responded by creating a time- or space-stamped dimension. Figure 6.16 represents a typical fragment

Product	Event	Date
Bats	Start	1/1/95
Gloves	Start	11/1/96
Hats	Start	1/11/97
Bats	Stop	1/1/98
Shoes	Start	2/2/98

Figure 6.16   A typical fragment of a time-stamped product dimension.

of a time-stamped product dimension. The product dimension is already in a type structure of form:

```
(Product.)~ Existence_start_time, Still_existent
```

That is to say, for every product that was ever carried, that product has a date associated with its coming into existence. (If this product type structure were fully normalized, the still_existent content would be applied to a location structure consisting of Product and Time.) In addition, as of the current time of the type structure, some of the products are still being carried and some have been discontinued. For those that have been discontinued whose value of still_existent is no, a separate type structure would record when the product was discontinued. (If you put the stop time in the same structure as the start time, you could create semantic ambiguity for those still existent products whose stop time would be blank but would mean not applicable versus those products that might have been discontinued but whose stop times are missing.)

Once the life span of an instance is time-stamped, you still have to figure out the basis by which you want to make comparisons. Unless you restrict yourself to comparing only those products that existed during the entire time period, you need to select some common denominator through which comparisons will be made. Although it may be that you translate the present into some form that resembles the past or the past into some form that resembles the present, you can also transform both into some framework that is appropriate for your analysis. Issues surrounding the maintenance of time-stamped dimensions and intertemporal comparisons based on past or present views have been well explored by Ralph Kimball.[10]

Even though the specific instances of the product or employee dimensions vary over time, when the comings and goings of the instances are tracked within a single type structure and all data sets being compared share the same multiversion type structure, you may think of the type structure as conformed in the sense that the capability to compare over time has been prepared for in advance.

What if there was no such forethought? What if what needs to be compared are two separate product lines from two different companies that were, perhaps, recently acquired by a single company? In these cases, the initial data sets may need to be coerced into a common framework. That coercion is likely to require some thought. Consider the case of two sales cubes where both are dimensioned by product and time. On the surface they may seem to be immediately comparable. However, upon closer inspection, you may notice that, although both data sets have a time dimension with the same calendar and the same fiscal years, the time dimensions in the two cubes reflect different holidays and a different number of operating hours per week. The product dimensions are entirely different.

Before doing anything, you need to be clear about what you're trying to do. Assume the two data sets reflect product sales from two regional chains that operate in different regions but carry similar merchandise. Let's say you're trying to compare sales of products across the two chains so that you can decide which product types to grow and which to shrink or eliminate based on the relative performances across the two chains. Given this kind of analysis, you can probably ignore differences based on days and concentrate on time at the month level or higher (something you couldn't do if you

		Product Price Groups		
		Cheap	Medium	Expensive
Time Q₁ Variables	Sales_chain1 (sales_chain1, Product.pricegroup.all)	.2	.3	.5
	Sales_chain2 (sales_chain2, Product.pricegroup.all)	.6	.3	.1

Figure 6.17 Comparison of Ratios of Low- to High-Priced Products across Two Chains of Stores

were looking to compare absolute sales amounts or sales spikes based on specific hours or days). However, you do need to find a common denominator for products. The best way to do this is by looking for common attributes in your product dimension tables. The attributes you look for should reflect your intended analysis. So if you suspected that one of the newly acquired chains had a more naturally upscale clientele while the other was more successful with bargain hunters, you would want to use the price attribute from each of the product dimensions to create a common denominator in the form of a dimension based on product price groupings.

Thus, you would wind up with an integrated schema as shown next where the Sales chain1 variable represents data from one chain and the Sales chain2 content represents data from the second chain and where the product dimension has been segmented by the attributes:

```
(Time.Calendar_period. ⊗ Product.Price_group.) ~ Sales_chain1,
Sales_chain2
```

Specifically, you might want to compare the ratio of sales for each product price group as a percentage of total sales for the chain to determine if one of the chains had a significantly higher percentage of its sales coming from low- or high-priced products. Figure 6.17 illustrates what the results of such a calculation might look like for one quarter. The two relevant variables are the ratio of each product price group's sales to all price group's sales for each of the two chains as shown here.

```
Sales_chain1 ÷ (sales_chain1, Product.pricegroup.all)
Sales_chain2 ÷ (sales_chain2, Product.pricegroup.all)
```

Summary

In this chapter you saw why a so-called cube or hypercube represents a contiguous collection of facts or propositions, where the contiguity is defined in terms of the types used as locators in the cube. Every cell in a well-defined cube or populated schema or model can be true or false. You learned the steps you need to take to ensure your schemas are well defined. You learned how to distinguish between different types of invalid data and how to correctly process invalid data so as to avoid creating incorrect derivations. You were also shown how to identify and treat separately the naturally distinct domains in your data or models, and you learned how to bring them together when necessary into a multidomain model.

Multidimensional Formulas

In the same way that enzymes are a critical component of all the metabolic processes that occur in the human body, so too are formulas a critical component of all multidimensional analysis. All derived data values are defined in terms of formulas. Formulas are used for aggregating, allocating, comparing, analyzing, explaining, and inferring. For example, net sales may be defined by a formula such as gross sales minus returns, and sales of business products may be defined as the sum of sales of computer products, fax machines, and photocopiers. Next year's projected sales may be defined as the average sales growth multiplied by the current sales.

Not only are all derived data created through formulas, but, as is frequently the case, multiple interconnected formulas may be necessary to do the job.

This chapter is divided into two sections. The first section, explains how to think about formulas within a multidimensional context. The main formula-affecting complexities that need to be worked through are hierarchies, multiple overlapping formulas, application ranges, and multiple partially overlapping cubes. The second section provides you with a set of reusable formula building blocks that you can use to construct your own multidimensional models.

Formulas in a Multidimensional Context

Formula Hierarchies or Dependency Trees

As you saw in Chapter 5, most dimensions have a hierarchical structure. This is true even with a simple example. Consider the schema that follows and the figures that represent the hierarchies of the types used as locators in the schema:

```
(Store. ⊗ Time. ⊗ Product. ⊗ Account.) ~ Dollar_Amount
```

Figures 7.1 through 7.4 show all the members for each of the four locator dimensions. Stores and time have single hierarchies. Products, with two separate hierarchies, have the most complex structure.

What exactly do these hierarchies represent? In Chapter 5, I spoke about the way hierarchical dimensions facilitated calculating (especially aggregating) and navigating or referencing. For example, all the store-level sales data may aggregate up the store

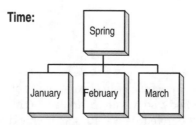

Figure 7.1   The dimensional structure for the time dimension.

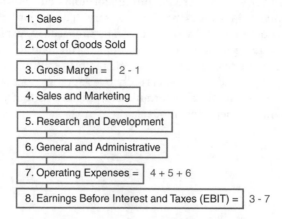

Figure 7.2   The dimensional structure for the account dimension.

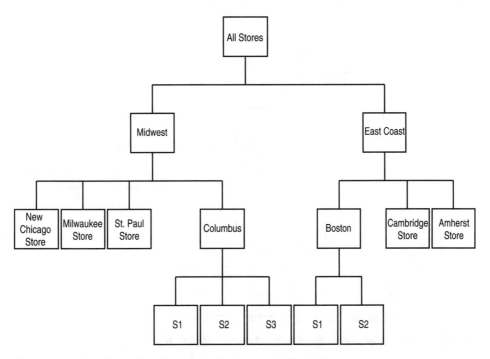

Figure 7.3 The dimensional structure for the store dimension.

dimension. You can refer to all the stores in a particular city (assuming that stores connect to cities) as the children or first-level members below that city. In other words, it seems that the hierarchical structure of a dimension determines both aggregations and referencing. Although this is frequently true, it is not always true. The way data is calculated within a hypercube need not share the same paths or structure as the way data is referenced. This is a very important point and one worth exploring.

The contents or data associated with the city Columbus in the store dimension of Figure 7.3, for example, is the sum of the data associated with the three stores in Columbus:

```
(Contents, Store.Columbus) = Sum (Contents , Store.(s1,s2, s3))
```

This is an example in which the calculation structure for a member is the same as the referential structure.

Now look at the "New Chicago Store" member of the store dimension in Figure 7.3. It represents a store that is being built but has not yet opened. Let's say you want to project what the revenues for this store might be. Figure 7.5 shows the formula for calculating the value of projected sales in the new Chicago store as the average of the known revenues for other nearby cities (perhaps modified by an appropriate weighting function). Notice that the dependency relationships for this formula also look like a hierarchy (otherwise known as a dependency tree). Thus, the formula hierarchy for a

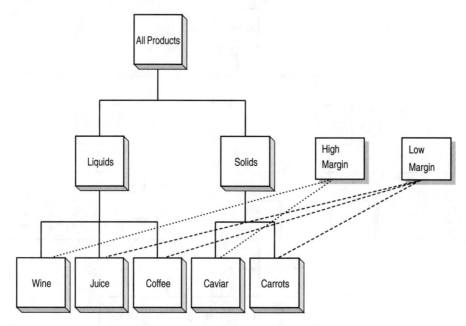

Figure 7.4 The dimensional structure for the product dimension.

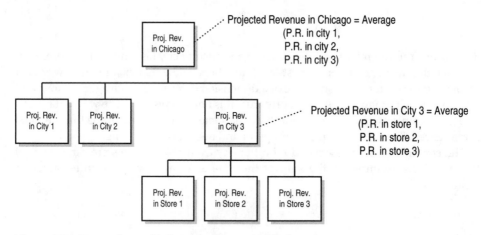

Figure 7.5 Dependency relationships form a hierarchy.

dimension member need not be the same as its referential hierarchy (that is, the formula for a member can use inputs that do not come from that member's children in the hierarchy).

Look closely at Figures 7.1 to 7.5. Can you spot another instance where the formula hierarchy for a member is not the same as the referential hierarchy? How about gross margin, operating expenses, and EBIT in the account dimension in Figure 7.2? Each of those account variables depends on other account variables in the accounts dimension yet all the account variables occupy a single dimension level.

When you define the parent/child relationships or hierarchies in the dimensions of whatever schema you are working with for an application, you are initially defining the referential structure of the dimensions. For all but your variables or variables dimension, that referential structure will frequently, though not always, be the same as the formulaic structure. In contrast, the formulas in the variables dimension may deviate substantially from their referential structure.

Finally, the dependency relationships between the members of a dimensional hierarchy may vary as a function of the other dimension members with whom they are intersecting. Notwithstanding the fact that many vendors and journalists loosely refer to input and derived members, the distinction between measured and derived applies to cells or data and not members. An extreme example of this is shown in Figure 7.6. For the variables "Direct Costs" the derivation path goes from the leaves to the root of the product hierarchy path. On the other hand, the variable "allocated indirect costs" takes the opposite derivation path, going from the root of the hierarchy toward the leaves because costs are allocated from the top down.

Given the variable nature of dependency relationships within a dimension, the most precise way to represent them is relative to actual data points. Figure 7.7 shows the relationship between input and derived values or data points.

Now that you've seen how the term *hierarchy* has both a referential and a dependency meaning and that formulas define dependency hierarchies, let us explore how formulas operate in a multidimensional environment.

Cell- and Axis-Based Formulas

In a traditional spreadsheet environment, the formulas in terms of which derived cells are defined apply directly to the cell. In Figure 7.8, the value for total sales appearing in cell F16 is defined in terms of a formula for the contents of cell F16; specifically,

```
F16 = Sum (F11 to F15).
```

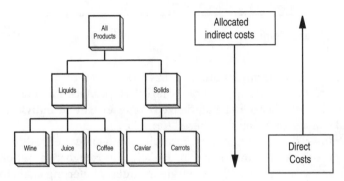

Figure 7.6 Derivation paths may flow in any direction.

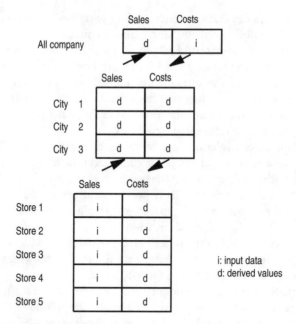

Figure 7.7   Input and derived values.

Sales of Ski Equipment by Region				
	C	**D**	**E**	**F**	
	West	North	East	Total	
skis	450	750	800	2000	11
bindings	150	300	250	700	12
boots	300	450	500	1250	13
poles	50	1251	00	275	14
goggles	75	2001	50	425	15
total	1025	1825	1800	4650	16
Every aggregated cell carries its own formula					
For example:					
The total in cell c13 = sum(c8:c1)2					
The total in cell d16 = sum(d1:d15)					

Figure 7.8   Cell-based formulas.

It is no secret that cell formulas can get numerous and messy as worksheets become complex. Given that OLAP applications can easily produce millions or billions of derived numbers (whether or not materialized), only an extreme individual would try to create and manage that many cell-based formulas.

In a multidimensional environment, formulas are usually defined in terms of the dimensions or axes. Axis formulas may be looked at as category- or set-based formulas. (Statisticians sometimes call these margin formulas.) Referring again to Figure 7.8, instead of creating one formula for the cell that defines the value of total sales for all

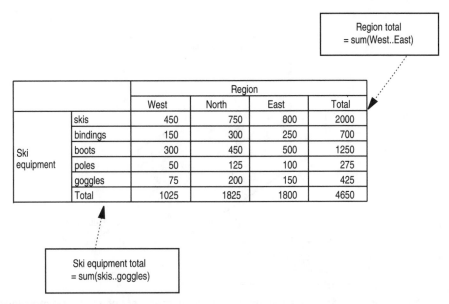

Region total
= sum(West..East)

		Region			
		West	North	East	Total
Ski equipment	skis	450	750	800	2000
	bindings	150	300	250	700
	boots	300	450	500	1250
	poles	50	125	100	275
	goggles	75	200	150	425
	Total	1025	1825	1800	4650

Ski equipment total
= sum(skis..goggles)

Figure 7.9 OLAP tools use margin or axis-based formulas.

products (that is, the formula for cell F16), you would define a formula for total sales in terms of each type of sale (along the variables dimension or axis) and a formula for all products in terms of individual products (along the product dimension or axis). The formula for total sales might be equal to the sum of direct plus indirect sales. The formula for all products might be equal to the sum of skis through goggles. The formula for total sales of all products is defined by the combination of the two separate formulas. An example of axis-based formulas is shown in Figure 7.9.

In a three-dimensional cube consisting of 10 members per dimension, a single formula applied to a single member, such as a formula for the allproduct member of the Product dimension, applies across all the cells in the cube that have an allproduct component. Specifically, this would amount to 100 cells. The number 100 is reached by taking the product of the number of members in each of the nonstore dimensions as shown in Figure 7.10.

Precedences

The formula for any particular cell is a function of the combination of all the dimension-specific formulas that apply to the cell. In other words, the value in a typical derived cell is the result of several interacting formulas. In many cases, as with the Figure 7.10, the order in which dimension-specific formulas are applied to a cell does not affect the result of the calculation because the calculation was defined purely in terms of sums. However, in other cases, where the individual formulas are not commutative, the order or precedence of calculation does affect the value of the cell. The remainder of this subsection explores the issue of calculation precedence.

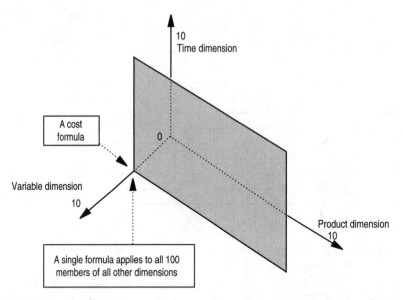

Figure 7.10   Formulas for a given member apply to all members of all other dimensions.

Columns before rows   Rows before columns

A. Pure summation

	Store 1	Store 2	Both Stores
Skis	80	30	110
Boots	40	60	100
BothProducts			**210**

	Store 1	Store 2	Both Stores
Skis	80	30	
Boots	40	60	
BothProducts	120	90	**210**

B. Pure differences

	Actual	Planned	Actual / Plan
Sales	120	90	**30**
Cost	60	30	**30**
Profit			**0**

	Actual	Planned	Actual / Plan
Sales	120	90	
Cost	60	30	
Profit	**60**	**60**	**0**

C. Pure ratios

	Actual	Planned	Actual / Plan
Sales	120	90	**1.33**
Cost	60	30	**2**
Margin			**0.67**

	Actual	Planned	Actual / Plan
Sales	120	90	
Cost	60	30	
Margin	**2**	**3**	**10**

Figure 7.11   Pure operations may be computed in any order.

The following series of examples in Figure 7.11 shows how sums, differences, and ratios may be taken in any order. The left panel in each case performs the calculation with the column dimension first. The right panel performs the same calculation with the row dimension first. Note that, in all cases, the same result is achieved.

When a cell is defined in terms of combinations of different operators, then the result of the calculation may depend on the order of the operations. In general, you can combine addition with subtraction in any order, and you can combine multiplication and division in any order, but you cannot combine addition or subtraction with division or multiplication without paying attention to the order. Consider the following examples that illustrate these principles.

Figure 7.12 shows actual sales, planned sales, and the difference between actual and planned for two products. Notice that whether we obtain the variance by first summing the actual and planned product sales and then taking the difference of the sums, or whether we obtain the variance by taking the difference of actual and planned sales for each product and then summing the differences, we get the same variance values.

Figure 7.13 shows the actual and planned total purchase price, tax rate and tax paid, and the ratio between the actual and planned values for each of these. Notice how, again, it doesn't make any difference whether we multiply the tax rate by the product price and then divide actual by plan, or we take the ratios of the actual and planned values first and then multiply them.

Figure 7.14 shows actual sales, planned sales, and variance in sales, except that this time variance is defined as actual divided by planned. Note how it does make a difference for the derived cell "variance in total costs" whether it was calculated as the ratio between total actual and total planned costs or whether it was calculated as the sum of the ratios of individual product variances.

Columns before rows

	Actual	Planned	Actual/Plan
Skis	120	100	
Boots	50	60	
BothProducts	170	160	10

Rows before columns

	Actual	Planned	Actual/Plan
Skis	120	100	20
Boots	50	60	-10
BothProducts			10

Figure 7.12 Mixing sums and differences.

Columns before rows

	Actual	Planned	Actual/Plan
Price	150	120	
Tax Rate	.3	.25	
Tax Paid	45	30	1.5

Rows before columns

	Actual	Planned	Actual/Plan
Price	150	120	1.25
Tax Rate	.3	.25	1.2
Tax Paid			1.5

Figure 7.13 Mixing products and ratios.

Columns before rows

	Actual	Planned	Actual/Plan
Skis	120	100	
Boots	50	60	
BothProducts	170	160	1.06

Rows before columns

	Actual	Planned	Actual/Plan
Skis	120	100	1.20
Boots	50	60	.83
BothProducts			2.03

Figure 7.14 Mixing sums and ratios.

Columns before rows

	Actual	Planned	Actual/Plan
Price	150	120	
Tax Rate	.3	.25	
Tax Paid	45	30	15

Rows before columns

	Actual	Planned	Actual/Plan
Price	150	120	30
Tax Rate	.3	.25	.05
Tax Paid			1.5

Figure 7.15   Mixing products and differences.

Finally, Figure 7.15 shows actual tax, planned tax, and variance in tax, except that this time variance is defined as the difference between actual and planned. Notice how it makes a difference whether the derived cell "variance in tax paid" was calculated as the difference of products or as the product of differences.

Measurements that derive from other quantities are frequently sensitive to the order in which they are calculated. Ratios (including *flows*, or measures of one type per unit of another type) aggregate percentages, normalized indicators, and multiplicatively combined variables are all sensitive to calculation order.

Ratios, aggregate percentages, and normalized indicators are usually calculated on summarized data and are averaged instead of summed. For example, if you had a data set describing the market penetration of your product in a variety of countries, you would not sum the percentages to a regional level to determine market penetration on a regional basis. You would either sum the data that went into computing the market penetration to the regional level and calculate market penetration at that level, or, if perhaps you possessed only market penetration figures, you would define the market penetration per region as the average of the penetrations per country. If you went with averages, they would most likely be weighted where the weighting was a function of the market size in each country. But this tendency is not a rule. For example, there may be instances where a ratio, such as profitability, is computed before being averaged. This produces an unweighted average profitability, which, in some cases, may be what you need.[1]

Multiplicatively related variables need to be combined before they are aggregated. For example, if you want to calculate the lost productivity across all workers in your organization as a result of local area network (LAN) downtimes—assuming you track downtime and system users—you would want to first multiply the length of downtime per system failure by the number of persons affected and then sum that number for lost productivity per failure across all system failures. You would get the wrong answer by first summing the number of downtime hours and the number of system users and then multiplying those two sums together.

Although tendencies exist, since almost any ordering of operations will produce a mathematically meaningful result, you really need to know what you are trying to calculate before assigning precedences to formulas.

Default Precedence Orders

Recall that formulas are typically associated with individual members of a dimension and then combined, by the tool, for the calculation of a cell. When using a multidimensional tool, if the value for a derived cell depends on the application order of the

ASSIGNING DEFAULT PRECEDENCE

Several complications are involved in algorithmically assigning the correct precedence for a series of dimension formulas that overlap at a cell. Before you can determine which dimension formula should be evaluated in which order, you need to assign some sort of precedence ordering to each dimension formula. In other words, there needs to be a table of precedences stating that addition comes before division (this being the type of rule that would enable a multidimensional tool to guess that an allproduct margin is to be calculated by taking the ratio of allproduct sales and allproduct costs, rather than the sum of individual product margins). However, dimension formulas may themselves be complexes of formulaic clauses. For example, the formula:

Variance = (Actual − Plan) / Plan

contains both a subtraction operator and a division operator. Given that subtraction and division have a different precedence, how do you assign a precedence to the formula as a whole? There is no right or wrong answer for the general case that vendors can use to ensure that the right thing happens in all cases. But somewhere (in the tool or in your head) there need to be rules for assigning precedence for dimension formulas that contain multiple formulaic clauses, each of which has a different precedence level. If you create complex formulas in your dimensions and if you are using a tool that does not force you to specify the order of calculation of the formulas, you should be aware of how the tool automatically assigns precedence levels to overlapping formulas. You should verify that aggregate values represent what you are trying to calculate.

What follows are some general classifications of formulas into precedence levels. The higher the level, the later the formula is calculated. These are listed in Table 7.1. Following the table, note the listing of several operators that cannot be assigned a precedence level without knowing what is being calculated. For example, the operator "max" has no

Table 7.1   General Rules of Thumb for Assigning Precedence Levels

OPERATOR	PRECEDENCE LEVEL
Input values for which there are no formulas	1
Count of nonmissing cells in a range	2
Multiplication, unary minus	3
Addition, subtraction, sum	4
Average	5
Division, exponentiation	6
Logical and relational operators such as equal to, not equal to; less than, greater than; and, or	7

(continued)

ASSIGNING DEFAULT PRECEDENCE *(continued)*

natural precedence level. Imagine that you keep track every month of which week during the month had the greatest sales. Each month would have a sales value for the maximum weekly sales. Suppose that you store this information in a simple cube composed of a variable and time dimension where time consists of weeks, months, quarters, and years. Furthermore, you define time so that all its members sum up to the next highest level. At the year level, the maximum sales could tell you two equally useful things, depending on its precedence level relative to the sum operator associated with the time dimension. If the summation operator of the time dimension were calculated first, it would tell you the greatest weekly sales value during the past year. But if the maximum operator were calculated first, it would tell you the sum of the 12 weekly maximums.

formulas that apply to the cell, you need some method for deciding which formulas to apply in which order. For example, precedence may be set on a dimension-wide basis (that is, time before products before variables) and then overridden on a member-by-member basis (as you will see in the next section).

There is no general rule for deciding what precedence order to apply in every case. In practice, of course, as with the previous example involving the sum of a set of ratios or percentages, rules of thumb can help you decide the order in which to compute aggregates, but once again, rules of thumb are no substitute for knowing what you are trying to calculate.

The practical methods offered by vendors vary widely. Some tools are fairly intelligent and do a good job of guessing the order in which to apply formulas. Other tools are not as intelligent, but offer a simple declarative method for users to specify the type of number any derived cell should contain. For example, by declaring that the cell for "all-product sales variance" is a ratio, the tool would know to calculate the variance ratio last. Still other tools, though flexible, are unintelligent and offer no more than a procedural approach for defining formula precedence.

Operators whose precedence level needs to be assigned on a case-by-case basis include the following:

- Max
- Min
- First
- Last
- Coefficient
- Variance
- Least squares intercept and slope
- Standard deviation

In practice, most multidimensional calculation engines apply only one rule to calculate a particular cell because the inputs to the derived cell are, relatively speaking, intermediate results from yet other calculations as opposed to raw data. (*In toto,* however, the cell's value is still the result of several chained formulas.) For example, as shown in Figure 7.14, the total variance cell (actual/plan), as seen in each of the two panels, is calculated in two different ways using two different single formulas each applied to a different input. In the left panel, it is calculated by applying the one formula "ratio" to the sum of actual product plus the sum of planned product sales. In the right panel, it is calculated by applying the one formula "sum" to the ratio of actual to planned ski sales plus the ratio of actual to planned boot sales.

Multidimensional Formulas

Now that you've seen how multidimensional formulas typically apply to dimension members, how they define their own dependency hierarchies, and how precedence issues need to be resolved when multiple noncommutative formulas apply to the same cell, you're ready to explore the various kinds or flavors of multidimensional formulas.

Unless you are building a very simple application, typical multidimensional models consist of systems of interrelated equations or formulas. My favorite metaphor for equation building is that of designing a bridge to span a river gorge. The job of the engineer is to span the gorge given whatever constraints apply to the solution, such as time to completion, cost, load, durability, or maintenance requirements. Once completed, the bridge creates a live, bidirectional link between the two sides of the gorge. Similarly, the job of a multidimensional application builder is to span the gap between data sources and end-user requirements, which lie on opposite sides of the gorge. Like the engineer, the application builder needs to design a system (to be constructed of equations rather than steel and cement) subject to whatever constraints apply to the solution, such as such as time to completion, cost, load, speed of execution, durability, or maintenance requirements. Like the bridge, once completed, the application creates a live, bidirectional link between the two sides of the gorge.

When the engineer confronts a new gorge project, he or she brings to it a grab bag or tool chest of prior project-based knowledge. Depending on the needs of the client, the engineer can design a variety of types of bridges to span the gorge and for any type of bridge (such as a beam, arch, or suspension), a variety of different flavors or styles. The same is true for a multidimensional application builder. There are a number of different kinds of formulas and a number of different kinds of flavors, styles, or complexities of formulas that any competent multidimensional application builder should have as a part of her or his grab bag of formula tools. Although the specific syntax and distribution of the formulas vary from tool to tool (that is, some tools may force you to put more of the formulas in calculation scripts; others may force you to be totally explicit about the calculation order), the essence of what you're doing does not. For example, if you know you need to take the ratio of the top and bottom quartiles of a multivariate index in order to derive a certain type of decision-oriented data set, you will need to create a multivariate index, calculate the quartile values, and take the ratio of the top and bottom quartiles regardless of the tool you happen to be using. If each of the variables that go in to defining the multivariate index is defined on a different set of units (for example, number of returns per month, revenue per employee, and employee turnover), you will have to relativize them in order to integrate them into a common index regardless of the tool you use.

The purpose of this section is to present you with a tool-neutral multidimensional formula tool chest. Although I've done my best to arrange the formula types in the most useful way I can, I do not consider the arrangement to be fixed in any way as the things that are being ordered are themselves complexes. Thus, so long as you retain, and can recall when required, the appropriate formulas for the task at hand, it makes no difference how you clump them. That said, I distinguish between formula types (conceived of bidirectionally) —such as aggregation/allocation, ratios/products, sortings/randomizings, and cross-dimensional, cross-cube and cross-source[2] selections— and formula complexities or flavors—such as simple, weighted, data or position conditional, overridden, ranged, and chained. As with the bridge metaphor, most every formula complexity can apply to any formula. In other words, formula kinds and formula flavors have an approximate M-N relationship with each other and thus are best thought of as belonging to two separate formula aspect dimensions.

Anatomy of a Multidimensional Aggregation Formula

Consider the increasingly familiar schema

```
(Store. ⊗ Time. ⊗ Product.) ~ Sales, Cost
```

where the leaves of Store, Time, and Product are connected in the usual fashion to the distinct members of the rows of their respective columns in a source table.

The first content formula, which should also be familiar by now, seeds the values of sales and costs from their respective columns (C4 and C5), in the source table, T3, as in the following manner:

```
Sales, L.leaf. << T3C4 Row.
Cost, L.leaf. << T3C5 Row.
```

Now consider the first aggregation formula that you might express:

```
Expression 7-1      Sales, L.leaf.above. = Sum(Sales, L.leaf.)
```

In words, it says that the value of Sales for all locations above the leaves is equal to the sum of the sales values in the leaf locations under the nonleaf location being evaluated.

Expression 7-1 illustrates the basic principles that you need to keep in mind regardless of the type or complexity of formulas you may be trying to write.

First, every type or variable in every formula has an associated application or existence range. In Chapter 6, I spoke of the application range for a variable, which you can see here is the location range associated with the left-hand side of the equation. The equation is telling us how to calculate the value of sales for those locations that are nonleaf. You can also see that there is a location range associated with the right-hand side of the equation. In other words, the values for sales at nonleaf locations are taken from the values for sales at leaf locations. (The values for sales at leaf locations were taken from the values of a certain column in a certain table.)

Most OLAP tools adhere to the convention that, unless otherwise stated, the application range of the left-hand side of the equation is all locations and the location range for all right-hand side terms is the same as that of the left-hand side, unless otherwise stated. When the location range of any of the right-hand side terms is different from that of the left-hand side term, that differencing, as with any computer programming, can be relative or absolute. Since equations get executed on a cell-by-cell basis, typically speaking the data used to calculate the value of the left-hand side of the equation is taken from the same intersection of all location dimensions, or the cell, that is being calculated. Of course, there are many exceptions to this. When, as I will get into later, you are working with even reasonably complex equations, especially when the data is sourced from multiple cubes, just figuring out the appropriate location range for the left-hand side of the equation can take a substantial amount of effort and is prone to error. As a result, I strongly advocate that even if the tool you are using doesn't force you to explicitly declare all location ranges, that you be explicit in writing your equations until you are sure they are working properly. Thus, for the remainder of this section, I will frequently write out the location range for all the types in the equation.

Second, as discussed in Chapter 5, every type in every equation has an associated metric or units. Although I know of no OLAP tool that forces you to declare your units, when working with systems of equations it is all too easy to create nonsense by mixing units. Your tool's compiler may not complain since as far as it is concerned all your types may be defined as floating point integers or decimals. But you should be careful. We highly recommend that when writing equations, you identify the units associated with every type and, separately from the expression of the equation in your tool's dimension and/or variable definition space, you record the units of each term in the equation and the operations connecting them and verify that the operations when applied to the units on the right-hand side of the equation create a type whose units are what you specified on the left-hand side.

Of course, as shown in expression 7-2 , adding units to expression 7-1 seems almost too obvious. The sum of a set of dollar values is of course "surprise!" another dollar value, but, I assure you, it is good practice and, as with location ranges, is equally prone to error as the equations get complex.

```
Expression 7-2    Sales {$} , L.leaf.above. = Sum(Sales {$}, L.leaf.)
```

For the remainder of this book, I will identify units within curly parentheses { } following the type name as done previously.

Given that there are three levels in each of the three locator dimensions, Store, Time, and Product, there are 27 distinct aggregation combinations for the schema as a whole. And given that the Location.leaf level is one of those combinations, expression 7.2 applies to 26 distinct aggregation levels. Thus, for example, the combination of Geography.Region, Time.Quarter, and Product.brand denotes an aggregation level that is at L.leaf.above, so the aggregation formula for sales applies and is executed.

Formula Types

If you are already familiar with one or more OLAP tools, then you know that most tools distribute calculations between the dimension definitions where, typically speaking, simple arithmetic is employed, and calculation scripts where more complex and sometimes procedural calculations are defined. There are several reasons for this, not the least of which is tradition. Early tools such as TM1 began their life as fast and flexible aggregation machines. Other types of calculations were not supported in the tool. Rather, it was anticipated that users would define additional calculations in client-side tools, typically spreadsheets.

There is no logical or application developer reason why this needs to be the case; therefore, I will, in this section, ignore those distinctions of where the calculation is defined and focus instead on the calculations themselves. In Chapter 19, however, I explore some of the main differences in the method of formula specification between OLAP products will be explored.

Selection Formulas

Although you may not think of them as formulas, selections are formulas. They are commands to retrieve some subset of a set of values based on some criteria. In fact, all formulas that return values (as opposed to just assigning them) are selection formulas. As such, selection formulas range from the extremely simple to the extremely complex.

Against our by now illustrious schema of

```
(Store. ⊗ Time. ⊗ Product.) ~ Sales, Cost
```

we can query for `Sales`, which selects all sales values. We can query for all sales values that meet some constraint such as sales of certain products as with the query

```
Sales, Product.Toys
```

Or we can query for sales of certain products for some time period as with

```
Sales, Product.Toys, Time.year.2000
```

Unless you are building scripts with an OLAP tool, you would rarely resort to writing out a statement to perform a simple selection. Most client tools directly provide this kind of functionality through their interface. You would typically point and click against a matrix view or a tree view of a dimension.

Cross-Dimensional Selections

The next stage of complexity for selection formulas is to select the members of one dimension based on the values of some other intersecting dimension. For example, you might wish to see those stores of a particular size, those customers who live in a certain area, or those products that are most often bought by certain customers or that are most often bought at certain times of the year.

```
Expression 7-3

P/E {Ratio}, Stock {Name}, Stock.(Marketcap > 1Billion). , Time.Year.
```

This formula asks for the price earnings ratio and associated stock on a year-by-year basis for those stocks whose market capitalizations on a year-by-year basis are greater than one billion.

```
P/E.decile {Decile} , Stock {Name}, Time.2000 , Stock.(P/E.decile.1,
Time.1999).
```

This formula asks for the year 2000 price/earnings decile and stock name for those stocks that were in the top decile in 1999.

```
P/E {Ratio}, Stock {Name}, (P/E.Time.2000 ÷ P/E.Time./1999 > 2).
```

This formula asks for the price/earnings ratio and stock name for those stocks whose year 2000 price/earnings were more than double their year 1999 price/earnings.

Allocation Formulas

Allocation formulas take some data at higher levels in a multidimensional hierarchy and distribute them down the hierarchy as a function of some other data value already at the lower level. If in addition to the sales and costs previously defined in expression 7-3, imagine you also had a total marketing budget defined, possibly by manual input or through a statement like

```
Marketing_Budget {$}, Geog.all, Time.Year.this, Product.all = $1 Million
```

which says that the total marketing budget is defined for all regions (Geog.all) for this year and for all products. An allocation formula would take the $1,000,000 and distribute it or allocate it to, for example, the individual products for all stores and for this year. If there are 1,000 individual products, the $1,000,000 will be split 1,000 ways. The question is: How will it be split? What's the allocation function? With our schema, a natural allocation function would be to allocate this year's marketing dollars as a function of last year's sales. If a product accounted for 5 percent of last year's sales, it would receive 5 percent of this year's marketing budget (a rather Darwinian marketing strategy). The following formula would define such an allocation strategy:

```
Marketing_Budget {$},
        Geog.all,
        Time.Year.this,
        Prod.individual.  =
        ((Sales {$} , Time.Year.(this-1) )/
        (Sales {$} , Geog.all, Time.Year.(this-1), Product.all))
        *  (Marketing_Budget {$},  Product.all)
```

It says the marketing budget for any individual product across all stores for this year is equal to the sales for that product last year divided by the sales for all products last year (this defines the ratio of total marketing budget to be allocated to the product) multiplied by the marketing budget for all products for this year. Notice how I only added the location specifier for a type when the range, on a type-specific basis, was different from that of the left-hand side of the equation. Notice how the ratio of two dollar amounts yields a rational that when multiplied by a dollar returns a dollar.

Allocation functions can be defined on every dimension. So it would have been possible to allocate marketing resources as a function of how well the products sold and as a function of how well each geography fared.

Ratio and Product Formulas

There are two main kinds of ratio functions that mirror the two main types of adjacencies within hierarchical dimensions. Ratios can be taken between cells that are hierarchically separated, which I call resolutional ratios, or not hierarchically separated, which I call positional ratios. The previous allocation example made use of a resolutional ratio. Any kind of ratio of some value to an ancestor's value as with the ratio of an individual product's sales to all products sales, the ratio of an individual company's earnings to its industry's earnings, or the ratio of a single employee's payroll to that of his or her company is an example of a resolutional ratio. *Since resolutional ratios are part-whole ratios, no resolutional ratio can ever be greater than one.*

Any kind of ratio between members or instances that are treated as contents and are not hierarchically related is a positional ratio. For example, the productivity ratio between two firms, the salary ratio between two employees, or the distance ratio between two ski jumpers are all examples of positional ratios. If you return to the formula schema and add a derived content to it called margins and set it equal to the ratio of Sales to Costs as shown here in two alternate definitions, you can see syntactic examples of positional ratios:

```
Margin {R},
        Geog. ,
        Time. ,
        Product. =
        Sales {$} / Cost {$}

Margin {R},
        L.leaf. =
        Sales {$} / Cost {$}
```

Positional ratios can assume any rational value. Note the ratio of two dollar-denominated variables yields a rational number. If Margin had been defined as the difference between Sales and Costs, then it would have been denominated in dollars.

```
Margin {$},
        L.leaf. =
        Sales {$} - Cost {$}
```

Whether you need to see comparisons as ratios or differences depends on what you intend to do with the resulting information. For example, with a variety of companies, in identifying which company may provide a better return on investment, you probably want to look at margins as percentages, since the absolute size of the company is independent of the company's profitability. However, if you are interested in determining which company has the resources to penetrate a new market, you probably want to look at absolute dollar margins since the resource requirements are absolute dollars.

Ordering Formulas

Ordering operations pervade analytical applications. Every time you query for the top 10 customers (as defined by earnings per customer), the bottom 5 products (as defined by sales), or the top 6 skiing sites (as defined by the average annual snowfall), you're performing an ordering operation—actually an ordering followed by a selection. The typical reasons why you would order or transform the order of the instances of a type are as follows:

- For queries, as in querying for the top or bottom N stocks
- For pattern detection, as in looking for a correlation between stock price volatility (the stock's beta coefficient), and the log of the market capitalization of the company
- For integration of disparate data, as in creating composite indexes
- For visualization, as in creating a surface plot of earnings per share varying over two dimensions defined by industry and companies_ordered_by_size

As described in Chapter 5, any nominal dimension can be ordered through its association with another already ordered variable. Thus, a nominal type such as Store can be ordinally or cardinally arranged by size or profitability; a nominal type such as customers can be ordered by duration and a nominal type such as products can be ordered by cost. This ordering of nominal types through their association with cardinal types is most frequently performed within the context of a dimension specification and leads to a named ordering for the dimension such as Store.salesorder.

Furthermore, any cardinal variable can be transformed or reordered for analytical purposes. Thus, the instances of the cardinal type per capita income can be ordered according to the log of their value so as to facilitate comparisons between countries of widely disparate per capita incomes. Although from an operational perspective, and as presented in this section, ordering operations are ordering operations regardless of the context; typically speaking, the reordering of cardinal types or quantitative variables is done by analysts within the context of defining formulas whether in an OLAP or statistical package, the latter offering far more types of orderings than an OLAP product.

Methods of Ordering

The three main methods for creating orderings are rank-based, normalization-based, and rank-preserving transformation-based. To illustrate the differences between these orderings, consider the following simple base schema relative to how the orderings are created is

```
(Product. , Time.all) ~ Sales
```

Table 7.2 illustrates one set of possible values.

It is best to think of ordering as a two-part process. One part, which is necessary, is the creation of the ordering based on some already ordered dimension. This is the ranking or normalizing. The other part, which typically, but not necessarily, occurs is the arrangement of the instances of a nominal dimension according to the ordered instances of the ordering dimension. This is the arrangement of products according to their ordered sales.

Rank-style orderings assign a rank number to the dimension value or type instance. They are ordinal in nature. If there are N elements in a dimension, each one will be assigned a value from 1 to M, which is $< = N$. Ties are typically given the same value with the appropriate number or rank-numbers skipped afterwards. Rank-style orderings are useful for all kinds of top and bottom N queries. Table 7.3 shows the top-to-bottom sales rankings and the associated product name and sales, and may be thought of as resulting from the following query:

```
Descending Rank (Sales) {Rank}, Product {Name} ,Sales {$}, Time.all
```

Normalization or one-based orderings map a set of dimension values to a value between zero and one. Since gaps are preserved in one-based orderings, they result in a cardinal series. Again, there are different ways of creating one-based orderings, but typically the difference between the minimum and maximum value is calculated and set to near one (this allowing for new values to appear that are greater than the current

Table 7.2 Alltime Sales per Product

PRODUCT	SALES {$}, TIME.ALL
A	500
B	750
C	250
D	2000
E	1500
F	3000
G	750

Table 7.3 Sales Rank and Associated Product Name and Sales Amount

RANK	PRODUCT NAME	SALES {$}
1	F	3000
2	D	2000
3	E	1500
4	G	750
5	B	750
6	C	500
7	A	250

Table 7.4 Sales Normalization Ordering and Associated Product Name and Sales Amount

NORMALIZATION ORDERING	PRODUCT NAME	SALES {$}
1	F	3000
.64	D	2000
.45	E	1500
.18	G	750
.18	B	750
.09	C	500
0	A	250

maximum). Every other value is then assigned an offset from zero to one. Table 7.4 shows the top-to-bottom one-based sales ordering, and the associated product name and sales and may be thought of as resulting from the following query:

```
Descending Normalization ordering (Sales) {Rank}, Product {Name} Sales
{$}, Product.*, Time.all
```

Rank-preserving (RP) transformation orderings transform a dimension value by some function to another value without changing the rank of the value. The most common form of RP transformation ordering is logarithmic. The reason for applying a log function (typically natural, base 2, or base 10) is to facilitate a comparison between clumps of widely disparate values whether the disparities represent company sizes, personal incomes, numbers of customers, or amounts of pollution. If you didn't apply some form of transformation, the cost of seeing some range of values clearly would be the inability to see other ranges clearly. For exa mple, if you wanted to compare the evolution of the Dow Jones Industrial Average and the NASDAQ Composite index by looking at average quarterly values for the past 15 years and you didn't first perform some type of transformation, you would either have a hard time seeing differences at the low range because all values would look like zeros (as illustrated in Figure 7.16), or at the high range because all values would like they were increasing to infinity.

Table 7.5 shows the natural log of sales in descending order and the associated product name and sales and may be thought of as resulting from the following query:

```
Descending Natural Log (Sales) {Log}, Product {Name} Sales {$},
Product. , Time.all
```

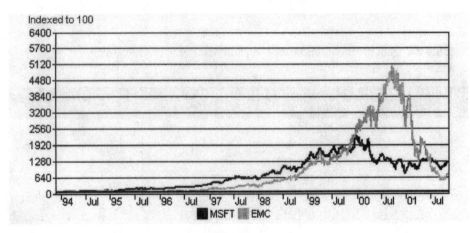

Figure 7.16 EMC versus MSFT Composite highlighting high-range differences.

Table 7.5 Natural Log of Sales, Associated Product Name, and Sales Amount

NATURAL LOG OF SALES	PRODUCT NAME	SALES {$}
8.01	F	3000
7.60	D	2000
7.31	E	1500
6.62	G	750
6.62	B	750
6.21	C	500
5.52	A	250

Aggregate Orderings

Binning, bucketing, and the creation of quartiles, pentiles, sextiles (sounds like a rock band), and deciles are all examples of aggregate orderings. Within an OLAP environment, the most typical use of aggregate orderings is the creation of aggregation levels within a dimension, based on the cardinal attributes of the dimension (or the cardinal types that are in a one-to-one association with the type for which the aggregate ordering is being created). Thus, the members of a customer dimension and an associated sales per customer type could be used to create an aggregate ordering for customers defined in terms of 10 ranges of equal value called deciles. Such groupings are typically either defined in terms of equal value ranges, in which case the number of customers per group may vary, or in terms of equanumerous groupings, in which case the value ranges for each group may vary.

As illustrated next, aggregate groupings can be referred to just like any other type instance set.

```
Avg(P/E) {R} , Time.2000, Stock. P/E.decile.1
```

This queries for the average P/E for all stocks in the top decile of P/E for 2000.

```
Avg (P/E.decile.1){R} / Avg(P/E.decile.2){R} , Time.2000
```

This queries for the ratio of the average P/E for companies in the first versus the second decile for the year 2000.

Creating a Composite Indicator

There are many reasons why you may want to create a composite indicator. From the Dow Jones Industrial Average, to the government's index of leading economic indicators, to United Nations measures of global well-being, to any kind of organizational metric such as a balanced scorecard or value imperative, indicators represent attempts to combine individual values that were sourced from multiple variables into a single composite variable or indicator. Over the years I have worked on numerous indicator projects. They can get very complex with hundreds of variables funneling through several levels into a single indicator or collection of indicators.

Regardless of whether there are 2, 200, or 2,000 variables merging into an indicator, anyone creating indicators needs to figure out how the individual variables are going to be weighted as they merge into that single indicator (set). As the astute reader will by now have guessed, it is the relative weighting where all the action takes place.

A simple example of a customer service quality indicator starting with five underlying variables is shown in Table 7.6.

Given these underlying variables, you need to order them in some way. Typically you would use a normalization-based ordering, thus mapping them into a value between zero and one. Finally, you need to assign each normalized variable a weight relative to the other variables going into the indicator. These two additional columns are shown in Table 7.7.

Table 7.6 Underlying Variables for a Composite Customer Service Quality Indicator

VARIABLES	MEASURED UNITS
Time to respond to customer	Seconds
Usefulness of info given	1-10
# customers seeking service	Integer/time
Sales	$/time
Usefulness of info learned from customers	1-10

Table 7.7 Addition of Normalizing Values and Weights

VARIABLES	MEASURED UNITS	NORMALIZED VALUE RANGE	WEIGHT
Time to respond to customer	Seconds	0-1	.3
Usefulness of info given	1-10	0-1	.3
# customers seeking service	Integer/time	0-1	.1
Sales	$/time	0-1	.1
Usefulness of info learned from customers	1-10	0-1	.2

Once you have the normalized values and weights, and assuming this indicator applies to a set of departments over time (and defining the metric indicator as {Ind}), you can define the Customer Service Quality (CSQ) indicator in the following way:

```
CSQ {Ind}
        Dept.,
        Time. =
        (.3 * Time_to_Respond + .3 * Usefulness_info_given +
        .1 * Customers_Seeking_Advice + .1 x Sales +
        .2 x Usefulness_of_Info_Learned)
```

Once you have the CSQ indicator, you can analyze departments in terms of CSQ with the following query that asks for the department chief of each of the top five departments in terms of CSQ:

```
Department_Chief, Department.(CSQ.Rank.1-5).
```

Of course, the department chiefs of those departments not in the top five, and especially those in the bottom ranks, will no doubt protest that the composite indicator does not adequately reflect their particular customer philosophies as evidenced by the way in which the individual variables were weighted. An analytically savvy department chief might point out that if the weighting for Time_to_Respond were lowered to 0.1 and the weighting for Customers_Seeking_Advice were raised to 0.3, then her or his department's ranking would increase from 25 to 5. Thus, if you ever find yourself creating composite indicators, be prepared to analyze the change in ranking (in this case for a particular department) as a function of changes in the relative weighting of the variables. Although there are a variety of approaches to performing sensitivity analysis on the weightings of composite indicators, regardless of the approach, there are a few steps that must be taken. Continuing with the previous example, let's assume that the analytically savvy department chief convinced the COO that the relative variable weightings were biased and that a more balanced weighting, as expressed in an alternative indicator definition, would look as follows:

```
NEW_CSQ {Ind},
        Dept.,
        Time. =
        (.1 * Time_to_Respond + .3 * Usefulness_info_given +
        .3 * Customers_Seeking_Advice + .1 x Sales +
        .2 x Usefulness_of_Info_Learned)
```

The next step is to recalculate every department's indicator value and then rank departments on the basis of their NEW_CSQ value as shown:

```
Rank {Int} , Dept {Name} , NEW_CSQ.Drnk.1-5
```

Let's say that this department does indeed rise to number five under the new indicator. How would the COO convince himself or herself that the new weighting was appropriate? One way is to look at the departments that were the most affected by the change in the indicator weighting definition, as with the following expression:

```
Dept {Name} , (CSQ.rank - NEW_CSQ.rank).rank.1 to 5
```

If the departments that gained or lost the most under the new indicator definition appear, ex-post-facto, to be deserving of their new rankings, then it stands a good chance that the analytically savvy department chief was right in asking for different weightings. If the COO strongly disagrees with some of the new sinkers or swimmers, then chances are the COO won't agree with the reranking of the department in question.

Cross-Cube

As shown in Chapter 6, most real-world data sets consist of multiple partially overlapping hypercubes. Therefore, as an application builder or analyst, you need to know how to create formulas that reference data across multiple cubes of nonidentical dimensionality. As you will see in Chapters 13 through 17, cross-cube formulas can get

SALES

		January	February
Neptune	Price {$/kg}	15	20
	Sales {kg}	100	150
	Revenue {$}	1500	3000
	Costs {$}		
Poseidon	Price {$/kg}	10	15
	Sales {kg}	200	300
	Revenue {$}	2000	4500
	Costs {$}		

MANUFACTURING RULES

		Tuna	Salmon
Neptune	Fish Requirements {G/kg}	750	250
Poseidon	Fish Requirements {G/kg}	250	750

MATERIAL COSTS

		Jan	Feb
Tuna	Price {$/kg}	10	15
Salmon	Price {$/kg}	5	10

Figure 7.17 A simple fishcake manufacturing schema and model.

pretty complex. Here you are introduced to the basics of cross-cube formulas. Consider the example schema and model in Figure 7.17. It represents a highly simplified data set for a producer and seller of fishcakes. There are three given cubes: one for product sales, one for manufacturing rules, and one for materials cost.

The sales cube is composed of six types in the following LC schema:

```
(Fishcake. ⊗ Time.month.) ~ Price {$/Kg}, Sales {Kg} ,   Revenue {$} ,
Cost {$}
```

As you can see in the figure, there is input data for price and sales, and easily calculated data for revenues. As an analyst, your goal is to calculate the cost of fishcakes sold, making appropriate use of the data in the other two cubes.

The manufacturing rules cube is composed of three types in the following LC schema:

```
(Fishcake. ⊗ Fish.) ~ Requirements {Grams/Kg}
```

The materials cost cube is also composed of three types in the following LC schema:

```
(Fish. ⊗ Time.) ~ Price {$/Kg}
```

A simple way to calculate the cost of fishcakes sold per month is to define it as the sum of the cost of fish consumed per fishcake per month over all fish. The cost of fish consumed per fishcake per month can then be defined as the sum of the quantity of each fish consumed in a month times the price of the fish that month, again over all fish.

This method of chunking the problem results in the definition of the two intermediate variables, Fish_Consumed{Kg}, and Cost_of_FishConsumed{$} defined against an intermediate cube as shown in Figure 7.18.

```
(Fishcake. ⊗ Fish. ⊗ Time.) ~ Fish_Consumed {Kg},
Cost_of_Fish_Consumed {$}
```

Where

```
Fish_Consumed {Kg} =
      [Manufacturing Rules]: Requirements {G/Kg}     x
      [Sales]: Sales {Kg}

Cost_of_FishConsumed {$} =
      Fish_Consumed {Kg}     x
      [Material costs]: Price {$/Kg}
```

The cost variable in the sales cube is then defined as

```
Cost {$} =
[Intermediate cube]:  (Cost_of_Fish_Consumed, Fish.all)
```

The appropriate filled-in cost values are shown in Figure 7.19.

Even though this was a simple example (actually the simplest example that could illustrate the point), it highlights the basic principles and semantic ambiguity of cross-cube formulas that occur over and over again no matter the complexity of the application.

FISH COST

			Tuna	Salmon
Neptune	Jan	Fish consumed {kg}		
		Cost of fish consumed {$}		
	Feb	Fish consumed {kg}		
		Cost of fish consumed {$}		
Poseidon	Jan	Fish consumed {kg}		
		Cost of fish consumed {$}		
	Feb	Fish consumed {kg}		
		Cost of fish consumed {$}		

Figure 7.18   An intermediate cube.

SALES

		January	February
Neptune	Price {$/kg}	15	20
	Sales {kg}	100	150
	Revenue {$}	1500	3000
	Costs {$}	875	2062
Poseidon	Price {$/kg}	10	15
	Sales {kg}	200	300
	Revenue {$}	2000	4500
	Costs {$}	1250	3375

Figure 7.19   The sales cube with filled-in cost values.

As regards this semantic ambiguity, the astute reader may be wondering what principle allowed me to connect:

- Sales data, which is not dimensioned by fish, with the Fish_Consumed variable, which *is* dimensioned by fish
- Manufacturing rules data, which is not dimensioned by time, with the Fish_Consumed variable, which is dimensioned by time

Is it as simple as plugging in a dummy single instance for every type otherwise missing from a variable, thus adding a Fish.all member to the location structure of the sales variable and a Time.all member to the location structure of the requirements variable as follows?

```
(Fishcake. ⊗ Time. ⊗ Fish.all) ~ Sales {Kg} ,

(Fishcake. ⊗ Fish. ⊗ Time.all) ~ Requirements {G/Kg}
```

Although the calculation of Fish_Consumed will turn out correctly by adding dummy dimensions to sales and requirements, the introduction of a new dimension has implications that may not be true. The dangerous implication is that a variable, once defined for any member of a dimension may subsequently be allocated or otherwise calculated for other members of the dimension.

Thus, the requirements variable that originally was not dimensioned by time could now be thought of as varying by time. That is pretty straightforward. Recipes change over time. In retrospect, one can see that the absence of the time dimension from the original formulation of requirements didn't mean that requirements were not dimensioned by time, just that requirements were constant over time.

But what about the Fish dimension as it pertains to the sales variable? Is sales dimensioned by fish? For every instance of sales, there is an associated fishcake and time, but there is no associated fish. It is not accurate to think of fishcake sales as being constant over fish in the same way that requirements are constant over time. You would be creating nonsense to relax the assumption of constancy and let fishcake sales vary over fish.

So how does one define a Fish_Consumed variable without getting into potential nonsense? Luckily, the principle of joining dissimilar cubes by taking the shared or intersecting dimensions as locators and each collection of nonshared or disjunct dimensions as contents, which I described in Chapter 6, is all you need to work through this problem.

The only dimension shared between sales and manufacturing rules is fishcake, so you can rewrite the sales, requirements, and materials cost schemas as follows:

```
Sales: (Fishcake.) ~ (Time. ~ Sales)
Manufacturing Rules: (Fishcake.) ~ (Fish. ~ Requirement)
Materials Cost: (Fishcake.) ~ ((Time. ⊗ Fish.) ~ Fish_Consumed)
```

The formula for Fish_Consumed looks as follows:

```
Fish_Consumed {Kg},
          Time.,
          Fish.,
          Fishcake. =
           (Sales {Kg} , Time.) *
           (Requirements {G/Kg}, Fish.)
```

Figure 7.20 shows how for each location defined by an individual fishcake (the common denominator) there exists an array A of time-specific sales values, an array B of fish-specific requirements values, and an array C of fish- and time-specific Fish_Consumed values. Note how no additional dimensions were ever attributed to either the sales or requirements variables.

From the preceding example you can see there are three basic principles to the construction of cross-cube formulas consisting of a single underlying constraint and two consequences.

The fundamental constraint in cross-cube formulas is that *at the moment of interaction* between two or more variables or contents that originate in different cubes, all contents must share the same location dimensions. As you saw earlier when defining calculations across multiple cubes with differing dimensionalities, this was accomplished in two ways: either by defining an intermediate cube join consisting of the union of all dimensions and assigning a dummy dimension to every variable lacking in any of the dimensions in the union, or by creating a join cube whose dimensions consist of only the intersecting dimensions and whose contents consist of each collection of nonshared dimensions.

The two consequences are that data are either distributed or aggregated across cubes of dissimilar dimensions (assuming that the data isn't selected from a single member). Thus, you saw that the fishcake sales data were distributed across the requirements data to calculate Fish_Consumed and the fish costs data were aggregated to calculate the fishcake costs.

Formula Complexities

Now that you've seen the basic types of formulas—selection, aggregation and allocation, ratio and product, ordering, aggregate ordering, and cross-cube—it is time to see

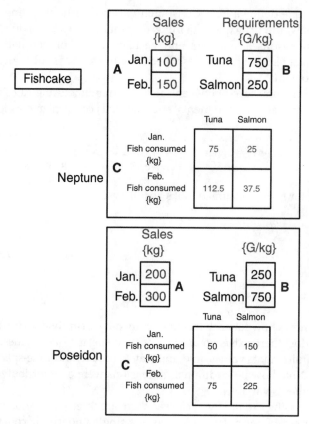

Figure 7.20 Dimensioning fishcake.

how any of these basic formulas can be modified, altered, or otherwise adopted through the application of weighting, ranges, conditionals, manual overrides, and finally chaining.

Weighted Formulas

Any time you modify the values of the terms or variables in an equation to reflect some additional factor (as with the composite indicator example used previously), you are weighting the terms in the equation by that factor. Typically, the weighting factor is expressed as a resolutional ratio and is intended to reflect the relative proportion of the additional factor possessed by each variable.

Thus, one might weight the average per capita caloric intake given for each country by the relative population of the country in order to calculate an average value for per capita caloric intake at the regional or continental level weighted by the relative population in each country. If you don't assign a population-based weighting to each country, each country's per capita caloric intake will be treated equally for the purposes of calculating the continental average. Thus, if the per capita caloric intake for China were

2,000 and for Bhutan 1,600 (and assuming them to be the only two countries in Asia), without weighting, one would calculate the average for Asia as 1,800, whereas with weighting by population, and assuming the population of China to be 100 times that of Bhutan, the weighted average would be 1,996.

Given a geography dimension with the two levels, Continent and Country, the LC formula for the overall per capita caloric intake for each continent might look as follows:

```
Weighted_PC_Caloric_Intake {Calories/Day},
     Geog.Continent. =
     Sum ((PC_Caloric_Intake, Geog.continent.Ccountry.) * (Population,
     Geog.Country. /
     Population, Geog.country.Continent))
```

You can see by inspection that the weighting factor (Population, Geog.Country. / Population, Geog.country.continent) is a resolutional ratio.

Ranged Formulas

The most common examples of range queries are running or moving averages and cumulative totals. Thus, we speak of three-month moving averages or sales to date (a cumulative total), or the ratio of sales to date for this year versus last year. Range queries require at least an ordinally ordered dimension for the range specification. By far and away the most common dimension against which to create ranges is time. As you should recall from Chapter 5, any dimension with ordinal properties can support range referencing. The following examples of range queries are defined against the simple schema *(Time.) ~ Sales* where the structure of the time dimension is illustrated in Figure 7.21.

A Cumulative_Sales_to_Date content or variable could look as follows:

```
Cumulative_Sales_to_Date ,
        Time.day. =
        Sum (Sales , Time.(Year.this).Day.(first to this))
```

LEVEL NAMES	INSTANCES PER LEVEL
Year	(2000, 2001, 2002 . . .)
Quarter	(1st, 2nd, 3rd, 4th)
Month	(January, February, March . . .)
Day	(Jan 1st, Jan 2nd, Jan 3rd . . .)
Hour	(9 am, 10 am, 11 am . . .)
Minute	(1, 2, 3 . . . 60)

Figure 7.21 Figure of time dimension structure.

Notice how the previous formula defines a cumulative sales variable on a year-by-year basis [that's the *Time.(Year.this)* fragment]. When triggered, it looks for the year value of the time dimension of whatever model it is defined in, and then within that year creates up to 366 distinct cumulative sums [as defined by the *Day.(first to this)* fragment]. Since after December 31, a new year begins, this particular cumulative sum function will start over again. How would you change this formula so that it never stopped accumulating?

A three-month moving average sales would look as follows:

```
Three_month_moving_avg_sales,
        Time.Month. =
        Avg(Sales , Time.Month.((this-2) to this)
```

Notice how the range specification in the previous formula, *Time.Month.((this-2) to this)*, unlike the one before, is always three months. Unfortunately, (and even though the SQL/OLAP extensions do support range queries), some OLAP products still do not directly support range queries. For those that don't, the user is typically forced to create a custom aggregation per distinct range. In other words, it could require up to 366 separately defined cumulative sum formulas to calculate the range of cumulative sums defined above for a single year.

Conditional Formulas

Conditional formulas can be categorized by the type of condition involved and whether the condition applies to the definition of the right-hand side of the equation or to the execution of the formula. For conditional expressions that affect the definition of the right-hand side of the formula, the two basic types of conditions that affect the right-hand side are position-based and data-based.

Position-Based

There are many occasions when a single-named formula, such as indirect costs, needs to have several different right-hand side equations depending on where in the multi-dimensional model the formula is being applied. The single-named variable indirect costs may be calculated differently in different countries or for different product lines or at different times of the year.

Regardless of the dimension(s) in which the definition of the formula varies, and regardless of the tool being used, you need to identify each position-based conditional. This may be done with a series of if/then statements, case statements, or separate application range-specific formula declarations (one per right-hand side declaration), as used here:

```
"Indirect costs" ,
        Geography.France = Total salary / 2

"Indirect costs" ,
    Geography.Spain = Direct costs / 4
```

A robust multidimensional system should also let you specify the positional conditions with any combination of relative dimensional referencing, such as "if member x is the child of member y," or "if member x has any children," and so on. For example, the indirect costs for producing furniture may be different from the indirect costs for producing clothing; using relative referencing, a solid multidimensional language would allow for formulas that express the following:

```
"Indirect costs" ,
        Product.furniture.atunder = Total salary / 2

"Indirect costs" ,
        Product.clothing.atunder = Direct costs / 3
```

Conditional formulas frequently have both an application range-specific set of formulas and a single general formula. For the previous example, this would amount to the existence of a single general formula for indirect costs, say *Total salary / 1.5*, intended to cover all those positions for which no specific positional override has been defined. Typically, you would like to give preference to position-based conditionals as a function of the narrowness or specificity of the declared application range. Thus, any specific position-based conditional should take precedence over a single general formula. For example, a position-based conditional that applies to Europe will be overridden by a position-based conditional that applies to Denmark. OLAP-enabled tools differ substantially in the way you need to ensure that local ranges override more general ones. For those tools that do not distinguish differing degrees of locality of reference, you may need to put each application-range-specific conditional in a particular order in your formula space (such as specific formulas before general ones) to ensure that the appropriate condition is triggered.

Data-Based

The other major type of conditional formula is data-based. Formulas for prices, costs, and physical depreciation often vary as a function of some data-driven conditional. For example, product prices charged to regular customers may vary as a function of yearly cumulative sales for that customer. Electricity costs may vary as a function of the number of kilowatt hours consumed per month. And the physical depreciation of a bridge as measured by the needed maintenance costs per month may vary as a function of the average daily load on the bridge.

Consider the formula for the pool of funds available for bonuses that may be conditioned on the percentage variance in direct sales between actual and plan.

A formula for this type data-driven conditional would look something like the following:

```
"Bonus pool" ,
      "variance of actual to plan direct sales" < 0.95,= 0

"Bonus pool" ,
            "variance of actual to plan direct sales" > 0.95 and < 1.2, =
            0.0001 * "total direct sales revenue"
```

```
"Bonus pool" ,
            "variance of actual to plan direct sales" >= 1.2,=
            0.1 * "total direct sales revenue"
```

Both position-based and data-based types of conditional formula exceptions are required for any reasonable OLAP solution.

Formula Triggering Conditionals

In addition to conditioning the right-hand side of a formula on specific data or position states, the triggering of a formula may also be conditioned on various system states. In an aggregation-style reporting application where many aggregates are created, a common business rule is to condition the triggering of an aggregation on the existence of a certain percentage of the underlying cells defined ether in terms of quantity or in terms of some weighting rule that has data to be aggregated. For example, in an international economics application one might condition the triggering of a continent-level aggregation based on the existence of more than 75 percent of the population-weighted countries having data. Those continents where less than 75 percent of the underlying country populations have data would show as missing. As is common with relational databases, formulas may also be triggered by the existence of certain events.

Overridden Formulas

Overridden formulas are akin to event-based conditionals where the event is the manual override of a derived value. Take, for example, the following schema:

```
(Time. ⊗ Geog.) ~ Sales
```

Imagine that you are the eastern regional sales manager and you need to submit your regional sales figures for the first quarter of this year. The sales model has been in production for several years and store-level data, once entered by the store managers, automatically rolls up to regions and countries. So at the regional level, sales is a derived variable as follows:

```
Sales, Geog.Region. = Sum (Sales , Geog.Store.)
```

Now imagine that all the stores in the company except for a few stores in your region have reported their sales and you have not implemented a missing data inferencing routine. You have a pretty good idea what the sales figures should be for the missing stores and are willing to input proxies for them, but you can't alter the store-level base data. What's a regional manager to do? Well, the astute manager would want to manually override the regional sales value for his or her region, thus temporarily blocking the aggregation of the store-level data from his or her region until all stores had reported. Then the overridden value could be aggregated with the rest of the regional sales values. Another reason why the regional sales manager might want to override an otherwise derived value is if it becomes known that some input value that can't be changed in the short term was incorrect. Several OLAP tools support manual overrides.

Chained Formulas

It is common for analytical queries in business or other domains to be composed of recursive collections or chains of formulas. In words (and LC), examples include the following:

- A financial analyst who wanted to compare the aggregate price earnings ratios between two portfolios for a given year, given a holdings dimension with individual stocks as leaves and portfolios as (possibly overlapping) groupings of individual stocks:

```
"The ratio of overall P/E between portfolios one and two" =
    Sum((P/E, Portfolio1.Stock.) *
    ((Number_of_Shares_Held * Price_per_Share ),
    Portfolio1.Stock.)) ÷
    Sum((P/E , Portfolio2.Stock.) *
    ((Number_of_Shares_Held * Price_per_Share),
    Portfolio2.Stock.))
```

- A sales analyst who wanted to compare the change in average earnings over the past year accruing to the top five selling products in each of the top five selling stores with the change in average earnings over the past year accruing to the five most average selling products for those same stores:

```
"Ratio of top selling to average selling products" =
        (
        (Avg(Earnings), Time.Year.this., Product.(Sales.Drnk.(1
        to 5).(Store, Sales.Drnk.(1 to -5) , Store.all
        Time.Year.this))
        /
    (Avg(Earnings) , Time.Year.(this-1), Product.(Sales.Drnk.(1 to
        5).(Store, Sales.Drnk.(1 to 5), Store.all Time.Year.(this-
        1))))
        /
        (Avg(Earnings) ,  Time.Year.this,
        Product.(Sales.Distance_from_mean.Arnk.(1 to 5).(Store,
        Sales.Drnk.(1 to 5), Store.all, Time.Year.this))
        /
        (Avg(Earnings), Time.Year.(this-1), Product.(Sales.
        Distance_from_Mean.Arnk.(1 to 5).(Store, Sales.Drnk.(1 to
        5), Store.all ,Time.Year.(this-1))))
        )
```

Summary

In the first section of this chapter, you saw that formulas operate in a more abstract fashion in a multidimensional environment than in a traditional spreadsheet environment. And rather than attaching to columns as with SQL databases, multidimensional formulas can apply to any member or instance of any dimension in a model. Because there can exist one formula per member per dimension, frequently more than one formula applies to a particular cell. In these cases a precedence rule needs to be invoked to determine which formula (or ordering of formulas) will be evaluated for the cell. In the second section, you were exposed to various kinds of reusable multidimensional formula building blocks including aggregations, allocations, ratios, products, and cross-dimensional and cross-cube formulas, as well as the ways in which they get weighted, conditionally modified, overridden, and chained. The formula building blocks you saw and the ways in which they may be modified will be of value to you regardless of the particular OLAP environment you may work with.

Links

Cubes need some linkage to the external data world if they are going to receive data. Those linkages may be as simple as a table import facility that is periodically invoked. All data processing products, from spreadsheets to statistics packages, have these capabilities. Unlike typical end-user applications, however, OLAP products are regularly called upon to process large amounts of periodically refreshed data. A manual approach to maintaining synchronicity between data sources and cubes is unacceptable in the long run. OLAP systems need to have the capability to establish persistent links with external sources of data (and dimensions and attributes), such that when changes occur in the external data sources or on a timed basis, they are automatically brought into the cube. Any dimension modifications or data calculations need to be automatically and incrementally performed.

Because OLAP products and applications are generally separate from the systems that input external data (in other words data-generating events connect to a host of operational systems that in turn may connect to a data warehousing environment that finally connects to an OLAP system), links also serve as transformation functions. They indicate how to transform table- or spreadsheet-formatted data and meta data into dimensional data and meta data.

At the time of this writing, it is still the case that in a typical OLAP application where the data is not being sourced from a well-designed data warehouse, over half (and frequently two-thirds to three-quarters) of the total energy spent on building a solution is spent on designing and implementing the input links! This is because the way data is modeled in source systems may be quite different from the way it's modeled in the OLAP system. As yet, no easy methods or tools exist for performing the necessary schema transformations.

Whether the tools that you use support links that you can just declare and have work, or whether you need to code the transformations by hand, the transformations would be the same. If your tool supports the ability to declare links without procedural code, then the functions it provides should map cleanly to the ones described here. If you need to code a script or program by hand, then the descriptions of link types can serve as its high-level design. Though I was involved in designing an OLAP product in the mid-90s that had as one of its goals the creation of extensive link capabilities, as of this writing, few OLAP tools offer such links.

Links can be read only or read/write. Although I focus here on the traditional read aspects of links, there is certainly a need for bidirectional links. As OLAP systems become more integrated with transactional systems, the results of analyzing data, such as finding an optimal price point for a product, will want to be fed back into operational systems, or at least the data warehouse, if there is one. Some products do support read/write links.

Links can be static or dynamic. Static links are not capable of processing changes made to the source. They are used only by the multidimensional tool when it loads or refreshes its information from the source. Dynamic links maintain an open connection between the source and the cube wherein changes to the source are propagated to the cube.

Links provide a persistent infrastructure for importing and exporting data and meta data. They vary as a function of the type of information brought into the cube and the type of data structure from which the information is obtained. The limiting factors for linking are the OLAP model's ability to process small amounts of change efficiently and the link processor's ability to detect changes efficiently. As illustrated in Figure 8.1, change may come from a variety of sources. The remainder of this chapter focuses on table links.

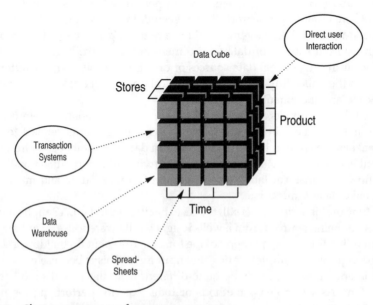

Figure 8.1   Changes may come from many sources.

Types of Links

There are three basic kinds of links:

- Structure links
- Attribute links
- Content links

A *structure link* is used to extract structural information for a dimension, identifying the members and their referential or hierarchical structure (if any). An *attribute link* is used to map attribute information to the members of a dimension. *Content links* are used to map data into the cube. Figure 8.2 shows a classification scheme for links. (They will be treated in depth later in this section, but Figure 8.2 should help you get a sense of them for now.)

Tables that contain structural information (member identity and hierarchical relationships) are linked to a dimension with structure links. A structure link connects a dimension with one or more structuring columns in a table. Two basic forms of such tables follow from the two basic types of hierarchies described in Chapter 5. In a parent-child table, a member may appear as the child of another member in one row and as the parent of other members in other rows. In a level table, there may be two or more columns that identify members at different hierarchical levels. Structure tables are described in more detail later in this chapter. It is possible (particularly for variables) that no hierarchy is specified. In this case, having all the members and being able to tell them apart is as much structure as is required from the table. Figure 8.3 shows structure links between a parent-child table representing the product dimension and the product dimension of the model. Note the hierarchical members of the product dimension. Figure 8.4 shows structure links between a lookup table and the levels of a dimension.

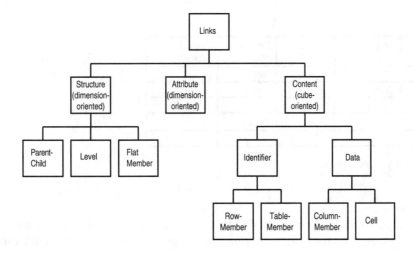

Figure 8.2 Classification of link types.

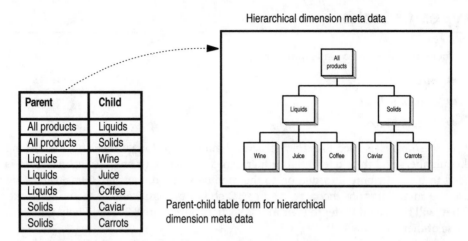

Hierarchical dimension meta data

Parent	Child
All products	Liquids
All products	Solids
Liquids	Wine
Liquids	Juice
Liquids	Coffee
Solids	Caviar
Solids	Carrots

Parent-child table form for hierarchical
dimension meta data

Figure 8.3 Parent-child structure inputs to hierarchical dimension of an OLAP model.

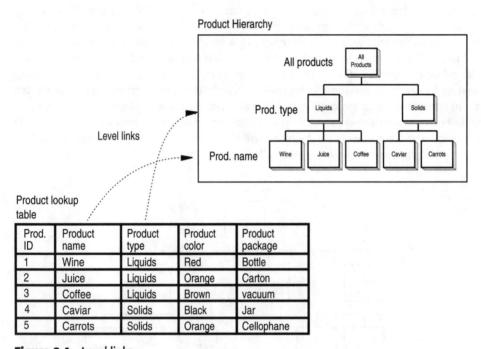

Product Hierarchy

Level links

Product lookup
table

Prod. ID	Product name	Product type	Product color	Product package
1	Wine	Liquids	Red	Bottle
2	Juice	Liquids	Orange	Carton
3	Coffee	Liquids	Brown	vacuum
4	Caviar	Solids	Black	Jar
5	Carrots	Solids	Orange	Cellophane

Figure 8.4 Level links.

Tables containing information other than structural relationships that are associated with members can have that information brought into the OLAP model through attribute links. Frequently, this attribute information will be part of a meta data table that also contains structural information, and the one table would be connected to the multidimensional model with both types of links. Each attribute link will connect an attribute associated with the members of a dimension to a column identifying the members and a column identifying values for the attribute. Attribute links are shown in Figure 8.5.

Tables containing values for variables in the hypercube's dimensional space need to be attached with content links. While the structure and attribute links connect a dimension and a table independently of any cube, the content links all connect to a table in the context of a cube. Two different types of content links are required to connect a table to a cube[1] because different links extract member identifiers and variable values from rows.

Figure 8.6 shows the content links between a multidimensional model and an input table.

Tables may require aggregation prior to entry in a cube. For example, a multidimensional model that has weeks as its lowest level of time may need to link to a data source that has daily summaries or individual transaction information. In this case, the necessary aggregations would be included in the overall link information. In general, if there end up being duplicate combinations of members in the rows, the data-bearing fields should be aggregated. For example, take a cube with sales variables and store, time, and product dimensions, and a linked data table containing transaction number, store, time, product, quantity, and sale price. One would not typically link the transaction number field into the OLAP model. (Although there are times when you want to maintain transaction level connections, which I describe in the application section of this book within the context of BatchID tracking.) Because one would expect more than one sales transaction for many store, day, and product combinations (there may be six different records that all contain *Store 3*, *May 11 2001*, *Dom Perignon*), one would want

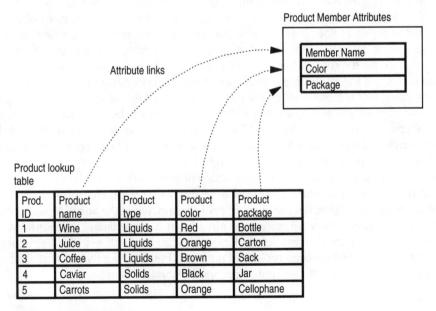

Figure 8.5 Attribute links.

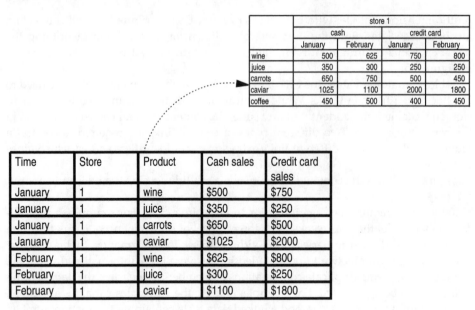

	store 1			
	cash		credit card	
	January	February	January	February
wine	500	625	750	800
juice	350	300	250	250
carrots	650	750	500	450
caviar	1025	1100	2000	1800
coffee	450	500	400	450

Time	Store	Product	Cash sales	Credit card sales
January	1	wine	$500	$750
January	1	juice	$350	$250
January	1	carrots	$650	$500
January	1	caviar	$1025	$2000
February	1	wine	$625	$800
February	1	juice	$300	$250
February	1	caviar	$1100	$1800

Figure 8.6   Content links from an input table to a cube.

to specify the summing of the quantity and averaging of the sale price fields as part of the links.

It is also possible to link data and hierarchical meta data from the same table, as illustrated in Figure 8.7. Certainly, if this is the form of your data tables, a multidimensional tool should be able to make use of the information. However, it is not recommended to maintain your data tables in this form because any organizational changes to your source data, such as reorganizing your product groups or changing the reporting structure for the corporation, will result in a need to define new links between the input tables and the multidimensional cube. This occurs because the columns—that is, stores, cities, and regions—define the particular form of the hierarchy. Any change to the hierarchy, such as adding a new product group, needs to be reflected in a change to the column structure of the input tables, which in turn requires a redefinition of the links between the cube and the input tables. It does provide a convenient form for packaging a client-sized cube of data, though.

Even if the table is providing multiple kinds of information, each link is to one kind of information only (structure, attributes, or content). One reason for this is that a structure link is used to define the members of a dimension, while the attribute and content links extract information for members already in a dimension. Procedurally, the dimension must be constructed before data values can be identified with its members. In some notation, a single construct could represent both, but we would say that it represents the combination of a separate structure link and content link.

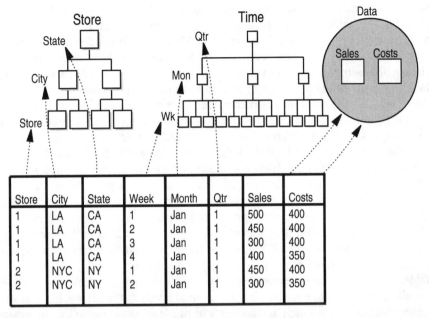

Figure 8.7   Linking data and meta data from the same table.

Structure Tables and Links

Because the variety of links mirrors the variety of source data forms, I frequently discuss link types and data source form types together. The two basic forms of structure tables and links, as mentioned previously, are parent child and level.

A *parent-child* table can define any type of member hierarchy, symmetric or asymmetric, and it is the easiest type of table for maintaining dynamic meta data definitions. All the information about the hierarchical structure of the dimension is defined in terms of the values of rows in the parent-child table, so a hierarchy can be completely rearranged just by tweaking the rows of the table. (The dimension tables in a star schema may contain a column for parent member, providing the necessary information for a single hierarchy. In this case, they function as a parent-child table as well as providing other attribute information.)

A parent-child table connects to a dimension via a single parent-child structure link between the dimension and the parent and child columns. Variations on the basic parent-child link can occur, as required by specific tools. For example, if a tool required hierarchies to be named, then each link would also need to connect to the named hierarchy of the dimension (if all rows of the table were for the same hierarchy) or to a column of the table whose field values contain the appropriate hierarchy name.

Recall the discussion of dimension hierarchies in Chapter 5. Note that parent-child relationships alone do not indicate semantic levels such as month/year or store/city. They can indicate that January, February, and March are all children of Quarter One; but they cannot define January, February, and March as months that collectively share a relationship with quarters and with days. Thus, the table columns in a pure parent-child table cannot fully specify levels in a multidimensional model.

A *level* table is a table of model structure information (such as a lookup or dimension table of the kind we saw in Chapter 2) that contains separate columns wherein each column is connected to a different level in a leveled hierarchy. For example, separate columns for City, State, and Region, or Company Name, SIC Code, and Industry can clearly identify not just hierarchical relationships between members, but also how the levels relate to each other. In this type of table, the names of the columns involved in identifying hierarchy levels will correspond to the levels in the multidimensional model. While these are flexible enough for moving members around in a given set of levels, they are less flexible than parent-child tables for adding and removing levels of hierarchy. Of course, the flexibility of the parent-child tables comes at the expense of not being able to express interlevel relationships adequately.

Tables containing named levels need level structure links, one link for each level. If the levels in the table are not mapping into named levels in the dimension, but simply a member hierarchy, then each link connects from a level's column to the dimension. If the levels in the table correspond to named levels in the dimension, then each level link connects from a level's column to the corresponding level in the dimension.

Occasionally, a dimension simply won't have any hierarchy (for example, a dimension of scenarios, or sales channels, and so on). If it is necessary to link this dimension to a table, then a level link for a single level will suffice. For a table containing only two named levels, like county and state, that is connected to a dimension without named levels, parent-child and level links can be used interchangeably.

The hierarchy pseudolevels described in Chapter 5 may be represented in a parent-child link table because they are described in terms of parents and children. Defining pseudolevels through parent-child links may significantly add to the number of parent-child links in the table because each member that is part of a pseudolevel will have a record for its connection to the pseudolevel root member as well as a record for its referential hierarchy. (Fortunately, using encoded values to identify members means each parent-child record is quite small.)

Data Tables and Content Links

Four different types of content links are required to connect any table to an OLAP schema for the purpose of mapping data into the cube:

- Row-member
- Column-member
- Cell
- Table-member

Row-Member Links

Row-member links are required to associate member names contained in each row of the table with the right members in the model. A row-member link connects a dimension of the cube and a column in the table whose field value in each row contains the name of a member in that dimension. If the dimension is a variable dimension, then it is quite likely that the table is a type zero table and that a cell link would also be used (see Figure 8.10, later in this chapter). It is also possible to see a type one table with the variable names occupying their own column. It is most likely a grave semantic error to make more than one member link between a particular field and any cube, as this would mean that the data is associated with members in two dimensions that share the same name.

Variations on the basic member links may be required from time to time. For example, denormalized data warehouse summary tables may contain multiple levels of members, one per column. For example, *Company, SIC Code,* and *Sector* would each be in their own column. Rows containing company-level summary data will have values in each of these columns. Rows containing an SIC-code-level summary will have a NULL company name and values for each SIC code and sector, and rows containing sector-level summaries will have NULL in both the Company Name and SIC Code fields. There may be an additional column that gives the name of the level to which the summary data pertains. This would assist a SQL programmer to query the table. The column containing the relevant member name varies from row to row in the table, and a member link that conditionally examines fields (perhaps based on the level name contained in another field) would be used.

Column-Member Links

Whereas row-member links associate columns with dimensions and the field values with members, a *column-member link* is required to associate a table's column with a particular variable and its field values with values for that variable. Each column-member link will connect a member of a dimension and a column in a table bearing data for a particular variable. Examples of such columns would be ones named *Number of Units Sold, Total Sales,* and so on. Column-member links are used to identify the data-bearing fields in type one or type two tables. Column-member links and cell links are mutually exclusive (because a table cannot be both a type zero and a type one); if a cube uses even one column-member link to connect to a table, then it cannot use a cell link, and vice versa. If a table has columns that do not correspond to one variable, but rather to a multidimensional intersection (type two tables), then one column-member link per dimension is required. For example, to link a table containing the columns *Actual Sales, Planned Sales, Actual Costs,* and *Planned Costs* to a model that had a scenario dimension with Actual and Planned members requires two column-member links for each of these columns. Each column would have a column-member link to the appropriate scenario member and a column-member link to the appropriate variable.

Figures 8.8 and 8.9 show member and column-member links connecting two different types of type one tables to a cube.

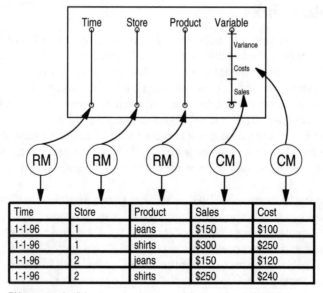

Figure 8.8 A typical type one table attached to a cube by row-member and column-member links.

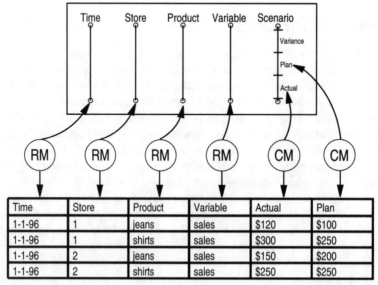

Figure 8.9 A less typical type one table attached to a cube by row-member and column-member links.

Cell Links

Sometimes, the column bearing data in a table will not correspond to any dimension that you have defined in the model, and all of the dimensions of the cube link to the table with member and table-member links (see Figure 8.11). Even the variable names are in a column. This would correspond to a type zero table. In order to associate the values with the variables, you need to create a *cell link*. A cell link connects the cube as a whole to a table column whose field values are data for cells that are otherwise completely specified by the other links. (Logical implications to this were explored in Chapter 4.) Figure 8.10 shows a type zero table connected to a cube via row-member links and a cell link.

Table-Member Links

One more type of link is required to connect data-bearing tables to a cube—a link that represents information that isn't in the table at all! Let's call this a *table-member link*. What kinds of information wouldn't be in a table? Well, a data table extracted from an operational system will generally contain actual values from the operations. (I hope!) If this is feeding into a planning cube that contains a scenario dimension having Plan, Actual, and Variance members, then the entire table is associated with the actual member in that cube. But there is nothing in the table, probably not even in its name, that we can use to assign it to its place in the model. Hence, we need this fourth type of link. It may be that more than one table-member link is required to connect a table to a cube.

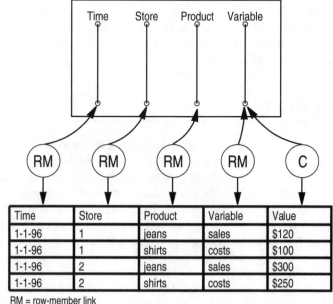

RM = row-member link
C = cell link

Figure 8.10 A type zero table attached to a cube by row-member links and a cell link.

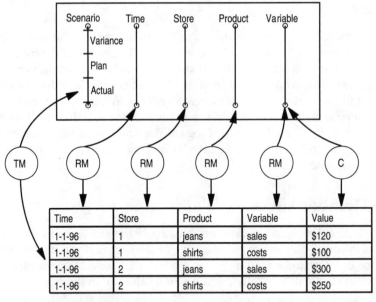

Figure 8.11 A type zero table completely connected using a table-member link.

For example, each table may contain the actual data for an individual line of business within the corporation, and the cube consolidates their results into the planning model. Figure 8.11 shows a type zero table of actual values connected to a cube containing scenarios using a table-member link.

Preaggregation

If the table being linked needs to be aggregated during the process of reading, then the aggregation can be specified as an extension to the linking process. The aggregation should be specified as part of the linking to ensure that the same aggregation is performed each and every time the links are used. However, the aggregation operation to be performed is not strictly a part of the link. Think of it as an attachment to the linked field or fields. All that needs to be specified is the aggregation operator (sum, average, and so on) on each field to be aggregated. The fields to be aggregated are the data fields. If you have already established links, they are the ones with either a column-member link or a cell link.

The reason aggregation operations need to be kept separate from individual links is most apparent when considering the column-member links of a type two table. For a type two table, which will have two column-member links connecting each table column to members in two different dimensions, it would be inconsistent to specify one preaggregation for one dimension and a different preaggregation for the other. What is being aggregated is the data of a column. It makes more sense to attach the aggregation to the columns of the table rather than to any specific link.

Summary

Links between multidimensional decision support and source systems are a fact of life. They define the method for maintaining a persistent (uni- or bidirectional) connection between a multidimensional schema and changing external data sets. I discussed content links, structure links, attribute links, and mixed-type links. I focused on the import capabilities of links in this chapter because they are the most critical and because most commercial OLAP environments are import oriented. Nevertheless, links will become more bidirectional as the results of multidimensional processing get automatically fed back into production databases. Although there is nothing inherently multidimensional about links, the need to have robust dynamic links and the ability to incorporate incremental changes efficiently into an OLAP schema are important features for successful multidimensional systems. Multidimensional systems deal with sufficiently large quantities of data that a manual approach to maintaining synchronicity between data sources and schemas is unacceptable in the long run. As of the time of this writing, most of the multidimensional vendors were working hard to improve the seamlessness of the links between their schemas and the typical relational database as source.

When a linked data table is read, the process of using the links can be summarized as follows: Any table-member and column-member links determine a set of model members that stays the same throughout the entire reading of the table. These members may be extracted from the model side of the link for use in identifying values of variables. Then, for each row, the fields for each column linked by a row-member link are examined and the members that they name determined. If the table has a cell link, then that column contains a single identified value for the variable identified through one of the row-member links, and the variable's value can be extracted from this field. If the table has column-member links instead, then for each column containing a column-member link, the members for its link (or links, in case of a type two table) are collected, and an identified value for a variable can be extracted from the column's field.

A schema cannot be considered fully linked to a data table until the following occurs:

- Each dimension of the schema either is directly connected to a column or has some member connected to either a column or to the table itself.

- Each meta data field and each data field of the table, deemed relevant to the schema, have been connected.

Given the types of links discussed in this chapter, you should be able to describe how to move virtually any type of data from tables to multidimensional models (or populated schemas).

Analytic Visualization

Data visualization is a complex multifaceted subject. On the technology end, data visualization includes

- Graphics accelerators
- Graphics libraries
- Graphic controllers
- Graphic development environments
- Graphic applications

On the research end, it includes

- Visual perception
- Rendering and representation algorithms
- Exploratory data analysis

Many excellent articles and books have been dedicated to it, a number of which are cited in this chapter.

The reason I included a section on data visualization in the first edition of *OLAP Solutions* and the reason I include a substantially expanded treatment of visualization here is because for most—if not all—decision support applications data visualization is an extremely valuable resource. You need to tap into data visualization if you are going to get the most value out of your applications (with the ultimate goal of making better decisions faster).

- Appropriate visualization can improve your ability to discover patterns or relationships in your data, which leads to better predictions that, when combined with the goals of the business, lead to more successful business decisions as measured by the degree to which the goals are achieved.

- For all the available literature on data visualization, there is still a lack of objective information about the appropriate uses of data visualization for decision support applications. (Supporters, frequently vendors, tend to exaggerate its usefulness.)

Consider how quickly we visually recognize common everyday objects. We identify doors, hallways, furniture, people, and places with ease. To our visual cortex, these objects of everyday experience are actually complex visual patterns that our brains discriminate from vast amounts of raw visual input equivalent to many megabytes of numeric or textual data per object. Luckily our brains are much faster at processing visual information than numeric data, or we could spend days just trying to recognize ourselves in the mirror.

If our brains are so adept at processing visual information, why do we still spend so much time in the business world thinking with numbers? Is it that some tasks are better performed with numbers as opposed to charts and graphs? Are we missing huge opportunities to operate more efficiently? As you'll discover by reading this chapter, both answers are yes.

This chapter will answer the following questions:

- What is visualization anyway?

- When is visualization appropriate?

- How does visualization work to convey meaning?

- What are typical decision-oriented things to visualize?

- How do you select the appropriate visualization for the job?

- How does one visualize higher-dimensional data?

- What are some typical business examples of higher-dimensional data visualization?

Along the way, I've included a variety of images selected from several of the popular visualization packages available on the market. On my companion web site, you will find a resource page pointing you to most of the visualization vendors with whom I am familiar.

What Is Data Visualization?

Before jumping into the topic of data visualization, I want to be clear about what I mean when using the term visualization or data visualization. Towards that end, it is useful to distinguish between two broadly different types of visualization: analog visualization and symbolic visualization.

The key factor with analog visualization is that the image or visual representation is an analog or topology-maintaining transformation of the original object or event that is represented. Photographic images, such as Figure 9.1, and control windows are examples of analog visualization. Because they attempt to capture as much visible detail as can be seen in the original thing or event, we call them realist.

Maps, such as the one in Figure 9.2, are also classic examples of analog representation, but because they only attempt to capture certain details or features (such as city

Figure 9.1   Photographic image of FCI's Lulu and Thor.

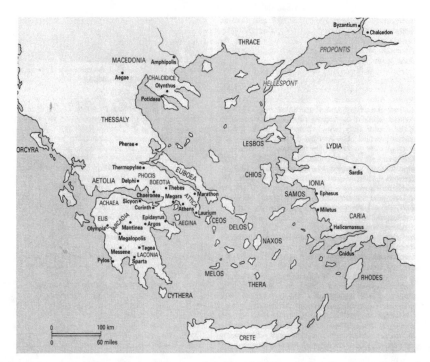

Figure 9.2   Map of Greek city states and their neighbors during the time of Herodotus.

locations and the boundaries between land and sea), we call them abstracted. Although neither form of analog visualization corresponds to what we typically think of when we use the term data visualization, maps are useful for business analysis of spatial relations such as the selection of new sites for retail outlets, and thus we treat them in this chapter as a part of the overall data visualization arsenal. Realist analog representations include medical imaging, product display, environmental monitoring, and package design.

Most standard business visualization, including bar charts, line graphs, and pie charts, falls under the category of basic symbolic representation. For example, although the pie chart representation of a corporation's assets in Figure 9.3, preserves critical information (namely, the ratios between the assets), the asset ratios do not literally exist next to each other, much less in a circular shape as depicted in the pie chart. This is why the pie chart is called a symbolic representation.

The rich 3D representation of web site activity in Insert I.1 is also symbolic, but the image itself is more complex in that it shows substantially more information than the pie chart in Figure 9.3. Likewise, other complex renderings such as parallel coordinates, nested charts, multiattribute pie charts, and 3D glyphs fall under the guise of rich symbolic representations.

Thus, this chapter focuses on symbolic representations—both basic and sophisticated—and abstracted analog representations. Realist analog representations since they are rarely used in general business applications, are not discussed.

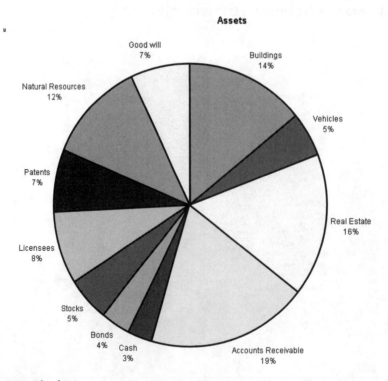

Figure 9.3   Pie chart.

The Semantics of Visualization

In Chapter 3, you saw how higher-dimensional data sets could be represented in terms of multidimensional matrices. Although multidimensional grid-based views are more powerful and more flexible than their spreadsheet antecedents, they are still composed of grids of data, primarily numbers. Grid-based number representations satisfy many business uses where the emphasis is on knowing how much or in seeing exact values —in essence, traditional reporting.

Whether in business or in science, traditional analyses are concerned with such things as finding upper and lower ranges (such as top and bottom quartiles), group attributes (such as means and modes), correlations, and trends. When end-user emphasis is on performing analysis—especially exploring relationships within the displayed data—graphical views are more popular and more productive than numeric views.

Why do graphical displays work better than tabular, numeric ones for exploring analytical relationships? This section explores the difference between graphic and tabular visualization.

Graphic versus Tabular-Numeric Representation

The term graphical has been used in a variety of ways, so I need to spend a little time distinguishing these meanings before defining the relationship between graphical and tabular displays.

Edward Tufte, in his seminal book *The Visual Display of Quantitative Information*, defines data graphics in the following way: "Data graphics visually display measured quantities by means of the combined use of points, lines, a coordinate system, numbers, symbols, words, shading and color."[1] In other words, for Tufte, everything visual qualifies as graphics—not necessarily good graphics, but graphics nonetheless. Although I agree that all forms of visual expression should come together in the graphical presentation of information, this definition is too broad to help us distinguish graphic displays, for which we all have an intuitive feel, from tabular displays.

A little less broadly, you may interpret graphics as visual displays that contain no numbers or words. Although numbers and words frequently make their way into the header and legend of a graphic, this definition holds for the body of most business graphics. Pie charts, bar charts, line graphs, and the like are composed of lines, points, colors, symbols, and shapes. We will come to use this definition by the end of the section, but to understand the essence of why graphics work, we need to begin with a more restrictive definition.

In its most restrictive form, graphics may be interpreted as visual displays that contain only points and sets of points (such as lines, shapes, areas, and volumes). Graph theory operates within these bounds, as do unadorned maps and typical geometric plots. We will begin our discussion with this definition because the essence of what makes graphical displays better for certain types of information may be found by exploring the properties of points and lines.

Points and Lines

To see how much easier it is to spot analytical patterns when data is graphically portrayed, and to see why this is so, consider Figures 9.4 and 9.5. Each of the figures is divided into two panels: an *a* panel that represents a tabular display and a *b* panel that represents a graphic display of the same data.

Figure 9.4 shows sales data in conjunction with cost data for the purpose of break-even analysis. See how much easier it is in the b panel to identify the changing relationship between sales and costs over time when the information is portrayed graphically. Although your eye might be able to scan the table in Figure 9.4 (a) to discover that break-even occurred in July, it is unlikely that you would notice from just looking at the numbers that at the break-even point, costs were leveling off while sales were accelerating.

It is easier to describe the relationship between sales and costs over time from a graphic perspective because with the graphic display, the relationship information is explicitly given. For example, a natural description of the line segment between points P and Q on the cost curve panel in Figure 9.4 (b) would say something like "Costs are continuing to increase, but at a diminishing rate of increase." You would never see this relationship at a glance from looking at the rows between P and Q in the table in Figure 9.4 (a). In contrast to looking for relationship information, if your goal were to know for any particular time the exact value of sales or costs, that information would be more immediately given with a tabular-numeric display. For example, to see what the company costs were in September, you would have to draw a line from September to the cost curve to find the cost point for September (shown by the dotten line in panel b), and then draw another line from that point on the cost curve to the y axis to see the dollar value of the costs at that time. In the tabular display, you would locate the row for September and immediately read the associated cost value.

a

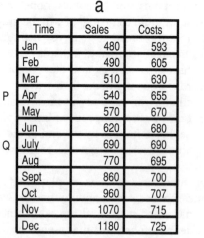

Time	Sales	Costs
Jan	480	593
Feb	490	605
Mar	510	630
P Apr	540	655
May	570	670
Jun	620	680
Q July	690	690
Aug	770	695
Sept	860	700
Oct	960	707
Nov	1070	715
Dec	1180	725

b

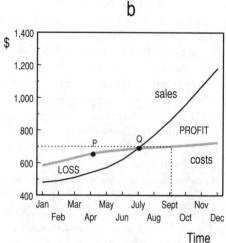

Figure 9.4   Break-even analysis.

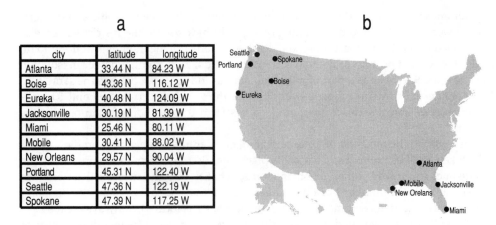

city	latitude	longitude
Atlanta	33.44 N	84.23 W
Boise	43.36 N	116.12 W
Eureka	40.48 N	124.09 W
Jacksonville	30.19 N	81.39 W
Miami	25.46 N	80.11 W
Mobile	30.41 N	88.02 W
New Orleans	29.57 N	90.04 W
Portland	45.31 N	122.40 W
Seattle	47.36 N	122.19 W
Spokane	47.39 N	117.25 W

Figure 9.5 Cities with high sales growth.

Let us look at another example. Figure 9.5 shows cities in the top quartile of sales growth with their corresponding longitude and latitude. Once again, simple inspection of the tabular view in the figure does not reveal any pattern to the cities with sales growth in the top quartile. In contrast, with the graphical view panel, recognizing the pattern (location relationship between the cities) that sales are growing fastest in the Northwest and Southeast is trivial.

Why is it so much easier to see location relationships with a graphic map display than with a tabular numeric display? There are three reasons:

- The map display uses locations on the computer screen to display location information about the data.

- The dimensionality of the location information about the data is preserved in the dimensionality of the location information on the computer screen. In other words, the two-dimensional longitude/latitude relationship between cities is preserved in a two-dimensional map display, but lost in a one-dimensional tabular one. For example, with the map display, moving vertically on the screen corresponds to moving in latitude; moving horizontally corresponds to moving in longitude. With the tabular display, however, there is no correspondence between moving up and down rows and moving in either longitude or latitude. This dimensional preservation is sometimes (and in this book will be) called an analog, as opposed to symbolic, representation. See the sidebar "Graphical Misrepresentations" for more information.

- The quantitative properties of the map display, such as the relative distance between points, which can be processed with minimal effort by the brain, correspond to quantitative properties of the data. For example, the distance between Jacksonville and Atlanta, which appears to be about the same on the map as the distance between Jacksonville and Miami, represents the fact that those distances are, in reality, roughly equivalent.

Summarizing this short excursion into the difference between graphic and numeric displays, we can say that the meaning of a graphical token (in the restrictive sense as described earlier) is its location on the display screen. The meaning has nothing to do with the content or form of the token. In other words, each point, whether in isolation as in Figure 9.5 (b) or as a part of a line segment as in Figure 9.4 (b), has the same content or internal structure or form. Every point is the same as every other point. The difference in meaning between the points comes from the location of the point on the screen.

In contrast, the meaning of a numerical token is entirely dependent on the form of the token and has nothing to do with its placement on the screen. Every number token is distinct from every other. In other words, what makes the number 2 different in meaning from the number 1 or the number 3 is just that the form or shape of the number 2 is distinct. It doesn't matter where the number 2 is located; it always means 2.

Thus, there are two fundamentally different ways of using tokens to represent or convey meaning on a display screen: using screen location and using screen content or form. Numbers convey meaning by virtue of their form. Graphic tokens convey meaning by virtue of their location. A token may represent two fundamentally different types of expressions: value and relationship. As we saw in Figure 9.4, numeric tokens represent their values more directly than the relationship between their values, while graphic tokens represent the relationships between their values more directly than their actual values. Figure 9.6 summarizes these key distinctions.

Colors and Shapes

Colors and shapes, although frequently associated with graphical displays because they show relationship information more easily than value information, work like numbers in that they derive their meaning more from their form on the screen (that is, the particular color or particular shape) than from their location. They were left out of the initial discussion because they have attributes of both numbers and graphics, as shown in our next example.

Figure 9.7 shows another map of the United States, this time colored on a state-by-state basis according to per-capita income quintiles. (In the world of geographic information systems, or GIS, these are called *thematic maps*.) As stated in the legend, the lowest quintile is shown by the lightest shade of gray, the next lowest quintile by the

	Represents Values	Represents Relationships
Location-based Meaning		Points, Lines
Form-based Meaning	Numbers	

Figure 9.6 The key distinctions between numeric and graphic displays.

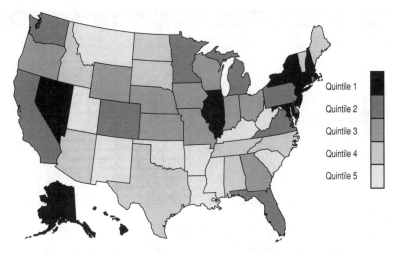

Figure 9.7   U.S. per capita income by state (shades based on quintiles).

GRAPHICAL MISREPRESENTATIONS

A serious problem associated with graphical representations is the ease with which they can misrepresent the underlying data.[3] Two major causes of misrepresentation are described here and both are avoidable.

1. Collapsing multiple data dimensions into a single location-based display dimension, as shown in Figure 9.8. When the graph and the data do not share the same structure, the graph can create false impressions about the data.
    The apparent periodic dip in sales across the x axis in Figure 9.8(b) is caused by the collapse onto one dimension of two dimensions worth of locator information: stores and months. By representing the data in two locator dimensions as a series of line graphs with one for each store, as shown in Figure 9.8(c), or as a plane in the z dimension, as shown in Figure 9.9, it is easy to see a constant upward trend over time for all stores.

2. Using any display technique, especially areas, that changes apparent value in amounts or proportions that are different from the changes to the underlying data. Tufte illustrated his book with many fine examples of misleading graphics. Figure 9.10 purports to show changes in sales of apples using the height of an apple to represent the sale of apples. Note how much larger the apple looks for 1996 than for 1995 even though sales just doubled. It is because the area of the apple quadruples when its height doubles.

(continued)

GRAPHICAL MISREPRESENTATIONS *(continued)*

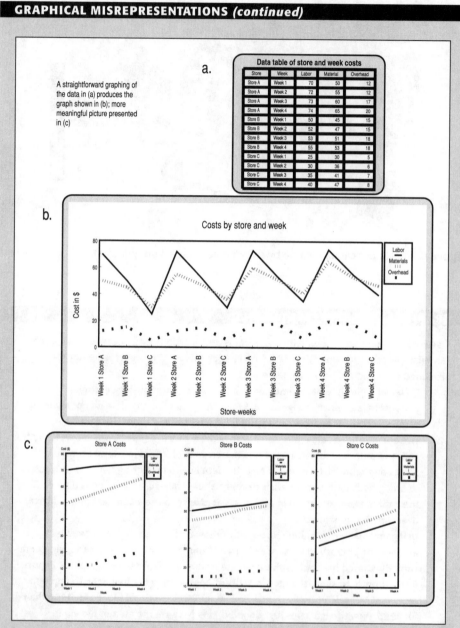

A straightforward graphing of the data in (a) produces the graph shown in (b); more meaningful picture presented in (c)

a.

Data table of store and week costs

Store	Week	Labor	Material	Overhead
Store A	Week 1	70	50	12
Store A	Week 2	72	55	12
Store A	Week 3	73	60	17
Store A	Week 4	74	65	20
Store B	Week 1	50	45	15
Store B	Week 2	52	47	15
Store B	Week 3	53	51	18
Store B	Week 4	55	53	18
Store C	Week 1	25	30	5
Store C	Week 2	30	36	6
Store C	Week 3	35	41	7
Store C	Week 4	40	47	8

Figure 9.8 False graphical impressions.

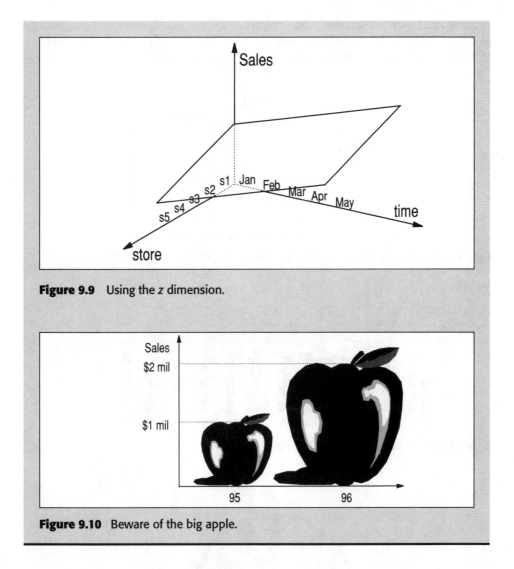

Figure 9.9 Using the *z* dimension.

Figure 9.10 Beware of the big apple.

next lightest shade of gray, and so on. Light gray in Georgia means the same as light gray in Montana. The meaning of each shade is independent of the location of the shade on the map. Instead, it is entirely a function of the shade itself. The shades are directly analogous to groupings or low-order numbers, in this case quintiles. However, unlike numbers, it is easy to detect relationships between states by looking at shades. In this example, it is easy to see that zones of high per-capita income occur in clusters along the East Coast, the West Coast, and the Great Lakes. In this sense, shades are analogous to points and lines. Figure 9.11 shows a version of Figure 9.6 updated to reflect the properties of shades, shapes, and symbols.

Looking back over the previous figures, you should notice that although Figures 9.4 (b) and 9.5 (b) were both graphical, they seemed to convey different kinds of information. Figure 9.4 (b) answered a comparison question. It used two lines in an *xy* plot to accomplish that. In addition to *xy* plots, bar graphs and pie charts (like the ones in Figures 9.12 and 9.13) are useful for showing comparisons between values.

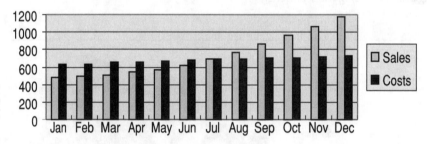

	Represents Values	Represents Relationships
Location-based Meaning		Points, Lines
Form-based Meaning	Numbers	Shades, Colors, Shapes

Figure 9.11 The key distinctions between numeric, graphic, and colored displays.

Figure 9.12 Comparison of sales and costs over time.

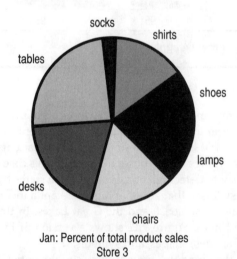

Jan: Percent of total product sales
Store 3

Figure 9.13 Comparison of product sales as a percentage of total sales.

Figure 9.5 (b) identified certain cities that met particular criteria by using a map to display city indicators. In addition to maps with symbolic indicators, topographic maps (and isosurfaces) like the one shown in Figure 9.14 are useful for identifying value ranges. The topographic map is ideal for identifying peaks, valleys, flat areas, and steep areas. Note, by the way, that any variable, not just geoaltitude, can have peaks and valleys and steeps and flats. The map could just as easily portray sales volume per booth in a large trade show, or pollution levels, or economic zones.

In addition to comparing and identifying values and value ranges, it is common to want to identify value changes over space and time. "What part of our network has the most bottlenecks during the course of a typical day?" is a question about value changes over space and time. "Where do our products go after they leave the warehouse?" is a question about the direction and volume of shipments over space and time. Arrows and directed graphs (especially when superimposed on maps), such as the one shown in Figure 9.15, are useful for showing value changes over space and time. Figure 9.15 shows, for each of PTT's warehouses, the relative volume of product shipments in each direction. Arrow locations represent where the shipments go, and arrow thickness represents the transported tonnage per month.

Abstract Grid Maps

Finally, let's look again at grid displays in the light of the previous discussion. Grid displays, like colors, bear some of the characteristics of graphics. For example, Figure 9.16 represents a data set of store profits by store and time. In the table display, the rows are ordered by time and within time, by store. For the graphical display, the stores on the store axis are arranged in descending order of average customer traffic per unit area of store space. The time axis is ordered chronologically. In both panels the store times with highest profitability are highlighted.

Looking at the grid panel in Figure 9.16 (b), it is easy to see that profitability is highest around December and around medium traffic stores. You would never detect this

Figure 9.14 Topographic map of the Lost River Valley.

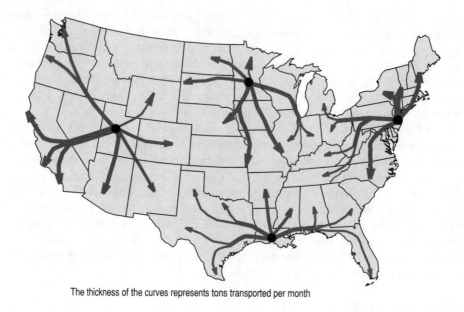

The thickness of the curves represents tons transported per month

Figure 9.15 The volume per path of PTT product shipments.

A

Time	Store traffic	Profit margin
Aug	1	2.0%
Aug	2	2.4%
Aug	3	2.6%
Aug	4	2.9%
Aug	5	2.7%
Aug	6	2.5%
Aug	7	2.2%
Sept	1	2.4%
Sept	2	2.7%
Sept	3	2.9%
Sept	4	3.2%
Sept	5	2.8%
Sept	6	2.6%
Sept	7	2.3%
Oct	1	2.8%
Oct	2	2.9%
Oct	3	3.1%

B

Store	Aug	Sept	Oct	Nov	Dec	Jan	Feb	Mar	Apr
1									
2									
3									
4									
5									
6									
7									

Note: cells representing profit margins of less than 3% are not colored

Figure 9. 16 Store profits by store and time.

in the table panel in Figure 9.16 (a). Why is that? As long as the two dimensions in the grid represent two key dimensions of the data, and as long as the grid dimensions are ordered according to some meaningful criteria, such as the chronological and store traffic criteria shown in the grid panel of Figure 9.16 (b), the grid behaves like an abstract map or coordinate system. (The exact properties of the grid are a function of the ordering characteristics of the dimensions, such as whether the dimensions are ordinally or cardinally ordered. This is addressed in Chapter 5.)

Picking the Appropriate Visualization Forms

Now that you've seen how visualization works and why graphical images, for some types of queries, convey more meaningful information than numeric grids, you may be feeling that although it's a great idea to use visualization, it is just too hard. Tools are pretty manual and force you to pick a visualization metaphor. What's a good way to pick the visualization?

There are several criteria. One is that the logical form or underlying type structure of the information should correspond with the logical form or underlying type structure of the visualization. Well how do you figure that out? If you've read this book to this point, you have the tool set. It is time to apply what you've learned about type structures to the classification of visual forms.

The two tables that follow describe the underlying type structure of different visual forms typically offered by vendors. Table 9.1 describes the logical structure of entire forms such as line graphs, pie charts, and so forth. The two essential descriptors are the number of types in each form and the combinatorial relationship between the types.

The purpose of assigning type structures to visual forms is that the same type structures are used to parse queries. This is what gives you the ability to select the appropriate visual form for the display of an analytical query result.

Table 9.2 describes the internal structure of each type within each form. In other words, once you know how many types are used in a visual form and their relationship, more information remains to be known about each type. How many instances or members can it support and are these instances nominal, ordinal, or cardinal? Once again, this type of information can be ascertained from a data source either through querying the schema files or through direct inspection.

NOTE Parallel coordinates have an interesting form that warrants further explanation. With parallel coordinates, every instance of every associated type is shown—these are the vertical segments and are represented by the T.-style types in the first type structure shown in Table 9.1 for parallel coordinates. The trailing type is a binary type, either on or off for any possible combination of vertical segment instances. In this sense, parallel coordinates are an N-dimensional abstraction of a scatterplot. However, the various instances are shown alongside each other and in a situation where, for example, you had three locator dimensions with 100 instances each, they would form a

Table 9.1   The Type Structure of Different Visual Forms

REPRESENTATION NAME	NUMBER OF TYPES	TYPE STRUCTURE	ROTATABILITY
Line graph	2	T1. ~ T2	No
Pie chart	2	T1. ~ T2	xy
Bar chart	2	T1. ~ T2	No
1D tiled bar chart	3	(T1. ⊗ T2.)~T3	No
Superimposed line graph	3	(T1. ⊗ T2.)~T3	No
Surface plot	3	(T1. ⊗ T2.)~T3	xyz
Scatter plot	3	(T1. ⊗ T2.)~T3	xy
Event trails	3	(T1. ⊗ T2.)~T3	No
Colored line graph	3	(T1.) ~ (T2, T3)	No
3D pie chart	3	(T1.) ~ (T2, T3)	xyz
2D tiled bar chart	4	(T1. ⊗ T2. ⊗ T3.)~T4	No
Colored surface plot	4	(T1. ⊗ T2.)~(T3, T4)	xyz
1D tiled superimposed line graph	4	(T1. ⊗ T2. ⊗ T3.)~T4	No
Colored 3D pie chart	4	(T1.) ~ (T2, T3, T4)	xyz
Parallel coordinates *	4-N	(T1.,T2.,T3.,T4.)~T5	No
	4-N	(T1.)~T2, T3, T4, T5	

dimensional space of 1,000,000 cells that in turn could support a 1,000,000-row fact table while the parallel coordinate representation would only show 300 instances. It's spatially economical, but not fully representational.

Parallel coordinates are ideally suited for data sets that have many contents, but only a small number (one or two) of locator dimensions. In the case where there is only one locator, the number of facts is equal to the number of instances in the locator, and content-content relationships are most clearly shown.

Table 9.2   The Type Structure of the Types in Each Visual Form

NAME	TYPE	CARDINALITY	ORDERING
Line graph	1. L - X axis	High	Cardinal ordinal
	2. C - Y axis	High	Cardinal
Colored line graph	1. L	High	Cardinal, ordinal
	2. C1	High	Cardinal, ordinal
	3. C2	Low	Nominal
Superimposed line graph	1. L1 - X axis	High	Cardinal
	2. L2 - lines	Low	Nominal
	3. C - Y axis	High	Cardinal
1D tiled superimposed line graph	1. L1 - X axis	High	Cardinal
	2. L2 - lines	Low	Nominal
	3. L3 - tiling	Low-medium	Nominal, ordinal
	4. C - Y axis	High	Cardinal
Pie chart	1. L slice number	Low	Nominal
	2. C area per slice	Medium	Cardinal
3D pie chart	1. L slice number	Low	Nominal
	2. C1 area per slice	Medium	Cardinal
	3. C2 height	Medium	Cardinal, ordinal
Colored 3D pie chart	1. L slice number	Low	Nominal
	2. C1 area per slice	Medium	Cardinal
	3. C2 height	Medium	Cardinal, ordinal
	4. C3 color	Low	Nominal, ordinal

(continued)

Table 9.2 The Type Structure of the Types in Each Visual Form *(continued)*

NAME	TYPE	CARDINALITY	ORDERING
Bar chart	1. L - X axis	Low-medium	Nominal, ordinal
	2. C - Y axis	Medium	Cardinal, ordinal, not nominal
1D tiled bar chart	1. L1 - inner X axis	Lowest	Nominal
	2. L2 - outer X axis	Low-medium	Nominal, ordinal
	3. C - Y axis	Medium	Cardinal, ordinal
Surface plot	1. L1 - X	High	Cardinal, ordinal
	2. L2 - Y	High	Cardinal, ordinal
	3. C - Z	High	Cardinal, ordinal
Colored surface plot	1. L1 - X	High	Cardinal, ordinal
	2. L2 - Y	High	Cardinal, ordinal
	3. C1 - Z	High	Cardinal, ordinal
	4. C2 - color	Low	Nominal, ordinal
Scatter plot	1. L1 - X	High	Cardinal, ordinal
	2. L2 - Y	High	Cardinal, ordinal
	3. C - points	Low	Binary
Parallel coordinates	1. L - locator segment	Low-medium	Cardinal, ordinal
	2. C1 - segment	Medium	Cardinal, ordinal
	3. C2 - segment	Medium	Cardinal, ordinal
	4. C3 - segment	Medium	Cardinal, ordinal

Other kinds of structural information that can be taken into account include whether the visual form can be rotated or whether a type can be scrolled, as well as nonstructural heuristics (such as previously used visual forms and individual preferences) that, while important and should ultimately be considered, are not crucial to the present understanding and thus will not be treated here.

Using Data Visualization for Decision Making

Given that visualization is most useful for decision-support-style decision making, the question remains, "Where does visualization fit into the decision-making process?" To answer that question, recall from Chapter 1 how data-driven decisions are made. Goals are a function of human factors. In most cases, the goals of a corporation are set by its board of directors and senior executives. Data visualization does not play a significant role in goal setting.

In contrast, predictions are a function of correlations, relationships, or patterns between descriptions. As we saw in the previous section, visualization is crucial to the discovery of patterns or relationships between data elements or facts.

Business Pattern Analysis

The discovery of patterns or relationships is an essential step in the prediction-making process. Patterns are local, slowly changing regularities whose validity needs to be continually monitored. In any domain with which a user has acquired some familiarity, the user is actually thinking in terms of patterns. Thus, wool buyers are familiar with the visual and textural patterns that define good wool, cocoa futures traders are familiar with the buying patterns that indicate good times to buy or sell, and national campaign managers are familiar with the demographic patterns that indicate good regions to perform test marketing.

The two figures that follow illustrate common patterns superimposed on collections of data or facts. Figure 9.17 illustrates exponential growth and Figure 9.18 illustrates linear growth. Note how the patterns in each case represent a central tendency or trend about which the data points vary.

The interplay between pattern and data points represents the concepts of curve fitting and variance. Seeing data within the context of a pattern enables characteristic values, variances, and extremes to be highlighted. Good visualization can show the approximate variance in the data points around a central tendency and how the variance may change over time.

Although analysts frequently look for patterns as part of a decision-support process, in any established domain, certain relationships need to be understood ahead of time. In these situations, many activities revolve around monitoring the degree to which new events fit established patterns. Typical activities include classification and exceptions tracking. Thus, an insurance analyst who is already familiar with patterns of fraudulent behavior might superimpose new claim data on a known pattern to see whether a new claim looks suspicious. This is illustrated in Figure 9.19.

Patterns in one collection of data can also be correlated with other patterns to highlight understood behaviors. In the figures that follow, the seasonal pattern of large household appliance purchases is seen to have evolved from resembling the purchasing pattern for small appliances (Figure 9.20) to resembling the known pattern of purchasing for luxury goods, as seen in Figure 9.21.

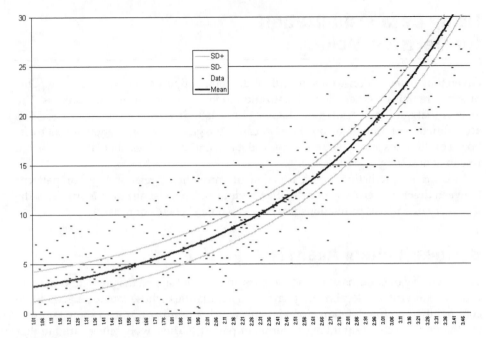

Figure 9.17 Exponential growth.

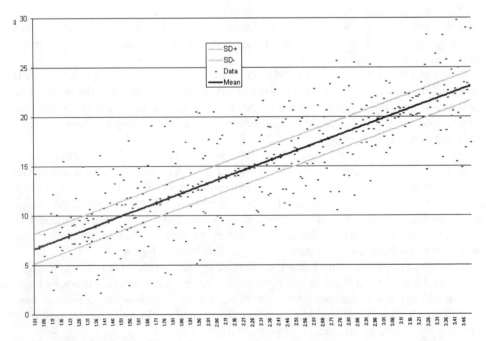

Figure 9.18 Linear growth.

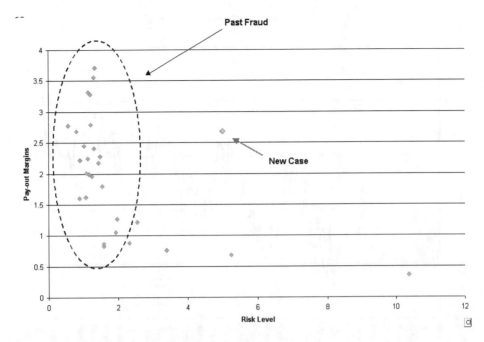

Figure 9.19   Patterns of fraudulent behavior.

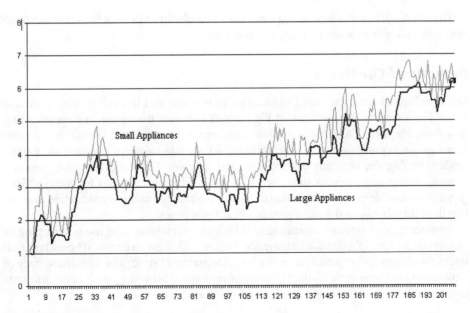

Figure 9.20   Small versus large appliances.

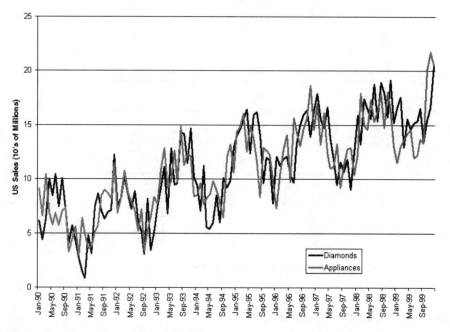

Figure 9.21 Correlation.

The remainder of this section explores how visualization depicts the common business patterns of constancy, change, and context.

Patterns of Constancy

Relationships of constancy tend to be some of the first and last relationships we discover. For example, the distance in Figure 9.22 between the upper line representing new computer prices and the lower line representing the prices of 18-month-old computer prices is easily seen in the graph and appears to be fairly constant over time. Understanding the constant price differential between first- and second-generation computers, for any point in time, helps to predict future revenues for today's first-generation machines, and thus guide decisions regarding machine production and the length of time between different generations of machines.

Another type of constant relationship is brought out through the use of grouping or clustering. Instead of a constant difference, Figure 9.23 shows a constant boundary that traces the movement of a customer in a large department store. The 52-minute trace of a customer indicates three distinct clusters of time spent browsing, with equal amounts of time in three specific areas: electronics, books, and furniture.

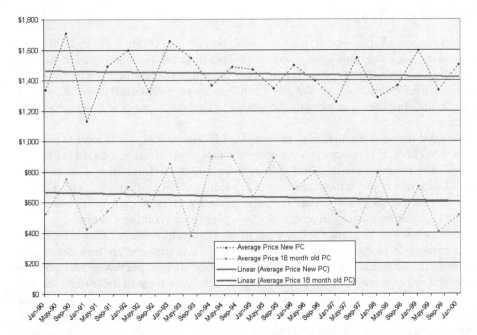

Figure 9.22 PC prices.

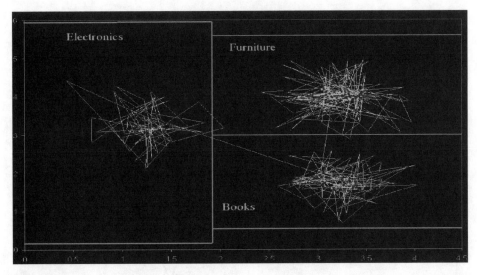

Figure 9.23 Constant boundaries.

Patterns of Change

Understanding change—be it relative costs, employees, product lines, underlying technologies, tax and trade laws, or consumer spending habits—is essential to business growth. The more accurately we can assign a pattern to that change, the better we are able to predict future changes. Patterns of change are sometimes called *trends*. The two main kinds of change that visualization helps to depict are periodic and nonperiodic changes.

Seasonal demand fluctuations, as illustrated in Figure 9.24, are typical of periodic change. A clothing store owner who opened a new shop in the fall might experience strong sales for three months, and then notice a slowdown in January. Knowing that sales had a seasonal periodic shift would instill confidence that sales will pick up again. Knowing how to visualize the sales to date and estimated future sales cycle would help determine how much product to order for the coming months.

Although the stock market follows the up and down movement of business cycles, stock market prices do not vary seasonally (as retail sales do) and are considered to be nonperiodic. Technical traders use analytical visualization to portray stock trade volumes and prices across time as shown in Figure 9.25. Regardless of the trading strategy employed, visualization allows movements of and relationships between key indicators to be highlighted. If, for example, the given strategy recommends selling as volume plateaus, now might be a good time to sell.

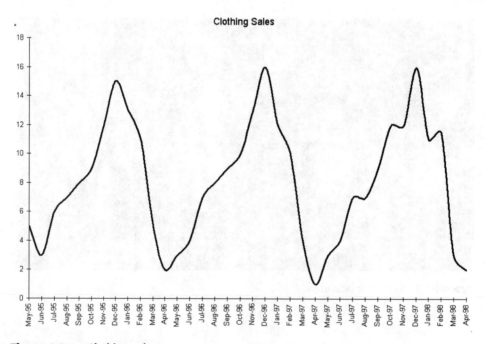

Figure 9.24   Clothing sales.

S&P500 Index Last 12 Months

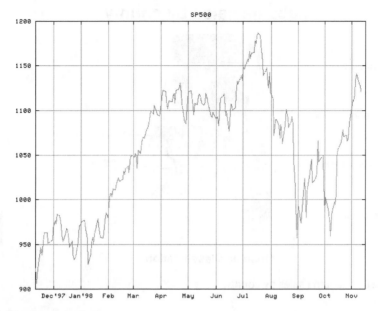

Figure 9.25 Stock market.

Contextual Patterns

Another attribute of visualization is the ability to clearly show multiple levels of context or resolution at once. Our eyes automatically perform aggregation with visual images, as shown in the examples that follow.

As illustrated in Figure 9.26, the display of local sales information within a map of regional sales information is a typical example of showing level relationships. Note how easy it is to see that although local sales are high relative to the surrounding region indicated by the county labeled A, the surrounding region sales in the area labeled B are low relative to their national region. This extra context information suggesting there may be regional problems, could lead to a decision to visit regional headquarters to learn why things are going so poorly.

In this section, we briefly explored how visualization can be used to highlight the most commonly recurring business patterns. Table 9.3 summarizes these uses with typical applications for the retail sector, several examples for which were included previously, and for the utilities sector.

Visualizing Multidimensional Business Data

Basic graphics, such as line graphs and pie charts, show at most two or three dimensions of information. Yet most business users routinely work with OLAP data sets composed of five or more dimensions. For example, a campaign management data set

Alabama sales by county

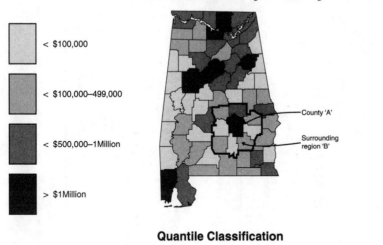

- < $100,000
- < $100,000–499,000
- < $500,000–1Million
- > $1Million

County 'A'

Surrounding region 'B'

Quantile Classification

N

Figure 9.26 Alabama sales by county.

Table 9.3 Examples of Commonly Occurring Business Patterns

	RETAIL	UTILITIES
Pattern Discovery		
Constancy	Margins	Fixed costs
Change		
More periodic	Seasonal fluctuations	Daily and seasonal demand
Less periodic	Interest rates	Variable costs
Context		
Hierarchical	City/state sales	City demand/state demand
Location relations	Top 10 stores	Top 10 energy consuming centers
Fact/pattern relationships		
Classification	Upscale market	Preusage spike
Pattern/pattern relationships		
Correlations	Appliances/luxuries	Urban/rural

might be composed of the following dimensions: product, time, channel, sales representative, and promotion type. This raises the question of the best way to graphically visualize more than two or three dimensions of the data.

This section describes some of the main techniques for graphically visualizing multidimensional business data and they are summarized as follows:

- Use basic graphics to visualize small slices or subsets of your data.

- Replicate or tile a basic graphic element in one or two screen axes with one or more nested dimensions per axis.

- Use a more complex visualization technique.

Subsetting

Even though typical business data may have six or more dimensions, it is always possible to take a slice or subset of the data and use basic visualization techniques for the lower dimensions. For example, as shown in Figure 9.27, a basic line graph may represent sales by time for a five-dimensional data set consisting of stores, times, products, scenarios, and variables.

Although the pattern for the Ridgewood store sales is easily visualized, and may well satisfy your needs if your sole responsibility is for a particular product-store-customer combination, relative to the underlying data set consisting of many products, stores, and customer types, the information contained in this basic visualization represents a very small subset of the underlying data and is analogous to the information retrieved by sticking a glue-tipped needle into a haystack.

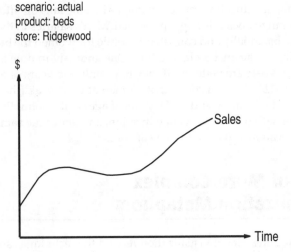

Figure 9.27 Sales by time.

Repeating or Tiled Patterns

What if you were interested in how changes in sales across stores and products varied across time? You might be trying to spot products for which there was less seasonal variance in sales. To do this, you would need to visualize a much greater percentage of your data. If you still wanted to look at lower dimensional images, it would take many of them in a repeating or tiled pattern to display the relevant information.

Insert I.3 shows a tiled image of dollar sales over a 15-week period. The image is divided into bins by food type and store number. An additional measure is added with coloring indicating certain kinds of promotions.

There are many insights one can immediately glean from this image. For example, salty snacks and frozen foods account for a much larger part of the sales than candy and soft drinks. We can see that the sea green promotion seemed to help some for soft drink sales in all stores, but more so for store number 1. The light green promotion seems to have had a follow-through effect in the third week in store number 2, but not in the other stores. The red promotion seems, at best, to have added no value.

Some of the weekly profiles look different for different stores. Salty snacks seem to rise and then fall over this period for store 2, but seem far less predictable in the other stores. One can also note that the sales seem to complement each other. Taken singly, sales would be quite variable, but together total sales are far more even.

The tiled image in Insert I.4 shows multidimensional nesting. The sex dimension splits the sample into two charts, one for males and one for females on the x-axis. This in turn is split into seven age ranges for each: 21–25, 26–30, 31–35, 36–40, 41–45, 46–50, and 51–55. Education is further nested on the x-axis with colors corresponding as follows: yellow for 3–5 years, green for 6–8 years, aqua for 9–11 years, blue for 12 years, red for 13–15 years, and violet for 16–18 years. The y-axis gives the income with the mean at the middle of the bars and one standard deviation at the ends of the bars.

Several interesting patterns are highlighted by this image. Men make more money than women in all categories. More education is generally better. Incomes generally go up with age, but for all education ranges, women's income falls off after 51. Only in the lowest education range does this happen for men. Men's salaries in the highest education range grow substantially and consistently, while for women the bars clearly decelerate as if bumping up against a glass ceiling. One anomaly to note is that women in the fifth age range, 41–45 are better off if they have only 3–5 years of education than if they have 6–8 or 9–11. We can also see that women at their peak (the highest earning bar at 16–18 years of education and 46–50 years of age) make about the same as a man 51–55 years of age with only 12 years of education, and about the same as a man with 13–15 years of education, but only 36–40 years old.

Examples of More Complex Data Visualization Metaphors

Most uses of multidimensional visualization rely on the techniques shown in the previous two sections. Keeping dimensions as pages serves to simplify the multidimensional space so that it can be visualized with normal-dimensional visualizations.

Repeating a normally dimensioned graph across a grid serves to extend the dimensional reach of a display. In contrast, higher-dimensional visualization techniques show multivariate, multidimensional relationships in a single nonpartitioned image. The examples below are all taken from real business applications. They can all be implemented with today's standard desktop hardware and widely available data visualization packages.

Product Sales Analysis

For most organizations, product sales analysis is a classic OLAP application. Ideally, as a user you would like to be able to look at several variables or contents at once while retaining a multidimensional and hierarchical perspective.

Inserts I.2 and I.5 represent sales and pricing data dimensioned by product, store and time. For the two insert views, *Stores* are represented as pages. The hierarchies in the *Product* and *Time* dimension are visible to the user, and in addition to the 3D bars in the cells, the back panels show aggregate sales values in each of the two dimensions. In the cell portion of the view, the height of each of the bars represents median product price. The color of each bar represents sales in dollars. For the back panel portion, the height of each bar represents the sales value. (This is why the height of the food bar on the back panel of I.2 is so much taller than the other bars.) Thus each view shows two contents across two levels of each of two dimensions.

In Insert I.2, you can see an initial view of the data with *Time* on the X-axis broken down by *Quarters* and *Product*, on the Y-axis broken down by *Food, Drink,* and *Nonconsumables*. The image illustrates a mouse brushing over the Food Sales for Q2 resulting in the Sales figure being shown. Insert I.5 shows the drill-down on Q1 and Nonconsumables with the mouse brushing over the Household Sales for the month of March.

The visualization style shown in these two inserts is a natural extension to numeric grid-based OLAP views and allows for dynamic visual analysis of multi-variate, multidimensional data (so long as the dimensions have a reasonably small cardinality), with a minimal increase in the complexity of the basic visual metaphor (in this case bar charts). One could also imagine tiling these images to provide for higher dimensional representation.

Credit Card Application Analysis

Insert I.6 uses glyphs in a three-dimensional space to show the results of analyzing credit card applications. Colored spheres show approved cardholders. In the original application, historical information on each cardholder could be obtained by clicking on each of the spheres. The three axes show application information—debit ratio, net worth, and work duration. The size of the sphere represents the salary and the color represents the credit limit for that cardholder. A white sphere, used to depict a new applicant's credit limit, can be assigned a credit limit by the 3D position of that sphere relative to the historical data base information.

We can see, for example, in Insert I.6 that the credit applicant has a debt ratio of about .25 and has worked for about 10 years. We can also see that most of his/her neighbors are colored green with some blue, so we would expect the applicant to be assigned about a $1,700 credit limit. There are a number of interesting things you can see from this visualization. Work duration seems to be the most important variable for determining the amount of credit offered. This is because the left-to-right movement along the work duration axis approximates the color shading from blue to red of credit offered. Salary level (the size of the balls) has far less effect than you might expect. You can tell that salary is not a major determinate of credit because the largest balls appear at all credit levels. You can also see an interesting exception or outlier: There is a blue ball with one of the largest ball sizes, representing salary, at about the 12-year work duration mark, with a debt ratio of only .12, and a comparatively low net worth. This individual is surrounded by green balls, all of whom have a lower salary, and who are given credit limits on the order of $2,500 to $3,000, while the outlying individual with the big salary only gets about a $500 credit limit. Clearly, the bank knows something about this customer that does not show up on this chart, though trouble is hinted at by the person's comparatively low net worth.

Web Site Traffic Analysis

Inserts I.7 and I.8 illustrate how a collection of several related visual perspectives can be used to analyze web traffic. A solid analysis needs to explore which promotions stimulated the most buyers, when buyers bought the most, and what path they took to complete their purchase. The data in this example comes from the e-commerce site for a large catalog retailer.

Insert I.7 shows the initial display for a promotional study, with color tied to promotion type. The large blue bar in the focus bar chart shows that the vast majority of the visitors came via *Catalog*, the company's own catalog. The correlation bar chart shows that most visitors were *Browsers* who did not buy anything; a small fraction were *Abandoners*, visitors who put items in their shopping basket, but did not complete the checkout process. Finally, the *Buyers* represent about 5 percent of the total number of visitors. The time dimension bar chart shows visitors by day for the one-week snapshot under study. The upper-left bar chart in Insert I.8 shows that after selecting and excluding visitors who come from the company's own catalog, the four top-producing banner ads were on *Yahoo, FreeShop, DoubleClick*, and *AOL*. Proceeding further by changing the correlation bar chart to show visits by country, selecting and excluding the *.coms, .nets,* and *.edus*, the upper-left bar chart in Insert I.8 shows that Canada and Italy are the two foreign countries that have sent the most visitors. By switching the time dimension to show hits by hour, the lower left graph in Insert I.8 shows that visitors followed a two-hump (or bimodal) daily traffic pattern. Activity is lowest during the early morning hours, peaks around dinnertime, decreases slightly, and peaks again at 2 A.M. This pattern suggests that many visitors are shopping from work in the early afternoons and late into the early morning. Alternatively, the surge of late evening traffic may be foreign shoppers in other time zones. The lower right chart shows a detailed listing of the *Abandoners*.

One important goal for web site traffic analysis is to understand why some shoppers abandon the buying process. Focusing on the Entry_URL and Exit_URL columns, the most common entry points for Abandoners are index.html, head.html, and vnav.html. The most common exit point is cgi-bin/showBasket.html and cgi-in/finit.asp. This suggests that customers are abandoning because they do not like what's in their basket, or perhaps because the *Show Basket* command executes too slowly, or because the search routine is too complex. Perhaps the interface to remove shopping basket items needs to be simplified.

In this section, you have seen several successful snapshot examples of business visualization in use. In each case, the visualizations highlighted key patterns that were essential to the business problem at hand and allowed the analyst to work with new information in terms of how it relates to previously detected patterns.

Summary

In this chapter you learned:

1. Points and lines convey meaning in terms of their location whereas numbers, colors, and shapes convey meaning in terms of their form.

2. Points add lines, and colors and shapes represent relationships better than direct values, whereas numbers represent direct values better than relationships.

3. How to analyze the information representation capabilities of different visual forms and connect them with the information representation needs of analytical query results.

4. The part of the decision making process most affected by visualization is the discovery and use of patterns or relationships for classifying new events; creating groupings of events; identifying exceptions, constants, and trends; and forming predictions.

5. How to think in terms of different types of classically occurring patterns such as consistency, periodic and nonperiodic change, and context.

6. When basic business graphics are offered in an interactive environment and combined with the ability to tile images, they can help business users understand many multidimensional business patterns.

7. About some more advanced methods of visualization that are available to represent complex analytical patterns.

Physical Design of Applications

If it were possible to store unlimited amounts of data, and if it were possible to perform any search, external data fetch, or computation in an instant, there would be no need for end-users or administrators of multidimensional information systems to pay any attention to the physical design of their applications. This is because the physical design of a system affects its performance, not the truth of its input or derived data.

Of course, no matter how fast the hardware or how many bytes we can cram on a disk, we always seem to come up with applications that require even more data and more calculations that need to run blazingly fast. Memory in all forms, processor speed, and bandwidth will always be relatively scarce, and product vendors and application developers will always have the incentive to create reasonably efficient physical system designs (although many software products and applications are less efficient than their ancestral versions in the 1970s when there were severe system resource constraints).

The tricky thing about physical design is that there are myriad system levels that impact physical performance. Although decisions that impact the state of the art at each level (such as the discovery of new materials for making computers or new configurations of L2 cache and CPUs for SMP machines) come from specialists in each field, decisions about which combination from the available choices results in the best total physical design of a decision-support application could all be made by, or fall under the jurisdiction of, one person.

For example, the CTO of a well-funded high tech start-up in the process of building its IT infrastructure would be responsible for making (or approving) decisions regarding the choice of hardware components (such as processor and memory type because the fastest is not always the best choice), hardware configuration (such as SMP versus MPP for the enterprise servers), operating systems (such as UNIX or Windows 2000), enterprise system architecture (such as client/server versus peer-to-peer), application software (such as Oracle RDB/MDDB versus Microsoft RDB/MDDB or Oracle RDB/Hyperion MDDB), and application design (such as using a larger number of simpler cubes with more query-time cube joins or using fewer, more complex cubes with fewer query-time cube joins).

There are at least seven distinct system levels that affect total system performance:

- Materials: Gears (the materials of Babbage's first difference engine), vacuum tubes, individual transistors, micro transistors etched in silicon, gallium arsenide, upcoming optical computers, quantum computers

- Hardware configuration: MPP, SMP, uniprocessor, processor speed, main memory size, L2 cache size, processor width, bus speed, disk speed

- Operating systems: Thread management, partition management, file caching

- Enterprise system architecture: Network topology, bandwidth, protocols

- Application software: Threadedness, disk/RAM based, cache intelligence

- Application development: Cube design, sparse dimension combination selections

- End use: Formula creation, query load

Typically speaking, by the time the application developer gets to make physical design decisions about the application—such as where to store low-level data, how many derived values to precalculate, and so forth—the company's enterprise architecture (including network topology and the distribution of source data), the operating system, and the enterprise hardware exist as fixed or reasonably fixed constraints. Given the user requirements and the system constraints, the application developer may then get to select the software vendor whose product can best meet those constraints. I suspect that many of you have been in situations where you were asked to optimize the physical design of the application layer for a decision-support system where the biggest performance impediment was a poorly designed network or inappropriate hardware and/or software.

Notwithstanding the limited range of decision making enjoyed by a typical application developer (although the decisions the application developer make can have a huge impact on performance), it is useful to know the spectrum of choices that can, at least in theory, be made to affect physical performance. Therefore, this chapter is organized in terms of how data storage (with associated index methods) and calculations can be distributed for optimum performance. The chapter looks at data distribution within a machine, across machines, across applications, and across partitions. It also looks at calculation distribution across time, across application tiers, and across applications. Within each area, where appropriate, it identifies who, along the decision spectrum, typically gets to make the choices.

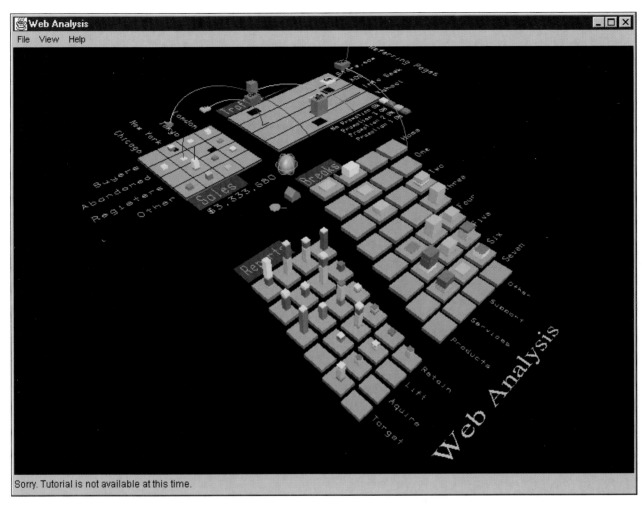

Insert I.1 Web site activity analysis. Created by Stephen G. Eick, Visual Insights.

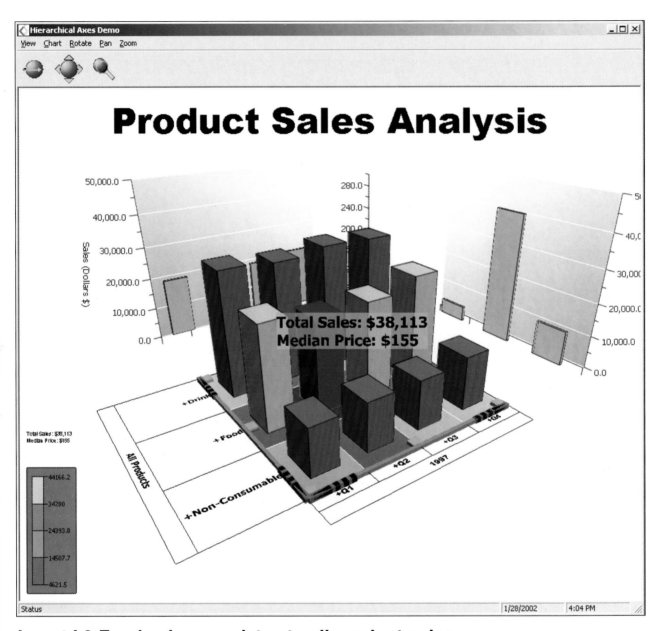

Insert I.2 Food sales as relates to all product sales. Courtesy of Syed M. Ali, Advanced Visual Systems, Inc. Copyright © 2002 Advanced Visual Systems, Inc.

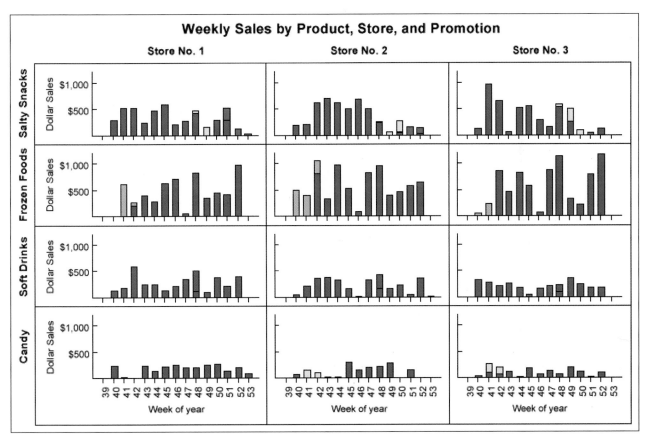

Insert I.3 Weekly sales by product, store, and promotion. CrossGraphs, Courtesy of PPD Informatics.

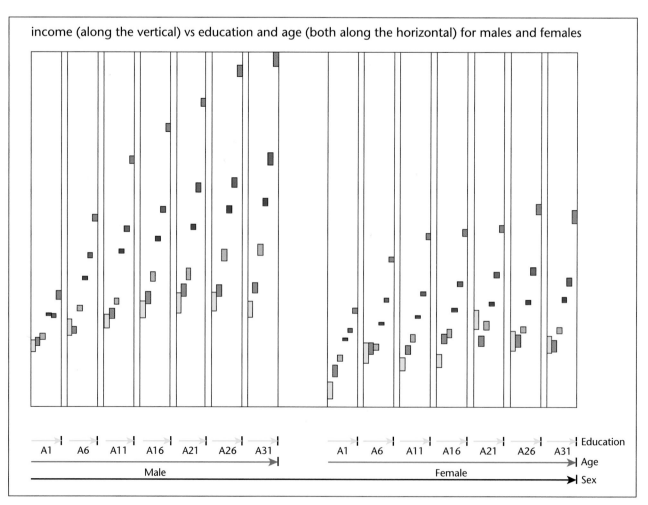

Insert I.4 Income versus education and age for males and females.

This image was generated using TempleMVV software from Mihalisin Associates Inc. TempleMVV is based on US patent no. 5,228,119, issued in July 1993, and Re. 36,840 issued in August 2000.

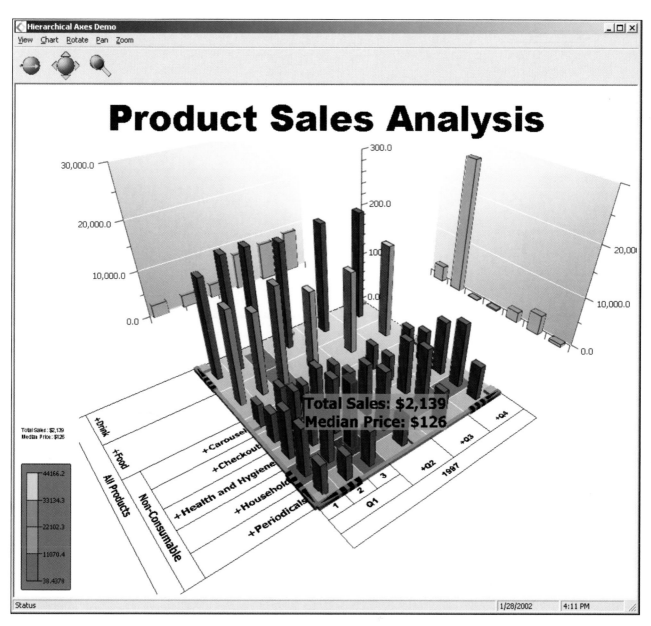

Insert I.5 Drilling down on non-consumable product sales. Courtesy of Syed M. Ali, Advanced Visual Systems, Inc. Copyright © 2002 Advanced Visual Systems Inc.

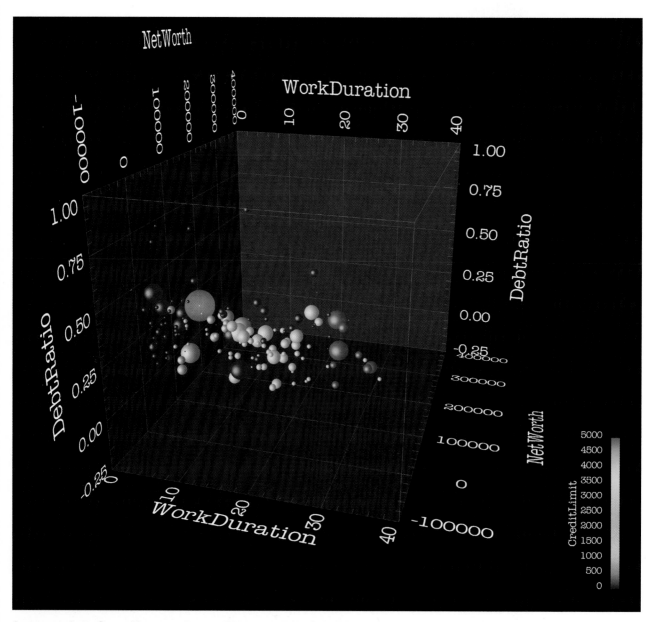

Insert I.6 Credit card applicant analysis. Image created by Frank Suits at the IBM T.J. Watson Research Center using the Data Explorer visualization environment, www.research.ibm.com/dx

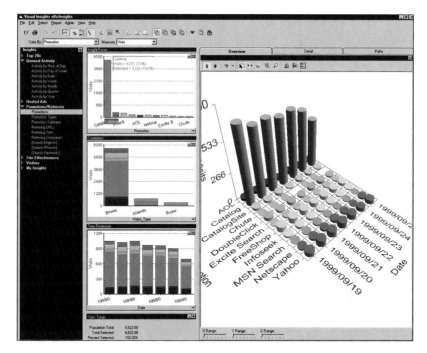

Insert I.7 Web site promotional study. Created by Stephen G. Eick, Visual Insights.

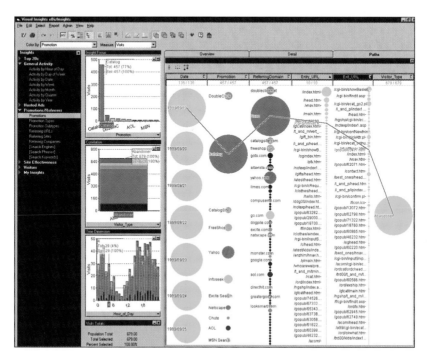

Insert I.8 E-commerce Web site promotional study traffic pattern analysis.
Created by Stephen G. Eick, Visual Insights.

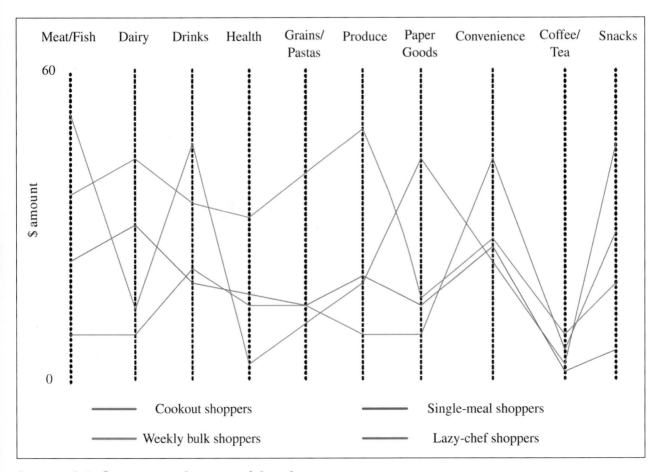

Insert I.9 Computed centroid values.

Data Distribution

Within Machines

Given a query, a data set and application against which the query is posed, and a machine on which the data and application reside, there are basically three places in the machine where the data that satisfies the query can exist: disk, main memory, and L2 cache. Each of these places has a different natural speed of retrieval. Currently, typical disk access speeds are on the order of 10 milliseconds; typical main memory speeds are on the order of 100 megahertz, and L2 cache is on a par with the CPU itself, thus hovering around the gigahertz range.

Although we're used to talking in terms of milliseconds for disk speeds, when you realize that milliseconds are equivalent to kilohertz and tens of milliseconds are equivalent to centihertz (if there is such a term), by far the largest jump in access time is between disk and main memory. The relative time difference to respond to two queries where one can be answered entirely from memory and the other from disk can be as much as 1,000,000 to 1! That's right; main memory can be 1,000,000 times faster than disk. To be fair, if the disk-resident data is well clustered, a single disk access may retrieve thousands of query-responding data elements and the disk access overhead will be distributed across all the data elements, thus reducing the average time difference between disk and memory access to something on the order of 100 or 1,000 to 1— still a huge difference. Of course, in real-world situations many other components affect total query time, such as screen rendering and network access time whose overheads may be hundreds of times larger than that of any disk access and which can apply to both memory-based and disk-based queries, thus effectively erasing the performance difference between the two mediums.

Issues regarding L2 cache, such as its size, its mapping to CPUs (some SMP configurations have multiple CPUs sharing a single L2 cache), and algorithms for deciding what to keep in L2 cache are determined by the hardware manufacturer. If your decision support system is otherwise physically optimized, the testing we have done in our lab suggests that using hardware with more and faster L2 cache (such as Xeon versus non-Xeon processors within Intel's Pentium family) can improve performance by up to a factor of two.

Issues regarding the use of disk versus memory for the storing of data in use are made by the software vendors and by application developers, and are discussed later in this chapter. From the moment data is accessed, manipulated, and persistently stored; some disk, some main memory, and some L2 cache are bound to get used. Thus, all OLAP products use all three forms of memory. Distinctions should be made in terms of relative emphases.

All analytical software products (at least all the ones I'm aware of) have some concept of active, live, accessible, or otherwise in-use data that is typically called a model, database, file, or even world. Many OLAP and other analytical software products, especially those where end-users are assumed capable of directly using the software, were designed to operate in main memory, typically on the end-users' machines.

Spreadsheets work this way, as do the client-side versions of several OLAP products such as TM/1 and FreeThink. The only time the disk was accessed was when models were loaded from or saved to disk, or if virtual memory was being used.

Assuming you have sufficient memory to hold all your base data and indexes, and plenty of head room for dynamic calculations, a memory-based application will always outperform a disk-based one. If your entire application easily fits in memory and there isn't too much data, many physical performance issues become less important. There is less of a need to optimize which derivations are precalculated, although you will still notice a lag in response time once the number of cells touched per calculation is in the millions or tens of millions. *Thus, even in a RAM-only environment you may still benefit from creating and storing some intermediate aggregations.* The lessened need to optimize the design of RAM-resident models means it is easier to build an application, and the reduced need to precalculate aggregates means it is faster to build the model, and the model will consume less disk space because less precalculated aggregates are stored. However, it may be slower to activate the model since all that data will need to be loaded from disk, and the money you saved on disk space will be more than chewed up by the additional money you will need to spend on RAM.

Even if you can afford all the memory that money can buy, you simply can't buy enough memory to store all the data associated with an enterprise-sized OLAP application whose raw data may consist of tens, hundreds, thousands, or even millions of billions of data values that, with indexes, can easily consume several terabytes (or petabytes) of addressable space. Thus, in-memory OLAP applications may be either too expensive or insufficiently scalable to meet your company's needs. From my experience, the most common reason in-memory OLAP solutions don't work is because there is simply too much data to manage.

Since many applications are based on more data than can fit in memory, those applications need to keep some of the data—typically the vast majority—on disk. Although not constrained by memory, disk-resident applications still need plenty of memory for storing indexes, performing calculations, and keeping a cache of recently used data.

Some of the more complex OLAP products allow the data storage and indexing structures to be chosen at the partition level. A single database may use a variety of storage and access methods on disk and in memory. Usually, this choice is transparent to the application and can be easily altered after the application has been built. This enables expert tuners to determine which parts of the application are RAM based, which parts are disk based, and which parts are RDBMS based, or which parts are combinations of all of them. This flexibility may seem attractive (and ceteris paribus, I would always opt for having more rather than less flexibility), but tuning facilities are a double-edged sword: They require effort to use, and it is just as likely that they will be used incorrectly as optimally. The ideal is for the system to provide intelligent defaults and plenty of manual tuning capabilities.

This may seem complex enough, but in the real world of computer hardware, the distinction between disk and RAM is often fuzzier than you might expect. Since all disk-based OLAP products use some form of data caching, the astute reader may be wondering what the difference is between an in-memory OLAP product and the cache portion of a disk-resident product. If the cache portion of a disk-resident product performs like an in-memory product, why buy an in-memory product? The former would appear to be a superset of the latter. It turns out that not all caches are created equal.

Most data caches found in OLAP products are *lightly indexed*, and read only or incrementally addable to (meaning that a new piece of information can be added to the cache such as a new day's sales figures, but data in the cache cannot be changed), and even then only for a single user. By contrast, most in-memory OLAP products provide multiuser read/write access and full editing capabilities with edit results appearing for all users.

Within an Application

Within a machine and within an application, there are many options for how data is distributed. The two types of options that you need to be aware of are storage and indexing options for the data (as provided for by your tools), and the mapping of any particular schema to a particular set of storage and indexing options (the use you make of your tools). There can be order-of-magnitude performance differences between different choices for both options. Since most OLAP products have only a small number of methods—possibly only one method—for storing and indexing data, when you buy an OLAP product, you are effectively selecting that small number of methods for storage and indexing from the dozens or more commercially available options and the hundreds of methods that have been written about, but never implemented. This is why you will typically be best served by understanding the physical needs of your application before choosing software.

Making Use of Storage and Indexing Options

The two major goals of developers of multidimensional database storage and access routines have been fast access and efficient storage of sparse data. As a result, most multidimensional databases store data in sets of small, relatively dense arrays, and indexes into the arrays. For example, given our standard schema of

```
(Geog. ⊗ Time. ⊗ Product.) ~ Sales, Cost
```

one approach might store collections of time-ordered arrays of sales and costs with existent combinations of stores and products used to define the indexes. The array approach contrasts with the table approach that stores all the data as tables and adds, for access purposes, additional purely indexical information.

Since many of the real-world decisions that you are likely to make as an application developer in the area of storage and access methods can be described in terms of tradeoffs between the number and density of stored arrays, and since the choices you make can have a substantial impact on the performance of your application, let's explore in more detail some of the choices you are likely to encounter.

By now, many readers are proficient at thinking in terms of the LC language. I illustrate the difference between the table and array approaches in LC next. The indexed array approach can be represented as follows:

```
((Time, Store) , Content.p) ~ (Content.(Prod.order).)
```

The subexpression on the left ((Time, Store) , Content.p) says to take every combination or tuple of Time and Store for which there exists at least one content or variable, in this case sales or costs. For every one of those combinations, associate an array of contents ordered by product. If there are 10 products and 2 contents, there will be 20 content values composed of 10 2-value pairs with the pairs ordered in terms of some default product ordering.

In contrast, the table approach looks like the following:

```
(Row.) ~ (((Time, Store, Prod) , Cont.p) ~ (Cont.))

(Store.) ~< row.store.n
(Time.)  ~< row.time.n
(Prod.)  ~< row.prod.n
```

The top expression describes the fact table and says there exists one row for each Time-Store-product tuple where at least one content has a value. For each of those rows, some value (including perhaps null) is attached for each content. If the existence of any one content means that all the other contents are likely to have a value, then the fact table will be pretty dense. The three minischemas underneath describe each of the dimension indexes into the fact table. Each one says that for each unique value in the dimension there are N nonoverlapping rows where the value of the dimension in the fact table is the same as in the dimension table.

Now that you've seen the essence of the difference between table and array-based storage approaches, let's continue drilling down into the options for array storage. Consider the following schema:

```
(Geog. ⊗ Time. ⊗ Product. ⊗ Scenario.) ~ Sales, Cost
```

What are your choices for storing and accessing this data in array form? What are the trade-offs? Think about it.

You have 16 choices for distributing the four dimensions across the outer index and the inner arrays, as shown in Figure 10.1.

How do you choose? What are, or should be, the factors guiding your choice?

There are basically three types of factors with many, many permutations. Those factors are as follows:

- Storage space
- Response time
- Total cost (dollars spent on the system including human time setting it up and managing it)

Although the ideal solution, as articulated by the wishful thinking department, takes no space, provides instantaneous responses, and is free, reality diverges considerably from this ideal. Nonetheless, these three dimensions govern most data distribution decisions. Assuming you are trying to improve on an existent physical design, you will certainly snag all options that take less space, are faster, and cost less; and you will certainly avoid all options that take more space, are slower, and cost more. Of course,

No. of dimensions in the index	4	3	2	1	0
No. of dimensions in the arrays	0	1	2	3	4
No. of combinations	1	4	6	4	1

Options

Option Number	Index dimensions	Array dimensions
1	G, T, P, S	
2	G, T, P	S
3	G, P, S	T
4	T, P, S	G
5	G, T, S	P
6	G, T	P, S
7	G, P	T, S
8	G, S	P, T
9	T, P	G, S
10	T, S	G, P
11	P, S	T, G
12	G	T, P, S
13	T	G, P, S
14	P	G, T, S
15	S	G, T, P
16		G, T, P, S

Figure 10.1 Storage distribution options.

there aren't too many options like that. Most options represent trade-offs in these three dimensions.

Typically speaking, you are trying to improve some factor while minimizing the degradation to the other factors. Thus, you may be trying to improve storage space efficiency for a minimum loss in response time and cost. Or you may be trying to improve response time for a minimum degradation in storage efficiency or cost. Or you may be trying to improve cost for a minimum degradation in storage efficiency and response time. Figure 10.2 illustrates a typical time/space trade-off for some cost constraint.

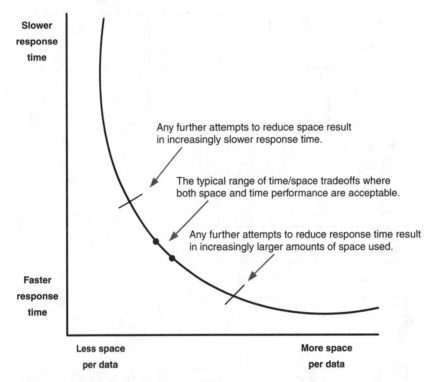

Slower response time

Any further attempts to reduce space result in increasingly slower response time.

The typical range of time/space tradeoffs where both space and time performance are acceptable.

Any further attempts to reduce response time result in increasingly larger amounts of space used.

Faster response time

Less space per data

More space per data

Figure 10.2 A typical time/space trade-off.

The largest issues affecting the choice of how to store data are the patterns of sparsity and the most likely use scenarios. Although the mechanisms differ, a number of disk-based products let you control which dimensions to put in the arrays in what nesting order, and which to put in the indexes.

Typically, the arrays all have the same shape. This is why you can avoid storing the dimension values. For example, if there are 100 geographical sites and 100 time periods dimensioning the variables sales and costs, and times are nested within stores, the array itself will only store values for sales and costs. It's the offset into the array that determines which geog/time combination is referred to. Obviously, this can only happen if all the arrays are dimensioned in exactly the same way. Since every array will have a slot for a sales and costs value for each of the 10,000 geog/time combinations, any missing or inapplicable sales or costs still need to be stored in their appropriate slot, though with a token indicating missing or not applicable. (Strictly speaking, this isn't true since it is possible to compress most of the emptiness out of the arrays. Compression may slow the operations down or speed them up in some cases, depending on when and how the compression is done.)

Since the arrays don't typically compress out sparse cells (at least when they are decompressed into memory), the ideal physical design defines the arrays so that they are relatively dense. The sparsity is brought out to the indexes because only actual dimensional intersections ever become an index entry. Striving towards dense arrays tends to make them smaller and more numerous. Since spatial and response time over-head are associated with accessing each array, the ideal physical design also minimizes the number and increases the size of arrays subject to the first constraint. Clearly, the two ideals are mutually conflicting. *Thus, physical design is a problem of constrained opti-mization that frequently produces a set of equally good, yet differently optimized solutions.*

In addition to the array size and numerosity issue, there is also an issue of dimen-sion nesting within an array. The ideal physical design will nest dimensions so that the innermost dimensions, which are the ones whose instances are most physically adja-cent in storage, are the ones most likely to be accessed at the same time. If a set of 1,000 data values comes from 1,000 adjacent slots in an array, there is a far greater likelihood that all that data will fit on a single disk page and be accessed in a single disk access. On the other hand, if those 1,000 data values were spread out across vast regions of a large array, it could take up to 1,000 disk accesses to retrieve that same data. For example, if the time dimension is the outermost dimension, performing a period-to-period comparison may require accessing two different pages. Now consider the same schema we looked at previously, but with the following data existence pattern descriptions:

- There are 100 stores, 100 times, 1,000 products, 3 scenarios, and 300,000 instances of each sales and cost variable.

- Most products are only sold at a few sites for any one time.

- Most stores only carry a third of the overall products.

- For the products carried by a store, they are sold about half the time.

- If there are actual values of sales or costs for a product, there are almost always planned values.

- The overall data sparsity is 99 percent.

Incidentally, data existence patterns like the simple one described previously, are something that as an application developer you need to know and frequently need to discover on your own before you can make physical design decisions.

Since we know that the data is very sparse, it wouldn't make any sense to store all the dimensions in one large array because of all the wasted space it would create. Nor would it make any sense to store all the dimensions in the indexes because it would take up a huge amount of index space and because it would create 100,000 data arrays. Since the products sold vary by time for a given store and by store for a given time, there's no way to define a reasonably dense array using the product dimension, so it probably belongs in the index. If we kept just products in the index and left Geog, Time, and Scenarios in the arrays, we would still have pretty sparse arrays because there would be one array with a full set of Store-Time-Scenario slots for every product that sold at least once—which we assume is every product. So actually, this design wouldn't compress out any of the sparsity. The same could be said of any design that puts only one dimension in the indexes, so long as each instance of the dimension is used at least once in the data set.

Since putting only one dimension in the index didn't generate any sparsity reduc-tion, how about putting three dimensions in the index? There are four possibilities.

Two of them, namely Time-Geog-Scenario and Time-Product-Scenario, do not reduce sparsity much. The first combination would only eliminate an intersection if some store sold no product for some time, which is unlikely. The second combination would only eliminate those intersections where a product was never sold in any store under any scenario, which is also unlikely.

The other two possibilities, Time-Geog-Product and Scenario-Geog-Product, both significantly reduce sparsity. Time-Geog-Product reduces sparsity wherever a particular product is not sold at a particular time for a particular store. Scenario-Geog-Product reduces sparsity wherever a particular product is never sold. The first of these two will compress out more sparsity than will the second. However, since there are 300,000 instances of each variable and it is assumed that the Scenario dimension is dense against all the others (a pretty realistic assumption), the first option will create 100,000 dense teeny-weeny arraylets that use the Scenario instances to order the slots for sales and costs. Although Scenario-Geog-Product will leave more sparsity in the arrays because about half the arrays will have sales of some product for some store for some time, but not for other times, there will be far fewer arrays—closer to 1,000.

If minimizing sparsity is your goal, then the optimal choice would be placing Time-Geog-Product in the index as no two-dimension combination of dimensions in the indexes can possibly reduce more sparsity. However, if you are willing to accept some sparsity, or if your software has good array compression algorithms, or if the benefit of strong sparsity reduction is overcome by the cost of maintaining and of computing with so many arraylets, then your choice may be the second of the three dimension options, namely Scenario-Geog-Product. If that is the case, then there is a two-dimension option that should work even better. Since the Scenario dimension is known to be very dense against all other dimensions, there would be a decrease in the number of arrays without any loss of sparsity reduction by combining the Scenario with the Time dimension in the arrays and leaving the Geog and Product dimensions in the indexes.

Thus, out of 16 possible ways of laying out four dimensions, two ways of slightly different characteristics emerge as equal contenders depending on the constraints of the application.

Different OLAP products offer different capabilities for designing efficient storage and access methods. For example, Hyperion's Essbase lets the application developer designate certain dimensions as sparse or dense with the union of the sparse dimensions being used as indexes. Oracle's Express lets the application developer declare combinations of dimensions as sparse to form indexes into dense arrays, or to merge sparse dimension combinations into a single so-called conjoint dimension, which is then used to dimension other dense arrays. Microsoft's Analysis Services uses a compressed record-based storage that is more akin to RDBMS storage. Applix's TM/1 lets the application developer specify the nesting order of dimensions. However, regardless of the specific techniques offered by a vendor and as evidenced by the previous example, you, the application developer, need to know the distribution of data across the various dimensions of your application before you can make informed choices about the best method to organize those dimensions for storage and retrieval.

Now that you've learned how to think about storing multidimensional data, let's turn to some of the storage and access methods offered by the vendors.

Storage and Access Methods

Although researchers into and developers of multidimensional databases have created many innovative storage and indexing routines over the years, they are leveraging the same body of principles as any other database researchers and developers. A classic text on database internal methods for both multidimensional and general databases is *Readings in Database Systems, 2nd ed.*[1]

What follows is just enough information for you to

- Appreciate some of the challenges faced by product developers.

- Ask the right questions when talking to vendors.

- Select the appropriate type of indexing for your needs, either by selecting the product that offers what you need or by selecting a method within a product that offers more than one.

MULTIDIMENSIONAL INDEXING

Multidimensional indexing has been an active area of research for a long time for geographic and spatial systems, for knowledge bases, and for other domains with multiple independent keys. The basic B-tree index has been extended to multiple dimensions with Kd-trees and R-trees, for example. Efficient multidimensional hashing can be implemented using grid files, and BANG files (balanced and nested grid files) form a tree-like hash index.

Merging the structures for indexing with computation processes, the hierarchical cube forest structure stores aggregate values in a clustered index (an index structure that contains the actual data as opposed to pointing to the data in a separate table), but also determines a storage/computation trade-off in a fashion similar to that described in "Implementing Data Cubes Efficiently."[2]

While these may be implemented in a specialized multidimensional database, they are just indexing techniques similar to those in use in all commercial RDBMSs. They index records in the same way that simple B-trees and one-dimensional hash indexes do already, so they could be applied and accessed through SQL in an RDBMS. Even when records are Z-ordered or Hilbert-numbered, as described next, the clustering is spread out, but not eliminated.

In Z-ordering, a single numerical key is synthesized from each dimension's member key to form a number that assists range searching in a hypercube. Rather than combining the keys one after another, the bits that compose the keys from each dimension are interleaved to form a binary-coded *Z-number*. Z-numbering tends to cluster records that are near each other in the dimensional spaces that are near each other on the disk, in all dimensions. This technique was first developed to support spatial querying for geographic and image databases. The clustering has the interesting property that no dimension is poorly clustered, and no dimension is ideally clustered either. (Contrast this with one-dimensional arrays, which do a great job of clustering on one dimension, but

(continued)

MULTIDIMENSIONAL INDEXING *(continued)*

provide no clustering on any other dimension). All points within a subcube are found between the corner of the hypercube with the lowest Z-number and the corner with the highest Z-number. With Z-ordering, certain types of multidimensional range queries will get more optimal access than they would with arrays, and no dimension should suffer badly compared with other sortings of records. However, there will be some bias towards the dimension that appears first in the order of interleaving, and some bias away from the last dimension in the order of interleaving.[3]

Hilbert numbering is conceptually similar and has been proven to more evenly cluster records, but is computationally more intensive to perform. Instead of a Z-number formed from interleaving bits, a Hilbert number represents a step in a fractal walk through the dimensional space. It is called a Hilbert number because the walk is in the form of a *Hilbert curve*. Hilbert numbering has been part of a considerable body of research and development on multidimensional indexing.[4]

Another specialized storage and access method that works only when your database has a time dimension, which is nearly always, treats the time series as the fundamental unit to be indexed. (This is akin to putting all the nontime dimensions in the index and storing a collection of compressed time series arrays.) Accrue's Pilot Decision Support Suite (formerly Pilot's Analysis Server) for example, understands time as a series and can automatically do time conversions across a variety of different calendar systems. But there is a cost associated with storing time series as entities. It is slower to perform cross-section (that is, cross-array) calculations.

Since disk storage is ultimately two dimensional and memory is ultimately one dimensional, multidimensional products cannot treat different dimensions as physically equivalent, even though from a computational perspective they may be treated as logically equivalent. There will always be some dimensions across which data are more easily retrieved than others. Given a particular set of data elements to be stored, the basic trade-offs are minimizing average seek time versus minimizing worst-case seek time versus minimizing best-case seek time. Storage is more typically optimized for the first two options.

Depending on the database, there may be choices to be made about the indexing technique to be used. Most multidimensional databases handle this automatically, but the system designer sometimes has a choice.

Table 10.1 is a partial list of the basic multidimensional structures found in commercial OLAP products. This list starts with the most basic multidimensional structures and moves to some of the more unusual, dynamic structures.

Across Machines

Many, but certainly not all, OLAP applications are deployed for multiple users to share within a departmental or an enterprise framework. Thus, there are typically a variety of machines existing in some kind of network topology and the OLAP data needs to be appropriately distributed. The issues surrounding the optimal distribution of data

Table 10.1   Commercial Multidimensional Structuring Techniques

BASIC STRUCTURE	COMPRESSION OR INDEXING TECHNIQUE	SPEED EFFICIENCY	SPACE EFFICIENCY	COMMENTS
Array	None	The fastest possible method for read and write, regardless of the number of dimensions.	Suitable for small or dense structures (>30 percent density). No overhead for keys or indexes.	*Well suited for complex modeling calculations with modest quantities of data. Often used for data temporarily held in RAM.*
Array	Empty pages suppressed	Very fast for read, good for write.	Suitable for "clumpy" data on disk. Good for density >10 percent.	*A typical mainframe database technique where large pages of data could be moved rapidly between disk and memory.*
Array	Strings of repeated values compressed	Slow for read, very slow for write. Unsuitable for random access.	Good for planning data (with many repeated or empty values), less good for actuals.	*A good way of handling disk-based dynamic compression with block transfers and unpacking in memory.*
Fixed record table	Hashing	Good for read and write with moderate data quantities.	Efficient dynamic sparsity in all but one dimension.	*Good dynamic sparsity handling in all but the columns dimension.*
Fixed record table	B-tree	Good for read and write.	Good for moderately sparse data without too many dimensions.	*Good for moderate data quantities.*
Fixed record table	Bitmap	Good for read and write.	Good for moderately sparse data with more dimensions than B-tree.	*Good for moderate to large data quantities.*
Fixed record table	Sorted	Good for read, very bad for write. Unaffected by sparsity.	Best with small numbers of dimensions.	*Good for large, very sparse, read-only data sets.*

(continued)

Table 10.1   Commercial Multidimensional Structuring Techniques *(continued)*

BASIC STRUCTURE	COMPRESSION OR INDEXING TECHNIQUE	SPEED EFFICIENCY	SPACE EFFICIENCY	COMMENTS
Fixed record table in an RDBMS	As used in the RDBMS	Acceptable for occasional read and write. Can be slow for bulk storage.	Effectively no net space used if the data was stored in the RDBMS anyway.	*Good for integration with other systems and warehouses, and for using the RDBMS's data management facilities.*
Variable length record structure	Sorted and compressed records	Acceptable read, very slow write.	Excellent data compression of randomly sparse data on disk.	*An excellent way of storing, but not processing, very sparse data on disk.*
Variable length record structure	Sorted records, with only incremental differences stored	Slow to read, completely unsuitable for write; updates must be stored separately and merged occasionally.	Highly flexible storage of tagged individual cells. Efficient for applications with up to a few million cells.	*A specialized technique for storing mixed data types multidimensionally.*

Adapted from Pendse and Creeth (1995).

across machines for OLAP applications are largely the same as for any other complex application. The major complicating factors that you need to keep in mind when optimizing the distribution of data across machines in OLAP applications is the massive amount of latent data and data reduction operations, the occasional pocket of data expansion operations, the existence of low bandwidth links—especially wireless—and the existence of many remote users who only occasionally connect to a network.

Basically, there are three choices for storing data:

- Source sites
- Use sites
- Intermediate sites

The major factors that influence decisions of how best to distribute data across machines are as follows:

- Machine functionality
- Bandwidth over different links in the network
- Machine location(s) of the major sources of data
- Machine location(s) of the major queries for data
- Locations of firewalls

Machine Functionality

The classic distinction everybody makes is between thick and thin hardware clients. In the old days, the distinction was between mainframe computers and dumb terminals. The thinner the clients, the more data and processing needs to happen on a server. Although thin-client strategies are common in web applications, I find that they inhibit all but the most rudimentary browse queries. One reason for this is that analytical sessions are composed of sets of context-maintaining queries while the HTTP-based query model is stateless.

It is also useful to distinguish between degrees of server functionality—especially when deciding whether an OLAP application and its associated data should reside on the same physical machine as a source application, typically relational, or whether the OLAP application should reside on a separate machine. The former case obviously demands a more powerful machine while the latter requires fast transfer rates between machines. The emergence of storage area networks may also have an impact on these decisions.

Bandwidth over Different Links in the Network

Clearly, you need to be careful about the transfer speed of the network connections between machines that routinely transfer large amounts of data. Although typical corporate LANs transfer data at 100 mps, the burgeoning number of wireless connections are still 1,000 times slower, and we still haven't eliminated modem connections from hotel rooms. So, the queries that work fine at the office may fail miserably in a WAN environment. You may want to adopt different data distribution strategies for different network types. For example, you may provide more replicated data for remote clients, assuming they can occasionally plug in to a LAN so that their remote queries require less data transfers. Or you may even reduce the number of cells returned in a query.

The Machine Location(s) of the Major Sources and Uses of Data

If your OLAP applications are getting most of their base data from an enterprise warehouse, and if there are multiple departments all using OLAP applications, and there are lots of users, you will probably get better performance by creating department-specific OLAP stores or marts. However, if you are using departmental stores, you need to be aware of the amount of data that is likely to be transferred between the enterprise warehouse and the departmental store. You may want to precalculate many derived cells at the departmental level (which you can do during off hours), to avoid having end-user queries trigger requests to the enterprise warehouse that require large data transfers during high-traffic business hours.

The Location of Firewalls

The major impact of firewalls in an enterprise is to define a security layer, limiting access from one side of the firewall to the other. The access control can be simple or sophisticated, and the technical capabilities are advancing quickly. Firewalls help to divide networks into separate security areas, or to bridge two or more separate networks together. As such, they are commonly associated with TCP/IP internetworking and with accessing data across the Internet. Two of the most common uses of a firewall are to prevent one side from initiating certain types of communications with the other, and to allow many devices on one side to access a small range of TCP/IP addresses on the other side.

Every OLAP system whose components can communicate over TCP/IP networking is capable of being distributed across the Internet. In practice, the use of firewalls complicates this, as firewalls typically are set up to block external access to all but a few well-known logical ports, whereas the OLAP system was probably attempting to use other, more obscure ports in its native communications in order to avoid conflict with the well-known ones. Many network administrators are reluctant to open ports, even if only to be used by a particular application, for fear that this will open unknown security holes.

However, there is most often at least one port open from the outside to the inside, and that is the port that web servers listen to for HTTP traffic (port 80). Accessing data outside a firewall is, for many users and administrators, synonymous with providing web (HTTP) access to the data.

Across Applications (ROLAP and HOLAP)

Traditionally, OLAP products have used their own proprietary databases, optimized to suit the particular applications for which the products were intended to be used.

Although an organization's data may be held in SQL tables, the SQL tables are a part of the organization's analysis-based decision-oriented information processing system and not a part of its operational systems. Thus, even if an OLAP application stores all its data in a relational database, it will be working on a separate copy of the data, not the live transaction database. This allows it to be physically optimized for decision support.

In principle, it is not difficult to store multidimensional data in SQL tables; after all, this is often how the data originated. The problem is to provide fast access and flexible multidimensional manipulation. (Recall that we looked at the problems of defining multidimensional aggregations and analyses in Chapter 2.)

The most common form of relational storage used for OLAP is commonly referred to as a *star schema*. (Recall the discussion of star schemas in Chapter 2.) Star schemas and their associated variants (such as snowflake schemas) are essentially methods of optimizing SQL database storage for data access purposes. Rarely are real-world applications constructed out of a single fact table. If there are many variables, it may not be possible to store them all in a single fact table because of column limits in the underlying relational database. It may also be inefficient because the sparsity may differ greatly between groups of variables, or all the dimensions might not apply to all the variables; and the data may also come from multiple applications, making updates to a single large table inefficient. Thus, in large applications, it is quite common to partition the fact table between groups of variables based on their sparsity, which dimensions apply to which variables, and where the data comes from.

Once the table layout has been designed, the base tables populated, and the summary tables created, the problem of multidimensional manipulation still needs to be resolved. The major impediment, as we saw in Chapter 2, is that standard SQL is not equipped to specify multidimensional operations.

The chart from the OLAP Report in Figure 10.3 shows the optimum storage strategy for different application sizes and sparsities. Of course, the scales are only approximate guides and will depend on the hardware being used. Applications and products can be mapped into this space and the degree to which an application fits a product's capacity and style can be checked. Products that allow multiple or hybrid structures cover more of the area and some might cover the whole surface, although other factors (not least, price) may still make them unsuitable for some applications.

The area of the chart in which memory-based applications are the best fit is based on the reckoning that a memory-based system will always outperform (and provide more dynamic calculations than) a disk-based system whenever it can hold everything in real RAM. However for very dense examples, disk-based products are nearly as good, but require less RAM and are therefore cheaper. Conversely, for very, very sparse applications, a hybrid solution of memory plus disk and/or RDBMS is probably best. This is because very sparse data typically has a higher overhead for indexes and pointers, as the sparsity is driven by high dimensionality, so there are simply more pointers. Even if held in memory, the available RAM capacity is consumed faster.

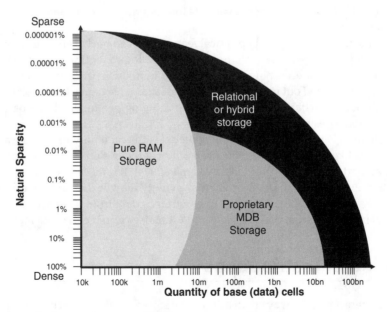

Figure 10.3 Optimum storage architecture across applications.

The area of the chart in which proprietary disk-based systems are recommended reflects their ability to handle medium to large quantities of data most efficiently. For fairly large, but very sparse data or very, very large databases, a RDBMS storage strategy may be the only feasible option, possibly boosted by memory and MDB-based storage of some of the most frequently used information. Even if it is desired that most data be kept in RDBMS storage, some memory-based structures are desirable for good performance. The option to keep some data in a proprietary structure allows intermediate or temporary results to be held within the OLAP application with better access performance than would be possible with the RDBMS alone, and also allows more application control over data structures that do not need to be shared with other applications.

It is not a bad idea to map any proposed early application into the chart, just to check that you understand it and how it relates to OLAP. Note that the log scales used on both axes make the memory area look somewhat larger than reality and the other two areas are somewhat compressed; however, this is not misleading because there are far more small than large OLAP applications. The horizontal axis shows the number of real *base* data cells stored, not the theoretical number that could be stored or those that are calculated from the base data. The position of the scale will depend on the amount of RAM available, so the scale should be regarded as an approximate guide, not a precise measure.

Across Partitions

Some OLAP products that are designed to handle larger quantities of data have implemented techniques to manage the data by dividing storage into partitions. Each partition provides a separate storage area for a subset of the data. In addition, most RDBMSs have the ability to logically partition tables into two or more separate storage areas. This can provide a number of benefits for querying, loading data, and maintaining the database.

Ideally, partitioning is a purely physical feature that can be driven by the logic of the overall model, but otherwise does not impact the logic. Partitions may be defined based on data load patterns, how data is accessed in frequent queries, or how different calculations are carried out in different regions of a larger schema. OLAP servers differ in their support for what can be partitioned and the degree to which the partitioning affects the model design.

The benefit of being able to partition the model is the capability to concentrate information that is likely to be used together into physical regions on disk (and memory and CPU when partitions are distributed across machines). If data can be loaded into only one partition out of a database, the total disk activity may be less and the efficiency of disk activity may be higher. If a query only retrieves data from one partition, then the number of bytes read from disk to locate and ultimately retrieve the data may be less.

Calculation Distributions

Although there are many ways to distribute the storage of data, the choices are all spatial. In contrast, calculations can be distributed across space and across time.

Temporal

The bottom line question you need to answer is which, if any, derivations do you calculate in advance of any particular query and which, if any, do you calculate only in response to a user's query? The fact that there can be thousands of times as much derivable data as input data is a strong disincentive against blindly precalculating everything. The fact that single queries for high-level aggregates may derive from billions of input data cells is a strong disincentive against calculating everything at query time. Thus, the majority of OLAP applications perform best when you precalculate some, but not all, derivations.

As far as precalculation is concerned, there are a few choices of event-based times. The earliest time you can calculate is at load time. Many applications offer the choice of performing aggregations at load time. Typically, load-time aggregating is good for bulk, simple aggregations where the dependency trees for the calculations match those of the dimensions. (Please see Chapter 7 for the description of dependency versus referential dimension trees.)

Batch update-based precalculation is a variant of load time. Frequently, large applications are updated in a batch process on either a daily or weekly basis during a fixed update window. Unless the organization maintains shadow cubes, which is necessary for 24/7 (3+ continent) operations, cube browsing will be unavailable during the update window, so the more calculations are performed at update time, the longer the downtime will be.

User update-based precalculation is much closer to request time, but not quite the same. Whenever users are entering data for planning and simulation purposes, small updates to the data may translate into many updates to derived values. Whole enterprise planning scenarios can be driven by a few numbers. The impacted derivations haven't been queried for yet, so calculating them is a form of precalculation.

Finally, calculations can be made when the user requests them. The user may not know that a particular value, such as Eastern region total margins in dollars, hasn't yet been calculated. The user simply has to request it. The request then triggers the calculation.

Optimizing the management of aggregate tables in an SQL database is an area of active research. Aggregate tables take up storage space, and reduce the time it takes to return aggregated results to a query. Given some knowledge of how big the base and aggregate tables are, a judicious compromise between storage and computation can be made. The ideal location of this knowledge would be in the SQL optimizer itself, but

---

SAMPLING

An alternative to speeding up queries by calculating a derivation in advance is to calculate a sample-based aggregation at request time. For some users, a result that is nearly exact will be good enough, especially given a high enough speedup. Sample-based aggregates are supported in some RDBMSs and some OLAP tools. Unfortunately, multidimensional sample-based aggregates are more difficult to calculate than one might think.[5]

this would require either extending SQL to describe the relationships between the aggregated views and the base table, or overhauling the internal catalog and optimizer to automatically recognize these relationships. However, this knowledge is also useful to products that know the structure held in the tables and generate their own SQL. The paper "Implementing Data Cubes Efficiently" by Harinarayan, Rajaraman, and Ullman[6] was an important description of research results for optimization techniques.

Other temporal considerations include the following:

- How often data needs to be updated, and whether this is in large batches or individual cells. (Batch updates are simple because only a single task has to be run and all the updates can be merged in at once, and any database restructuring can occur at the same time; individual cell updates are much more complex because they need fast random write access, even to hitherto empty cells, which not all tools can support.)

- How often the database dimensions change. (This will affect the extent to which the dimensions are made data driven.)

Across Applications and Utilities

In addition to being able to distribute calculations over time, in a typical decision support architecture you also need to decide which applications you are going to use for certain calculations. Relative to an OLAP application, the basic issues are deciding which calculations, if any, are to be performed on your source database, which are to be performed in any data transformation software, and which, if any, are to be performed on a supplementary analytic tool. The source database may be relational, or a mainframe database, or a real-time process historian. Frequently, data is aggregated and other simple calculations are performed during the process of transforming the data between systems in an ETL (*extract, transform,* and *load*) step. The OLAP tools provide varying degrees of computational ability, but more advanced analytical calculations may require the services of a statistical package or other specialized system.

Using the RDB

If SQL Group By operations are to be used to generate derived values, it is most efficient not to mix multiple levels of consolidation together in a table. This means that for each combination of hierarchical level in each dimension that is deemed to be worth precalculating, a separate summary table will be needed. However, these in turn are likely to be partitioned on the same lines as the base tables, so the potential number of precalculated summary tables can rise very rapidly. The largest applications can include thousands of summary tables. These need to be kept in line with the data and comprehensively revised if, for example, product structures change.

Calculations in ETL Packages

Some ETL packages can perform aggregations and simple calculations on data as the data is moved from source to target. Simple row-wise calculations (multiplying two fields, or converting a NULL to a zero if some condition is true) are readily performed. They may also provide light aggregation of data as well—for example, collapsing a set of similar transaction lines to a single line representing all the units of a single product.

Special-purpose sorting packages, frequently used as part of the overall ETL process, can sometimes also produce larger-scale aggregates as well. These packages are typically not considered ETL products in and of themselves, but can be critical to the overall process of getting data loaded and indexed for analysis.

Client Application versus Server Calculations

The client application a user sits down to may in fact add even more layers of software on top of whatever OLAP server and client components already exist. For example, some systems use a spreadsheet interface to OLAP client components that in turn access relational or MD servers. Additional calculations may be embedded in spreadsheet formulas to act on retrieved analytical results. Alternatively, custom C++ or Java code may perform further manipulations of data in other client interfaces. Such additional calculations are usually performed either for user convenience (the user knows spreadsheet formulas, but lacks the knowledge to alter the queries that filled the spreadsheet in the first place), or because the underlying OLAP system lacks the technical ability to perform the calculation in a timely fashion.

Common Configurations

So far in this chapter, you've seen a variety of ways and some of the decision heuristics for distributing data and calculations in an attempt to optimize, or at least satisfice[7] the physical design of your application. In this last section, you will see some of the most common application distribution configurations I've seen adopted by organizations who've implemented OLAP solutions. From a wide brush stroke perspective, they differ as a function of whether they are departmental or enterprise solutions, whether they are purely multidimensional or mixed-multidimensional relational, whether they are thick-client or web-browser based, and whether they are internal or cross the firewall.

Departmental: Relational Data Mart with a Multidimensional Client

Many corporations have relationally based departmental data marts to which they have given end-users data access through OLAP query tools. Although the query tools differ as a function of whether they reside purely on the client or whether a part of the query tool is server resident, the tools typically create single user query result caches, which means that the more end-users there are, the more server memory is needed to store each of the user's query results. Products will differ as a function of whether some or all of that cache is client resident and whether the cache is incrementally modifiable.

Since the source data is relational and since there is no significant multidimensional processing done on the server, this type of configuration does not lend itself to sophisticated client calculations beyond those whose required data is small enough that it can be efficiently sent across the network to the client.

There will typically be 5 to 30 users in 1 to 3 job functions that need to access reports swiftly to assist their managers.

There is likely only one server involved for the data mart, which will usually be dedicated to running the RDBMS. In a smaller situation, the RDBMS may be used for other applications besides the data mart. Each user will have his or her own client computer to access the data. The multidimensional client software can be based on the client tier or based on the server and accessed through a web interface. In the event of client-tier multidimensional software, end-user computers are likely to be slightly more powerful than the standard computer (or at least have more RAM) owing to the client-side multidimensional processing.

By far, the most frequent type of derivation is summation. Some number of differences and ratios will also be used. Simpler dimensional referencing is common along the Time dimension, for example, to perform period-to-period comparisons.

Departmental: Multidimensional Server and Client

Many OLAP solutions, especially in the financial sector or function, replaced or complemented what were previously spreadsheet-based applications with source data coming directly from users as with budgeting and planning, or with source data coming from financial transaction systems. In these situations, the solution configuration typically contains a multidimensional departmental server connected to a set of multidimensional clients.

Whether the client and server tiers are serviced by a single multitier product or by two products communicating through an API (which is typically public, though not necessarily published), the multidimensional server typically provides robust dimensional structuring and calculations. It is usually possible for end-users to specify calculations on the client that are executed on the server with the appropriate result set (or a cursor into a server-resident query result cache) funneled back to the client.

This type of configuration is especially useful when end-users actually need to perform sophisticated analyses, and not just view and drill down on previously created result sets.

The number of users will still be in the range of 5 to 35. The reporting needs will be similar to that of other departments, except that when financial reporting is involved there tends to be less of a need for user interaction and more of a need to lay reports out in a complex and precise fashion owing to management needs.

The calculations performed in a departmental solution with a multidimensional server are typically more involved than those performed with a multidimensional client to a relational data source. More types of dimensional referencing are provided and used—for example, many flavors of allocations, cumulative and rolling sums, and averages.

Enterprise: Relational Warehouse, Multidimensional Midtier Server, and Multidimensional Client

As more and more corporations have deployed enterprise data warehouses and as many corporations have deployed some form of departmental OLAP solutions, it is also common to see multidimensional clients connecting to multidimensional servers acting as midtier intermediaries. An enterprise analytical system may have from 100 to 5,000 users in this type of architecture. The users will be spread across a spectrum of job responsibilities and divisional areas, including finance, marketing, production, distribution, customer relations, and more. Each department of the organization will have a user profile and application needs similar to the departmental scenarios described earlier. In addition, senior management will likely have a simplified interface to a set of indicators drawn from all areas of the organization and a set of more advanced analysts in one or more of the departments.

The relational warehouse may be in one or several large servers, most likely high-end UNIX boxes. There are likely to be several multidimensional midtier servers, still likely to be on midsized servers that may be running UNIX or a Windows NT derivative. The multidimensional servers draw data from one or more of the RDBMS warehouse servers as needed. Each end-user has his or her own client computer, a higher-end PC.

While the warehouse can be very large, the specialized OLAP application systems are usually directed at strategic subsets of interest in the different functional and departmental areas. The data warehouse itself performs some of the OLAP functionality. For example, summary tables are maintained, frequently by a package that specializes in sorting and aggregation (as opposed to by SQL SELECT queries). The warehouse itself is fed by an ETL system that lightly aggregates records together as transactions are retrieved from source systems.

As with the other configurations, the majority of calculations are aggregations, along with a number of differences and ratios. Traditional statistics and nonparametric statistics are likely performed on separate application servers, as the capabilities of the database servers are likely reserved for the relational and OLAP systems.

Enterprise: Relational Warehouse, Multidimensional Midtier Server, Web Server, and Multidimensional Thin Client

The situation of an enterprise warehouse and multidimensional midtier server(s) with web servers and thin multidimensional clients is largely similar to the preceding enterprise warehouse scenario. The very same multidimensional servers may be involved in supporting both cases.

Extending the system with a web server and thin-client software enables a set of additional users and usage scenarios. It facilitates the use of the warehouse to internal users at remote locations, such as in hotel rooms. Portal applications become possible as well. Suppliers and customers can access analytics to assist them in supply chain decisions. Some organizations have also created or shifted to providing analytical portals as their primary business.

From the point of view of physical distribution of the software, the thin-client approach is more compelling in an enterprise than in a single department. Software upgrades are localized to a smaller set of servers rather than a large number of desktops. Thin-client software is not always as robust as client-side software, though, and there is additional latency and consumption of server and network resources in producing and transmitting the HTML, XML, and image files as necessary to web browsers. (Note that when components or Java applets are activated on the client side, the client cannot really be considered thin anymore. Web deployment can still require clients as thick as any other.)

Summary

In this chapter, you saw how data storage, with associated index methods, and calculations can be distributed for optimum performance. You were exposed, by way of example, to the reasoning associated with selecting some storage form over another for a particular data set, and you learned that you need to know something about the data's sparsity before you can make appropriate storage decisions. The chapter also explained how data can and ought to be distributed within a machine, across machines, across applications, and across partitions. You learned how calculations should be distributed across time, across application tiers, and across applications. Finally, you were exposed to a variety of common physical configurations.

PART

Three

Applications

_All our faculties can never carry us farther than barely to observe
that particular objects are constantly conjoined together
and that the mind is carried by customary transition from
the appearance of one to the belief of the other._

DAVID HUME

Practical Steps for Designing and Implementing OLAP Models

There are many tasks associated with the design and implementation of a multi-dimensional information system. At a high level, they can be summed up as problem definition, tool selection, and solution implementation. In an idealized world, tool selection should follow problem definition because, as we saw in Chapter 10, tools are generally optimized for particular uses.

Some tools, for example,

- Work exclusively as a client or server
- Need to load all data into main memory
- Assume that persistent data is stored in an SQL database
- Have built-in knowledge of time, accounting, or currencies
- Assume that certain dimensions—such as time, location, and/or products—are present
- Have less functionality, but are simpler to use within their intended domain
- Are harder to use, but are more general in their applicability

In reality, however, tool selection may precede a full understanding of the problem and be a function of many things that have nothing to do with the logical or physical aspects of that problem, including tool price, the geographical representation of the vendor, the friendliness of the salesperson, the size and reputation of the vendor, the quality of the vendor's collateral, and the existence of vendor champions within the organization. Thus, your tool selection process may affect how you design and implement your Online Analytical Processing (OLAP) model.

Regardless of the factors that influenced tool selection, regardless of whether you are building a model for yourself or others, and regardless of whether you are rapidly prototyping a solution or designing a logical model prior to implementation, you still need to go through the distinct steps of defining cubes, dimensions, hierarchies, members, formulas, and data links. Let us call these model-building steps. While it is true that there are substantial differences between tools in terms of the way you think through and perform these steps, the way the steps are chunked, and the order in which they are performed, you still need to pass through the same basic steps.

This chapter describes and explains the practical steps associated with designing and implementing OLAP models. It is written more as a guide than as a methodology. As such, it is not meant to generate any of the partisan fervor typified by proponents of methodologies such as De Marco, Yourdon, Martin, Rumbaugh, Booch, Shlaer-Mellor, and so on. The guidelines should serve you regardless of the tools you are using or the type of multidimensional system you are implementing.

So, for whom are these guidelines written? These guidelines are written for the designer and implementer of the OLAP model. They make no assumption about the relationship between the designer/implementer and the end-user(s). In other words, you may be designing a model to be used by others, or you may be designing a model for yourself. In either case, you need to design and implement it, and should define the core of the model before defining any ad hoc additions. The guidelines also make no assumptions about whether tool selection has or has not yet occurred. While on average, it may be that tool selection has already occurred and you are now ready to design and implement an actual solution (which may not be your first), you may want to first define your problem space and then specify the requirements that the tool you select needs to fulfill.

The guidelines are more detailed about the attributes of a well-constructed model than the order in which a model is constructed. As you will see, there are multiple starting points and sequences for building models, and different tools encourage you to build models in different orders as well. Only the specifics of a situation can serve to identify which starting point makes the most sense in that situation. *In general, you want to begin where you are most confident of what is or what needs to be done and work out from there.* For example, it might be that you are most confident of the data sources, but you are not yet sure of all the purposes people will use them for. This would result in a more bottom-up, data-to-function modeling approach. It might be that you know the types of calculations that need to be performed, but are less confident of the data sources to feed those computations. This is more of a top-down, function-to-data approach. You may have invested in datawarehousing and want to explore the value-add to your end-users of defining an OLAP layer on top of your relational star schemas. You may be coming from a spreadsheet environment where you have been performing some calculations and have some data, but want to generalize the calculations for model extensibility.

What is critical is that you design a properly connected structure. In this sense, there is no right or wrong starting point. Rather, there are right and wrong connections. (Software model construction enjoys a relative freedom of sequencing in comparison to physical model construction where you cannot, for example, build a skyscraper from the top down.)

Nevertheless, this chapter needs to be in some order. To correspond with what is typically the easiest way to learn about an OLAP solution, this guideline chapter is presented in an essentially top-down fashion, starting with cubes and ending with formulas that attach to members. The guidelines take you through the major steps of designing and, to a much lesser degree, implementing a multidimensional information system.

At a high level those steps include the following:

- Understanding the current and ideal data flow
- Defining cubes
- Defining dimensions, members, and links
- Defining dimension levels and/or hierarchies
- Defining aggregations and other formulas

Physical issues are addressed, whenever relevant, together with logical issues.[1] The reason implementation issues are only slightly addressed is because many of them are extremely tool specific.

Finally, these guidelines are presented as a series of descriptions as follows:

- Things that typically occur
- Things you need to do and watch out for
- Rules of thumb for making certain decisions
- Questions that you should ask either yourself or those for whom you are designing the system

User Requirements

Understand the Current Situation

Regardless of how you go about designing a model, you first need to understand the problem situation for which you are attempting to provide a solution, in terms of what is actually going on and in terms of what ought to be going on.[2] As you saw in the last section, there are logical and physical aspects to what is going on. You need to be aware of both.

From a tool perspective, there could be any number of different initial situations, such as

- A bunch of analysts accessing the same worksheets or many separate partially redundant worksheets
- A data warehouse database or several linked databases from which analytical data is directly accessed or perhaps staged in a data mart
- Several legacy databases running operational programs from which extracts are taken through the use of homegrown routines

- Only an SQL database serving as data warehouse with a bunch of SQL report writing tools on the client side, probably with a large supporting IT shop

Regardless of the specific tools being used, you need to learn about the user's schemas and any schemas relevant to the source data. You also need to gain an understanding of relevant business rules such as rules about performance thresholds, data access, or the event-based distribution of information. The rules might be encoded or in the minds of key personnel.

As a solution provider, you need to talk with all the persons who have something to do with the system that existed at the time you arrived on the scene, as well as everyone who has a part in the system you are going to design and implement. These may include power end-users, casual end-users, data entry operators, system administrators, persons responsible for the data sources, and management. You will need to discover not only what people are currently doing, but also what they would like to be doing.

As you learn about the situation, you will identify problems and loosely classify them according to whether they have more to do with the availability of data, needed derivations, or representation forms (in which case they are more logical), or whether they have more to do with speed of access, amount of storage required, maximum number of concurrent users, operating system problems, network jams, or where the data is coming from (in which case they are more physical).

If you are the kind of person who was brought in to put out fires or stop hemorrhaging (pick your metaphor), there's typically an immediately apparent problem such as wrong budget totals or multihour response time for what should be multisecond queries. In these cases, you can jump over the problem definition and go straight to solution design.

Useful Questions to Ask

In any real situation, there is a dynamic that will exist between you and those for whom you are trying to build a solution (assuming those are different people). That dynamic will largely determine the degree to which you can ask questions of your choosing or insist that the eventual solution consumers respond to your questions once asked. This is especially true when the person(s) you are questioning or interviewing is a client of yours or closer to your CEO than you.

Also, once you are in a dialogue, information may be forthcoming in an unpredictable manner. A question about the number of users may trigger a response about slow response times, difficulties logging on, or weaknesses in data integrity. Since problems tend to occupy peoples' minds, it is not uncommon for interviewees to jump right into their problems while you're still trying to understand the context. You may only get a chance to learn about the context, or actual situation, after the fact.

Thus, the following questions about the actual situation, problems, and constraints on a solution should be taken as rough guidelines that highlight the types of information you eventually need to have, rather than a recipe that needs to be followed in a particular order.

Questions about the Actual Situation

1. With what frequency do which types of users use the system? (Questions 1.1 through 1.7 pertain to each type of user.)

   1.1 How many users are there for each type?

   1.2 What kinds of dialogue does each type of user have with the system?

   1.3 How much data does each type of user examine during a typical session?

   1.4 How much data travels across the network in response to typical queries for each type of user?

   1.5 What are the categories of information typically browsed by each type of user?

   1.6 What kind of end-user tools are being used to browse and analyze the data?

   1.7 How many distinct views are needed per type of end-user?

2. Overall, how much data is input to the system?

3. How many distinct data sources are there?

   3.1 For each source, what is its schema?

   3.2 How much data is there?

   3.3 At what rate are the links refreshed?

   3.4 What integration and refinement issues were involved with the source data?

4. What ad hoc computations are typically performed on the server?

5. What computations are preperformed on the server?

6. What computations are typically performed on the client?

7. What machines, operating systems, and network configuration(s) are used?

At this point, you should be able to draw or fill in a sources and uses diagram like the one shown in Figure 11.1. It is a convenient way to picture important information. The sources and uses diagram represents what is important for sources and end-users. It shows what kinds of data enter the system and who is using the data. It is, in effect, a simple logical model capable of summarily portraying the current situation.

Questions about Problems

You need to gain an understanding of problems that users are experiencing. As stated elsewhere, although it is useful to chunk problems into the two rough categories of logical and physical, be aware that many specific problems will have a mixture of logical and physical components. An easy way to cull out the most physical problems is to ask yourself if the problem would go away if only there were an infinite amount of infinitely fast hardware of infinite bandwidth. If the answer is yes, the problem is largely physical; if the answer is no, the problem is largely logical.

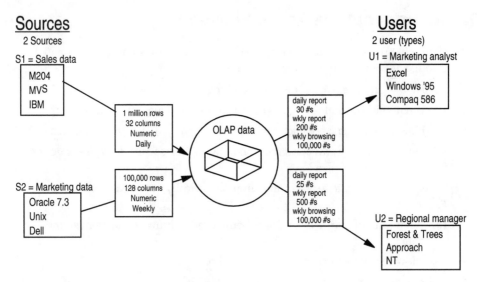

Figure 11.1 A sources and uses diagram.

Logical Problems

For each of the following questions to which your respondents answer yes, there exists a logical or physical problem:

- Is it hard to define certain multidimensional calculations such as profitability by product, market, and time? If so, how are they currently defined?
- Is it hard to drill down from summaries to underlying details?
- Is it hard to change views once they are created?
- Are users stuck with hard-to-interpret names?
- Is a lot of end-user intelligence required to operate the application programs?
- Are the graphics lacking?
- Are reports filled with zeros?
- Is there any inconsistent data?
- Does text need to be, without currently being able to be, associated with data?

Physical Problems

- Is end-user data access fast enough? How fast does it need to be?
- Can end-users generate queries without too much IT support?
- Is there enough hardware and software capacity at the server and client ends?

- Is a lot of client or server processing required for what seem like simple queries?

- Is there a lot of network traffic in response to client queries?

- Does the system support an adequate number of users for read/write operations?

Information about Constraints

Some of the relevant information you need in order to propose a solution may be expressed by participants in the form of constraints on a solution. For example, the users for whom you are working to provide a solution may not think of their operating system as a problem, but if they want to use an OLAP tool that needs to run on NT while the relevant database source is running on UNIX, then the OS could be a problem.

A typical solution might include the following types of physical system constraints:

- Type of large-scale machine: SMP or MPP

- Type of end-user machines: uni processor or dual processor

- Operating system: Windows 2000 or Solaris

- Network topology: client server or peer-to-peer

- Other software that needs to interact with the solution: GIS, statistics packages or Visualization

- Number of system users: tens, hundreds, thousands, and so on

- Data set sizes on the server: gigabytes, terabytes, and so on

- Application refresh rates: every minute, hour, day, or week

- Valid data types (numeric and non-numeric)

Requirements Documentation

If you have passed through the previous stages and can answer most or all of the questioned contained therein, you have learned what the situation looks like at the source and for the end-users. You have learned about logical and physical problems with the current state of affairs, and you have learned about various constraints on a solution. You are ready now to learn about and suggest the user requirements that need to be met.

All application projects should have some form of user requirements documentation. User requirements, or simply requirements, represent a description of what any model must do in terms of logical or physical capabilities in order to successfully solve the identified problems. There are as many different kinds of requirements as there are applications.

Any measurable attribute of an application, such as the following, can be a part of the user requirements:

- The identification of data sources
- The number of end-users given concurrent access
- The specific calculations or views supported
- The speed of calculation
- The specific algorithms used for data encryption
- The data transfer rate over a network

User requirements are an indispensable tool for communication between users, developers, and managers whether that communication takes place before, during, or after development. The only way to resolve disputes over the degree to which some developer(s) did or did not build the agreed-upon application to some agreed-upon set of characteristics is to have mutually agreed-upon documentation (that is, the user requirements) defining those characteristics. For medium to large organizations and medium to large projects, user requirements may take months to create. Lots of politics may be involved. There are likely to be several iterations. A final document can easily be over 100 pages.

Since any and every aspect of a multidimensional model can be included in a requirements document and since user views and specifications of data sources typically are included, it is tempting to say that user requirements and solution design are one and the same. However, this would be incorrect. As detailed as they might be, it is always possible, and typically probable, that in order to meet all the user requirements, some unanticipated model structures not otherwise mentioned in the requirements documentation—this can be any combination of dimensions, cubes, variables, or data sources—will be required.

Since user requirements documentation is not specific to OLAP solutions and the items covered in a requirements document are also covered in a model design, and since the purpose of this chapter is to teach you how to build solutions, I have not included any specific examples of requirements documentation here.

Solution Design

Logical Model Definition[3]

Given an understanding of the current situation, known problems, user requirements, and constraints on a solution, how do you define a multidimensional model to meet the user requirements within the given constraints and solve all known problems? Is there a specific order to the steps for defining a multidimensional model? Are there certain things that must be specified?

From the 100,000-foot perspective, you need to define your model in terms of one or more cubes such that data sources (or links to data sources) and derived data outputs (or user views) are represented within the cubes, and all derived data are definable in

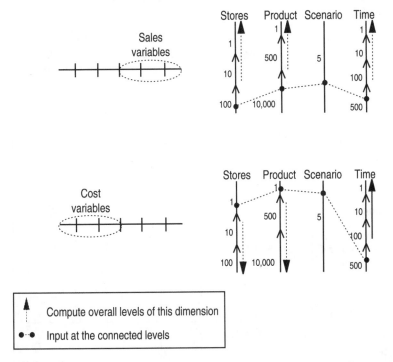

Figure 11.2 Multidimensional type structure (MTS) represents data transformations.

terms of input data. This ensures that it is possible to generate the data outputs from the data sources. Figure 11.2 shows a version of the multidimensional data structures presented in Chapter 3, which are used here to represent data transformations. The vertical line segments still represent dimensions, but this time each segment represents a granularity level rather than an individual member. The connected points represent the specific granularity levels where the data entered the cube. The arrows represent the direction of calculation. For example, in the top panel, sales data can be seen entering the base level of the cube and aggregating upwards. While in the lower panel, cost data can be seen entering the top levels of store and product and the lowest level of time, and can be seen being allocated down stores and products but aggregated up in time.

So how do you define such cubes? There are a variety of steps that can be followed in a variety of orders. Figure 11.3 summarizes the main items that need to be defined, how often each item needs to be defined, and the order in which each item type should be and is typically defined as a function of the design environment (OLAP software versus some documenting repository) and for each design environment, the particular starting point. There are three different kinds of starting points per environment.

The sequences in Figure 11.3 should not be taken as absolute. Rather, they are rough examples of real differences in sequencing that frequently occur on at least the first pass through model creation. Since the entire process is iterative (requirements understanding, solution design, and implementation), the differences between the starting points may fade after the first iteration. Nevertheless, I think it is useful to realize why

Definition coverage: How frequently items are defined	Items defined	Environment				
		OLAP software			Repository/design	
		Working from data		Working from a model	Top-down / bottom up	User-back / source forward
		In an RDB with a star schema	In a spreadsheet			
Per application	Cubes: source and/or use	3	**4**	1	1	1, 4 /3, 4
Per cube	Dimensions	2	3	3	1	1, 4 /3, 4
Per dimension	Dimension members and hierarchies	2	2	1	4	2 /3, 4
Per cube	Variables	4	3	1	1	1, 4 /3, 4
Per cube	Aggregations	**5**	5, 7	3	2	1, 4 /3, 4
Per cube	Other derivations	6	7, 5	2	3	1, 4 /3, 4
Per cube	Links	2	6	**4**	4	3 /2
Per application	Source data	1	1	**4**	4	2 /1

Figure 11.3   A sample variety of sequences for defining an OLAP model.

NOTE For those sequences defined in OLAP software, the earliest point at which the cubes(s) could be processed is indicated by the **bold font** used for the sequence number.

there are different starting points and perhaps, most importantly to understand that it is possible and useful—and unfortunately not common practice—to create a design document prior to and alongside any tool-specific model implementation.

Since the rise of datawarehousing beginning in the early 1990s, the most common sequence for defining OLAP solutions has been working directly in OLAP software from data in a relational database (RDB) with a star schema. There, most typically, data is identified in one or more fact and associated dimension tables. Then working from within an OLAP environment, the warehouse data is linked into an OLAP model where links are created between dimension tables and OLAP cube dimension definitions. This linking usually defines most of the dimensional hierarchies as well. In many products, one would process the dimensions at this point and create a product-specific internal and persistent representation of the dimensions and hierarchies. The dimensions are combined into cubes. The cubes may also be instantiated by the software. Then variables are defined with default aggregation routines in place. At this point, the cubes' data can be processed, which is to say the links can be activated and data can be brought into the cubes and aggregated. Finally, while working from within the OLAP environment, additional derivations may be defined and calculated.

The next most common sequencing is working with OLAP software from data in a spreadsheet. This frequently occurs in financial applications where the current state is defined by small groups of users struggling to share worksheets for a common application. The main difference between working from an RDB-based star schema and working from spreadsheets is that star schemas, because they are already regularized, map cleanly to OLAP cubes. (Of course, the more complicated the star schema, the more complicated the cube structure.) In contrast, spreadsheet models can be (and often are) arbitrarily irregular. Thus, when working from spreadsheets, one typically needs to spend time analyzing the worksheets looking for sets of row and column names that could be OLAP dimensions. Once these are found, variables are picked out of the cell values and combined with sets of dimensions—typically but not necessarily all present along with the cell values—to form cubes of variables. Then, typically, aggregations are defined within the OLAP environment, links to the worksheets are created, data is read in, and further derivations are defined. Alternatively, the derivations are defined before the links are created and the aggregations are created afterward.

Although it occurs in scientific research, working from models prior to data is uncommon in the business world with the possible exception of demo creation where models are built first followed by the loading in of some data that is typically disguised and expanded to fill the needs of the demo.

Currently, it is not common practice for organizations to create a repository for their OLAP designs independent of the software environment within which the design is implemented. OLAP solutions are still being built like spreadsheet solutions. This is unfortunate because implemented models (aka applications) of any reasonable degree of complexity are usually not self-explanatory. Typically, there isn't even a full script of the application in the software. Rather, key design decisions are reflected in disjoint outline structures, dialogue boxes, radio buttons, and other mouse clicks. Once the application is built, any disputes about derivations or other functionality may be difficult to resolve because the requirements were insufficiently specified. Then, after a few years have gone by and everyone who built the original models has moved on, anyone subsequently charged with altering the model may be in for an unpleasant foray into application archeology.

The good thing about design repositories is that the basic technology for creating and maintaining them is available in word processors, charting tools, and simple databases. Given all the energy that goes into developing and then fixing analytical applications, I believe that full model design documentation should be a requirement for projects of any reasonable degree of complexity—if only to maintain clarity of communication between developers, users, and management. In this respect, there are two basic types of path directions: top down or bottom up, and user back or source forward. Of course, they may be combined. A design may proceed top down for a bit, then proceed from the user back, then drill down a bit more, then incorporate source information, then go bottom up, and so on.

Since the purpose of this section is to make sure you can think through the various issues surrounding the design of an OLAP solution, since I openly advocate the use of design documentation as a part of the solutions process, and since the top-down approach is frequently the easiest one to understand for communication purposes, I use it to organize this section.

HIGH- AND LOW-LEVEL LOGICAL MODELS

A logical multidimensional model spans several levels of abstraction that, if you are coming from the relational world, might be thought of as different things. A high-level logical model represents the essential elements of the model as understood by its users. For example, a typical entity relationship diagram represents a high-level logical model outlining the basic entities, attributes, and relationships in a model. This is illustrated in Figure 11.4.

A low-level logical model contains sufficient detail to design a physical model. For example, the set of normalized relations shown in Figure 11.5 contains all the logical elements of the model. Every key and nonkey attribute as well as every datum or data point is represented in this low-level logical model.

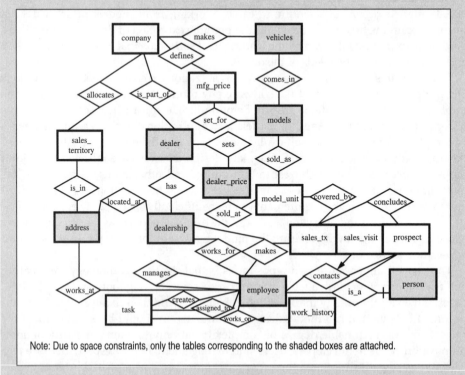

Note: Due to space constraints, only the tables corresponding to the shaded boxes are attached.

Figure 11.4 A typical entity relationship model.

dealer

dealer_no	dealer_name	number_of_dealerships
integer4	varchar(30)	integer
1	versailles ford	2

address

address_no	civic_address	city	zip	state	country	tel	fax
integer4	varchar(30)	vhar(30)	char(10)	char(3)	char10	char12	char12
1	123 street 1	city1	123	CA	USA	111.213.3333	111.1112222

dealership

dealership_no	dealer_no	address_no	dealership_name
integer4	integer4	integer4	name
1	1	1	varchar(30)

dealer_price

dealer_no	price_class_no	start_date	end_date	price
integer4	integer4	date	date	money
1	1	1/1/19	1/1/40	$2,000

vehicles

vehicle_no	company_no	vehicle_line_name	launch_date
integer4	integer4	varchar(30)	date
1	1	Cadilac	1/1/89

models

vehicle_no	model_no	model_name	model_options
integer4	integer4	varchar(30)	varchar(30)
1	1	DeVille	OptionPack111

person

person_no	SSN	Lname	Fname	Gender	Age
integer4	varchar(10)	char(30	char(30)	char	integer
1	111-1111-111	Antonuk	Ferengi	M	35

employee

person_no	dealership_no	employee_no	manager_no	hire_date
integer4	integer4	integer4	integer4	date
1	1	1	1	1/1/90

Figure 11.5 A low-level schema.

Whereas entity relationship models and table schemas are typically considered to be different models, the high- and low-level logical views that they define are all a part of any one logical multidimensional model. In the multidimensional world, cubes, dimensions, and hierarchies form the high-level, user-oriented picture of the model. Members, their relationships, and formulas paint the low-level logical picture. Furthermore, typical relational schemas whether high- or low-level do not depict the data transformations that take place. In contrast, a multidimensional model more explicitly represents the entire data transformation process.

Cubes and Dimensions

The first thing you need to design is the logical cube and dimension structure for the model. Even if you are using a hypercube product, which may force you to put all data that needs to interact in a single physical cube, it is useful to see the logical cube structure of your data. The benefit to seeing the logical structure is that it reveals more about the representation, transformation, and viewing of data than any physical structure.

Although one can talk about designing cube structures without mentioning variables and although OLAP tools let you create dimension structures and connect them to form cubes absent of any information about the variables, since the purpose of the dimensions (or types used as locators) is to individuate the values of the variables, you need to think about the variables in order to properly identify the dimensions. Variables (or types used as contents) are what get represented, stored, accessed, manipulated, and otherwise vary according to some set of dimensions. The way to proceed is to identify the variables or types of things tracked, measured, or otherwise calculated, and group them according to the locator dimensions by which they vary.

For example, while keeping things to single domain models, with a sales application, the variables might include sales, costs, and units sold, while the dimensions might be time, market, and product. With a financial application, the variables might include account balance and credit rating, while the dimensions might be account number, branch number, account type, and time. With a budget planning application, the variables might include projected revenues, head count, overhead, and allocated expenses, while the dimensions might be organizational unit, time, and scenario. If you are talking to users, they should be able to tell you what the basic contents are and how they vary.

If you are looking at data sources in a table form consisting of key columns and attribute columns, look for the nonkey attributes as indicative of the variables and look for the keys as indicative of the dimensions. If all the data seems to be in one column, which would likely be called a *data* or *value column*, then look for one of the columns (generally immediately to the left of the value column) to be a variables dimension consisting of names of variables.[4]

If your starting point includes base tables, you can pull some, if not all, the basic dimensions from the base tables using links. (Recall from Chapter 8 that there may be dimensional information that is table wide and thus not captured in any table.) For example, if you are given a table with stores, time, product, sales, and costs, you would most likely define stores, times, and products as dimensions, and define sales and costs as members of a variables dimension. The only differences between the types of tools are whether you define stores, time, and products as dimensions in an OLAP system or as lookup table dimensions with an SQL database, and whether costs and sales are members of a variables dimension or are treated as individual variables to be dimensioned by stores, time, and product. Either way, they mean the same thing. Some OLAP products even build the cube for you once you have the source data in table form. That table form may vary between vendors, but will generally be either type zero or type one.

Sometimes a base table holds the leaf-level data and some other tables hold hierarchy information so the source tables get connected to the leaf level of the dimensions as defined in the hierarchy tables.

If there are multiple tables, look at them and ask yourself whether the facts in each table belong with each other. Is there some key, like time, place, or scenario, that is implicit in one table but explicit in the other? Are the key columns between the tables related to each other in a way that it would make sense to have them combined into a single cube? Does one table deal with the Northwest while another table describes the

South? If there are multiple tables and you cannot figure out how to merge their key structures, and the data between the two tables cannot be brought into a common set of dimensions, chances are the tables should be modeled as separate cubes. To be sure, you should perform the density test that was introduced in Chapter 5.

If your source data is in spreadsheets, think about how the dimensions are expressed in the spreadsheets. Are there pages or worksheets, or distinct areas within a worksheet? The values that identify each page, sheet, or file may form a dimension. For example, each page may represent a separate store. Spreadsheets need not be so regular, however. A single worksheet may contain multiple axes, levels of granularity, and even cubes worth of data. See the PDF appendix "Building an OLAP Solution from Spreadsheets" on the companion Web site.

Building an OLAP solution is like building a bridge connecting two sides of a gorge. One side has user requirements in the form of use cubes; the other side has data sources in the form of source cubes. The model is the bridge connecting the two sides. When working on what is clearly a multicube model where there may be multiple source cubes, multiple intermediate cubes, and multiple end-user cubes, I nearly always start with one of two endpoints: sources or uses. It reduces the chance for error.

Recall from Chapter 6 that when there are multiple cubes, those cubes need to be joined along identically structured common dimensions for any kind of cross-cube analysis. Sometimes, especially if the OLAP work follows a datawarehousing program, the common dimensions used for joining different cubes will be or have been identically structured, in which case they are typically called *conformed*. But what do you do when those common dimensions are not identically structured?

I prefer to model all variables that share the same dimensions—even when they do not share the same cells—as a part of the same cube. This kind of logical reduction reduces the number of cubes in my model. (Some multicube models that employ five or ten physical cubes can be logically represented as one or two cubes. In these cases, the physical cubes come closer to representing physical partitions than information content differences.) Assuming one can create derivations of the different variables that map them to the same locations within the cube, it highlights the fact that data residing in the same cube can be meaningfully compared. (This is why the schemas shown throughout the application section of this book are written in a staggered fashion with contents that vary in a subset of the schemas' total set of dimensions—but are applicable to all the dimensions—shown indented and below those contents that vary in all the dimensions.)

For example, consider modeling a data set consisting of international sales data and macroeconomic information. Imagine that the sales data is collected at the store level every week, while the macroeconomic information is collected at the national level every month. Depending on the multidimensional tool you were using, you may wind up creating a different cube for each data set. But logically speaking, when designing a model, I would always find it simpler to define them as a part of the same cube. Furthermore, being in the same cube, it is easy to see how I can compare the sales data with the macroeconomic data by aggregating my store and week level sales data to the country by month level and then meaningfully compare changes in national level sales with changes in macroeconomic indicators.

Although data may belong in the same logical cube, performance considerations such as refresh requirements, cube-necessitated network transfers, or data set sizes, combined with the fact that a memory-based tool may force you to load an entire model into memory, may dictate keeping the data in separate physical cubes.

You also need to be aware of what are called *attributes*. Recall from Chapters 5 and 7 that an attribute is just a content that varies mostly—but not entirely—as a function of the members of one dimension. They are usually found in lookup tables associated with, or as a part of, dimension tables. Most applications make heavy use of attributes. OLAP tools differ significantly in their support for attributes. (See the guideline questions in Chapter 18.) In a retail model where stores, time, product, and variables are dimensions, there will be many facts about the members of each of the dimensions. With stores, for example, the facts might include square footage, rent, address, manager names, phone number, and so on. Logically speaking, these variables or facts belong at the all-product-by-store-by-sometime level of the cube. They belong at the store level because facts like address vary from store to store. They belong at the all-product level because the address of a store is independent of the products carried by the store, but they belong at the sometime or not-totally-specified time level because the facts can change over time. Addresses change, managers change, rents change, and square footage can change, and you may want to keep a history of the values.

Depending on how tightly integrated your OLAP solution is to a backend data warehouse, you may simply leverage the warehouse attribute tables, you may want to create separate attribute cubes, you may load the attributes as constants (but be prepared to convert them to yearly or quarterly variables as they change), or if tracking the changes are important, you may want to maintain them in a time-stamped attribute table.

The thing to keep in mind is that given a set of dimensions cross-joined in a schema, contents may and frequently do vary by any combination of the dimensions (as with fourth normal form relations and what are called *M to N relations* in the datawarehousing world (see Chapter 16). So make sure you are open to seeing contents vary by any combination of dimensions. If, after that, you see that there are large numbers of contents that, for the purposes of the model you are building, effectively only vary in one dimension, and you like the term attribute, then by all means use it.

At the end of this step, you should be able to identify all the cubes that define the model and all the dimensions that make up each cube. Figure 11.6 illustrates what a cube structure may look like. Notice, this is a high-level logical view of a model. It shows the number of variables, the number of locator dimensions, and the approximate number of members in each dimension. It does not show any information about the number of levels per dimension or any information about data flows. Figure 11.7 shows the same high-level information for a multicube model.

Before moving onto the next step, you should also create a dynamic image of the proposed solution. In addition to knowing the cube-defining collections of dimensions and variables, you also need to have an understanding of the data flows between the cubes and a rough idea of the amount of data each cube represents. Figure 11.8 shows the same kind of high-level information displayed in Figure 11.7, plus information about flows, sparsity, and data set sizes. The view in Figure 11.8 shows that exchange rate information from the exchange cube is used to calculate derived values in the pur-

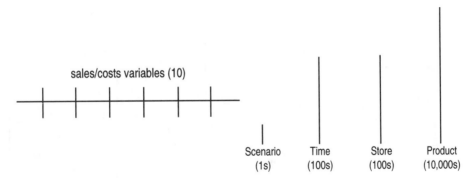

Figure 11.6   A high-level view of your model.

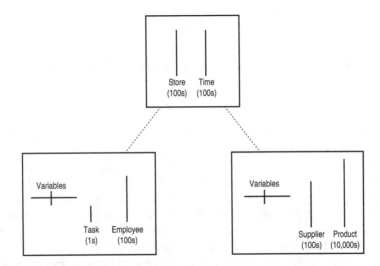

Figure 11.7   A high-level MTS view of a multicube.

chases cube (presumably converting input local prices to derived dollar prices) and that information from the recipe cube is used to determine how much inventory is required to meet given amounts of production. The figure shows purchases flow into inventory, which flow into production, and that the amount of data held in the exchange and recipe cubes is smaller than for the other three.

Refining the Number of Dimensions

Whether you defined your cubes based on existing data sources or whether you defined them based on what you think you want to model, you should spend some time reviewing the dimensional choices you made before proceeding to solidify them

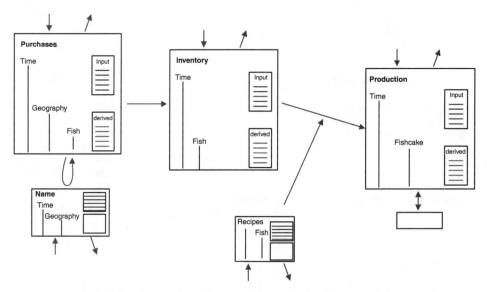

Figure 11.8 A high-level MTS view of a multicube with data flows and data set sizes.

with hierarchies and members. The main way you modify the dimensional structure of a cube is by adding and subtracting dimensions.

If one or more cubes are very sparse and the dimensional combinations that produce the sparsity are nominal, and if the tool you are working with does not provide automatic support for sparsity management, you may want to combine two or more dimensions whose intersections are not everywhere meaningful into a single dimension composed exclusively of valid intersections and a higher cardinality than either of the two original dimensions. The benefit of combining dimensions is to eliminate meaningless values and lower the growth of derived data in the cube. The main downside of combining dimensions is the loss of efficiency when dealing with changes that occur in a single dimension (such as needing to make multiple formula entries in a dimension where one entry would have sufficed if the dimensions would have been broken out).

The two main reasons for adding dimensions are

- To take into account some factor that was previously unaccounted for, such as time or place

- To represent co-factors present in a single list of elements with separate dimensions that can vary independently of one another

As for unaccounted-for information, your source data may come from multiple tables where each table represents a different time or place. In such cases, the time or place of the data may be implicit to the data and thus not explicitly included in any fields associated with the table (other than, perhaps, the table name). There is no real downside to taking this information into account. If you didn't, you would not be able to put it into a single cube.

Regarding co-factors, you might have a table whose attribute columns are labeled *actual direct sales, actual indirect sales, actual salaries, actual material costs, actual other costs, planned direct sales, planned indirect sales, planned salaries, planned material costs,* and *planned other costs.* All your sales and cost information is either actual, planned, or a calculated variance. Every actual and planned value is for a sales value or a cost value. Sales and costs, which can be thought of as members of an accounts dimension, are thus co-factors along with actuals and plans, which can be thought of as members of a scenario dimension. By representing this information in terms of the two dimensions accounts and scenario, it is easier to define formulaic relationships that pertain to accounts or scenarios and it is easier to visually represent accounts and scenarios along separate axes on a display screen. If the number of original members is very large, say, one million, and if the number of members in each of the two created dimensions is roughly equivalent, then the number of members in each of the two new dimensions will be approximately equal to the square root of the number of original dimension members. In other words, one dimension with 1,000,000 members could be represented by two dimensions with 1,000 members per dimension.

When Dimensions Change over Time

There is a Buddhist saying that the only thing constant is change. The real question for each dimension is, What is the rate of change? At one extreme, some dimensions may not change during their lifetime in a single model, especially if that model is a single server-based application of short duration. But for models that evolve with the users, change in at least one dimension is certain. The most dramatic changes usually occur with product dimensions, organization dimensions, employee dimensions, and marketing geography dimensions. For example, products are added and subtracted, product lines are reorganized, employees come and go, and corporations change their reporting hierarchies.

There is no one right way to model these changes. You can keep multiple copies of dimensions and build separate cubes for each dimensional version. You can keep a single dimension in a single cube that represents the union of each dimension version. You can also keep explicit dimension versions in a single cube. The second and third options require direct support from a product. The first you could implement with most any product.

The datawarehousing world has long dealt with changing dimensions. Ralph Kimball wrote about various methods for tracking these changes.[5] An OLAP application that works with changing dimensions whose definition resides in external tables, typically data-warehouse-based, needs to refresh its dimension structures from those tables. However, you still need to decide how the OLAP application is going to handle comparisons that involve the dimensions in two or more states.

For example, if the changing dimension in question is a product dimension and you want to perform any kind of time-based analysis, you need to decide how to deal with the fact that some products that existed for the early time periods were discontinued and some products that didn't exist during the early time periods were subsequently introduced.

Clearly, there will be some kinds of questions that are meaningless given the changing dimension. For example, any query for a growth rate in sales over the time period in question for a product that did not exist for the entire time period will be meaningless. (It violates the application range of the sales variable.) Although queries about specific products may be meaningless, a way to make use of the sales information about all the products that did not exist for the full length of time is to abstract the individual products that do not exist for the full time range into groups that do, and then perform inter-temporal comparisons on the groups. Thus, for example, while specific women's shoes may have been introduced and discontinued over time, the category women's shoes remained stable. Queries about the growth rate of women's shoes are perfectly mean-ingful even though the specific shoes that comprise the category have changed.

Links

Assuming that you can identify the source data, that the source data corresponds to the leaf level of the model, and that there are no references to higher levels of aggregation in the source tables, it is useful to give the links from the cube to the data source a trial run at this stage.

> **NOTE** If your source tables have aggregation levels defined in them or if some of the source data represents aggregate information, you will need to have defined these levels in the cube prior to linking, or you will need to use a tool capable of defining levels through the linking process.

The good thing about bringing in some or all of the data at this stage is that it gives you the ability to test the dimensionality of the model you have created before you have defined a lot of other structures that might all have to be revised in the event that the dimensionality of the model needs to be changed. Since the data is there, it also lets you define and test variable formulas. With most of the hierarchies not yet present, there should be no danger of a time- and storage-consuming database explosion com-plicating the picture.

The more you are sure of the hierarchies that need to be created in each dimension as well as of the dimensions themselves, the less difference it makes whether you define the links and bring in data before or after defining the hierarchies.

Dimension Hierarchies

As you saw in Chapter 5, dimensions may, but do not necessarily, have a hierarchical structure. For example, products, time, and place usually have hierarchical structures. Scenario typically does not have a hierarchical structure. The question remains: What kind of hierarchical structure do the dimensions have? Again, as you saw in Chapter 5, most hierarchies have more of a ragged or leveled nature. Most tools have either a ragged or leveled bias.

If you are working from hierarchical source tables, the types of dimension hierar-chies may already be given to you. If you are working from data tables and there are levels in the tables, they will be found as the names of columns in the base data tables or in lookup or dimension tables associated with the base tables. Any levels that were used in the situation as you found it have to be accounted for somewhere in the system. It also may be the case that users want you to implement levels that were not a part of their base data. If this is so, you need to learn the parent/child relationships that define each level. For an initial pass, it will suffice to know the dimension to which a level applies and its relative hierarchical position. In other words, region as a geographical level may be defined as in between cities and states. If your source tables are ragged, look for specific parent-child tables to use to define the dimension hierarchy.

If you know that hierarchies need to exist in the OLAP model that do not exist in the source tables, ask yourself what those hierarchies are based on. Frequently, they are based on attribute groupings such as price, color, size, or weight for a product dimension. They may also be based on business requirements not yet electronically encoded as, for example, with a marketing analyst's new way of grouping competitors or channels.

At the end of this second stage, you will still have a high-level logical model, but it will contain more detail relative to the end of the first stage. Think of the process as similar to increasing the magnification on a microscope that is focused on an onion skin. Starting from a relatively high level where many cells are in view, as the magnification is increased, at first everything blurs, but then a new, more detailed view of the interior of a cell comes into focus. There are fixed levels of detail at which interesting structures appear. The same is true with a dimensional model.

Multiple Hierarchies

When the instances of a dimension need to be aggregated by different groupings, you need to create multiple hierarchies. Most tools allow for multiple aggregation paths. The grouping principle for each path should be identified and the hierarchies named. (Even in a dimension with a single hierarchy, the principle should be identified.) For example, products may be grouped by generalizations of product type, by classifications of size or color, by demographic groups they are targeted to, and so forth.[6] Attributes associated with the members will provide clues to useful hierarchies. Tools vary substantially in their support for multiple hierarchies.

Since tools may support different types of hierarchy structures depending on the type of dimension, identifying the aggregation paths needed will help to form the strategy later on for expressing the structure and computations. Some tools require the designation of one of the hierarchy paths as the consolidation path; other paths can exist to organize members, but do not play the same role in computing aggregations.

When forming the hierarchies, depending on a tool's structuring capabilities, you may need to decide whether to create multiple root members to define the hierarchies. For example, you may consider the typical grouping of products by levels of generalization of product type to be the primary aggregation path of interest, and may be interested in aggregating up to an all-product member. In the same dimension, you could have other aggregation paths that group products by the demographic group for which they are designed by pricing or size categories, for example. If all leaf members feed into the product-by-price-category path, then an all-product-by-price-category member will generate an aggregation redundant with the all-product-by-type member's. However, the highest-level by-price-category members will appear in the model to each be a separate path, practically indistinct from the highest-level by-size-category path members as well.

Deciding between Multiple Levels in a Dimension and Multiple Dimensions

Imagine a data table whose columns consisted of products, stores, and product groups. Clearly, you would keep products and stores as separate dimensions. But would you do the same with product groups? What would make you decide? Generally, you want to examine the cardinality relationship between the members of the columns, in this case, product groups and products. The more that relationship is M to N, the more it makes sense to treat product groups as a separate dimension. In contrast, the more their relationship is 1 to N, the more it makes more sense to treat product groups as a separate level of the products dimension.

Cardinality relationships, like dimensionality, are sometimes in the eye of the beholder. Look at the following data set, shown in Table 11.1, for an imaginary company that produces six products belonging to three categories.

At first, it may seem that a 1-N relationship exists between product categories and products, specifically that there are two products for every one product category, and thus that product categories belong as a level within an overall product dimension. But notice that there is the same number of products within each product category. *Instead of thinking of each product as an individual with a unique name, you could think of each product as a relatively numbered member of a product category.* This is shown in Table 11.2.

Table 11.1 Products and Product Categories

PRODUCT	PRODUCT CATEGORY
Triglets	Foobars
Spiglets	Foobars
Derbots	Doobars
Berbots	Doobars
Crumpets	Goobars
Flumpets	Goobars

Table 11.2 Relative Numbering of Products

PRODUCT	PRODUCT CATEGORY
1	Foobars
2	Foobars
1	Doobars
2	Doobars
1	Goobars
2	Goobars

Table 11.3   Products and Categories as Separate Dimensions

		CATEGORY		
		FOOBARS	**DOOBARS**	**GOOBARS**
PRODUCT	1			
	2			

By re-representing the products as relatively numbered within each category, we have converted a 1-*N* relationship between product categories and products into an *M-N* relationship. As an *M-N* relationship, products and product categories could be represented as two separate dimensions (see Table 11.3).

The thing to watch out for is whether the lower-level members—in this case, individual products—can be beneficially represented as relatively enumerated items within a higher-level grouping. To answer yes, there should be some similarity between products that have the same relative enumeration per category. Perhaps products are organized within each category by price or margin, so that it makes sense to talk about products 1 or 2 in general. Also, if adding a product 3 at a later time would mean adding a product 3 to each product category, then products and categories make better candidates for separate dimensions.

One of the potential benefits (assuming you answered yes to the previous question) of splitting up levels into separate dimensions is the ability to represent them on separate axes of a display screen. In other words, most OLAP tools are not able to display two levels of one model dimension in two dimensions on a computer screen. You also need to ensure that there are roughly the same number of relatively enumerated items in each higher-level grouping; otherwise, you will generate a lot of meaningless intersections. Time is an example of a dimension whose levels are frequently represented as separate dimensions, especially weeks and months where weeks are cast as the first, second, third, and fourth week of the month.

Disconnected Hierarchies

So far, the dimensions we have looked at in this book have either been loose collections of elements, such as those found in a variables dimension, or they have been composed of one or more hierarchies. The implicit assumption with hierarchical dimensions that contain multiple hierarchies is that the hierarchies are connected through at least some of the members. You should be aware that this need not be the case. *A single product dimension with a hierarchical structure sometimes splits into two or more disconnected hierarchies.* This could be the result of a product reorganization where, for some period of time, a new product division did not feed into the main product root. It could also be the result of a mistake; perhaps an intermediate product category was inadvertently deleted. In either event, a situation would be produced where the root member of the dimension did not connect to all the leaf nodes in the dimension. This may not be apparent with large dimensions. So when you are working with large dimensions, you need to verify that either all the leaf members do indeed connect to the root member or that the dimension contains an intentionally disconnected hierarchy.

When a Dependent Member Is a Parent versus a Peer

How should you represent a dependent member, such as a total cost that depends on a variety of particular costs? Should you represent it as a parent of the individual costs or as a sibling to the individual costs? Does it make any difference? Most of the time with dimensions like time, products, geography, and employees, you define levels within a dimension and portray dependent members as relative parents within a hierarchy. The biggest single reason why it is worth the effort to define hierarchies is because they funnel the masses of individual members into the higher-level categories that we think about for decision making. In a product dimension with 30,000 individual products, 100 product categories, and 10 brands, it is easier and more natural to think about and define rules for the 100 product categories and 10 brands that are the basis for most of our decision making than to think about and define rules that explicitly consider the 30,000 individual products.

When there are not too many members in the dimension, you will have more flexibility if you represent them. This commonly occurs in variables and scenario dimensions. For example, some OLAP products make it difficult to have data enter at a nonleaf level. If you have some data that is not normally provided at the most detailed level or you need to enter estimates by hand for some of the dependent members for which you do not yet have data, it would be easier if the member was a leaf-member rather than a nonleaf member. Also, it may be easier to compute members without needing to override built-in aggregation formulas if the members are all peers.

Figure 11.9 shows a simple variables dimension in two forms. Figure 11.9a shows all the members as peers and Figure 11.9b shows the dependent members as parents.

a. All members as peers

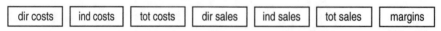

Easier when: more irregular edits, more complicated formulas, fewer of them.

b. Dependent members as parents

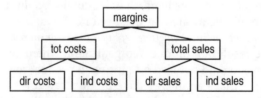

Easier when: more regular edits, simpler formulas, more of them.

Figure 11.9 Showing dependents as parents or as peers.

Dimension Members

If you want to think of a dividing line between higher- and lower-level multidimensional models, a good place to imagine that line is at the boundary between hierarchies and individual members. In a dimension like products or customers, there may be five or ten levels or generations, while there may be thousands or even millions of base-level members. A diagram of all 2,000,000 customers serves no practical purpose, certainly not as an abstraction. There are too many members. A useful model needs to be a scaled-down version of the real thing, not a replica.

It may be useful to list a representative sample of the members of a dimension to make sure that there is no confusion, or it may be useful to define a test model with a sample list of members. But when it comes to working with all the members in a dimension with many members, the best you can do is assure yourself that the member list is sufficiently clean. If it is a customer list, for example, you want to be confident that the same customers are not listed multiple times. As discussed in Chapter 1, data (or in this case what some would call meta data) cleansing is a part of the warehousing process. To reiterate, the techniques presented in this book on multidimensional systems assume that the base data exists and is of good quality.

In a typical large model, no more than one or two dimensions have such high cardinality. This means that most cubes have one or more low-cardinality dimensions. Scenario and market dimensions are generally of low enough cardinality that it is useful to enumerate all of their members. For example, there may only be ten markets into which a particular group of products is sold or there may only be four scenarios for the purposes of budgeting.

In addition to distinguishing between low- and high-cardinality dimensions, it is useful to keep the variables dimension separate from all the others—assuming you are using a tool that purports to treat all dimensions generically and keeps the names of contents or variables in a variables (or more properly variables name) dimension. Remember, the members of the variables dimension, whether there are 5 or 500, will have most of the nonsummation formulas in the cube. They are, after all, the things whose values you are tracking in the model. Even if there are 500, as with a large chart of accounts, whoever is using that information will need to be aware of each of the 500 accounts. Variables usually need to be dealt with on an individual basis.

Looking over the base tables, there are two basic ways (as shown in Chapter 8) that the dimension member information can be represented: embedded within data tables, in which case the dimensional information will be represented by column headings in a level-based way, or free standing in parent-child tables.

The cells defined by the intersections of dimension members times the number of variables per cell will be at least as numerous as the number of base data points to enter the system. In cases where the source data represents transactions such as actual products sold, the number of data points brought in to a model may only be a small percentage of the total number of cells in the model. The cube in this situation would be called sparse.

Relationships between Members

For each of the dimensions in the cube you are designing, how do the members relate to each other? Assume you are working with a stores dimension. What is the relationship between stores? Are they simply enumerated members in a list, or is there some additional information that serves to differentiate them? The reason you would want to capture this information is for the purpose of pattern searches, extrapolations, and other analyses. (Recall the distinctions made in Chapter 5 between nominal, ordinal, and cardinal orderings and the analysis distinctions in Appendix D for Chapter 11.) For example, if you know how your sales have changed by month for the past three years, you could make a projection for the next month based on past experience. This is because time intervals are cardinally ordered. You can define a formula that says

```
sales , time_{x+1} = (sales , time_x)+ (projected change in sales , time_x)
```

You could not define such a formula for a dimension where the members were just nominally ordered elements of a list. Nor could you explore correlations between variables unless your identifier dimensions were cardinally ordered.

Changing Names of Members

Sometimes dimension members have coded names, like SKU codes, in the source tables that end-users do not want to be forced to work with. You should verify for all the dimensions whether the member names need to be given aliases for the benefit of end-users. If you feel it is necessary, you should make sure that aliases are supported by whatever OLAP tool you invest in and check to see what the impact is of changing names on your existing model structures. For example, with some products, you would need to manually change all formulas that depend on members whose names have changed. In such cases, you want to define your aliases as early in the model design process as possible.

The Decision Context

The previous steps have led to a dimensional structure for your data. The task of defining formulas remains. Before launching into them, you may want to step back for a minute and ask yourself, perhaps more thoroughly than you have before, the following questions: What is the purpose of the model you are building? What kinds of formulas are you defining to achieve that purpose? Are you trying to construct a picture of what is going on in your company or organization? Are you trying to analyze certain events such as the decrease in market share of your product in order to discover what may have been the cause? Are you trying to predict how sales, costs, and margins are going to evolve over the next twelve months? Are you, perhaps, trying to come up with policy recommendations?

Recall the discussion in Chapter 1 of the four stages of decision functions: descriptive, explanatory, predictive, and prescriptive. Although OLAP tools were seen to focus on derived descriptions, your application needs may require additional decision functions. Assuming a single domain model, you would build all decision functions within a single cube. The movement from descriptive formulas to prescriptive formulas represents a series of incremental increases in analytical complexity within the same cube. Prescriptive formulas rely on inferential or predictive formulas that rely on explanatory formulas that rely on descriptive formulas. There is no way to build a predictive formula that does not contain, implicitly or explicitly, an explanatory formula and a descriptive formula. All formulas may share the same cube-defined dimensional structure. Of course, if you are working with a multidomain model, there may be many cubes in general, and your decision functions may be spread across all of them.

Formulas

A major factor that affects the analyses you will need to create is whether you are the end-user or whether you are defining a system for end-users to perform their own analyses. If you are preparing a system to be used by others, your goal should be to create an environment that facilitates analysis. If you are the end-user, you will still want to perform your ad hoc analysis on top of more basic, preparatory analysis. Either way, you need to perform basic aggregations and analysis.

A key component of multidimensional modeling is the definition of formulas or derivations, especially aggregation formulas. A formula can be as simple as the sum of two numbers of a single variable organized according to a single dimension or as complex as a multicube system of chained, conditionally weighted equations. For most applications, the majority of formulas are basic sums and averages. Figure 11.10 shows an MTS view of simple aggregation formulas across three hierarchical dimensions for data entering at the leaf level.

There is no a priori calculation order for models. As you saw in Chapter 7, you need to know what you are trying to calculate in order to determine precedence order on a formula-by-formula basis. Thus, although you will typically perform aggregations before other types of calculations, and they are presented first in the text that follows, there are so many exceptions to this ordering. I wouldn't even call it a rule of thumb. Be careful, however, if you know that you need to perform leaf-level derivations prior to aggregating. Not all products support leaf-level calculations.

Aggregation Formulas

When creating a logical model, you need to identify all the dimensions that are principally used for aggregation. With the exception of scenarios (and variables if using a

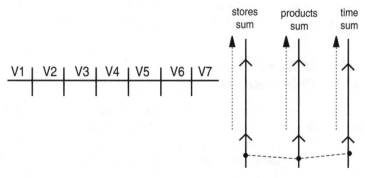

Figure 11.10   Showing aggregation dimension formulas in the MTS.

variables dimension), most dimensions, such as products, customers, time, geography, and departments, are hierarchical and responsible for generating simple aggregations. A typical aggregation definition that you might find or have occasion to define in an OLAP tool for the dimension products might state that all products sum into their parents. Recalling that derivation is an attribute of data and not of members, you should realize that this actually means that all data (in the absence of overriding formulas) sums across products.

Since OLAP models can become quite complex, I recommend incrementally verifying them (and if need be, debugging them). Toward that end, I suggest that you test out the basic aggregation functions before putting in the fancier stuff. A good way to do this is to compute aggregates along dimensions for which the aggregation function is a pure and simple function, like sum, for variables (that is, members of the variables dimension) that have no attached formula.

Basic Variables and Other Nonaggregation Formulas

Once you have assured yourself that the basic aggregation functions are working, it is time to add any further formulas that are a part of the core model. The core model in this sense means any data that

- Most users will want to look at
- Is most frequently queried
- Is a part of your first deliverable
- Might feed further analysis

Typically, such formulas are found in the variables (dimension) as ratios, products, and differences. They can also occur in the time dimension where it is not unusual to see interperiod ratios.

Unless your formulas are complex within single dimensions, you may not want to test them on a dimension-by-dimension basis except for verifying that the syntax is correct and that they say what you think they are supposed to say. Of course, it is possible to run aground anywhere, but it is more likely that if problems are going to arise, they will arise when formulas in one dimension intersect with formulas in another dimension (as discussed in the section on formula precedence in Chapter 7).

Functions Attached to Dimensions versus Functions in Rules/Scripts

The decision to attach functions to the members of a dimension as opposed to in a separate calculation rule or script is related to the product that you use, but exists for all products. If the computation you want to express is summation, then the choice is likely arbitrary since all products support summation in the hierarchies and could be driven by performance considerations. If the computation is a ratio or involves several terms with different operators, it may not be possible to express this in the dimension structure as opposed to a script.

Qualified Referencing of Data

As you are writing formulas, be aware of all the hierarchically qualified references. For example, the formula Margin = Sales − Cost in a two-dimensional cube whose other dimension is geographical involves nonhierarchical references. At the store level, store margins are calculated in terms of store sales and costs; at the city level, they use city sales and costs. You should also keep in mind when you are making relative hierarchical references—as is the case with the term parent—and when you are making absolute hierarchical references—as is the case with any named level such as cities or brands.

Consider the formula Contribution = Sales/ (Sales, Geog.parent). At the store level, in a hierarchy where cities follow stores, this formula calculates the ratio of one store's sales to all the sales made in the city. Conceptually, it is straightforward, but unless you've been writing OLAP applications before, it is easy to introduce a mistake. There may be cases in an asymmetric hierarchy where stores connect to cities in some places, but to states or regions in others. If what you want to calculate at the store level is the contribution of the store to the city, then you will get the wrong answer for stores that connect directly to states. (The correct answer would be the number one as opposed to the fraction of state or regional sales accounted for by the store.) In such a case, you would want to either add a city node to your geography hierarchy or define a conditional formula for contribution.

Calculation Precedence

Recall from Chapter 7 that the need to decide calculation precedence arises whenever the formulas that originated in different dimensions produce different results as a function of the order in which they are applied. The common case is a summation formula in one dimension intersecting with a ratio formula in another dimension. The sum of a set of ratios is not equal to the ratio of a set of sums. It is easy to make mistakes here. On the positive side, when mistakes are made, numbers are usually thrown off by a large factor and are therefore easy to spot as erroneous when performing a manual check. You should initially look for incorrect results in a trial calculation by reviewing aggregates whose values you can associate with a particular range. For example, an average employee age may need to fit between 18 and 65. A value of 2,500 would signal an aggregation error. The most common error is due to incorrect precedence. Frequently, a variable that needed to be averaged got summed.

As described in Chapter 7, there are many operational combinations such as summing and dividing where the operational precedence makes a difference. Unlike the testing of simple aggregations where the aggregation function is given by the formula attached to the aggregation dimension, the aggregation function needs to be determined in cases where operational precedence is an issue. I suggest working through the calculation of a small number of cells when there is doubt.

Formula Complexities

Unlike formula precedence issues that can arise in an otherwise exceptionless cube, formula complexities generally arise from the existence of known exceptions to the regularity defined by a cube. For example, the market value of a stock means something different for a private portfolio (where it is a function of the number of shares held in the stock multiplied by the price per share) than for an industry basket such as the Dow Jones Industrial Average or the S&P 500 (where it is a function of the number of shares issued and outstanding of the stock multiplied by the price per share). Certain managers may need to be alerted if a flow indicator drops below a certain level. The price charged to a customer might be a function of the cumulative sales to that customer. In cases of missing values for some variables and not others, tests for existence may be required to combine them or aggregate correctly. A pool of bonus funds may only be available if actual sales exceed plans by a certain amount. Some members of a particular dimension, such as the shirt member of a product dimension, may have values for attributes, such as color, that do not apply to other members of that dimension, such as wrenches.

As you saw in Chapter 7, there are many types of formula complexities, and errors here will usually be more subtle than with incorrect precedence so you should manually verify, at least for a few cases, that any formula complexities are working properly.

Deciding When and Where to Compute

This topic was discussed in Chapter 10 and it is one of the areas where there is a large divergence between types of tools. Tools that work with SQL databases, for example, generally handle issues of pre-aggregation differently from MDDB tools. You may need to create tables of aggregates in SQL and then connect the aggregate tables to the associated OLAP tool. Several tools provide aggregation materialization assistance. Most OLAP tools—with the exception of those tools that operate entirely on dynamically calculated results—provide an option that lets you define certain aggregations to be performed at request time.

Whatever tool you use, you will want to give some thought as to which aggregates need to be precalculated and which do not.

More Complex Aggregations and Analysis

As stated at the beginning of this chapter, there are many different ways you can sequentially proceed with the design and implementation of an OLAP model. Depending on your situation, you may or may not need to think through more complex issues. On average, however, you will most likely have to first work through all the issues of basic aggregation. The issues placed in this section were the ones that I felt arise for some of the people some of the time. This section does not discuss analytical techniques such as how to create a decision tree, perform a cluster analysis, or define a constrained optimization. Rather, it focuses on issues of derived descriptions that appear in multidimensional environments and can hinder the analytical process.

Nonleaf Input Data

Data does not always enter a cube at the leaf or base level. In Chapter 7, we looked at some examples of cost allocations running down the same product hierarchy for which sales information was aggregated. The cost data entered the cube at the top of the hierarchy (in the form of total allocatable costs) and was allocated downwards. Remember that the attributes input and derived are a function of data and not dimension members.

From a practical perspective, you need to be able to spot data that does not enter the cube at the base level, and you need to know when formulas rely on input data that come from a nonleaf level, especially when leaf-level data exist.

One reason for being aware of data that need to enter at a nonleaf level is that not all products are equally graceful at accepting nonleaf level input data. As discussed earlier in this chapter, there are many occasions where data that all share the same dimensional structure do not all share the same aggregation levels. Recall the example of a sales cube where sales data were entered at the store level and where macroeconomic information was entered at the national level. Assuming your product can handle nonleaf level inputs, there shouldn't be any problem here so long as the data only enters at the nonleaf level.

Things get trickier when data for the same variable enter at both a leaf and nonleaf level. Think about a sales model where sales data normally enters a cube at the store level and aggregates upwards. Now imagine that the VP of sales needs to make a presentation that includes current figures for all regional sales and their aggregates, but that all of the relevant store level data has not yet entered the system. The easiest solution is for each regional sales manager to manually enter a best guess for the regional sales totals and then aggregate those regional sales guesstimates to the national level. To do this properly, an multidimensional system would need to be able to aggregate sales from the regional level only where the estimates were placed; if the system took the base-level data it had and ignored the estimates, it would get incorrect results.

You may also need to suppress the aggregation of base-level sales data until all stores have reported their sales. Again, you need to be sure that it is important to you that the tools you use offer this option.

When formulas need to access data from multiple levels within the cube, I find it useful to write formulas, if only for my own mental model, that include the aggregation level of the inputs to the formula. For the previous example, I would write the following formula:

```
Sales , Geography.countries. = Sum (Sales , Geography.regions.)
```

Nominal versus Ordinal versus Cardinal Analysis

In a cube with a store, time, product, and sales variables dimension, you could compare sales across any combination of stores, products, and time. In this sense (and as we saw in Chapter 7), the analysis of variables takes place relative to the cube's dimensional structure. The question remains: What about more sophisticated analyses?

Your ability to perform more sophisticated analyses, such as correlations, regressions, clusterings, and projections, is limited by the quantitative structure of your dimensions and your data. (Please see Chapter 20 for a discussion of dimensional analysis.) In other words are your data and dimensions nominal, ordinal, or cardinal? Typically, with the exception of a time dimension that generally has a cardinal or quantitative structure, all your dimensions are nominal. This means that there is no quantitative relationship between the members of the dimension. In contrast, and with the exception of ranks and other groupings, all of your numeric data will be cardinal. Since nominally, ordinally, and cardinally ordered data look the same, you need to be careful.

The most important thing is to make sure that you do not try to perform an analysis that requires cardinal dimensions and data, such as a regression, with anything other than cardinal dimensions and data. For example, you would not want to run a regression of sales against costs along a typical nominally structured product dimension. You would get a result, but it would be meaningless.

Sparsity

Most multidimensional models contain some sparsity. Sparsity was treated in Chapter 6. When designing and implementing an OLAP system, you need to know the following information:

- How sparse is the data?
- Which dimensional combinations are the sparse ones; which are the dense ones?
- What kind of sparsity exists?

Depending on the tool you are using, you may or may not have to deal with the first and second questions. Some tools automatically figure out the amount of sparsity in the data and adjust the storage accordingly (see Chapter 10). Other tools make you decide whether or not your data is significantly sparse and if so, which dimensional combinations are the most sparse.

You can answer the first question by calculating the number of intersections at the base level of the model (which equals the product of the number of leaf elements in each dimension times) and dividing that into the number of data points at the base level per variable. This will give you the sparsity at the base level of the model on a variable-by-variable basis.

The second question is tougher to answer, and may not have a clean answer. Another way of phrasing it is as follows: What dimensions can you use to partition the cube such that you are left with relatively dense subcubes? The dimensions of the dense subcubes are then called the *dense dimensional combinations* and the dimensions used for partitioning are called the *sparse dimensional combinations*. In any event, it helps to have an understanding of the data in order to address the question.

You can take a stab at the third question by finding the sparse entries, substituting the terms zero, missing, and not applicable, and seeing which one makes the most sense. As with the second question, you may need to know something about the data in order to figure out what the sparsity means. In a retail model, for example, where you might see a sparse intersection at widgets, January, Florida, and sales, you might guess that the sparsity meant the number zero. It probably would. But without a meta data description defining the meaning of sparse intersections, it could have meant anything. It could be that widgets are not sold in Florida or that the data for widgets or Florida is missing or that zero widgets were sold in Florida in January.

Typically, for retail data, sparse intersections refer to zeros. If, however, there is a customer dimension, the sparse intersections will most likely denote not applicable. This is because most customers only do business with a small number of outlets. With financial data, sparse intersections frequently refer to nonapplicable indicators such as change in share price over the last 12 months for a company that has only been public for 6 months. In marketing and transportation models sparsity is also frequently a measure of nonapplicability. There may be certain products that are not sold through certain channels and transportation segment combinations for which no transportation exists. In socioeconomic models, sparse intersections frequently denote missing data.

Make sure you understand any assumptions made by your tool regarding the interpretation of absent cells and zero-valued cells. Products that don't distinguish between zero and meaningless can run into problems when batches of data whose value is zero are loaded into the system as an update or correction to previously loaded data for the same set of cells whose initially loaded value was not zero. (Imagine loading on Friday afternoon corrections to home furnishings product sales entries made Friday morning where, for some home furnishings, sales of $2,000 were incorrectly reported, and the correct value of zero was keyed in later that day.) The product may treat the zero-valued cells as meaningless and ignore them and thus fail to overwrite the initially entered nonzero valued cells.

Here again, if you are not sure of what you are doing, first check to make sure that there is sparsity in the data. Whereas for storage purposes, you can ignore sparsity of less than 30 percent or so, for calculation purposes, even one sparse cell can throw off your calculations. Since some products assume that sparse intersections mean a zero value, you need to verify what they really do mean.

Then after you have defined your aggregation functions, manually verify that the aggregates make sense. Since you need to look at every input number to perform a manual check, you should carve out a small enough slice that you can check each number. Once you have carved out a working slice, check to make sure that if sparse cells are nonapplicable, they were left out of the calculation. This means that they do not enter the denominator in a calculation of averages. In a calculation of sums, you should also do a count of meaningful cells so that the viewer of the aggregate results knows what percentage of the underlying cells went into the aggregate. If working with missing data, check to make sure that proxies were used for the missing values or that the missing values were eliminated from the calculation.

Auditing

The last topic that will be dealt with is the creation of auditable models. When someone is using the model, you want her/him to be able to easily discover for any piece of data whether it is input or derived.

- If it is input, ask the following questions:
  - Where did the data originate?
  - Are there multiple sources?
  - Are there conflicts between sources?
  - How often is the source data refreshed?
  - Who has write authority for that data?
  - Who has read permission?

- If it is a derived data value, ask the following questions:
  - Who defined the formulas?
  - What is the type of formula?
  - What kind of formula complexity is there?
  - What kind of change history for the formula is there?

You will want to know if there are any comments related to any part of the model, such as dimensional structures, hierarchies, aggregation formulas, and so on.

The best thing you can do is keep track of all relevant meta data as you are designing the model, and be aware of the meta data you lack and how you intend to acquire it. Since not all products offer the same support for auditing and annotation, you should check to see whether your product offers audit trails in the form of dependency tracking and, if so, to what level of detail dependencies are tracked. (Dependency tracking is the tracing of inputs to a particular cell and/or outputs from a particular cell.)

Summary

You have by this point defined the logical schema for the multidimensional model that will serve as the basis of your proposed solution. During the course of defining the model, you have figured out, or generated the necessary information to figure out, how many distinct cubes will be required, how much base data there is per cube, how much data will be derived, the sources for the base data, how often the base data will be refreshed, how many calculations will be performed, how many of the calculations will be complex, and how much sparsity is at the base level. You have also prepared to document the formulas and the pedigree of your data as it flows through the model.

## CHAPTER 12

Introduction to the Foodcakes Application Example

Preface to the Second Edition

Those readers who are familiar with the first edition of *OLAP Solutions* may recall that it used actual software against real data sets and took the reader through a keystroke-by-keystroke tutorial in each of the application chapters. In this edition, by contrast, there is no such live tutorial.

Although many readers enjoyed the hands-on tutorials (and I am a firm believer in connecting theory and practice), there are enough major differences in the way Online Analytical Processing (OLAP) products work that it is difficult to teach the fundamentals of OLAP application design (such as dimension, hierarchy, and multidomain formula definitions) while using any one product. I tried in the first edition to encourage the reader to abstract from the specific steps taken in the product used for that book. But without the existence of different OLAP products to use for contrast, the hands-on tutorials, though certainly better than no hands-on experience at all, were closer to a product lesson than a technology lesson. These days, there is an increasing number of after-market OLAP tool-specific books, at least for the more popular products.

In this edition, I have tried to provide the best of both worlds: product-neutral application descriptions (defined in the Located Contents [LC] language), which should hone your application building skills *if you think along with the dialog* (in Chapters 13 through 17) and comparisons of some of the major products and languages commercially available (in Chapter 19).

Towards that end, the next several chapters take you through the major steps and concomitant thought processes of designing an enterprisewide OLAP solution for a vertically integrated international producer of foodcakes. Chapter 17 (the answers to which are on the companion Web site) is one big fully integrated multicubelet calculation example. (Here *cubelets* are multidimensional cubes with all the structural complexity of full cubes, but with just enough dimension members and data points to support a small number of manually performable calculations.) The chapter takes you on a cross-enterprise journey from an activity-based management perspective beginning with product sales and ending with materials purchasing in order to calculate the earnings or losses incurred by a company during the sale of a particular product. In contrast, each of Chapters 13 through 16 represents the working through of the dimension and cube design and the key formula creation for a particular business process (specifically sales and marketing, purchasing, materials inventory, and activity-based management). Each of these chapters begins with basic issues and moves on to more advanced topics. Because the more advanced application material builds on the simpler material that precedes it, I suggest that advanced readers at least skim the early sections of each application chapter, so they have sufficient context to follow at whatever entry point they choose.

Introduction to the Foodcakes International Application

Foodcakes International (FCI) is a privately held, vertically integrated company that produces and sells two lines of foodcakes: fish based and vegetarian. FCI purchases raw materials in over 20 countries, has manufacturing facilities on 3 continents, and has 300 distribution centers in over 75 countries from where it sells its products to over 10,000 stores. Last year, for the first time, FCI's annual revenues topped $500,000,000 (U.S.). The company has a well-known, reputable brand image and good market penetration in most of its operating countries. FCI would like to go public.

However, product quality is inconsistent, the company is slow to adopt to changing markets, and earnings are erratic relative to other packaged food-producing companies of similar size. The company was warned that until they improve the consistency of their operations, the public would be unlikely to support an IPO.

In an effort to improve the company's operating performance consistency prior to going public, FCI initiated a datawarehousing project. All facets of the company were involved in the project. Operational systems from purchasing, materials and product inventory, production, materials and product distribution, human resources, sales and marketing, customer relations, and financial management contributed in an orderly fashion to FCI's data warehouse.

Some of the queries that the data warehouse was intended to support, and the subject area in the warehouse from which the query is answered, are as follows:

Purchasing:

- How much raw material was purchased per time period?
- How much raw material was purchased per market?

Materials inventory:

- How much of some raw material is there in inventory for some date?

- How much raw material arrived in inventory on some date?

- How much of some raw material left inventory during some time period?

Production:

- How much of some binder ingredient was consumed during some time period for some manufacturing plant?

- How much of some fish was consumed producing some kind of fishcake in all plants for some time period?

- How much of some kind of veggie cake was produced in some plant for some time period?

Distribution:

- How long does it take to transport foodcakes between some production facility and some distribution center?

- When did a particular shipment of foodcakes leave inventory?

- How much quality deterioration happens with fish transported from some market to some inventory center?

Sales:

- How many kilos of some foodcake were sold for some time period?

- How many kilos of foodcakes were sold to some group of stores for some time period?

- How much revenue occurred for some foodcakes for some time period?

During the course of the datawarehousing project as FCI analysts and managers continued to share their information requirements with the application developers, it became clear to at least one senior manager, whom we'll call Jane, that many of the important questions that FCI needed to, but could not answer, were multidomain derivations that crossed business processes, time, and space. These questions included "How much does FCI actually earn from the sale of a particular foodcake?" and "What are the major drivers of production cost variance?"

Although the basic query and reporting tools that were a part of the original warehousing project specification provided minimal OLAP functionality in the form of pivot tables and drill-down capabilities, Jane knew they were not capable of providing all the information that FCI decision makers needed. As soon as she realized there were important classes of queries whose support was not anticipated in the initial design (and recognizing that now wasn't the time to voice her concerns), she got together quietly with her senior analysts and did some brainstorming on important decisions that the company needed to make before floating an IPO and on the types of information that would help to improve those decisions. Some of those decisions and associated information requirements are found in the list that follows:

Important, More Regularly Occurring Decisions Include

Decision type   How to distribute fish purchases across markets

- **Information requirements**   Factors influencing the relative cost of fish
- **Sources**   Purchasing, exchange rates, materials distribution , production requirements
- **For example**   Should we temporarily stop buying sole from France?

Decision type   How to reduce inventory waste

- **Information requirements**   Track fish aging and sales by fish
- **Sources**   Purchasing, production, inventory, sales
- **For example**   What fishcakes do we need to increase production of, and which can we sell for the highest margins, so as to use up the most cod?

Decision type   How to improve production employee productivity

- **Information requirements**   Track employee type and production qualitys
- **Sources**   Human resources, mill level production process, production Quality Assurance (QA)
- **For example**   Which employees have the greatest positive impact on veggie cake production costs?

Decision type   How to reduce earnings volatility per foodcake

- **Information requirements**   Sales volume and discounts, distribution costs per fishcake, production costs, inventory costs, purchasing costs, exchange rates, labor and physical asset depreciation
- **Sources**   All subject areas
- **For example**   Which fishcakes should we stop regularly producing because of unacceptably high volatility in earnings?

Important, Less Regularly Occurring Decisions Include

Decision   Where to build the next product distribution center

- **Information requirements**   Product transportation costs, growth trends for stores
- **Sources**   Production, distribution, sales, and marketing
- **For example**   Should we increase the size of our distribution center in Hartford or build a new distribution center, and if so where?

Decision   Where to seek new outlets

- **Information requirements**   Dynamic market characteristics, production and distribution costs

- **Sources**   All subject areas
- **For example**   Should we look to sell to stores in Brazil though we have no distribution center near that part of the world or should we expand our presence in Japan?

Given how clearly Jane and her analysts could see that FCI desperately needed solid multidomain query and analysis capabilities, Jane asked the CEO for permission to engage in a skunk-works project whose goal was to implement a working prototype of a full-fledged, enterprisewide, activity-based-management-style OLAP solution. Once completed, it would be demonstrated to the senior management team. Assuming the prototype is a success, it would then be fully implemented as a part of FCI's overall datawarehousing environment. The CEO was thrilled and gave Jane and her team his full support.

As Jane and her team knew that FCI managers need, above all, to understand the drivers of earnings volatility (whether a function of raw materials chosen, purchasing site, production method, distribution, marketing, or sales), the application developers will need to fully connect all links in the corporate value chain so that top-level questions can be answered on a timely and accurate basis.

With no room for error, Jane contacted FCI's two most senior and respected application developers, Lulu and Thor, and made them equally responsible for designing and implementing the prototype solution. Because Lulu and Thor typically work as senior design architects with sole design responsibility, they are not used to having to work on an equal footing with a colleague. As a result, they frequently took and argued for different approaches during the prototype design process. You, the reader, will learn the most from these application chapters by following along with their dialogue and reasoning through the issues on your own, especially when the text tells you to think about it.

Because the purpose of this section is to illustrate how OLAP technology can be used across the enterprise and to help you think more effectively about modeling both single and multidomain areas (as opposed to working through a detailed treatment of all subject areas as would be necessary if this were a data model resource book), I have tried to maintain a balance between detail and illustration.

Of the nine modules identified as a part of FCI's enterprise schema, which are illustrated in Figure 12.1 (and which are already a simplification over what would exist in reality), I selected four modules for detailed treatment in this section:

- Sales and marketing
- Purchasing and currency exchange
- Inventory throughput and costing
- Activity-based management

Because the activity-based management analysis depends on data derived from all of the other eight modules, I included summary treatments in that chapter for each of the business processes not given a chapter of its own, namely

- FCI's raw materials transport from purchasing sites to materials inventory co-located with production centers

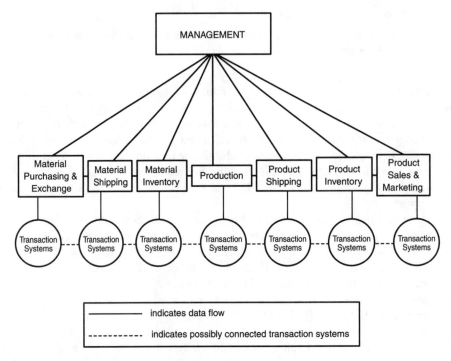

Figure 12.1   FCI's business process relationships.

- FCI's machine-level production
- FCI's product distribution from production center to distribution center
- FCI's finished product inventory at its distribution centers
- FCI's product distribution from its distribution centers to its customers, the retail stores

The criteria for deciding whether a module was to be given full or passing treatment was based on length and relevance. For reasons of length, I could only afford to include four detailed modules at the most. As to relevance, I picked for detailed treatment those four modules that I believed would be the most relevant to the reader in terms of developing OLAP problem-solving skills.

As to working through the examples, because I included a fully computational model of FCI in Chapter 17 (at least as it relates to calculating the total costs and earnings for a particular batch of foodcakes sold on a particular day in a particular store), the other chapters in this section rely on numerical illustrations. Keep in mind that the formulas are correct (or at least are intended to be), so you will be able to apply what you learn in these chapters to your own design efforts. I simply didn't include enough numerical data points for you to manually calculate the variety of query results whose query formulations are described in Chapters 13 through 16. Thus, the data in the result set views that follow most of the queries in Chapters 13 through 16 are illustrative.

## CHAPTER 13

Purchasing and Currency Exchange

Background Issues

Foodcakes International (FCI) purchases fish in over 100 markets in 20 countries. Fish are purchased in local currency for which local bank accounts are established. Currently, expenditures are reported in local currency on a monthly basis and converted to dollars at headquarters using average monthly exchange rates. Although local purchasing agents are attuned to the day-to-day price fluctuations of fish and other materials, FCI corporate managers realize that the total purchasing cost of fish is a function of the local price and the exchange rate relative to U.S. dollars, and that day-to-day fluctuations in exchange rates can be just as large as the daily movements in local currency-denominated material prices. Furthermore, they also realize that local purchasing agents maintain local currency-denominated bank accounts whose cost relative to U.S. dollars is more a function of the price at which the currency was bought than of the exchange rate on the day the currency was spent. Thus, FCI wants to add a currency exchange module that distinguishes exchange rates from cost of currency. The exchange rate used needs to be the same one used by the local banks with which FCI's purchasing agents conduct business. When implemented, the module will enable corporate managers to compare relative material prices across countries and markets, and make corporate decisions to shift purchasing between locations on a timely/daily basis.[1]

Data Sources

Purchasing

The two sources of purchasing data are bills of sale that record actual purchasing trans-actions and exchange rate tables that record official exchange rates. Since FCI initiated its data warehousing project, it has transformed the bill-of-sale data from a collection of transaction header and detail tables to the purchasing fact table, and associated dimension tables shown in Figure 13.1.

Note how the process of transforming the bill-of-sale data added location informa-tion. This is because out on the wharf where FCI's purchasing agents are scrambling for the best fish they can find, the bills of sale they exchange with local fishermen do not include such obvious information as town and country. Location information, which is implicit at the source, clearly needs to be incorporated into the system for sub-sequent use. In contrast, every bill of sale includes the name of the supplier, such as Max's Fishing Boats, which is left out of the purchasing table because FCI typically buys fish from several sources in each town where it conducts business, and physically aggregates all the fish for each type of fish purchased before sending the fish to its materials distribution center. So from a business process perspective, FCI is not capa-ble of tracking the supplier for a particular day's purchase. FCI does perform quality testing at the docks, however, and has always felt comfortable with its ability to iden-tify quality problems from specific suppliers before the fish is aggregated with the fish of other suppliers. The key point to take away here is that many information-modeling decisions reflect underlying business processes. You can't always change one without changing the other.

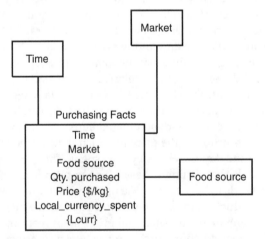

Figure 13.1 Global purchasing fact table.

Exchange Rates

Building an exchange rate cube is a new endeavor for FCI. Prior to this warehousing initiative, FCI only kept a table of current exchange rates at HQ for accounting purposes. In order to implement the currency exchange module as described, FCI needed to input daily purchases for local currency relative to $US, from each of the banks with whom FCI buys and sells currency.

Purchases Cube

Since FCI is starting with a fact table, there is already an explicit LC structure that we can leverage for defining a purchases cube. As you can see from the purchases fact table, there are three locator dimensions: *Time, Market,* and *Foodsource.* The three measured contents are *quantity purchased, price per kilogram* in the local currency, and *local currency spent.* These are discussed in the following sections.

Locator Dimensions

Time

Although Time is by nature a cardinally ordered type, for FCI there are enough hierarchies and attributes associated with Time that are not formulaic (and which thus need to be explicitly stored), such as the dates of holidays and the demarcation of fiscal periods (which change from country to country), that FCI treats Time as an explicit dimension by storing actual instances of time at all levels of granularity. This enables FCI to store irregular attributes in a classic time dimension attribute table. FCI also chose to represent time as a date data type with formulaic extension capabilities, rather than as a character string, thus enabling it to define time-based formulas that rely on time's inherent cardinal properties.

The central accounting department is responsible for the maintenance of all fiscal period definitions. (Parts of FCI's business resulted from acquisitions of companies that continued to be run as wholly owned subsidiaries with their own fiscal periods.) Corporate human resources (again, in conjunction with the appropriate local divisions) is responsible for the maintenance of holiday periods.

Geography

Since the Geography dimension is composed of the names of places as opposed to their longitude and latitude, FCI represents it as an explicit, nominally ordered dimension called Geog.Market. Figure 13.2 lists a few of the attributes that FCI associates with its geography dimension.

Geog.Market
Name_of_Agent
Address_of_Agent
Phone_Number_of_Agent
Population
Currency

Figure 13.2   Geog.Market attributes.

Foodsource

FCI started its life as a fishcake manufacturer whose daily purchases were predominantly fish. It's not that they didn't use flour and flavorings, but these ingredients were purchased from a much smaller number of suppliers and locations, and because these other ingredients did not spoil so readily, they were purchased on a much more infrequent basis as well. Then, FCI expanded production to include vegetarian cakes whose ingredients, while not fish, were still often exotic, purchased from many different countries, especially the spices, and were more time-sensitive than other filler ingredients. Thus, the food_source dimension represents the union of what had been the fish dimension plus an earlier materials and later vegetarian dimension. Although most of the dimension is explicitly defined, FCI has traditionally maintained a formulaically defined alternate hierarchy based on price. A few of the attributes FCI maintains for its Foodsource dimension are listed in Figure 13.3.

With the three purchasing dimensions defined and with their instance sources explicitly defined, FCI can create an empty cube with the following schema.

```
(Geog. ⊗ Foodsource. ⊗ Time.) ~
```

Foodsource
Calories
Fat
Vitamins
Carbohydrates
Seasonal

Figure 13.3   Foodsource attributes.

Input Contents

There are three contents normally input into the purchases cube: *local price, quantity purchased,* and *local currency spent*. Each of the contents is defined in the following code. Following standard practice, Thor defined the content's source first. Each content or variable definition includes on the first line the name of the content in double quotes (as is standard with SQL), and the root metric or units in curly braces { }. Subsequent lines, which are indented one tab, define the application range restriction with one type's restriction per line. On the same line as the last application range restriction, the identity or linking function is included with the source.

```
"Local_price" {Lcurr/kg},
    Time.day. ,
    Geog.market. ,
    Fish.individual_fish., << Purchasing Table

"Qty_purchased" {kg},
    Time.day. ,
    Geog.market. ,
    Fish.individual_fish., << Purchasing Table

"Local_currency_spent"  {Lcurr},
    Time.day. ,
    Geog.market. ,
    Fish.individual_fish. , << Purchasing Table
```

Each of the input formulas states that the values for the variable being defined come from the purchasing table and are linked to the leaf level of each of the cube dimensions. Note that although Local_price, Qty_purchased, and Local_currency_spent are all three input, they are interdeterministic, so that a filter could be run on them (as will be shown later) to make sure there were no mistakes in inputting data or spending currency. Figure 13.4 shows some representative prices paid for fish.

Basic Derivations

Aggregations

With the dimensions and input variables defined, Thor went on to define basic aggregations. As with formulas beyond input source declarations, there now exists a right-hand side of the equation. Thor, in continuing the same style of formula writing, places one right-hand side variable expression (that is, a content plus any location modifiers) per line and indents them all one tab relative to their left-hand side location ranges. For example, aggregations for local price were defined as follows:

```
"Local_price" {Lcurr/kg},
    L.leaf.above. =
        Sum(Price {Lcurr /kg}, L.leaf.)
```

				Feb 1	Feb 2	Feb 3	Feb 4
		Salmon	Price {Lcurr/kg}	7.25	8.00	7.00	8.50
	Vancouver	Cod	Price {Lcurr/kg}	7.75	6.50	7.00	6.95
		Bass	Price {Lcurr/kg}	7.25	8.00	8.50	7.00
		Trout	Price {Lcurr/kg}	9.00	10.75	9.25	10.00
	Prince Rupert	Shrimp	Price {Lcurr/kg}	9.50	9.00	9.25	9.75
		Tuna	Price {Lcurr/kg}	9.50	8.50	9.25	9.00

column

Time.Day

row

Geog.Market.

Foodsource.Fish.

Variable { }

Figure 13.4   Representative fish prices.

This says that local prices are summed across all dimensions, which is a typical default in most OLAP products. Figure 13.5 shows a representative view of aggregate prices. Compare the values in Figure 13.5 with those of Figure 13.4. **What do you think?**

Luckily, Lulu was awake and realized something was wrong before any of Jane's analysts saw the view. She told Thor he made a mess of his first aggregation and that aggregate prices needed to be averaged, not summed. Furthermore, she pointed out, local prices can't average between different currencies so local price doesn't apply above the country level of the Geography dimension. Finally, when local prices are averaged, they need to reflect or be weighted by the relative amounts of foodsource purchased. What do you think the aggregation formula for local prices should look like? **Think about it.**

Lulu rewrote the aggregation formula for local prices as follows:

```
"Local_price" {Lcurr/kg},
    Time.leaf.above.,
    Foodsource.leaf.above.,
    Geog.(leaf.above and country.atunder). , =

        Sum(
        ("Local price" {Lcurr/kg}, L.leaf.) x
        ("Qty_Purchased" {Kg} , L.leaf.) /
        ("Qty_Purchased" {Kg})
        )
```

				column			
				Time.Day			
				Feb 1	Feb 2	Feb 3	Feb 4
	Canada	Salmon	Price {Lcurr/kg}	200	210	190	185
		Cod	Price {Lcurr/kg}	190	195	201	213
row		Bass	Price {Lcurr/kg}	175	178	182	169
Geog.Market.	Mexico	Trout	Price {Lcurr/kg}	199	201	213	189
Foodsource.Fish.		Shrimp	Price {Lcurr/kg}	162	191	187	200
Price { }		Tuna	Price {Lcurr/kg}	167	181	159	193

Figure 13.5 Aggregate prices.

This says that local prices average according to the relative amounts of foodsource purchased at each price, up the whole time hierarchy, and up the whole fish hierarchy, but only up the Geography hierarchy until they reach the country level. Note the weighting factor:

```
(Qty_Purchased {Kg} , L.leaf.) / (Qty_Purchased {Kg}).
```

The denominator in the expression (*Qty_Purchased {Kg}*) needs to reflect the dimension within which the aggregate is being created. Thus, for example, if weighted average local prices were being sought for a particular market over time for a particular fish, at any aggregate level of time, the expression (*Qty_Purchased {Kg}*) would be evaluated for that same aggregate level of time and thus would pick up the appropriate denominator to create the weighting expression.

Figure 13.6 shows a representative view of corrected aggregate prices.

Humbled (slightly) by his mistake with a deceptively easy derivation, Thor decided to proceed more slowly with future derivations and, at the risk of belaboring the obvious, always double-check the aggregation function and the application range restrictions. All readers are encouraged to follow Thor's example.

So how would you aggregate quantity purchased? Does it have any restrictions? Thor couldn't think of any. He could imagine asking for how many kilos of raw food material FCI purchased last year or last month or yesterday. He could imagine asking for how many kilos of fish were bought from South American markets last month or

				column			
				Time.Day			
				Feb 1	Feb 2	Feb 3	Feb 4
	Canada	Salmon	Price {Lcurr/kg}	7.25	7.00	8.00	7.00
		Cod	Price {Lcurr/kg}	7.75	8.50	8.00	7.75
row		Bass	Price {Lcurr/kg}	7.00	7.25	7.50	7.25
Geog.Market.	Mexico	Trout	Price {Lcurr/kg}	10.00	9.75	9.50	10.25
Foodsource.Fish.		Shrimp	Price {Lcurr/kg}	9.25	9.25	9.50	9.25
Variable { }		Tuna	Price {Lcurr/kg}	9.00	8.75	9.00	9.25

Figure 13.6 Corrected aggregate prices.

how many kilos of whitefish were bought from around the world. It does seem to genuinely sum, without restriction across all dimensions. Thus, the aggregation formula for quantity purchased is as follows:

```
"Quantity purchased" {Kg}
     L.leaf.above. =

          Sum("Quantity purchased" {Kg}, L.leaf.)
```

What about the aggregation formula for local currency spent? Does it have any restrictions? It seems to sum appropriately. But, like local prices, it only applies to the country level and lower in the Geography dimension. Its formula is as follows:

```
"Local currency spent" {Lcurr/kg} ,
     Time.leaf.above.,
     Foodsource.leaf.above.,
     Geog.(leaf.above. and country.atunder.). =

          Sum("Local currency spent"{Lcurr/kg}, L.leaf.)
```

Other Calculations

Thor was heartened by his recent aggregation successes and wanted to continue creating useful analytic derivations. First let's define a calculation to spot all purchasing events where the money spent is inconsistent with the stated prices and quantities purchased. Lulu proposed defining a formula that she called Data_check that is assigned the value 0 if everything is consistent and otherwise is assigned the value 1, as follows (noting the use of the assignment operator ⊨):

```
"Data_check" =

    If (
    "Local currency spent" {Lcurr} ÷
    ("quantity bought" {Kg} x
    "Local Price" {Lcurr/Kg})
    ) = 1
      ⊨ 0
    Else   ⊨ 1
```

Now it is easy to count the number of times that purchasing data may contain an error as, for example, with the following formula:

```
Cnt(Data_check.1)
```

If you're looking to identify those markets that seem to be plagued with the greatest number of inconsistencies, a formula fragment like the following will catch it:

```
Market.(Cnt(Data_check.1)).Drank.(1 to 5)
```

This formula will identify those markets across all fish and times with the greatest total counts of inconsistencies.

Now what about looking for sources of volatility? Lulu suggested looking for fish (actually fish names, which is why the stated metric for fish is {N} for names or nominal), with the greatest price swings over the year with a query formula like the following:

```
"Fish" {N}, "Country" {N},
  (("Local Price" {Lcurr} , Time.year.this).max -
  ("Local Price" {Lcurr}, Time.year.this).min).Drank.(1 to 5)
```

This should return the five fish-country tuples with the greatest price swing over the year. What do you think? Thor noticed a fatal problem. There is no way to meaningfully compare price changes across countries without first relativizing them in some way. Depending on an OLAP tool's defaults, a formula like this will either not compile or it will return those countries with the smallest denominated currencies like those shown in Figure 13.7.

The obvious way to look for the fish-country tuples is to convert all local currency measurements into dollars and then compare. But Lulu and Thor don't have access to

Page
Time.2000
((Price, Time.year.this).max -
(Price, Time.year.this).min)

Column
Variables { }

	Foodsource.Fish {N}	Country {N}
1	Swordfish	Italy
2	Catfish	Japan
3	Bass	Ecuador
4	Tilapia	Mongolia
5	Salmon	Madagascar

(Drank)

Row
Drank.1-5

Figure 13.7   Results of initial volatility query.

the exchange rate cube yet. So what else can they do? Lulu pointed out that she can create a relative price for each fish-country tuple by dividing the actual price paid for any specific time by the average for the year for that country as with the following formula whose domain is that of the decimals {D}:

```
"Relative price" {D},
     Time.leaf. ,
     Foodsource.Fish.leaf. ,
     Geography.Market., =

     "Local Price" {Lcurr} ÷
     ("Local Price" {Lcurr}, Time.Year)
```

Figure 13.8 shows a set of local currency fish prices, the yearly average price, and associated relative prices.

Armed with relative fish prices, we can go on to look for those fish with the greatest relative price movements during the year, those countries with the greatest relative price movements across all fish during the year, and those country-fish pairs with the greatest relative price movements.

To calculate those fish with the greatest relative price movements, Thor said it is first necessary to combine fish purchases across different countries, which requires weighting the relative price movements by the amount of fish purchased as with the following formula :

Page
Time.Feb2
Geog.Market.Canada.LM5

Column
Variables { }

		Price {Lcurr/kg}	(Price {Lcurr/kg},Time.1999)	Relative Price {D}
	Salmon	11.77	5.56	2.12
Row	Tuna	12.94	6.75	1.92
Foodsource.fish	Bass	11.75	6.34	1.85

Figure 13.8   Local and relative fish prices.

```
"Relative price" {D},
Foodsource.fish.leaf. ,
Geog.all ,
Time.year. =

    Sum (
    ("Relative price" {D} , Geog.leaf.) x
    (("Quantity purchased" {Kg} , Geog.leaf.) ÷
    ("Quantity purchased" {Kg}))
        )
```

Recall that a weighted average is a sum of weighting factors times the item to be averaged, which is why the weighted average relative price is calculated as a sum. Also note how the calculation context shifted for Geography during the course of the formula. Thus, we began with the all level of Geography on the left-hand side of the equation. This made it necessary to explicitly state that we wanted to sum relative prices from the leaf level of geography. Since the context was set by the left-hand side, we again needed to qualify Geography in the clause ("Quantity purchased" {Kg}, Geog.leaf.) but finally, for the denominator, since we wanted *quantity purchased* for all countries (this being a resolutional ratio) we didn't have to add any qualifier since the context, as set by the left-hand side, was already all countries.

What do you think of the preceding formula? Can you think of a way to express the same formula that requires fewer operations? Lulu can. Why are you creating all those ratios, she asked Thor. Why not just sum the series of products of *price* and *quantity_purchased* and then divide the entire sum, just once by the total *quantity purchased*? The formula looks like this:

```
"Relative price" {D},
    Foodsource.fish.leaf. ,
    Geog.all ,
    Time.year. =
```

```
Sum (
("Relative price" {D} , Geog.leaf.) x
("Quantity purchased" {Kg} , Geog.leaf.)
      ) ÷
"Quantity purchased" {Kg}
```

Thor admitted that Lulu's version was more efficient, but when working with small amounts of data, and especially when performing spot calculations by hand, he preferred his form of expression because it showed the weighting factor:

```
(("Quantity purchased" {Kg} , Geog.leaf.) ÷
("Quantity purchased" {Kg}))
```

as a discrete ratio for each term. With Lulu's more efficient version, the individual weighting ratios are not calculated.

Thor went on to calculate the fish with the greatest relative price movements as with the following formula, the results of which are shown in Figure 13.9.

```
"Fish" {N},
    Geog.all ,
    (("Relative price" {D} , Time.year.this).max -
    ("Relative price" {D} , Time.year.this).min).Drank.(1 to 5)
```

Lulu asked Thor whether the formula has to apply to the all member of the Geography dimension or whether it could apply lower down the hierarchy as well. **What do you think?**

It depends on what you're trying to do, replied Thor. If FCI wants to know the fish with the greatest relative price movement in the world, then the formula stands as it is.

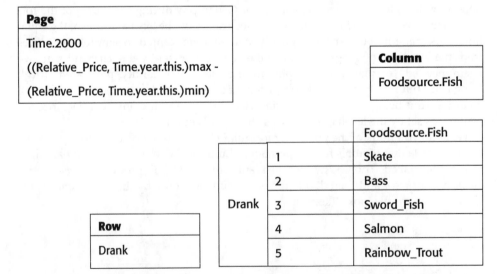

Figure 13.9 Top five ranked fish by weighted relative price change.

However, if FCI took a more decentralized approach to purchasing, it would want to know for each purchasing region (however defined) which fish had the greatest relative price movements per region. So how would you define the formula in a way that left the geography unspecified, asked Lulu. **Think about it.**

Two formulas need to generalize. First, the formula for relative prices that works for the all level of the geography dimension needs to be generalized to work for any level above the leaf as shown here:

```
"Relative price" {D},
     Foodsource.fish.leaf. ,
          Time. =

     Sum (
     ("Relative price" {D} , Geog.leaf.) x
     ("Quantity purchased" {Kg} , Geog.leaf.)
          ) ÷
     "Quantity purchased" {Kg}
```

Then the formula for finding the fish with the greatest relative price movements needs to be generalized in the same way. The resulting formula, shown next, will list the fish with the greatest relative price movements for any geographic territory above the market level. The query results are shown in Figure 13.10.

```
"Fish" {N},
     Geog.leaf.above. ,
     ((Relative price , Time.year.this).max -
     (Relative price , Time.year.this).min).Drank.(1 to 5)
```

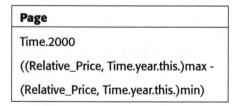

Figure 13.10   Fish with greatest relative price movements.

Although Lulu and Thor realize they will need to analyze the exchange rate cube before they can fully answer their questions of cost fluctuation, there are still a number of purchasing cube-specific derivations whose results will help them in their analysis.

FCI knows that one of the secrets to stabilizing their input cost structure is to diversify their input sources. The first step to doing that is to know their current state of diversification and concentration. The following items are illustrative (though by no means exhaustive) of the kinds of calculations needed for FCI managers to have a solid understanding of their current state of concentration and diversification:

- The countries from which FCI buys the most number of different fish over the year
- The countries from which FCI buys the most of some particular fish, such as shrimp
- The fish that are bought from the greatest number of different countries

How many countries are we looking for, asked Thor. Think about it, replied Lulu. The purpose of these queries is to give FCI purchasing managers a better handle on foodsource volatility. We don't know whether there's 1 country or 50 countries from which FCI purchases a lot of different kinds of fish. One way to approach the problem is to generate a graph of the number of distinct fish purchased by country for all countries and, through visual inspection, select those countries that are at or near the top in terms of the number of distinct fish bought per year. Another way is to start someplace, say with the top five countries, look at them, and then depending on the drop off between the top-ranked and the fifth-ranked country either restrict, enlarge, or simply keep that selection.

Since I don't have my graphing module running right now, let's take the second approach, said Thor. What you have to do is calculate for each country the number of different fish for which the quantity purchased is greater than zero and then select the top five ranked countries in terms of the number of distinct fish bought (see the following formula). For starters, let's look at how countries fared in 2000. The results are shown in Figure 13.11. Incidentally, said Thor, I'm going to use two separate expressions —one to calculate the distinct number of fish bought per country and the second to rank countries by the distinct number of fish bought. For the record, I could have combined both in a single expression, but it would have been harder to understand or reuse.

```
"Distinct_number_of_fish_bought"{Integer I},
Time.year.2000 ,
Foodsource.all ,
Geog.country. =

Cnt("Foodsource.leaf"{N} ,(Quantity purchased {Kg}  > 0))

"Drank" , "Country"{N} ,"Distinct_number_of_fish_bought" {I} ,
    Distinct_number_of_fish_bought.Drank.(1 to 5) , Time.year.2000
```

Hey, wait a minute, said Lulu. In your first expression on the left-hand side of the equation, you set the application range in the Foodsource dimension to the all member. But then on the right-hand side you set it equal to the leaves. What's that about? Good

Page		Column
Time.2000		Variables { }

		Country {N}	Distinct_number_of_fish_bought {I}
	1	Ecuador	81
	2	Mexico	79
Drank	3	South Africa	75
	4	Australia	73
	5	Spain	71

Row
Drank

Figure 13.11   Top five countries in terms of the number of distinct fish bought per country.

question, replied Thor. If you look closely, you'll notice that on the left-hand side of the equation, the type Foodsource is being treated as a locator or dimension, and, yes, the application range in the Foodsource dimension is set to the all member. After all (no pun intended), for each country per year there can be only one value for the distinct number of fish bought. However, on the right-hand side of the equation, the same type of Foodsource is being used as a variable or content. In other words, we are not setting it to some value in order to constrain something else, rather we are looking for its value, or rather a function of its value, based on other constraints—in this case that the quantity purchased is greater than zero. Since we're using Foodsource as a content on the right-hand side of the equation, we needed to identify it as such by surrounding the term in double quotes as we do for all types used as variables and by including its metric or units, in this case simply {names}. Thanks, said Lulu. Now let me write the second formula, the results of which are shown in Figure 13.12.

```
"Country" {N} ,
    Time.all ,
        ("Quantity purchased" {Kg} , Geog.country. , Foodsource.shrimp).max
```

Parsing the expression from the inside, it says take the quantity purchased of shrimp for each country:

```
("Quantity purchased" {Kg} , Geog.country. , Foodsource.shrimp)
```

Take the maximum quantity purchased from that:

```
("Quantity purchased" {Kg} , Geog.country. , Foodsource.shrimp).max
```

Then take the country associated with the maximum:

```
"Country" {N}, Time.all , ("Quantity purchased" {Kg} , Geog.country ,
Foodsource.shrimp) .max
```

		Country {N}
	1	United States
	2	Ecuador
Drank	3	Italy
	4	Japan
	5	Australia

Figure 13.12   Top five countries for shrimp purchases.

Thor insisted on writing the formula for three. He began with the following:

```
"Distinct_number_of_countries_from_which_fish_is_bought" {I},
     Foodsource.fish.leaf. ,
     Geog.all ,
     Time.year.atabove. =

            Cnt("Geog.country" {N} ,
            ("Quantity purchased" {Kg} > 0))
```

Thor added, before we can list the fish that are bought from the greatest number of countries we need to be able to count the number of countries from which fish is bought. So that's what I did. Lulu furled her brow. Your formula doesn't correspond to the item in number three, said Lulu. Why did you define an application range in terms of years when the original item made no reference to time? Shouldn't you be defining the formula at the all-time level? **What do you think?**

From my experience, replied Thor, end-users do not always fully specify exactly what they need to have calculated. Typically, the specification of formulas whose outputs satisfy their requirements takes a few iterations with the end-user(s) involved at each iteration. I considered applying the formula for getting the distinct count of countries to the all-time level, but believed that if the FCI manager who initially made this request were present and if we had had the chance to speak, she or he would have almost certainly agreed that the distinct count of countries variable is even more useful if calculated at the year level in addition to the all-time level. Don't forget, I didn't just apply the formula to the year level, but rather to the year and above level. So my formula specification will return a superset of what was originally asked for.

Thor continued. The top five fish in terms of the number of different source countries and that number of source countries are shown in Figure 13.13 by year and time levels as a result of the following query:

```
"Foodsource.Fish.leaf" {N} ,
     Distinct_number_of_countries_from_which_fish_is_bought.Drank.(1to5)
       ,  Time.year.
```

Page
Time.2000

Column
Drank.
Foodsource.Fish
Variables {   }

	Foodsource.Fish {N}	Distinct_number_of_countries_ from_which_fish_is_bought {I}
1	Tuna	32
2	Salmon	28
3	Shrimp	25
4	Trout	20
5	Whitefish	17

Row
Drank

Figure 13.13 The top five fish in terms of the number of different source countries and that number of source countries by year and all-time.

Suddenly, without warning, Jane walked in. So what have you learned, she inquired? We've learned that some of the fish that FCI relies on most heavily for production have relatively high price volatilities as defined by changes in local currency prices. Furthermore, some of those heavily used fish are only sourced from a small number of different countries. Interesting, said Jane. I like the way this project has gone so far and suspect that by the time it's finished we'll have created lots of empirically grounded suggestions for ways that FCI can reduce the volatility of its cost structure.

Exchange Rate Cube

The Dimensions

Prior to this warehousing initiative, FCI only kept a table of current exchange rates at HQ for accounting purposes. Thus, building an exchange rate cube is a new endeavor. At first glance, the dimensions of the exchange rate cube should be a subset of the dimensions of the purchases cube—namely Geography and Time. Exchange rates, after all, should not vary as a function of the raw material purchased.

However, since in many countries FCI negotiates with several different institutions in an attempt to get the best exchange rates, it would seem that the geography dimension of the Xrate cube should have a leaf level composed of financial institutions. Of course, by the same reasoning, if the Geography dimension of the Xrate cube has leaf-level members composed of financial institutions, then why shouldn't the Geography dimension for the purchases cube have a leaf level composed of raw material suppliers. In this case, should there be one or two different Geography dimensions? **Think about it.**

Thor is a big fan of Einstein anecdotes, especially that models should be as simple as possible but no simpler. He says there is no inherent difference between financial institutions and fishermen—both are suppliers. Thus, there should only be one Supplier_Geography dimension that includes all suppliers.

Lulu is also a big fan of Einstein, but thinks that Thor's solution, while simple from a dimension definition standpoint leads to overly complex formulas because the financial formulas won't apply to the raw material suppliers and the raw materials purchasing formulas won't apply to the financial institutions. This means that every formula will have to have a location range qualifier such as the following:

```
"Dollars per local currency" {$/Lcurr} ,
      Geog. businesstype.bank. = Some formula
```

Lulu pointed out that regardless of whether the qualifier is based on an attribute table as with the inferred Businesstype attribute table, or whether the qualifier is based on defining specialized nodes within the Supplier_Geography dimension and then referring to all members under the financial or raw materials node, some qualification will have to take place for every formula.

The increased simplicity of the Supplier_Geography dimension is more than overcome by the increased complexity of the purchasing and exchange rate formulas. Thus, the simplest overall approach would be to define a single Geography dimension for countries and their groupings, a single markets and raw materials supplier dimension, and a single bank dimension. Then, for the application, one would join the markets and raw materials suppliers to the countries for the purchases cube, and join the banks and the countries for the exchange rate cube. (This is how the dimensions are defined in the calculation example in Chapter 17.) Thor conceded.

Now what about the cube itself? FCI would like to do bidirectional currency translation because sometimes it buys dollars with local currency and sometimes it buys local currency with dollars. (Keep in mind that the exchange rate cube will eventually be used to calculate how local currency received for selling foodcakes translates into U.S. dollars.) Lulu figured that the From-To concept popular with shipping models would apply to currency translation and suggested an exchange rate cube that used a From and To currency defined as follows:

```
(Time. ⊗ Geog.From. ⊗ Geog.To.) ~ "Exchange rate" {R}

    Where
    If Geog.From = Geog.To
    Then Exchange rate = n/a
```

She added the where clause because exchange rates are not applicable for a country selling its own currency to itself. Since there's a From and a To country, there's no need to use a separate content for currency purchases and currency sales. Both concepts are subsumed under the single content "Exchange rate" as illustrated in Figure 13.14.

Page				
Time.Feb.19.2000				

Column
Geog.To

	Canada	France	Mexico	US
Canada	n/a	4.05	0.90	0.13
France	0.25	n/a	0.22	0.53
Mexico	1.12	4.52	n/a	0.12
United States	7.65	1.89	8.54	n/a

Row
Geog.From

Figure 13.14   Lulu's view of the exchange rate cube.

Thor was impressed, but felt obliged to point out that FCI wasn't interested in analyzing currency exchanges between any two countries, but only between any one country and the United States. Thus, not only is the diagonal not applicable, but all the cells except those along the two edges defined by the United States crossed with all other countries would be empty as illustrated in Figure 13.15. Since they were empty, aggregation formulas would either have to define specific application ranges or lots of defaults for aggregating missing data values. Either way, it's a lot of unnecessary and error-prone work.

Thus, Thor proposed that for FCI it would be simpler to use only a single Geography dimension and to use two separate contents: Dollars per local currency, which captures the exchange rate for buying U.S. dollars with a particular local currency from a particular bank, and local currency per dollar, which captures the exchange rate for

Page				
Time.Feb.19.2000				

Column
Geog.To

	Canada	France	Mexico	US
Canada				0.13
France				0.53
Mexico				0.12
United States	7.65	1.89	8.54	n/a

Row
Geog.From

Figure 13.15   Thor's view of the exchange rate cube.

buying a particular local currency from U.S. dollars at a particular bank. Thor's schema looks as follows:

```
(Geog. ⊗ Time.) ~ "Dollars per local currency"{$/Lcurr} , "local
currency per dollar"{Lcurr/$}
```

Input Contents and Aggregations

Given Thor's proposed schema, which Lulu was forced to admit was the more useful, there were two base variables that they both agreed needed to be input by the banks on a daily basis. At this point, you should be able to easily define their associated aggregation formulas.

```
"Dollars per local currency" {$/Lcurr} ,
     Time.day. ,
     Geography.bank. << source..

"Dollars per local currency" {$/Lcurr} ,
     Time.day.above. ,
     Geog.(bank.above and Country.atunder). =

     Avg ( "Dollars per local currency" {$/Lcurr} , Time.day. , Geog.bank. )

"Local currency per dollar" {Lcurr/$} ,
     Time.day. ,
     Geography.bank. << source

"Local currency per dollar" {Lcurr/$} ,
     Time.day.above. ,
     Geog.(bank.above and Country.atunder). =

     Avg ("Local currency per dollar" {Lcurr/$} , Time.day. , Geog.bank. )
```

Lulu agreed with the basics, but pointed out that Thor's model was underspecified. What, she asked, was going to be input by the banks on a daily basis: average rates, opening rates, or closing rates? When each day were the banks going to submit their information: at the start of the day, at some arbitrary time or times during the day, or at the end of the day? Thor replied that the banks were to submit their numbers once at the end of every day and that the exchange rates represented the average for the day. This is because FCI had requested daily-level tracking. Thor pointed out that should FCI management want, it would be easy to add an opening rate and a closing rate content (effectively transaction-level information), or a high and low rate for that matter, for each of the two exchange rate variables, as shown in Figure 13.16.

Given this full suite of contents, the expression, whose result set is shown in Figure 13.17, which returns, for example, the lowest closing exchange rate for dollars per local currency for each country for the past year would look as follows:

```
"Country" {N} , "Day" {N} , "Dollars per local currency_closing" {D},
     (Dollars per local currency_closing , Time.year.this.day.)min
```

Country		
Bank		
Day		
Local currency per dollar	Opening	
	Low	
	High	
	Closing	
	Average	
Dollar per local currency	Opening	
	Low	
	High	
	Closing	
	Average	

Figure 13.16   Thor's proposed exchange rate table.

Country	Day	Dollars / local currency
France	Jan 5	0.13
Japan	Feb 9	0.008
Canada	March 15	0.61

Figure 13.17   Low closing exchange rate per country.

However, unless FCI specifically wanted to track opening and closing rates at the transaction level, it was easy enough to see, down to the day level, the opening and closing (average daily) positions for time levels above the day. For example, as shown in Figure 13.18, the opening and closing average daily exchange rate for the month is simply the average exchange rate for the first day of the month and the average exchange rate for the last day of the month.

Derived Contents

Recalling that FCI ultimately wants to compare cost fluctuations across time, countries, and fish, and that the total cost fluctuation is a function of local price changes and exchange rate changes, Lulu and Thor need to define some relative exchange rate

Page
Time.2000

Column
Time.
Variable { }

			Day		Month
			June 1	June 30	June
			{$/Lcurr}	{$/Lcurr}	{$/Lcurr}
France	Opening		0.131	0.150	0.141
	Closing		0.135	0.148	0.142
Japan	Opening		0.008	0.010	0.009
	Closing		0.009	0.011	0.010
Canada	Opening		0.612	0.613	0.613
	Closing		0.609	0.614	0.612

Row
Country
Variable {$/Lcurr}

Figure 13.18   Opening and closing exchange rates.

formulas. Like the relative prices in the purchasing cube, the next two formulas create ratios between the exchange rate on any one day and the average exchange rate for the year.

```
"Relative local currency per dollar" {D} ,
     Time.Day. ,
     Geography.bank. =

          "Local currency per dollar" {Lcurr} ÷
          "local currency per dollar" {Lcurr/$}, Time.Year


"Relative dollars per local currency" {R} ,
     Time.day. ,
     Geography.bank. =

          "Dollars per local currency" {$/Lcurr} ÷
          "Dollars per local currency" {$/Lcurr}, Time.Year
```

As stated at the beginning of this chapter, FCI knew that the actual cost of local currency was not determined by the exchange rate on the day of the materials purchase, but rather on the exchange rate that was utilized to acquire the currency that was used to buy the materials. The model, as it stands now, is akin to FCI invoking a currency exchange function at the moment of purchase, whereas FCI, as described by its managers, stated that they maintain a local currency reserve in every country with which they conduct business. So how best to model it?

Thor suggested he add currency purchased and currency on hand variables to the exchange rate cube, which now might be better called a currency cube. Lulu pointed out that by modeling currency on hand, currency was being treated like a product with its own inventory. So why not add these currency-purchasing variables to the purchases cube? What would you do?

Given that the geography dimension was separated from both the raw materials and the currency providers, it wouldn't make sense to add currency purchasing to the purchases cube unless FCI wanted to adopt Thor's original unified supplier dimension. Since that unified dimension was already rejected because of the unnecessary increases in formula complexity and since the dimensions of currency purchasing matched the dimensions of the exchange rate cube, Thor persuaded Lulu that the overall model would be simpler if the currency purchases were added to the exchange rate cube, the variables for which are shown in Figure 13.19.

By tracking actual currency purchases, said Lulu, you can calculate a weighted average exchange rate that applies to all the currency on hand for any particular day that is used to calculate the effective rate that applies to any one day's purchase. How would you define such a calculation? Lulu took a stab at it with the following formula:

```
"Effective exchange rate" {Lcurr/$} ,
     Geog.country. ,
     Time.day. =

          Sum ( "Local currency purchased" {Lcurr}) ÷
          Sum ("Dollars spent per local currency purchased" {$})
```

Before she could put her marker down, she realized that that formula would never work. Of course, it's not the amount of local currency purchased today that matters,

Contents
Dollars per local currency {$/Lcurr}
Local currency per dollar {Lcurr/$}
Local currency purchased {Lcurr}
Dollars spent per local currency purchased {$}
Dollars purchased {$}
Local currency spent per dollars purchased {Lcurr}

Figure 13.19 Combined contents for currency purchases and exchange rates.

but the cumulative amount of local currency purchased and the dollars spent acquiring it. So she amended her formula as follows. **What do you think?**

```
"Effective exchange rate" { Lcurr/$} ,
    Geog.country. ,
    Time.day. =

        Cumsum("Local currency purchased" {Lcurr} , Time.day.first-
this) ÷
        Cumsum ("Dollars spent" {$} , Time.day.first-this)
```

Thor pointed out that this formula only works until the first time local currency is actually spent acquiring raw materials, which, given the expectation that raw materials are purchased almost every day, means the formula is not acceptable.

You need some additional contents to make the calculation, he said, and suggested that they first list the variables that play a role in the calculation of an effective exchange rate before trying to write out the formulaic relationships.

An effective exchange rate is a function of some measure of the following factors:

- Cumulative local currency purchased
- Cumulative dollars spent acquiring the local currency
- Local currency spent acquiring raw materials
- Local currency on hand

The first two measures can be combined to create a transaction-oriented exchange rate. The third measure combined with the first two should give a measure of local currency on hand. Of course, as with other stock measures, one needs to specify the part of the day to which the measure applies. In this case, Lulu and Thor agree they want a currency on hand variable defined for the beginning of the day with a formula as follows.

```
"Lcurr on hand_opening",
    Geog.country. ,
    Time.day. =

        (("Local currency purchased" {Lcurr} -
        "Local currency spent" {Lcurr}),  Time.day.this-1) +
        ('Lcurr on hand_opening', Time.day.this-1)


        "Lcurr on hand_opening",
        Geog.bank.
        Time.day.first = X
```

This says that the currency on hand at the beginning of the day is equal to the currency on hand at the beginning of the previous day plus additions minus subtractions. Of course, as with any other time-lagged formula, some initial value needs to be assigned to a designated first time.

Now, what about the effective rate? From the way "Lcurr on hand_opening" was calculated, it seems that the effective rate should also be a time-lagged function with today's effective rate a modification of the previous day's rate. Thor suggested the following:

```
"Effective rate" {Lcurr/$},
    Geog.bank. ,
    Time.day. =

            ("Lcurr on hand_opening" {Lcurr} ÷
              ("Lcurr on hand_opening" {Lcurr}  +
                "Lcurr purchased" {Lcurr}) x
                  ("Effective rate" {Lcurr/$} , time.day.this-1)
                  + "Lcurr purchased" {Lcurr} ÷
              ("Lcurr on hand_opening" +
                "Lcurr purchased") x
                  ("Lcurr purchased" ÷ "Dollars spent" )
```

In words, this says that the effective rate for purchases made during the day is the weighted average of the effective rate that applied to the local currency on hand at the beginning of the day and the exchange rate that applied to the currency bought that day prior to the expenditure of the local currency on hand. Thor added an extra level of indent to the exchange rate variables so as to highlight the essential structure of the formula as a weighted average.

Lulu had taken accounting and wasn't so ready to let Thor have the last word. She pointed out that if you're going to take the inventory approach, why not go all the way and use either a FIFO or a LIFO approach? Thor admitted that such an approach could work, but that the cost of implementing it might not be worth the benefit to FCI.

With a better modeling of effective exchange rates under their belts, Lulu and Thor finally feel that they sufficiently understand the inner working of the purchasing and currency exchange processes to begin effectively combining them to look at total cost fluctuations for FCI.

Combined Purchasing and Exchange Rates

The first thing Lulu and Thor want to do is define a relative total cost variable that reflects changes in local prices and effective exchange rates. Where does this variable belong—in the purchasing cube, in the exchange rate cube, in both places, or yet somewhere else? Where would you put it?

Thor pointed out (as was described in Chapter 6) that from a logical perspective you want to put a variable in a cube of appropriate dimensionality. If one of the source cubes has the dimensionality of a new derived variable, then that variable belongs in the corresponding source cube. But Lulu was quick to add that it is common for derived variables to be dimensioned by a combination of dimensions that do not correspond to any of the source cubes. When this is the case, she said it is best to define a new derived cube to serve as the schema for the new variables. In either event, most OLAP tools force you to think one way or the other.

Since dollar prices are dimensioned by Time, Geography.Market, and Foodsource, it would seem they belong in the purchases cube. For clarity of exposition, Thor said he likes to include the cube name associated with the defined variable on the left-hand side of the equation as shown here:

```
[Purchasing]: "Dollar price"{$},
    Time.day.,
    Geog.Market.,
    Foodsource.leaf. =

        "Local price" {Lcurr} X
        [Currency Exchange]: "Effective Rate" {$/Lcurr}, Geog.Country
```

Hey, said Lulu, shouldn't the Geog.country term on the last line of the formula have a dot at the end of it? Isn't it working as a locator? **What do you think?**

Thor replied that he had meant exactly what he wrote. The dollar price for a fish at a market is going to be the local price at the market times that country's effective exchange rate, and the way to reference the country for some market is *Geog.country* without the period. *Geog.country.* would have meant for every country and been meaningless in that expression. He went on to explain that since local price comes from the purchases cube, there is no need to add the reference. Similarly, the effective exchange rate is being pulled from the same day for which the dollar price is being calculated and so no further qualifier is needed. Only the exchange rate needed to be qualified.

Looking for sources of cost variance, Thor decided to look at the fish most bought by FCI. After all, the erratic performance for FCI wasn't going to be affected by fish that were hardly bought, rather by the fish that accounted for a major portion of FCI's fish expenditures. The way to express this is as follows:

```
"Foodsource.Fish".("Dollars_Spent" {$}, Time.Year.this).Drank.(1 to 5)
```

This says select those fish for which the dollars spent on those fish across all countries this year was in the top five. But you also need to decide how you want to see the results, says Lulu, who suggested the expression result be represented as a simple table as shown in Figure 13.20.

According to Lulu, it's easy to see that FCI spends the most money on salmon, shrimp, tuna, cod, and whitefish. Then Thor pointed out that dollars spent isn't the same thing as volatility. Total volatility is a function of dollars spent and fluctuations in dollar prices. How would you calculate FCI's hot volatility spots? (This exercise is left for you.)

Page						
Time.2000						

Column
Drank

		1	2	3	4	5
	Foodsource. Fish {N}	Salmon	Shrimp	Tuna	Cod	Whitefish

Row
Variables { }

		1	2	3	4	5
	Dollars_Spent {$}	540,000	510,000	480,000	460,000	420,000

Figure 13.20   The top five fish by money spent.

Summary

Lulu and Thor learned that FCI has significant room for improving the stability of its purchasing costs both in terms of which fish it buys and in terms of the countries from which it makes its purchases. In gaining that understanding, they had to wrestle with a number of modeling and analysis issues: tradeoffs between dimensional simplicity and formula complexity, time-recursive formulas, upper hierarchical limits on aggregation, nested ranking expressions, aggregating opening and closing balances, weighted average exchange rates, and relative values.

Materials Inventory Analysis

In this chapter, by following Lulu and Thor within the context of materials inventory analysis, you will learn how to model stocks and flows, how to add a new dimension to a cube, how to map data from the prior cube to the new one with the added dimension, how to calculate the quantity on hand of raw materials when those materials age (which is a function that is recursive in two dimensions), how to calculate when shortages in one center are more than offset by overstocking in other areas, how to calculate which age buckets are used up and what remains after daily orders are sent to production, how to handle inventory sparsity, how to create variables with restricted application ranges, and how to calculate the costs and productivity of storing materials per weight and time period.

Foodcakes International (FCI) maintains an inventory of food source materials in cold storage facilities co-located with its production centers. It currently has 10 inventory and production centers in 7 countries on 3 continents. Fish and other food source materials arrive on a daily basis from the myriad markets where FCI does its purchasing. As a general rule, when materials are acquired from multiple sources, they are shipped to the nearest inventory center, subject, of course, to variations in production requirements.

Although FCI historically lumped all inventory costs into general overhead, in Jane's skunk works effort to empirically understand the major reasons for FCI's erratic earnings, she asked Lulu and Thor to measure, within reason, the activity-based cost of inventory in order to understand the degree to which it varies by site, fish, employee, or any other important factor—ultimately in order to make appropriate inventory decisions affecting cost (and quality).

Food source materials arrive in a variety of forms such as palettes of boxes, individual cartons, and 20-kilo bags. As each unit of food source is unloaded from its truck, it is tagged with an arrival date. FCI has always tracked the flow of materials into and out of inventory. With the exception of statistically random partial inventory audits, actual stocks have historically been derived. Once a year, FCI does a complete inventory audit and reconciliation. The interdependency between inventory stocks and flows is the same as the interdependency shown in Chapter 13 between food source quantities purchased, prices, and currency spent. Any two constrain the third. (Flows received plus quantity on hand determines flows out, flows received plus flows out determines quantity on hand, and flows out plus quantity on hand determines flows received.)

Although many of FCI's vegetarian food sources are as perishable as fish, Jane decided in this pilot phase to have Lulu and Thor concentrate on improving FCI's ability to assign activity-based inventory costs to fish, their most perishable of raw food sources.

In order to keep fish moving, FCI uses a first-in, first-out or FIFO method for honoring fish requests from production. This ensures that all requests are met by using up the oldest fish first. When packers are fulfilling fish requests, they check fish quality in two ways:

- By comparing the arrival date with that day's date. (Any fish that has spent more than six days in inventory is put aside to be sold on a secondary market for pet food.)

- By sniffing the fish, a practice for which the packers have a highly developed skill.

The Inventory Throughput Cube

Data Sources

The four main data sources for the inventory cube are data collected from food materials arriving at the inventory site, data collected while shipping out food materials to meet production requests, data collected from unexpected damage reports, and data collected when auditing the inventory. An example of each of these data sources is shown in Figures 14.1, 14.2, 14.3, and 14.4.

Date	Material	Qty received {Kg}	Qty rejected {Kg}
1/1/01	Cod	100	0
1/1/01	Tuna	200	5
1/3/01	Cod	500	15
1/3/01	Perch	200	10

Figure 14.1   Food_source shipment arrival table for FCI Vancouver.

Date	Material	Qty tent to production	Qty over age	Qty spoiled
1/1/01	Cod	200	10	10
1/1/01	Tuna	500	20	0
1/2/01	Perch	100	0	0
1/2/01	Cod	200	25	10

Figure 14.2 Food_source sent to production table for FCI Vancouver.

Date	Material	Qty damaged {Kg}	Reason for damage
1/1/01	Cod	100	Dropped fish on ground
1/1/01	Tuna	20	Supervisor's cat snuck into freezer
1/2/01	Cod	10	Spilled grease

Figure 14.3 Unexpected Food_source damage table for FCI Vancouver.

Date	Material	Qty derived on hand	Qty counted on hand	Reconciliation
1/1/01	Cod	250	250	0
1/1/01	Tuna	100	110	10
1/1/01	Perch	500	495	(5)

Figure 14.4 Annual reconciliation table for FCI Vancouver.

As with the purchasing data, FCI maintains inventory data in its data warehouse where missing dimensions such as site are added.

Dimensions

Thor wanted to use three dimensions for modeling inventory: *Food_source*, *Time*, and *Site*. *Food_source* and *Time* are identical with the versions you saw for purchasing. Since *Site* is yet another geography-style dimension, Thor defined and maintained it as a separate unilevel nominal list and then appended its members as children of the country level of the country geography dimension as shown in Figure 14.5 (and in Chapter 17).

Geog.MarketSite	Country
Guadalajara	Mexico
Gloucester	United Kingdom
Seattle	United States
Miami	United States
Vancouver	Canada
Barcelona	Spain
Hamburg	Germany
Marseille	France

Figure 14.5   Appending sites to the country level of the geography dimension.

Lulu asked about all the countries in which they conduct purchasing but where there are no inventory sites. FCI purchases fish in over 50 countries, she said. Why not keep track of them in the new Geography dimension? Won't that make it easier to join the inventory cube with cubes from other FCI business processes down the road? **What do you think?**

Thor shook his head. You're forgetting about the sparsity, he said. No, I'm not, Lulu replied. If we use the full country dimension, we'll be able to see all those countries where we buy fish but don't have any inventory and production facilities. For those countries, we'll just see zeros that we won't even store. Nor will we have to see those zeros on the screen as our client tools all have suppress zero functions. So the amount of extra disk space consumed for maintaining the complete reference list of countries in the inventory cube is insignificant.

Don't be too sure, Thor said. Either you're going to have to restrict the application ranges of all the inventory variables to just the seven countries where FCI currently has inventory facilities, which will needlessly increase the complexity of their definition, or there are going to be a lot of sites with the value zero for amounts of fish received, amounts of fish on hand, and amounts of fish sent. Lulu broke in, but the application won't store those values, Thor. They won't affect anything.

What about queries for the average amount by site of fish received or of fish on hand? asked Thor. Won't the application count all the zero-valued sites in the denominator thus throwing off all measures of average stocks or flows? Maybe the OLAP tools in your department lack the appropriate sophistication, said Lulu, but in our department we standardized on an OLAP tool that will simply ignore all those meaningless zeros. So queries for average amounts of stock or flows will be correctly calculated.

Thor smiled and said, what about the meaningful zeros? What about all the occasions when sites received no fish, sent no fish, or otherwise have no fish on hand? Those zeros must be counted. If they are ignored, your calculations will be incorrect! I challenge you to show me a way to distinguish meaningful zeros from meaningless zeros without defining an application range (as was described in Chapter 6) that sets the boundary between meaningless and meaningful intersections, cells, or locations relative to a given set of dimensions with their potential intersections, and one or more variables that share the same application range. Lulu conceded.

Input Contents

There are 10 different input contents to the inventory cube coming from the 4 sources mentioned. Seven of them are described in the following sections, relative to the Inventory dimensions described previously and shown here in schema form:

```
(Foodsource. ⊗ Site. ⊗ Time.)~
```

Declaration of Content Sources

The input variables are grouped in their definition by the external table they are sourced from.

```
"Qty received" {Kg} ,
"Qty rejected at receipt" {Kg}),
         L.leaf.  << Food_source shipment arrival table

"Qty over age" {Kg} ,
"Qty sent to production" {Kg} ,
"Qty spoiled" {Kg} ,
       L.leaf. << Food_source sent to production table

"Qty damaged" {Kg},
       L.leaf. << Unexpected Food_source damage table

"Qty counted at audit" {Kg} ,
       L.leaf. <<Annual reconciliation table
```

Declaration of Basic Aggregations

All contents sum up all hierarchies except *Qty counted at audit,* which doesn't sum in the time dimension.

```
"Qty counted at audit" ,
       Geog.Site.above. ,
       Food_source.leaf.above. ,
       Time.day. =

              Sum("Qty counted at audit" ,
              Geog.Site.leaf. , Food_source.leaf.)
```

Compared to the purchase and exchange rate cubes, the inventory cube seems like a piece of cake. With the exception of the annual audit, every input content has a unit metric of kilograms, is measured at the leaf level of all dimensions, and sums up all dimensions. Are we missing anything? Thor wondered. Well, said Lulu, we could track the type of container for each kind of fish. Some come in boxes on pallets; others come in individual cartons. Still others come in sacks. There may be a correlation between the type of container in which the fish arrives and either the cost of its handling in inventory or the likelihood of damage, as from dropping. How would you track container type?

Shouldn't container type be stored in the fish dimension table as an attribute? said Thor. That depends, replied Lulu. How does container type vary? Yes, that is the key question, said Thor. You only want to store it as a dimension attribute if it essentially only varies by fish. I could just as easily imagine that container type varies by fish, purchasing market, and even time. Some weeks we receive Salmon from Juneau in 100-pound crates; other weeks we receive it in 50-pound plastic sacks.

Thor continued. Assuming for the moment that container type varies in all three dimensions, how would you model it, Lulu? Would you create a container type dimension? Would you create a new variable per container type? What would you do? **Think about it.**

I wouldn't use any of your options, Lulu told Thor. I would create a single new variable called received container type whose values were the possible container types. Then I would apply that variable to the leaf level of the inventory cube. If FCI changes container type for fish once they're in inventory, I would create one container type variable for each stage of inventory; otherwise, I would use just one. The values of the container type variable would be a nominal string derived from whatever supply contracts have the container type information. Then I would create a dimension table for the container type variable and associate any relevant properties such as capacity, strength, cost, and so forth. But since we don't have access to that supply information now, let's leave that modeling for after the pilot is completed.

Viewing Basic Aggregations

Now that you've seen the basic dimensions and variables, let's look at a few simple aggregations to get a feel for the inventory throughput cube.

Figures 14.6 and 14.7 show the results of some basic aggregations. Figure 14.6 illustrates a typical aggregate view of quantity received by site and by quarter for all fish, as follows:

```
"Qty received",
        Geog.site. ,
        Time.quarter. ,
        Foodsource.all
```

Page
Qt_Received {kg}
Foodsource.all

Column
Geog.Site.

		United States		Canada	France	
		Miami	Seattle	Vancouver	Marseille	La Rochelle
	2001 Q2	25150	31400	48130	8500	2070
Row	2001 Q1	20040	24620	34100	7620	2510
Time.quarter.	2000 Q4	22580	25180	39280	7920	2460

Figure 14.6   Aggregating Qt_Received.

Figure 14.7 shows the following:

```
"Qty sent to production" {Kg},
        Geog.all ,
        Time.quarter. ,
        Foodsource.fishtypes.
```

Page
Qt_Sent {kg}
Foodsource.all

Column
Geog.Site.

		United States		Canada	France	
		Miami	Seattle	Vancouver	Marseille	La Rochelle
	2001 Q2	25150	31400	48130	8500	2070
Row	2001 Q1	20040	24620	34100	7620	2510
Time.quarter.	2000 Q4	22580	25180	39280	7920	2460

Figure 14.7   Aggregating Qty Sent to production.

Enough with this easy stuff, said Thor. Let's do something challenging. Not so fast, replied Lulu. Even with just the basic input contents, there are many useful aggregation-style queries that can now be answered and whose answers may help us understand how FCI can improve its materials inventory throughput processing. What aggregation-style queries would you pose of the inventory cube? **Think about it.** What follows are seven of Lulu's queries first in words and then in code, with each query accompanied by an illustrative view of the result set.

1. Total fish lost last month (see Figure 14.8):

```
"Total fish lost" {Kg},
        site. ,
        Food_source.all ,
        Time.month.prev =

                "Qty rejected" +
                "Qty over aged" +
                "Qty damaged" +
                "Qty spoiled"
```

Page
Time.2001.July
Foodsource.all

Column
Geog.Site.

	United States		Canada	France	
	Miami	Gloucester	Vancouver	Marseille	La Rochelle
Qty rejected	4,000	2,000	1,200	3,000	2,500
Qty over aged	3,000	3,000	1,500	2,000	3,200
Qty damaged	2,000	1,000	1,400	3,200	3,300
Qty spoiled	4,000	3,000	1,500	2,300	2,000
Total fish lost	13,000	9,000	5,600	10,500	11,000

Row
variables { }

Figure 14.8 Total fish lost.

2. The fish that perished the most this quarter (see Figure 14.9):

```
"Fish" {N} , "Site" {N} ,
        Time.quarter.prev ,
        Total fish lost.max
```

Page					
Time.2001.Q2					

Column
Geog.Site.

	United States		Canada	France	
Row	Miami	Boston	Vancouver	Marseille	La Rochelle
Total_fish_lost.max	Salmon	Shrimp	Salmon	French Sole	Tuna

Figure 14.9 The fish that perished the most.

3. The site that processes the largest quantity of fish (see Figure 14.10):

```
"Site" {N} ,
        Time.year. ,
        Food_source.all ,
        Fish received.max
```

Page
Qty_Received.max
Foodsource.all
InventorySite

Column
Time.year

1998	1999	2000
London	Hong Kong	Vancouver

Figure 14.10 The site that processes the largest quantity of fish.

4. The site that processes the largest number of kinds of fish (see Figure 14.11):

```
"ProductionSite" {N} ,
        Time.year. ,
        Foodsource.all
        Count(Foodsource.Fish. ,
        (Qty_Received > 0)).max
```

Page
Foodsource.all

Column
Time.year

Row	1998	1999	2000
Production Site	Vancouver	Hong Kong	Vancouver

Figure 14.11 The site that processes the largest number of kinds of fish.

5. The site with the least amount of losses (see Figure 14.12):

```
"Site" {N} ,
        Time.year. ,
        Foodsource.all ,
        Total_fish_lost.min
```

Page		
Total_Fish_Lost.min		
Foodsource.all		

Column
Time.year

Row		1998	1999	2000
Inventory Site		Buenos Aires	Hong Kong	Vancouver

Figure 14.12   The site with the least amount of losses.

6. The site with the greatest amount of variance in the quantity of fish throughput during the year (see Figure 14.13):

```
"Site" {N} ,
        Time.year,
        variance.(Foodsource.all).max
```

Page		
Variance.(Foodsource.all)		

Column
Time.year

Row		1998	1999	2000
"Site" {N}		Detroit	Nice	Cologne

Figure 14.13   The site with the greatest amount of variance in the quantity of fish throughput during the year.

7. The site that processes the most salmon (see Figure 14.14):

```
"Site" {N} ,
        Time.year. ,
        Foodsource.salmon ,
        Fish_received.max
```

Page		Column	
Qty_Received.max		Time.year	
Foodsource.Salmon			

Row	1998	1999	2000
InventorySite	Marseille	Miami	Boston

Figure 14.14   The site that processes the most salmon.

It looks like inventory sites vary considerably in terms of the regularity of their throughput, the number of kinds of fish throughput, and the amount of losses. It also looks like fish vary in terms of the average amount of losses. For some reason, there seems to be a lot of damaged salmon.

What about quantity on hand, said Thor, and what about losses as a percentage of throughput? Those are excellent questions, said Lulu, and it's about time we started trying to answer them.

More Analytical Derivations

Losses as a percentage of throughput are pretty straightforward to calculate, said Thor. Impress me, replied Lulu. How would you calculate by site and year the fish with the greatest relative losses? Thor's answer is as follows (see Figure 14.15):

```
"Fish" {N} ,
        Site. ,
        Time.Year.  ,
        Food_source.Fish.all ,
        (Qty rejected + Qty damaged + Qty spoiled + Qty over
        aged) / Qty received).max
```

Quantity on Hand

How would you calculate the quantity on hand, asked Lulu? Remember, notwithstanding inventory audits, we don't directly measure stocks. That's easy, replied Thor. The quantity on hand is just the difference between flows in and flows out. I wrote the formula out. Do you agree with Thor? **Think about it.**

```
'Qty on hand' {Kg},
        L.leaf. =

                Qty received -
                (Qty rejected +
                Qty over aged +
                Qty damaged +
                Qty spoiled +
                Qty sent to production)
```

Page
Time.2001
Foodsource.Fish.all
(Qty rejected + Qty damaged +
Qty spoiled + Qty over aged) /
Qty received).max

Column
Geog.Site.

	United States		Canada	France	
Row	Miami	Boston	Vancouver	Marseille	La Rochelle
"Fish" {N}	Tuna	Salmon	Salmon	French Sole	Shrimp

Figure 14.15 Losses as percentage of throughput.

So you see, said Thor, you just take all the inflows, namely the quantity received, and subtract out all the outflows, namely fish lost for any reason, plus fish sent to production, and you're left with the quantity of fish on hand. Is that so, said Lulu. I think you're forgetting something. **What do you think?**

Isn't the Qty on hand also a function of the previous day's Qty on hand? Surely, the formula needs to be recursive in time. As long as I'm criticizing your formula, can you tell me what time of day Qty on hand applies to? Is it Qty on hand at the beginning of the day, at the end of the day, the average for the day, or the Qty on hand after every change in quantity? Your formula isn't just wrong, Thor; it's also unclear. Lulu offered to take a stab at it.

First, said Lulu, I would make Qty on hand refer to the quantity on hand at the beginning of the day. It could have referred to any time, but I had to choose some time, and I felt it would be most useful to know the amount of fish on hand at the beginning of every day. Thus, all the additions and subtractions to the quantity of fish on hand that happen later on during the same day affect the next day's value for Qty on hand. The additions and subtractions to the quantity of fish on hand that affect any particular day's value represent events that happened the day before. Finally, the recursive property of Qty on hand, depending on its previous day's value, can only hold true for days other than the first day in the model because obviously there's no day that is previous to the first day. Thus, the recursively defined Qty on hand only applies to days 2 thru N, and the formula for Qty on hand for day 1 is a simple input as shown:

```
"Qty on hand" {Kg},
     Site. ,
     Food_source.fish.leaf. ,
     Time.day.first.after =
```

```
              (Qty on hand , Time.day.this-1) +
              (Qty received - (Qty rejected + Qty over
              aged + Qty damaged + Qty spoiled + Qty
              sent to production) , Time.day.this-1)

"Qty on hand" {Kg},
    Site. ,
    Food_source.fish.leaf. ,
    Time.day.first << input
```

So the quantity on hand at the beginning of any given day is equal to the previous day's quantity on hand plus new receipts minus the sum of material sent and all lost materials that previous day.

Stock Management

What about stocking issues, asked Thor? How can you tell when a food_source is out of stock? Is there enough information to judge whether a food_source that was out of stock in one place was available in others and how often that occurs? Is it a total rarity or does it occur with enough frequency that something needs to be done about it? Those are good questions, said Lulu. So long as we're on the topic, I would also like to know which food sources are about to run out so that any necessary changes can be made before the stock runs dry.

Thor proposed the following out of stock variable:

```
"Out of stock" ,
    L.        =
    "Qty on hand" - "Qty requested"
```

Does this make sense to you? It didn't to Lulu. She pointed out that the concept of out of stock was a condition that represented a certain relationship between Qty on hand and Qty requested, namely that the latter was greater than the former. Thus, out of stock should be treated as a condition or binary variable: true if Qty on hand is less than or equal to Qty requested, and false otherwise.

```
Out of stock.true = (Qty on hand - Qty requested < 0)
Out of stock.false = (Qty on hand - Qty requested >= 0)
```

How would you figure out when fish that was out of stock in one site was available elsewhere? asked Thor. This is a tougher query, replied Lulu. I need to think about the desired result form first as shown in Figure 14.16 with some hypothetical data.

Lulu continued. The query breaks down into several components:

- Determining every date-site-fish tuple that experienced a shortage
- Determining every other site that had at that time and for that fish an excess greater than or equal to the amount of the shortfall
- Determining the amount of that excess

Date	Site	Fish	Shortage {Kg}	Sites available	Excess per site
January 5	Vancouver	Salmon	500	Boston	800
				Nuremberg	750
				Seattle	900
January 12	Seattle	Tuna	300	Boston	350
				San Diego	450
				Nice	400

Figure 14.16   Desired result form for out of stock query.

I will address them in that order.
The first query component

```
"Time" {N}, "Site" {N}, "Fish" {N} ,
        L. ,
        Out of stock.true
```

returns the set of time-fish-site tuples where some fish was out of stock for some time for some site.

The second query component itself has multiple subcomponents of which the first

```
"Time" {N}, "Site" {N}, "Fish" {N} ,
      "Shortage" AS (Qty requested - Qty on hand),
            L. ,Out of stock.true
```

returns the amount of shortage defined within the query as Qty requested and Qty on hand.

Thor was impressed. That's pretty good, Lulu, but how would you figure out the other sites that had appropriate excess capacity? Lulu was clearly thinking about the problem. What would you do? **Think about it.**

After a few minutes, Lulu went up to the white board and wrote out the following query formula:

```
"Time" {N}, "Site.n" {N}, "Fish" {N} , "Shortage" {Kg} ,
        (Site.n̄). , (Qty requested - Qty on hand , Site.n) <
        (Qty on hand - Qty requested  , Site.n̄)
        L. ,
        Out of stock.true
```

In words, it says to return the time-site-fish tuples where some shortfall as defined by Out of stock.true exists, and to return along with each tuple the name of every other site or Site.n̄) where the excess capacity for the same fish on the same day defined as

(Qty requested − Qty on hand, Site.n) < (Qty on hand − Qty requested, Site.n was greater than the shortfall in the original site.

Thor's eyes were starting to glaze over. What's wrong? asked Lulu. I'm not sure about your last query, replied Thor. I understand what you're doing, but you may be concatenating too many query fragments. The cardinality of the time-site-fish tuples where some shortfall as defined by Out of stock.true exists may be quite different from the cardinality of sites with excess capacity as defined by (Site.n̄, (Qty requested − Qty on hand, Site.n) < (Qty on hand − Qty requested, Site.n̄). In other words, for every instance of a time-site-fish tuple there may be several other sites where excess fish was available. Doesn't it make sense to separate those fragments into two queries and then join them? **What do you think?**

Lulu responded. Although it would indeed be easy to separate the fragments into two separate queries, the information value comes from seeing the shortage tuples joined with the excess tuples, and by defining two separate queries, I will still have to create a join to connect them in a single analytical view; the effort required to join the results of the two queries will be at least as difficult as the effort required to join them in a single view within one query. Thus, so long as my tool set lets me define single complex queries whose result sets are defined by collections of tuples of potentially unequal cardinalities, I will do just that. So as to make it a little more concrete, Thor, let me show you how I expect the result to look. (See Figure 14.17.)

Finally, Lulu said, now that you're comfortable with this kind of query, we can see the amount of excess capacity for each other site with the following query. The bold subexpression *Qty on hand − Qty requested* is what returns the data we are looking for. Basically, it says that in addition to the name of every site.n that has excess capacity where site.n has a shortage, the query also needs to return the amount of that excess capacity. The final query is shown next and in Figure 14.18.

```
"Time" {N} , "Site.n" {N}, "Fish" {N} , "Shortage" {Kg} ,
          (Site.n̄ , Excess AS 'Qty on hand - Qty requested' ,
(Qty requested - Qty on hand , Site.n) <
(Qty on hand - Qty requested , Site.n̄)
L. ,
Out of stock.true
```

After analyzing the data, Lulu and Thor felt they had found a disturbing amount of inventory throughput management problems ranging from chronic overcapacity in some fish for some sites to sporadic undercapacity in other fish for other sites. Even worse, they found areas, such as the ones just noted, where the shortfall in one site was more than compensated for by excess capacity in the same fish for one or more other sites.

Systematic Age Tracking

It was pretty clear that Lulu and Thor needed to find a better way to systematically track fish aging, and that way was going to consist of changes to FCI's business processes and concomitant changes to their dimensional model. Hopefully, Jane was going to agree with their assessment of the need. Look again at the inventory cube.

Shortage tuples	Excess sites
Salmon, January 5, Vancouver, 500 Kg	Boston
	Nuremberg
	Seattle
Tuna, January 12, Seattle, 300 Kg	Boston
	San Diego
	Nice

Figure 14.17 Single complex queries whose result sets are defined by collections of tuples.

Shortage tuples	Excess Sites	Excess amounts {Kg}
Salmon, January 5, Vancouver, 500 Kg	Boston	800
	Nuremberg	750
	Seattle	900
Tuna, January 12, Seattle, 300 Kg	Boston	350
	San Diego	450
	Nice	400

Figure 14.18 The final query.

What would you do to systematically track aging? FCI already assigns a date of arrival to each shipment of received fish. But that information is only used by the packers so they can follow the FIFO inventory practice and discard overaged fish. How could this information be better leveraged? Would you add a date variable to the inventory cube? **Think about it.**

Changing the Cube

Lulu pointed out that regardless of how it was done, the quantity on hand variable was going to have to be differentiated by age. That is to say, FCI needs to know not just how much fish they have in stock, but how much of each age of fish they have in stock. Thor suggested, and Lulu agreed, they need to define an aging dimension and add it to the inventory cube. There are three basic steps to adding and using an Age dimension:

1. Define the dimension and add it to the existing location structure, void of data.

2. Do whatever rework is required to map the old data into the new location structure.

3. Add any appropriate new formulas defined in the new age-tracking inventory cube.

The Age dimension in itself is simple, they thought. It should be defined as a cardinal type with the same number of leaf-level instances as the maximum number of days that fish can age in inventory before needing to be gotten rid of. This is shown in Figure 14.19.

Before proceeding any further, Lulu wanted to know what the entire process looked like. What are the steps, which, once taken will result in a new age-tracking inventory cube? Practically speaking, said Thor, adding a new dimension is not like adding a new variable. Because the dimensionality of data is central to its definition, to its physical layout in storage, and to its method of access, nearly every OLAP tool forces you to reload and recalculate the data, essentially rebuild a cube, as a result of changing its dimensionality.

So, Thor continued, the process of adding a new dimension consists of defining the new dimension and adding it to a new version of the old schema. In other words, defining a new and empty cube. Then you redefine the old inventory formulas taking into account the new dimension and being careful to associate the formulas with the right member(s) of the Age dimension in the newly dimensioned cube. Once you've tested the newly defined cube you can then map the data from the old inventory cube (or its sources) into the new inventory cube. When that has been done successfully, you can connect the new inventory cube to all the cubes that were connected to the old inventory cube. This includes both cubes that referenced the old inventory cube and cubes previously referenced by the old inventory cube. Again, all links will need to reflect the new dimension. When the new inventory cube has been shown to correctly process new input data, including new fish received, intermediate losses reported, new requests, and fish sent to production, as well as correctly calculate all derivations and correctly connect to all appropriate cubes, then and only then can the old inventory cube be safely deleted.

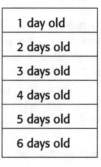

| 1 day old |
| 2 days old |
| 3 days old |
| 4 days old |
| 5 days old |
| 6 days old |

Figure 14.19   The Age dimension.

Having defined the new Age dimension, it is time to redefine the inventory variables given the new Age dimension. This can also be used to test whether the Age dimension is properly defined. Let's begin with Quantity received, recalling first its definition in the old inventory cube:

```
"Qty received " {Kg} ,
          L.leaf. << Input

"Qty received" ,
          L.leaf.above. =
                    Sum("Qty received " , L.leaf.)
```

Redefining Quantity Received

The first question, said Thor, is where does Qty received connect in the Age dimension? Where would you make the connection? **Think about it.**

That's easy, said Lulu. Fish are received as one day old. This is shown as follows:

```
"Quantity received",
          Time.day. ,
          Geog.site. ,
          Food_source.fish.leaf. ,
          Age.1 << input
```

The metric is the same for the old and the new Qty received. But what about aggregating? Does Qty received sum over the Age dimension? **What do you think?**

Lulu and Thor both agreed it doesn't. On the contrary, given FCI's current business model where fish arrives from purchasing within 24 hours, the variable Qty received only applies to the one-day-old member of the Age dimension. However, Thor pointed out, by adding an Age dimension, FCI could, in the future, differentiate between different ages of fish as they arrived at inventory. This would point to date-tagging the time of purchase, but would only be useful if some fish took more than 24 hours to arrive at inventory. Then, with that business process, Qty received would aggregate over the Age dimension as well.

Redefining Quantity Requested

The next variable they looked to redefine was Qty requested, the amount of fish requested by production to be sent from inventory. Recall from the old inventory model that Qty requested can be larger than quantity on hand, in which case there's a shortage. To which member of the Age dimension does Qty requested connect? Lulu was tempted to say it connects to Age.1 just like quantity received, but she knew that wasn't quite right. After all, lots of fish stay in inventory and, when sent, have several possible ages between one and six days. Thor was pondering the question. What do you think?

Thor eventually said that Qty requested doesn't connect to any of the Age members because there's a mistake in the Age dimension. It lacks an all member. When the folks at production are requesting fish, they aren't requesting fish of any particular age. Subject only to the FIFO inventory management principle, the folks at production don't dimension their requests by age. So after amending the Age dimension to reflect the all member, Thor wrote down the definition of the Qty requested variable.

```
"Qty requested" ,
        Time.day. ,
        Geog.site. ,
        Food_source.fish.leaf. ,
        Age.all << input
```

Redefining Quantity Sent

The next variable to redefine was Quantity sent. Now that FCI is systematically tracking fish age, they need to specify for every collection of fish sent to production how much of each age of fish was sent. So how do you put that in a formula? Think about it. It may be trickier than you suspect.

Thor said, it's a good idea—especially when a formula looks complex—to write out a formula prototype to identify the variables upon which the formula is defined. So what are the input variables for Quantity sent? To abstract away the extraneous, he noted that the formula should be the same for all fish and for all dates and for all sites. So those dimensions can be safely ignored for the moment. The real game seems to take place between the inventory variables mentioned and the Age dimension. Lulu agreed with Thor and started writing the following prototype function:

```
"Quantity Sent" = F(( Quantity requested , Age.all) , Quantity on hand )
```

Then, to help her think through the formula, she worked through the calculation in her mind. The quantity requested comes in at the all member of the Age dimension. Since FCI uses a FIFO method, the quantity requested then needs to be compared with the oldest quantity on hand, namely the six-day-old fish. If there is enough fish in the six-day-old bin to satisfy the requirement, then the quantity sent from the six-day-old bin is equal to the quantity requested at the all level. Putting this fragment in LC, she wrote the following:

```
If ("Qty on hand" {Kg} , Age.6)  >= ("Qty requested" {Kg} , Age.all)
Then ("Qty sent" {Kg} , Age.6) = ("Qty requested" {Kg} , Age.all)
```

But what if the six-day-old Qty on hand is less than the quantity requested? How is that handled? Well, for sure, the six-day-old bin would be cleaned out and the remaining quantity needed to fulfill the request would be compared with the quantity on hand of five-day-old fish. Thor suggested the following:

```
If ("Qty on hand" {Kg} , Age.6)  < ("Qty requested" {Kg} , Age.all)
Then ("Qty sent" {Kg} , Age.6) = ("Qty on hand" {Kg} , Age.6)
```

and

```
If ("Qty on hand" , Age.5) >=  ("Qty requested", Age.all - Qty sent,
Age.6)
Then "Qty sent" , Age.5 = ("Qty requested", Age.all - "Qty sent", Age.6)
```

and

```
If ("Qty on hand" , Age.5)  < ("Qty requested", Age.all - "Qty sent",
Age.6)
Then "Qty sent" , Age.5 = "Qty on hand" , Age.5
```

and

```
If ("Qty on hand" , Age.4) >=  ("Qty requested", Age.all - ("Qty sent",
Age.6 + "Qty sent" , Age.5))
Then "Qty sent" , Age.4 = ("Qty requested", Age.all - ("Qty sent", Age.6
+ "Qty sent" Age.5))
```

and so on until we get to Qty on hand, Age.1 at which point if there isn't enough fish in the one-day-old bin, there isn't enough fish in inventory and there exists a shortage.

Even Lulu was impressed with Thor's formulation. She suggested, and this is good practice, to write out the inputs and outputs for a relevant piece of formula in a simple table or worksheet or cubelet so the workings of the formula can really be thought about, as shown in Figure 14.20.

Thor had several comments once he got a chance to look at an example of the formula workings. In the formula, there is a decrementing term, namely the Qty requested minus the sum of quantities sent of different ages. This quantity, which is what's compared with the amount in every bin of some age, is a type of intermediate quantity. Even though no one is interested in looking at just that quantity, it might be easier to define an intermediate or working variable to capture the notion so as to avoid having to write a separate formula clause for each day of age in the Age dimension. What would happen, for example, if FCI wanted to track aging for all the more slowly perishable vegetarian ingredients and added 90 days to the Age dimension? In its current form, the formula would get unwieldy pretty quickly.

Age	Qty on hand {Kg}	Qty requested	Qty sent {Kg}
1	0		0
2	0		0
3	500		250
4	300		300
5	450		450
6	200		200
All	1450	1200	

Figure 14.20 The throughput for a formula cubelet.

Lulu suggested the following:

```
For Age.this = max  to min

While "Qty sent" , Age.this = "Qty on hand" , Age.this
And
While Sum ("Qty sent" , Age.max-this) < "Qty requested" , Age.all

If "Qty on hand" , Age.this >=  ("Qty requested" , Age.all -
Sum("Qty sent" , Age.max-this))

Then "Qty sent" , Age.this = ("Qty requested" , Age.all -
Sum("Qty sent" , Age.max-this))

Else

"Qty sent" , Age.this = "Qty on hand" , Age.this
```

And what about the remainders, asked Thor? We are, after all, modeling a depletion transaction. Where does the new Qty on hand get represented? Is it captured on the next day's balance? Or do we need to represent it with an additional variable, such as a post deletion Qty on hand?

Lulu replied that the answer depends on FCI's business processes. If we assume that Quantities received and requested come in only once per day (as we are assuming here), then, even if users are querying the system around the clock, FCI can calculate a quantity on hand at beginning of the day variable based on the previous day's transactions as soon as the day's quantities sent, quantities lost, and quantities received have been registered. Since no transaction will alter those quantities until the following day, FCI has the data to calculate the next day's Quantity on hand at the beginning of the day. So FCI doesn't need to create post-transaction balances.

Redefining Quantity on Hand

So, said Lulu, what is the new definition of Quantity on hand? Thor replied, let's first recall the old definition stripped of the complexities of the various sources of lost fish:

```
"Qty on hand" {Kg},
        Site. ,
        Food_source.fish.leaf. ,
        Time.day.first.after. =

                ("Qty on hand" , Time.day.this-1) +
                ("Qty received" -
                ("Qty lost for any reason" + "Qty sent to
                production") , Time.day.this-1)

"Qty on hand" {Kg},
        Site. ,
        Food_source.fish.leaf. ,
        Time.day.first << input
```

All you need to do, said Thor, is add the Age dimension to each of the two formulas, as I've done next, making sure to refer to Age.leaf since there's also an Age.all. What do you think of Thor's formulas?

```
"Qty on hand" {Kg},
        Site. ,
        Food_source.fish.leaf. ,
        Time.day.first.after. ,
        Age.leaf. =
                ("Qty on hand" , Time.day.this-1) +
                ("Qty received" -
                ("Qty lost for any reason" + "Qty sent to
production") , Time.day.this-1)


"Qty on hand" {Kg},
    Site. ,
    Food_source.fish.leaf. ,
    Time.day.first ,
    Age.leaf. << input
```

Lulu pointed out several problems with the new definitions as stated. First of all, in the new cube, Quantity received is input solely at the 1 member of the Age dimension. Quantity sent does happen on a day-old-by-day-old basis so that part of the formula remains. But then how do additions occur? asked Thor. Good question, said Lulu. Think about it.

Additions to fish of some age occur through the aging process itself. This implies that Quantity on hand for any age fish needs to be a recursive function in two dimensions: Time and Age, as shown here and in Figure 14.21:

```
"Qty on hand",
    Site. ,
    Food_source.fish.leaf. ,
    Time.day.first.after. ,
    Age.1.after. =
        ("Qty on hand" , Time.day.this-1 ,
          Age.this-1) -
        ("Qty lost for any reason" + "Qty sent to
          production") , Time.day.this-1)
```

Furthermore, said Lulu, there are two separate starting cases that you need to be aware of and which I show you next: the first day, which happens once for the whole cube, and the first day of age, which happens for every fish as it is received:

```
"Qty on hand" {Kg},
        Site. ,
        Food_source.fish.leaf. ,
        Time.day.first ,
        Age.1 << input
```

```
"Qty on hand",
Site. ,
Food_source.fish.leaf. ,
Time.day.first.after. ,
Age.1 = Qty received, Age.1
```

Redefining the Loss Variables

Now we can add back the various loss variables. Quantity rejected at receipt, like Quantity received, is input for the one-day-old member of the Age dimension.

```
"Quantity rejected at receipt" ,
        Time.day. ,
        Geog.site. ,
        Foodsource.fish.leaf. ,
        Age.1 << input
```

			Jan 23	Jan 24	Jan 25
Vancouver	Whitefish	Qty_Sent {kg}	2,000	2,100	2,050
		Qty_Received {kg}	1,900	2,200	2,250
		Qty_Lost {kg}	100	125	75
		Qty_On_Hand {kg}	1,600	1,575	1,700
	Tuna	Qty_Sent {kg}	1,500	1,400	1,450
		Qty_Received {kg}	1,400	1,450	1,500
		Qty_Lost {kg}	100	75	125
		Qty_On_Hand {kg}	1,400	1,375	1,300
Boston	Bass	Qty_Sent {kg}	1,720	1,620	1,670
		Qty_Received {kg}	1,620	1,670	1,720
		Qty_Lost {kg}	175	150	200
		Qty_On_Hand {kg}	1,620	1,520	1,370
	Tuna	Qty_Sent {kg}	1,845	1,745	1,795
		Qty_Received {kg}	1,745	1,795	1,845
		Qty_Lost {kg}	200	175	225
		Qty_On_Hand {kg}	22,650	22,775	22,950

Figure 14.21 Inventory variables by fish, site, and time.

Quantity over age is equivalent to a seven-day-old quantity on hand variable. Lulu even suggested that a seventh day be added to the day-old dimension where all quantities on hand on the seventh day are shipped to a secondary market. But Thor responded that adding a seventh day to the Age dimension would mean that all the depletion formulas that start with the oldest fish first would now have to start with the second oldest. Besides, he said, there's an easy way to express over-aged fish. So what should be the formula? **Think about it.** Thor suggested the following:

```
"Overaged fish",
        Time.day. ,
        Site.leaf,
        Material.leaf. ,
        Age.6 = "Quantity on hand"  - "Quantity sent"
```

This basically says that any six-day-old fish left over after whatever fish is to be sent to production has been sent is (given there's only one transaction per day) over age. (This formulation, and assuming no fancy use of the Naturals as the domain, thereby eliminating the possibility of negative integers, will produce zero-valued and negative numbers for all cases where no fish is overaged.) What about quantity damaged or spoiled? asked Lulu. Fish can be damaged or spoiled at any time. You can just show me the formula for quantity damaged.

```
"Quantity damaged" ,
        Site.leaf. ,
        Time.day. ,
        Foodsource.fish.leaf. ,
        Age. << input
```

So now we're ready to define the full equation for Quantity on hand given the method of depletion and the various ways that fish are lost as shown here:

```
"Qty on hand",
    Site. ,
    Foodsource.fish.leaf. ,
    Time.day.first.after. ,
    Age.1.after. =
    ("Qty on hand" , Time.day.this-1 ,
    Age.this.-1) - ("Quantity damaged" + "Quantity spoiled" +
    "Qty sent to production" , Time.day.this-1 , Age.this.-1)

"Qty on hand",
    Site. ,
    Food_source.fish.leaf. ,
    Time.day.first ,
    Age.1 << input

"Qty on hand",
    Site. ,
    Food_source.fish.leaf. ,
    Time.day.first.after. ,
    Age.1 = "Qty received", Age.1
```

Auditing

Relative to basic inventory tracking, auditing is straightforward, said Lulu. Although we calculate the quantity of fish on hand based on measurements of flows input and output, we could audit those numbers by measuring any and all quantities on hand. FCI decided to perform random sample audits in addition to the year-end audit. All audits have the following form:

```
"Quantity on hand audited" {Kg} ,
     Time.day. ,
     Site.leaf. ,
     Foodsource.fish.leaf. ,
     Age.leaf. << input

"Reconciliation" {Kg},
     Time.day. ,
     Site.leaf. ,
     Foodsource.fish.leaf. ,
     Age.leaf. = "Quantity on hand" - "Quantity on hand audited"
```

Derived Variables

Now that we've mapped the basic inventory variables from the ageless inventory cube to the age-tracking cube, said Thor, I, for one, am ready to create some analytically useful derived variables. Lulu and Thor then proceeded to take turns writing out analytical formulas and showing sample views of their results as follows (see Figures 14.22 through 14.25).

1. Oldest fish and freshest fish sent to production

```
("Fish", Age.min), ("Fish" , Age.max),
       Foodsource.all,
       Time.Day.,
       Geog.MaterialsInventorySite.,
       ("Qty sent to production", Time.Day.this > 0)
```

Time.July1	United States		Canada	France	
	Miami	Boston	Vancouver	Marseille	La Rochelle
Fish, Age.min	Tuna	Salmon	Salmon	Swordfish	Cod
Fish, Age.max	Bluefish	Whitefish	Catfish	Bass	French Sole

Figure 14.22 Oldest fish and freshest fish sent to production.

2. Average fish age in materials inventory:

```
(Sum(Qty on hand × Age, Age.) ÷ (Qty on hand, Age.all)),
Foodsource.Fish.all, Geog.MaterialsInventorySite., Time.Day.
```

Alternatively, and to accentuate the sum-of-series aspect to the weighted average, they wrote the following:

```
Sum ((("Qty on hand" ÷ ("Qty on hand , Age.all)) x Age) , Age.) ,
Foodsource.Fish.all, Geog.MaterialsInventorySite., Time.Day.
```

Time.July1	United States		Canada	France	
	Miami	Boston	Vancouver	Marseille	La Rochelle
(Sum(Qty on hand × Age.this, Age.) ÷ (Qty on hand, Age.all))	4.2	4.5	4.9	3.5	3.7

Figure 14.23 Average fish age in materials inventory.

3. Fish most needed to be used to avoid throwing any away:

```
("Fish" {N}, Qty on hand.max),   "Qty on hand" {Kg}
Age.6,
Foodsource.Fish.,
Geog.MaterialsInventorySite.,
Time.Day.
```

Time.July1 Age.6	United States		Canada	France	
	Miami	Boston	Vancouver	Marseille	La Rochelle
Fish, Qty on hand.max	Bluefish	Whitefish	Catfish	n/a	n/a
Qty_on_hand {kg}	75	65	70	0	0

Figure 14.24 Fish needed to be used to avoid throwing any away.

4. Material inventory sites with the greatest waste/throughput ratio:

```
"MaterialsInventorySite", "Rank",
        Time.day.,
        Age.all,
        Food_source.all ,
        ("Qty lost" /"Qty_Throughput"), Geog.all).Drnk.(1 to 3)
```

		July 1	July 2	July 3
Drank.1	Material Inventory {N}	Vancouver	Boston	London
Drank.2	Material Inventory {N}	San Francisco	Detroit	Nuremberg
Drank.3	Material Inventory {N}	Nice	Hong Kong	Nice

Figure 14.25 Material inventory sites with the greatest waste/throughput ratio.

Costing

The two major differences in granularity for which inventory costs can be calculated are site by time-aggregated costs and employee-task-level costs. The basic framework for the former method of tracking costs consists of a two-dimensional location structure defined by time and site and all the relevant cost variables such as energy, financial, maintenance, and labor. Once tracked, costs can then be compared with the inventory throughputs achieved by site and by time in order to calculate the costs per unit of fish moved through inventory and to calculate the true, activity-based cost of fish as it arrives at a production facility.

The latter method of tracking costs requires the measurement of what each inventory employee is doing at a particular time, in effect, treating the inventory process as a project to be managed. The time dimension would have to be resolved to the hour or even minute level. Site-specific employees would have to be connected to specific tasks at specific times such as loading and unloading fish. Once in place, this would allow FCI to calculate, among other things, fish losses by employee group, perhaps finding that employees with certain attributes are more or less likely to drop fish or misevaluate spoiled fish.

As useful as this information may prove to be, FCI did not think that it was as important as creating an employee-level understanding of production. So, forced to prioritize, FCI took a breadth first approach to the company-wide performance indicators it was creating and was willing to leave the detailed inventory employee mapping project to a later time.

Site by Time-Level Costing

All right, said Thor, where do we begin? Lulu replied that the two dimensions needed for inventory costing, site-based geography, and day-based time are identical with the versions already being used for throughput analysis. So we only need to think about the input variables. Lulu went on to say that the basic strategy is straightforward. Collect all cost variables at their natural level of time granularity and combine them into a total cost variable at some appropriately fine level of time granularity. Then compare fish throughput with total costs for that same level of time granularity.

After talking to the folks in accounting, Lulu was given the following month-level summary of cost accounts pertaining to every inventory site:

- Number of employees {int}
  - For each paygrade
    Number of employee hours per pay grade {int}

- Maintenance costs {$}

- Facility costs {$}

- Energy costs {$}

For the analyst's purposes, each of the variables was input at the site-by-month level. Figure 14.26 shows representative data for three sites. Note that all sites have three different paygrades, though the dollar amounts per paygrade vary considerably

Variable	Site 1	Site 2	Site 3
Month/rent	5,000	6,500	6,000
No. of employees	19	22	20
Hrs paygrade 1	2,400	2,600	2,000
$/hr paygrade 1	17	19	22
Hrs paygrade 2	600	800	550
$/hr paygrade 2	38	42	45
Hrs paygrade 3	50	100	40
$/hr paygrade 3	60	75	85
Maintenance	5,000	6,000	5,000
Facility	10,000	14,000	12,000
Energy	5,000	4,000	4,000
Total costs	86,600	114,500	93,150

Figure 14.26 Costs by site.

from site to site. This is because base labor rates vary substantially across continents. All sites report in terms of U.S. dollars based on average monthly effective exchange rates.

We are now ready to assign operating costs to throughput. Thor suggested bringing the cost data into the throughput cube since the throughput cube was already performing most of the calculations and it was a good idea to have specialized calculation cubes. Lulu said, you want to balance the calculations and so it's better to put the combined formulas in the cost cube. How would you do it? Would you bring operating costs into the inventory throughput cube or vice versa as our analysts suggested? Or would you build a new cube? More importantly, how would you decide? **Think about it.**

Remember, whenever you are defining multicube calculations, the best way to avoid confusion is to stay focused on what you're trying to do. The way to do that, is to begin by specifying the dimensionality of the result set and then working backwards to join up with your starting data sets.

Lulu began drawing out a table representation of the two multicube variables she was interested in calculating (see Figure 14.27).

The top expression, *$cost, Asset.all*, comes from the Cost cube and represents the aggregation of all the line item costs. The bottom expression, *Qty thruput, Food_source.all, Age.all*, represents the sum of all fish of all ages throughput. Although there are a variety of ways of defining throughput, a simple method based on averaging the quantity of fish received and sent was used.

Thor said, so long as the multicube expressions are correctly dimensioned by site and by time it doesn't make any logical difference whether the cost data is brought into the throughput cube or vice versa, or whether all the data is put into a new cube. (When it does make a difference—seen often in the cube calculation exercise in Chapter 17—is when the dimensions of the new variable do not correspond to the dimensions of any existing cube and thus some join or merge cube is required.) Practically speaking, since many front-end tools make it easier to view the contents of a single cube at a time, you would typically define the multicube variable in that cube whose other variables are most likely to be queried at the same time. In this case, FCI is most likely to query for

Time.month/ Geog.site		Site1		Site2
January	V1	$cost, Asset.all	V1	$cost, Asset.all
	V2	Qty thruput, Food_source.all, Age.all	V2	Qty thruput, Food_source.all, Age.all
February	V1	$cost, Asset.all	V1	$cost, Asset.all
	V2	Qty thruput, Food_source.all, Age.all	V2	Qty thruput, Food_source.all, Age.all

Figure 14.27 Combining costs and throughput.

V1 = variable one. V2 = variable two.

cost per kilo of fish information at the same time it queries for other costs so the multi-cube cost per kilo variables were defined in the cost cube as shown here:

```
[Materials Cost]: "Cost per kilo of fish processed in inventory"{$/Kg} ,
    Geog.site. ,
    Time.month. =
        "Total costs" / [Materials Throughput]: "Quantity
        thruput" , Age.all , Foodsource.fish.all
```

Other subtotal cost variables, such as labor, management, or utility, can be defined in the same way. Thor noted that productivity variables also have the same structure as with the following:

```
[Materials Cost]: "No. of labor hours per kilo of fish processed in
inventory" {Hrs/Kg} ,
    Geog.site. ,
    Time.month. =
        (Paygrade 1 hours + Paygrade 2 hours + Paygrade 3
        hours) / [Materials Throughput]: Quantity sent ,
        Age.all , Foodsource.fish.all
```

Lulu was underwhelmed with Thor's formulas. You got it right, Thor, she said, but those aren't the most riveting formulas I've seen today. Can't you show me something exciting? Thor replied that they didn't have access to any of the detailed employment information that would be required to connect actual employees to specific tasks. But Lulu persisted. Isn't there any other derivable and useful information that can be gleaned from the data? **Think about it.**

Thor was still working on the problem when Lulu said that even though they don't have access to activity-level data, they can still approximate the daily storage cost of fish. This can be done by allocating inventory costs to the day level and then combining daily storage costs with daily throughput quantities to estimate the cost in dollars to store one kilogram of fish for one day. Then they can leverage the data based on the Age dimension to figure out on a day-by-day and fish-by-fish basis the total cost of storing some particular type of fish based on its number of days spent in inventory.

Clearly, the inventory cost per kilo of fish that remained in storage only one day is less than the cost per kilo of fish that remained in storage six days. Even if all the employee's time is allocated to processing fish received and fish sent, we can still assign some storage cost through the facility, maintenance, and energy bills. Assuming here that one-third of the site is dedicated to loading and unloading and the rest is dedicated to storage, Lulu said we can create a rough formula for assigning incremental time-based storage costs as follows:

```
[Cost]: "Cost per kilo of fish processed in inventory" {$/Kg} ,
    Geog.site. ,
    Time.day. =
        (2/3 (Costs , Asset.all) / [Throughput]: (Quantity sent
        + Quantity received)/2, Age.all , Material.all
```

Not bad, said Thor. However, I don't think you've correctly captured the total costs of inventory. Do you agree with Thor? If so, what is he referring to? Lulu wasn't sure.

Thor continued. You need to loosen up on your formula and lump all costs together (that is, not pretend to capture loading and unloading), in which case your formula simplifies to the following:

```
[Cost]: "Cost per kilo of fish processed in inventory"{$/Kg-day} ,
    Geog.site. ,
    Time.day. =

        (Costs , Asset.all) / [Throughput]: (Quantity sent +
        Quantity received)/2 , Age.all , Material.all
```

As written, this formula enables you to assign a daily cost of inventory to the day's throughput of fish. That cost is expressed in terms of dollars per kilogram-day. The total cost of storing any fish for any amount of time is thus the sum of the costs per kilogram-day times the amount of fish in storage per day for every day the fish in question is in storage.

However, as written, the formula does not distinguish storage costs from loading and unloading costs. If, for example, the costs of loading and unloading were significantly higher than the costs of storage, then the average cost per day would be highest for fish that spent the least amount of time in storage. Or if there were a discrete cost-generating event that occurred at the receiving or sending end, your formula, as written, would not pick it up. Rather those discrete loading and unloading costs would be combined with the overall storage costs. Lulu chimed in, so how should we calculate those costs, Mr. Fancy Pants? How would you?

Blushing, Thor continued, if you want to differentiate storage costs from the costs of loading and unloading, you first of all need to track loading costs separately from unloading costs. FCI is not currently doing this, so my approach cannot be implemented at the current time. Assuming for the moment that FCI does track these costs separately, my approach requires breaking up the total inventory cost into three components: cost of receiving, cost of storing, and cost of sending. The tricky part is that the method of calculating the inventory cost of fish sent to production is different than calculating the inventory cost of fish received. Can you say why that is?

Calculating the inventory cost for a particular lot of fish of a particular age is much simpler than calculating the inventory cost of fish for a lot of fish entering inventory. This is because a single lot of fish of a single age, sent to production, can trace back to a single lot received on a single day, whereas a single lot received on a single day may be sent out on multiple days. Since the concept is the same, let me just focus on calculating backwards from quantities sent to production. Given a quantity of a particular type of fish, Fish.x, of a particular age, Age.x, (greater than or equal to one day old since fish arrives one day old) sent to production on a particular day, Time.day.x , and leveraging the previous formula for calculating storage cost of fish on hand, the total inventory cost for that fish may be calculated as follows.

```
("Qty sent" , Time.day.x , Foodsource.fish.x , Age.x) / ("Qty sent" ,
Time.day.x , Foodsource.all , Age.all)  X ("Sending costs" , Time.day.x)    +


If "Age" , Foodsource.fish.x > = 1 then
(
("Qty on hand" , Foodsource.fish.x  , Age.x , Time.Age.(1 to x)) /
("Qty on hand" , Foodsource.fish.all , Age.all ,Time.(Age.(1 to x) ,
Foodsource.fish.x) )    X    ("Storage costs" , Time.Age.(1-x))
)
Else 0


+
("Qty received" , Time.day.Age.1) / ("Qty received" , Foodsource.fish.all)  X
("Receiving costs" , Time.day.Age.1)
```

If the fish was sent out the same day it was received, then the middle cost expression drops out, added Thor. I see where you're going, said Lulu. But could you explain the middle term in more detail? Sure, replied Thor. The top two lines evaluate as an array of ratios between the quantity of fish.x on hand and the total quantity of all fish on hand. There exists one ratio per day that fish.x is in storage. The term that gives us that array is the Time.Age.(1 to x). In words, it says to take the set of times for which the age (of fish.x) ranges from one day old to x days old where x days old is the age of fish.x at the time it is sent to production. Then for the same set of dates, that ratio is multiplied by the total costs of storage, and the resulting set of daily storage costs per fish. x is then summed to generate the total cost of storage for fish.x.

Although I appreciate your clear explanation, said Lulu, it's interesting to note that even here, you can't really assign elemental cost events to the right fish. For example, if there's a cost spike due to any unforeseen event that affects any receiving of fish on a particular day, that cost increment, though captured, is evenly assigned to all fish received that day. If you want the ability to track the ultimate sources of dips and spikes, then you need to maintain a connection to your event tracking or transaction database.

As useful as it is to track costs, even if they're not totally elemental, said Lulu, I think that in all this rush to detail we left out some interesting cost-like derivations. Maybe we can use the differing amounts of time spent in inventory, the differing amounts of fish on hand, and some measure of inventory capacity to come up with a measure of overall inventory productivity as with the following formula beginning with its prototype:

```
Inventory productivity = F( 1/time spent in inventory , percent
utilization of storage facilities as defined by the maximum fish on hand
for the year)
```

In other words, the more productive a site, the less time fish spends in inventory and the more fish, as a percentage of the maximum amount of fish storable, is on hand. Since there are two distinct productivity measures, it makes sense to define them separately. One such formulation and corresponding result set looks, for each, as follows (see Figure 14.28):

```
"Inventory volume productivity" {R},
      Time.month. ,
      Geog.site. =

            Avg
            ("Quantity on hand" , Time.day. /
            "Quantity on hand.max" , Time.day.this.year)
```

Time.July	United States		Canada	France	
	Miami	Boston	Vancouver	Marseille	La Rochelle
Inventory Volume Productivity	0.73	0.81	0.89	0.79	0.69

Figure 14.28   Inventory capacity productivity.

In words, the volume productivity of inventory space is defined as the average ratio of daily quantity on hand divided by the maximum day's quantity on hand for the year. The formula for inventory turns is shown as follows (see Figure 14.29):

```
"Inventory turn productivity" {R},
            Time.month. ,
            Geog.site. ,
            Foodsource.fish. =

                Avg
                ((Quantity sent, Age.1 / Quantity sent , Age.all) ,
                Time.day , Foodsource.fish.)
```

Time.July	United States		Canada	France	
	Miami	Boston	Vancouver	Marseille	La Rochelle
Inventory Turn Productivity	0.15	0.13	0.25	0.19	0.10

Figure 14.29   Inventory turn productivity.

In words, the inventory turn productivity is defined as the average percent of fish sent out that is one day old. Note that the evaluation of inventory turns creates a calculation for every fish-month-site tuple.

Summary

In this chapter, FCI's analysts figured out how to model inventory stocks and flows, how to add a new dimension to a cube, how to map data from the prior cube to the new one with the added dimension, and how to calculate the quantity on hand of raw materials when those materials age (which is a function that is recursive in two dimensions). They also figured out how to calculate when shortages in one center were more than offset by overstocking in other areas, how to calculate which age buckets are used up and what remains after daily orders are sent to production, how to handle inventory sparsity, how to create variables with restricted application ranges, and how to calculate the costs and productivity of storing materials per weight and time period.

## CHAPTER 15

FCI's Sales
and Marketing

In this chapter, you will learn how an OLAP solution can be brought to bear on sales and marketing. By following Lulu and Thor as they wrestle with whether to model package type as a dimension or a variable, you will see different ways of aggregating variables that don't simply sum in all dimensions. You will learn about different ways of inputting data that has gaps in it, and will see how to perform mix variance analysis for sales in multiple dimensions. You will learn about the best way to model a marketing expenditure variable that captures source expenses at different levels of granularity, how to aggregate marketing expenditures, and how to allocate them to the product level and compare allocated costs with sales. You will also learn how to create a customer value state model.

Foodcakes International (FCI) needs to understand how and why sales of their products vary by time, by store, by customer type, and by foodcake. The company knows that in order to accomplish this, it needs to gain insight into the ultimate consumers of its products. After all, FCI does not sell its products directly to consumers. Rather, it sells its foodcakes to stores who, in turn, sell them to consumers. In order to get a chance to analyze its final customers, FCI proposed, as a part of its warehousing initiative, and nearly all its client-stores agreed, to create a store-resident extranet supply chain application that exposed the client-store foodcake transaction data, with minimal delay to FCI. With appropriate security, each client store, by contributing its own data could see FCI-generated analyses of its future sales and comparisons of its sales with aggregates of other similar stores. No store's actual data were visible to any entity other than FCI. In addition, FCI offered to sponsor some comarketing activities with the stores. The stores therefore expected to benefit from additional sales and better

Date	Time	Register	Transaction ID	Total amount{$}
Jan 8, 2001	09:11	4	90821	43.21
Jan 8, 2001	09:12	2	30111	62.18
Jan 8, 2001	09:14	4	90823	12.06

Figure 15.1 Transaction summary.

Transaction ID	Item name	Price {$/unit}	Qty_Sold {unit}	Total_ Revenue {$}	Discount {$}
90814	Gourmet Fishcakes Sea Supreme 8-pk	12.95	3	38.85	5.00
90818	Gourmet Fishcakes Poseidon 8-pk	11.95	3	35.85	4.00
90821	Diet Fishcakes Neptune 8-pk	10.95	3	32.85	3.00

Figure 15.2 Detail records.

inventory management. To kick off this effort, FCI's skunk works sponsoring manager, Jane, sent Lulu and Thor (in their role as customer-facing consultants) to their sole client store in Cambridge, Massachusetts.

The first thing shown to FCI was the summary and detail transaction records for Cambridge as illustrated in Figures 15.1 and 15.2. When asked if they needed to see anything beyond the foodcake transactions, FCI responded that in addition to gaining access to the detailed foodcake transactions, they would need to see the transaction summaries to understand what percentage of the customer's food basket was dedicated to foodcakes. Beyond that, if they were going to understand the basket of products likely to be purchased at the same time as foodcakes—knowledge that is necessary in order to design effective sales promotional campaigns—they would have to see the entire set of detailed transactions. The Cambridge store understood this, but responded that for now FCI should focus on understanding sales of foodcakes.

To get the ball rolling, Lulu wanted to build a straightforward cube to calculate the various rollups of the store's sales data.

Cube Dimensions

The sales and marketing cube has four dimensions (described in more detail in Chapter 13) that interrelate in a standard Cartesian product:

- **Time.**   Lulu used FCI's standard time dimension that is level-based, begins with days on the lowest level, and has a week rollup and a month quarter year rollup. The dimension covers three years' worth of days.

- **Geography.**   Consistent with earlier design decisions, Lulu joined the FCI-maintained list of stores with the FCI-maintained country-based geography dimension to create a store-based geography dimension.

- **Foodcakes.**   Currently, FCI sells 30 different kinds of foodcakes broken out into three types: Gourmet, Diet, and Vegetarian.

- **Scenario.**   FCI's standard reporting includes three scenarios: Plan, Actual, and Variance.

Cube Input Variables

The data collected at the stores that is now being funneled to FCI is composed of the input variables described in the following sections.

Number of Packages Sold: Qty_Sold{pkg}

The stores track sales by package. FCI produces two different package types: four-packs and eight-packs. Lulu asked at this point whether it made more sense to treat the difference between four-packs and eight-packs as a variables difference or a dimension difference. **What do you think?**

Dimension or Variable?

After thinking about it for a minute, Thor said that if all foodcakes are sold as either four- or eight-packs and given only one kind of quantity sold variable, then it was more efficient to treat the pack type distinction as a variables distinction rather than a Foodcake dimension distinction. This is because if the pack type distinction were to be defined on the Foodcake dimension, it would require doubling the number of leaf-level elements in that dimension. From a process perspective, they would need to either add a new level to the foodcake dimension called the SKU or package level where each combination of two- and eight-packs rolls up to what are the now existing leaves or every current leaf would have to be edited to become either a two- or eight-pack and then the other kind of package would have to be added alongside. In either event, a minimum of 60 new declarations would have to be performed.

In contrast, continued Thor, tracking the distinction between package types in the variables can be done by creating two quantity sold variables for the one they currently have in place. However, if FCI sold different kinds of packages for different kinds of foodcakes, this variable-based strategy wouldn't work. They would either have to define additional variables with foodcake-based constrained application ranges or they would have to represent package distinctions on the leaves of the foodcake dimension. Do you agree with Thor?

The Package Dimension[1]	
Package.all	Package.4pack
	Package.8pack

Figure 15.3 Pack dimension.

Lulu responded, I like your reasoning, Thor, and I agree that adding two new variables is better than adding 60 new leaves, but you left out an important and ultimately, I think, the best option: adding a new package-type dimension to the cube. That's really the most efficient way to go. The problem with adding the two new variables is that over time the cube is likely to expand in the number of base variables and thus the two variables will eventually become 20 or 40 variables. In contrast, if we add a new, package-type dimension, it will be unaffected by increases in the number of things we track. Rather, it will only grow if FCI adds new package types, which is a less likely scenario.

I guess the most important decision factor is knowing the likely sources of future variance, said Thor. The less that is known about future variances, the less can be said about what constitutes an optimal method of modeling the present. At this point, we're only arguing about different physical ways of representing the same logical schema. I'm okay with treating the distinction between package types as a dimension distinction defined in terms of two leaf-level instances: four-pack and eight-pack that connect in a Package.all root instance as illustrated in Figure 15.3.

After rebuilding their sales and marketing cube, Lulu and Thor continued with the process of defining variables.

Return to Qty Sold {pkg}

Qty_sold is input at the leaf level of time, foodcake package type, and geography. Its metric is defined as Integer number of packages {pkg}. Actual data are input for the actual member of the scenario dimension; plan data are input at the plan element.

```
"Qty_Sold" {pkg},
        Geog.leaf.,
        Time.leaf.,
        Foodcake.leaf.,
        Package.leaf.,
        Scenario.actual <<      [input from store tables summed to the
                                day level]

"Qty_Sold" {pkg},
        Geog.leaf. ,
        Time.leaf. ,
        Foodcake.leaf. ,
```

```
Package.leaf. ,
Scenario.plan <<
[input from FCI planning data summed to the day level]
```

Both actual and planned Qty_Sold {pkg} sum up all but the scenario dimension. The exclusion of the scenario dimension from aggregation is handled differently as a function of how the OLAP tool used lets the user define dimensions. If the tool forces the user to define an all member for every dimension, then the user needs to find a way to exclude the scenario dimension from any aggregations. This could be done with a formula as simple as the following:

```
"Qty_Sold" {pkg},
    Geog.leaf.above. ,
    Time.leaf.above. ,
    Foodcake.leaf.above. ,
    Package.leaf.above. ,
    Scenario.actual =

Sum( Qty_Sold {pkg}, Geog.leaf., Time.leaf., Foodcake.leaf. ,
         Package.leaf. )
```

In other words, the application range of the variable is restricted to the actual member of the scenario dimension. Alternatively, if the OLAP environment allows for dimensions to be defined without an all member, then the scenario dimension can be ignored for the purposes of aggregation as with the following formula:

```
"Qty_Sold" {pkg},
    Geog.leaf.above. ,
    Time.leaf.above. ,
    Foodcake.leaf.above. ,
    Package.leaf.above. =

    Sum( Qty_Sold {pkg}, Geog.leaf, Time.leaf, Foodcake.leaf,
                 Package.leaf )
```

List Price per Package {$/pkg}

The list price per package is the suggested retail price for a package of FCI's foodcakes. FCI is very conscious of its brand image and although it regularly runs promotions on its products in conjunction with its client-stores, the company does not typically allow retailers to initiate discounts on its foodcakes.

Managing Price Changes

FCI maintains price change information in a Type 2 dimension as illustrated in Figure 15.4.

Thor noticed right away that it was going to take a bit of transformation to bring the data into the cube. Can you see what the problem is? Thor explained that the problem

Foodcake	Date	Wholesale_Price {$}	List_Price {$}
Neptune.4pack	Jan 02	5.75	6.90
Neptune.4pack	Jan 31	5.60	6.55
Neptune.8pack	Jan 02	11.35	13.10

Figure 15.4 Price change table.

arises because in the pricing table, package type information was a part of the item description. This is equivalent to defining package type as a leaf-level element of the foodcake dimension. Unfortunately, neither the relational nor the OLAP tool was well equipped for this kind of transformation.

Thor figured he needed to transpose the pack suffixes currently part of the foodcake name with the Wholesale (W) and List (L) price columns, effectively creating two columns for every one that existed before. But was it that simple? Lulu didn't think so. She told Thor that his ability to perform the transposition was a function of whether FCI changed its prices for both package types at the same time. To illustrate her point, she showed what FCI's price table would look like if transposed according to Thor's design.

Lulu's illustration of Thor's proposed design is shown in Figure 15.5.

There's bound to be a lot of sparsity in this type of table design, she said. A row is going to have valid values in either the 4pack columns or the 8pack columns but not both. Thor agreed, but with the qualification that if FCI changed its prices for both types of packages on the same dates, then the table would be dense and hence appropriate. True enough, said Lulu, but currently FCI's business process creates price changes for each package type independently, and FCI shouldn't change its business process just to make their job easier.

Thus, given the way the Foodcake dimension was defined in their sales model, the analysts were left with two basic choices. On the one hand, they could replicate pricing data and keep it all in a single table like the previous table. The advantage of this approach is that there is just one table to maintain and link with. The disadvantage is that it is harder to tell when prices have changed since there is a row for all package types whenever any one of them has changed. On the other hand, they could create a

Foodcake	Date	4pack W price	4pack L price	8pack W price	8pack L price
Neptune	Jan 02	5.75	6.90		
Neptune	Jan 31	5.60	6.55		
Neptune	Jan 02			11.35	13.10

Figure 15.5 Thor's proposed design.

separate table for each package type. The advantage with this approach is that every row in both tables represents a genuine price change and the tables are in fourth normal form, thus less susceptible to update anomalies. The disadvantage is that there are more tables to link to. Since for FCI, now, there are only two different package types, no one felt that having two pricing tables was a hardship and so they chose to use a different pricing table for each package type, as shown in Figures 15.6 and 15.7.

After they'd created the two tables and looked at them, Lulu wondered aloud, you know, Thor, I'm not sure that breaking up the package changes is the right way to go either. What happens if FCI creates more package types? It could be hard to maintain. Isn't there a way we can have the best of both worlds? Can't we leverage the package type dimension we created? **What do you think?**

I got it, said Thor! Why not make package type a column header, thus implicitly using it as a dimension? That's it, said Lulu. I don't know why we didn't think of that before. This is illustrated in Figure 15.8.

To bring the pricing information into the sales cube, Thor designed the following input formula:

```
"List_price"{$/pkg},
      Foodcake.leaf. ,
      Time.day. ,
      Geog.all ,
      Package. ,
      Scenario.actual <<
              [Price change table]: L price
```

Foodcake	Date	4pack W price {$}	4pack L price {$}
Neptune	Jan 02	5.75	6.90
Neptune	Jan 31	5.60	6.55
Poseidon	Jan 31	5.25	6.15

Figure 15.6 Four-pack price change table.

Foodcake	Date	8pack W price {$}	8pack L price {$}
Neptune	Jan 15	6.25	8.75
Poseidon	Jan 15	7.25	9.50
Neptune	Feb 05	5.75	8.15

Figure 15.7 Eight-pack price change table.

Foodcake	Package type	Date	W price {$}	L price {$}
Neptune	4 pack	Jan 02	5.75	6.90
Neptune	8 pack	Jan 15	6.25	8.75
Poseidon	8 pack	Jan 15	7.25	9.50
Neptune	4 pack	Jan 31	5.60	6.55
Poseidon	4 pack	Jan 31	5.25	6.15
Neptune	8 pack	Feb 05	5.75	8.15

Figure 15.8   The Foodcake price change table.

This should work, he said. All the formula needs to do is pull the right values out of the price change table. Do you agree? Lulu didn't. Wait a minute, she said. How is this going to work? It seems like there are two distinct cases:

- When leaf members of the time dimension match a date value in the price change table
- When leaf members of the time dimension do not match any date value in the price change table

The first case is easy. That's when you want to input the appropriate row. But what about the second case. As stated, the cube would register a missing value for all those dates where there was no new pricing information in the table. But what you want is to keep the most recent value until such time as it changes. Lulu suggested the following approach, which works for both types of packages:

```
"List_Price" {$/pkg},
      Foodcake.leaf. ,
      Time.day. ,
      Package. ,
      Geog.all ,
      Scenario.actual <<
                  [Price change table]: L price

Else If missing
        List_Price {$/pkg},
        Time.day.this =
           List_Price {$/pkg}, Time.day.-1
```

In other words, for any particular day, if there is a value in the price change table, it gets inserted into the cube. But if there is no such value (that is, there was no price change that day), then the price value in the cube is set equal to what it was the day before.

Retail Dollar Sales {$}

Retail dollar sales is also an input variable defined as follows:

```
"Retail dollar sales" {$} ,
     Time.leaf. ,
     Foodcake.leaf. ,
     Geog.leaf.,
     Scenario.actual <<
                 input [Sales Fact table]: Retail dollar sales
```

The variable sums in all dimensions except scenario as defined here:

```
"Retail dollar sales" {$} ,
     Time.leaf.above. ,
     Foodcake.leaf.above. ,
     Geog.leaf.above. =
         Sum( "Retail dollar sales", Time.leaf.,  Foodcake.leaf.,
             Geog.leaf., Scenario.actual)
```

Discount {$}

Promotions of any kind are registered as discounts in the stores' detailed transaction records as shown in Figure 15.1.

```
"Discount"{$} ,
     Time.leaf.,
     Foodcake.leaf.,
     Geog.leaf.,
     Scenario.actual <<
                 [input transaction detail summed to the day level]
```

The variable sums in all dimensions except scenario as defined here:

```
"Discount"{$},
     Time.leaf.above.,
     Foodcake.leaf.above. ,
     Geog.leaf.above. =
         Sum(Discount{$}, Time.leaf.,  Foodcake.leaf., Geog.leaf.,
             Scenario.actual)
```

Discount Share {R}

In order to keep track of the reason why a certain discount was in effect and how to apportion the discounted dollars between client-store and FCI, store-clients also kept track of the discount share. The value of the discount share is a fraction denoting the discounted revenue accruing to the store. A value of one means that the store assumes all of the lost revenue. A value of zero means that FCI assumes all of the lost revenue.

Everything in between identifies each party's relative share. Since FCI does not allow its client-stores to independently run promotions, there aren't any discount shares with a value of one. But there are several in between. Lulu said it's easier to see algebraically and so wrote out the following equation:

```
(Wholesale price - (FCI's Discount Share × Discount)) + (Markup -
(store's Discount Share × Discount)) = List price - discount
```

In other words, using the fact that wholesale price plus markup equals list price, we can subtract the discount from both sides wherein on the left-hand side, the discount is broken down into FCI's share of the discount and the client store's (inverse) share of the discount.

Aggregating Moving Percentages

So how would you aggregate the *Discount_Share* variable, asked Thor? Certainly you wouldn't just sum it. We all know you don't sum percentages. I guess it depends on what kind of aggregate information you're looking for, said Lulu. It would seem that FCI management needs to know aggregate amounts of discounted dollars, which is to say for any given amount of store sales, how many more dollars would have been taken in if there had been no discount? Also, FCI needs to know on average how much discounts represented as a percentage of sales. FCI also needs to know of the discounts given, on average, what percent of the discount was assumed by FCI? This last figure, Lulu proposed, needed to be weighted by total sales. Do you agree? Thor didn't. Why total sales? Why not total discount, asked Thor?

Since either calculation can be made, you really need to think for a minute about the decisions that need to be made with the information. If you weigh aggregate promotion type by total sales, you will skew the aggregate towards stores that have large amounts of sales. However, you will be missing the fact that different stores offered different amounts of discounts. The dollars lost from list price sales are not reflected in total sales. Since *Discount_Share*, as a variable, is intended to capture the percent of the discounted revenue assumed by FCI versus the store, *Discount_Share* should be weighted by total discount and not total sales. This is illustrated in Figure 15.9.

Thor was convinced that *Discount_Share* needed to be weighted by total discount, but now saw that this weighted average needed to be calculated from the transaction level on out. In other words, the same weighted average calculated by FCI in the OLAP environment had to begin with each store's transaction data.

Store	Total_Revenue ($)	Total Discount ($)	Discount_Share
Cambridge	$1000	$100	20%
Boston	$1000	$500	40%
Massachusetts	$2000	$600	30% or 36.7%

Figure 15.9   Two different weighting schemes.

Dollars Owed to FCI

The *Dollars_Owed_FCI* are a function of the wholesale price, the number of packages sold, the total amount of discount, and the percentage of discount assumed by FCI. Lulu suggested the following formula that she generalized to accommodate all package types:

```
"Dollar_Owed_FCI" {$} ,
     Geog.store. ,
     Time.week. ,
     Foodcake.all ,
     Package.all ,
     Scenario.actual =
          Wholesale_Price {$/pkg} X
          Qty_Sold {pkg} -
          ( Discount {$} X    ( 1 - Discount_Share {R} ) )
```

Do you think Lulu got it right? Thor didn't. He said that she did a good job representing the deductions from the simple product of wholesale price and quantity of packages sold that FCI, in essence, needed to reimburse to each store. With a dense array of data, such a formula would come up with the right answer as shown in Figure 15.10.

Combining Time-Lagged Flows

In practice, there was always going to be a time lag between the sales of foodcakes from FCI's distribution center to the stores and the sales of foodcakes from the stores to final customers. This is because every client store maintains an inventory and the foodcakes they sell during any particular week reflect purchases they made from FCI some time before. Thus, to calculate dollars owed FCI for the purposes of invoicing client stores, what was agreed on between FCI and the stores who resell its foodcakes is for FCI to combine the current week's sales of foodcakes from its distribution centers to the stores (Wholesale price {$/pkg} × Qty_Sold {pkg}) with FCI's current week's contribution to retail discounts (accruing from sales to the store from some time in the past).

In addition, Lulu knew she had to convert the package-based quantities into kilograms, as the rest of FCI was based on quantities in kilograms of raw materials and

Store	Whole-sale price {$/pkg}	List price	Qty_ Sold {pkg}	Total revenues	Total discount	Dis-count share	Discount dollars owed store	Dollars owed FCI
Cambridge	5.50	6.95	100	595	100	20	20	530
Allston	5.50	6.95	50	250	50	50	25	250
Brighton	5.50	6.95	200	1100	200	0	0	1100

Figure 15.10   Foodcake.Neptune, Package Type.4pack, Scenario.actual.

finished foodcakes. For the present analyses, Lulu was happy to populate the OLAP model with daily aggregates from relational transaction tables as shown here:

```
"Qty sold" {pkg},
    L.leaf.  <<
            Select Qty sold
            From join Summary, Detail transaction tables
            Group by Day , Foodcake
```

Analyzing Sales

Now that Lulu and Thor have set up the basic framework, they want to generate some of the typical aggregate reports that FCI senior management expects from them. Given the basic framework, Lulu feels that these aggregate reports are straightforward to define as illustrated in the next six panels, Figures 15.11 through 15.17, comprised of a word description of a query, the associated Located Contents (LC) expression and sample view of the result.

1. Total revenue of foodcakes by store, month, and package type:

```
"Total_Revenue" {$} ,
Store. , Time.month. , Package. , Foodcake.all
```

Page
Foodcake.all
Total_Revenue {$}

Column
Time.month

		April	May	June
Cambridge	4pack	25,700	27,400	26,100
	8pack	34,400	35,300	35,200
Boston	4pack	33,300	32,400	32,800
	8pack	31,800	30,600	31,000
Allston	4pack	19,100	20,700	20,800
	8pack	22,700	21,300	20,200

Row
Geog.Store.
Foodcake.Package.

Figure 15.11 Total revenues 1.

2. Total revenue of foodcakes by foodcake and by month:

```
"Total_Revenue" {$} ,
Foodcake., Time.month. , Package.all , Store.all
```

Page
Store.all
Package.all
Total_Revenue {$}

Column
Time.month

	April	May	June
Neptune	18,000	20,100	19,900
Poseidon	17,500	22,000	18,900
Seabreeze	19,000	21,000	20,200
SailorsdeLite	13,500	15,400	16,000

Row
Foodcake.

Figure 15.12   Total revenues 2.

3. The top five stores in terms of monthly revenue, and their monthly quantity sold:

```
"Store", "Qty_Sold" {kg},
Foodcake.all, Time.month., Total_Revenue.Drank.(1 to 5)
```

Page
Foodcake.all
Total_Revenue {$}

Column
Time.month.
Geog.Store.Variable { }

	April		May	
	Store	Qty_Sold {kg}	Store	Qty_Sold {kg}
1	New York	28,000	Hong Kong	28,500
2	Hong Kong	27,550	New York	27,250
3	London	25,300	London	24,900
4	Sydney	24,900	Mexico City	24,800
5	Mexico City	24,000	Sydney	24,000

Row
Drank.

Figure 15.13   Total revenues 3.

4. The top five selling foodcakes for each of the top three stores in April:

```
"Store.(Total_Revenue, Foodcake.all).Drank.(1 to 3)",
"Foodcake.(Qty_Sold, Store.this).Drank.(1 to 5)",
Time.month.April
```

Page
Time.month.April

		1	Neptune	
		2	LibertyWave	
1	New York	3	Seabreeze	
		4	MarinerDiet	
		5	GourmetLite	
		1	SailorsdeLite	
		2	Poseidon	
2	Hong Kong	3	YoshisDream	
		4	SushiLite	
		5	NeptuneGourmet	
		1	Seabreeze	
		2	Poseidon	
3	London	3	DrakesDiet	
		4	GourmetLite	
		5	HenrysFish	

Row
Drank.
Store.
Drank.
Foodcake. {N}

Figure 15.14 Top three stores.

Could you parse that last one for me, Lulu? asked Thor. I liked your use of nested expressions. Sure, replied Lulu. The query starts by asking for the top three stores in terms of total_revenue and for each of those stores the top five selling foodcakes. Lulu continued with her analytical formulas.

The stores with the lowest variance in monthly sales are defined as follows:

```
"Store" , "Total_Revenue" {$}, "Variance",²
Time.month.,
Variance(Total_Revenue, Foodcake.all, Time.month.this).min
```

Page
Variance(Total_Revenue, Foodcake.all, Time.month.this).min

Column
Time.month

Row
Geog.Store
Variables { }

	April	May	June
Geog.Store.	Plymouth	Cancun	Kinshasa
Total_ Revenue {$}	4,000	3,000	3,750
Variance	3,000	1,000	1,000

Figure 15.15 Min variance.

5. The stores with the highest variance:

```
"Store", "Total_Revenue" {$}, "Variance",
Time.month.,
Variance(Total_Revenue, Foodcake.all, Time.month.this).max
```

Page
Variance(Total_Revenue, Foodcake.all, Time.month.this).max

Column
Time.month

Row
Geog.Store
Variables { }

	April	May	June
Geog.Store.	New York	Hong Kong	London
Total_ Revenue {$}	240,000	245,000	23,500
Variance	1,200,000	1,495,000	1,330,000

Figure 15.16 Max variance in revenues.

6. The stores with the greatest variance in dollars owed to FCI:

```
"Store", "Dollars_Owed_FCI","Variance",
Time.month.,
Variance(Dollars_Owed_FCI {$}, Foodcake.all, Time.month.this).max
```

Page
Variance(Dollars_Owed_FCI {$}
Foodcake.all, Time.month.this).max

Column
Time.month

	April	May	June
Store.	New York	Hong Kong	London
Dollars_Owed_FCI {$}	200,000	199,000	198,000
Variance	1,160,000	1,395,000	1,220,000

Row
Geog.Store
Variables { }

Figure 15.17 Max variance in dollars owed to FCI.

Marketing

Comfortable with their analysis of FCI's sales, Lulu and Thor turned their attention to FCI's marketing. The first thing they wanted to know was FCI's percentage of market share. How do you think we should go about it? asked Thor, who had only limited experience in market analysis. What would you do?

Market Share

The first thing we need to figure out is the granularity, based on available data sources, at which we are defining the markets, Lulu responded. This applies to geography, products, and time. Are we talking about national markets, regional markets, or even local markets? Is there data for fishcakes broken out from vegetarian cakes? Is there maybe data for diet cakes? Or are we going to have to make inferences about the market size for each of our product lines of foodcakes based on available data for generic food patties? For the moment, I'm assuming that we can leverage existing market data. If I'm wrong, we may have to commission a market study.

Luckily, Lulu's assumption was correct. Market data existed for fishcakes and for vegetarian cakes by region. The following formulas are used to calculate FCI's share of the vegetarian foodcakes market on a regional and monthly basis.

```
"Market size"{$} ,
         Foodcake.vegetarian ,
         Time.month. ,
         Geography.region.,
         Scenario.actual << [Source marketing data]

"FCI market share"{R} ,
         Foodcake.vegetarian ,
         Time.month. ,
         Geography.region.,
         Scenario.actual =
                  Sales {$} /
                  Market size {$}
```

The formulas look simple enough, said Thor. But why are you restricting the application range of the FCI market share variable to vegetarian foodcakes? Shouldn't the formula apply to all foodcakes? You're right, replied Lulu, in that the formula for market share applies to all foodcakes for which there is market data. However, for the moment we only have data for vegetarian cakes. If we omitted the Foodcake.vegetarian application range restriction, we might create a lot of incorrect zeros for market shares in those foodcake products for which we have sales data but for which no market sizing data is available. Do you agree with Lulu?

Thor wasn't convinced. But, Lulu, I thought that by restricting the application range of market size in its definition to vegetarian foodcakes the ratio of sales to market size in the market share definition would automatically be restricted to the application range of the denominator, in this case, vegetarian foodcakes. Good point, Thor, replied Lulu. Different tools will handle this differently. There are three types of relevant sparsity complications here: market size is blank, sales is zero, or sales is missing.

In the first case, where market size is blank as with the market size for fishcakes, we want the formula for market share to return a not applicable if queried for any fishcake locations. Most tools will insert a zero or a blank that becomes a zero in calculation for the market size variable for those cells for which no data was loaded (the fishcake cells). In this case the calculation of market share becomes a ratio between some nonzero number and a zero. You might get a divide-by-zero error or simply NA if querying for market share for nonvegetarian foodcakes. This result is acceptable.

In the second case, where actual sales is zero (as there may be pockets of regions in the world where people do not consume either fish or vegetarian foodcakes), the calculation of market share should correctly return a zero.

However, in the third case, where, for some reason, the stores in a region or the region itself has not reported its sales, so that sales is missing but forthcoming, most tools without further logic would erroneously coerce the blank sales cell into a zero and thus incorrectly return a zero market share value where the correct answer would have been missing. Again (recalling the discussion on sparsity from Chapter 6), only by defining an application range can a tool correctly interpret when a blank cell refers to not applicable and when a blank cell refers to missing. Furthermore, the distinction between empty or nonexistent cells that denote missing and empty or nonexistent cells that denote zero can only be made on a schema-by-schema basis.

Marketing Expenditures

FCI has traditionally engaged in marketing at a brand, product line, and store level. For this prototype effort, Jane had asked Lulu and Thor to come up with a rough estimate of the amount of dollars spent in active marketing on a per-product basis. Jane had made available FCI's marketing expense data. Since the marketing expense data was dimensioned by the same dimensions (though not all the same members or levels) as the sales data, it was loaded into the same cube.

How do you want to load in the data? asked Lulu. Should we create a distinct variable for each kind of marketing expense or should we load all the different marketing expenses into a single marketing expense variable? What do you think? How would you decide?

Thor responded that his decision was based on whether there would be any occasions when the different marketing expenses would not aggregate together. If the brand, product line, and store marketing expenses always sum together whether for purposes of aggregation or for allocation to the product level, then I would prefer to load all the marketing expenses into a single variable. But what about differences in measurement processes? said Lulu. What if the way that FCI calculates brand marketing expenses makes certain assumptions that aren't made for product-line marketing expenses? Thor replied that any annotations that needed to be made could be made within a single variable on a location-range-by-location-range basis. The central issue, continued Thor, is whether the values for each of the marketing expenses can be freely combined. Are total marketing expenses equal to the sum of brand, product line, and store marketing, yes or no? If the answer is no, then whatever transformations need to occur to enable the aggregation of expense data need to occur regardless of whether the expense data resides in a singe variable or in three variables. Do you agree with Thor?

Lulu didn't. You're missing something, Thor. You're going to have problems aggregating if you map all the input data to a single variable. Let's assume that you did load all the inputs into different location ranges of a single variable as shown here:

```
"Marketing expenses"{$} ,
     Geog.store. ,
     Foodcake.all ,
     Time.month. << [input from store by month store marketing data]


"Marketing expenses" {$},
     Geog.region. ,
     Time.month. ,
     Foodcake.all << [input from region by month brand marketing data]


"Marketing expenses",
     Geog.region. ,
     Time.month. ,
     Foodcake.(vegetarian + fish). <<
               [input from region by month product line marketing data]
```

Now when it comes to aggregating, you might try writing a formula like this one:

```
"Marketing expenses" ,
    Geog.store.above. ,
    Time.month.above. ,
    Foodcake.(vegetarian + fish).atabove. =
        Sum( Marketing expenses, Geog.store., Time.month.,
            Foodcake.(vegetarian + fish))
```

The problem is that you can't really aggregate the variable marketing expenses because the higher level inputs—in this case brand—interferes with the aggregation of lower-level data—in this case store and product line. (Mapping distinct inputs into differing location ranges of an OLAP variable works when the location ranges are not hierarchically related.) Any aggregation function would want to put the value of the sum of store and product line data into a region by all product cell except that it will find the input value for brand expenses in those cells. You could treat the brand-level data as manual overrides of the other expenses or you could overwrite the brand-level data, but there's no way to combine the store and product-line data at the appropriate region by month by allproduct level with the brand data entered there within a single variable. You're right Lulu, Thor conceded; I guess I really don't have that much experience working with marketing data.

So let's do it right this time, said Lulu. We need to bring in each kind of input data into a separate variable as shown here:

```
"Store_Marketing expenses" ,
    Geog.store. ,
    Foodcake.all ,
    Time.month. <<
     [input from store by month store marketing data]

"Brand_Marketing expenses" ,
    Geog.region. ,
    Time.month. ,
    Foodcake.all <<
        [input from region by month brand marketing data]

"Product line_Marketing expenses" ,
    Geog.region. ,
    Time.month. ,
    Foodcake.(vegetarian + fish) <<
        [input from region by month product line marketing data]
```

Then we need to combine the variables. The simplest way is to define the aggregations for each variable separately and then combine the variables at any aggregation level through summation as shown next:

```
"Store_Marketing expenses" ,
    Geog.store.above. ,
    Time.month.above. ,
    Foodcake.all =
        Sum( Store_Marketing expenses, Geog.store., Foodcake.all ,
            Time.month.)

"Brand_Marketing expenses" ,
    Geog.region.above. ,
    Time.month.above. ,
    Foodcake.all  =
        Sum( Brand_Marketing expenses , Geog.region. ,  Time.month.,
            Foodcake.all )

"Product line_Marketing expenses" ,
    Geog.region.above. ,
    Time.month.above. ,
    Foodcake.all =
      Sum( Product line_Marketing expenses , Geog.region. ,
            Time.month. , Foodcake.(vegetarian + fish).)
```

Now we can define the combined marketing expenses as follows:

```
"Combined marketing expenses" ,
    Geog.store. ,
    Time.month.atabove. ,
    Foodcake.(vegetarian + fish).atabove. =
        Sum ( Store_Marketing expenses +
          Brand_Marketing expenses +
          Product line_Marketing expenses )
```

Allocating Marketing Expenses to Product Sales

We need to allocate all the incurred marketing expenses to the sale of foodcake products, said Lulu. How would you handle it, Thor? I would like to allocate the combined marketing expenses to the store by product by month level, but I suspect I'm leaving out a step. Do you agree with Thor? **What do you think?**

Lulu replied, you're right, Thor. You are leaving something out. Unfortunately, we can't reuse our combined marketing variable. The problem with the combined marketing variable is that it, properly, combines product-type-specific (product line) and product invariant (brand and store) marketing expenses, whereas we need to allocate each of these expenses separately to their respective product categories. We don't want to count fishcake marketing expenses in our calculation of marketing expenses for vegetarian cakes!

Also, to be clear, given the granularity level of our marketing expense data, I would suggest that we calculate marketing expenses on a per-product basis commensurate with the product line distinctions. Thus, our results will show marketing costs as a percentage of product sales per store averaged by month and by product type—fishcake or vegetarian cake.

Lulu said, I would suggest the following formula with its result set shown in Figure 15.18.

```
"Marketing costs as a percentage of product sales" ,       Geog.store. ,
      Foodcake.(Fish + Vegetarian). ,
      Time.month =

           ( Store_Marketing expenses /
               Total_Revenue {$}, Foodcake.(Fish + Vegetarian) )
           +
           ( Brand_Marketing expenses {$}, Geog.store.region. /
                 ( Count(Region.down1.) X
     Total_Revenue {$}, Foodcake.(Fish + Vegetarian). ) )
           +
           ( Product line_Marketing expenses {$} , Geog.store.region. /
                 ( Count(Region.down1.) X
                   Total_Revenue {$}, Foodcake.(Fish + Vegetarian) ) )
```

Value States[3]

Thor asked Lulu if she thought that Jane would be satisfied with what they've done. Why wouldn't she? replied Lulu. We did everything she asked us to do for sales and marketing. But I have the feeling that there's more that we could be doing. It must be possible to leverage the sales data we collect and the costs data we're generating (as described in the product costing section of Chapter 16) to come up with a measure of earnings per transaction and then to use earnings per transaction to look at customers in terms of their earnings profile. I think you're talking about value state models, said Lulu. They're a useful way of looking at sales and customers over time; I just attended a class about them. What exactly are value state models? Thor asked. Lulu proceeded to explain.

Quality, Thor, unlike death and taxes, is not a constant. This applies to everything and everybody whether customers, products, suppliers, workers, or managers. One year's profitable customer or product is another year's money loser. Suppliers who are reliable one quarter may be unreliable another.

Since quality varies, it is possible to track changes in quality over time and classify things or processes (whatever it is whose quality we are measuring) by the way their quality is changing or not changing. Classifying and tracking quality changes is a necessary first step to creating any kind of analysis of the causal factors that promote increases, decreases, or stability in quality over time. The most systematic way to look at quality changes is by creating what may be called a quality or value state model.

Page

Scenario.actual

Column

Time.month
Variable: { }

Row

Geog.Store.
Foodcake.

		January			February		
		Total_Revenue ($)	Mkt_Expenses ($)	Mkt_Expenses/Total_Revenue	Total_Revenue ($)	Mkt_Expenses ($)	Mkt_Expenses/Total_Revenue
Cambridge	Fishcakes	39,000	1950	5.0%	38,500	1886.5	4.9%
	Veggie	21,000	1071	5.1%	21,900	1116.9	5.1%
Allston	Fishcakes	29,400	1441	4.9%	28,500	1425	5.0%
	Veggie	13,300	638	4.8%	14,000	658	4.7%

Figure15.18 Marketing expenses.

Thing or process being tracked	Time 1	Time 2
1	High	High
2	Medium	Medium
3	Medium	Medium
4	High	Medium
5	Medium	Low
6	Low	Medium

Figure 15.19 A traditional view.

From/To	Low	Medium	High
High		T_4	T_1
Medium		T_2, T_3	
Low	T_5	T_6	

Figure 15.20 A value state view.

To illustrate the difference between tracking quality per thing or process over time, and tracking the identities of things or processes by their quality changes, Thor, consider the following diagrams shown in Figures 15.19 and 15.20.

In the first diagram, Figure 15.19, you can see what I call the traditional view where quality is treated as a measure that varies by thing or process and time. Notice how the measures of quality—in this case, High, Medium, and Low—are the contents of cells defined by the intersection of time and thing or process. The basic schema in the traditional view is as follows:

```
(Thing. ⊗ Time.) ~ Quality
```

So far, Lulu, you're not impressing me, said Thor. There's nothing new about tracking quality. But I realize you're itching to show me the next diagram. That's right, said Lulu. Hold on to your seat while you look at Figure 15.20. This is the value state model view. Notice how we're treating the identities of things (or processes) labeled as T_n as measures that vary in terms of the way their quality is changing. The basic schema in the value state view is as follows:

```
((Fromtime , value). ⊗ (Totime , value).) ~ Thing {Name}
```

I think I'm getting it, said Thor. I understand, for example, that we would be treating customers as the so-called things that exist in value space. So instead of just looking at specific customers and analyzing their quality using a value state model, we could also look at the pattern of movement of customers over time and see, for example, that in the last year the number of customers who remain high quality for more than 12 months has dropped or increased by 25 percent, or that there are twice as many high-quality customers who drop to average as there are average customers who rise to high quality. Still, could you get into a little more detail? We really should build one for FCI.

Sure, replied Lulu. At its simplest, a customer value state model requires some collection of customer- and time-specific quality values. However, since the most common and fungible quality indicator is earnings (notwithstanding the various accounting tricks that can artificially manipulate earnings), I will talk specifically about earnings-based customer value state models.

The information requirements for building an earnings-based customer value state model include access to sales transaction data for which fully discounted revenue per item per customer is recorded (that is to say, stated revenue net any discounts) and for which the total costs (including all attributable overhead) per item per customer are also recorded. These are shown in Figures 15.21 and 15.22. Otherwise, it is impossible

Transaction ID	T123
Date and time	10/19 /2001 :10:10AM
Location	Cambridge
Total revenues	$150
Customer ID	C456
Total costs	$130
Total earnings	$20

Figure 15.21 Transaction summary table.

Transaction ID	T123
Item	Smiling Buddha 6-pack Veggie cakes
Total cost per item	$4.50
List price	$5.95
Discount	$0.45
Qty of item sold	3
Item revenue	$16.50
Item transaction earnings	$3.00

Figure 15.22 Transaction detail table.

to derive earnings per customer, transaction, and products. These earnings derivations are necessary for the creation of any earnings-based customer value state model. Luckily we've been creating just this kind of information during our skunk works project for Jane. (The calculation of total costs is shown in Chapter 16 and is also the focus of the calculation exercise in Chapter 17.)

The major steps for creating an earnings-based customer value state model include:

1. Calculate and assign a total cost to every item sold.

2. Subtract any discounts, explicit or hidden, to arrive at a net value for revenues in the transaction detail table.

3. Sum the costs and revenues from the detail table into the summary table.

4. Calculate earnings per transaction per time per location.

5. Sum the costs and revenues along the time dimension of the summary table to that level of time required to see a single time-specific value state of the customer.

The fifth step requires knowledge of FCI. Basically, we need to figure out the time granularity over which a customer value state is applicable. So here's a question for you, Thor. Who are the customers? What are our choices? What do you think?

Thor replied, we have two basic choices: stores as customers or final foodcake purchasers as customers. Since we're already doing a comarketing study with these stores, I suggest we get their approval to jointly create a value state for the final foodcake purchasers. We can always create a store-based value state model afterward. With final purchasers as customers, I think that the appropriate level of granularity is monthly. Lulu agreed and continued.

At the end of step 5, you have an intermediate, still traditional-looking customer value model that uses customer ID and time as dimensions and that uses customer value as its measure. The steps continue as follows:

6. For any n time periods of interest at the granularity chosen in step 5, create at least three ordering bins that correspond to high, medium, and low earnings per customer per time period; assign each customer to an earnings bin. This is illustrated in Figure 15.23.

Cust ID	Time	Earnings bin
1	1	Medium
1	2	Medium
2	1	Medium
2	2	High
3	1	High
3	2	Medium

Figure 15.23   Intermediate traditional view.

Keep in mind that there are several different flavors of ordering bins to choose from. If you pick a relative ordering such as ranking, you are sure to get some customers in every ordering group you create. Like a curved exam in school, a relative ordering will guarantee that some customers are always high valued, some medium valued, and some low valued. Furthermore, the numeric definition of the boundaries between the different bins may change over time. For me, said Lulu, this is less useful than using a fixed-boundary ordering. Why is that, asked Thor? Think about it.

Lulu responded, if we use a relative ordering, customers will be evenly distributed in value space. But we're trying to analyze the differences in distribution such as the lack of long-term, high-value customers or the fact that three-fourths of the customers who drop from high to medium quality eventually rise to high value again. Thus, we want an absolute value-based ordering wherein the number of customers for any particular value bin may vary and even be zero.

The steps continue as follows:

7. Build a dimensional model out of any two-to-n time-specific earnings bins used as dimensions.

Here's where the inversion happens, Thor. Up until now, earnings have been treated as a derived variable, and earnings bins were groupings of a derived variable. To create our value state model, we need to treat two or more time-state-specific earnings bins as low-cardinality dimensions relative to which we will analyze a variety of customer behaviors.[4] Value state models are a concrete class of application that rely on dimensional symmetry. Since our tool set doesn't provide native support for dimensional symmetry, we need to create a satellite analytical fact table that uses earnings bins as dimensions and counts of customers as measures. From this new fact table we can create our value state model for which a view is shown in Figure 15.24.

Looking at things in terms of a value state makes it easy to see that slightly more than a third of the customers have been and are continuing to provide only medium value. Furthermore, that is over three times the number of customers in any other value state. Over half the customers either were of medium value or have become medium in value.

Naturally, knowing just the number of customers in each value state isn't enough to make key decisions. You also need to know things like the dollars sold to each category of customer, average transaction size, and so forth. A small number of customers can account for a large share of the revenue. As shown in Figure 15.25, there are many vari-

From/To	Low	Medium	High
High	2	10	10
Medium	10	35	10
Low	11	11	1

Figure 15.24 Earnings-based customer value state model with percentage counts of customers in each state.

From/To	Low	Medium	High
High	4	20	60
Medium	30	75	20
Low	15	15	0.01

Figure 15.25 Earnings-based value states with sales {$100s} in each state.

ables for which it is useful to view their values in terms of how they vary in value state space.

Here you can see that although only 10 percent of FCI's customers maintained a high value state over the last two time periods (as shown in Figure 15.25), they accounted for about a quarter of the company's sales.

I really like this way of looking at things in terms of value states, said Thor. But I think you're missing something. How do you deal with the transition between being a customer and being a noncustomer? Good question, replied Lulu. I learned about that, too. By creating a no-value bin in the earnings dimension, it is possible to explicitly model these noncustomers. Of course, there remain the business decisions, especially on the ex-customer side of defining the difference between a highly inactive customer and a noncustomer. FCI management needs to make those decisions. Regardless of how those definitions are made, you will wind up with a value state model like the one illustrated in Figure 15.26.

Once you've gotten your data into a value state model, there are myriad queries to pose of the newly structured information, such as the following:

- What percentage of FCI's customers are stable high value?
- What percentage of FCI's customers have changed from high to medium value?
- What percentage of FCI's sales accrues to stable medium-value customers?
- What percentage of FCI's total earnings is accounted for by stable high-value customers?

From/To	Noncustomer	Low	Medium	High
High		2	8	8
Medium		8	35	9
Low	6	8	11	1
Noncustomer		4		

Figure 15.26 Earnings-based customer value state model that includes noncustomers with percentage counts of customers in each state.

- What percentage of FCI's customers are improving in value?

- What are the attribute characteristics of these customers?

- Which customers are declining in value?

- What are the attribute characteristics of these customers?

Once FCI management has gained new insights into its customers and their changing value states, they are armed with the appropriate information to take decisive actions, such as:

- Sending different kinds of mailings to customers in different value states

- Offering special discounts to customers who recently transitioned from a high-to a medium-value state

- Offering long-term service relationships to customers who transitioned from low to medium value several periods ago and have stayed medium value since then

- Analyze the attributes of customers in each value category and build a predictive model of customers likely to increase or decrease in value and then use that model to identify customers for focused marketing activity

Thanks, Lulu, said Thor. You've really clarified in my mind what value state models are, why they are valuable, and how to build them. I can see that by using value state models we can help management to classify customers according to the dynamics of their relationship with FCI, make targeted decisions about how to treat different value-classes of customers, and better leverage CRM investments that they may have already made.

Summary

You've now seen how an OLAP solution can be brought to bear on sales and marketing. In this chapter you've seen Lulu and Thor wrestle with whether to model package type as a dimension or a variable, you learned different ways of aggregating variables that don't simply sum in all dimensions, you've seen different ways of inputting data that has gaps in it, you were shown how to perform sales mix variance analysis in multiple dimensions, you watched Lulu and Thor argue about and resolve the best way to model a marketing expenditure variable that captures source expenses at different levels of granularity and then aggregating it, you've seen how to allocate marketing costs to the product level and compare allocated costs with sales, and you've learned how to create a customer value state model.

## CHAPTER 16

FCI's Activity-Based Management

In this chapter you will learn how to model an entire value chain by creating and then combining a business asset dimension with a business process dimension. You will see that management can be represented both within each business process and at the all-process level. You will learn how to combine batch-level production tags with the leaf level of a product dimension to create a cross-value-chain product-batch-tracking capability. You will learn how to calculate the incremental activity-based costs on a per business process and per kilo basis for product distribution, product inventory, product shipping, batch level production, materials inventory, materials shipping, and purchasing. Along the way you will learn about the need to create hybrid batch-containing join cubes for calculating materials inventory and shipping costs on a per batch basis. You will see many different kinds of multicube formulas including formulas whose time values depend on variable-constrained events from other cubes, and formulas that create sets of moving cumulative ranges. You will see how to model different kinds of input-output situations depending on the combinatorial relationships between the inputs and the outputs. And you will learn about modeling *M/N* relationships.

Most of the FCI managers had been with the company since its early days. Their familiarity with the company's inner workings was based on hands-on experience. Most of the managers had an intuitive feel for their customers and suppliers. They all knew fish; not all were as familiar with the vegetarian side of the business. If everyone does his or her part, the founder said, the company as a whole will thrive. Their stove-piped reporting was consistent with this management philosophy. Each business function manager acted as a semi-autonomous agent. HQ only received high-level activity summaries. So long as FCI managers had intimate knowledge of each business function and so long as business was booming, this stove-piped approach worked fine, but as FCI grew, and as FCI was exposed to more dynamic market forces, it was harder and harder for the managers to make the right decisions, or sometimes even see the problems, given only high-level business function reporting. On the other hand, it didn't make any sense for management to simply immerse themselves in the details of each business function. That, after all, was the responsibility of the business function managers, and there was so much detailed activity data that decisions based on anything short of full-time devotion to the details was bound to miss the mark. What's a corporate manager to do?

One day at a regular corporate management meeting, Jane, one of the new technical managers, said she had a confession to make. She said that for the past five months she had been secretly working with many of the business function managers to implement an enterprisewide OLAP layer on top of their data warehousing system. The prototype was now sufficiently complete to show to FCI's senior executives. The purpose of the system, said Jane, was to solve FCI's top management information problems. Those problems were

- The inability to compare and analyze cost, throughput, and quality information at differing levels of granularity across time, space, employees, capital, business functions, and other appropriate business dimensions

- The inability to equate activity-based costs and quality with revenues

Who, asked Jane rhetorically, can state with precision the total activity-based cost of manufacturing a particular kilo of foodcake sold on a particular day at a particular store? Which business function is responsible for the greatest amount of cost volatility? What is the principal source of product quality problems? What impact would employee training have on product quality or costs? Who can quantify the volatility in FCI's customer base? How can we claim with a straight face to be doing customer analytics without being able to quantify the marginal contribution to earnings made by a customer on a transaction-by-transaction basis? If we can't quantify the customer's marginal contribution, how can we pretend to be able to quantify the customer's total contribution?

Everyone nodded when Jane said that these and other similar questions are often raised by FCI's managers, but due to inappropriate information systems, their answers have remained beyond the purview of management—until now.

Jane went on to say that she may have been the instigator and funder of this project, but she didn't do the work. All the credit for this effort should go to Lulu and Thor (see Figure 9.1), two of FCI's rising stars who designed and implemented the prototype enterprise OLAP layer. Since they were the brains behind the project, Jane said she had invited them to come at this time so that if any managers had questions beyond her grasp of the application, Lulu and Thor would be there to provide an appropriate response.

Jane's Presentation

As much as we love to see people eating our foodcakes, said Jane, at the end of the day if we couldn't make money at it, we would have to be doing something else. Making money means that on average we receive more money from the customer—which for us is a store who buys our foodcake—than it costs us to produce that same foodcake. So, isn't it only natural that we should want to know how much it costs to produce a particular foodcake and how much we make or lose on the sale of that foodcake to a store/customer?

That's not how we do things today. Even though we all see monthly reports detailing how much money we earned, which reports are broken down by parts of the world and by foodcake, and even though we see reports detailing how we did compared to the plan, the calculations in those reports are based on standard values for foodcake production costs and standard values for operating expenses, which includes everything from shipping to inventory costs. Can anyone tell me the formula for calculating standard earnings that we use in our mix variance analysis for sales? It's based on the average earnings per foodcake for the previous year. So how does FCI track the earnings differences between foodcakes, asked one of the managers. We do it by taking the average foodsource cost over the year, which is our material cost of goods sold, and subtracting it from the average product sales price for the year to come up with the average gross margin. Then we subtract total overhead, which is a fancy word for all other expenses including production, inventory, and distribution, apportioned over the total volume of production. The result is our standard earnings per product per year.

How are we supposed to make informed decisions to reduce our earnings volatility if we assume away the volatility in our cost structure by using year-level aggregate costs for foodsources and assuming all other costs are the same for all foodcakes sold? Why not use standard values for revenues? The managers laughed at that one. That's right, Jane said. It's as ludicrous to use standard values for costs as it is for revenues.

For the next 60 minutes that our CEO has been gracious enough to let me use, I will do my best to show you how our prototype implementation of an enterprise OLAP layer enables us to track corporate activity, analyze the sources of erratic cost and quality performance, figure out total product costs, equate activity-based costs with revenues, and finally apply that knowledge to the modeling of customer behavior. Towards that end, I will say a few words about the business approach we took and take you through a cost discovery journey that begins with product sales and crosses every business process in FCI, ending with the purchasing of raw materials..

The Approach

As a first step toward calculating the earnings we make or lose on a kilo of foodcake, Jane said, I want you to think about the result set. Assuming we could calculate the dollar value of the earnings[1] for a particular kilo of foodcake, how would those earnings be dimensioned? The CFO raised his hand. That's easy he said, earnings should be dimensioned by time, by foodcake, and by store (as shown in the following schema and illustrated in Figure 16.1).

```
(Time.day. ⊗ Foodcake. ⊗ Geog.store.) ~ earnings
```

		Jan15	Jan16	Jan17
Hartford	Labor	912	912	912
	Maintenance	50	50	50
	Facility	200	200	200
	Energy	100	100	100
	All	1,262	1,262	1,262
Palo Alto	Labor	901	901	901
	Maintenance	45	45	45
	Facility	190	190	190
	Energy	95	95	95
	All	1,231	1,231	1,231

Figure 16.1 Foodcake earnings by time, foodcake, and store.

Is that so, said Jane. Why not dimension earnings by production facility or production machine or by inventory center? Don't you want to be able to calculate how the earnings you made on a foodcake were affected by the facility where it was produced? She drew the relevant schema on the white board.

```
(Time.day. ⊗ Foodcake. ⊗ Geog.store. ⊗ Production Facility. ⊗ Machine.
⊗ Inventory center.) ~ earnings
```

Well for one thing, replied the CFO (who had some experience in data modeling), there doesn't exist the same sort of M/N relationship between production facilities, machines, and inventory centers as there does between time, foodcakes, and stores. However, I would like to see how earnings are affected by the particular route followed by a foodcake through production and distribution. How can you let me see the impact of various business processes on costs without over dimensioning earnings?

Business Process and Asset Dimensions

Jane was still parsing the question when she nodded at Lulu to take over. That's a great question, said Lulu. In order to calculate the impact of various business processes on costs, FCI needs to create a general business process dimension and a general asset dimension. The business process dimension is composed of each of the business processes carried out by FCI (as shown in Figure 16.2).

Hey, wait a minute, exclaimed one of the managers. Aren't you forgetting something? Where are we? Doesn't management count as a business process? That's a good question, replied Lulu. Don't think that I'm making any political statements here. Of course management counts. The issue is how best to represent it for analytical pur-

FCI Business Processes
Foodsource purchasing and currency exchange
Foodsource shipments
Foodsource inventory
Production
Product transport to distribution centers
Product inventory
Product distribution to stores
Product sales and marketing

Figure 16.2 FCI business process dimension.

poses. Although, as you can see, I chose not to represent management as a business process, it would be easier for us to discuss how I did represent management after I explain how assets were modeled.

FCI assets include everything that gets used by any business process. The main asset categories that form the basis of FCI's asset dimension are listed in Figure 16.3.

Assets and business functions exist in an M/N relationship with each other, said Lulu. For every one of FCI's business processes, whether it be purchasing or distribution, we can calculate the amount of physical resources and the dollar value of the resources used for each type of asset on any particular day. Over the past couple of months, one of the things we made sure to do for each business process, which I will show you shortly, was to calculate the dollar value of assets used per day per kilogram of throughput.

It all sounds fine, said one of the managers, but I still don't see management as you'd promised.

FCI Assets
Throughput
Facilities
Equipment
Labor
Utilities
Financial
Other

Figure 16.3 Top-level members of FCI's asset dimension.

I didn't promise to highlight management as a distinct dimension member or Type instance. I promised to explain where management fits in and now I will. Although management is a crucial business function and although managers are crucial employees, it doesn't make sense to represent them as either a separate leaf-level element of the business process dimension or as a separate type of asset. There are several reasons for this.

Most management activity either occurs within or is directed to a particular business process. For example, in addition to the VP of products who sits at corporate headquarters, every production facility has a production manager and several line managers on site. All these people are performing management activities. The energy they expend should be accounted for in the business process for which they expend their energy, here it's production. The reason their activity doesn't seem to occur as a separate asset utilization in the Asset dimension is simply because we only represented the top level of assets in the Asset dimension. If we drill down one level (for most asset categories), it would look like Figure 16.4.

FCI Assets
Throughput:
Fish Vegetarian Binders Flavors Foodcakes
Material Supplies
Facilities: Stationary Moving
Equipment: Stationary Moving
Labor: Low skilled Technical Midmanagement Senior management
Utilities: Electricity Phone Water Gas
Financial
Other

Figure 16.4 A drill-down view of FCI's asset dimension.

By not creating a separate asset structure for corporate offices and by not creating a separate leaf-level business function for management, it encourages us to try to apportion as much as possible of management's time and assets to specific business processes. What about finance and legal or business relationships? It seems arbitrary to map them to a particular business process, said one of the managers. I still think you need a separate business process for management.

Lulu smiled and said, you are right in the sense that there are management activities that do not belong to any one business process. However, the way to represent that isn't by creating a separate leaf element called management in the Business Process dimension, but by leveraging the multilevel representation capabilities inherent in a dimensional model, and thus representing those management activities that don't belong in any one business process as belonging to the All level of the Business Process dimension. The cost of FCI's management is thus the cost of labor, utilities, facilities, supplies, and equipment used for the management of each specific business process plus the cost of all the assets used for the All process.

Calculating Total Cost of Goods Sold

Now we can begin to answer the first question that Jane posed a few minutes ago. The first thing to recognize is that revenues and costs, as the components of earnings, are each dimensioned differently at the source. Measured revenues, rather than earnings as someone had suggested, are dimensioned by store, time, and foodcake.

```
(Time. ⊗ Store. ⊗ Foodcake.) ~ Revenue
```

Measured costs are dimensioned by business process, asset, and time.

```
(Time. ⊗ Business process. ⊗ Asset.) ~ Costs
```

So how do we connect these two cubes in a way that allows us to calculate costs per foodcake when the only dimension they seem to share is Time? Think about it. What else can we track both at the time of sale and through other business processes?

Tracking Batchids at the Point of Sales

How about batch number, said Lulu? Isn't that what connects everything? When a particular foodcake is being produced on a specific machine at a specific time, it is given a batch number. We know, for example, through our transaction systems that batch 123 refers to a batch of Neptune fishcakes produced in Vancouver on January 16 between 9:00 A.M. and noon. We also know that batch 123 was shipped to Cambridge on the afternoon of January 16 and arrived in Cambridge the morning of January 17 where it was added to the store's stock. The store uses a FIFO inventory principle and so, based on the stores sales records, the last 25 packages of Neptune from the 150 packages sold on January 17 came from batch 123.

So how do you add batch number to the revenue and cost models? Batch number gets added in several different places on the revenue side: shipping received, stock on hand, and transaction-level sales. When a store receives its daily shipment, the shipment has a unique identifier. Furthermore, each shipment has a detailed inventory list of batchids included in the shipment and the quantity of, and type of foodcake included in the batch.

Thus, for example, when the Cambridge store acknowledges the receipt of its shipment on the morning of January 17, it explicitly represents the batch identity of all foodcakes received. But how does it do that? What are the options? Lulu explained that they are currently building a dynamic hybrid Foodcake-Batchid dimension from delivery and sales transaction data, and then reprocessing the sales cube every night. But they are also looking into other options as well. A glance around the room revealed enough glazed eyes to make Lulu put out an example.

Currently, Lulu said, FCI creates a modified Foodcake dimension wherein for each leaf in the foodcake dimension on a day-by-day and store-by-store basis, there is inserted the id numbers of every batch that was either received, remains on hand, or was sold on that day for that store.

In LC, the expression for such a modified dimension is as follows:
Define the new dimension Foodcake-Batch as

```
Foodcake.leaf.(Time.day.this , Store.this ,(Qty received or Qty sold or
Qty on hand) >0) ~< Batchid
```

The schema is then

```
(Time.day. ⊗ Geog.store. ⊗ Foodcake-batch.) ~
Qty received , Qty sold, Price, . . .
```

An example view of sales data that incorporates Batchid as a dimension can be found in Figure 16.5.

Figure 16.5 shows that on January 17 the Cambridge store received 100 units of Neptune from batch 123 and 50 units of Poseidon from batch 161. It also shows that 100 units of Neptune were sold from the previous batch 142, which exhausted that batch, and 80 units of Poseidon from the previous batch 188 were sold, as well as 10

Jan17, Cambridge	Neptune		Poseidon	
	B123	B142	B161	B188
Qty received	100	0	50	0
Qty sold	50	100	10	80
Price	5.95	5.95	5.50	5.50
Revenue	297.50	595	297.50	0
Qty on hand	50	0	40	0

Figure 16.5 Tracking Batchids of sales in Cambridge.

units from the newly arrived batch 161. It is important to realize that the identities and number of batchids attached to the leaves of the foodcake dimension are constantly changing. Thus, if we were to look at the same view from a neighboring store, it might resemble Figure 16.6.

So how do you build such a hybrid dimension, asked one of the managers. I understand the definition you put up on the white board, but what kind of information do we need to actually create it? Good question, said Lulu. You need access to your transaction figures for shipping and sales, and you have to either leverage or create some kind of relation between foodcakes and batchids.

Using the batch identifier information, FCI can track the age of different batches at the stores and even order the batchids by age. Since each batchid can (but doesn't have to) change from day to day and from store to store, it doesn't make any sense to pose queries about how some variable with a particular value for some batchid changes its value across time or stores because the batchid won't exist. In other words, queries like "How does Qty received for Neptune batch 213 change from Arlington to Cambridge" don't make any sense because the batchid 213 only exists for Arlington on that day.

Most of the managers were impressed, but the CFO pressed on. How does the model handle foodcakes for which no batches were shipped or exist in inventory? For example, how would you ask for the price of a foodcake on a particular day for which no batches were on hand in any store? Lulu was thinking through how to respond when Thor stepped forward. He thanked the CFO for pointing out a whiteboard simplification that needed to be dealt with in the actual application. The way we handle cases where no batches are present in the system is by distinguishing those foodcakes for which some batch exists and those for which no batch exists. The hybrid dimension definition above only applied to the case where batches exist. The complete definition of the hybrid dimension is thus:

Define the new and complete Foodcake-Batch dimension "Hfoodcake" as

```
Foodcake.leaf.(Time.day.this , Store.this ,(Qty received or Qty sold or
Qty on hand) >0) ~< Batchid
Union
Foodcake.leaf.(Time.day.this , Store.this ,(Qty received and Qty sold
and Qty on hand) = 0) ~ Batchid.n/a
```

Jan17, Arlington	Neptune		Poseidon		
	B213	B102	B209	B165	B276
Qty received	100	0	50	0	50
Qty sold	50	100	10	80	0
Price	5.95	5.95	5.50	5.50	0
Revenue	297.50	595	55	440	0
Qty on hand	50	0	40	0	50

Figure 16.6 Tracking Batchids of sales in Arlington.

Batchid.n/a, meaning not applicable (the token that was introduced in Chapter 5), is reserved for those locations where there are otherwise no foodcakes received, sold, or on hand. This is illustrated in Figure 16.7.

But if the batchid leaf is not applicable for Poseidon cakes, how can there be any prices or quantities, asked one of the managers. Thor responded that all the variable values applied equally well to the foodcake level of the Hfoodcake dimension. For example, the number 0 in the Qty received row under Poseidon cakes means that no Poseidon cakes were received. Furthermore, the stated price of $5.50 refers to the stated price of Poseidon cakes as listed in the Price attribute of the Fishcake dimension figure and which is true regardless of whether there are any Poseidon cakes in stock. Lulu added that the screen is less than fully perspicuous as the regularity of the dimension representation forces us to show a nonapplicable batchid leaf as opposed to showing nothing at all (as with the following recasting of the same screen representation, which took a little custom user interface work to create). Lulu's version is shown in Figure 16.8.

Jan18, Arlington	Neptune		Poseidon
	B213	B102	B.NA
Qty received	100	0	0
Qty sold	50	100	0
Price	5.95	5.95	5.50
Revenue	297.50	595	0
Qty on hand	50	0	0

Figure 16.7 Thor's version of tracking not-applicable Batchids in Arlington.

Jan18, Arlington	Neptune		Poseidon
	B213	B102	B.NA
Qty received	100	0	0
Qty sold	5	10	0
Price	5.95	5.95	5.50
Revenue	29.75	59.5	0
Qty on hand	95	13	43

Figure 16.8 Lulu's version of tracking not-applicable Batchids in Arlington.

ORDINAL BATCH

The only down side of this approach, said Thor, is that the sales cube needs to be reprocessed every day because one of its dimensions, the hybrid foodcake dimension, changes every day. Also, if you're trying to look at batch management across time or stores, as with queries such as

- What is the average amount of foodcake in each existent batch?
- How often are foodcakes sold without following the FIFO principle?

it can be awkward to formulate because there is no general concept of batch. One way to make it easier to compare batches across time and store, and avoid the need to reprocess the cube every day is to create an ordinal batch dimension and treat Batchid as a variable as shown in the schema below.

```
(Time. ⊗ Store. ⊗ Foodcake. ⊗ Batchordinal.) ~
        Batchid , Qty received, Qty sold , Qty on hand
```

The creation and use of the Batchordinal dimension, said Lulu, is very much like the creation and use of the Age dimension in inventory. The number of ordinal batches in the Batch dimension should be picked to reflect the maximum number of batches for any foodcake that any store is likely to have on hand at the same time. Since foodcakes are perishable, since the stores get daily shipments, and since they use a FIFO inventory principle, a five-member Batchordinal dimension should be sufficient. Batches arrive at a store in Batchordinal order with the youngest batch being assigned the batch1 position. Unlike the inventory Age dimension where all fish of some age increases one day in age per day, with an ordinal batch dimension, batches only age in terms of their ordinal bin number, with the arrival of younger batches.

Thor concluded, and the management seemed to nod in agreement, that the batch-specific Foodcake dimension finally allows FCI to connect changes in sales and marketing with changes through the entire value chain in FCI and beyond.

The hybrid Foodcake-Batch dimension also enables FCI to exert finer control over product quality management than ever before. For example, said Lulu, it is now straightforward to query for such things as the variance in quality attributes between different batches of the same foodcake.

Calculating Total Costs

Introduction

Now that you've seen how to maintain Batchid information right up to the point of sale, we can return to our primary question of calculating the total cost of production. All of the groundwork has been laid, said Thor. During these past months, we built an analytical layer on top of every major business process transaction system at FCI including purchasing, currency exchange, materials transport, materials inventory, production, distribution, marketing, sales, and yes, even management.

The basic strategy we used was to measure all quantities of asset utilization, prices per quantity of asset utilization, and costs of asset utilization within each business process as accurately as possible at whatever granularity the measurements naturally occur. For example, some labor costs are measured by the hour while some financial costs are measured by the month. Then we allocated all costs across whatever unit of process was appropriate. For example, distribution costs were calculated for kilograms of material or product moved one kilometer, while inventory costs were calculated for kilograms of material or product stored for one day. Production costs were calculated for kilograms of foodcake produced per machine per batch. Finally, we aggregated total costs per business process and per asset type.

Though most of the audience looked pleased about the prospects of analyzing their business in such detail, the VP of Foodsources raised his hand. I don't see how you can talk about batches across all FCI business processes, he said. Aren't fish treated as a homogeneous commodity? Can this system really tell me where the Salmon came from that appear, for example, in the Neptune fishcakes sold on January 17 in Cambridge?

Lulu thanked the VP for going straight to FCI's tracking limitations and, by association, the limitations of this analytical system. (You can't manage what you don't measure, Thor murmured to himself.) For those of you who didn't follow the question, let me explain. FCI attaches a Batchid to every discrete batch of foodcake that is produced. The Batchid identifies the production facility, the machine, the start and end time, and the foodcake produced. FCI does not track the foodsources that go into our foodcakes with the same concept of a batch. We do track, at materials inventory, how much of each type of foodsource came in on any day and the weighted average price paid per kilo of foodsource. We also track the cargo id for the shipment on which the foodsource arrived.

But we lose track of the actual foodsource in three different places:

- At the market where the foodsource is bought
- In the transport vessel
- In inventory

Historically, FCI operates this way because once fish passed the inspection of our on-site purchaser, it was thought to be sufficiently homogeneous not to need any further distinction beyond its age. Thus, our South American materials inventory site does not distinguish between three-day-old Argentinean Bass and three-day-old Chilean Bass. Since FCI begins mixing fish as far back in the business process as the pier, FCI also mixes fish prices, appropriately weighted by relative quantities purchased. If FCI thought that it needed to be able to figure out for any foodcake sold not only the weighted average price per kilo per foodsource and its date of origin, but also the specific shipment or shipments of foodsource (such as French Bass bought in Marseilles from Pierre's fishing fleet), the company would need to substantially change not only its business practices, but also its fixed-asset structure. For example, instead of using fish transport vessels with one bin per fish type, FCI would need to use transport mechanisms with one bin per fish type per supplier. Instead of keeping date-tagged bins in materials inventory, FCI would need to maintain separate supplier-tagged bins for every fish type and age in inventory. These practices would add a significant cost to FCI's total cost of purchasing, distribution, and inventory. It isn't clear at this time that such an improvement to the company's foodsource tracking capabilities would be recouped through enhanced sales, reduced costs, or improved management. From my perspective, added Thor, the reasons FCI might eventually want to add such levels of tracking would be to improve quality control rather than costs. Source-level tracking would enable us to connect a bad batch of foodcakes with a particular supplier. It would also enable us to figure out which batches of foodcakes are affected by some specific foodsource if we were to learn of problems with that foodsource.

But your question was so insightful and to the point, continued Lulu, that I propose we illustrate the benefits of the enterprise OLAP layer we created by showing everyone in this room how to calculate and trace the incremental contributions to total earnings for two sets of foodcakes from two particular batches of the same kind of foodcake sold at two different stores in the same region on the same day.

Before launching into the exercise, Thor offered a few words of caution. To those of you (and I'm really referring to the readers here) who intend to follow along with us on a step-by-step basis, especially when we write out expressions, let me just say that beyond the confines of this pedagogically oriented exposition, it would be unusual to write such expressions so as to follow the path of just one or two batches. Rather, it would be far more typical to query for and view sets of batches across ranges of times, locations, products, distribution paths, and so on.

Thus, given our game plan of tracking and analyzing across all of FCI's business processes the incremental costs associated with two different batches of the same kind of foodcake, I will take the liberty of mixing up expressions and views, sometimes showing the results from a narrowly defined query and sometimes showing additional view context.

Please keep in mind that, although you will see many of the calculations required to determine the total costs of foodcake production, you will not see all of them. Given time constraints, I think showing you representative calculations from across FCI's value chain is just as instructive and is a more efficient way to learn. (Remember, if you want to follow every single step with a pencil and perform every single calculation yourself, there is a full computational exercise in Chapter 17.)

Also, since we are taking you through this cost-tracing odyssey on a cube-by-cube basis, you might get the false impression that someone needs to manually bring context into every business process. All the business processes are interconnected. We could have written a single expression to calculate the total activity-based costs and earnings accruing to any sales of any foodcakes in any stores at any time. For pedagogical reasons, we feel it is more beneficial to you, the managers (and readers), to be able to follow each business process independently.

The Enterprise Asset Utilization and Cost Cube

The first things we need to do, said Lulu, are define a business process and a business asset dimension and assemble them in a cost and activity-tracking schema as loosely defined in the following code (that is, mentioning types of variables rather than defining specific variables):

```
(Time.day. ⊗ Business_process. ⊗ Asset. ) ~
        physical throughput and financial cost variables
```

Thor continued, as you all understand how various asset utilization costs are calculated, I think it is most valuable for you to see how global asset and business process costs are calculated. Since we began this exercise by trying to figure out how much we earned or lost selling two different batches of the same kind of foodcake on a particular day at two different stores in the same region, we will follow the cost trail backwards beginning with sales and marketing.

Sales and Marketing

There are two basic pieces of information that FCI needs from the stores who sell its foodcakes: How many packages were sold (net any returns) and how much money is owed FCI. Recall that the amount of money owed FCI is a function of the wholesale price of the foodcakes and FCI's share in whatever discounts are applied to the foodcakes.

For simplicity, let's assume that discounts are day wide and customer invariant, so we don't have to look at actual transaction data at this point. The relevant schema (with derived variables underlined) is

```
[S&M] Schema:
(Time.Day. ⊗ Geog.Store. ⊗ Hfoodcake.) ~
        Qty_Sold{pkg}, List_Price{$/pkg}, Wholesale_Price{$/pkg},
        Discount{$/pkg}, Discount_Share{R}, Total_Revenue{$},
        Dollars_Owed_FCI{$},  Effective_Wholesale_Price{$/pkg},
        Dollars_Owed_FCI_per_kg{$/kg}
```

Given this schema, let's estimate what we earned or lost for those foodcakes for which we sold the greatest number of packages from two different stores on a particular day, in a particular zone (say the Boston zone), on some specific day, such as January 18. To see the result set in context, we'll query for the most popular foodcakes from the days surrounding January 18 as well. The query results are shown in Figure 16.9.

```
"Foodcake", "Geog.Store" ,
        Time.Jan.(17 to 19) ,
        Geog.Zone.Boston_Area,
        Qty_Sold.max
```

Page
Geog.Zone.Boston_Area
Qty_Sold.max

Row			
Time.Day.	Jan17	Poseidon.8packs.	Glouchester
Foodcake {N}	Jan18	Neptune.4pack.	Cambridge
Geog.Store {N}	Jan19	SailorsDelite.4pack.	Boston

Figure 16.9 Qty_Sold Max.

Neptune four packs turned up as the hottest selling foodcake in the Boston zone on January 18. Next, we asked for the top two selling batches of Neptune four packs and the stores in which they sold with the following query, whose results are shown in Figure 16.10.

```
"Hfoodcake.leaf", "Geog.Store" ,
     Time.(Jan17 to Jan19) ,
     Geog.Zone.Boston_Area ,
     Product.Neptune.4pack.(Qty sold.Drank1-2)
```

Page
Geog.Zone.Boston_Area

Row				
Time.Day.	Jan17	1	Neptune.4pack.B.90	Boston
		2	Neptune.4pack.B101	Wellesley
	Jan18	1	Neptune.4pack.B123	Cambridge
		2	Neptune.4pack.B101	Allston
Drank.Hfoodcake {N} Geog.Store {N}	Jan19	1	Neptune.4pack.B156	Newton
		2	Neptune.4pack.B.95	Boston

Figure 16.10 Top two selling batches of Neptune foodcakes.

The result turned up Neptune four packs from batch 123 sold in Cambridge and Neptune four packs from batch 101 sold in Allston as the hottest selling batches of

Neptune foodcake; both sold on January 18. Next, we asked for the associated financial data with the following query, whose results are shown in Figure 16.11 and 16.12.

```
[S&M]: "Qty_Sold"{pkg}, "List_Price"{$/pkg}, "Wholesale_Price"{$/pkg},
"Discount"{$/pkg}, "Discount_Share"{R}, "Total_Revenue"{$},
"Dollars_Owed_FCI"{$},  "Effective_Wholesale_Price"{$/pkg},
"Dollars_Owed_FCI_per_kg"{$/kg},
Hfoodcake.Neptune.4pack.(B123 and B101),
Time.Jan18,
Geog.(Cambridge and Allston)
```

Page		Column
Time.Jan18		Store.Hfoodcake.

		Cambridge	Allston
		Neptune.4pack. B123	Neptune.4pack. .B101
	Qty_Sold {pkg}	50	45
	List_Price {$/pkg}	6.95	6.95
	Wholesale_Price {$/pkg}	5.50	5.50
	Discount {$}	1.00	0.75
	Discount_Share {R}	0.50	0.50
	Total_Revenue {$}	298	279
	Effective_Wholesale {$/pkg}	5.00	5.13
Row	Dollars_Owed_FCI {$}	250	231
Variables { }	Dollars_Owed_FCI_per_kg {$/kg}	10.00	10.25

Figure 16.11   [S&M] cube view.

Business Process	Hfoodcake.	Costs {$/Kg} , Asset.All	Wholesale Revenue {$/Kg} , Asset.all
Sales & Marketing	Neptune.4pack.B123. (OrderID.0169)	1.00	11.00
	Neptune.4pack.B101. (OrderID.0170)	0.75	11.00

Figure 16.12   Activity-based costs of sales and marketing.

So, Lulu said, you can see that by counting FCI's promotion share and targeted marketing (described in Chapter 15) as costs, FCI spends nearly $1 per kilogram of Neptune fishcake on sales and marketing activities. I submit that the fundamental activity-based management question for FCI to answer is, "What was the total cost on a per kilogram basis for FCI to deliver those 50 packages of Neptune fishcakes to Cambridge for which it received $250, and the total cost to deliver the 45 packages to Allston for which it received $231?"

Transportation from Product Inventory to Stores

Working backwards, the next business process is the transportation that brought the foodcakes from the Hartford distribution center to the Cambridge and Allston stores. FCI owns and operates its own distribution centers. Furthermore, every distribution center can be stocked with any foodcake that any store may want. So, any particular store receives its foodcakes from one and only one distribution center. The relevant distribution schemas are as follows:

```
[Travel] Schema:
((Time.Day. ⊗ Geog.ProductInventorySite.) ~< Geog.Zone.) ~
        VehicleID{integer}, Total_Distance{km}, Fixed_Cost{$},
        Vehicle_Travel_Cost{$},  (Delivery_PlanID{integer} ~<
            Geog.Store{N}, Time.Hour.Quarter{qtr_hour}, Trip_Share{R},
            OrderID{integer}, Order_Travel_Cost{$},
            Travel_Cost_per_kg{$/kg})
```

```
[Vehicle] Schema:
(Time.Day.atabove. ⊗ VehicleID.) ~
    Cost_per_km{$/km}
```

```
[Order] Schema:
(OrderID. ⊗ Hfoodcake.) ~
    Qty{kg}
```

To figure out the cost per kilogram of transporting each of the two sets of Neptune fishcakes, Lulu said, we need to figure out the cost of the trip (assuming that both batches of foodcakes were delivered on the same day) and the share of the trip's costs attributable to the delivery made to Cambridge/Allston, and the share of the Cambridge/Allston delivery costs attributable to the Neptune fishcakes delivered. All the managers nodded in approval.

The expression for total trip cost is

```
[Travel]: Vehicle_Travel_Cost{$}=
        Fixed_Cost{$} +
        Total_Distance{km} x
        [Vehicle]: (Cost_per_km{$/km})
```

The query basically says that vehicle travel cost is equal to the fixed cost associated with the [Travel] schema plus a variable cost defined as the distance times the cost per kilometer, where the cost per kilometer is associated with a separate [Vehicle] schema.

The query to calculate the travel cost for the vehicle that our Neptune fishcakes traveled in is

```
[Travel]: Vehicle_Travel_Cost{$},
          Time.Jan18,
          Geog.ProductInventorySite.Hartford,
          Geog.Zone.Boston_Area
```

The result set and its components are illustrated in Figure 16.13.

Page
Geog.ProductInventorySite.Hartford
Time.Jan18
Geog.Zone.Boston_Area

Column
Variable { }

Row		Total_Distance {km}	Fixed_Cost {$}	Vehicle_Travel_Cost {$}
VehicleID	VehicleID. 60	400	150	250

Figure 16.13 Vehicle travel costs.

One of the managers asked why the cost per kilometer was put in a separate VehicleID cube as shown in Figure 16.14. Why wasn't it included in the Travel cube? Good question, said Thor. The reason we put VehicleID in a separate cube is because vehicles are not tied to routes. The vehicle that makes the Boston run one day may make the Springfield run another. However, the cost of operating the vehicle is a function of the vehicle and not the route. Thus, from a normalization perspective, it makes more sense to maintain VehicleID, and associated vehicle properties, in a separate cube. Of course, if the source data emanating from warehouse figures is already denormalized, and robust rules are in place for working with missing and meaningless data, and so long as the schema is more for read than write purposes, maintaining a denormalized schema may be perfectly fine from a logical perspective. From a physical perspective, it may lead to much improved query performance.

In order to find out the Cost_per_km for all vehicles on the day that our Neptune fishcakes were transported, you could use a query like this

```
[Vehicle]: "Cost_per_km", VehicleID., Time.Jan18
```

Sample results of this query are shown in Figure 16.14.

Lulu could see that questions were still lingering in some managers' heads. What do you think of the three distribution cubes?

Page		Column	
Time.Jan18		Cost_per_km {$/km}	

			Cost_per_km {$/km}
		VehicleID. 21	0.25
		VehicleID. 35	0.25
		VehicleID. 60	0.25
Row		VehicleID. 56	0.30
VehicleID.		VehicleID. 67	0.30

Figure 16.14   Vehicle costs per kilometer.

Another manager then asked why the delivery plan information was embedded in the Travel cube (using the ~< or $1/N$ operator defined in Chapter 4)? If it makes sense to break out the VehicleID information, why not the delivery plan information? Lulu responded that they could have broken out the delivery plan information into a separate cube, but decided that since the same department responsible for maintaining the Travel cube was responsible for maintaining the Delivery cube, and since delivery plan ids are unique identifiers that occur only once in the [Travel] schema whereas the VehicleID occurs every time the vehicle is used, and since the delivery plan information is only accessed through the [Travel] schema (yes, she admitted that with a unique identifier it would certainly be possible to access delivery plan information directly, but so far no one thinks in terms of delivery plan ids but rather the dates) and ship from and ship to locations—which after all is how the unique identifiers are generated—they decided to keep delivery plan information embedded within the [Travel] schema.

As if these weren't enough questions, another manager asked why the $1/N$ correlation that existed between Geog.ProductInventorySite and Geog.Zone locations was placed outside of the cross product of Time and Geog.ProductInventorySite. In other words, as he showed on the white board, why does the expression look like

```
((Time.Day. ⊗ Geog.ProductInventorySite.) ~< Geog.Zone.)
```

and not like

```
(Time.Day. ⊗ (Geog.ProductInventorySite. ~< Geog.Zone.))
```

What do you think? Thor responded to this question by saying that the reason ~< *Geog.Zone* was included outside the parentheses was because although the set of ship to zones always maintained a $1/N$ relationship with ship-from locations, the particular set of ship-to zones associated with any one ship-from location changes over time. As new outlet stores came on board and as new distribution centers were created, the optimal mapping of distribution centers to retail outlets varied accordingly.

Returning to the calculation at hand, the order travel cost and the order travel cost per kilogram are expressed in the following way:

```
[Travel]: "Order_Travel_Cost"{$},
          OrderID. =

                     Tripshare{R} x
                     Vehicle_Travel_Cost{$}

[Travel]: "Travel_Cost_per_kg"{$/kg},
          OrderID. =

                     Order_Travel_Cost{$} +
                     [Order]: Qty{kg}, Hfoodcake.all
```

Notice how the formula definition for Travel_Cost_per_kg {$/kg} makes a reference to the [Order] schema to obtain the total quantity of kilograms in each order. Knowing that our foodcake packages, from Hfoodcake batches Neptune.4pack.B123 and Neptune.4pack.B101, arrive at their relevant stores through Delivery_PlanID.D36 in OrderID.0169 and OrderID.0170 respectively, we can express the query for the order travel cost and the order travel cost per kg as follows:

```
[Travel]: "Order_Travel_Cost"{$},
                   OrderID.(0169 and 0170),
                   Time.Jan18,
                   Geog.ProductInventorySite.Hartford,
                   Geog.Zone.Boston_Area,
                   Geog.Store.(Cambridge and Allston)
[Travel]: "Travel_Cost_per_kg"{$/kg},
                   OrderID.(0169 and 0170)
```

The result set, with surrounding context is shown in Figure 16.15.

Kilograms per order from the [Order] schema for the Neptune batches of interest are shown here in Figure 16.16.

Now, we can see how trips with a high tripshare or with large distances to travel or with high vehicle operating costs could have a substantial impact on the transportation costs between the product inventory site and the stores. Furthermore, the quantity in each order impacts the Travel_Cost_per_kg {$/kg}. Total costs per kilogram of distributing foodcake packages in these orders from our batches is shown in Figure 16.17.

Page
Time.Jan18
Geog.ProductInventorySite. Hartford
Geog.Zone.Boston_Area

		Store	Cambridge
D36	0169	Time	6:00 A.M.
		Trip_Share {R}	0.25
		Order_Travel_ Cost {$}	62.5
		Travel_Cost_per_ kg {$/kg}	0.25
	0170	Store	Allston
		Time	6:30 A.M.
		Trip_Share {R}	0.2
		Order_Travel_ Cost {$}	50
		Travel_Cost_per_ kg {$/kg}	0.22

Row
Delivery_PlanID.
OrderID.
Variables { }

Figure 16.15   Calculating travel cost per kilogram.

Column
Qty {kg}

			Qty {kg}
	169	Neptune.4pack.B123	80
		Neptune.8pack.B127	75
		SeaBreeze.8pack.B43	90
		All	250
	170	Neptune.4pack.B101	85
		SeaBreeze.4pack.B25	75
		Poseidon.8pack.B120	65
		Hfoodcake.	

Row
OrderID.

Figure 16.16   Quantity of fish per order.

Business Process	Hfoodcake.	Costs{$/Kg} , Asset.All
Product Distribution to Stores	Neptune.4pack.B123.(OrderID.0169)	0.29
	Neptune.4pack.B101.(OrderID.0170)	0.15

Figure 16.17 Activity-based costs of product distribution.

Product Inventory Costs

What about the time spent in Hartford? How much cost can we attribute to the time those foodcakes spent in inventory? As is typical across the enterprise, there are two relevant schemas: one for throughput or activity labeled [PI Throughput] and one for costs labeled [PI Cost].

```
[PI Throughput] Schema:
(Time.Day.atabove. ⊗ Geog.ProductInventorySite. ⊗ Hfoodcake.
 ⊗ Age.) ~
        Qty_Sent{kg}, Qty_Received{kg}, Qty_On_Hand{kg},
        Qty_Throughput{kg}, Cost_per_kg{$/kg}


[PI Cost] Schema:
(Time.Day.atabove. ⊗ Geog.ProductInventorySite. ⊗ Stuff.NonFoodAsset.) ~
        Cost{$}
```

The main things we need to figure out are how long did those specific Neptune cakes remain in inventory and what was the cost per day of their stay for those specific days? To address the first question we need to pose the following query that leverages our knowledge of when the foodcakes were shipped to the Boston area:

```
[PI Throughput]: "Age",
        Time.Jan18,
        Geog.ProductInventorySite.Hartford ,
        Hfoodcake.Neptune4pack.(B123 and B101)
```

In words, it asks for the age of the Neptune four pack foodcake packages at the Hartford product inventory site on the day they left inventory and were shipped to the Boston area. Another way to look for the answer is by querying for the arrival date for the foodcakes as with the following query:

```
"Time.day" ,
    Geog.ProductInventorySite.Hartford ,
    Age.1 , Hfoodcake.Neptune.4pack(B101, B123)
```

Page	Column
Time.Jan.18.	Age.

			Age.1	Age.2	Age.3	Age.4
		SeaBreeze.8pack. B205	Jan16	Jan17	n/a	n/a
		Neptune.4pack. B123	Jan16	Jan17	Jan18	n/a
Row	Hartford	Neptune.4pack. B101	Jan15	Jan16	Jan17	Jan18
Geog.Product InventorySite.		SeaBreeze.8pack. B41	Jan15	Jan16	Jan17	Jan18
Hfoodcake.		Poseidon.4pack. B99	Jan17	Jan18	n/a	n/a

Figure 16.18 Viewing inventory age at time of shipping.

Since foodcakes arrive at inventory as one day old, as illustrated in Figure 16.18, foodcakes in batch 123 destined for Cambridge spent two days in Hartford, while the foodcakes in batch 101 destined for Allston spent three days in inventory.

```
"Time.day" ,
    Geog.ProductInventorySite.Hartford ,
    Age.1 , Hfoodcake.Neptune.4pack(B101, B123) =
        Jan15, Jan16
```

These are the answers we were expecting, said Thor, so we move along in our analysis. Next we need to find out the inventory costs during the time period that each set of Neptune cakes was in storage. First let's get a feel for the cost structure associated with product inventory. This can be accomplished with the following query whose results in context are shown in Figure 16.19:

```
[PI Cost]: "Cost"{$},
            Time.Jan.(15 to 17),
            Geog.ProductInventorySite.(Hartford and Palo Alto),
                Stuff.NonfoodAsset.
```

In words, the query asks for the cost in dollars of all nonfood assets for two inventory sites and three dates. Next we can query for the specific inventory costs associated with each of the two batches of foodcakes. In words, the query asks for the costs for all nonfood assets in Hartford spent on the foodcakes in our two batches for the time

			Jan15	Jan16	Jan17
		Labor	912	912	912
		Maintenance	50	50	50
	Hartford	Facility	200	200	200
		Energy	100	100	100
		All	1,262	1,262	1,262
		Labor	901	901	901
		Maintenance	45	45	45
	Palo Alto	Facility	190	190	190
		Energy	95	95	95
		All	1,231	1,231	1,231

Page

Cost {$}

Hfoodcake.all

Age.all

Column

Time.Day.

Row

Geog.ProductInventory.
Site.

Stuff.NonFoodAsset.

Figure 16.19 Cost of product inventory.

period ranging between January 18, the day both sets of foodcakes shipped out, and the particular date on which each subbatch (that is, each set of foodcakes produced in the same batch; remember that each batch is split up and sent to multiple inventory sites after leaving production) of foodcakes was one day old.

```
[PI Cost]: Cost {$},
           Time.Day.(Jan18 to (Time.day.Age.1),
           Hfoodcake.(B123, B101),
           Geog.ProductInventorySite.Hartford,
           NonFoodAsset.All
```

Since the inventory dates are not the same for each batch, we needed to refer to the time period by the date range defined by the period between the common ship out date, January 18, and their distinct arrival dates, defined by the day on which each subbatch was one day old. The results are shown in Figure 16.20.

The next step, said Lulu, is to calculate the inventory cost for each of the two sets of foodcakes. We need to figure out how much product was throughput during each of the two time periods. There are several ways to do this. Recall from our in-depth discussion on inventory (in Chapter 14) that we decided to use the average of quantities

Hfoodcake.	Time.day.(Jan18 to (Time.day.Age.1))	Costs {$}, Asset.All,
Neptune.4pack.B123	Jan 18 to 16	2,524
Neptune.4pack.B101	Jan 18 to 15	3,786

Figure 16.20 Cumulative inventory costs.

Hfoodcake.	Time.day.(Jan18 to (Time.day.(Age.1)))	Qty_Throughput {kg}
Neptune.4pack.B123	Jan 16 to 18	45,150
Neptune.4pack.B101	Jan 15 to 18	30,200

Figure 16.21 Cumulative product inventory throughput.

sent and received as a measure of quantity throughput. Thus, the formula for throughput is as follows: (The results are shown in Figure 16.21.)

```
[PI Throughput]: "Qty_Throughput" {kg},
        Time.Day.(Jan18 to (Time.Day.(Age.1))),
            Hfoodcake.Neptune.4pack.(B123, B101),
        Geog.ProductInventorySite.Hartford,
        Hfoodcake.all,
        Age.all =

                ( Qty_Sent {kg} +
            Qty_Received {kg} ) ÷ 2
```

Lulu added that they could have also defined measures of quantity throughput and cost on a day-to-day basis, and then summed the individual costs per throughput per day. Hey wait a minute, said one of the managers. Aren't costs per throughput per day ratios? I thought you weren't supposed to sum ratios. Excellent question, said Lulu! The sum of the ratios (as shown in Chapter 7) is not equal to the ratio of the sums. However, we are not looking for the average cost per day, but rather the sum of the costs per day (effectively, a sum of numerators divided by a sum of denominators). If something costs $10 per day one day and $20 per day another day, it costs $30 per two days or ($10 + $20) / (1 day + 1 day). Finally, said Lulu, we can define a new variable to calculate the costs of storing each of the subbatches of Neptune foodcakes by multiplying the ratio of quantity throughput per batch to total throughput multiplied by the total costs for that time period as follows:

```
"Cost of storing Neptune foodcakes from batches 101 and 123 in orders
556 and 567" =

          [PI Throughput]: (Qty_Sent {kg},
          Hfoodcake.Neptune.4pack.(B123, B101), Time.Jan18)
          ÷
          (Qty throughput {Kg} , Time.day.(Jan18 to (Time.day ,
          Age.1 , Hfoodcake.4pack.(B123 +B101).)), Hfoodcake.all)
          ×
          [PI Costs]: Cost {$} , Time.day.(Jan18 to (Time.day ,
          Age.1 , Hfoodcake.Neptune.4pack.(B123 + B101).)),
          Geog.ProductInventorySite.Hartford, NonFoodAsset.all
```

In words, the cost of storing the foodcakes from each of the Neptune batches during their slightly different length stays in Hartford is equal to all the costs incurred by Hartford inventory during those days multiplied by each of the ratios for the amount of Neptune batch 123 or 101 foodcakes throughput divided by the total number of foodcakes throughput in Hartford during that same time.

Lulu tapped Thor on the shoulder; I think you're forgetting something, Thor, she said. What do you think? Just then, one of the managers raised her hand. Are you sure this is right? Aren't you assuming that all of the relevant Neptune cakes stored in inventory are sent to Cambridge or Allston? Don't we need to find the ratio of each batch of Neptune cakes sent to Cambridge or Allston, to all the Neptune batch 123 or 101 cakes received and stored? Couldn't we have done that directly in the formula above?

You are absolutely right, replied Thor. I was hoping someone would catch that planted mistake. So let's write that formula over again using the right quantity values for each of the Neptune batches.

```
"Cost of storing Neptune foodcakes from batches 101 and 123 in orders
556 and 567" =

          [S&M]: ²(Qty_Sold {kg}, Hfoodcake.Neptune.4pack.(B123 +
          B101) , Time.Jan18), Geog.Store.(Cambridge, Allston).
          ÷
          [PI Throughput]: (Qty_Throughput {kg}, Time.day.(Jan18 to
          (Time.day ,Age.1 , Hfoodcake.Neptune.4pack.(B123 + B101)))
          , Hfoodcake.all)
          ×
          [PI Costs]: Cost {$}, Time.day.(Jan18 to (Time.day, Age.1,
          Hfoodcake.Neptune.4pack.(B123 + B101))),
          Geog.ProductInventorySite.Hartford , NonFoodAsset.all
          ×
          (Age - 1), Time.Jan18, Hfoodcake.Neptune4pack.(B123 +
          B101).
```

In words, it says to take the quantity sold from the sales and marketing cube and divide it into the total inventory throughput as calculated in the product inventory

Hfoodcake.	(Age-1) , Time.Jan18	Qty_Sold {kg}	Cost {$}
Neptune.4pack.B123	2	25.0	3.76
Neptune.4pack.B101	3	22.5	5.66

Figure 16.22   Cost of storing foodcakes.

		Cost {$/Kg} , Asset.			
FCI_Business_Process.	Hfoodcake.	All	Labor	Facility	Utilities
Product Inventory	Neptune.4pack.B123	0.15	0.06	0.06	0.03
	Neptune.4pack.B101	0.25	0.10	0.09	0.06

Figure 16.23   Asset costs of product inventory on a per kilogram basis.

throughput cube for each of the two time periods corresponding to the time period that batch 123 spent in inventory and the time period that batch 101 spent in inventory, and multiply each of the two ratios by the total costs of inventory over the time period each foodcake was in inventory. This yields cost per kilogram per day, which then needs to be multiplied by the number of days spent in inventory as was done in the bottom expression. The results are shown in Figure 16.22.

Finally, we have the information to calculate the cost of product inventory on a per kilogram basis as shown in Figure 16.23.

Transport from Production to Product Inventory

The cost of the transport from FCI's production facilities to the Hartford distribution center is similar to the cost of the transport from the distribution center to the stores. But there are some differences. Can anybody suggest what they are, asked Lulu. What do you think?

Think about the business differences, said Lulu. Since not all foodcakes are produced in all production facilities, a single distribution center may receive foodcakes from more than one production facility. How would you reflect that difference in the design of the [Distribution] schema, asked Lulu?

I suppose I would define an M/N or Cartesian relationship between the ship from (Geog.ProductionSite.) and ship to (Geog.ProductInventorySite) dimensions rather than the $1/N$ relationship used in the final distribution to the stores, said one of the managers. Great answer, said Lulu. That's exactly right. So the schemas for product shipping would look like the following:

```
[Distribution] Schema:
(Time.Day. ⊗ Geog.ProductionSite. ⊗ Geog.ProductInventorySite.) ~
Method {N}, Total_Distance{km}, Fixed_Cost{$}, CargoID {I},
Arrival_Time{qtr_hour}, Cargo_Distribution_Cost{$},
Distribution_Cost_per_kg{$/kg},

[Transport Method] Schema:
(Time.Day.atabove. ⊗ Method.) ~
      Cost_per_kg_km{$/(kg*km)}

[Cargo] Schema:
(CargoID. ⊗ Hfoodcake.) ~
      Qty_Shipped{kg}
```

Although the Geog.ProductionSite. and Geog.ProductInventorySite. relationships are more complex here than in the final product distribution, the CargoID is simpler than its equivalent in final distribution because each vehicle only makes one stop, namely to the product inventory site. Thus, the costs of transporting the Neptune cakes is the multiplicative product of the cost per kg*km for the transportation method of their respective CargoIDs and the quantity {kg} of Neptunes sold. Of course, since the two batches traveled on two different days, possibly using two different methods, the actual costs may be different for each batch. Since we have limited time, I'm just going to show you the specific formulas for calculating distribution costs per kilogram of product sold for one of the two batches, namely the Neptune cakes sold in Cambridge. Of course, the general formula for calculating distribution costs is the same for both batches; the only difference is the date of shipment. The Neptune cakes destined for Cambridge traveled on January 16; those destined for Allston traveled on January 15.

```
[Distribution]:
"Cargo_Distribution_Cost"{$}=
            Fixed_Cost{$} + (Total_Distance{km} ×
            [Cargo]: (Qty_Shipped{kg}, Hfoodcake.all) ×
            [Transport Method]: (Cost_per_kg_km{$/(kg*km)}))
            Time.Jan16, Geog.ProductionSite.Vancouver,
            Geog.ProductInventorySite.Hartford
```

In words, the formula says that cargo distribution costs for the Neptune cakes destined for Cambridge are equal to fixed costs, taken from the Distribution cube, plus variable costs defined as distance times quantity shipped times the cost per kilogram and kilometer as taken from the Transport Method cube. The formula further specifies Vancouver as the ship-from location, Hartford as the ship-to location and January 16 as the arrival date. That cost is then combined with the ratio of kilograms of Neptune cakes sold taken from the Sales and Marketing cube to the kilograms shipped for all of CargoID.567 as defined in the formula fragment that follows:

```
[S&M]: (Qty_Sold {kg}, Hfoodcake.Neptune.4pack.B123 ,
Time.Jan18,Geog.Store.Cambridge)
÷
```

```
(Qty_Shipped {kg}, CargoID.567) ×
[Distribution]: (Cargo_Distribution_Cost {$} , Cargoid.567)
```

Hey wait a minute, said one of the managers. I understand the formula, but where did you get that CargoID number? Lulu responded, good observation! I got that number from perusing the Product Distribution cube and knowing what date(s) I needed. If, however, I didn't know the CargoID, I could have asked for it in a relative way as with the following query:

```
[Distribution]:  "CargoID" {I},
    Geog.ProductionSite.Vancouver ,
    Geog.ProductInventorySite.Hartford ,
    Time.[PI Throughput]:(Time.day.this-1 , Age.1 ,
    Hfoodcake.Neptune.4pack.B123)
```

Could you explain how you derived CargoID, asked one of the managers. Sure, said Thor. Remember, in the [Distribution] schema CargoID is a variable. For every unique date, production site, and product inventory site, there is exactly one CargoID. We know the production site and the product inventory site, but the dates, unless we want to manually pluck them from product inventory, need to be derived. Since it takes one day for products to be shipped from the production facility to the distribution center, the shipping date in the Distribution cube is one day prior to the day that the products arrived in inventory, which we track as the day on which the products are one day old. Thus, we're asking for the CargoID that corresponds to the date in the Inventory cube that is one day prior to the day when the batch was one day old.

Figures 16.24 through 16.26 show that the distribution costs per kilogram are similar between the two different batches.

			Column
			Qty {kg}

			Qty {kg}
	CargoID. 567	Neptune.4pack.B123	205
		Neptune.8pack.B127	150
		SeaBreeze.8pack.B43	190
		All	7,000
	CargoID. 556	Neptune.4pack.B101	210
Row		SeaBreeze.4pack.B25	175
CargoID.		Poseidon.8pack.B120	165
Hfoodcake.		All	8,500

Figure 16.24 Quantity transported per unique cargo shipment.

	Column
	Time.Day

			Jan15	Jan16
Row	MethodID.Truck	Cost_per_kg_km {$/(kg x km)}	0.000089	0.000089
	MethodID.Plane	Cost_per_kg_km {$/(kg x km)}	0.000160	0.000170
MethodID. Variables { }	MethodID.Train	Cost_per_kg_km {$/(kg x km)}	0.000120	0.000110

Figure 16.25   Cost per kilogram and kilometer per method of transport.

Page
Geog.ProductionSite.Vancouver
Geog.ProductInventorySite.Hartford

Column
Time.Day

		Jan15	Jan16
	MethodID	Plane	Plane
	Total_Distance {km}	5,000	5,000
	Fixed_Cost {$}	275	275
	CargoID	556	567
	Arrival_Time	Jan15	Jan16
Row	Cargo_Distribution_Cost {$}	7,075	5,875
Variables { }	Distribution_Cost_per_kg {$/kg}	0.832	0.839

Figure 16.26   Distribution costs by day.

As compared with the costs of final distribution, the costs of product shipment are substantially higher getting them from the production site to the product inventory site than from the product inventory site to the store. That's because these two batches of Neptune cakes traveled by plane from Vancouver to Hartford as compared with the cake's final journey by delivery truck from Hartford to the Boston zone. The total cost per kilogram for foodcakes in each batch is shown in Figure 16.27.

FCI_Business_Process.	Hfoodcake.	Cost {$/Kg} , Asset.all
Transport from Production to Product Inventory	Neptune.4pack.B123	0.839
	Neptune.4pack.B101	0.832

Figure 16.27 Transport costs per kilogram.

Production

So far we've traced our Neptune cakes back from the Boston zone where they were sold on January 18 to Vancouver where Neptune batch 123 was put on a plane on January 16 and Neptune batch 101 was put on a plane on January 15. Our next task is to determine how much it cost to produce each of the two batches of Neptune cakes. Are you all still with me, asked Lulu? Most everyone nodded yes. One of the managers raised his hand. I don't mean to ask a silly question, but can you reinforce for me the reason, as I can see from the blackboard you're about to do again, why you show us all these schemas. Before Lulu could respond, the CEO stepped in. May I, he said. Certainly, said Lulu.

What Lulu and Thor are so ably doing is showing you, probably for the first time, the inner engine of our business. FCI is engaged in many activities in order to sell food-cakes. Although we don't have to know every last detail of every process, it is essential that all of us in senior management understand how the activities we engage in relate to one another. The schemas are a succinct way of showing, for each business process, the major variables or facts we measure or track, and the major variables we need to derive in order to have the information required to make appropriate decisions. The formulas are then the specific way we calculate those derivations. I think you should all understand by now that the combination of the schemas and formulas reflect our current business practices at both a tactical and a strategic level. If there are changes that we think need to be made in our business, we can simulate them in our business model. For example, before this presentation is over, we may come to the conclusion that some business processes that we currently perform ourselves, such as product shipping, would be more efficiently performed through outsourcing or vice versa.

Lulu then continued. There are two schemas we use to represent the production process. These are shown with the relevant variables. Note the reemergence of a batch ordinal or sequencing dimension (as discussed earlier in this chapter).

```
[Production] schema

(Time.Day. ⊗ Geog.ProductionSite. ⊗ Stuff. ⊗ Process. ⊗ BatchOrdinal.) ~

        Qty_Input{kg}
        Qty_Output{kg}
        Production_Cost{$}
        Production_Cost_per_kg{$/kg}
```

```
(Time.Day. ⊗ Geog.ProductionSite. ⊗ Stuff.all ⊗
Process. ⊗ BatchOrdinal.) ~

              Start_Time {qtr_hour},
              End_Time  {qtr_hour},

              (Time.Day. ⊗ Geog.ProductionSite. ⊗ Stuff.all
              ⊗ Process.all ⊗ BatchOrdinal.) ~

              BatchID {string }
```

[Batch] Schema:

```
BatchID. ~
MachineID, Time.Day, Geog.ProductionSite, BatchOrdinal,
(Start_Time, End_Time, Process.leaf.)
```

To calculate the total costs of production, we need to sum the dollar value of all the nonfoodsource assets consumed, which costs have already been allocated to the day level, such as electricity, capital equipment, labor, and so forth. Why aren't we counting the foodsource costs, asked one of the junior managers? Because that would be double counting, answered Thor. Foodsource costs are accounted for at purchasing time. The key thing to keep in mind is that some of the costs are directly measurable at production time, such as electricity used. But many other costs, such as capital costs and labor costs, are not measured on a daily basis, but only at the weekly or monthly level. Those costs then need to be allocated down to the minute level since production times are measured in minutes.

Isn't that a little over precise, said one of the junior managers, somewhat sarcastically. Not at all replied one of the senior production managers. Foodcake production is very capital intensive; 85 percent of the nonfoodsource costs are for capital depreciation. It costs almost $1,000 per hour per machine, whether it's running or not; that's almost $17 per minute, per machine. The senior production manager put it very succinctly, said Thor. Notwithstanding unplanned repairs, machine costs are essentially fixed. It's because those costs are so high that FCI management, I believe, has been toying with the idea of moving from two shifts per day to three.

Another manager then asked what this Stuff dimension was all about. Why are you talking about stuff instead of foodsources? Good question replied Lulu. Can anyone venture a guess? What do you think?

When no one raised his or her hand, Lulu continued. One of the interesting things about production is that the output of one process is the input to another. Furthermore, during production most everything that FCI would call a foodsource or a nonfood asset or a supply or a product is either input or output or both. We toyed with the idea of creating separate variables for every kind of stuff input to or output from production, but that would have resulted in lots of confusion from such an abundance of variables. Since the input and output values are dimensioned the same regardless of whether its fish input or electricity input, or whatever it is input or output, you don't want to treat different kinds of stuff as separate dimensions or as distinctions between variables. Thus, we choose to combine all the types of stuff that are either input to or output from any production process and call the combined dimension Stuff.

Okay, I understand what this Stuff dimension is all about, said one of the managers. But I still don't follow your production schema. Why is there only one Stuff dimension? During my career, I have built many input-output models, and though I didn't use multidimensional tools to do my modeling, what I did was multidimensional and I always treated inputs and outputs as separate dimensions. The classic case is probably the input-output model of the economy that allows us to see which outputs of which economic sectors are used as inputs in others. If it were up to me, I would have created a [Production] schema with the following basic form:

```
(Time.Day. ⊗ Geog.ProductionSite. ⊗ Process. ⊗ BatchOrdinal. ⊗
Stuff.input. ⊗ Stuff.output.) ~
                        Qty{kg}
```

Do you agree with this manager? What do you think? Lulu was polite in her response. Yes, she said, you can certainly model some input-output equations by making an explicit input and output dimension, but you need to understand the combinatorial relationships between the inputs and the outputs before deciding on a schema form. In the same way that you've seen there are differences in the relationship between origin and destination in transportation schemas (we've seen both MxN and 1xN relationships), there are differences in the input-output relationships in production processes. With the exception of fish, which are both input and output in the cleaning process, most stuff is either input only, such as the nonfood assets or fish in mixing, or output only, such as foodcakes in mixing. By making the input-output distinction in the variables rather than in the dimensions, we were able to model this fact more easily by making the appropriate adjustments to our application ranges. The most difficult part was creating specialized location ranges for the input and output variables in terms of stuff and process. In other words, Qty_input {kg} for Stuff.foodcakes only applies to Process.freezing&packing, and Qty_ output {kg} for Stuff.fish only applies to Process.cleaning. (These application range restrictions were not shown previously.) But there's no way around that if you want a useful model.

Anyway, said Lulu, let's calculate what it cost to produce our two batches of Neptune foodcakes, beginning with finding the machine that produced the foodcakes and the date and time of production. She typed into her laptop the following query, whose output was projected on the wall, and shown in Figure 16.28:

```
Time.day , Geog.ProductionSite , Machineid , (Start time,
Process.Cleaning) , (End time , Process.Packing) ,
Foodcake.Neptune.(B123 , B101)
```

		Time.day	Site	Machine	Start time, Process.cleaning	Stop time, Process.packing
Batch	101	Jan15	Vancouver	4	3:00 P.M.	7:00 P.M.
	123	Jan16	Vancouver	1	9:00 A.M.	12:00 P.M.

Figure 16.28   Processing time by day and machine.

Already we can see that for some reason the Neptune foodcakes produced on Machine 4 on January 15 consumed 33 percent more time than the foodcakes on January 16. Since we all know that each batch produces about 1,000 kilograms and that each machine costs about $1,000 per hour, we can already guess that the cost of production for batch 101 was around $1 per kilogram higher than the cost of production for batch 123! Was that a one-time event, asked one of the managers, or is there some pattern based on the machine or day or employees that makes some batches systematically more expensive to produce than others?

Good question, replied Lulu. Since we know where and on what machine each of the two batches was produced, we need to query for their relative production costs, as well as the relative production costs for the two machines in general.

The general formulas for calculating total production costs and production costs per kilogram are straightforward and presented as follows:

```
[Production]: "Production_Cost"{$}, L.leaf.above. =
            Sum(Production_Cost{$}, L.leaf.)

[Production]: "Production_Cost_per_kg"{$/kg} =
            Production_Cost{$} ÷ (Qty_Output{kg}, Process.Packaging)
```

Applying those formulas to the specific batches, we create the views shown in Figure 16.29.

We can see that indeed the cost of production on a per kilogram basis was $0.88 higher for batch 101 than for batch 123! That's a huge difference. Furthermore, nearly the entire cost differential was attributable to the increased capital costs for running

Page							Column
Geog.ProductionSite.Vancouver							Asset.

			Capital	Labor	Facility	Utilities	All
	Machine 1 Hfoodcake. B123	Production Cost {$}	2870	250	100	300	3520
Row		Avg. Cost of Production cost per Kilo {$/kg}	2.87	0.25	0.10	0.30	3.52
	Machine 4 Hfoodcake. B101	Production Cost {$}	3640	290	120	350	4400
MachineID ~ Hfoodcake.leaf Variable {}		Avg. Cost of Production cost per Kilo {$/kg}	3.64	0.29	0.12	0.35	4.40

Figure 16.29 Production costs by machine and batch.

Machine 4 the extra hour. By summing our production data to the quarter level and looking at average production time, number of machine stoppages, and average cost of production per kilogram, we can see if the high production cost for batch 101 was a one-time event or whether it is symptomatic of higher production costs in general for Machine 4. Figure 16.30 shows this information for the previous few quarters.

It looks like a little of each, exclaimed one of the managers. Average production costs for Machine 4 are indeed higher than for the other machines in Vancouver, however, not nearly as high as they were producing batch 101. Maybe Machine 4 is prone to major problems. In any event, said the production manger, something needs to be done. The total costs per kilogram of processing our two batches are shown in Figure 16.31 and broken out by asset.

Page							Column
Geog.ProductionSite.Vancouver							Time.Year.Qtr

			2000.Q1	2000.Q2	2000.Q3
	1	Avg. Production Time {hrs}	3.0	3.1	3.0
		Number of Machine Stoppages {N}	12	14	13
		Avg. Cost of Production {$/kg}	3.50	3.63	3.68
Row	4	Avg. Production Time {hrs}	3.5	3.3	3.4
MachineID.		Number of Machine Stoppages {N}	15	14	14
Variable { }		Avg. Cost of Production {$/kg}	3.90	3.82	3.75

Figure 16.30 Quarter-level average production time, number of machine stoppages, and average cost of production.

FCI_Business_ Process.	Hfoodcake.	Variable {}	Asset.				
			All	Labor	Facility	Utilities	Capital
Production	Neptune. 4pack.B123	Costs {$/kg}	3.52	0.25	0.10	0.30	2.87
	Neptune. 4pack.B101	Costs {$/kg}	4.40	0.29	0.12	0.35	3.64

Figure 16.31 Cumulative production costs by batch.

Materials Inventory

As someone pointed out earlier, and as I then explained, FCI does not track batchids before production. But though we can't tell which market the fish came from or which boat or supplier we bought it from, we do know how many lots of fish or other food supplies there are per batch produced and the ages of each lot and (from looking at the purchasing data) the weighted average price of each lot, and thus of all the foodsources used during production.

We can figure out the relevant foodsource information by looking at the outflows from materials inventory. This is because all the foodsources used during production on any particular day came from that production center's materials inventory. Can anyone offer a logical consequence of this fact?

After a minute's silence Lulu continued. This means that the inventory costs and the weighted average price of any foodsource used is the same for all production on a given day for a given production facility. Consider now the description of the materials inventory schemas.

Materials Inventory Schemas:

```
[MI Throughput] Schema:
(Time.Day.atabove. ⊗ Geog.MaterialsInventorySite. ⊗ Stuff.Foodsource.
⊗ Age.) ~
    Qty_Sent{kg}, Qty_Received{kg}, Qty_On_Hand{kg},
Qty_Throughput{kg}, Storage_Cost_per_kg{$/kg},
Cumulative_Qty_Throughput{kg},
Cumulative_Storage_Cost_per_kg{$/kg}


[MI Cost] Schema:
(Time.Day.atabove. ⊗ Geog.MaterialsInventorySite. ⊗
Stuff.NonFoodAsset.) ~
    Storage_Cost{$}, Cumulative_Storage_Cost{$}


[MI Batch] Schema:
(Stuff.Foodsource. ⊗ Age. ⊗ BatchID.) ~
Qty_Used_in_Batch{kg}, Storage_Cost_in_Batch{$},
Storage_Cost_per_kg_in_Batch{$/kg}
```

The first thing we need to know is the amount of each type and age of fish sent to production on January 15 and 16 that was used in the production of those Neptune foodcakes. This is illustrated with the following query (which is for batch 123 produced on January 16 only):

```
[Material Inventory Thruput]:
"Fish" {N},"Qty sent to production" {Kg},
        Age.,
        Time.Jan15 ,
        Geog.Vancouver ,
        [Production]:  "Qty input" {Kg} , ((Machine, Start
        time.(process.cleaning)). [Batch]: Batchid123) > 0
```

Age/Fish	Tuna	Salmon	Cod
1	0	0	0
2	0	0	0
3	0	0	0
4	200	300	200
5	150	200	250
6	50	0	0

Figure 16.32   Fish sent to production in Vancouver on January 15 that were used in batch 123 on January 16.

In words, it says to find the fish and the quantities that were sent to production on January 15 in Vancouver for every age bin from inventory where the quantity of fish input into the specific machine and process time used for the production of batch 123 was greater than 0. Alternatively stated, for every kind of fish that was used in the production of batch 123, what was the total amount of that fish sent that day to production by age bin. The results are illustrated in Figure 16.32.

Could you slow down a bit Lulu, asked one of the managers. I'm trying to follow and everything made sense, but that seemingly innocent query just pulled in data from three different cubes. Going forward, could you explain your steps in a little more detail? Thor stepped in. I wasn't as close to the material inventory calculations as Lulu; I think I can move forward at a slower pace.

Now that we know the fish sent to production for batch 123 (and as easily for batch 101), we can calculate the inventory cost of storing those fish, and then figure out what percentage of that cost accrues to the fish used for each of our batches of Neptune foodcakes. How would you calculate inventory costs? How would you express those calculations? Think about it.

There are several cubes that all have information relevant to figuring out inventory costs for batch 123 (and 101): the Materials Inventory cube, the Production cube, and the Batch cube. In words, we want to represent the total cost of inventory for the foodsources for batch 123 as the sum of the inventory costs of each of the age groups of foodsources (where each of those costs is determined as the ratio of the amount of foodsource per lot to the total inventory costs for the time period each lot was held times the percentage of each lot used by batch 123). Can anyone tell me why I don't care about fish type? Think about it.

Because inventory costs vary by the quantity of fish stored and the amount of time that fish was stored, but not by the type of fish stored, one of the managers replied. Yes, said Thor. That's exactly right.

You can all see from Figure 16.33 that there are three different age groups from which fish was sourced: six-day-old, five-day-old, and four-day-old. I think we need to multiply the cost per kilogram per day of storing fish by the number of kilograms held per amount of time stored, said one of the managers. Do you agree? Thor didn't.

		Age.4	Age.5	Age.6
Page				
Cumulative_Storage_Cost_per_kg {$/kg}				
Geog.MaterialsInventorySite.Vancouver				
Time.Jan18		**Column**		
Foodsource.all		Age.		

		Age.4	Age.5	Age.6
Row	Neptune.4pack.B123	0.43	0.53	0.64
Hfoodcake.	Neptune.4pack.B101	0.39	0.43	0.53

Figure 16.33 Cumulative storage cost per kilogram per batch.

If we did that, said Thor, it would be equivalent to using a standard cost for inventory. While admittedly, for this example where we are combining fish stored on similar days, January 9–15 (January 10–15, and January 11–15), we want to as much as possible allow for the chance of differential costs at the base level of our model. For example, if weekend labor rates are substantially higher (and January 9 and 10 fell on a weekend), that would show up. If there were a sudden jump in electrical rates on January 11, or if we negotiated a new labor contract, these changes to our cost structure would not appear if we assumed them away by adopting standard costs. Also remember, our mission is to ferret out the sources of erratic cost variances for FCI.

Therefore, we calculate the cost of inventory for each age lot separately, and then sum them together. The first thing we need to do is figure out the cost of storage per day that applies to all fish of all ages, basically everything that was in house per day as with the following expression. Keep in mind that [MIT] refers to the Materials Inventory Throughput cube and [MIC] refers to the Materials Inventory Cost cube.

```
[MIT]:  "Storage_Cost_per_kg"{$/kg},
        Foodsource.all,
        Age.all,
        Time.Day. =
                [MIC]: (Storage_Cost{$}, NonFoodAsset.all) ÷
                Qty_Throughput{kg}
```

Next, we need to calculate the cumulative quantities of fish put through inventory (Qty_Throughput) and the cumulative storage costs for each of the time periods that each of the fish age groups spent in inventory. The general formula for cumulative quantity throughput is as follows:

```
[MIT]:  "Cumulative_Qty_Throughput"{kg},
        Time.Day.,
        Age. =

        Sum( Qty_Throughput{kg}, Time.Day.((this+1-Age.) to this) )
```

Nearly all the managers immediately raised their hands. What does the clause Time.Day.((this + 1 − Age.) to this) mean, they all asked? Good question, replied Thor. Can anyone describe what we're doing if not the exact parsing of the clause? It looks like a range specification, said one of the managers. That's right, said Thor. We're using the range of fish ages sent to production to select a set of days for which we're calculating quantities throughput. Since fish enters materials inventory at an age of one day, we need to add one day to the current day (Day.this). In words, the clause says to take that set of days that ranges from Time.Day.((this + 1 − Age.), keeping in mind that the period (.) at the end of the term Age means to take every age, thus ages 1 to 6. Thus, we're summing the throughput of fish in inventory for five ranges of days: January 10–15, 11–15, 12–15, 13–15, and 14–15.

Next, we need to figure out the cumulative storage costs, which we do with the following formula. As you can see, the method of calculating the appropriate dates is the same as for the previous formula.

```
[MI Cost]: "Cumulative_Storage_Cost"{kg},
           Time.Day.,
           Age. =

                   Sum( "Storage_Cost"{$}, Time.Day.((this+1-Age.) to
                   this) )
```

The next step is to combine quantities throughput and costs to figure out the cumulative storage costs per kilogram as is done with the expression that follows:

```
[MIT]: "Cumulative_Storage_Cost_per_kg"{$/kg},
       Foodsource.all,
       Time.Day.,
       Age. =
                 Sum("Storage_Cost"{$} ÷
                 "Qty_Throughput"{kg}){$/(kg*day)} x
                 ("Age"{I} , Time.day.this)
```

What's that multiplication doing at the end, asked one of the managers? Thor replied that they needed to do that because the ratio of cumulative costs per throughput yields an average cost per kilogram per day whereas we need to know the total cost of storage per kilogram for all the days that each age group spent in inventory. Figure 16.33 shows the costs for each of the three ages of fish inventory used for batch 123 (and 101).

Thor asked the managers, so how do we get from knowing the cost per kilogram for each age bin of fish used to make those Neptune cakes to knowing the cost for the fish actually used to make each particular batch? Can't we just multiply the cost for each age lot by the ratio between the quantity used for batch 123 and the entire lot, asked one of the managers. That would give us three calculations—one each for Age.6, Age.5, and Age.4. Thor seemed okay with this tactic; Lulu furled her brow. What do you think?

You almost got it, Lulu said. You're right that the cost of fish storage is a function of the quantity of fish and the dates it is in storage, and thus is independent of the type of fish. So we only need to make three calculations: one for each age of fish used in production (6-, 5-, and 4-day-old fish). However, what we need to calculate for each age of fish used in production is the weighted average of the cost of storage per kilogram (which we calculated earlier) where the weighting is based on the ratio of fish used in production of that age divided by all the fish used in production. To do that, however, requires one extra manipulation, namely the creation of a hybrid cube [MI Batch] that joins the Materials Inventory Throughput cube and the Batch cube. There are still several formulas required, so I just wrote out one of the main and representative ones (the full listing of formulas is in Chapter 17) and the final view result (see Figure 16.34).

```
[MI Batch]: "Storage_Cost_in_Batch"{$}, Foodsource.all, Age.all =
            Sum( (Cumulative_Storage_Cost_per_kg{$/kg},
            Time.([Batch]:(Time.Day.(this-1), BatchID.)) x
            Qty_Used_in_Batch{kg}), Age. )
```

Materials Shipping

FCI, as you all know, currently outsources its materials shipping (from the food markets to the production facilities inventory) to Food Transport International, FTI. Our deal with FTI is simple: They charge us $0.10 per 100 kilograms per kilometer, and they guarantee that all of our foodsources are delivered from anywhere in the world to any of our production inventory facilities within 24 hours. Although we've always felt this was a good deal, now that we are calculating the true costs of doing business, we can compare what we pay FTI with what it costs us internally to ship our products from our production centers to our distribution facilities and from our distribution facilities to the stores.

Even though they do all the shipping, we still maintain our own shipping records. On any given day, we know how much of each type of food is being shipped from every market and the production inventory center where the shipment is going. We also know the distance traveled on each route, the weight of each shipment, and the cost, to us, of each shipment. FTI's records of what they are shipping are reconciled both at the food markets from where they depart and at the production inventory center where they arrive.

Row		Hfoodcake.		Asset.			
				All	**Labor**	**Facility**	**Utilities**
FCI_Business_Process HFoodcake. Cost {$/Kg}	Materials inventory	Neptune.4pack. B123	Cost {$/Kg}.	0.48	0.15	0.23	0.10
		Neptune.4pack. B101	Cost {$/Kg}.	0.50	0.15	0.25	0.10

Figure 16.34   Inventory activity costs per kilogram.

We've already established that FCI does not track specific purchases of fish and so we can't know exactly what the transportation costs were. However, we feel we can get pretty close. What would you do, Lulu asked, looking straight at one of the managers, to calculate the cost of transporting the foodsources that went into a particular batch of Neptune cakes so as to make the best use of available information? Think about what FCI does know.

FCI knows, for any given foodsource, every market in every country where that foodsource was purchased. FCI also knows the relative amount of that foodsource purchased in every market where it was purchased. Also, FCI knows the distance from every purchasing market to every production site inventory location.

So, for example, the transportation cost of the six-day-old salmon used for any cakes produced in Vancouver on January 15 (and thus also the cakes in Neptune batch 123) is a function of the relative amount of salmon purchased in each market on January (15 minus 6) 9 and the distance traveled from each purchasing market to Vancouver. The total transportation costs for all the foodsources used in batch 123 is then the sum of the transportation costs for each food and age.

There are over 10 distinct types of calculations that need to be performed to figure out the cost per kilogram of each of the batches of Neptune foodcakes produced. So I'll just show you two representative ones that get you all thinking, and then jump (like in those Julia Child cooking shows) to the calculated value for cost of transportation for each of our two batches of Neptune foodcakes. (Again I encourage you to work through all of the calculations as presented in Chapter 17.) First, you should all look at the relevant schema as shown here:

Materials Shipping Schema

```
[MS Distribution] Schema:
(Time.Day. ⊗ Geog.Market. ⊗ Geog.MaterialsInventorySite. ⊗
Stuff.Foodsource.) ~
Qty_Sent{kg}, Shipping_Cost{$}

          (Time.Day.all ⊗ Geog.Market. ⊗
          Geog.MaterialsInventorySite. ⊗  Stuff.Foodsource.all) ~
          Distance{km}, Shipping_Cost_per_kg_km{$/(kg × km)},
          Shipping_Cost_per_kg{$/kg}
```

Before I continue, can anyone suggest an approach to calculating material shipping costs? What's the first thing we probably need to do? I'll give you a hint. It's similar to what we had to do to figure out the cost of materials inventory. What would you do?

Don't we need to join our Batch dimension with the materials shipping schema, asked one of the managers? Yes that's right, replied Lulu. The only way we can calculate material shipping costs for particular batches of foodcakes produced is by maintaining the links between production batches and material shipping. Here's the [MS Batch] schema.

```
[MS Batch] Schema:
(Time.Day.atabove. ⊗ Geog.Market. ⊗ Stuff.Foodsource. ⊗ BatchID.) ~
          Qty_Shipped_in_Batch{kg},
```

```
Shipping_Cost_in_Batch{$},
Shipping_Cost_per_kg_in_Batch{$/kg},
Foodsource_Cost_in_Batch{$},
NonFoodAsset_Cost_in_Batch{$},
Foodsource_Cost_per_kg_in_Batch{$/kg},
NonFoodAsset_Cost_per_kg_in_Batch{$}
```

```
(Time.Day.all ⊗ Geog.Market.all ⊗
Stuff.Foodsource.all ⊗ BatchID.) ~
Geog.MaterialsInventorySite {N}
```

Another manager had a question. Why do we have to create a new schema? Why can't we just calculate shipping costs per fish used in some batch straight in the materials shipping schema? Good question, said Lulu. The reason, and this applies to why we needed to create a Materials Inventory Batch cube, is because the resources consumed and the costs associated with the shipping vary by time, geography, fish, and batch. The fact that we are creating derived variables that vary according to a Batch dimension means that we need to associate them with a schema that has those same dimensions. Thus, we need to create batch-containing schemas.

Now, how would you calculate the cost of fish shipped per batch-specific production? Let's assume you've already calculated the cost of shipping per kilogram per purchasing market with the destination of materials inventory in Vancouver. Also, let's assume you already know how much fish purchased in each market on each relevant day was actually sent to Vancouver.

After no one offered an answer, Thor spoke up. First, I'd calculate the total shipping cost from each purchasing market to Vancouver. Then I'd divide that amount by the amount of fish sent from each market to Vancouver to obtain the cost per kilogram of fish shipped. I would then multiply that number by the amount of fish used in the batch-specific production of Neptune cakes to figure out the total cost of shipping for each type of fish of each age used, as with the following expression:

```
[MS Batch]: "Shipping_Cost_in_Batch"{$} =
          [MSD]:(Shipping_Cost{$}÷ Qty_Sent{kg},
       Geog.Market.all, [MSB]:(Geog.MaterialsInventorySite)) x
       Qty_Shipped_in_Batch{kg}
```

So, jumping straight to the punch line you can see (as shown in Figure 16.35) that there was almost a 15 percent difference in the cost per kilogram of materials shipping between our two batches of Neptune foodcakes.

FCI_Business_Process.	Hfoodcake.	Costs {$/Kg} , Asset.All
Materials Shipping	Neptune.4pack.B123	.84
	Neptune.4pack.B101	.95

Figure 16.35 Activity cost for materials shipping.

Purchasing Costs

Thor began, total purchasing costs have three main components:

- The cost in local currency of the foodsource purchased
- The cost of local currency as determined by exchange rates and the local money that FCI's supplier has in stock
- The asset utilization costs associated with purchasing operations

Since nearly all of you attended the FCI purchasing seminar earlier this morning (and readers hopefully read Chapter 13 on purchasing and exchange), I don't want to go over territory already covered.

Rather, I would like to discuss the information contained in the business process by Asset Cost cube that is now completed for both batches 123 and 101 and shown in Figure 16.36. Thor and Lulu, said the CEO, I'd like to take over from here. Thank you very much for a job extremely well done. And thank you, Jane, for championing the whole project. I look forward to your prototype becoming fully operational so that FCI can get the grip it needs on its cost (and quality) volatility, and succeed with its business and its public offering.

I should add for the record that I was skeptical at first about the value of the information we were going to find through this process. I wasn't sure that the benefit was worth the cost. If it hadn't been for Jane's insistence, I probably never would have given the okay. So now it is time for me to publicly admit that not only is the information provided by this enterprise warehousing and OLAP solution of extremely high value for everyone from middle management on up to and including senior management and myself, but I actually learned some things about this business along the way. Although I always knew that everything was connected across our entire value chain, it was only by working through the flow of derivations during some late-night sessions with Lulu and Thor that I came to appreciate the quantity and pattern of interdependencies in our business.

The cost per kilogram of carrying out currency exchange and purchasing materials is shown in Figure 16.36.

So now that we've got this incredibly informative view of our company, let's think about what it says, starting with the bottom line differences between the two batches. Whereas we made $0.75 per kilogram of Neptune batch 123 sold, which is still below average for FCI, we *lost* almost $0.50 per kilogram of batch 101! That's an amazing difference for two batches of the same product produced in the same facility on two successive days and sent to the same inventory facility and sold in the same area on the same day for the same price!

You can also see that while over 50 percent of our costs come from purchasing material and production, amazingly almost 40 percent of our costs are tied up in distribution and inventory of various forms. We definitely need to improve the turn efficiency of our materials inventory. And it looks like our internal cost of final product distribution is substantially less than the prices we're paying for outsourcing our materials shipping. We may want to consider internalizing some of our materials shipping.

In addition to showing costs, the cube view highlighted in bold those costs that were more than one standard deviation form the mean. You can see that several of the

	Costs {$/Kg}	
FCI Business Processes	**B101**	**B123**
Purchasing & Currency Exchange	**.50**	.25
Materials Shipping	.95	.84
Materials Inventory	.50	.48
Production	**4.40**	3.52
Transport from Production to Product Inventory	.832	.839
Product Inventory	**.25**	.15
Product to Stores	.15	**.29**
Sales & Marketing	.75	1.00
Management	.25	.23
Revenue	11.00	11.00
EBIT	(.48)	.75

Figure 16.36 A summary of costs by business process combined with revenues.

specific costs for each of our two batches were more than one standard deviation from the mean! That's a huge amount of volatility. But now that, thanks to our OLAP solution, we can identify from where the volatility is arising, I am confident that we can take the appropriate actions to reduce it.

Legal Issues: A Reader Exercise

During the course of Lulu and Thor's skunk works project, Peter, the General Council for FCI, while working on a new case of importance to FCI, came across a company reference to Lulu and Thor as resident analytical experts. Peter approached the two and asked them for help in modeling and analyzing a current legal situation for FCI.

According to General Council, an unscrupulous tofu vendor was suing FCI for breach of contract claiming that FCI had committed to purchasing 2,000,000 kilograms of tofu during the recently ended calendar year, whereas they had in fact only purchased 1,000,000 kilograms. The vendor was requesting 150 percent of the contract amount with the last 50 percent going for punitive purposes. An adverse judgment could cost FCI several million dollars. Peter clearly didn't want to lose, nor did he think FCI deserved to lose the case. He countered that there were several provisions in the contract they signed that allowed FCI to reduce the amount of tofu it actually purchased.

Absent an out-of-court settlement between the parties, FCI was preparing to go to court as a defendant and wanted to analyze past court cases to see if there were any identifiable patterns between court locations and/or times and/or judges and opinions, and thus if there were any courts, times, or judges that should be especially sought or avoided. In addition, FCI needed to track the hours used by its in-house attorneys, as well as the hours billed to FCI by external lawyers.

As soon as Peter stepped out of the room, Thor confessed to Lulu that he had never modeled any legal process before. Lulu replied that she too had no experience. Before either of them could panic, Thor mentioned that he did have experience modeling healthcare provision from his previous job and that many of the issues they wrestled with in healthcare, including the multiplicity of doctors, diagnoses, and treatments associated with a single patient visit, were mirrored by the legal process they were about to model and analyze.

For example, in a typical healthcare provision application, a single patient encounter at a single time in a single location may involve multiple physicians, each offering multiple diagnoses for which some treatment or set of treatments then needs to be established, followed through, and tracked.

In a typical legal caseload application, there are for each case at some particular time and place, possibly several associated judges, lawyers, defendants, and plaintiffs. There can even be multiple times and places associated with a case. When monetary verdicts are reached, the dollar amounts must be properly allocated across those involved. Hours spent by attorneys must be properly aggregated across time and space without over or under counting. From a modeling perspective, the legal process is an absolute M/N mania.

The naïve OLAP approach treats each person present at a case at some time in some place as an independent dimension. Everything works smoothly when there is just one person from each role associated with a case, as illustrated with the following schema:

```
(Case. ⊗ Time. ⊗ Courthouse. ⊗ Judge. ⊗ Defense attorney. ⊗
Prosecuting attorney. ⊗ Defendant. ⊗ Plaintiff.) ~ Judgement
```

The problem then arises when more than one judge or attorney or defendant is present at the case. It is better to plan for multiple instances of judges, lawyers, and defendants to be present from the beginning. The best way to achieve that is to store your data in fourth rather than third normal form. In fourth normal form every unique dimensional combination for which any data is associated is represented.

The schema for one such solution is as follows:

```
(Case.) ~ when opened , Case attributes , Current status ,
(Case.closed.) ~ Judgment

(Case.) ~< (Times , courthouses , Judges , Defense Lawyers ,
Prosecuting Lawyers, defendants , plaintiffs)

(Judges.)  ~  who appointed by , salary , yrs prior experience

(Lawyers.)  ~ who retained by ,

(defendants.) ~  personal information
```

```
(plaintiffs.) ~ personal information

((Case. ⊗ Time. ⊗ Courthouse.) ~< Judges)  ~  billable hours

((Case. ⊗ Time. ⊗ Courthouse.) ~< Defense attorneys)  ~ billable hours

((Case. ⊗ Time.all , Courthouse.all) ~< Defense attorneys)  ~
billable hours , share of proceeds

((Case. ⊗ Time. ⊗ Courthouse) ~< Prosecuting attorney)  ~  hours spent

((Case. ⊗* Time. ⊗* Courthouse) ~< Defendants) ~ hours appeared

((Case. ⊗ Time. ⊗ Courthouse) ~< Plaintiffs) ~ hours appeared
```

Given these legal schemas, what formula(s) would you define for counting the number of billable hours per FCI (or other grouped) attorney? What formula(s) would you create for allocating judgments across different attorneys? What formula(s) would you create to compare judgments of particular types of cases with judges, attorneys, and courthouses? The schema for one such solution is illustrated in Figure 16.37.

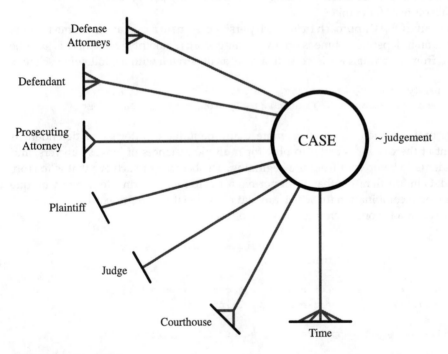

Figure 16.37 Legal.

Summary

In this chapter you've learned how to model an entire value chain by creating, and then combining a business asset dimension with a business process dimension. You saw that management can be represented both within each business process and at the all-process level. You learned how to combine batch-level production tags with the leaf level of a product dimension to create a cross-value-chain product-batch-tracking capability. You learned how to calculate the incremental activity-based costs on a per business process and per kilogram basis for product distribution, product inventory, product shipping, batch-level production, materials inventory, materials shipping, and purchasing. Along the way you learned about the need to create hybrid batch-containing join cubes for calculating materials inventory and shipping costs on a per batch basis. You learned about many different kinds of multicube formulas, including formulas whose time values depend on variable-constrained events from other cubes, and formulas that create sets of moving cumulative ranges. You've also learned how to model different kinds of input-output situations depending on the combinatorial relationships between the inputs and the outputs.

A Computational Example

The purpose of this chapter is to provide a fully computational example of one of Foodcakes International's (FCI) most important queries, namely calculating the positive or negative earnings accruing to FCI for a particular transaction. The calculation is based on what it actually costs across the entire value chain to produce some particular foodcake (with the exception of management), in this case batch 123 of Neptune fishcakes, sold on January 18 at a particular store in Cambridge, Massachusetts, combined with the revenues actually due to FCI net any discounts. I chose this type of query as the basis for the computational example in this chapter because it touches on every business process in FCI.

Even though I simplified the cube structure somewhat as compared with the level of detail described in Chapters 13 through 16, the example in this chapter still contains 19 different cubelets across 9 different business process cubes. It is a serious multicubelet example. The cubelets are shown in the order that is required to answer the top-level query beginning with the sales and marketing cube and working backwards to materials purchasing.

The cost information is accumulated in a special management cube that shows asset utilization and costs by business process and by time and product. The fact that this example dwells on costs should in no way be taken to imply that only costs deserve to be treated in such a holistic fashion. Several cross-business-function variable categories deserve equal treatment, including quality and productivity. There was simply no room in this book for a more comprehensive example.

Each of the cubelets is shown as a view where the specification of the view is given in LC and where the specific contents shown are sufficient to resolve the top-level query. Every variable shown is defined in the same section as where the cube view is given. The data values for all input variables are given. The formulas for all derived variables are given as well. The sequence of operations that you need to perform to evaluate every derived variable is also given. It is your job to calculate the values of all the derived variables.

The answers to all the exercises, that is to say the values for all the calculated variables are available on my companion Web site. In addition, you can also find a more challenging version of the exercise, one I highly recommend you try, where only the names of the derived variables and the sequence of operations are specified, but you are left with the task of defining the formulas in addition to evaluating them.

You can think of this chapter as a big exercise in Online Analytical Processing (OLAP) of multidimensional algebra. Working through the OLAP problems by hand is like calculating a least squares correlation coefficient by hand so you understand how the process works before relying on statistics packages where after loading a data table you simply press a button.

Before jumping into the exercises you should review all the contextual information:

- Dimension definitions
- Schemas
- Mapping of dimensions to cubes
- Business rules

The dimension definitions tell you the names of all the dimensions used in the cube calculation exercise and they give you a flavor for the kinds of elements or instances that exist for each dimension (or type). The schemas describe each of the 19 cubes organized by business process and presented in sequential order starting with sales and marketing and working backwards to materials purchasing. Please note that the schemas in the cube calculation exercise do not exactly match the schemas created and used in the four preceding application chapters, though they are extremely similar. This is because the cube calculation exercise represents a somewhat simplified version of the schemas presented in the application chapters. In contrast with Chapters 13 through 16 where a large part of each chapter was the working through of the modeling complexities of adding dimensions or deciding whether to model something as a dimension or a variable, here you will actually be calculating. The somewhat simplified schemas made for substantially simpler calculations.

Originally, I tried to keep the numbers simple enough that all the calculations could be done in your head, but as with any reasonably realistic example, there were too many additions and divisions to keep from needing to use a calculator.

How to Work through the Exercise

The way to work through the exercises is to start with the first equation in the first chunk in the section titled "FCI Cost-Revenue Analysis Calculation Steps." That equation is for total revenues in the sales and marketing cube. You will notice that the business process header "Sales and Marketing" also identifies the figure number (or numbers) for which the equation is associated Thus, the way to proceed is to carry out the equation listed as equation number 1 relative to Figure 17.2a, which is the associated view of the sales and marketing cube. That view contains all the raw data you need, such as wholesale price, list price, and so forth, required to perform the calculation. When you have performed the required calculation, write your answer down in the appropriate cell (or download a copy of the exercise from my companion Web site and mark that up), and at the end of your calculations for each business process, write your answer for the cost per kilogram per business process in the management costing cube view, as seen in Figure 17.1.

If you have already perused the exercise, you may have noticed that the business processes between production and sales are substantially less complicated than the processes between materials purchasing and production. This is not to say that pre-production processes are inherently more complicated than post-production processes, but as far as tracking production batches is concerned, and as was discussed in Chapter 16, prior to production, there is no product that exists so costing takes place relative to the collection of materials that eventually become a product. Substantial, real-world complexity was left in the exercise. Thus, you will need to calculate raw materials costs as a function of purchases made in a variety of markets at different times in different countries with different currencies and with different shipping methods and costs.

I apologize in advance for the cumbersomeness of having to refer back and forth in the book between the calculation steps, the schemas, and the views. When I use this material for teaching, I give students a separate workbook for each of the schemas, calculations, and cube views, as well as the contextual information comprised of the business rules, the dimension definitions, and the mapping of dimensions to cubes. Then they spread each of the workbooks out on a desk where they can easily see all of them at the same time. Again, I have made most of this material available on my companion Web site.

FCI Dimension Definitions

The following dimensions are used in the exercise. Example members are shown in parentheses:

Geog.Continent	(Europe, North America, Asia . . .)
Geog.Country	(U.S., Canada, France, Mexico . . .)
Zone	(Boston Zone, New York Zone . . .)
Store	(Cambridge, Boston, Plymouth . . .)
Bank	(Local Bank 1, Local Bank 2 . . .)
Market	(Local Market 1, Local Market 2 . . .)
MaterialsInventorySite	(Vancouver, Boston, Nuremberg . . .)
ProductionSite	(Vancouver, Boston, Nuremberg . . .)
ProductInventorySite	(Hartford, Palo Alto, Chicago . . .)
Time.Year	(2000, 2001, 2002 . . .)
Quarter	(1st, 2nd, 3rd, 4th)

Month	(January, February, March . . .)
Day	(Jan 1st, Jan 2nd, Jan 3rd . . .)
Hour	(9 am, 10 am, 11 am . . .)
Minute	(1, 2, 3 . . . 60)
BusinessProcess	(S&M, Product Inventory, Distribution, Production . . .)
Production.Process	(Cleaning, Mixing, Freezing, Packaging)
Stuff.	(Foodsource, Product, NonFoodAsset.atunder)
Foodsource.MajorType	(Fish, Vegetables, Filler, Flavor . . .)
Fish	(Tuna, Salmon, French Sole, Bass)
Vegetables	(Carrots, Tofu, Lentils . . .)
Filler	(Flour, Bread, Cheese . . .)
Flavor	(Salt, Pepper, Cumin, Cardomon . . .)
Product.Foodcake	(Fishcake, Veggiecake)
Fishcake	(Neptune, Poseidon, Sea Breeze)
Package	(4pack, 8pack . . .)
Veggiecake	(Yoshi's Dream, Drake's Diet)
NonFoodAsset	(Labor, Capital, Energy . . .)
Hfoodcake	(Neptune.4pack.Batch123, Poseidon.8pack.Batch456 . . .)
MachineID	(1, 2, 3, 4 . . .)
VehicleID	(1, 2, 3, 4 . . .)
CargoID	(1, 2, 3, 4 . . .)
BatchID	(1, 2, 3, 4 . . .)
OrderID	(1, 2, 3, 4 . . .)
BatchOrdinal	(1, 2, 3, 4 . . .)
Age	(1, 2, 3, 4 . . .)

Global Business Rules

The following rules are used, where appropriate, in calculations. For example, the rule that nothing is ever 0 days old means that wherever a business process has an age dimension, such as materials inventory and product inventory, either materials or product arrives in inventory at an age of 1 day old:

- **Age:** Nothing is ever 0 days old; inventory and purchasing ages begin at the age of 1 day.

- **Inventory:** Throughput is calculated by summing quantity received and quantity sent and dividing by 2. This is not *the* formula for calculating throughput; there are many. But it is the one used in this exercise.

- **Transit:** [PI-Stores]: Products leave product inventory in the evening and arrive in stores the next day; they are counted as part of inventory on the day they leave. [Prod-PI]: Products are sent to product inventory the evening they are produced, arriving the next day. They are counted as inventory (age 1) the day they arrive. [MI-Prod]: Materials leave materials inventory in the morning and are used in production the same day; they are *not* counted as inventory the day they leave, nor is their inventory-age incremented on that day. [Purch-MI]: Materials arrive in materials inventory 1 day after the day they are purchased; they are counted as part of inventory, with age 1, the day they arrive.

- **Stores:** Each store receives shipment of at most one incoming product order per day.

- **Production:** During production, fish inputs are well-mixed, so the age-ratio of fish output is the same as the age ratio of the (larger-quantity) input which produced it.

- **ProductionSite:** All materials inventory output is input to production at the same site: [MI]: (Qty_Sent, Time.Day.this) ≡ [Production]: (Qty_Input, MachineID.all, BatchID.all, Time.Day.(this+1))

FCI Schemas

The following conventions were adopted for the description of the schemas. First, the distinction was made (as first described in Chapter 6) between contents that vary in all dimensions and contents that vary in only some dimensions. Where this is the case, as for example with the Sales and Marketing schema, you will notice that all the contents that vary in all dimensions are listed first followed by a description of whatever subset of dimensions serves as the location structure for those contents that vary in some but not all dimensions.

Second, all contents whose values you will derive are underlined.

Third, cube name abbreviations are shown in square brackets at the top of each schema declaration.

Business Process Schemas

Sales and Marketing

```
[S&M] Schema:
(Time.Day.atabove ⊗ Geog.Store.atabove ⊗ Hfoodcake.atabove) ~
            Qty_Sold{pkg}, Total_Revenue{$}, Dollars_Owed_FCI{$},
            Dollars_Owed_FCI_per_kg{$/kg}

(Time.Day. ⊗ Geog.Store. ⊗ Hfoodcake.) ~
            List_Price{$/pkg}, Wholesale_Price{$/pkg},
            Discount{$/pkg}, Discount_Share{R},
            Effective_Wholesale_Price{$/pkg},
```

Transportation from Product Inventory to Stores

```
[Travel] Schema:
((Time.Day. ⊗ Geog.ProductInventorySite.) ~< Geog.Zone.) ~
          VehicleID{I}, Total_Distance{km}, Fixed_Cost{$},
          Vehicle_Travel_Cost{$}, (Delivery_PlanID{I} ~<
          Geog.Store, Time.Hour.Quarter{qtr_hour},
          Trip_Share{R}, OrderID{I}, Order_Travel_Cost{$},
          Order_Travel_Cost_per_kg{$/kg})


[Vehicle] Schema:
(Time.Day. ⊗ VehicleID.) ~
    Cost_per_km{$/km}


[Order] Schema:
(OrderID. ⊗ Hfoodcake.) ~
    Qty_Ordered{kg}
```

Product Inventory

```
[PI Throughput] Schema:
(Time.Day.atabove ⊗ Geog.ProductInventorySite.atabove ⊗ Hfoodcake.atabove
⊗ Age.atabove) ~
          Qty_Sent{kg}, Qty_Received{kg}, Qty_On_Hand{kg},
          Qty_Throughput{kg}, Cost_per_kg{$/kg}


[PI Cost] Schema:
(Time.Day.atabove ⊗ Geog.ProductInventorySite.atabove ⊗
NonFoodAsset.atabove) ~
          Cost{$}
```

Transportation from Production to Product Inventory

```
[Distribution] Schema:
(Time.Day. ⊗ Geog.ProductionSite. ⊗ Geog.ProductInventorySite.) ~
          Method, Total_Distance{km}, Fixed_Cost{$},
          CargoID{I}, Arrival_Time{qtr_hour},
          Cargo_Distribution_Cost{$},
          Distribution_Cost_per_kg{$/kg},


[Transport Method] Schema:
(Time.Day.atabove ⊗ Method.) ~
    Cost_per_kg_km{$/(kg * km)}


[Cargo] Schema:
(CargoID. ⊗ Hfoodcake.) ~
    Qty_Shipped{kg}
```

Production

```
[Production] Schema:
(Time.Day.atabove ⊗ Geog.ProductionSite. ⊗ Stuff. ⊗ Process. ⊗
BatchOrdinal. ⊗ MachineID.) ~
                Qty_Input{kg}, Qty_Output{kg}, Production_Cost{$},

(Time.Day. × Geog.ProductionSite. ⊗ Stuff.all ⊗ Process. ⊗
        BatchOrdinal. ⊗ MachineID.) ~
        Start_Time{qtr_hour}, End_Time{qtr_hour},
        Production_Cost_per_kg{$/kg}
(Time.Day. ⊗ Geog.ProductionSite. ⊗ Stuff.all ⊗
        Process.all ⊗ BatchOrdinal. ⊗ MachineID.) ~
                BatchID{I}


[Batch] Schema:
    (BatchID.) ~
                MachineID{I}, BatchOrdinal{I}, Time.Day,
                Geog.ProductionSite
```

Materials Inventory

```
[MI Throughput] Schema:
(Time.Day.atabove ⊗ Geog.MaterialsInventorySite. ⊗ Stuff.Foodsource. ⊗
Age.) ~
                Qty_Sent{kg}, Qty_Received{kg}, Qty_On_Hand{kg},
                Qty_Throughput{kg}, Storage_Cost_per_kg{$/kg},
                Cumulative_Qty_Throughput{kg},
                Cumulative_Storage_Cost_per_kg{$/kg}


[MI Cost] Schema:
(Time.Day.atabove ⊗ Geog.MaterialsInventorySite. ⊗ NonFoodAsset.) ~
    Storage_Cost{$}, Cumulative_Storage_Cost{$}


[MI Batch] Schema:
(Stuff.Foodsource. ⊗ Age. ⊗ BatchID.) ~
                Qty_Used_in_Batch{kg}, Storage_Cost_in_Batch{$},
                Storage_Cost_per_kg_in_Batch{$/kg}
```

Materials Shipping

```
[MS Distribution] Schema:
(Time.Day. ⊗ Geog.Market. ⊗ Geog.MaterialsInventorySite. ⊗
Stuff.Foodsource.) ~
                    Qty_Sent{kg}, Shipping_Cost{$}
            (Time.Day.all ⊗ Geog.Market. ⊗
        Geog.MaterialsInventorySite. ⊗ Stuff.Foodsource.all) ~
                Distance{km}, Shipping_Cost_per_kg_km
                {$/(kg ⊗ km)}, Shipping_Cost_per_kg{$/kg}
```

```
[MS Batch] Schema:
(Time.Day.atabove ⊗ Geog.Market. ⊗ Stuff.Foodsource. ⊗ BatchID.) ~
                 Qty_Shipped_in_Batch{kg},
                        Shipping_Cost_in_Batch{$},
                        Shipping_Cost_per_kg_in_Batch{$/kg},
                        Foodsource_Cost_in_Batch{$},
                        NonFoodAsset_Cost_in_Batch{$},
        (Time.Day.all ⊗ Geog.Market.all ⊗ Stuff.Foodsource.all ⊗
BatchID.) ~
                        Geog.MaterialsInventorySite,
                        Foodsource_Cost_per_kg_in_Batch{$/kg},
                        NonFoodAsset_Cost_per_kg_in_Batch{$/kg}
```

Currency Exchange

```
[Currency] Schema:
(Time.Day.atabove ⊗ Geog.Country.) ~
                Local_Currency_Spent{Lcurr},
                Local_Currency_Purchased{Lcurr}
(Time.Day. ⊗ Geog.Country.) ~
                Local_Currency_on_Hand_Opening{Lcurr},
                Local_Currency_Remaining{Lcurr},
                Daily_Exchange_Rate{$/Lcurr},
                Effective_Rate{$/Lcurr},
                Dollars_Spent_for_Local_Currency_Purchased{$}
```

Purchasing

```
[Purchasing Activity] Schema:
(Time.Day. ⊗ Geog.Market. ⊗ Foodsource.) ~
                Price{Lcurr/kg}, Qty_Purchased{kg},
                Local_Currency_Spent{Lcurr},  Dollars_Spent{$},
                Foodsource_Cost_per_kg{$/kg}

[Purchasing Cost] Schema:
(Time.Day.atabove ⊗ Geog.Market.atabove ⊗ NonFoodAsset.) ~
                NonFoodAsset_Cost{$}, NonFoodAsset_Cost_per_kg{$/kg}
```

Cubes

Dimensions \ Cubes	Sales & Marketing [S&M]	Transp. from Product Inv. to Stores [Travel]	[Vehicle]	[Order]	Product Inventory [PI Throughput]	[PI Cost]	Transp. from Production to Product Inv. [Distribution]	[Transport Method]	[Cargo]	Production [Production]	[Batch]	Material Inventory [MI Throughput]	[MI Cost]	[MI Batch]	Material Shipping [MS Distribution]	[MS Batch]	Purch. & Currency Exch. [P. Activity]	[P. Cost]	[Currency]
Geog_Zone	X																		
Geog_Store		X	X																
Geog_Bank	X																		X
Geog_Market															X		X	X	X
Geog_MaterialsInventorySite												X	X		X				
Geog_ProductionSite							X			X	X		X		X				
Geog_ProductInventorySite		X			X	X	X	X		X	X	X	X		X	X	X	X	X
Time_Day	X	X	X		X	X	X	X		X	X	X	X		X	X	X	X	X
Stuff										X									
Stuff_Product_Foodcake																			
Stuff_FoodSource																	X		
Stuff_NonFoodAsset						X				X		X	X	X	X	X		X	
MachineID								X		X									
Method							X	X											
VehicleID		X	X				X		X										
CargoID							X		X										
BatchID										X	X			X		X			
OrderID			X																
Production_Process										X	X								
BatchOrdinal										X	X								
Hfoodcake	X			X	X							X							
Age					X	X			X			X		X					

Figure 17.1 Mapping of dimensions and queries to cubes.

Cube Views

Sales and Marketing

Page:	HFoodcake.

Row:	Geog.Store.
Row:	Variables { }

Column:	Time.Day.

		Jan17	Jan18
Store.Cambridge	Qty_Sold {pkg}	55	50
	List_Price {$/pkg}	6.95	6.95
	Wholesale_Price {$/pkg}	5.50	5.50
	Discount {$/pkg}	1.00	1.00
	Discount_Share {R}	0.45	0.50
	TotalStore_Revenue {$}	327	
	Effective_Wholesale {$/pkg}	5.05	
	Dollars_Owed_FCI {$}	278	
	Dollars_Owed_FCI_per_kg {$/kg}	10.10	
Store.Boston	Qty_Sold {pkg}	80	85
	List_Price {$/pkg}	7.15	7.15
	Wholesale_Price {$/pkg}	5.50	5.50
	Discount {$/pkg}	1.00	1.00
	Discount_Share {R}	0.50	0.55
	Total_Revenue {$}	492	523
	Effective_Wholesale {$/pkg}	5.00	4.95
	Dollars_Owed_FCI {$}	400	421
	Dollars_Owed_FCI_per_kg {$/kg}	10.00	9.90

Figure 17.2a   [S&M] Cube view.

Product	Weight
Neptune, eight pack	1,000 grams
Neptune, four pack	500 grams

Figure 17.2b Product Attribute view.

Transportation from Product Inventory to Stores

Page:	**Geog.ProductInventorySite.Hartford**
Page:	**Time.Jan18**

Row:	**Geog.Zone.**
Row:	**VehicleID.**

Column:	**Variables { }**

		Total_Distance {km}	Fixed_Cost {$}	Vehicle_ Travel_ Cost {$}
Geog.Zone. Boston_Area	VehicleID. 41	400	160	
Geog.Zone. NewYork_Area	VehicleID. 67	300	140	230
Geog.Zone. Providence_Area	VehicleID. 56	160	120	168

Figure 17.3a [Travel] Cube view.

Page:	Time.Jan18

Row:	VehicleID.

Column:	Variables { }

	Cost_per_km {$/km}
VehicleID. 21	0.25
VehicleID. 35	0.25
VehicleID. 41	0.30
VehicleID. 56	0.30
VehicleID. 67	0.30

Figure 17.3b [Vehicle] Cube view.

Row:	OrderID.
Row:	Hfoodcake.

Column:	Variables { }

		Qty {kg}
OrderID. 0179	Neptune.4pack.B123	80
	Neptune.8pack.B127	50
	SeaBreeze.8pack.B43	90
	All	250
OrderID. 0180	Neptune.4pack.B123	55
	SeaBreeze.4pack.B25	75
	Poseidon.8pack.B120	65
	All	300
OrderID. 0181	Poseidon.4pack.B133	60
	Neptune.8pack.B132	65
	Neptune.8pack.B127	70
	All	160

Figure 17.3c [Order] Cube view.

Page:	Time.Jan18
Page:	Geog.ProductInventorySite.Hartford
Page:	Geog.Zone.Boston_Area

Row:	Delivery_PlanID.
Row:	OrderID.
Row:	Variables { }

Delivery_ PlanID.D25	OrderID.0179	Store	Cambridge
		Time	6:00 am
		Trip_Share	0.33
		Order_Travel_Cost {$}	
		Travel_Cost_per_kg {$/kg}	
	OrderID.0180	Store	Boston
		Time	6:30 am
		Trip_Share	0.29
		Order_Travel_Cost {$}	81.20
	OrderID.0181	Travel_Cost_per_kg {$/kg}	0.27
		Store	Plymouth
		Time	7:15 am
		Trip_Share	0.20
		Order_Travel_Cost {$}	56.00
		Travel_Cost_per_kg {$/kg}	0.35

Figure 17.3d [Travel] Cube view.

Product Inventory

Page:	Time.Day

Row:	Geog.ProductInventorySite.Hartford
Row:	Hfoodcake.

Column:	Age.

		Age.1	Age.2	Age.3
ProductInventorySite.Hartford	Neptune.4pack.B123	Jan17	n/a	n/a
	Neptune.8pack.B127	Jan17	Jan18	n/a
	SeaBreeze.8pack.B41	Jan16	Jan17	Jan18
	Poseidon.4pack.B99	Jan16	Jan17	n/a
	SeaBreeze.8pack.B05	Jan16	Jan17	Jan18

Figure 17.4a   [PI Throughput] Cube view.

Page:	Cost {$}

Row:	Geog.ProductInventorySite.
Row:	NonFoodAsset.

Column:	Time.Day.

		Jan16	Jan17	Jan18
ProductInventorySite. Hartford	Labor	912	912	912
	Maintenance	50	50	50
	Facility	200	200	200
	Energy	100	100	100
	All	1,262	1,262	1,262
ProductInventorySite. Palo Alto	Labor	901	901	901
	Maintenance	45	45	45
	Facility	190	190	190
	Energy	95	95	95
	All	1,231	1,231	1,231
ProductInventorySite. St. Louis	Labor	990	990	990
	Maintenance	70	70	70
	Facility	230	230	230
	Energy	120	120	120
	All	1,410	1,410	1,410

Figure 17.4b   [PI Cost] Cube view.

Page:	Age.all
Page:	Hfoodcake.all

Row:	Geog.ProductInventorySite.
Row:	Variables { }

Column:	Time.Day.

		Jan16	Jan17	Jan18
ProductInventorySite. Hartford	Qty_Received {kg}	15,000	15,350	14,900
	Qty_Sent {kg}	14,900	15,200	14,950
	Qty_On_Hand {kg}	300	450	400
	Qty_Throughput {kg}	14,950		14,925
	Cost_per_kg {$/kg}	0.084		0.085
ProductInventorySite. Palo Alto	Qty_Received {kg}	14,800	15,050	15,000
	Qty_Sent {kg}	14,700	14,900	15,050
	Qty_On_Hand {kg}	300	450	400
	Qty_Throughput {kg}	14,750	14,975	15,025
	Cost_per_kg {$/kg}	0.083	0.082	0.082
ProductInventorySite. St Louis	Qty_Received {kg}	14,800	15,050	15,000
	Qty_Sent {kg}	14,700	14,900	15,050
	Qty_On_Hand {kg}	300	450	400
	Qty_Throughput {kg}	14,750	14,975	15,025
	Cost_per_kg {$/kg}	0.096	0.094	0.094

Figure 17.4c [PI Throughput] Cube view.

Transportation from Production to Product Inventory

Page:	Geog.ProductionSite.Vancouver

Row:	Geog.ProductInventorySite.
Row:	Variables { }

Column:	Time.Day.

		Jan16
	MethodID	Plane
	Total_Distance {km}	5,000
	Fixed_Cost {$}	275
ProductInventorySite.Hartford	CargoID	567
	Arrival_Time	Jan16
	Cargo_Distribution_Cost {$}	
	Distribution_Cost_per_kg {$/kg}	
	MethodID	Plane
	Total_Distance {km}	5,300
	Fixed_Cost {$}	300
ProductInventorySite.Houston	CargoID	568
	Arrival_Time	Jan17
	Cargo_Distribution_Cost {$}	7,508
	Distribution_Cost_per_kg {$/kg}	0.88
	MethodID	Train
	Total_Distance {km}	1,000
	Fixed_Cost {$}	250
ProductInventorySite.Seattle	CargoID	569
	Arrival_Time	Jan18
	Cargo_Distribution_Cost {$}	1,150
	Distribution_Cost_per_kg {$/kg}	0.15

Figure 17.5a [Distribution] Cube view.

Column:	Method.

Row:	Variables { }

	Truck	Plane	Train
Cost_per_kg_km {$/(kg x km)}	0.0000890	0.0001600	0.0001200

Figure 17.5b   [Transport Method] Cube view.

Row:	CargoID.
Row:	Hfoodcake.
Row:	Variables { }

		Qty {kg}
CargoID. 567	Neptune.4pack.B123	80
	Neptune.8pack.B127	50
	SeaBreeze.8pack.B43	90
	All	7,000
CargoID. 568	Neptune.4pack.B123	55
	SeaBreeze.4pack.B25	75
	Poseidon.8pack.B120	65
	All	8,500
CargoID. 569	Poseidon.4pack.B133	60
	Neptune.8pack.B132	65
	Neptune.8pack.B127	70
	All	7,500

Figure 17.5c   [Cargo] Cube view.

Production

Column:	Process.

Page:	Time.Jan16
Page:	Geog.ProductionSite.Vancouver
Page:	Machine.1

Row:	Stuff.(Qty_Input or Qty_Output or Qty_Discarded or Production_Cost > 0)
Row:	Variables { }
Row:	BatchOrdinal.

BatchOrdinal.1

Process.Cleaning		Process.Mixing		Process.(Freezing & Packaging)		Process.all	
(Qty_Input, Stuff.Tuna) {kg}	400	(Qty_Input, Stuff.Tuna) {kg}	360	(Qty_Input, Stuff.Neptune.4pack.B123) {kg}	900	BatchID	123
(Qty_Input, Stuff.Salmon) {kg}	400	(Qty_Input, Stuff.Salmon) {kg}	360			(Production_Cost, Stuff.NonFoodAssets.all) {$}	3165
(Qty_Input, Stuff.FSole) {kg}	200	(Qty_Input, Stuff.FSole) {lg}	180			Production_Cost_per_kg {$/kg}	3.52
(Qty_Output, Stuff.Tuna) {kg}	360						
(Qty_Output, Stuff.Salmon) {kg}	360						
(Qty_Output, Stuff.FSole) {kg}	180	(Qty_Output, Stuff.Neptune.4pack.B123) {kg}	900	(Qty_Output, Stuff.Neptune.4pack.B123) {kg}	900		

Figure 17.6 [Production] Cube view.

	Process.Cleaning	Process.Mixing	Process.(Freezing & Packaging)	Process.all
BatchOrdinal.1	(Qty_Discarded, Stuff.all) [kg] 100			
	Time Started 9:00 am	Time Started 10:00 am	Time Started 11:00 am	
	Time Stopped 10:00 am	Time Stopped 11:00 am	Time Stopped 12:00 pm	
	(Production_Cost, Stuff.NonFoodAssets.Energy) {$} 30	(Production_Cost Stuff.NonFoodAssets.Energy) {$} 35	(Production_Cost, Stuff.NonFoodAssets.Energy) {$} 40	
	(Production_Cost, Stuff.NonFoodAssets.Labor) {$} 120	(Production_Cost, Stuff.NonFoodAssets.Labor) {$} 120	(Production_Cost, Stuff.NonFoodAssets.Labor) {$} 120	
	(Production_Cost, Stuff.NonFoodAssets.Capital) {$} 800	(Production_Cost, Stuff.NonFoodAssets.Capital) {$} 900	(Production_Cost, Stuff.NonFoodAssets.Capital) {$} 1,000	
BatchOrdinal.2	(Qty_Input, Stuff.Bass) [kg] 500	(Qty_Input, Stuff.Bass) [kg] 490	(Qty_Input, Stuff.Poseidon. 8pack.B124) [kg] 1,200	BatchID 124
	(Qty_Input, Stuff.Salmon) [kg] 500	(Qty_Input, Stuff.Salmon) [kg] 489		(Production_Cost, Stuff.NonFoodAssets. all) {$} 3,165
	(Qty_Input, Stuff.Cod) [kg] 250	(Qty_Input, Stuff.Cod) [kg] 245		Production_Cost_ per_kg {$/kg} 2.64

Figure 17.6 [Production] Cube view. (*continued*)

BatchOrdinal.3			
(Qty_Output, Stuff.Bass) [kg]	490		
(Qty_Output, Stuff.Salmon) [kg]	489		
(Qty_Output, Stuff.Cod) 245 [kg]			
(Qty_Discarded, Stuff.all) [kg]	26	(Qty_Discarded, S.all) [kg]	24
Time Started 12:00 pm		Time Started 1:00 pm	Time Started 2:00 pm
Time Stopped 1:00 pm		Time Stopped 2:00 pm	Time Stopped 3:00 pm
(Production_Cost, Stuff.NonFoodAssets.Energy) [$] 30		(Production_Cost, Stuff.NonFoodAssets.Energy) [$] 35	(Production_Cost, Stuff.NonFoodAssets.Energy) [$] 40
(Production_Cost, Stuff.NonFoodAssets.Labor) [$] 120		(Production_Cost, Stuff.NonFoodAssets.Labor) [$] 120	(Production_Cost, Stuff.NonFoodAssets.Labor) [$] 120
(Production_Cost, Stuff.NonFoodAssets.Capital) [$] 800		(Production_Cost, Stuff.NonFoodAssets.Capital) [$] 900	(Production_Cost, Stuff.NonFoodAssets.Capital) [$] 1,000
		(Qty_Output, Stuff.Poseidon.8pack.B124) [kg] 1,200	(Qty_Output, Stuff.Poseidon.8pack.B124) [kg] 1,200

Figure 17.6 [Production] Cube view. *(continued)*

Materials Inventory

Page:	Geog.MaterialsInventorySite.Vancouver
Page:	Storage_Cost {$}

Row:	Stuff.NonFoodAsset.

Column:	Time.Day.

	Jan10	Jan11	Jan12	Jan13	Jan14	Jan15	Jan16
Labor	1,820	1,820	1,820	1,820	1,820	1,820	1,820
Maintenance	200	200	200	200	200	200	200
Facility	900	900	900	900	900	900	900
Energy	500	500	500	500	500	500	500
All	3,420	3,420	3,420	3,420	3,420	3,420	3,420

Figure 17.7a [MI Cost] Cube view.

Page: **Geog.MaterialsInventorySite.Vancouver**

| | Column: | **Time.Day.** |
| | Column: | **Foodsource.** |

Row: **Variables { }**

Row: **Age. 4–6**

		Jan.10	Jan.11	Jan.12	Jan.13	Jan.14	Jan.15			
		Foodsource. all	Foodsource. all	Foodsource. all	Foodsource. all	Foodsource. all	Foodsource. Tuna	Foodsource. Salmon	Foodsource. Fsole	Foodsource. all
Qty_Sent {kg}	Age.1	870	930	900	960	1,020	0	0	0	990
	Age.2	2,030	2,170	2,100	2,240	2,380	0	0	0	2,310
	Age.3	4,350	4,650	4,500	4,800	5,100	0	0	0	4,950
	Age.4	9,860	10,540	10,200	10,880	11,560	2,900	3,000	800	11,220
	Age.5	8,410	8,990	8,700	9,280	9,860	2,200	2,700	900	9,570
	Age.6	3,480	3,720	3,600	3,840	4,080	500	0	0	3,960
	Age.all	29,000	31,000	30,000	32,000	34,000	5,600	5,700	1,700	33,000
Qty_Received {kg}	Age.all	33,500	33,000	32,000	32,000	31,000	5,700	6,000	1,800	33,000
Qty_Onhand {kg}	Age.all	44,500	46,500	48,500	48,500	45,500	5,500	6,300	2,100	44,500
Qty_Throughput {kg}	Age.all									
Storage_Cost_ per_kg {$/kg}	Age.all									

Figure 17.7b [MI Throughput] Cube view.

Page:	BatchID.123
Page:	Qty_Used_in_Batch {kg}

Row:	Foodsource.

Column:	Age.

	Age.6	Age.5	Age.4
Foodsource.Tuna			
Foodsource.Salmon			
Foodsource.FSole			
Foodsource.all			

Figure 17.7c   [MI Batch] Cube view.

Page:	BatchID.123
Page:	Foodsource.all

Row:	Variables { }

Column:	Age.

	Age.6	Age.5	Age.4
Storage_Cost_in_Batch, BatchID.123 {$}			

Figure 17.7d   [MI Batch] Cube view.

Page:	BatchID.123
Page:	Foodsource.all
Page:	Age.all

Row:	Variables { }

Storage_Cost_in_Batch {$}	
Storage_Cost_per_kg_in_Batch {$/kg}	

Figure 17.7e   [MI Batch] Cube view.

Materials Shipping

Page:	Geog.MaterialsInventorySite.Vancouver
Page:	Foodsource.all
Page:	Time.Day.all

Row:	Geog.Market.
Row:	Variables { }

			Jan9	Jan10	Jan11
Market. Canada.	LM1	Shipping_Cost_per_kg_km {$/(kg x km)}	0.001	0.001	0.001
		Distance {km}	50	50	50
		Shipping_Cost_per_kg {$/kg}			
	LM2	Shipping_Cost_per_kg_km {$/(kg x km)}	0.001	0.001	0.001
		Distance {km}	500	500	500
		Shipping_Cost_per_kg {$/kg}			
Market. France	LM1	Shipping_Cost_per_kg_km {$/(kg x km)}	0.0005	0.0005	0.0005
		Distance {km}	8,000	8,000	8,000
		Shipping_Cost_per_kg {$/kg}			

Figure 17.8a [MS Distribution] Cube view.

Page:	Geog.MaterialsInventorySite.Vancouver

Row:	Geog.Market.
Row:	Foodsource.
Row:	Variables { }

Column:	Time.Day.

				Jan9	Jan10	Jan11
Market. Canada	LM1	Foodsource.Tuna	Qty_Sent {kg}	803	829	893
			Shipping_Cost {$}			
		Foodsource.Salmon	Qty_Sent {kg}	331	341	368
			Shipping_Cost {$}			
	LM2	Foodsource.Tuna	Qty_Sent {kg}	268	276	298
			Shipping_Cost {$}			
		Foodsource.Salmon	Qty_Sent {kg}	992	1,024	1,103
			Shipping_Cost {$}			
Market. France	LM1	Foodsource.FSole	Qty_Sent {kg}	126	195	210
			Shipping_Cost {$}			

Figure 17.8b [MS Distribution] Cube view.

Page:	BatchID.123
Page:	Qty_Shipped_in_Batch {kg}

Row:	Geog.Market.all
Row:	Foodsource.

Column:	Time.Day.

		Jan9	Jan10	Jan11
Market.all	Foodsource.Tuna			
	Foodsource.Salmon			
	Foodsource.FSole			

Figure 17.8c [MS Batch] Cube view.

Page:	BatchID.123
Page:	Geog.MaterialsInventorySite.Vancouver

Row:	Geog.Market.
Row:	Foodsource.
Row:	Variables { }

Column:	Time.Day.

				Jan9	Jan10	Jan11
Market. Canada	LM1	Foodsource.Tuna	Qty_Shipped_ in_Batch{kg}			
		Foodsource.Salmon	Qty_Shipped_ in_Batch{kg}			
		Foodsource.all	Qty_Shipped_ in_Batch{kg}			
		Foodsource.all	Shipping_Cost_ in_Batch{$}			
	LM2	Foodsource.Tuna	Qty_Shipped_ in_Batch{kg}			
		Foodsource.Salmon	Qty_Shipped_ in_Batch{kg}			
		Foodsource.all	Qty_Shipped_ in_Batch{kg}			
		Foodsource.all	Shipping_Cost_ in_Batch{$}			
Market. France	LM1	Foodsource.FSole	Qty_Shipped_ in_Batch{kg}			
		Foodsource.all	Qty_Shipped_ in_Batch{kg}			
		Foodsource.all	Shipping_Cost_ in_Batch{$}			

Figure 17.8d   [MS Batch] Cube view.

Page:	BatchID.123
Page:	Foodsource.all
Page:	Time.all
Page:	Geog.Market.all

Row:	Variables { }

Shipping_Cost_in_Batch {$}	
Shipping_Cost_per_kg_in_Batch_ {$/kg}	

Figure 17.8e   [MS Batch] Cube view.

Currency and Exchange

Row:	Geog.Country.
Row:	Variables { }

Column:	Time.Day.

		Jan8	Jan9	Jan10	Jan11
Country. Canada	**Local_Currency_on_Hand_ Opening {Lcurr}**	25,000			
	Effective_Rate {Lcurr/$}	2.00			
	Local_Currency_Spent {Lcurr}	20,000	20,000	15,000	20,000
	Local_Currency_Remaining {Lcurr}				
	Local_Currency_Purchased {Lcurr}	20,000	20,000	20,000	15,000
	Dollars_Spent_for_Local_ Currency_Purchased {$}				
	Daily_Exchange_Rate {Lcurr/$}	2.00	1.75	2.00	1.85
Country. France	**Local_Currency_on_Hand_ Opening {Lcurr}**	75,000			
	Effective_Rate {Lcurr/$}	7.60			
	Local_Currency_Spent {Lcurr}	50,000	50,000	30,000	50,000
	Local_Currency_Remaining {Lcurr}				
	Local_Currency_Purchased {Lcurr}	25,000	40,000	50,000	40,000
	Dollars_Spent_for_Local_ Currency_Purchased {$}				
	Daily_Exchange_Rate {Lcurr/$}	7.60	7.40	7.10	7.50

Figure 17.9   [Currency] Cube view.

Purchasing

Row:	Geog.Market.
Row:	Variables { }
Row:	NonFoodAsset.

Column:	Time.Day.

				Jan9	Jan10	Jan11
Market Canada	LM1	NonFoodAsset_Cost {$}	Rent	55	55	55
		NonFoodAsset_Cost {$}	Utilities	25	25	25
		NonFoodAsset_Cost {$}	Labor	455	455	455
		NonFoodAsset_Cost {$}	Other	75	75	75
		NonFoodAsset_Cost {$}	All	610	610	610
		NonFoodAsset_Cost_ per_kg {$/kg}	All			
	LM2	NonFoodAsset_Cost {$}	Rent	60	60	60
		NonFoodAsset_Cost {$}	Utilities	30	30	30
		NonFoodAsset_Cost {$}	Labor	560	560	560
		NonFoodAsset_Cost {$}	Other	70	70	70
		NonFoodAsset_Cost {$}	All	720	720	720
		NonFoodAsset_Cost_ per_kg {$/kg}	All			
Market. France	LM1	NonFoodAsset_Cost {$}	Rent	60	60	60
		NonFoodAsset_Cost {$}	Utilities	25	25	25
		NonFoodAsset_Cost {$}	Labor	450	450	450
		NonFoodAsset_Cost {$}	Other	80	80	80
		NonFoodAsset_Cost {$}	All	615	615	615
		NonFoodAsset_Cost_ per_kg {$/kg}	All			

Figure 17.10a [Purchasing Cost] Cube view.

Row:	Geog.Market.
Row:	Foodsource.
Row:	Variables { }

Column:	Time.Day.

				Jan9	Jan10	Jan11
Market. Canada	LM1	Foodsource. Tuna	Price (L/kg)	4	5	4
			Qty_Purchased {kg}	803	829	893
			Local_Currency_Spent {Lcurr}			
			Dollars_Spent {$}			
			Foodsource_Cost_per_kg {$/kg}			
		Foodsource. Salmon	Price (L/kg)	5	4	6
			Qty_Purchased {kg}	331	341	368
			Local_Currency_Spent {Lcurr}			
			Dollars_Spent {$}			
			Foodsource_Cost_per_kg {$/kg}			
		Foodsource.all	Qty_Purchased {kg}	2,000	1,900	1,800
	LM2	Foodsource. Tuna	Price (L/kg)	6	4	6
			Qty_Purchased {kg}	268	276	298
			Local_Currency_Spent {Lcurr}			
			Dollars_Spent {$}			
			Foodsource_Cost_per_kg {$/kg}			
		Foodsource. Salmon	Price (L/kg)	6	6	5
			Qty_Purchased {kg}	992	1,024	1,103
			Local_Currency_Spent {Lcurr}			
			Dollars_Spent {$}			
			Foodsource_Cost_per_kg {$/kg}			
		Foodsource.all	Qty_Purchased {kg}	1,600	1,900	1,800

Figure 17.10b [Purchasing Activity] Cube view.

				Jan9	Jan10	Jan11
Market. France	LM1	Foodsource. Fsole	Price (L/kg)	30	30	33
			Qty_Purchased {kg}	126	195	210
			Local_Currency_Spent {Lcurr}			
			Dollars_Spent {$}			
			Foodsource_Cost_per_kg {$/kg}			
		Foodsource.all	Qty_Purchased {kg}	1,500	1,300	1,200

Figure 17.10b   [Purchasing Activity] Cube view. *(continued)*

Page:	BatchID.123

Row:	Geog.Market.
Row:	Foodsource.
Row:	Variables { }

Column:	Time.Day.

				Jan9	Jan10	Jan11
Market. Canada	LM1	Foodsource. Tuna	Qty_Shipped_in_Batch {kg}			
			Foodsource_Cost_per_kg {$/kg}			
			NonFoodAsset_Cost_per_kg {$/kg}			
		Foodsource. Salmon	Qty_Shipped_in_Batch {kg}			
			Foodsource_Cost_per_kg {$/kg}			
			NonFoodAsset_Cost_per_kg {$/kg}			
	LM2	Foodsource. Tuna	Qty_Shipped_in_Batch {kg}			
			Foodsource_Cost_per_kg {$/kg}			
			NonFoodAsset_Cost_per_kg {$/kg}			
		Foodsource. Salmon	Qty_Shipped_in_Batch {kg}			
			Foodsource_Cost_per_kg {$/kg}			
			NonFoodAsset_Cost_per_kg {$/kg}			
Market. France	LM1	Foodsource. FSole	Qty_Shipped_in_Batch {kg}			
			Foodsource_Cost_per_kg {$/kg}			
			NonFoodAsset_Cost_per_kg {$/kg}			

Figure 17.10c [MS Batch] × [Purchasing Activity] Cube view.

Page:	BatchID.123
Page:	Foodsource.all
Page:	Time.Day.all
Page:	Geog.Market.all
Row:	Variables { }

Foodsource_Cost_in_Batch {$}	
Foodsource_Cost_per_kg_in_Batch {$/kg}	
NonFoodAsset_Cost_in_Batch {$}	
NonFoodAsset_Cost_per_kg_in_Batch {$/kg}	

Figure 17.10d [MS Batch] x [Purchasing Activity] Cube view.

Costs Summary

Module	Calculated Cost or Revenue	Revenue	Cost
Rev[S&M]	Wholesale_Price {$/kg}		
[S&M]	Wholesale_Price {$/kg} − Effective_ Wholesale {$/kg}		
[Travel]	Travel_Cost_per_kg {$/kg}		
[PI Cost]	Cost_per_kg {$/kg}		
[Distribution]	Distribution_Cost_per_kg {$/kg}		
[Production]	Production_Cost_per_kg {$/kg}		
[MI Cost]	Storage_Cost_per_kg_in_Batch {$/kg}		
[MS Batch]	Shipping_Cost_per_kg_in_Batch {$/kg}		
[MS Batch]	Foodsource_Cost_per_kg_in_Batch {$/kg}		
[MS Batch]	NonFoodAsset_Cost_per_kg_in_Batch		
Total	Revenue for Batch123{$/kg}		

Figure 17.11 Cost summary of all business processes.

FCI Cost-Revenue Analysis Calculation Steps by Schema

Since each business process is treated separately, from a formulaic standpoint, context, such as identifying the particular day that a particular batch arrived in inventory, is established at the beginning of each business process-specific set of calculations. These calculations are generally labeled 0 within each business-process-specific set of calculations. These context setting calculations are typically just queries for arrival dates or batch numbers and I frequently give the answer to the query below the statement of the query. When I felt it was instructive for the reader to follow a context-setting query, I wrote "see view" at the bottom of the query.

Also, if you were implementing these formulas as a part of an enterprise OLAP solution, you would no doubt define fairly general formulas such as formulas for calculating inventory cost in general, and then look up or navigate to the specific inventory costs for a particular batch of product. I tried to maintain the same style by defining formulas for calculating the various derived elements in general followed by, typically, a query for the specific cells associated with the specific batch of product being tracked in this exercise. I used italics to identify the queries for the calculated cells whose general formula would have appeared immediately above. For example, formula number one in the sales and marketing business process articulates a general formula for calculating total revenue given the sales and marketing schema shown previously. Formula 1q is the specific query to return the specific cells associated with batch 123.

Sales and Marketing (see Figures 17.2a-b)

1. Daily revenue for a given store on a given day by package type

```
1) [S&M]: "Total_Revenue"{$},
     Time.Day.,
     Geog.Store.,
     Hfoodcake.leaf. =
                 Qty_Sold {pkg} ×
               ( List_Price {$/pkg} -
                 Discount {$/pkg} )
```

1q) [S&M]: "TotalStore_Revenue"{$},
   Time.Jan18,
   Geog.Cambridge,
   Hfoodcake.Neptune.4pack.B123

2. FCI's revenue per package from a given store on a given day

```
2) [S&M]: "Effective_Wholesale_Price"{$/pkg},
     Time.Day.,
     Geog.Store.,
     Hfoodcake.leaf. =
```

```
                           Wholesale_Price{$/pkg} -
                         ( Discount{$/pkg} ×
                           Discount_Share{R} )
    2q) [S&M]: "Effective_Wholesale_Price"{$/pkg},
         Time.Jan18,
         Geog.Cambridge,
         Hfoodcake.Neptune.4pack.B123
```

3. Daily revenue for FCI from a given store on a given day by package type

```
    3) [S&M]: "Dollars_Owed_FCI"{$},
         Time.Day.,
         Geog.Store.,
         Hfoodcake.leaf. =
                 Effective_Wholesale_Price{$/pkg} ×
                 Qty_Sold{pkg}
    3q) [S&M]: "Dollars_Owed_FCI"{$},
         Time.Jan18,
         Geog.Cambridge,
         Hfoodcake.Neptune.4pack.B123
    4) [S&M]: "Dollars_Owed_FCI_per_kg"{$/kg}, Daily revenue per kg for
    FCI from a given store on a given day, by package type
         Time.Day.,
         Geog.Store.,
         Hfoodcake.leaf. =
                 Effective_Wholesale_Price{$/pkg} ÷
                 [Foodsource]: Foodcake.Neptune.4pack.Weight{kg/pkg}
    4q) [S&M]: "Dollars_Owed_FCI_per_kg"{$/kg},
         Time.Jan18,
         Geog.Cambridge,
         Hfoodcake.Neptune.4pack.B123
```

Transportation from Product Inventory to Stores (see Figures 17.3a-d)

0. Given that the order ID for Neptune four-pack b123 = 0179

```
    0q) "OrderID",
         Time.Jan18,
         Geog.ProductInventorySite.Hartford,
         Geog.Zone.BostonArea,
         Geog.Store.Cambridge
             =0179
```

1. Cost of transportation from an inventory site to a delivery zone along the delivery route for a given day

```
    1) [Travel]: "Vehicle_Travel_Cost"{$},
         Time.Day.,
```

```
      Geog.ProductInventorySite.,
      Geog.Zone.  =
            Fixed_Cost{$} +
            Total_Distance{km} ×
            [Vehicle]: (Cost_per_km{$/km})
1q) [Travel]:" Vehicle_Travel_Cost"{$}, Time.Jan18,
Geog.ProductInventorySite.Hartford, Geog.Zone.BostonArea
```

2. Transportation cost attributed to a given order

```
2) [Travel]: "Order_Travel_Cost"{$},
      OrderID.,
      Time.Day.,
      Geog.ProductInventorySite.,
      Geog.Zone. =
                  Tripshare{R} ×
                  Vehicle_Travel_Cost{$}
2q) [Travel]: "Order_Travel_Cost"{$},
      OrderID.0179,
      Time.Jan18,
      Geog.ProductInventorySite.Hartford,
      Geog.Zone.BostonArea
```

3. Transportation cost per kg for a given order

```
3) [Travel]: "Order_Travel_Cost_per_kg"{$/kg},
      OrderID.,
      Time.Day.,
      Geog.ProductInventorySite.,
      Geog.Zone. =
                  Order_Travel_Cost{$} ÷
                  [Order]: (Qty_Ordered{kg}, Hfoodcake.all)
3q) [Travel]: Order_Travel_Cost_per_kg{$/kg},
      OrderID.0179,
      Time.Jan18,
      Geog.ProductInventorySite.Hartford,
      Geog.Zone.BostonArea
```

Product Inventory (see Figures 17.4a–c)

0. When did Neptune b123 arrive in product inventory?

```
0q) [PI Throughput]: "Time.Day",
      Geog.ProductInventorySite.Hartford,
      Age.1,
      Hfoodcake.Neptune.4pack.B123
          see view
```

1. What was total inventory cost that day?

```
1q) [PI Cost]: "Cost"{$},
    NonFoodAsset.all,
    Time.Jan17,
    Geog.ProductInventorySite.Hartford
        see view
```

2. Quantity passing through an inventory site over a given period of time

```
2)  [PI Throughput]: "Qty_Throughput"{kg},
    Time.Day.atabove,
    Geog.ProductInventorySite.atabove.,
    Hfoodcake.atabove.,
    Age.atabove. =
                ( Qty_Sent{kg} +
                Qty_Received{kg} ) ÷ 2
2q) [PI Throughput]: "Qty_Throughput"{kg},
    Time.Jan17,
    Geog.ProductInventorySite.Hartford
```

3. Daily storage cost per kg

```
3)  [PI Throughput]: "Cost_per_kg"{$/kg},
    Time.Day.,
    Geog.ProductInventorySite.,
    Hfoodcake.all,
    Age.all =
[PI Cost]: (Cost{$}, NonFoodAsset.all) ÷ Qty_Throughput{kg}
3q) [PI Throughput]:"Cost_per_kg"{$/kg},
    Time.Jan17,
    Geog.ProductInventorySite.Hartford
```

Transportation from Production to Product Inventory (see Figures 17.5a-c)

0. From which product site on which date was Neptune b123 shipped to Hartford?

```
0q) [Distribution]: "Geog.ProductionSite", "CargoID", "Time.Day",
    Arrival_Time.Jan17,
    Geog.ProductInventorySite.Hartford,
    [Cargo]:(Qty_Shipped{kg}, Hfoodcake.Neptune.4Pack.B123 > 0)
        Vancouver, 567, Jan16
```

1. Cost of distributing cargo from a production site to an inventory site

```
1)  [Distribution]: "Cargo_Distribution_Cost"{$},
    Time.Day.,
    Geog.ProductionSite.,
```

```
         Geog.ProductInventorySite. =
                  Fixed_Cost{$} +
                  ( Total_Distance{km} ×
                  [Cargo]:(Qty_Shipped {kg}, Hfoodcake.all) ×
                  [Transport Method]: Cost_per_kg_km {$/(kg*km)} )
```

1q) [Distribution]: "Cargo_Distribution_Cost"{$},
Time.Jan16,
Geog.ProductionSite.Vancouver,
Geog.ProductInventorySite.Hartford

2) [Distribution]: "Distribution_Cost_per_kg"{$/kg},
   Time.Day.atabove.,
   Geog.ProductionSite.atabove.,
   Geog.ProductInventorySite.atabove. =
         Cargo_Distribution_Cost{$} ÷
         [Cargo]: (Qty_Shipped{kg})

2q) [Distribution]: "Distribution_Cost_per_kg"{$/kg},
CargoID.567

Production (see Figure 17.6)

0. When, where, and on what machine was batch 123 produced?

```
0q) [Production]: "Geog.ProductionSite"{N}, "Time.Day", "MachineID"{I},
"BatchOrdinal"{I}, BatchID.123
        Vancouver, Jan16, 1, 1
```

1. Total production costs

1q) [Production]: "Production_Cost"{$},
Time.Jan16,
Geog.ProductionSite.Vancouver,
MachineID.1,
BatchOrdinal.1,
Stuff.NonFoodAsset.all,
Process.all =
Sum (Product cost, Stuff.NonFoodAsset., Process.leaf.)

2. Nonfoodasset cost per kg of producing foodcakes

2) [Production]: "Production_Cost_per_kg"{$/kg},
Time.Day.atabove.,
Geog.ProductionSite.atabove.,
Stuff.all,
Process.all,
BatchOrdinal.atabove. =
Production_Cost{$} ÷
Qty_Output{kg}, Process.Freezing&Packaging

2. Nonfoodasset cost per kg of producing Neptune b123

> *2q) [Production]:* `"Production_Cost_per_kg"`*{$/kg},*
>   *Time.Jan16,*
>   *Geog.Vancouver,*
>   *MachineID.1,*
>   *BatchOrdinal.1*

3. Find all the fish used to make Neptune b123

> *3q) [Production]:* `"Qty_Input"`*{kg},* `"Stuff.Foodsource."`*{N},*
>   *Time.Jan16,*
>   *Geog.Vancouver,*
>   *MachineID.1,*
>   *BatchOrdinal.1,*
>   *Process.Cleaning,*
>   *(Qty_Input{kg} > 0)*

Materials Inventory (see Figures 17.7a-e)

0. When did b123 leave inventory using rules?

> 0q) [Batch]: `"Geog.ProductionSite"`{N}, `"Time.Day.(this - 1)"`,
>   BatchID.123
>   Vancouver, Jan15

1. Quantity passing through an inventory site over a given period of time

> 1) [MI Throughput]: `"Qty_Throughput"`{kg},
>   Foodsource.all,
>   Time.Day.atabove.,
>   Geog.ProductionSite.atabove.,
>   Age.all =
>   (Qty_Sent{kg} +
>   Qty_Received{kg}) ÷ 2
> *1q) [MI Throughput]:* `"Qty_Throughput"`*{kg},*
>   *Time.(Jan10 to Jan16).,*
>   *Geog.MaterialsInventorySite.Vancouver*

2. Daily storage cost per kg

> 2) [MI Throughput]: `"Storage_Cost_per_kg"`{$/kg},
>   Foodsource.all,
>   Time.Day.,
>   Age.all,
>   Geog.ProductionSite. =
>
>   [MIC]: (Storage_Cost{$}, NonFoodAsset.all) ÷
>   `Qty_Throughput`{kg}

3. Total storage cost per kg for fish of a given age

```
3) [MI Throughput]: "Cumulative_Storage_Cost_per_kg"{$/kg},
       Foodsource.all,
       Time.Day.,
       Age. =
            Sum( Storage_Cost_per_kg{$/kg},
              Time.Day.((this+1 - Age.) to this) )
3q) [MI Throughput]: "Cumulative_Storage_Cost_per_kg"{$/kg},
       Time.Jan15,
       Age.(4,5,6).
```

4. Quantity of fish from inventory used in a given batch

```
4) [MI Batch]: "Qty_Used_in_Batch"{kg},
       Foodsource.,
       Age.atabove.,
       BatchID. =
                  [Production]:(Qty_Input{kg}, Process.Cleaning,
       BatchID.) x
                  [MI]:( (Qty_Sent{kg}, Age. ÷
                         Qty_Sent{kg}, Age.all), [Batch]:Time.Day.
                         this-1) )
4q) [MI Batch]: "Qty_Used_in_Batch"{kg},
       Foodsource.,
       Age.,
       BatchID.123,
       (Qty_Sent{kg} > 0)
```

5. Cumulative cost of storing fish used in a given batch

```
5) [MI Batch]: "Storage_Cost_in_Batch"{$},
       Foodsource.,
       Age.atabove.,
       BatchID. =
            Sum( ( Cumulative_Storage_Cost_per_kg{$/kg},
                  [Batch]:Time.Day.(this-1)) ×
                  Qty_Used_in_Batch{kg} ),
                Age. )
5q) [MI Batch]: "Storage_Cost_in_Batch"{$},
       BatchID.123
```

6. Cumulative cost per kg of storing all fish in a given batch

```
6) [MI Batch]: "Storage_Cost_per_kg_in_Batch"{$/kg},
       Foodsource.all,
       Age.all,
       BatchID. =
                  Storage_Cost_in_Batch{$} ÷
                  [Production]:(Qty_Input{kg}, Process.Cleaning)
6q) [MI Batch]: "Storage_Cost_per_kg_in_Batch"{$/kg},
       BatchID.123
```

Materials Shipping (see Figures 17.8a-e)

```
0.1q) [MI Batch]: "Time.Day.(this - Age.)",
      Foodsource.all,
      (Qty_Used_in_Batch{kg}> 0, BatchID.123)
            Jan9, Jan10, Jan11
0.2q) [MS Distribution]: "Geog.Market",
      Geog.Vancouver,
      Foodsource.all,
      BatchID.123
            Canada.LM1, Canada.LM2, France.LM1
  1) MyGrouping = Geog.(Canada.LM1, Canada.LM2, France.LM1)
```

2. Cost per kg of distributing materials from a market to an inventory site

```
  2) [MS Distribution]: "Shipping_Cost_per_kg"{$/kg}
     Time.Day.,
     Geog.Market.,
     Geog.MaterialsInventorySite.,
     Foodsource.all =
                Shipping_Cost_per_kg_km{$/(kg*km)} ✕
                Distance{km}
  2q) [MS Distribution]: "Shipping_Cost_per_kg"{$/kg},
      Time.(Jan9 to Jan11).,
      Geog.Market.MyGrouping.down1.,
      Geog.MaterialsInventorySite.Vancouver
```

3. Total cost of distributing material from a market to an inventory site

```
  3) [MS Distribution]: "Shipping_Cost"{$},
     Time.Day.,
     Geog.Market.,
     Geog.MaterialsInventorySite.,
     Foodsource. =
                Shipping_Cost_per_kg{$/kg} ✕
                Qty_Sent{kg}
 3.1q) [MS Distribution]: "Shipping_Cost"{$},
       Time.(Jan9 to Jan11).,
       Geog.Market.MyGrouping.down1.,
       Geog.MaterialsInventorySite.Vancouver,
       Foodsource.(Tuna,Salmon,Fsole).,
       (Qty_Sent{kg} > 0)
```

4. Quantity of fish shipped from all markets in a given batch

```
  4) [MS Batch]: "Qty_Shipped_in_Batch"{kg},
     Time.Day.,
     Geog.Market.all,
     Foodsource.,
```

```
            BatchID.  =
[MI Batch]:( Qty_Used_in_Batch, Age.([Batch]:Time.Day.(this-1) -
                                [MS Batch]:Time.Day.this )  )
```

4a. Quantity of fish shipped from a given market in a given batch

```
4a) [MS Batch]: "Qty_Shipped_in_Batch"{kg},
     Time.Day.,
     Geog.Market.,
     Foodsource.,
     Age.,
     BatchID. =
                 Qty_Shipped_in_Batch{kg}, Geog.Market.all ×
                 [MS Distribution]:(Qty_Sent{kg}, Geog.Market. ÷
                 Qty_Sent{kg}, Geog.Market.all)
```

4.1 Qty shipped in batch from each market by fish type

```
4.1q) [MS Batch]: "Qty_Shipped_in_Batch"{kg},
      Time.Day.,
      Geog.Market.,
      Foodsource.,
      BatchID.123,
      (Qty_Shipped_in_Batch{kg} >0)
```

4.2 Total qty shipped in batch from each market

```
4.2q) [MS Batch]: "Qty_Shipped_in_Batch"{kg},
      Time.Day.,
      Geog.Market.,
      Foodsource.all,
      BatchID.123,
      (Qty_Shipped_in_Batch{kg} >0)
```

5. Cost to ship fish used in a given batch

```
5) [MS Batch]: "Shipping_Cost_in_Batch"{$},
    Time.Day.,
    Geog.Market.,
    BatchID.
    Foodsource. =
                 Qty_Shipped_in_Batch{kg} ×
                 [MS Distribution]: (Shipping_Cost_per_kg{$/kg})
5q)[MS Batch]: "Shipping_Cost_in_Batch"{$},
    Foodsource.,
    Time.Day.,
    BatchID.123,
    (Qty_Shipped_in_Batch{kg} >0)
```

6. Cost per kg to ship all fish in a given batch

```
6)  [MS Batch]: "Shipping_Cost_per_kg_in_Batch"{$/kg},
        Time.all,
        Geog.Market.all,
        Foodsource.all,
        BatchID. =
                    Shipping_Cost_in_Batch{$}÷
                    Qty_Shipped_ in_Batch{kg}
6q) [MS Batch]: "Shipping_Cost_per_kg_in_Batch"{$/kg}, BatchID.123
```

Currency Exchange (see Figure 17.9)

1. Currency available in a country at the start of a given day

```
1)  [C]: "Local_Currency_on_Hand_Opening"{Lcurr}
        Time.Day.,
        Geog.Country. =
                    (Local_Currency_Purchased{Lcurr} +
                    Local_Currency_Remaining{Lcurr}), Time.Day.(this-1)
1q) [C]: "Local_Currency_on_Hand_Opening"{Lcurr},
        Time.(Jan8 to Jan11).,
        Geog.(Canada, France).
```

2. Currency remaining in a country after expenditures on a given day

```
2)  [C]: "Local_Currency_Remaining"{Lcurr}
        Time.Day.,
        Geog.Country. =
                    Local_Currency_on_Hand_Opening{Lcurr} -
                    Local_Currency_Spent{Lcurr}
2q) [C]: "Local_Currency_Remaining"{Lcurr},
        Time.(Jan8 to Jan11).,
        Geog.(Canada, France).
```

3. Dollars spent on currency in a country on a given day

```
3)  [C]: "Dollars_Spent_for_Local_Currency_Purchased"{$}
        Time.Day.,
        Geog.Country. =
                    Local_Currency_Spent{Lcurr} +
                    Daily_Exchange_Rate{Lcurr/$}, Time.Day.this
3q) [C]: "Dollars_Spent_for_Local_Currency_Purchased"{$},
        Time.(Jan8 to Jan11).,
Geog.(Canada,France).
```

4. Effective exchange rate utilized for currency on hand at the start of a given day

```
4) [C]: "Effective_Rate"{Lcurr/$},
    Time.Day.,
    Geog.Country. =
                    Local_Currency_on_hand_opening{Lcurr},
            Time.Day.this ÷
                ( ( Local_Currency_Remaining{Lcurr} +
                        Effective_Rate{Lcurr/$} +
            Dollars_Spent_for_Local_Currency_Purchased{$} ),
            Time.Day.(this-1) )
4q) [C]: "Effective_Rate",
    Time.(Jan8-Jan11).,
    Geog.(Canada, France).
```

Purchasing (see Figures 17.10a-d)

1. NonFoodAsset cost per kg of foodstuff purchased

```
1) [Purchasing Cost]: "NonFoodAsset_Cost_per_kg"{$/kg},
    Time.Day.atabove.,
    Geog.Market.atabove.,
    Foodsource.atabove. =
                NonFoodAsset_Cost{$} ÷
                [Purchasing Activity]: (Qty_Purchased{kg})
1q) [Purchasing Cost]: "NonFoodAsset_Cost_per_kg"{$/kg},
    Time.(Jan9 to Jan11).,
    Geog.Market.MyGrouping.down1.,
    Foodsource.all
```

2. Daily expenditure on a given food item at a given market

```
2) [Purchasing Activity]: "Local_Currency_Spent"{Lcurr},
    Time.Day.,
    Geog.Market.,
    Foodsource. =
                Price{Lcurr/kg} ×
                Qty_Purchased{kg}
2q) [Purchasing Activity]:  "Local_Currency_Spent"{Lcurr},
    Time.(Jan9 to Jan11).,
    Geog.MyGrouping.down1.,
    Foodsource.(Salmon, Tuna, FSole).
```

3. Expenditure per kg for foodstuffs purchased

```
3) [Purchasing Activity]: "Dollars_Spent"{$},
    Time.Day.,
    Geog.Market.atabove.,
    Foodsource.atabove. =
```

```
                    Local_Currency_Spent{Lcurr} ÷
                    [C]: (Effective_Rate{Lcurr/$},
                    Geog.Market.Country)
3q) [Purchasing Activity]: "Dollars_Spent"{$},
    Time.(Jan9 to Jan11).,
    Geog.MyGrouping.down1.
```

4. Expenditure per kg for foodstuffs purchased

```
4) [Purchasing Activity]: "Foodsource_Cost_per_kg"{$/kg},
    Time.Day.atabove.,
    Geog.Market.atabove.,
    Foodsource.atabove. =
                    Dollars_Spent{$} ÷
                    Qty_Purchased{kg}
4q) [Purchasing Activity]: "Foodsource_Cost_per_kg"{$/kg},
    Time.(Jan9 to Jan11).,
    Geog.Market.MyGrouping,
    Foodsource.(Salmon,Tuna,Fsole).
```

5a. Quantity of fish shipped from a given market in a given batch

```
5a) [MS Batch]: "Qty_Shipped_in_Batch"{kg},
    Time.Day.,
    Foodsource.atabove.,
    Geog.Market.,
    BatchID. =
                Qty_Shipped_in_Batch{kg}, Geog.Market.all x
                [MS Distribution]:(Qty_Sent{kg}, Geog.Market. ÷
                                Qty_Sent{kg}, Geog.Market.all)
```

5q. Qty shipped in batch from each market by fishtype

```
5q) [MS Batch]: "Qty_Shipped_in_Batch"{kg},
    Time.Day.,
    Geog.Market.,
    Foodsource.Fish.,
    BatchID.123,
    (Qty_Shipped_in_Batch{kg} > 0)
```

6. Total expenditure for foodstuffs used in a given batch

```
6) [MS Batch X Purchasing Activity]: "Foodsource_Cost_in_Batch"{$},
    Time.Day.,
    Foodsource.,
    Geog.Market.all,
    BatchID. =
```

```
        Sum( ( [Purchasing Activity]: (Foodsource_Cost_per_kg{$/kg}) x
                 Qty_Shipped_in_Batch{kg}),
              Geog.Market.)
6q) [MS Batch]: "Foodsource_Cost_in_Batch"{$},
    BatchID.123,
    Geog.Market.all,
    Time.Day.all,
    Foodsource.all
```

7. Total expenditure per kg for foodstuffs used in a batch

```
7) [MS Batch]: "Foodsource_Cost_per_kg_in_Batch"{$/kg},
   Time.Day.all,
   Geog.Market.all,
   Foodsource.atabove.,
   BatchID. =

              Foodsource_Cost_in_Batch {$} ÷
              Qty_Shipped_in_Batch {kg}
7q) [MS Batch]: "Foodsource_Cost_per_kg_in_Batch"{$/kg},
    BatchID.123,
    Time.Day.all,
    Foodsource.all,
    Age.all
```

8. Total nonfood asset cost of foodstuffs used in a given batch

```
8) [MS Batch]: "NonFoodAsset_Cost_in_Batch"{$},
   Time.Day.atabove,
   Geog.Market.atabove.,
   Foodsource.atabove.,
   Age.,
   BatchID. =
        Sum( ( [Purchasing Cost]:(NonFoodAsset_Cost_per_kg{$/kg}) X
                 Qty_Shipped_in_Batch{kg} ),
              Geog.Market. )
8q) [MS Batch]: "NonFoodAsset_Cost_in_Batch"{$},
    BatchID.123,
    Time.Day.all,
    NonFoodAsset.all,
    Age.all
```

9. Nonfood asset cost per kg of foodstuffs used in a batch

```
9) [MS Batch]: "NonFoodAsset_Cost_per_kg_in_Batch"{$/kg},
     Time.Day.atabove.,
     Geog.Market.atabove.,
     Foodsource.atabove.,
     Age.,
     BatchID. =

               NonFoodAsset_Cost_in_Batch{$}÷
               Qty_Shipped_in_Batch{kg}
9q) [MS Batch]: "NonFoodAsset_Cost_per_kg_in_Batch"{$/kg},
     BatchID.123,
     Time.Day.all,
     Geog.Market.all,
     NonFoodAsset.all
```

Further Issues

Why should it be possible to have grounds for believing anything if it isn't possible to be certain?

LUDWIG WITTGENSTEIN

Multidimensional Guidelines

The purpose of these feature guidelines is to describe the key areas of multidimensional functionality in terms of feature categories that any tool must provide and in terms of features that tools may or may not provide. When appropriate, within each category, features are ordered in terms of how basic or advanced they are. Although any tool should support basic features in all categories (and most do), it is not necessary for any tool to provide advanced functionality in all areas.

Rather, it is important that you evaluate your needs and align those needs with the features offered in a tool. If your application is budgeting, you may require nonleaf level data entry and efficient incremental updating capabilities. If your application is route analysis for a shipping company, you may require very large dimension support and excellent sparsity management. If your application involves financial reporting across a basket of currencies, you may wish to use a tool that understands currency translations.

You will benefit the most from these guidelines if you have read the chapters in Part 2 and thought about some of the questions that you can ask yourself to assess your needs. The descriptions and questions in this chapter are meant to fine-tune your awareness.

The guidelines are divided into two broad categories: predominantly logical features and predominantly physical features. Logical features can be described independently, without regard to any particular hardware platform, operating system, number of users, physical storage methods, or network properties. How a product defines dimensions, hierarchies, formulas, links, and views are examples of logical features.

Physical features can be described independently, without regard to any particular model that might be defined or analyzed. Physical features include how a product distributes computations across a network, the methods used to store and retrieve data, and the speed and spatial efficiency attained, as well as what hardware and software platforms it can run on. Of course, as with most binary schemes, these classifications are rough labels covering what would be more accurately described as a spectrum, with the schema definition being most logical and the clumps of charge in the transistors being the most physical, which is why I inserted the term predominantly in the previous paragraph. Support for multiple users, for example, has both logical and physical implications. In addition, even though different features of products can be grouped into being more physical or more logical, there are many times when the natural and immediate follow-up question to a key logical attribute is a physical question, typically performance-related. Thus, from time to time I insert natural follow-up questions in the guidelines, regardless of the type of question.

Outline

At an overview level, the guidelines are structured as follows:

- **Logical**
  - Core
    Structure
    Operations
    Representations
  - Application
    Knowledge-oriented
    Process-oriented

- **Physical**
  - Storage/access
  - Computation
  - Optimization
  - Security
  - Tiering
  - Platform

Core Logical Features

The three principal categories of core logical features described here are *structure, operations*, and *representations*. How models and dimensions are defined and the types of relationships that can exist between members of a dimension are examples of structural issues. How data flows through a cube, the types of links that can be created, and the types of formulas that can be defined are examples of operational issues. How multidimensional data is displayed and browsed in either matrix or graphic form are examples of representational issues. This organization is similar but not identical to the relational model that is usually defined in terms of data structure, data operations, and data integrity.[1]

Please note that wherever I use the term maximum (as in the maximum number of members per dimension or the maximum number of dimensions per cube or the maximum number of data cells per cube), I mean it in the spectral sense of a sliding scale of practical maximums that vary as a function of hardware and other factors. So if you are using these guidelines to formulate questions, always connect your questions about tool limits with some measure of contextualized performance, such as, "On a dual-processor Pentium III with 2GB of memory, with a single user directly accessing the machine, what is the maximum number of base data values from which the tool can calculate aggregates and other derivations in under 10 seconds when the inputs are all held in memory?" This is especially necessary where the tool's performance depends on certain data or meta data being in memory and where your circumstances may not permit all the appropriate data to reside in memory. In these cases you will need to find out how performance drops when key regulating information needs to get paged in and out of memory or conversely what kind of hardware investment will be required to guarantee the kind of performance you are looking for.

Structure

Dimensions

General

1. Does the tool support formulaically defined dimension members , such as using a date stamp for time?
2. Does the tool support derived dimensions?
3. Are dimensions fully symmetrical?

   3.1 If not, what kinds of dimensions does the tool define?

      3.1.1 What are the different attributes for each kind of dimension?

Hierarchies

1. Does the tool support hierarchical dimensions?
2. If so, is it level-based, ragged hierarchy-based, or both?
3. If level-based, can it simulate raggedness through dummy members?

   3.1 If both, does it support both types of hierarchical relationships within a single dimension?

   3.2 Can it support multiple hierarchies within a single dimension?

      3.2.1 If so, is navigation supported equally across all hierarchies equivalent or is there a principal hierarchy?

4. Do all the members of a dimension hierarchy have to be connected or can they be unconnected?

Cardinality

1. What is the maximum number of dimensions that may exist in a database?
2. For each type of dimension recognized by the tool:
   2.1 How many members can it contain?
   2.2 If the dimension type is hierarchical:
      2.2.1 How many levels or generations can it contain?
      2.2.2 How many children can each parent have?

Versioning

1. Does the tool support aliases for dimension members?
2. Can different subsets of the same dimension be used in different cubes?
3. Can those different versions be updated at different times?
   3.1 Think about the case where the marketing department is responsible for maintaining the official list of products and this list changes every quarter. Sales analysts can't analyze the quarter's sales until the quarter has ended. So ideally they work on last quarter's product dimension until they have finished their analysis at which point their product cube is updated to reflect the changes made by the marketing department.

Dimension Orderings

1. Can dimensions be ordinally or cardinally ordered?
   1.1 If so, can the orderings be named?
   1.2 Can you write formulas that involve the notion of the following?
      1.2.1 Previous member, next member
      1.2.2 First member, last member
      1.2.3 Distance between two members (cycle length = distance between min and min)
   1.3 If so, can you do it for dimensions other than time?

Cubes

1. Is the tool fully symmetrical? If not:
   1.1 Does the tool distinguish measures and dimensions?
      1.1.1 To what degree can they swap roles?
   1.2 Does it define a measures dimension?
   1.3 What extra capabilities are defined for the members of the measures dimension such as data typing or aggregation function exceptions?
2. What is the maximum number of dimensions per cube?

3. What is the maximum number of intersections or cells per cube?

4. What is the maximum number of input data cells per cube?

5. What is the maximum number of total stored data cells per cube?

6. Which factors most affect cube performance?

   6.1 Can cubes be defined in terms of other cubes?

      6.1.1 If so, what is the maximum number of input cubes per derived cube?

      6.1.2 How long can the chain of derived cubes be?

         6.1.2.1 Can a derived cube contain a mixture of input and derived data?

Further Issue: Regularity

1. Can subsets of the cube have different dimensionality (additional or fewer dimensions) relative to the rest of cube?

2. Can a cube be composed of subsets of defined dimensions as opposed to entire dimensions?

Models and Databases

1. Is the model or database composed of a single hypercube or of multiple interactive cubes?

   1.1 If multiple interactive cubes, how are dimensions shared between cubes?

      1.1.1 For multicube architectures, can cubes be joined along dimensions that are not identical?

         1.1.1.1 If so, how are the dimension member differences reconciled? (Lookup table . . .)

         1.1.1.2 What are the performance issues?

2. How are application ranges defined?

   2.1 Are all variables in a cube dimensioned in the same way?

   2.2 How are location ranges for terms on the right-hand side of an equation determined?

   2.3 Does the tools formula language support multiple calculation contexts per expression?

Data Types or Domains

1. What is the range of numerical types supported?

2. Does it support character strings or other media such as images as data values?

3. Does it support data types on a variable-by-variable basis?

4. Does it recognize nominal, ordinal, and cardinal series?

   4.1 If so, is it just that sorting is an option for formatting?

   4.2 If so, does it apply to individual variables or to the cube as a whole?

Further Issues: Data Types

1. Does the tool support user-defined data types?

   1.1 If so, are they user-defined enumerated values, constrained forms of built-in types, or others?

   1.2 Can they be composites of multiple types, as in relations or objects?

   1.3 Can there be user-defined operations on those types?

   1.4 Can the data types inherit operations from other types?

Operations

Queries

1. Does the tool support selection based on dimension members or on characteristic attributes?

   1.1 Can the tool show the distinct values for an attribute?

      1.1.1 What advance work has to be done by a DBA?

2. Does the tool support selection based on an expression?

3. Does the tool support aggregations based on member attributes?

4. Does the UI or API support drilling down a hierarchy?

   4.1 Does the tool support the definition of custom drill paths?

      4.1.1 Does it display the path when in use?

5. Does the tool let the user create manual grouping of items in a dimension?

Iterative Query Capabilities

1. Does the tool support iterative queries?

   1.1 What kinds of iterative queries?

   1.2 Ranking/sorting/filtering of result set?

   1.3 Can set operators be used?

   1.4 Further computation using the result set?

      1.4.1 Is the further query executed against the previous result set?

      1.4.2 Where is that result set maintained?

2. Can the tool save queries and reuse them in an iterative process?

Formulas and Calculations

1. Does data have to enter at the leaf level of dimensions?

2. If not, and formulas exist for rolling up the leaf-level data, can the user control when these aggregation formulas are overridden by manually entered data?

3. Can formulas reference data from multiple cubes?

    3.1 How is multicube referencing specified?

4. Can a formula reference data from a mixture of cubes and tables?

5. Are there any restrictions to the dimensional referencing within formulas?

6. If the tool distinguishes a measures dimension from other dimensions and forces every cube to have one measures dimension, and assuming the tool enables you to define formulas for the individual members of the measures dimension:

    6.1 Does the tool permit formulas to be added to nonmeasures dimensions?

        6.1.1 What are the restrictions on those formulas?

7. What numerical operations are provided?

8. Does it support range and conditional operators?

9. What logical operations are provided?

10. What set operations are provided?

11. What text operations are provided?

12. What other member operations are provided?

13. Is there a mechanism for extending the calculations with user-defined functions?

14. Can the formula compiler detect simultaneous equations?

    14.1 If they are detectable, can the system resolve them?

    14.2 If not, are they treated as circular?

        14.2.1 Can circular references be detected?

            14.2.1.1 If not, what happens?

15. Does the tool provide for point and click choices when creating statements or does the user have to write in functions? Where is the transition?

16. Does the tool provide a partial name-matching facility? Does it show you a list of possibilities when there are more than one?

17. How does the tool handle interdimensional precedence?

    17.1 Can you set precedence on a dimension-by-dimension basis?

    17.2 Can you override them on a cell-by-cell basis or member basis?

    17.3 Does the tool provide facilities for testing the impact of using different precedence?

18. How does the tool specify formula application ranges?

   18.1 Does the tool provide for formula exceptions?

       18.1.1 If so, what kinds?

       18.1.2 How are they defined? Member-based and/or tuple-based?

19. Are attributes treated as different entities than variables?

   19.1 If so, what data types may be used for attributes?

   19.2 Can attributes be used to construct dimension levels as well?

20. Can the tool distinguish between the following?

   20.1 Cube intersections whose data is missing and whose value is otherwise unknown

   20.2 Intersections for which data would be meaningless

   20.3 Intersections whose data, while not entered, is known to be equal to zero

       20.3.1 If yes, does the tool process missing data differently from meaningless data?

       20.3.2 Can the tool substitute data where data is missing? How is this done?

       20.3.3 Can the tool substitute meaningful variables where a variable is meaningless?

21. In a client/server implementation, can calculations be designed on the client? If so, what range of calculations can be client-defined?

22. Can an end-user create what-if modifications to the server-resident cube?

   22.1 Can those modifications be stored or shared?

       22.1.1 Can they be written back to the database?

Links

1. Can a dimension be defined in terms of parent-child tables?

2. Can a dimension be defined in terms of SQL tables where each column in the table represents a level in a dimensional hierarchy?

3. Can a dimension be defined in terms of a snowflake (members in snowflake form)?

4. Can a dimension be defined in terms of a star schema, constellation, or federation?

5. Can the product be customized to access data from proprietary (nonrelational) databases?

6. For products that distinguish between member attributes and cube measures:

   6.1 Can member attributes be defined on additional joined tables?

   6.2 If so, what are the limits to the joins that the member attribute tables can have to the dimension tables?

7. For each dimension definition, must all members be in one table, or can the members be created from more than one table (horizontal partitioning of dimension tables for a given level)?

8. Can data and meta data be brought into a model from a single table?

9. Can the links parse a type two table?

10. Can the links parse a type one table?

11. Can the links read measures from rows as opposed to columns?

12. Can the links contain expressions, or can they only contain column names?

13. Are the links persistent?

14. Can the system link to multiple fact tables for different sets of keys for the same nonkey information (horizontal partitioning of fact table information)?

15. Can the system link to multiple fact tables for different sets of nonkey information (vertical partitioning of fact table information)?

    15.1 If so, how are changes detected in the external data source?

16. Can formulas that are stored in external tables be referenced from within formulas in an MD model?

17. For products that create and manage their own nontabular data storage:

    17.1 Can data from external tables be aggregated in an MD model without first duplicating the data?

    17.2 Can data from an MD model be sent back to an external table?

    17.3 Can data from external tables be joined with data in cubes via a command/query sent to the cube?

18. For products that are defined purely from RDBMS tables:

    18.1 Can the system link to and recognize aggregate tables?

    18.2 Can the system link to and recognize aggregate values in the primary fact table?

Batch Automation

1. Can recomputes be scheduled?

    1.1 When multiple cubes and dimensions are scheduled together for recompute, is there an intelligent queue manager to optimize the ordering of recomputed items such as computing dimensions before cubes?

2. Can data automatically be fed into a cube via links and then (re)computed?

3. Can changes to model structure defined in external tables be brought automatically into a model and used for recomputation?

4. Are changes to member names automatically propagated throughout all formulas where the member name is used?

Optimizations and Efficiencies

1. How is cache coherency maintained when changes are made to the underlying data? What triggers a cache flushing?

    1.1 Can the cache be incrementally updated?

    1.2 Can the cache be edited?

2. Is it possible for the hypercube to be left in an inconsistent state as a result of a partial recalculation?

3. What is recalculated during a minimal recalc?

4. Does the tool enable an administrator to specify which aggregates get pre-computed and stored and which get computed at request time?

    4.1 Is this then transparent to the end-user?

5. Can the tool automatically figure out what aggregates are best to precompute and compute on the fly? What kind of algorithm does the tool use?

6. Can the tool figure out where a computation should take place—client or server or database?

Representations

When evaluating tools, make sure you sit down and use them. There are real differences in terms of how you browse and reorganize views. Most of these questions only apply to OLAP clients.

Views and Navigating

1. Does the application provide a standard matrix-style viewer?

    1.2 If so, does the matrix viewer enable multiple cubes (of similar or different dimensionality) to be viewed together?

      1.2.1 If so, can they be linked together for synchronized viewing?

2. If dimensions can be nested on a result matrix, can the user navigate by dimensions at the outer levels, or is navigation just at the lowest (cell) level?

3. Can the user seek or go to a particular member or cell in a report, or must the user scroll to every member or cell?

4. Does the matrix provide the capability to drill down and up without specifying a new query?

5. Where are result sets cached? Does every screen event generate a new query to the server or is there a local cache?

6. Does the viewer display descriptions (short or long) of elements?

7. Can the viewer set sections that will be sorted within sections for nonhierarchical data?

8. Can the tool save, post, recall, edit, and format reports?

9. What kind of output form manipulation is provided? Can users switch between different display metaphors? Can the user easily change from a table to a grid to chart display?

10. Does the OLAP tool support color coding based on the value of the data, such as color of text/number, cell, background, or report attributes?

11. Can the OLAP tool hide data in reports based on positional or value criteria?

12. Does the tool evaluate the response time or data load for a query and alert the user or stop the query when a query is long or large beyond some user- or system-defined limits?

    12.1 If the user still wants to and has the authority to execute a large query, will the tool begin displaying results as they arrive or will the user be forced to wait for the entire result set to arrive?

    12.2 For lengthy reports, can the user jump from one page to another with some form of goto command or does the user have to scroll through and wait for the display of every page in between?

Formatting

1. What options does the tool provide for default display formats to be associated with measures in the database?

2. What options does the tool provide for display formats to be associated with nonmeasures members?

3. Can it provide precedence for representation overlaps where they exist?

4. Can the suggested display formats be overridden at the browser?

5. Can the end-user change column width, a font for the heading, and/or the order of the columns?

6. Can report page headers be linked to the dimensional slices they represent?

7. What controls does the user have for specifying the display attributes of numeric values, such as page, model, variable, range, and so forth?

8. What kind of annotations are supported?

Noncore Logical

Knowledge-Domain

Time

Time is an aspect of any situation and most data sets.

1. Does the tool have any special time knowledge?

2. Does it understand calendars (fiscal, project, and retail)?

3. Can it compare time series of different periodicities?

4. Can it algorithmically generate time series positions?

5. If it offers time knowledge, can you still create your own time dimensions?

6. Can there be more than one time dimension in a single cube?

    6.1 If so, can they both (or all) use a date data type?

7. Can you specify current week, month, quarter, and/or year and have it come out with proper data when next refreshed?

8. Can the tool correctly determine the appropriate "same period last year"?

9. Does it have the capability to understand appropriate relative times (that is, understand "last 13 weeks," and reasonably determine comparable period from prior year for comparison)?

10. Special custom time periods to be defined (for example, high season might start and stop at different dates for different businesses)?

Currency

1. Does the tool recognize currencies?

2. Can it perform currency translations?

    2.1 Can it handle cost of exchange?

3. Can these be based on average exchange rate, last day, first day, lowest, and/or highest?

Personal Profiles

1. Can they be created?

    1.1 If so, what information is maintained?

    1.2 Is there an API to the profile?

Any Other Specialized Domains

1. Does the tool have prebuilt solutions or protosolutions for specific applications such as in retail, manufacturing, and/or finance?

What Languages Does the Tool Support?

1. For those languages that the tool supports, how much of the program is translated? Are the menu options, error messages, and help translated?

Process-Oriented Domains

Information Distribution

1. Alert members of a distribution list of the availability of a new report?
2. Store a client/user profile that can be edited by the distributor?

    2.1 What does the distributor need to set up for the user profile?

3. What kinds of information can be tracked about usage?

    3.1 How many times logged in?

    3.2 Average number of users working concurrently?

    3.3 What reports were run and how many times?

    3.4 Which pages were viewed?

    3.5 What datapoints were retrieved?

Application Building

1. What kind of application development environment is provided by the system:

    1.1 Does the tool provide its own application development environment?

    1.2 Does the tool leverage third-party application development environments (for example, Visual Basic, Enterprise JavaBeans, and so forth)?

2. What functions are covered by the application environment: analysis, links, model creation, and/or reporting?
3. To what degree is it declarative or procedural, textual or graphic?
4. Does it offer debugging facilities?
5. What templates or other prebuilt application fragments are provided?
6. Does the tool let you build miniquery applets?

    6.1 Link dynamic expressions for prompting purposes?

    6.2 Customize prompting?

Integrated DSS Capabilities

1. How well does the tool integrate with data-mining functions?

    1.1 Which vendors/tools work with the OLAP tool? How are the tools communicating? Is it through the OLAP tool's API?

2. Does the mining work with cube data alone, base data held in SQL tables alone, a combination of the two, or something else?

3. Do you need to perform any preliminary transformations (such as type conversion, normalization, or scaling) on the data?

4. Can the data mining leverage the hierarchical MD structure?

    4.1 For example, can a single data-mining operation such as association apply across multiple levels in, say, a product hierarchy?

5. Can OLAP dimensions be created from the outputs of data-mining operations?

    5.1 Can the OLAP tool be used to browse the output of a data-mining operation such as affinity analysis?

6. Can documents and numeric cube slices be joined within a common dimensional framework?

    6.1 For example, can the tool support searches for precanned reports by industry?

Agents and Exception or State Tracking

1. Does the tool offer agents or value tracking?

2. How are monitored values defined?

3. What kinds of values are tracked?

4. Can queries run in the background on the server?

5. How many background queries can run simultaneously (given a particular machine configuration)?

6. Can alerts be broadcast to a list of users?

7. Do broadcasts emanate from the server or does the client need to get involved?

8. Can attachments point to server-resident reports?

Friendliness Features

These features affect many areas from interfaces for browsing to defining formulas.

1. Does the tool enable you to form queries without executing them immediately?

2. Does the tool prompt the user for confirmation before performing large operations, such as deleting a cube?

3. Does the tool warn the user when an expensive query has been requested (for example, "This query will take 45 minutes to compute. Do you want to do this?")?

4. Can the user stop a query in progress?

5. Is there an undo button? How far back does it go?

6. Can the user have multiple interactive windows open simultaneously? Are changes made through one window propagated to the other windows?

7. Does the tool make good use of wizards?

Physical Features

Storage and Access

1. Is data in use stored on the client and/or server?

   1.1 If on the client, what is kept on the client:

       1.1.1 Dimensional information, cube cell data, and/or calculation results?

       1.1.2 What about for Web browsers?

2. For any caches:

   2.1 Can it be incrementally added to? (In other words, can a query that is partially answered by the existing cache use what is in the cache and only query the source for additional cells?)

   2.2 Can any portions be modified without flushing the entire cache?

   2.3 What aspects of server cache are multiread? For example, sometimes tools provide a multiread report cache, but otherwise have single user query caches.

   2.4 What changes to the underlying data sources require cache flushing?

3. For any MDB storage:

   3.1 What changes can be made without requiring a recalc of the MDB?

   3.2 For R/OLAP style tools, is there any kind of persistent storage? If so, what is stored, and what is the form of that storage?

4. For any machine on which the application is running, what are the options for how data in use is distributed between disk and RAM, and between data cells and indexes?

5. Do pointers/indexes need to be stored in RAM? If they do, what happens to performance when the pointers/indexes can no longer fit in RAM?

6. Does dimensional meta data originating from source DBs need to be stored in MD server RAM? How much, if any, needs to be stored on the client?

7. Can the OLAP application store data in an external, typically SQL application?

   7.1 If so, what aspects of the external application can be controlled?

8. Does the application support partitioned dimensions?

   8.1 If so, what can they be distributed in: drives, machines, operating systems?

9. Depending on the type of storage, how much overhead is there per stored number?

   9.1 Does this vary as a function of how much data and/or sparsity there is?

10. How are missing, meaningless, and zero-valued data stored?

11. How does the ratio of empty cells to actual values affect storage?

12. Can individual client queries be processed in parallel?

13. What specific functions are multithreaded?

14. Are there any access performance benchmarks that show how retrieval speed varies as a function of the number of datapoints against which the query is run?

Computations

1. What kinds of calculations must be performed prior to querying?

2. What kinds of calculations can be performed during the course of a query?

3. For calculations that can take place either before or during query processing, what facilities are there to figure out time-space tradeoffs?

4. Are there any performance benchmarks to show how long it takes to compute a screenful of numbers as a function of increases to the number of input cells per output cell and as a function of the total number of datapoints against which the query is run?

5. What happens to compute time when functions reference complex sets of inputs?

6. How much temporary storage is needed for server calculations?

    6.1 What are the determinants of the amount of space needed?

Multitier Distribution

1. Can the user/DBA control where calculations are performed?

2. For Internet browser-based applications, what kinds of calculations can be performed on the client?

3. What computations can be defined on the client to be performed on the server?

    3.1 What if the client is a thin browser?

4. Can the system figure out the most efficient way to distribute computations between the client, any middle tiers, and the server?

    4.1. What are the determinants in its calculation?

5. What is the maximum number of concurrent clients?

6. Can multiple clients share the same server data?

7. Can the administrator set the query cache sizes?

8. Are query caches persistent between requests?

9. For the tools that support multiuser write:

    9.1. Is updating multithreaded?

    9.2 What happens if two or more users attempt to write to the same cell(s) at the same time?

9.3 If one user is writing to a cube, at what level is the cube locked against further writes?

10. Can clients browse the data cube at the same time that the cube is being recomputed?

11. What levels of data isolation are available to the client?

Optimizations and Efficiencies

DBMS Facilities

1. What kind of backup facilities does the tool offer?

2. What happens if system software goes down?

3. What happens if there is a hardware failure?

4. Is there a transaction log? Can partially finished transactions be rolled back?

5. Can the system ever wind up in an inconsistent state?

Platform Issues

1. What platforms are supported?

2. How is browser functionality provided?

   2.1. Java applets, Active X?

3. How does client functionality compare with browser-based functionality?

4. How portable are applications across machines?

Multiuser Security

1. Does the tool offer security for both reads and writes?

2. Is security defined in a dimensional language?

3. To what level of granularity can security be defined: database/model, cube, dimension members, and cells?

4. If a data cell is secured to some level, are all its dependents automatically assigned the same level of security?

5. Can the system record when (and by whom) attempts were made to access or write secure data?

6. Can the user see the members for cells to which he or she has no access?

7. Is access granted or revoked or both?

8. Can security be associated with individuals and/or groups of individuals?

9. Can authentication be performed from the network identification?

Product Language Comparisons

As you can see from Chapter 18, there are literally hundreds of questions that can be asked of any OLAP product and its associated language. Even semidetailed write-ups of product analyses, such as the one created by my colleague George Spofford (from which an excerpt was used in this chapter) that compared Microsoft's first release of its OLAP product with Oracle's Express version 6.3.0, can easily run over 60 pages. User manuals for products typically run in the many hundreds of pages. Furthermore, the product landscape is constantly changing. By the time you read this book, it is likely that any representations made about a particular vendor's product language will have already changed.

Given these caveats, my reasons for including a chapter on product language[1] comparisons are as follows:

- To show you via concrete examples that, yes, every product language does need to provide some mechanism for the various core functions you learned about in this book, such as relative referencing, missing data handling, or application range specification

- To show you how to leverage your understanding of the Located Contents (LC) model to help you interpret dimensional formulas from different products

- To give you a relative sense or feel for, as well as to contrast, the variety of ways that different OLAP product languages accomplish the same thing

Toward that end this chapter uses examples where possible to describe the different ways that four OLAP product languages—namely those from Oracle, Hyperion, Microsoft, and TM1—provide for relative referencing, basic formulas, application ranges, logical sparsity management, and formula precedence. Where appropriate, the way of specifying the expression in LC will be shown as well. To avoid confusion and at the same time allow for a comparison of LC, which is just a language with a variety of product-specific languages, the column headings in the tables where language comparisons are made bear the titles "Language Name" and "Syntax." I have taken the liberty of referring to each commercially available product's language, within the confines of this chapter, by the name of its product, even though some vendors have given specific names to their product languages.

This chapter in no way pretends to do a full comparison between these product languages, even in the aforementioned areas. There are plenty of other areas where these products can but will not be compared, such as how dimensions are defined, how schemas can be linked to data sources, how many physical optimization controls are provided, how the products use disk and memory, how they set up user caches, how they provide for security, and how they integrate with relational databases.

Kickoff Example

To drive home the point that different OLAP environments provide for substantially different ways to accomplish the same thing, consider the following extremely simple schema and associated formula, where the name of the schema is Sales Cube and where the Geography dimension has a store, region, and all level:

```
(Geography.)~ Sales
```

Now let's say you want to define a new variable as the ratio of some store's sales to the sales in that store's region, and you want the calculation to apply only to the store level of the Geography dimension because it makes no sense at any other level in the dimension. In LC you could use the calculation that follows[2]:

```
"Region share" {R}  , Geography.stores. =
    Sales / (Sales , Geography.region)
```

In Essbase the calculation could look as follows:

```
If (@Curlev(Geography) = 0)
 "Region share" = Sales / @ParentVal (Geography, Sales)
Else
    "Region share" = #Missing
Endif
```

In Express, the calculation could look as follows:

```
Limit Geography to Store_level 'Store'
Region_share = Sales / Sales (Store_Region)
```

In TM1, the calculation could look as follows:

```
[Region share] =
If (ElLev ('Geography' , !Geography) = 0,
     [Sales] / DB('Sales Cube', ELPAR ('Geography' , !Geography , 1)), 0

)
```

In Microsoft, the calculation could look as follows:

```
CREATE MEMBER [Measures].[Region share] AS
'IIF (
     [Geography].CurrentMember.Level IS [Geography].[Store],
     [Measures].[Sales] / ([Measures].[Sales],
         Ancestor([Geography].CurrentMember, [Geography].[Region]) ),
         NULL
)'
```

Even without getting into syntax details, you should be able to see that each of the product languages dealt in some way with the issues of referencing the parent of the sales value in the Geography dimension, and limiting the application of the calculation to the store level of the Geography dimension and that the ways used by each of the product languages were considerably different. Since relative referencing is one of the cornerstones of dimensional applications, and since there are a variety of relative referencing functions that need to be provided for, let's look a bit more closely at how these product languages provide for it.

Sample Schemata

I will use two different schemata as the basis for illustrating the products' language and concepts. (For ease of reading, and when context is clear, I will use the otherwise slightly different-meaning terms "product language," "product syntax," "language," and "product" interchangeably in this chapter.) In order to provide a common basis for comparing product language elements, I will use the simple dimension structure outlined in Figure 19.1. This dimension will be called "Product" (with editorial hindsight, perhaps not an optimal choice). In order to illustrate product languages in use in an application, I will rely on the APB-1 schema, which is the only application schema I am aware of that has been publicly implemented by four different OLAP tool vendors.[3]

Referencing Examples

Each of these products' languages supports a different subset of OLAP dimension concepts, and also a different set of intradimensional referencing operators and semantics.

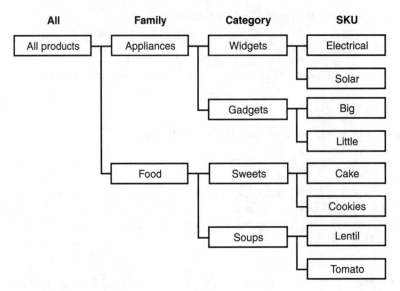

All	Family	Category	SKU

Figure 19.1   Sample product dimension outline.

Each of these products' languages supports referencing of members by name, and referencing relative to a member that is the current one in some calculation or query context. The ability to perform hierarchical referencing may be different for a product language depending on whether the point of reference is a specific named member or the current member in context.

Analysis Services 2000 (abbreviated to AS2K) uses the MDX language, which is supported to varying degrees by other servers as well. The examples here will use standard MDX to the degree possible, and I will note deviations to Microsoft-specific syntax.

Referencing a Specific Member

The simplest intradimensional reference is to refer to a specific member. For example, a formula may need to refer to the Widgets member. In some cases, the purpose may be to refer to the member; in other cases the purpose would be to refer to data at a cell that is associated with that member. In LC, referring to the member would be expressed as Product.Widgets. Each product language (or just language in the case of LC), provides a fairly straightforward way of doing this, as illustrated in Table 19.1.

The next simplest intradimensional reference is to refer to the current member in a calculation or query context. For example, Table 19.2 includes examples in each language of referencing the current member in the Product dimension in a context that is expecting or can handle a current member.

In TM1, the ! in front of a dimension's name indicates to return the name of the current member. This name is simply a string value and needs to be used in a context that will use the name to refer to the member. In Essbase, certain functions operate relative

Table 19.1 Referencing a Specific Member in a Dimension or Instance in a Type

LANGUAGE NAME	SYNTAX
LC	Product.Widgets
TM1	'Widgets'
Essbase	@Member ("Widgets")
AS2K/MDX	Product.Widgets
Express	'Widgets'

Table 19.2 Referencing the Current Member or Instance

LANGUAGE NAME	SYNTAX
LC	Product.this
LC	*no syntax, implicit*
TM1	!Product
Essbase	Product
AS2K	Product.CurrentMember
AS2K	Product *(The .CurrentMember function is implicit when omitted)*
Express	*No syntax, implicit*

to the current member of a dimension, and all that is required is to list the name of that dimension. In MDX, the .CurrentMember function returns a reference to the member. It is the default function for a dimension, so simply listing Product is adequate as well.

Referencing a Parent Member

An extremely common and usually simple type of reference is to refer to a parent member within a hierarchy. We will do that relative to the member Widgets in the Product dimension. Although parent in a hierarchy is a simple concept, using it in a product's language immediately brings to light some striking differences in these languages.

TM1, Essbase, and Analysis Services provide a single, hierarchical-dimension data structure. Members and hierarchical relationships between them are all contained within the dimension. Express, however, provides for hierarchies by associating a *relation* data structure to a dimension. Furthermore, there are two different ways of using relations to implement a hierarchy, and depending on which way you choose, certain functionality and syntax is available or denied. One way is to relate two or more dimensions through a relation. This allows for the cleanest expression of level-based dimensions: Each Express dimension corresponds to a different level of the application's dimension, and relations contain the 1-*N* relationships between the parents in one level and the children in another. However, as far as Express is concerned, each dimension is different, so the set of dimensions the application is modeling and the set of dimensions Express contains are different.

The other way to create a hierarchy in Express is to relate a dimension to itself. This allows an application's dimension to directly correspond to a single Express dimension. An application can use more robust hierarchical syntax that combines the dimension and the relations, and it can easily use members from more than one dimension. (Other differences will become apparent when we look at adjacency later on in this chapter.)

For the purposes of describing the Express language as used to define a dimension per level, we will use three dimensions: Prod_Family, Prod_Category, and Prod_SKU. The relation Fam_Cat_R will relate each category to its family, and the Cat_SKU_R relation will relate each SKU to its category. For the Express language in an embedded-total dimension, we will use one dimension called product, with a Parent_Prod_R relation that relates each product to its parent in the hierarchy.

Express provides both a simple syntax that can be used with relations, and a LIMIT() function that can be used to construct arbitrarily complicated sets of members. We will use both of these syntaxes when possible.

Essbase provides separate functions to retrieve data associated with a parent and to retrieve a reference to the parent member, (@ParentVal() and @Parent()). For this example, we are interested in accessing the parent member itself. In TM1, we need to provide an index for the parent, since a TM1 dimension is not strictly hierarchical. A member can have more than one parent, making it a network (directed acyclic graph) instead of a hierarchy (see Table 19.3).

Table 19.3   Referencing a Parent of a Specific Member

LANGUAGE NAME	SYNTAX
LC	Widgets.up(1) or Widgets.Parent
TM1	ELPAR('Product', 'Widgets', 1) *the 1 means "take the first parent"*
Essbase	@Parent (@Member ("Widgets"))
MDX	Widgets.Parent
Express (using levels, and a relation named ProdFamily_R)	Fam_Cat_R (Prod_Category 'Widgets')
Express (using embedded-total dimension)	Parent_Prod_R (Product 'Widgets')
Express (using embedded-total dimension)	Limit (Limit Product To 'Widgets') To Parents Using Parent_Prod_R

Table 19.4   Referencing a Parent of an Unspecified Member

LANGUAGE NAME	SYNTAX
LC	Product.up(1) or Product.Parent
TM1	ELPAR('Product', !Product, 1)
Essbase	@Parent(Product)
AS2K	Product.CurrentMember.Parent
AS2K	Product.Parent
Express (using levels, and a relation named ProdFamily_R)	Fam_Cat_R
Express (using embedded-total dimension)	Parent_Prod_R

Often, we want to retrieve the parent member relative to an arbitrary member in a calculation or context. Table 19.4 shows the syntax in each of the representative languages.

Referencing the Set of Children

Selecting the children of a member is also a common operation in OLAP systems. This is an operation that returns a set of members rather than a single member.

Unlike the other product languages described here, TM1 does not permit declarative access in its Rules language to the set of children for a member. It does permit access to the count of children and the Nth child, but no iteration primitives are provided to actually loop through the N children.

The syntax for each of the commercial products is found in Table 19.5.

Previous and Next Members (Lag and Lead)

Each of the product languages that we are contrasting makes the order of members explicit in a dimension. This ordering is available for use by an application and may be easier or more difficult to maintain. The ordering may be leveraged in a database and by expressions and queries. (For example, time-series analysis frequently makes use of the database ordering of members.) The simplest ordering-based operation is to access the previous or next member in the level, which assumes, as was shown in Chapter 5, at least an ordinal ordering.

Surprisingly, OLAP products and languages vary significantly in how they support ordering and ordering per level. In TM1, and in embedded-total dimensions in Express, all members of a dimension share a single numbering system, regardless of level. For example, in a time dimension, all days, months, quarters, and years are numbered

Table 19.5 Referencing the Children of a Member

PRODUCT	SYNTAX
LC	Product.Widgets.down(1) or Product.Widgets.Children
TM1	*not possible*
Essbase	@Children (Widgets)
AS2K	Product.Widgets.Children
Express (using levels, and a relation named ProdCategory_R)	Cat_SKU_R 'Widgets' *implicitly selects the SKU members related to Widgets*
Express (using embedded-total dimension)	Parent_Prod_R 'Widgets'
Express (using embedded-total dimension)	Limit (Limit Product To 'Widgets') To Children Using Parent_Prod_R

together in a flat dimension; the first 31 members might be days, the next member might be a month, the next 28 members days, the next member a month, and so on. Thus, simply saying "give me the next member" might not return a member from the same level; additional understanding needs to be built into the application logic to know when to access the next member and when to access some other member. In Express, using separate dimensions as separate levels of an application dimension avoids this issue.

In Essbase, you cannot refer to members relative to a member. You can, however, refer to data from an ordinally related member. The function that looks up the next or previous member can take an arbitrary ordered list of members in which to look up the next or previous member. If no list is provided, the member might come from another level in the hierarchy, but usually the list will include all members from the appropriate level.

In AS2K, ordinal relationships are maintained per level. This frees a developer from needing to consider the other levels of a hierarchy (see Table 19.6).

Referring to Ancestors

In addition to referring to parent members, we frequently need to refer to ancestor members above the parent. Each product provides some mechanism for this. Express can provide ancestor members at a particular named level within an embedded-total only if additional information is provided that specifies the level for each member. This can be accomplished in more than one way. One way would be to include an additional dimension that lists the levels of the modeled dimension (call this the *level dimension*) and a relation between the level dimension and the main dimension that relates each member of the main dimension to the level dimension member representing its level.

Table 19.6 Previous and Next Members

LANGUAGE NAME	SYNTAX
LC	Time.Dec2001.-1
TM1	DimIX('Time', 'Dec2001')-1 *requires logic to ensure that this index points to the correct level*
Essbase	@Prior ("Dec2001" @LevMbrs (Time, 3)) *cell value reference only*
AS2K	Time.Dec2001.PrevMember
Express (using levels)	Lag('Dec2001', 1, Months)
Express (using embedded-total dimension)	Lag('Dec2001', 1, TimePeriod) *requires logic to ensure that this index points to the correct level*

This is the approach that we will use when providing an example of choosing an ancestor member at a particular named level. The Express dimension whose members represent the product levels is called Product.Level, and the multidimensional relation between it and products is called ProdLevel_R (dimensioned by Product and Product.Level).

A similar approach can be used in TM1, using what are called *string cubes* in that product. The TM1 string cube is called ProdLevels. The dimension whose members represent the product levels does not need to be named in the expression that references the ancestor. Essbase and Analysis Services provide a direct ancestor mechanism within their hierarchy structures.

Table 19.7 shows the syntax in each of the commercial product languages.

The Essbase @Ancest() function only works on the current member of a dimension; it cannot be made to directly work on a named member. Essbase does provide the @Ancestors() function, which can work on a named member. However, @Ancestors() returns all ancestor members above the given member, so if you want one in particular, you need to strip away the unnecessary ones with the @Remove() function. Table 19.8 shows the syntax in each product.

The last example to illustrate referencing ancestors shows how to reference an ancestor at a named level, as opposed to some number of steps up. For the purpose of this example, we will reference the Family-level ancestor of the Lentil member. In Essbase, levels and generations can be assigned names, so that the Family level in our sample outline can be given the name Family. However, there is no direct syntax to determine the number associated with a name, nor are there functions that can indirectly arrive at the number of the next level down. By knowing the number corresponding to the depth or height in the hierarchy of Family members, though, we can use the numbers of the ancestors as shown in Table 19.9.

Table 19.7   Current Member Ancestors

LANGUAGE NAME	SYNTAX
LC	Product.up(2)
TM1	ELPAR('Product', ELPAR('Product', !Product, 1), 1) *impossible to do otherwise*
Essbase	@Ancest (Product, @CurGen (Product) - 2)
AS2K	Ancestor (Product.CurrentMember, 2) *this is a Microsoft extension, no way to access relative levels in standard MDX*
Express (using levels)	Fam_Cat_R Cat_SKU_R
Express (using embedded-total dimension)	ProdLevel_R ProdLevel_R
Express (using embedded-total dimension)	limit (limit (etproduct to parents using parent.etprod) to parents using parent.etprod)

Table 19.8   The Ancestor of a Particular Member

LANGUAGE NAME	SYNTAX
LC	Product.Big.Up(2)
TM1	ELPAR('Product', ELPAR('Product', 'Big', 1), 1) *impossible to do otherwise*
Essbase	@Remove(@Ancestors ("Big", @Gen ("Big") - 2), @Ancestors ("Big", @Gen ("Big") - 1))
AS2K	Ancestor (Product.Big, 2) *this is a Microsoft extension, no way to access relative levels in standard MDX*
Express (using levels)	Fam_Cat_R Cat_SKU_R 'Big'
Express (using embedded-total dimension)	ProdLevel_R ProdLevel_R 'Big'
Express (using embedded-total dimension)	limit (limit (limit (etproduct to 'Big') to parents using parent.etprod) to parents using parent.etprod)

Table 19.9 Named-Level Ancestor Referencing

LANGUAGE NAME	SYNTAX
LC	Product.Lentil.Family.
TM1	DB ('ProdLevels', DIMIX('Product', 'Lentil'), 'Family')
Essbase	@Remove(@Ancestors ("Lentil", 1), @Ancestors ("Lentil", 2))
AS2K	Ancestor(Product.Lentil, Product.Family)
Express (using levels)	Fam_Cat_R Cat_SKU_R 'Lentil'
Express (using embedded-total dimension)	ProdLevel_R (Product.Level 'Family' Product 'Lentil')

Descendants

The last form of hierarchical referencing I am going to explore in this chapter is referencing a set of descendants of a member. Two different collections of descendants are frequently referenced: all descendants of a member, and the leaf-level descendants. In the interests of chapter length, I won't go into the referencing of all descendants at a particular level.

Table 19.10 shows the syntax required in each of the languages.

To reference just the leaf-level descendants of the food, the Express embedded-total version of this selects all descendants and removes all parents within the list of descendants, leaving the leaf members. The Express level-wise version of this relies on knowing the number of intervening relations between Widgets and the leaf level. In order to

Table 19.10 Ragged Hierarchy Descendants Referencing

LANGUAGE NAME	SYNTAX
LC	Products.Food.AtUnder.
TM1	*not possible*
Essbase	@IDescendants (Food)
AS2K	Descendants (Product.Food)
Express (using levels)	*not possible*
Express (using embedded-total dimension)	Limit (Limit (Product To 'Food') To Descendants Using ProdTree_R

Table 19.11   Leaf Referencing

LANGUAGE NAME	SYNTAX
LC	Product.Food.Leaf.
TM1	*not possible*
Essbase	@Descendants (Food, 0)
AS2K	Descendants (Product.Food,,LEAVES) *this is a Microsoft extension*
Express (using levels)	Cat_SKU_R Fam_Cat_R 'Food'
Express (using embedded-total dimension)	Limit(Limit (Limit (Product To 'Food') To Descendants Using ProdTree_R) Remove Parents Using Using ProdTree_R)

perform the reference, the relations are chained together; from right to left, the categories corresponding to family Widgets are selected and then the SKUs corresponding to those categories are selected.

Table 19.11 shows the syntax required in each of the languages.

Although each tool provides syntax to perform most or all of the common referencing needs within a dimension, the structural and functional differences between products influence the implementation of the dimensions and as a result the syntax to employ as well.

Treatment of Missing and Inapplicable Cells (Instances)

Missing and inapplicable instances of types are handled in different ways between the products. Only one product that I am aware of even claims to handle the distinction between missing and inapplicable values (Media, from Speedware). Most products provide some recognition of nonvalues at cell locations. For example, Oracle Express uses NA, Hyperion Essbase uses #MISSING, and Microsoft Analysis Services has a NULL. Applix TM1 makes no distinction between nonvalue and 0; every cell in a cube has either a 0 or a nonzero value associated with it (unless the cube holds strings). But when a product does not provide the distinction between inapplicable and empty, you have no way to know what the lack of data signifies.

Empty cells frequently arise as a result of no transactions taking place where they are applicable, and hence a zero value can be imputed. This is a common, rudimentary data compression typically used in databases and is the case that TM1 was designed to handle. Other systems have techniques to make it easier to treat nonvalues as 0 or another value; generally speaking, some automatic conversion to 0 is provided. Microsoft's MDX automatically treats NULL as zero in most cases; the NASKIP and NASKIP2 options in Oracle Express control whether NA values are converted to zero.

Hyperion Essbase will treat #MISSING as either 0 or make the calculation result equal to #MISSING, depending on the operator or function it is being input to. Each of their languages provides one or more ways to test a cell for not having a value, so that function logic can be altered (for example, to ensure that the result of the calculation is itself not a value) or a substitution can be made.

Handling Calculation Precedence

All OLAP products provide some means of controlling precedence of dimensional calculations. Given that most products provide at least two different mechanisms for calculations, the control is not always straightforward. For example, if some cells are calculated on-the-fly in response to a query, while others are precalculated in advance, there may be procedural issues as well as precedence issues between the two types of calculations. However, precalculation scripts make precedence straightforward, as you can simply calculate some cells earlier and other cells later. Some products (not discussed in this chapter) provide heuristic algorithms to determine precedence based on the typical use of operators, such as taking ratios after calculating differences and sums.

Oracle Express has relatively simple control over dimensional precedence. Calculation procedures perform all calculations for stored variables in the order you list them in the script. Models, which can calculate variables using equations on more than one dimension, enlist a simultaneous equation solver that does not try to resolve precedence. Formulas, which are calculated on-the-fly, only have one formula, and hence issues of precedence are reduced to issues of which formula depends on which other formula.

Essbase provides straightforward precedence control in calculation scripts as well by the user or DBA ordering the calculations to be performed. However, if the DBA requests Essbase to simply calculate the database using the dimensional formulas described in the dimensional meta data, an intricate ordering is used based on the following factors:

- Whether the dimension is an account, a time dimension, or another dimension
  - Formulas associated with the members of an accounts dimension are resolved according to the order in which the account members are listed.
- Whether the dimension is treated as sparse or dense
- Whether the calculation should be carried out once or more than once ("two-pass")

Cells calculated on-the-fly in response to a query have a similar but not identical precedence as those that are precalculated.

TM1 provides a single ordered list of all calculation rules in a cube. The first rule that applies to a cell as the cell is being calculated is the rule used to calculate it. If there are general rules for larger regions of the cube, and exceptions to those rules for subregions of those regions, the exceptions need to be listed first to take effect. (This makes rule ordering and management critical to a TM1 developer.) Microsoft's AS2K uses a single list of calculation rules in a cube, where rules are ordered by a solve order number to determine their position in the list, and where ties in the list are resolved by the dimension's order in the cube.

Basic Formulas

To illustrate formulas, I will show them in the context of an application. As I mentioned earlier, the only standard application available is the OLAP Council's APB-1. The following is an illustrative section of the Oracle Express and Hyperion Essbase code implemented by the vendors themselves to perform the benchmark, along with an implementation of the benchmark schema that we performed at the DSS Lab in Microsoft's Analysis Services.

The APB-1 benchmark has six model dimensions: Time, Customer, Product, Channel, Measure, and Scenario. The most instructive way to highlight the differences between products is to look at how they handle the more complicated forecasting calculations. Figure 19.2 shows the dimensions and levels, and illustrates the calculation requirements for computing forecast measures.

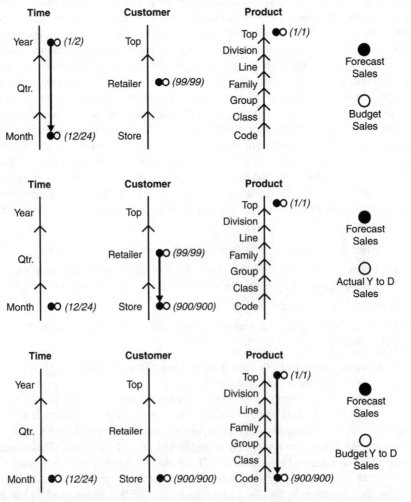

Figure 19.2   MDS of APB-1 allocation calculation application ranges.

The benchmark defines the forecasting requirements as follows:

"Calculate total 1996 forecast values by the retailer level of the customer hierarchy as the annualized values of the second half actuals of 1995 increased by 15 percent. Allocate to the months in 1996 based on the 1996 budget. Allocate to the stores from the retailer based on the year-to-date actuals. Allocate to products based on year-to-date budget." (Implicitly, the all level of the product hierarchy is in effect until the last step.)

As described there are three separate allocation steps. I will focus here on the last two time- and customer-based allocations. Also, I should mention that the total effort required to perform these calculations is distributed across the tools application logic. Some effort is put into the immediate formula; some is put into dimensional formulas; some is encoded directly into the dimensional structures; and some is dispersed throughout the application. I'll begin by looking at the immediate formulas.

Scope, or range specification, is a crucial concept for all OLAP applications. The calculation requirements include both formula requirements (annualized values increased by 15 percent, allocated values based on year-to-date actuals) and application range specifications (for example, 1996 values by retailer by all product, months of 1996 by retailer by all product, months of 1996 by store by all product). The product implementations of this benchmark application afford insights into different techniques for specifying application ranges.

The code of Figure 19.3 is a subset of the formula that is associated with the Forecast scenario member in the Essbase database. The IF clauses in this overall formula for the Forecast member set the application range for each equation within it. The first three IF clauses ensure that the formula is only being executed at the Channel member, the Product member, and either the Customer member or its children (the retailer members). Remember, in Essbase a dimension is identified by a member with the dimension's name, and that member is typically the All member in that dimension. The fourth IF clause checks to see if the time is the 1996 member that corresponds to the first clause of the requirement. The fifth IF checks to see that the measure is one of the additive measures that will be allocated.

For cells within this application range, data for the Forecast scenario is computed as 2.3 times the Q3 + Q4 values, which corresponds to annualizing that sum and increasing it by 15 percent. Note that specifying an intersection of members from more than one dimension is carried out by the -> operator in Essbase, so that "Actual->1995Q3" specifies data from (in LC) Scenario.Actual and Time.1995Q3.The first ELSE clause then checks to see, since the time member is not 1996, if it is either under 1996 or at the 199606YTD member (used for calculating year-to-date values); if either of those conditions are true, then the annualized value is multiplied by the ratio of the budget scenario's data to the budget scenario's data at 1996, which implements the allocation to the months, allocated down from the customer parent based on the ratio of the actual year-to-date value to the customer parent's actual year-to-date value.

The second ELSE now sets up the allocation to stores from retailers, since the formula is not executing at either a retailer or the Customer root member. The allocation references the data value at the parent of the current Customer member using the @ParentVal() function once for the forecast data and once for the actual year-to-date data.

All of this logic for the Forecast scenario member calculation uses conditional logic embedded within a formula to define application ranges. In calculation scripts, used to

```
IF(@ISMBR("Channel"))
  IF (@ISMBR("Product"))
    IF (@ISICH"ILD("Customer"))
      IF (@ISMBR("1996"))
        // annualized values increased by 15%
        IF (@ISMBR("Sales In Units", "Cost In Dollars", "Dollar
Sales"))
          Forecast = (Actual->"1995Q3"+ Actual->"1995Q4") * 2.3;
        ENDIF;
      ELSE
        IF (@ISDESC("1996") OR @ISMBR("199606YTD"))
          // allocate to the months based on 1996 budget
          Forecast =((Actual->"1995Q3"+ Actual->"1995Q4") * 2.3)
                   * (Budget->Channel / Budget->Channel->"1996");
        ENDIF;
      ENDIF;
    ELSE
      IF (@ISDESC("1996") OR @ISMBR("199606YTD"))
        IF (@ISMBR("Sales In Units", "Cost In Dollars", "Dollar
Sales"))
          // allocate to the stores based on year-to-date actuals
          Forecast=@PARENTVAL(Customer,Forecast) *
                 (Actual->"199606YTD" / @PARENTVAL(Customer,Actual-
>"199606YTD"));
        ENDIF;
      ENDIF;
    ENDIF;
  . . .
```

Figure 19.3 Essbase code from APB-1 forecast calculation.

precalculate portions of an Essbase database, other syntax is available to confine the application range of a formula.

Let us look now at Oracle's implementation of the APB-1 in Express 6.3. The relevant section of Express Stored Procedure Language (SPL) is shown in Figure 19.4.

Like the Essbase formula, Oracle's Express formula begins by identifying a scope and then defining the calculation to take place over that scope. Rather than being computed entirely on-the-fly through a run-time formula, Express is precalculating values. Thus, this is a script that is run, and the LIMIT command is being used to limit the scope within the script. This fragment of script uses entities that aren't necessary from a logic point of view but help increase its speed (this was a performance benchmark, after all), and we won't discuss them in detail. Note the statement limit CUST to CUST_LEVEL 'Retailer,' which sets the CUST dimension to all members corresponding to the retailer level; CUST_LEVEL is an Express relation that connects all members to their appropriate level.

```
    limit PROD to PROD_TOP_R
    limit CHAN to CHAN_TOP_R
    limit CUST to CUST_LEVEL 'Retailer'
    limit MEASURE to all
    limit TIME to '1996'
    _TimePer1 = '1995Q3'
    _TimePer2 = '1995Q4'


"       Compute first step of annualized second-half sales:

XFCST = ( ACTUAL( TIME _TimePer1) + ACTUAL( TIME _TimePer2) ) * 2
* 1.15


"       Compute CUST_TOP:
aggregate XFCST using FCST_C_AGG

limit CUST add CUST_TOP_R

 " 'Allocate to months, qtrs, ytd in 1996 based on the 1996
budget.'
limit TIME to descendants using TIME_TIME '1996'
limit TIME add '1996Ytd'
_TimePer1 = '1996'
XFCST = XFCST(TIME _TimePer1) * (BUDGET/BUDGET(TIME _TimePer1))

 " 'Allocate to the stores from retailer based current YTD
actuals.'
limit TIME add '1996'
limit CUST to CUST_LEVEL 'Store'
    push TIME
    limit TIME to '1996Ytd'
    T_RATIO_TC = ACTUAL/ACTUAL(CUST CUST_CUST)
    pop TIME
XFCST = XFCST(CUST CUST_CUST) * T_RATIO_TC
...
```

Figure 19.4 Oracle Express code from APB-1 forecast calculation.

After setting LIMITs on dimensions to the right scope, the first calculation step computes the value of an X_FCST variable to the annualized total of Q3 and Q4 increased by 15 percent. In this implementation, ACTUAL is an Express variable that represents all data for the actual scenario. The command aggregate XFCST using FCST_C_AGG then performs an aggregation of this to the all-customer level (from the retailers). Then, the top customer is added into the scope through the limit CUST add CUST_TOP_R statement, and the time members in scope are changed to those below 1996 and the year-to-date member. Within this scope, the first allocation stage is performed by another equation for XFCST. The scope is then modified by adding 1996 back in and re-setting customers to the store level only. The time scope is then saved, the ratio for actuals to 1996 year-to-date actuals is calculated, and then the time scope is restored and the ratio applied. Note in the last line of Express code that the XFCST(CUST CUST_CUST) refers to the XFCST data at the parent level of the current customer, which in this database is the associated retailer.

Although the syntax is different and the dimensional constructs also different, the operations and logic in one tool can be recognized clearly in the other.

Let us look at the same calculations in Microsoft's version of MDX. This implementation was created by us in the DSS Lab for our own use and, unlike the foregoing two examples, does not represent a vendor implementation. Microsoft provides a feature called cell calculations in their product, where each cell calculation specifies a formula to execute over a region of a cube. The initial calculation and the first two allocations are shown in MDX in Figure 19.5.

In each CREATE CELL CALCULATION statement that declares a calculation formula, the FOR clause at the beginning specifies the region of the cube over which the calculation is in effect. The calculation named [Step 1] is applied to the 1996 member of Time, the All members of Product and Channel, the retailer level of the Customer dimension, the forecast scenario only, and across all measures. (Cell calculations are subject to formula precedence in the same way as other calculations, so this doesn't mean that all measures will be calculated by this formula. The SOLVE_ORDER number at the end of the statement controls the precedence.) As with the other implementations, the number is calculated as 2.3 times the sum of actuals for Q3 and Q4 of 1995.

The calculation named [Step 2] is applied to all descendants of 1996 for retailers, forecast, across all measures, and the All members of the Product and Channel dimensions. It calculates its results as the 1996 value allocated by the ratio of budget to 1996 budget, as required. In order to draw its 1996 data from [Step 1], it uses Microsoft's CalculationPassValue() function to retrieve data from the prior calculation pass, which is the calculation defined in [Step 1]. It is defined as using CALCULATION_PASS_NUMBER 3, whereas [Step 1] uses CALCULATION_PASS_NUMBER 2, so it follows the calculation of [Step 1]. The calculation named [Step 3] is applied to the same range as [Step 2], except that it applies to the Retailer level of the Customer dimension, and it allocates data from the retailer-level ancestors of the customers according to actual year-to-date values. It draws from the results of [Step 3] by being placed in the next calculation pass (4) and using CalculationPassValue() to retrieve results from the [Step 3] pass (pass 3).

Application Ranges in Joined Cubes

For Microsoft's AS2K, within any regular cube, all measures are dimensioned in the same way. Within a virtual cube, while every measure appears in the meta data to be dimensioned by all of the dimensions of the virtual cube, data values will only be found within a space corresponding to their base cube's dimensionality.

For Express, each variable and formula represents a hypercube. A formula or other equation that incorporates a dimension that one of its component variables or formulas

```
CREATE CELL CALCULATION CURRENTCUBE.[Step 1] FOR
'(  {[Time].[1996]}, {[Product].[All Product]},
    [Customer].[Retailer].MEMBERS, {[Channel].[All Channel]},
    {[Scenario].[Forecast]}, {Measures.ALLMEMBERS}
)' AS
'CalculationPassValue (
   (   ([Time].[1995Q3], [Scenario].[Actual])
    + ([Time].[1995Q4], [Scenario].[Actual])
   ) * 2.3,
   -1,
   RELATIVE
)', SOLVE_ORDER = 10, FORMAT_STRING = '0.000',
CALCULATION_PASS_NUMBER = '2'


CREATE CELL CALCULATION CURRENTCUBE.[Step 2] FOR
'(  DESCENDANTS([Time].[1996]), {[Product].[All Product]},
    {[Customer].[Retailer].MEMBERS}, {[Channel].[All Channel]},
    {[Scenario].[Forecast]}, {Measures.ALLMEMBERS}
)' AS
'CalculationPassValue (
   [Time].[1996]
   * [Scenario].[Budget] / ([Scenario].[Budget], [Time].[1996]),
   -1,
   RELATIVE
)', SOLVE_ORDER = 10, FORMAT_STRING = '0.000',
CALCULATION_PASS_NUMBER = '3'


CREATE CELL CALCULATION CURRENTCUBE.[Step 3] FOR
'(  DESCENDANTS([Time].[1996]), {[Product].[All Product]},
    [Customer].[Store].MEMBERS, {[Channel].[All Channel]},
    {[Scenario].[Forecast]}, {[Measures].ALLMEMBERS}
)' AS
'CalculationPassValue (
   Ancestor (
     [Customer].CurrentMember,
     [Customer].[Retailer]
   )
   * [Scenario].[Actual]
   / ([Scenario].[Actual], [Time].[199606Ytd]),
   -1,
   RELATIVE

)', SOLVE_ORDER = 10, FORMAT_STRING = '0.000',
CALCULATION_PASS_NUMBER = '4'
```

Figure 19.5 MDX for APB-1 forecast calculation.

Microsoft's AS2K					
	All Return Reason	**Damaged**	**Wrong Size**		
	Sales	**Returns**	**Sales**	**Returns**	**Sales**	**Returns**
Jan 1999	2,519	137		37		100
Feb 1999	1,033	75		45		30
Mar 1999	1,180	48		21		27
Oracle Express					
	All Return Reason	**Damaged**	**Wrong Size**		
	Sales	**Returns**	**Sales**	**Returns**	**Sales**	**Returns**
Jan 1999	2,519	137	2,519	37	2,519	100
Feb 1999	1,033	75	1,033	45	1,033	30
Mar 1999	1,180	48	1,180	21	1,180	27

Figure 19.6   Application ranges for the Sales variable when combined with Returns.

does not have will access that data regardless of where in the dimension the data is accessed.

For example, Figure 19.6 shows the application range for the sales variable when it is combined with the returns variable across the return reason dimension. In OLAP services, sales is only available at the All Return Reason member of the return reason dimension, while in Express the same sales value is replicated across every return reason.

What does this mean for the consumer of the combined data? Each system has its pros and cons. In AS2K, if you want to be able to combine the sales amount from a return reason, you need to specially reference it (usually with Microsoft's ValidMeasure() function, which exists for this purpose). In Express, you don't need to do this. However, in Express, when you are referencing the sales value across the returns dimension, you have no clue (other than going back to the meta data) that sales was not dimensioned by the return reason dimension as well.

Summary

This chapter showed how different OLAP environments, regardless of their vendor of origin, need to deal with the same set of core issues such as providing for the following:

- Rich dimensional structuring and referencing
- Application ranges
- Ways to deal with sparsity
- Ways of specifying formula precedence

It also, by way of example, gave you a taste for the different ways that vendors have tried to solve the same set of problems. Although there are many other aspects to full-blown OLAP products that were not discussed, the differences in these core modeling areas impact any application you might ever build.

DSS Fusion

Chapter 1 described the various recursively linked functions that are required to connect data with decisions: descriptive, explanatory, predictive, and prescriptive. It then went on to show:

- How the core operations or data manipulation language (DML) of OLAP or multidimensional systems corresponds to what may be called derived descriptions

- That what is typically called data mining or statistics corresponds to the combination of explanatory and predictive modeling

- That what is typically called decision analysis or optimization corresponds to prescriptive modeling

Since all of these functions need to be performed in order to connect data with decisions, it should come as no surprise that single decision support applications [whether the product of a single vendor or of multiple vendors working through appropriate Application Programming Interfaces (APIs)] ought to provide for the entire suite of decision support functions. Furthermore, most classic business problems, such as capital budgeting, product marketing, customer relationship management, mix variance for production, site selection for physical premises, activity-based management, and the creation of key performance indicators, require a combination of *at least* OLAP, data mining, decision analysis, and visualization to be properly solved.

Although reasonable strides have been taken during the past 10 years, and more products are more integrated now than ever before, currently I am not aware of any publicly available fully unified decision support system. Perhaps the best example today is that of the family of DB products coming from the intelligent database laboratory at the University of Illinois at Urbana-Champaign under the direction of Jiawei Han.

In this chapter, I add four additional logical decision support dimensions to the recursive decision function dimension described in Chapter 1:

- Media
- Something that might be called the degree of data-versus model-drivenness
- Degree of relevance
- Level of abstraction or degree of inferenceability

The resulting framework (itself a multidimensional model) encompasses all decision support functionality, including what is more typically called knowledge management (which I subsume under the rubric of Decision Support System [DSS]). In other words, any particular decision support application covers some decision function for some media with some degree of data-versus model-drivenness at some level of abstraction with some degree of relevance and some internal and external physical design (physical design being another dimension in decision support applications, which was discussed in Chapter 10). Furthermore, one can speak of integration along the decision function dimension, along the media dimension, along the data/model dimension, along the abstraction dimension, along the relevance dimension, and/or along the physical dimension.

Since the need for and challenges of creating unified decision support applications is by far more logical than physical, I will focus on the five logical dimensions in this chapter. Since within the logical challenges, the industry is closest to providing for integration along the decision function dimension, and since I would like this chapter to point ahead but not too far ahead, I will spend the most time with decision function integration as well.

Thus, this chapter:

- Provides an overview of a unified decision support framework
- Shows a variety of small, concrete examples of partial integration
- Describes a single example, coming from retail sales, of more fully integrated decision support application

As there is still much work to be done in the decision support arena, the content of this chapter is a mix of things that are being done now and things that would be nice to do or see but are still a bit too cumbersome to perform using off-the-shelf tools.

Overview of a Unified Architecture

In this section, I present in incremental stages a unified framework for decision support. The framework leverages material presented in Chapters 1, 8, 9, and 11 through 17.

It will then be used to contextualize or explain the specific examples that follow in the subsequent sections.

The Decision Function Dimension

For compactness of representation (and in keeping with the spirit of MTS), let's portray the decision function dimension described in Chapter 1, as an annotated line segment. This is shown in Table 20.1.

The Media Dimension

To this we now add a media dimension (covering the main media found in decision support applications) and show in Table 20.2 the combination of the two along with some typical functions for those intersections that have them.

In Located Contents (LC), of course we have simply created the following schema:

```
(Decision function. ⊗ Media.) ~ Functions
```

The diagram shows how the decision function dimension is most fully represented along the decision function dimension for numeric media. This is true even though multiple kinds of products are required to cover the full set of decision functions and even though those products, as you will see in this chapter, are insufficiently integrated. (Recall the counterproductive relationship between OLAP and data mining vendors described in Chapter 1.) You can also see (as I showed in *Intelligent Enterprise*, November 1998, Volume 1, #2) how the functional boundaries in the figure need not correspond to product boundaries as product features may extend beyond their principal categories.

Table 20.1   The Decision Function Dimension

DESCRIPTIVE	EXPLANATORY	PREDICTIVE	PRESCRIPTIVE

Table 20.2   Combining the Decision Function and Media Dimensions

	DESCRIPTIVE	EXPLANATORY	PREDICTIVE	PRESCRIPTIVE
Numbers	Aggregation	Clustering	Model management	Monte Carlo
Text	Term extraction	Vectorspace dot product		
Images	Edge detection	Feature comparison		
Spatial Images	Polygon mapping			

Internal and External Representation Dimensions

Now let's add, as shown in Figure 20.1, two additional and orthogonal features described in Chapters 8 and 9:

- Physical design or internal representation
- Visualization or external representation

What this diagram shows is that representation is orthogonal to both decision function and media. Visualization, or more properly external representation, is not a function that can or should only occur at some point in a decision support application. Everything at all times can be (and to a large extent is) externally represented. As you learned in Chapter 9, sometimes it is best to use a diagrammatic or visual method of representation and sometimes it is best to use a numeric display. Whichever form of representation is being used, regardless of whether a person is interacting with it, something is being used. We can certainly speak of the method of representation used for any and all decision functions or media. You should realize that this means that the media chosen for external representation need not match the media of the data input. Thus, we can use words to represent pictures, pictures to represent words, pictures to represent sounds, or sounds to represent words. By the same token, physical design or internal representation is also independent of decision function and media while at the same time every combination of media and decision function must have some physical representation.

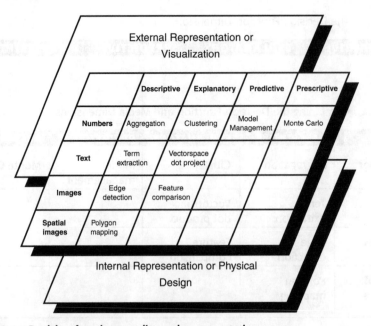

Figure 20.1 Decision function, media, and representation.

Source versus Derived Expressions

Now let's add, as shown in Figure 20.2, the distinction between source- or operations-oriented models and decision-oriented models that was made in Chapters 1 and 6 and relied upon in Part 3 (Chapters 11 thru 17). For simplicity of exposition I show only two source-oriented models connecting to a single decision-oriented model here.

The DEER Cycle

Now let's contextualize, as shown in Figure 20.3, the entire representation process (within limits and) within the decision-execution-environment-representation or DEER cycle introduced in Chapter 1.

What you can see from this diagram is that all of the decision support functions discussed so far belong to the representation stage of the DEER cycle. At the end of the day the information derived through all the decision support analyses is still only in support of a decision whose maker (that is the decision maker) may or may not follow the information derived. A manager, for example, is free to ignore any and all analytical reports. Once taken, the decision still needs to be executed, and its execution, occurring in an environment, may or may not produce the intended consequences that in turn need to be represented.[1]

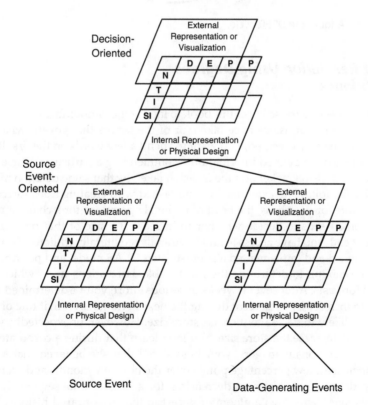

Figure 20.2   Source event versus decision-oriented modeling.

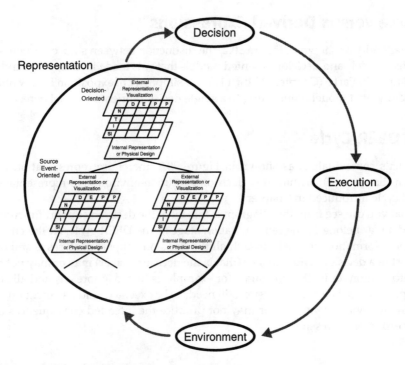

Figure 20.3   Adding the DEER cycle.

Conflict Resolution Using Degrees of Confidence

Although it is beyond the scope of this book to look at the various factors governing the proper execution of decisions once taken, or of the factors that govern what actually happens once they are executed, I do want to spend a few words on the first link: what happens between the derived information recommending a particular course of action to a particular decision maker and the decision taken by that same decision maker.

Consider the following example. You are tasked with creating sales forecasts for a particular store for your boss, the head of regional operations for a chain of retail outlets. Your boss needs to decide whether to increase the size of that particular store. Toward that end, you have access to and have analyzed literally trillions of data points. You've designed and implemented a sophisticated OLAP model and performed high-quality data mining to determine the most stable associations upon which to make your sales forecasts. After several weeks of serious effort, you've determined that sales are likely to increase by 20 percent during the next 12 months. At that rate of increase, your boss is likely to decide to increase store size. However, unexpectedly, your boss chooses not to increase the store size. You later learn that during a corporate meeting of regional operations managers, your boss stated that she believed that sales were going to increase a few percentage points over the next few months and then plateau, remaining flat and possibly even decreasing, for at least the subsequent 12 months. When questioned why such a gloomy forecast in the face of rapid historical growth, she replied, "My intuition tells me that Bill's Bargain Basement is going to open a competitive superstore in the empty mall a mile down road." Four months later, that's exactly what happened. Does your boss overriding your predictive model invalidate the notion of decision functions? **Think about it.**

To see why your boss's actions are consistent with the notion of decision functions, consider Figure 20.4, which uses a combination of the DEER cycle (showing just the representation and decision) and decision functions to represent the sequence of events just described. First you progressed through descriptive and explanatory functions to arrive at a predictive model for sales. This sequence is labeled A. At the same time, however, your boss was creating her own predictive model labeled B. So what happened is that there were two different predictive models: one you created that was data-driven, and one your boss had in her head that we'll call, for the moment, model-driven. Furthermore, these two predictions did not agree and your boss had more confidence in her prediction than in yours. As a result of going with a sales growth prediction of zero as opposed to 20 percent, your boss then made the decision to not expand the store size.

Reconciling Data- and Model-Driven Predictions

The existence of both data-driven and model-driven predictions reflects the fact that any decision function can be either data- or model-driven,[2] which is why it gets treated as a dimension of a unified decision support framework. Many people, whether in daily life or, for some, in their roles as managers, use anecdotal evidence, primitive assumptions, convictions, core beliefs, and axioms (not to mention such undesirable forms of model-driven behavior as prejudice and stereotyping) to supply either model-driven descriptions, explanations, or predictions.

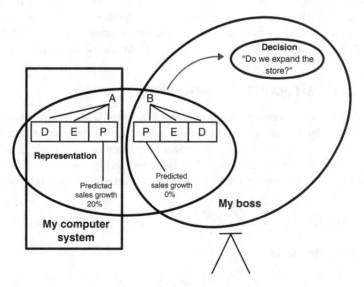

Figure 20.4 Reconciling data- and model-driven predictions.

When data- and model-driven expressions are the same, the decision support process can continue unfettered. But when data- and model-driven expressions do not agree, how are the source conflicts reconciled? When should model-based expressions override data-driven expressions? When should data-driven expressions override model-driven ones? There are no absolute answers here for the same reasons that nothing can be absolutely certain. That we need to treat some things as certain within the context of a particular argument or program or model is an entirely different matter.[3] However, before saying anything, we need to look a little more closely at what it means to be model-driven.

Model-Driven Is Knowledge-Based

A synonym for model-driven that I could have used but intentionally did not because of all its connotations was knowledge-driven or simply knowledge-based. The main connotation that gets in the way, but that will be dealt with now, is that of knowledge having something to do with text, whereas data has something to do with numbers. Although few readers may have ever found themselves saying these particular words, they are implicit in the data and knowledge management industries.

So-called knowledge management software, whether playing in the workgroup enabling space, the portal space, the personal information manager space, or the document management space, is geared more toward working with textual information, while business intelligence or decision support software is more focused on working with numbers. Can this be true? Is the relationship between data and knowledge roughly equivalent to the relationship between numbers and text? **Think about it.**

Since a real unification of decision support requires the integration of so-called business intelligence and knowledge management systems, I will use this section to show that the relationship between data and knowledge has nothing to do with the distinction between numbers and text. Rather, the distinction is the media and decision function invariant (which is why I treat it as yet another dimension in a unified decision support framework). The remainder of this section is based on a column I wrote for *Intelligent Enterprise* in April 2000 called simply "Data and Knowledge."

Levels of Abstraction Dimension

Consider the following example-pairs intended to show that the distinction between data and knowledge has nothing to do with whether the information is numeric or textual, or even visual. Each example pair shows a representative sample of what would typically be called data in the A section, and what would typically be called knowledge in the B section. The three example pairs represent numeric, textual, and visual media.

Numeric Media

Numeric So-Called Data

```
02/02/02 Sales Cambridge $10,000
```

This is a typical example of numeric data as it might appear in any query or reporting tool or spreadsheet. The $10,000 is the so-called numeric data, measure, fact, or variable; it represents the amount of sales in Cambridge on 02/02/02. Other examples include just about any fact table in a data warehouse: dollars spent as found in an expense report, budget dollars entered into spreadsheets, entries in the general ledger, and just about all filled cells in multidimensional databases.

Numeric So-Called Knowledge

$$\text{Sales}(t_n) = x_1 \times \text{Sales}(t_{n-1}) + x_2 \times \Delta \text{ interest rates} + x_3 \times \Delta \text{ prices}$$

Another, somewhat wordy, but still essentially numeric, example would be: "Stores with less than 10,000 products have top quintile earnings per product in areas where population density is less than 200 persons per square mile."

Most relationships as discovered through data mining or statistics represent numeric knowledge. This knowledge includes everything from sales forecasts, unemployment drivers, and price elasticity of demand to market-basket association coefficients, options pricing models, and customer segmentation analyses. Vast amounts of corporate knowledge are in numeric form.

Textual Media

Textual So-Called Data

- Customer Bob Jones had a bad encounter with service representative Charley Johnson at 3:00 p.m. on 02/02/02.
- The weather in Cambridge on 02/02/02 was sunny.

It's easy to see how each of these examples could have been portrayed as dimensional grids with a qualitative or text variable in the cells, namely the type of encounter in the first example and the type of weather in the second.

In fact, most qualitative attributes for the dimensions in a data warehouse would qualify as textual data. This includes, for example, package type, product color, the name of the store manager, customer address, sex, and family status.

Textual So-Called Knowledge

- All of our competitors that are growing faster than us have poorer customer service.
- All plants absorb CO_2 and emit O_2.

Snippets of wisdom, rules of thumb, business procedures, best practices, and customs typically find their expression in textual form. A lot of textual-form corporate knowledge goes up and down the elevators every day. Collecting and sharing it is more of a cultural than technical challenge.

Visual Media

Visual So-Called Data

Although the information in Figure 20.5 is visual and we typically think of visual information as portraying knowledge and insight, in this case it shows no more than two simple data points.

Visual So-Called Knowledge

In Figure 20.6, the visual information shows relationships between product prices, earnings, and location. This graph is a classic example of visually represented knowledge.

These examples show that data and knowledge can come in any medium or form. The term "data" does not mean numeric, and the term "knowledge" does not mean textual. So, medium plays no role in distinguishing data from knowledge, but what does?

From these examples, you can see that the concept of generality, abstraction, or inference support seems to play an important role in distinguishing knowledge from data.

Single facts or assertions such as, "The Paris store sold 100 pairs of shoes yesterday," would seem to have very low inference support and thus their support for decision-making would seem to be limited. Given only this sales figure, for example, the only decision you could make is how many shoes sold on that day in Paris. Regardless of

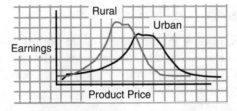

Figure 20.5 This information is visual, but not knowledge.

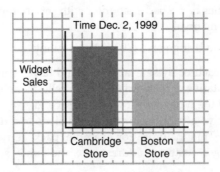

Figure 20.6 A classic example of visually represented knowledge.

the medium of expression, single facts or assertions with low inference support typically function in the context of decision-making as what we typically call data.

In contrast, statements of the type, "Women's shoes are selling much faster than expected in Europe," are far more general, applying to many situations. They could thus enable all sorts of stocking and drill-down decisions for those stores where women's shoes are not selling well.

General facts or assertions with high inference support typically function in the context of decision-making as what we typically call knowledge.

Data Versus Knowledge Dimension

Certainly, all of the preceding knowledge examples are more general in their scope than the corresponding data examples. So the degree of generality or abstraction does appear to be a factor in distinguishing data from knowledge. But is it *the* defining factor? Think about it as you consider the following two examples.

Imagine you are a midlevel analyst with a national security service and you witnessed some events including secret information being copied and handed over to foreign agents by the head of your agency. You now know that the head of the service is a secret agent for a foreign country. This piece of information is very specific; it has low inferencing capability, just like data. But it is very important.

This one simple fact—no more general than "Bob Jones is a loyal customer"—if believed, would generate an entire sequence of actions: secret meetings with associates, attempts to discover the scope of the infiltration, possibly an assassination attempt, and certainly a search for the real president. By any normal use of the term *knowledge*, the fact that the head of a national security agency is a mole would be considered vital, strategic knowledge and would deserve a place in your knowledge management system (albeit with tight access privileges). So a statement doesn't have to have high inferencing capability to be knowledge.

Now imagine you are VP of marketing for an automobile company and you've just attended a seminar (albeit a rather low-quality seminar) where you learned that "small children don't buy your products." This statement has an extremely high inferencing capability. There are a huge number of small children in the world. For every small child you might encounter, you could infer that that child will not buy your cars so don't waste your resources marketing to that child. However, it is fairly irrelevant because it would never apply to any decisions you are likely to make. I doubt you would store and manage this piece of information in your knowledge-management application.

Knowledge Defined

Thus, the notion of abstraction or generality is neither a necessary nor a sufficient condition for considering a piece of information as knowledge. In practical terms, in other words, you would not want to expend energy collecting, storing, verifying, or managing it for decision-making purposes.

I'm not trying to suggest that we load our knowledge bases with masses of specific facts or that high inference-supporting assertions aren't extremely useful. Rather, I am trying to bring home the point that pragmatically speaking, knowledge[4] should be thought of as comprising that body of assertions, both specific and general, that we believe to be true and that are most relevant to the decisions we need to make.

So the difference between data and knowledge is not a matter of media or abstraction. The difference is functional. Consider the following examples of knowledge-playing assertions used for decision-making.

Examples of Knowledge Used for Decision Making

- A set of rules for calculating the likelihood that a potential borrower defaults on a loan, which may have been generated with a data-mining package, is relevant knowledge for deciding whether or not to loan someone money. In practice, data about a person would be submitted and, through the use of loan knowledge, a decision would be reached regarding whether to loan the money.

- A set of formulas, which may have been created in an OLAP environment, for calculating how to determine the earnings a product generates is relevant knowledge for making decisions about whether to increase or decrease production of that product.

- A set of procedures, which may have been created in a marketing document, for displaying packages in stores is relevant knowledge for making decisions about where to display products or even which stores to work with.

Concluding Remarks on Data and Knowledge

Metaphorically speaking, the relationship between data and knowledge is akin to that between a river and its bank. The former is best represented as a continuously moving flow of information or assertions, while the latter is best represented as a set of constraints that at any given time determines the direction of that flow. Furthermore, over time, the river will change the form of the bank. Our knowledge is constantly being affected by new data, and if you look close, you will see that the river contains pieces of the bank and the bank contains water from the river. In that sense the concept of pure data or pure knowledge is as much a theoretical limit as the notions of pure river or pure bank. Thus, knowledge, especially the abstract component of knowledge that comprises the slowly changing local regularities derived from explanatory modeling, needs to be constantly tested and maintained. (Whether that testing is done hourly or yearly is, of course, a function of the specific domain.)

Knowledge is embedded in many different places within today's corporate information systems: formulas in OLAP systems, triggers in relational databases, visual patterns in GIS systems, predictive models in data-mining packages, classification rules and personal profiles in text engine-based applications, business procedures in rules-automation systems, and drivers in decision-analysis tools. All the various sources need to be integrated for unified decision support systems.

Concluding Remarks on a Unified Decision Support Framework

In this section, you've seen OLAP as defined by the data definition language (DDL) and DML described in this book contextualized within a larger decision support framework that includes the set of functions required to connect data to decisions, various media, degrees of abstraction and relevance, and differences between input and derived data, which itself was bundled within a DEER cycle that encompasses the representational activity within a cycle of decisions, executions of decisions, the environment, and representation.

Smaller, Multifunction Tasks

Although no product may provide fully integrated capabilities, many products and applications have provided for some integration across some dimension(s). A sample variety of discrete multifunction capabilities that are either directly provided by some products or that can be done using today's tools and a bit of elbow grease is briefly outlined in the following section. The discussion begins with functions that integrate OLAP and data mining or statistics.

Integrating OLAP and Data Mining or Statistics

Testing for Independence between Dimensions

In practice, we are always viewing and analyzing variables (y's) with respect to locator dimensions (x's). We may view the value of a sales variable for some product dimension value and some time dimension value, or we may analyze changes in sales as a function of changes in product or time.

All analysis can be built from these simple beginnings. Viewing or specifying the change in some variable as a function of changes in some dimension is equivalent to defining a partial derivative for the variables function. Add a little complexity and you can specify the second order derivative as the change in change of some variable with respect to the change in change of some dimension. Going further, one can specify the ratio, or change in ratio, or change in change of ratio between two or more variables, still for some dimension, change in dimension, or change in change in some dimension. In other words, all views and analyses of variables are relative to some dimension value or location. This location serves the role of framework for viewing and analysis.

Now what happens if you are trying to analyze for some customer how sales to that customer varied across stores in a sales data set where store and customer are identifier dimensions, and it turns out that customer and store are correlated? What would it mean to analyze how sales to a customer varied exclusively across stores? You might get an answer such as sales were at some value for one store, and zero for all other stores. But this isn't meaningful information about sales trends per customer. (Would you now go about trying to increase sales across the stores that experienced zero sales to that customer? Probably, you would not take such a course of action.)

Rather, the information confirms that the customer shops at a particular store (which is to say that customer IDs are correlated with store IDs), and that changes observed for the variable sales are not totally attributable to changes in store. You will not be able to look at an accurate partial derivative of customer sales on a store until the influence of the store's correlation with customers has been totally compensated for, or else eliminated.

For the purposes of dimension-specific analysis of variance, it is important that changes in the values of any locator dimension are uncorrelated with changes in the values of any other locator dimension. To the degree that the locators are interdependent, they can no longer serve as separable factors.

The independence or dependence between different locator dimensions is a function of the use of the dimensions in a particular data set. In other words, two dimensions that may be independent in one data set can be dependent in another. So the best way to look at the degree to which your dimensions are independent is to examine the data sets from whence they came.

In general, and always relative to a particular data set, two dimensions can be coexistent and independent, coexistent and interdependent, or noncoexistent. In order to discover the degree to which your dimensions are independent, I suggest drawing a diagram of the cross product of the two dimensions. If the two dimensions are totally independent, every one of the possible intersections will be valid as shown in Figure 20.7. If there are some dependencies between the two dimensions, this will show in a reduction of the number of valid intersections as depicted in Figure 20.8. If the two dimensions are totally dependent, their relationship will appear as a line within the matrix as shown in Figure 20.9. I also suggest using scatter plots and parallel coordinates to look at the dependencies between dimensions. Recall the use of parallel coordinates in Chapter 9.

Focusing for the moment on just two dimensions, if the dimensions are independent of each other, they can both be used as locators. When there is interdependence, any one should be used as a locator, and the other one as variable. For example, if store and

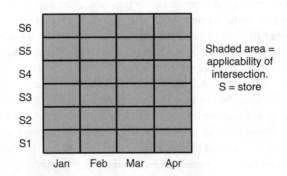

Figure 20.7 Independent dimensions.

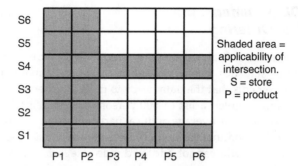

Figure 20.8 Some dependencies between dimensions.

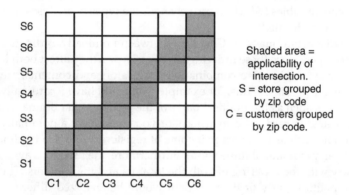

Figure 20.9 Interdependent dimensions.

customer are correlated, you can treat stores as the dependent dimension with customer as the independent dimension or vice versa. You might look at store facts per customer as a function of customer facts. This tells you information about the stores that different types of customers like. Alternately, you can treat customers as the dependent dimension with stores as the independent dimension. Here you would look at customer facts per store like the income and education distribution of the customers for store x.

By treating customer and store as interdependent, you succeed in squeezing a maximum amount of information from your data set. Of course, things get more complicated as the number of dimensions increases because the degree of independence of two dimensions may be a function of the values of the other dimensions. Furthermore, dimensions may only be independent of other dimensions for a subset of their possible values. Some products may be correlated with some stores. Some customers may be correlated with some products. Some store may be correlated with some times. Nevertheless, the principle of looking at interdependencies remains the same.

Combining OLAP Dimensions with Statistical Ordering

Regardless of the area, most analyses are performed with the aide of mathematics such as algebra, calculus, statistics, geometry, and sets. Different mathematical analyses have different requirements that the data needs to meet in order for the analysis to be performed. For example, given a list of 500 persons and their political affiliation, it makes no sense to calculate the average political party of the group. Political parties are values of a categorical or nominal variable. There is no way to take the average of a categorical variable because you cannot add or divide categories. You could, however, count the number of persons in each political party, create a histogram of those counts from which you could sort the political parties by their count, and identify the mode or political party having the highest count.

This section describes the interplay of ordering and statistical analysis.[5] It explores how the ordering of dimensions and variables affects the types of analyses that can be performed, and looks at how the process of analysis changes the ordering of the dimensions and variables (which in turn changes the types of analyses that can subsequently be performed).

Recall the distinction made in Chapter 5 between nominally, ordinally, and cardinally ordered types. Since these orderings apply to types, they affect both locators and contents. Since expressions are combinations of locators and contents, any combination of ordering is possible. Thus, for example, you could have a cardinally organized nominal variable, such as the political party of the president (a nominal variable) represented over time (a cardinal dimension), or you could have a nominally organized cardinal variable such as the average income of registered voters (a cardinal variable) per political party (a nominal dimension). Furthermore, the functions available to analyze data vary with the ordering of both the locators and the contents. Thus, the time series of the political party of the president would be analyzed differently from the party-organized income data.

Typical OLAP models are composed of nominally ordered locator dimensions such as products, stores (or rather the way products and stores are typically treated), one cardinally ordered dimension, time, and a set of cardinally ordered variables such as sales and costs. This is due to the domains where OLAP usage has sprung up and to the limitations of OLAP products. Looking ahead, OLAP environments will need to make greater use of cardinally ordered dimensions as well as nominally and ordinally ordered variables if they are to serve the needs of the enterprise business and analytical community. Cardinally ordered dimensions are critical for analysis of variance, and nominally ordered variables are commonly found in analytical models.

Orderings Change during the Analytical Process

An important part of the analytical process is the incorporation of newly learned information into the model. For example, you may start off with a nominally ordered list of countries and the per capita incomes in each country. Then, if you want to compute the per capita income for the region, you need to find out the population of each country so you can create correctly weighted average incomes. In doing this, however, you have added information to your country dimension. Instead of just a list of names you now have a list of cardinal values, the population figures, attached to those names. A list of population-weighted countries is a cardinal dimension for which you can quantify the relationship between any two countries. Country A is twice the size of country B, et cetera. This means for any variable you believe is correlated with country population, it makes sense to explore what that relationship is through the use of correlations and regressions. For example, it might be that you want to predict what the demand for roads or schools will be in some new country of a known population.

Sometimes, as was first described in Chapter 7, we need to transform variables by scaling the values of a variable so they fit between zero and one, or by taking the log of a set of values because that correlates better with something. For example, the log of a typical growing bacteria count has a linear relationship with time.

Sometimes these new weightings, scalings, or logarithms permanently stick to the dimension. When they become incorporated, we get to use the new ordering to view and analyze other information. Figure 20.10 presents a matrix of dimension or locator

		Locators or Dimensions		
		Nominal	**Ordinal**	**Cardinal**
Variables or Contents	Nominal	Majority political party by district .... Count histogram, mode	Majority political party by town income rank	Majority political party in town *x* by time .... Logistic regression (LR), multiple LR
	Ordinal	Party finish by town .... Ordinal rank Percentile rank Median Kruskal-Wallis test Wilcoxon two-sample test	Party finish by town income rank .... Kendall's correlation coefficient of rank	Party finish by time ....
	Cardinal	Sales by store .... Sum Chi-square test* Mean	Sales by store ranked by size .... Running mean	Sales by time .... Standard deviation Regression

*Note that means assume that the elements that were summed and whose count needs to be taken to complete the calculation of the mean are of equal size for the purposes of the calculation.

Figure 20.10 Ordering combinations and the analyses that work with them.

orderings by variable or content orderings. For each intersection, such as nominal dimension by ordinal variable, a data set that exhibits those characteristics is described in the upper region of the cell (above the dotted line) and the names of standard statistical analyses that require at least that amount of ordering (if there are any) are listed in the lower region (below the dotted line). The statistical terms are described below the table. (Note that statistical routines can always work on data sets that are more ordered than the minimum amount of required ordering.)

Here are descriptions of the analysis terms:

- **Count.**   Compute the number of instances of each value. This is perhaps the most general operation. It works with nominal data. You can count colors, genders, races, and religions. It doesn't assume anything about how the instances are ordered.

- **Histogram.**   Graphical technique of plotting the counts associated with each value. Ordinal and cardinal dimensions may indicate relevant relationships among the various counts.

- **Mode.**   Determines the most frequently occurring value.

- **Ordinal rank.**   Assigns a relative ranking to the data values (as in assigning medals to race times at a track meet).

- **Percentile rank.**   Like an ordinal rank, but carries additional proportion-of-set information, as the percentile rank for a value in the set is the percentage of values in the total set that the value of interest is greater than.

- **Median.**   Finds the middle value for the given values of the variable. The values of the variable generate the ordering required; hence, it can be used with nominally ordered dimensions.

- **Kruskal-Wallis test.**   Tests for differences in the rank location of data that are grouped by some single classification. This lets you see if there is some significance to the relative rankings that the values get, based on the classification.

- **Wilcoxon two-sample test.**   Tests to see if there are significant differences between two sets of data based on their ranks.

- **Kendall's correlation coefficient of rank.**   Computes a coefficient of correlation between ordinal data values and their ordinal position within a dimension. Any correlation activity is correlating values of a dependent variable with their locations along an independent dimension, hence the need for this operation to use ordinal data in an ordinal dimension.

- **Sum.**   Adds together all of the values for the variable. The ordering of the dimension should have no effect on the sum obtained.

- **Chi-square test.**   Tests the significance of differences in values of a variable distributed across nominally divided baskets. Note that if this is performed on variables organized by an ordinal or cardinal dimension, the dimension must be divided into essentially nominal sets for the test to work.

- **Mean.**   Computed by dividing the sum of the values by the count of the values. As with sums, the ordering of the dimension has no effect on the average obtained. However, when you are averaging aggregates of unequal size (like averaging per capita income across several countries), you will generally want to weigh the averages by the size-determining factor of the aggregates.

- **Standard deviation.**   Computed using the mean of the values and the values themselves. Describes the variation between the values. Since it depends on the mean, it requires its input values to be suitable for means.

- **Regression.**   Computes the coefficients of a function connecting the values of cardinal variables to their position along the dimension. The dimension needs to be cardinally ordered, so that change in variable per change in dimension position can make sense as an operation.

- **Logistic regression.**   Computes the correlation between changes in the values or state of nominal variables and a cardinal-independent dimension. Basic logistic regression assumes one binary state variable. Other forms work with multistate variables and multiple variables.

Multilevel Correlations

Most correlations can apply to more than one level of abstraction. For example, affinity coefficients can be evaluated at any level in any kind of product hierarchy. Financial account information can be obtained by almost any time granularity such as day, month, or quarter. This is a classic example of integration between OLAP and directed data mining for the purposes of predictive modeling.

Cluster Levels

Most types used as a dimension in some schema are associated with a significant number of attributes. A representative customer dimension and associated attributes are shown in Figure 20.11. When this is the case, and on a level-by-level basis, the dimension members can be clustered, as illustrated in Figure 20.12, according to patterns of similarity in their attribute values. The resulting grouping of dimension members can be used as a defining principle for both creating a set of members (the clusters) that represents a new level in the dimension, and for classifying new events as belonging to one new level member or another. The enhanced dimension with the cluster-defined

Customer	Age	Income	Occupation	Education	purchases
Bill T.	23	45	teacher	16	little
Jane D.	34	53	lawyer	16	lots
June R.	32	27	doctor	20	lots
Sam T.	43	75	singer	12	some
Jack E.	54	87	cab driver	20	lots
Dave S.	21	56	thrill seeker	12	none

Figure 20.11   Connecting less directed mining and OLAP.

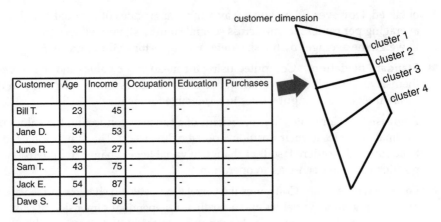

Figure 20.12 Using clusters for OLAP levels.

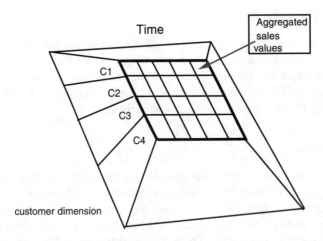

Figure 20.13 Aggregating data with cluster-based levels.

level can then be used, for example, to aggregate other data as illustrated in Figure 20.13. This is a classic example of integration between OLAP and undirected data mining for the purposes of alternate aggregations.

Business-Driven Analytical Segmentation

Most businesses that have been around for a while have, through accumulated knowledge, manually segmented their world in a number of dimensions and a particular set of members and hierarchies in those dimensions. These are typically the same ones they use for business analysis. In other words, a business that chooses to roll up their product dimension into three basic kinds of products—clothing, furniture, and accessories—has manually segmented their data into these three categories for reporting and analytical purposes. This manual segmentation accomplishes the same purpose as statistical methods such as clustering. When manually generated business segmentations are used to partition statistical models, it is a classic example of integration between OLAP and data mining. Ideally, there should be some interplay between the manual and statistically driven methods of segmentation.

MD Visualization

Traditionally, the province of scientific computing, the combination of data visualization and multidimensional meta data has begun appearing in some visualization products. For example, many visualization products provide for drill down and pivoting directly on the graphical representation (Sufer examples I_2, T_5). These capabilities are classic examples of integration between OLAP and data visualization.

MD Arrays for Text Retrieval

Documents are typically stored and retrieved using specialized text management systems. At the heart of any text management system is a method of calculating term and document relevance. These methods can be expressed, optimized, and run on relational and on multidimensional databases.

   Although running text analysis applications on relational databases provides for far superior data management and security features than are native to text systems, running those same text analysis applications on multidimensional databases provides for far more ways the original documents could be organized.[6]

MD Arrays for Data Mining

Jiawei Han showed in "Metarule-Guided Mining of Multi-Dimensional Association Rules Using Data Cubes" that association rules could be most efficiently mined when the data was kept in multidimensional arrays.[7]

A Single More Fully Integrated Example[8]

Since the most common examples of DSS integration leverage OLAP, data mining, and visualization, I will focus on these with this last example. Imagine you have recently been hired as director of marketing for a chain of grocery stores with the mission of increasing storewide sales through improved customer service. Although the company has implemented a data warehouse for which there is extensive point-of-sale (POS) data, many transactions are anonymous, so you don't know the identity of your customers. You do, however, have an OLAP system in place that store and product managers are using to report and analyze sales, and you'd like to add data-mining tools to your arsenal of DSS technology. All you need is a good business problem whose solution would benefit from the use of data mining.

After calling around, you learn that one store is already using data mining to design promotions. The store manager is applying *affinity analysis* on POS data to discover which products sell well together.[9] The results of affinity analysis may take the form of discovered rules or associations, such as: "If a customer buys tofu patties, there is a 60 percent chance that the customer will also buy buns." The support for this rule is 20 percent. Support refers to the ratio of the times tofu patties were purchased relative to the total number of transactions. Assuming that the store makes more money selling its own brand of bun than it does selling tofu patties, the affinity analysis may prompt the store manager to advertise a sale on tofu patties and put the buns near them.

You say to yourself, this information is useful, but it seems more tactical than strategic. Are there any broad patterns that you might be able to detect in your POS data that could lead you to a better understanding of your customers? How about trying to understand the reasons why customers shop at your store, as reflected in the collection of items they purchase in one visit? If you could understand your customers' goals when they enter your store, you might be able to help them fulfill their goals better and turn them into appreciative, loyal customers. After seeing how much you care about them, they might also be more willing to sign up for the customer cards you want to distribute. Because you don't know what buying patterns you're seeking—just that you want to find actionable, homogenous groups—you would probably want to use a less directed data-mining technique, a technique that doesn't need to be told what to look for. Traditional neural nets wouldn't work in this situation because they require some type of training pattern. A *k-means* approach, on the other hand, is relatively undirected; you can use it to cluster market baskets according to their similarities. Although there is no such thing as a wrong number of clusters, the patterns you discover and their usefulness to you are a function of the number of clusters you pick. So, even with a (supposedly) undirected algorithm, such as *k-means*, you must know something about your data (that is, you need to have already done some descriptive modeling before trying to mine it). If you are creating clusters purely for exploratory

---

K-MEANS

The *k-means* algorithm works as follows: Given a set of *k* initial-seed centroids (a kind of multidimensional mean) that can be composed of randomly chosen records, a *k-means* algorithm assigns each record to the cluster that is closest to it (as defined by the distance between the record and the centroid of each cluster). The centroid is, as you might expect, the spot at the center of the cluster. The algorithm makes a series of passes through the data. On each pass, it assigns every record to a cluster and recalculates the centroid of each cluster. Each new pass may change the cluster to which some records belong, and the process ends when the clusters no longer move between records.[10]

(Note that the preceding discussion assumed a particular type of *k-means* algorithm in which every record is assigned to one and only one cluster. These are sometimes called *hard* or *nonoverlapping* clusters. There are also *soft*, *overlapping*, or *probabilistic* clustering algorithms, which assign a probability function to each record so that it is assigned to every cluster with a different probability per cluster.)

analysis, you should be prepared to apply your clustering algorithm repeatedly using a different value for k each time.

So how do you apply this *k-means* algorithm to your POS data? Think about what you are trying to do: discover regular buying patterns that reflect different customer intentions. This is a pretty high-level pattern. To see this kind of pattern, you should work with partially aggregated data leveraging the aggregate members of your product dimension as defined in your OLAP application.

Your OLAP application has been aggregating POS data in as many ways as you can imagine. You can view sales by product, product category, brand, or by group for individual days, weeks, months, quarters, or years across individual stores or any combination of these. At one aggregate level of the product dimension, your OLAP environment distinguishes produce, meat, fish, cheese and dairy, coffee and tea, drinks, grains and pastas, convenience food, health products, and flowers. These are meaningful, high-level categories that represent business-driven segmentations of how your company reports and analyzes its data.

Before going any further, you need to segment your data into at least two parts: training and testing. Because you intend to use the groupings you discover through the *k-means* approach to track customer behavior, you should be sure that the detected clusters are representative of your data as a whole and will efficiently classify your customers' behavior. The most effective way to ensure this is to train the algorithm on one piece of your data, run it again on a second piece, and then compare the clusters found in the two trials. You can compare them with a multivariate, means-testing algorithm, such as Hotelling's.[11]

For our example in Figure 20.14, the data can be used without scaling or weighting because every variable is measured in dollars, and a dollar spent on any product is, for our purposes, as valuable as a dollar spent on any other. If you did scale the variables in this example, your results could be misleading because you would be treating dollar differences in flower purchases 10 times higher than dollar differences in meat purchases. (However, because the range between minimum and maximum dollar amounts spent on meat was 10 times the range of amounts spent on flowers, differences in meat purchases will probably account for more cluster boundaries than differences in flower purchases.) After applying scales and weights as necessary, you must choose how many clusters to use for your analysis. In our example, because you are looking for broad classes of customer behavior, a small k value, such as five, is appropriate. (Remember, you can always change k and run the algorithm again.)

Figure 20.15 lists six POS transactions and shows the amounts paid for products in each of the 10 categories. The sales amount within each product category can then be

Convenience	Paper Goods	Produce	Dairy	Meat/Fish	Total Purchases	Trans. ID
12	0	18	7	22	70	101
0	0	20	9	30	85	102
16	0	0	2	0	18	103
0	3	10	8	5	31	104
0	8	0	6	40	75	105
10	2	8	9	22	51	106

Figure 20.14 Sample of dollar amounts purchased per category per transaction.

Cluster	Meat/Fish	Dairy	Drinks	Health	Grains/Pastas	Produce	Paper Goods	Convenience	Coffee/Tea	Snacks
1	13	20	10	8	6	10	1	15	1	5
2	55	10	45	1	5	10	20	10	2	40
3	5	5	12	8	8	5	5	30	5	20
4	35	37	25	23	33	45	5	12	3	10

Figure 20.15 Centroid dollar values per customer.

treated as a separate variable for the purposes of clustering and used as input into a *k-means* algorithm. As you are preparing your data for analysis, you will need to decide whether to scale and/or weight your variables (as was discussed in Chapter 7). *K-means*, like most algorithms, is sensitive to these issues. For example, if you are creating a cluster on customer attributes and you have columns for age, income, marital status, and job description, you need to map each of the variables to a common scale (say a linear normalized scale of zero to one). In addition to scaling the data, you must also determine the importance of the attributes relative to one another, such as age versus income.

Figure 20.15 is a table of the computed centroid values for each category of product by cluster. Although you could analyze the clusters to see if there are discernible homogeneous purpose groups revealed through the clustering, the differences between the clusters (for reasons described in Chapter 9) are likely to show up better graphically than in a table of numbers.

Insert I.9 is a graphic representation of the computed centroid values. It makes use of a technique called parallel coordinates that represents the value scale for each variable with a separate vertical line. It's akin to the MTS diagrammatic method used to show variable values. Since, in our example, all the variables were measured in dollars, the segments don't have to be scaled or weighted.

If you look at the graphic image, you can identify distinct profiles that represent different inferred reasons for shopping. The line labeled A shows high values for meat and fish, drinks, paper goods, and snacks. Can you speculate what kind of purpose someone who bought those amounts of those items might have had? How about cookout parties? The line labeled B has high amounts for most categories and by far the highest amounts for produce. Maybe those are weekly shoppers. The line labeled C shows small amounts for everything but drinks and convenience foods. Maybe these are our lazy chefs! The line labeled D shows small amounts, though more than for the lazy chefs, for most items. Maybe these are single meal shoppers. (In practice, there would also be an E line representing market baskets whose profile was different from the four to which we could attach significance.)

Now that we've identified these clusters, we can use them as a new purpose dimension, in our OLAP environment, as shown in Figure 20.16 in order to further aggregate our sales data.

Next, you may want to mine this newly aggregated sales data to discover if there are any interesting correlations between dollars spent shopping and some combination of shopping purpose, time and/or store. Using an association rules algorithm, you may discover that most shopping by weekly shoppers occurs on the weekends while most single meal shopping occurs during the early evening near the end of the week and lazy chefs are most prominent in the urban areas. Taking what you've learned from

		C	D	E	F	G	H	I	J
			Actual	Product	Sales				
		Sunday	Monday	Tuesday	Wednesday	Thursday	Friday	Saturday	
4409	Weekly Stockup	1020	3824	1530	1912	2167	3314	7648	
	Cookout	2039	765	1224	1530	4334	4971	5099	
	Lazy Chef	863	3236	2589	4854	3667	1402	4314	
	Single Meal	2444	1528	3259	4583	3463	1456	2037	
	Other	2103	2629	2103	2629	2980	3418	3505	
4413	Weekly Stockup	999	3744	1583	2079	1989	3489	7425	
	Cookout	1842	823	1200	1394	3938	5186	4792	
	Lazy Chef	938	3170	2351	5189	3565	1409	4577	
	Single Meal	2419	1543	3147	4643	3144	1334	2121	
	Other	2188	2419	2065	2630	3158	3479	3531	

Figure 20.16   Sales per trip purpose.

your analysis, you may feel ready to begin to design a promotional strategy for your company.

Let's review for a minute what you've done. In support of a single business problem, namely promotion development, you used the following:

- An OLAP environment to partially aggregate transaction data according to your business-based aggregate product categories

- A data mining environment to cluster the partially aggregated data

- A data visualization environment to interpret the data mining results

- An OLAP environment to incorporate the cluster-based dimension for the purpose of aggregating the sales data

- A data-mining environment to look for patterns in the cluster-dimension aggregated sales data

In other words, you needed to use, at least, OLAP, data mining, and visualization to solve a single problem. I keep using the qualifier at least because in a real application there are even more technologies, as mentioned in the first section to this chapter, that can and ought to be brought to bear, even on this example of promotion development.

For example, in the retail world, there exists purchasable product affinity data (the result of extensive data mining), organized by what's called lifestyle segment where each lifestyle segment represents a different product affinity cluster. You can also get a hold of the count of families per lifestyle segment living in a particular area. Those areas can be quite small, such as census-sized block groups. To fully leverage this information, you would typically use a geographic information system to store the base data, calculate the predominant lifestyle segments per block group, calculate the distance each block group or more aggregated zone is from each store, and thus also calculate, given the types of products sold in your store, the areas of greatest concentration of families who have an affinity for the kinds of products you sell and who are close enough to your store to be or become customers. Figure 20.17, for example, shows the block groups surrounding three of your stores and the dominant lifestyle segment per block group.

Typically, you would bring calculated variables such as distance to store into your numeric warehouse environment where they would get picked up by either OLAP or data mining routines and used, for example, to create dimensional groupings representing either distances traveled (short, medium, long) and/or type of community (urban, rural), which in turn would get used for aggregations as illustrated in Figure 20.18. Thus, GIS should certainly be a part of your unified DSS infrastructure.

The appropriate use of decision analysis (mentioned first in Chapter 1) would also help you create effective promotions. For example, after discovering what you believe are reasonably stable patterns in your data so that you can create targeted promotions, you still need to figure out how to allocate limited marketing dollars to the suite of

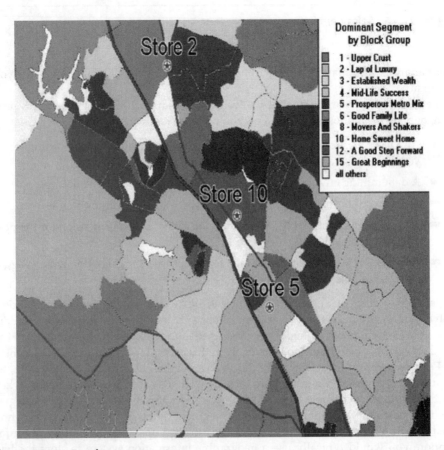

Figure 20.17 Dominant segments.

	A	B	C	D	E	F	G	H	I	J	K
1						Actual	Products				
2		3/31/97		4/1/97		4/2/97		4/3/97		4/4/97	
3		Avg Dist	Sales	Avg Dist	Sales	Avg Dist	Sales	Avg Dist	Sales	Avg Dist	Sales
4	Urban	1.04	291,362.05	1.04	277,200.85	1.05	305,648.97	1.06	325,587.40	1.06	288,132.11
5	Rural	4.94	272,248.34	5.03	291,618.37	5.00	257,805.76	5.01	226,706.25	5.04	244,696.30
6											
7											
8											

Figure 20.18   Sales by urban and rural.

promotions you could create so as to maximize the likely bang for the buck. Towards that end, you would need to take into account possible actions by competitors, possible changes in the price of supplies, the costs and effectiveness of different channels for promotion (newspaper, radio, flyers, and so forth), any discounts you may wish to apply, and so on. Figure 20.19 shows a typical view from a decision analysis package where you identify the endogenous variables that you control, the exogenous variables you don't control along with expected probability distributions for the possible outcomes for each of the exogenous variables, and the goal, in this case, profit.

After running a few simulations you may come to the conclusion that the best promotional strategy is to hand out flyers in small neighborhoods with high concentrations of lazy chefs, and use a combination of radio and in-store promotions to reach the weekly shoppers, cookout party makers, and single meal shoppers.

Summary

This chapter presented an overview of a unified architecture for decision support, described a variety of small, real-world examples of partial DSS integration, and finished by more deeply exploring a single example taken from retail sales. Within the chapter you learned that the distinction between OLAP, data mining, and decision analysis, made first in Chapter 1, represents only one of several dimensions that together describe decision support applications. The other dimensions included the kind of media, degree of abstraction, degree of relevance, and whether the data was

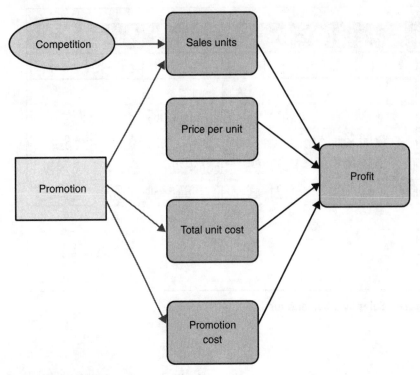

Figure 20.19 An influence diagram.

more source- or decision-oriented. Furthermore, the entire representational framework was subsumed in a single, representational stage of a holistic decision-making framework that included the decision made, the execution of the decision, and the environment within which the consequences of the executed decision occur in addition to the representation.

When all these pieces are in place and work smoothly together (whether through the heroic efforts of your end-user and/or IT organization or through the efforts of a single vendor or that of many), organizations will be able to fully represent all relevant aspects of their world and make optimal decisions that reflect their locality and slowly changing nature, as well as the sensitivity to current facts of that bundle of regular and multilevel patterns we call knowledge.

Standards in the OLAP Marketplace

Standard: **Something established by authority, custom, or general consent**
—Merriam-Webster's Collegiate Dictionary, Electronic Edition 1.5

As with many other areas of computing, different OLAP vendors' products were first created to serve different niches and were based on different underlying techniques. Within their individual niches, there was no need to do things in the same way as was done in other niches, and if two vendors were aware of each other in the same niche, they were not inclined to collaborate on anything. Standards were eventually put in place in many other areas of computing (networking, relational access languages, storage communication protocols, system busses, and so forth), but standards have continued to prove elusive within the OLAP space. The tide is changing and perhaps strong standards will be available by the time the third edition is written, but as of the writing of this second edition, only some rather contentious beginning steps have been taken.

What kinds of standards are relevant? Standards are most relevant in three key areas: data models, application programming interfaces (APIs), and benchmarks. A standard data model allows developers and users to work with applications without suffering from the incompatibilities between different vendors' tools, particularly in multivendor environments. A standard API allows programmers to build applications that can be run on the products from different vendors. (To be an effective standard, an API presupposes a good standard data model too.) Standard benchmarks allow organizations to effectively compare product offerings for tasks, and are also very helpful for assisting the physical implementation of a particular system.

Data Models

As described in Chapter 2, OLAP or multidimensional modeling and analysis products sprang up independently of any particular data model. Once established as products, individual vendors had little self interest looking for or supporting a model that might indicate functionality gaps in their products. As described in Chapter 4, there are numerous benefits to having a well-grounded model. The LC model used throughout this book (whose core modeling constructs existed well before the development of the industry buzzword OLAP) represents my best attempt to provide such a standard model. I hope you have found it useful in this book. Time will tell how well it (or some other attempt) succeeds.

APIs

Significant effort has been expended in API standardization, albeit with mixed results. The OLAP Council, an organization that was formed to promote awareness of OLAP and standards for it, released two iterations of an API specification (MDAPI) that worked hard to minimize the effort required for any vendor to implement it, but for various reasons was ultimately only implemented by one server vendor and one client vendor. Several members of the OLAP Council went on to form a Java Community Process working group for an API called JOLAP, which is a spiritual successor to the MDAPI. The process was begun in June 2000, and drafts of the API specification have not been made public as of October 2001.

The strongest effort towards standardizing APIs has been made by Microsoft, with its OLE DB for OLAP and XML for Analysis specifications. OLE DB for OLAP is an extension to Microsoft's OLE DB, and specifies data structures and function interfaces along with the MDX language for executing DDL and DML. As a COM-based interface, it will only run on Win32 platforms, which are predominant among end-users. The programmatic aspect of OLE DB for OLAP allows client applications to retrieve dimension and cube metadata, initiate the execution of queries and commands, and retrieve results from cube queries. The MDX language provides a rich set of primitives for dimensional navigation (examples which you saw in Chapter 19), and a data model that is in some ways tightly connected to the data model for Microsoft's Analysis Services, and in some ways expands on it. (However, even here Microsoft breaks the rules of its own MDX language specification in nontrivial ways.)

OLE DB for OLAP is a quasi- or near-standard in that, by general consent, a number of vendors are supporting to varying degrees on both the client side and, notably, the server side. It is a proprietary specification in that it is solely Microsoft's to keep or alter as it sees fit, but it is an open specification in that it is specified in detail and freely available for anyone to implement clients or servers for as they desire. (The specification is available at www.microsoft.com/data/oledb.) Microsoft has solicited input from vendors and end-users as it developed and evolved the specification, and the specification does have a few features in it that are not pertinent to its own products, but relevant to those from other vendors.

Currently, most OLAP tool use is by persons interacting with information. Circa 2000, the majority of these human beings were sitting down to computers running Microsoft Windows-family operating systems on Intel-based CPUs (*Wintel* machines). Going forward from 2001, more and more humans will be sitting down to non-Wintel machines (such as hand-held computers of many stripes). Additionally, more and more of the analytical functionality will not be accessed by humans, but by other computers, especially over the Internet. These machines will be running other operating systems for which the probability that Microsoft ports its APIs is essentially zero, including Solaris, Linux, HP/UX, AIX, and other Unix variants. To address these needs in one stroke, Microsoft together with Hyperion Software is also sponsoring the XML for Analysis specification as a standard.

XML for Analysis is essentially OLE DB for OLAP, where the data structures are expressed in XML format rather than binary format. It is based on the simple object access protocol (SOAP), which provides a generalized way to invoke operations on a remote service and retrieve results, all through the exchange of XML. Interestingly, SOAP doesn't depend on any particular lower-level transmission protocol, so while HTTP is the most likely protocol for sending and receiving, file transfer protocol (FTP) and simple mail transport protocol (SMTP) implementations exist, and others could be used if necessary. XML for Analysis may add features over time in comparison with OLE DB for OLAP; as this is written, the 1.0 specification exists and beta software exists, but there have been no commercial releases.

Benchmarks

Standard benchmarks are available in many areas of information processing. CPU performance is benchmarked in a number of ways, relational database performance benchmarked for different applications, desktop systems benchmarked for application suite performance, and so on. Some benchmarks have been specified through industry consortia, and others have been individually developed and become somewhat standard through wide application. The OLAP arena has had one significant effort to date to create a standardized benchmark, which has had some limited success.

Benchmarks are useful for at least three purposes:

- Ascertaining performance for a given hardware/software combination
- Validating the correctness of an application implemented in a given hardware/software combination
- Providing data points from which to estimate a suitable hardware/software combination

Standard benchmarks allow for different vendors' offerings to be compared within these three purposes. Note that the first and second purposes listed each have a different focus. Performance in terms of speed and bytes consumed is usually important (see Chapter 10 for considerations), and a great deal of attention sometimes needs to be spent in raising the speed and reducing the bytes. Equally important is whether or not the hardware/software combination can achieve the results at all as bogus results no matter how rapidly returned, are always unacceptable. Since running benchmarks can be time consuming, a scientific analysis of a few benchmark results can be used to achieve the third purpose.

In the relational database world, there are several standard benchmarks maintained under the auspices of the Transaction Processing Performance Council (TPC). The TPC-C benchmark is oriented towards transaction processing, while the TPC-H and TPC-R benchmarks (spinoffs of what was initially a single TPC-D benchmark) are oriented towards decision-support queries. The nature of the interaction with the database is different in each of the benchmarks, as they reflect different types of applications.

In the OLAP world, the only public standard benchmark to date has been the Analytical Processing Benchmark (APB-1), produced by the OLAP Council. The benchmark was the instrument of performance claims between Applix, Hyperion, and Oracle during the late 1990s, and subsets of it have been run by other vendors seeking to establish their performance rankings as well. The benchmark was also used by a number of vendors to determine whether they provided sufficient OLAP functionality to be able to brand themselves as OLAP product vendors.

The benchmark tests calculation and query performance for an OLAP server. Implementing the benchmark requires a server to be able to handle different structures of data in source tables, and to implement a moderately sophisticated set of allocations in the calculation logic. It uses a smaller number of dimensions (products, customers, channels, time, and scenario). The size of the dimensions can be varied for each run of the benchmark, and the density of the generated data can be adjusted as well. This allows different sizes of databases to be used. Additionally, the number of simultaneous client sessions can be specified. This allows testers to evaluate performance for large data set sizes independently from performance for large numbers of users. To be published according to APB-1 guidelines, the results of the benchmark must be audited, ensuring that the results are actually meaningful.

However, one benchmark is not enough, as there are many other types of applications and usage scenarios in addition to the one modeled in the APB-1. Additionally, the APB-1 specifies that calculations must take place on the server and not on the client tier, which reflects a desire to make it a benchmark of server performance, but limits its usefulness as an application benchmark. Real-world applications can require many other data structures and calculations than those reflected in the APB-1. For example, it is very common to have ranking queries (top 10 products) in the real world, to specify sorting of results, to specify data-based conditions for data retrieval, and to make use of lower dimensional data (like so-called attributes—such as customer address). Real-world application configurations are usually more sophisticated than simply relying on a single powerful server. For example, if an OLAP vendor's product distributes its processing on multiple tiers, including the client tier, then this should be allowable in an application benchmark. One of the notable aspects of the APB-1 benchmark has been that due to the requirements of the calculations, many OLAP-oriented servers have been unable to run the benchmark in its entirety. Many applications have less sophisticated requirements as well, and a benchmark that has fewer computational requirements would allow standard comparison of a greater variety of tools. Additionally, budgeting and forecasting is one of the oldest applications for OLAP tools. A real-world budgeting and forecasting system requires some degree of transaction processing within the analytical environment as well as perhaps sophisticated multidimensional calculations. It is my hope that standard benchmarks will emerge that more fully reflect the needs of real users across a wider variety of applications and domains.

LC Language Constructs

This appendix summarizes, without explaining, the LC syntax used throughout the book.

Operators and Markers

Unary

```
{T.}:   every instance of T .
```

Using dot notation, as introduced in Chapter 5, the specification of a member set may take place through the use of multiple term specifiers beginning with the name of the type followed by a dot followed by a further restriction such as the name of a level or specific instance. A dot at the end of a term specification string denotes the fact that what is specified, as for example with Geog.USA.atunder. is a set of instances and that all such instances are to be used/returned/considered. If the final token used to identify an instance set returns a single instance, there is no need to terminate the string with a dot.

```
{n/a,m,a,p} : logical status markers
```

As introduced in Chapter 6, it is important for an application to be able to distinguish between missing and meaningless data. The four logical LC status tokens accomplish this. Specifically

'n/a'   means not applicable

'm'   means missing

'a'   means applicable and

'p'   means present

They are appended to the end of a content specification and refer to whatever set of instances are specified to that point. For example, (Sales.m , Geog.USA.atunder.) says that sales values are missing for the USA and all its descendents.

```
{},  : Units or metric specifiers
```

As introduced in Chapter 7, it is good practice to specify the units of every variable. Commonly used units or metrics in this book were

```
Integers {I}
Rationals {R}
Nominals or names {N}
Dollars {$}
Currency {Curr}
Local currency {Lcurr}
Dollars per kilogram kilometer {$/Kg-Km}
Dollars per kilogram day {$/Kg-Day}
```

Binary Operators

■ **Assignment**

```
assignment (1-1, yields, fill with, equals)
```

{~} : The instances on the right-hand side of the operator are assigned a one-to-one correspondance with the instances on the left-hand side.

{>>} : The expression on the left-hand side yields the result on the right-hand side.

{<<} : The schema on the left-hand side is filled with values taken from the source on the right-hand side.

{=} : Standard equality

```
{F}  Standard assignment
```

■ **Arithmetic**

```
{+, -, *, / , < , >} : standard arithmetic
```

■ **Structuring**

{⊗} :   cartesian product

{~<} : The instances on the left-hand side are assigned a one-to-N correspondance with the instances on the right-hand side.

Intra-Type Referencing

Most of the intra-type referencing was introduced in Chapter 5.

- **Hierarchical**

  {L} refers to the combination of all types used as locators within the schema.
  Thus the expression (Sales , L.leaf.) << Table x says that the variable sales at the
  leaf level of all the dimensions used as locators in the schema is sourced from
  Table x.

  For ragged hierarchies:

  ```
  below, above, atbelow, atabove , down(N) , up(N) ,leaf , root
  ```

  For leveled hierarchies:

  ```
  instance.level, level.instances , uplevel(N) , downlevel(N),
  ```

- **Nonhierarchical**

  {this} refers to the current member.

  {this+ or - x} refers to referencing along an ordinally or cardinally
  arranged set of instances.

  {first , last} refers to the first or last member in an ordered sequence.

Ordering and Aggregating

- **Aggregations**

  ```
  {sum(   )}
  {count(    )}
  {avg(     )}
  {Type.min} or { Type.max}
  ```

- **Ordering**

  {Arank , Drank} Ascending and descending rank

Defaults and Conventions

Application range of left-hand side **(lhs)** : all locations.
   Location range of right-hand side **(rhs)** : inherited from **lhs**. If an **rhs** L-range is specified, it can be relative to the **lhs** range.

Aggregate: From the Latin term *aggregare*, meaning to collect in a flock. As a verb, it refers to the process of combining two or more data items into a single item. Summing a series of numbers is a typical example of aggregating. As a noun, it refers to any data item that is the result of an aggregation process, such as a total or average.

Algorithm: (n) 1699, either influenced by or borrowed from French *algorithme*, and perhaps separately formed in English as an alteration of *algorism* (the Arabic or decimal system of numerals), probably before 1200; influenced by Greek *arithmos*, or number.

Analysis: (n) Borrowing of Medieval Latin *analysis*, from Greek *ana'lysis*, a breaking up, from *analy'ein*, unloose (ana-up + ly'ein-loosen, untie). Like so many abstract terms, analysis traces back through Latin into Greek. It originally meant to take apart, as opposed to put together. Thinking required both analysis and synthesis. These days, it is common for the term analysis to refer to both traditional (decompositional) analysis and to synthesis.

Ancestor: Within a hierarchy, an ancestor of a member is found along the path between the member and the root (that is, parent, grandparent, and so on).

Antecedent: *See* ancestor.

API: Acronym for application programming interface. An API provides services that a software developer can write applications to use. Nearly all (if not all) OLAP products, and certainly all server products have an API. Some products are popular enough that their own API is used by a variety of other vendors and solution providers. Recently, Microsoft has promoted an API called OLE DB for OLAP as a standard API to which many client tools are supporting as consumers and several server vendors are supporting as providers. They generally consist of a specified set of callable functions and data structures that may be exchanged with the functions.

Applicable: Whether a variable makes semantic sense at a given coordinate (or location). For example, if a single hypercube's measure dimension contains members for both inventory and employee measures, and an organizational dimension contains members for both product categories and job classifications, the inventory measures are inapplicable at job-classification-related cells, and the employee measures are inapplicable at product-category-related cells. A variable or content can be considered missing only at a cell in which it is considered applicable.

Application range: The subset of a schema to which a formula applies. Absent some qualifications (which qualifications is specified differently in different products—as shown in Chapter 19), multidimensional formulas apply to the entire schema.

Array: (physical) A storage method where the elements of the array are placed sequentially in a contiguous region of storage (disk or RAM). Element 1 is followed by element 2, which is followed by element 3, and so on. When all elements are the same size (as is usually the case), then the location for any element in the array can be directly computed by multiplying the size of an element by the array index number for the element; it can then be accessed by skipping ahead that many units from the beginning of the array. This is a fundamental structure for computers; the memory of a computer is modeled as an array of bytes, pages of records in databases are frequently organized as an array of records, and so on.

Attribute: Information associated with an object, frequently with the members of a dimension. Address, for example, may be an attribute of a store dimension.

B-tree: A hierarchical indexing technique. Each node represents a range of indexed values, and each level of the hierarchy starting at the top focuses in on a progressively smaller set of index values, so an entry may be looked up by zeroing in on its value from the top down. Unlike a binary tree, a parent element in a B-tree can have many children. It has many variations, including the B+-tree and the B*-tree, which place index information differently within the same basic structure.

Buffer: A region of memory that holds information being transferred from one place to another. In database terms, a buffer can hold information transferred from the disk or other storage medium. Because a computer can operate only on data held in RAM, some form of buffer is required to operate on data in a database. *See also* cache.

Cache: A set of buffers or in-memory data structures that hold information that is either also on disk, is slated to be placed on disk, or has just been read from disk. The set of buffers is held in memory so that further accesses to the information will not require reading it from disk, but can simply be read from memory. OLAP products vary considerably in terms of the sophistication of the cache. On one extreme are caches that are user and query specific. At the other extreme are caches that possess most of the properties of a full-fledged in-memory database.

Calculate: (v) Circa 1570, probably in part a back formation from *calculation*, and in part borrowed from late-Latin *calculatus*, past participle of *calculare*, from Latin *calculus*, reckoning or account; originally, a small stone used in counting, diminutive of *calx* (genitive calcis), small stone, limestone; in the late 1500s and 1600s, *calculate* replaced earlier *calculen* (before 1378); borrowed from Old French *calculer* and late-Latin *calculare*. Another form, *calk*, Middle English *calken* (probably before 1400) existed originally as a shortened form of *calculen*, and was in use at least into the 1650s.

Calculation: (n) Before 1393, borrowed from Anglo-French *calculation*, from late-Latin *calculationem* (nominative *calculatio*) from *calculare*, calculate.

Cell: For OLAP vendors who model variables as members of a variables dimension, the intersection of one member from each dimension in a hypercube. Associated with a value.

Child: In a hierarchy with distinct leaves and roots, a child of a member is any member that is one hierarchical unit toward the leaves from the given member.

Cleansing: The process of discovering and repairing anomalous data within data tables.

Computation: (n) Around 1408, *computacion*, borrowed from Old French *computation*, learned borrowing from Latin *computationem* (nominative *computation*) from *computare*, to count, sum up (com-together 1 putare-count, reckon, consider).

Compute: (v) 1631, Borrowed from French *computer*, learned borrowing from Latin *computare*.

Consolidate: As a financial term, used to refer to complex aggregations that may involve internal transfers of physical and/or financial resources, intracompany transfer pricing as well as currency translations.

Content: Within the context of a query or schema, contents are those types whose values are sought after relative to a set of locations. In this sense, the term content is roughly equivalent to variable, or measure.

Descendent: Within a hierarchy, a given member's descendents include any members found along the path between the member and the hierarchy's leaves.

Dimension: A type used for locator purposes. A collection of instances, members, positions, or units of the same type. Synonyms from different disciplines include factor, axis, attribute, and variable. In a multi-dimensional data set, every data point is associated with one and only one member from each of multiple dimensions. Dimensions are frequently organized into one or more hierarchies in OLAP applications, though this is not a logical requirement.

Dimensional formula: A formula whose left-hand side is a dimension member. For example, give the term "profit" as a member of an accounts dimension the formulas Profit = Sales − Costs or Profit, L. = Sales − Costs are examples of dimensional formulas.

Domain 1. *Relational*: The data type from which an attribute is drawn. For example, Sales may be drawn from the domain of positive integers. A type is a highly structured domain.

Domain 2. *General and AI*: A topic or subject matter as in the domain of chemistry versus the domain of economics. The term *multi-domain* generally has this second sense as well.

Drill up/down: Navigating toward/away from the root of a hierarchy.

Form-based meaning: When the meaning of a symbol, such as a number, is a function of the form of the symbol.

Formula: (n) Before 1638, a set form of words used in a ceremony or ritual; borrowed from Latin *formula*, form, rule, method (literally, small form); diminutive of *forma*. The sense of prescription or recipe is first recorded in 1706, its use in mathematics in 1796, its use in chemistry in 1846.

Generation: A hierarchical distance measured from a member toward the leaves. *See also* level.

Granularity: *See* resolution.

Hash index: A technique whereby the key for a record in a database is converted to a number (through the use of what is called a *hash function*), which can then be used as an offset into an array of record locations to find the actual location of the record. Because all information in a computer (including text) may be treated as numbers, it becomes possible to treat the key values as a number or set of numbers that can be combined. This technique is much faster than using trees to index a set of records, but it scrambles the order; so it is not useful to, say, find all of the records whose product name begins with A and look them up in alphabetical order.

Hierarchy: An organization of members into a logical tree structure, with each member having at most one "parent" member and an arbitrary number of "children" members. The metrics associated with the instances of the the hierarchy all need to be quantitatively comparable or the hierarchy is illegitimate.

Hypercube: A multi-dimensional schema formed from the cross-product of a number of dimensions, the combination of which is in one-to-one association with some number of types used as contents.

Identifier: Within the context of a data set, dimensions can be used as identifiers or keys *or as variables or things that get tracked*.

Index: A structure used to facilitate the process of locating values. Optimum indexes vary as a function of many things including value set sizes, frequency of usage, and ratio of updates to accesses.

Inverted table: A table where all the fields have been indexed.

Leaf: Any bottom-most member of a hierarchy (a member without children).

Level 1. *Named set of equally weighted members:* The members are capable of being referenced as a group either from above or from below in the hierarchy. Multiple levels need to be fully connected otherwise they are named groups.

Level 2. *Measure of hierarchical distance*: In some OLAP products, a level is specified as the hierarchical distance or number of hierarchical steps from either a root member of the hierarchy or from the leaf members of the hierarchy to a particular member. These products may use the term *level* to mean members measured in one direction (from the hierarchy lead members or root) and *generation* to mean members measured in the other direction.

Location: Any set of tuples defined in terms of the union of the locator dimensions.

Location-based meaning: When the meaning of a symbol, such as a point, is a function of where it is on a display.

Locator: Within the context of a query or schema, locators are those types whose values are given as constraints relative to a set of contents to be evaluated or returned relative to that set of constraints. In this sense, the term locator is roughly equivalent to dimension.

Meaningless: Cells in a hypercube for which no data would ever exist are meaningless or inapplicable.

Measure: A unit-bearing data type. Though literally it refers to measured data such as measured temperature or measured sales, the term has been used by several OLAP vendors as synonymous with the term *variable*, which also includes the notion of derived or nonmeasured values. *See also* variable or content.

Member: An element, position, or instance within a dimension or type.

Meta data: Data about data. Meta data falls into several different categories. The most common categories are descriptive, usage, source, and structural. Ultimately, the distinction between data and metadata is functional.

Missing: Cells in a hypercube for which data is applicable, but does not currently exist.

Multi-cube: A multi-dimensional construct formed from two or more hypercubes that each share one or more dimensions in common.

Nest: With respect to row and column displays, nesting one dimension under another means that all the members of the nested dimension appear for each member of the nesting dimension. Another way to look at it is the nesting dimension represents the primary sort while the nested dimension represents a secondary sort.

OLAP: An acronym that stands for On-Line Analytical Processing. It is meant to contrast with OLTP. The key aspects are that OLAP is analysis-based and decision-oriented.

OLTP: An acronym meaning On-Line Transaction Processing.

Orient: The mapping of logical dimensions to the screen dimensions of row, column, and page.

Override: Manual substitution, dimensional formulas and precedences that apply to many cells sometimes need to be overridden for a subregion of cells.

Page (disk): A unit of information that can be read from a disk or written to a disk. While a disk is theoretically capable of transferring just a single bit at a time to or from memory, in practice bytes are written and read some multiples at a time. On IBM PC compatibles and UNIX systems, the operating system may transfer 512 bytes in one operation, while on a mainframe computer the number might be 8,192 bytes (8 KB). Because this has an impact on the efficiency of transferring information between memory and disk, database programs will transfer pages of information to and from disk as well. A database program may use pages of data that are the same size as the pages the operating system uses, or pages that are a multiple of the size of the operating system's.

Page dimension: The set of dimensions in a hypercube that are not displayed across either the rows or columns, but that are necessarily displayed as pages where one and only one member of each page dimension is displayed at a time.

Parent: In a hierarchy with distinct leaves and roots, the parent of a member is the member that is one hierarchical unit toward the root from the member.

Peer: In a hierarchy, all members at the same level are considered to be peers. Note the multiple definitions for *level*; depending on the definition of level used, the peer group will be different.

Pivot: Rearranging the orientation of logical dimensions on the screen at query time.

Precedence: When multiple formulas defined in different dimensions intersect at a cell, the precedence of each formula determines the order in which it is calculated, or in the case where only one formula is actually applied to the cell, which formula is applied.

Refinement: The integration of names, units, and forms required for the creation of global data sets.

Replication: A form of data duplication where only changes are propagated from place to place.

Resolution: A level whose members are defined in terms of a common scale or granularity.

Root: The top-most member of a hierarchy. In a dimension with multiple hierarchies, there will be multiple roots.

Scale: *See* resolution.

Siblings: All children of the same parent.

Star schema: An arrangement of tables in a relational database where a central fact table is connected to a set of dimension tables, one per dimension. The name star comes from the usual diagrammatic depiction of this schema with the fact table in the center and each dimension table shown surrounding it, like the points on a starburst.

Tree: Synonym for hierarchy. A binary tree is a tree where each node may have zero, one, or two children. A B-tree (see definition) is a hierarchically structured search index.

Type: The single underlying structure capable of accounting for hierarchies and formulas and whose differentiated use within the context of a query or schema corresponds to the terms locator or "dimension" and content or fact, variable and measure.

Type one table: A table where one dimension (usually the variables dimension) has its members placed across the columns as column headings, and all the other dimensions have their names as column headings and their members defined down the rows.

Type zero table: A table where all the dimensions have been placed as the headers of columns whose data runs down the rows and a value dimension becomes the heading for the one data column.

Value: The quantity for a single instance of a variable. For example, $30 could be a value for a sales variable.

Variable: A unit-bearing data type, either measured or derived. Sales, costs, profits, and interest rates are typical variables. Depending on the OLAP tool, variables may be treated on an individual basis and kept separate from the dimensions according to which they are organized, or they may be collected together in a single variables dimension.

Virtual memory: A technique for allowing software in a computer to address more memory than is installed in the system. This allows programs that require a large amount of RAM to operate on systems that have only smaller amounts of RAM. Data that will not fit into actual RAM is moved onto or off of disk as needed, without the software being aware that the disk was involved. Generally, this is a feature of the operating systems that is transparent to the programs running on it.

The Relationship between Dimensions and Variables

In Chapter 3, I discussed the multi aspect of multidimensionality more than the dimensional aspect. Remember how we distinguished between logical and physical dimensions? Angle-based dimensions as found in a cube were physical dimensions and spatially limited to three. In contrast, logical dimensions apply to any situation and have no inherent upper limits. So the key to understanding the multi aspect of multidimensionality is understanding the difference between logical and physical dimensions.

> **NOTE** The term orthogonal has been used in the industry to mean generic as in, if all dimensions are generically the same, they are orthogonal. This is an unfortunate misuse of the term. Especially because the term's real use, as defined by its mathematical origins, has to do with the concept of independence between dimensions, which, as we saw in the text, is an important concept in the OLAP world.

The dimensional aspect is just as important as the multi aspect. What makes something dimensional or a dimension? How do we identify the dimensional structure of a data set? Are columns in a flat file always dimensions? In a business sense, the term is frequently used to mean a perspective.

But what exactly is a perspective?[1]

All this could make it seem that a dimension is a property of the organization of a data set because, as we saw in Chapter 3, the same data can be organized in multiple ways. In which case the dimensionality is in the eye of the beholder. Or, is the dimensionality of a data set somehow a property of the data independent of how it is organized? It certainly seemed that dimensions were equated with groups of things such as all the departments, stores, or employees in a company, and that such things are to some degree observer independent. But if dimensions equate with groups, are all groups dimensions?

The purpose of this appendix (which represents a slightly revised version of section one from Chapter 15 of the first edition of *OLAP Solutions*) is to compliment the introduction to the LC model (from Chapter 14) and its particular take on the relationship between dimensions (or locators) and variables (or contents) with their common grounding in types by looking, somewhat informally, at that relationship from two different and popularly taken perspectives. First, we look at the difference between locators or dimensions and contents or variables. I will especially draw attention to the inconsistencies in positions that maintain that there is no distinction to be made. Subsequently, this appendix looks at the underlying sameness between locators and contents (what you learned to call types in Chapter 4). If you are happy with your current understanding of the relationship between locators and contents as coexistent, type-grounded functional distinctions found within any query or response, and are not interested in exploring it any further, you may safely skip this appendix.

The Basis for the Distinction between Contents and Locators

As we saw briefly in Chapter 3, the basis for the distinction between dimensions and variables arises from a combination of the activity of describing (and manipulating) events and the events themselves. Look at the urban commercial planning example in Figure E.1. It shows a table containing data about times, neighborhoods, stores, and sales. Can you visualize the data source? Let us say that the data came from a small-sized city neighborhood and the stores that do business within its boundaries. Figure E.2 shows a map of the neighborhood and the location of its stores and their type. The urban planning authorities monitor the neighborhood once a month.

Months	Neighborhood	Store	Sales	Foot traffic
Jan	Pearl Square	C1	200	4000
Feb	Pearl Square	C1	75	2000
Mar	Pearl Square	C1	125	2250
Apr	Pearl Square	C1	150	3000
:	:	:	:	:
:	:	:	:	:
Dec	Pearl Square	C1	225	5000

Figure E.1 Urban planning data.

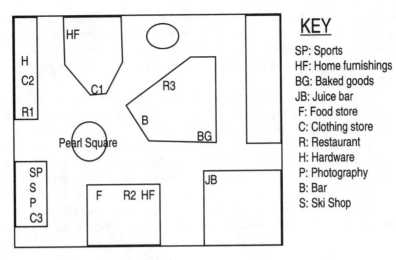

Figure E.2 Pearl Square neighborhood.

What You Need to Take into Account

If you had the responsibility for building a commercial monitoring system for a senior analyst with the urban planning authorities, what aspects, components, or factors of the neighborhood's situation would you need to know or take into account (assuming all the neighborhoods' businesses were cooperative)?

Contents or Variables

Certainly, you would have to take store sales into account or you couldn't talk about having a commercial monitoring system. Unless you are exceptionally clairvoyant, you can only do this by tracking, measuring, or otherwise recording the fact that something was sold for each time and place that a sale is made. Everything that you track in a situation is called a content or variable (in that situation). By way of comparison, in a financial situation, line items or accounts usually function as variables. In a manufacturing situation, worker productivity and error rates may serve as variables. In a transportation situation, passenger miles, cost, and revenue per passenger mile may serve as variables.

Note how the urban planner's variables reflect what the urban planner is trying to do. A different entity with different purposes may track different variables in the same situation. For example, given the same events within which the urban planner is tracking sales, a local resident might be tracking what stores s/he enters and how much money s/he spends per store.

Now let's say you've accumulated some instances of your sales variables and it is time to analyze and report on them. What might you want to know? You might want to know the value for a particular instance of a particular variable, say the sales variable for the dry cleaners in January. You might want to know how sales compared between two times, say last week and this week. You might want to know how many sales go to young customers compared with old customers. You might want to know which businesses are doing the best and the worst in the neighborhood. You might want to know many things.

But what could you ever know unless you could differentiate or identify specific instances or groups of instances of the variables you originally measured. You wouldn't be able to ask for the first measurement taken or the measurements taken from store x, or the measurements made Tuesday, or the measurements of product y sales, or even the first sequential measurement in data storage. You would never be able to formulate any questions about your variables, not even a question about their total or average. For even a question about totals assumes it is possible to differentiate the instances of one variable from the instances of another. So, strictly speaking, unless the instances of your variables can be individuated, your variables are totally and completely useless.

Locators or Dimensions

Of course, you would never measure a series of variables without retaining the ability to somehow identify their instances. If you were tracking sales in the example given in the previous section, it is likely that the specific instances of sales would be identified by time, store, and product. Each set of identifying factors—that is, the set of all stores or the set of all times, or the set of all products—is a locator dimension of the situation.

In contrast with variables, the locator dimensions of an information-generating situation have values that you already know. Refer back to Figure E.1, the simple row and column layout of commercial data, and ask yourself the following question, "What are the months for which I am tracking sales?" Don't you somehow know this? Don't you need to know this to specify a particular report? If Figure E1 was what you wanted to see, it must be that it represents the response to a command, such as "Show me the sales for January through June in the green neighborhood," or the answer to a question such as "What are the sales for January through June?" However phrased, the time value January through June identifies which sales instances you are interested in seeing. In other words, unless you are really doing data archeology, a typical data set can be looked at as a collection or set of answers to a given question. In Chapter 4, we showed how this looks in type language.

Since dimensions have values you already know, a stream of dimension values to which no other information was attached couldn't possibly tell you anything new. Dimensions are as meaningless without variables, as variables are meaningless without dimensions. Luckily, you would never think to build a model without including them both. (For a refutation of a pseudo-counter example, please see the following sidebar.)

Variables (or contents) and dimensions (or locators) are at the core of any MD modeling taxonomy, (regardless of whether or not variables are given any special status in the MD product that you use). As I showed in Chapter 4, locators and contents represent basic functions or roles that types may fill. Rules and scripts, objects, entities and relationships, generalized blackboards, and logic denote data modeling taxonomies in their respective domains. Modeling taxonomies are at the heart of what the AI community calls knowledge representation.[2, 3]

POSSIBLE COUNTER EXAMPLES TO THE NEED FOR DISTINGUISHING BETWEEN LOCATORS AND CONTENTS

Possible counter example 1:

As a possible counter example to the need for distinguishing locators (or dimensions) and contents (or variables), consider a situation where you are given a commercial model for which you didn't even know the dimensions, much less their values. You could start your queries into the model with the question "What are the dimensions of my model?" To which the response might be "months, stores, products, and customers." (Note, this is how the meta data discovery of any OLAP API typically works.) Following this, you could formulate the question "For what months do we have commercial data?" To which the response might be "January, February, and March." Thereafter, you could formulate more typical queries such as "What are the sales for January, February, and March?" While on the surface this might seem like a counter example to the assertion that we need to know the values of our dimensions, closer inspection reveals otherwise.

Recall that a dimension is only a dimension relative to a variable. Nothing is inherently a dimension or a variable. Time, which usually serves as a dimension, can just as easily serve as a variable. For example, in a model that tracks the average amount of time between feeding sessions for humans, time would be the variable, and age, culture, or geography might be dimensions.

When you asked the question "What are the dimensions of my model?" the term dimension was serving as a variable, and the term model was serving as a dimension. Imagine that you had several models, not just a commercial model. Questions such as "Are there any dimensions in my commercial model that are shared by my finance model?" or "What are the dimensions of my human resources model?" All these questions treat model as a locator or dimension for the term dimension, which is acting like a variable and whose unknown values are what these meta models are tracking.

When you asked the question, "What are the time values for which I have commercial data?" (Which could be rephrased as "What are the members of the time dimension in my commercial model?"), the term member was serving as a variable, and the term dimension was serving as a dimension. Here, in other words, you are tracking sets of member values as identified by their dimension name. The set of members in a dimension varies from dimension to dimension.

So, the counter example isn't a counter example because there isn't a single model. There are three models. Model one is the commercial model we've been talking about all along. Its variables are sales and costs; its dimensions are time, store, and product. To ask questions about particular sales values, you have to know the value of the time, store, or month whose sales values you want to know. Model two is a meta data model. Its variables are dimension members; its dimensions are dimension names. To ask questions about the members of a dimension, you have to know for what dimension you are asking the question. Finally, model three is also a meta data model. Its variables are dimension names; its dimensions contain model names. To ask questions about the names of dimensions in a model, you have to know for what model you are asking the question.

(continued)

**POSSIBLE COUNTER EXAMPLES TO THE NEED FOR
DISTINGUISHING BETWEEN LOCATORS AND CONTENTS** *(continued)*

Possible counter example 2:
Of course, one can imagine extreme cases where a seemingly pure one-dimensional
stream of dimension values constitutes useful information. For example, consider a
model that just tracked, for a moment in time, which products were being carried. Figure
E.3 shows such a model. It would appear to contradict the rule that both a variable and a
dimension are required for a useful model. Kimball, in his book *The Data Warehouse
Toolkit*, called this a factless fact table.[4]

However, the seemingly one-dimensional model is not really one dimensional. In
addition to the product dimension, there is an implicit second dimension bearing one
member that acts as a variable. That dimension might be called an existence dimension.
Its one member might be called status. The status variable has a Boolean variable
capable of two values: yes meaning the product is available, and no. The model consists
of the intersection of the product and the existence dimensions. The cell values would
thus contain the binary values: yes and no. This is shown in Figure E.4. Notice how all the
values are yes. In other words, the only products listed in Figure E.3 were the available

Products
Sniglets
Foozbars
Dingbots
Foodles
Smuglets
Grimples

Figure E.3   List of products carried.

Products	Status
Sniglets	Yes
Foozbars	Yes
Dingbots	Yes
Foodles	Yes
Smuglets	Yes
Grimples	Yes

Figure E.4   Revealing the existence dimension.

Products	Status
Sniglets	Yes
Tugles	No
Foozbars	Yes
Bonkles	No
Dingbots	Yes
Foodles	Yes
Jimbas	No
Smuglets	Yes
Grimples	Yes
Nerplas	No

Figure E.5   List of products and their status.

ones. It is this convention (as opposed to showing all products that did or could ever exist along with their existence value of yes or no) that eliminates the need to explicitly show the existence dimension. Figure E.5 shows what the model would look like with all products, available and unavailable.

The concept of an implicit dimension is analogous to the concept of an implicit part of speech. The interjection wow for example, seems to carry meaning when used in a real-world situation, yet apparently violates the need for a subject and predicate. Of course, implicitly, wow parses into a subject-predicate form meaning, approximately, this thing/event here now is unusual.

Benefits to Thinking in Terms of Variables and Dimensions

By this point you should be convinced that there is no escaping the distinction between variables and dimensions. But what would you be giving up by not making the distinction? Maybe it's no worse than not distinguishing Cabernet Sauvignon grapes from Merlot grapes when ordering wine. After all, you can still ask for red and get what you want.

As stated at the beginning of this appendix, the difference between dimensions and variables is going to be secured and then deepened. The reason for doing this is because all further development of MD analysis depends on this distinction. Since not all products single out variables, there is some feeling that variables are somehow optional or that they are just another dimension, like products. As I have mentioned elsewhere, you can ignore the distinction between dimensions and variables for the purposes of display, but not for analysis.

Better Connection to Logic and Analysis

Dimensions, as opposed to variables, provide the logical notion of uniqueness, identity, object, or reference. In database terms, this is called a key. The concept of key is a central, and logically grounded, tenet of the relational model. In fact, it is law number one in the relational model version 2.[5]

MD models need this distinction for the same reason that relational models need them. It provides criteria for meaningful and meaningless statements. In other words, a database, MD or relational, is just a fancy word for a big collection of statements capable of being true, false, missing, and meaningless. A necessary, though not sufficient, condition for meaningfulness is the coexistence of an identifier (or key) and a variable (or nonkey) attribute. Furthermore, when it comes to handling missing and meaningless data, keys or identifiers get handled differently from nonkeys or variables. (Missing keys, for example, are not allowed in the relational model whereas missing attributes are allowed.[6]) There is no way to properly handle missing and meaningless data without making the distinction at some point.

Dimensions and variables are to modeling behavior as gravity is to physical behavior. In the same way that you can live your life in cognitive ignorance of gravity, but your physical being cannot ignore or break the laws of gravity, you can live your life in cognitive ignorance of the difference between dimensions and variables, but your cognitive being cannot ignore or break the laws of dimensions (or locators) and variables (or contents). Incidentally, these kinds of laws should not be confused with politically based laws such as tax rates, gun control, abortion, and highway speed limits. You can only break human laws. What follows is a brief description of the benefits to thinking in terms of variables and dimensions.

The Common Grounding of Dimensions and Variables

You have just seen how dimensions and variables are both a necessary part of any OLAP model. At the same time, I kept mentioning that the distinction between dimensions and variables is one of function or role, and not one of kind. In other words (as I showed in Chapter 4), anything that can be used as a dimension in one query or calculation can be used as a variable in another and vice versa. Let's explore this common grounding further.

First of all, let's look at a simple two-column table of time and sales as shown in Figure E.6.

Figure E.6 represents a simple sales table. The time column is the key column or dimension. Sales is the attribute column or variable. The table shows how many sales were made for each time period. Normally, each column would be defined in terms of a previously declared data type as illustrated in Figure E.7.

What about a more objective criteria for differentiating locators (or dimensions) and contents (or variables) within the context of a data-generating event? Is there one? It

Identifier: Time (hour)	Variable: Sales (100s of dollars)
10:00	5
11:00	3
12:00	4
13:00	4
14:00	4
15:00	6
16:00	3
17:00	3
18:00	4
19:00	2

Figure E.6   A simple sales table.

Possible Time Values	Possible Sales values
Any integer > 0 representing a number of minutes	Any integer > 0 representing sales in dollars

Figure E.7   Meta data definition of the time and sales dimension.

turns out that there is a more public or objective way of distinguishing between dimensions and variables that is consistent with the common sense definition given earlier.

Within the context of a data-generating event, the mapping of types to the roles of variable and dimensions can be objectively made based on the relationships between the distribution of their values in a data set and their definition at the meta data level. In most cases, there is a clear difference in the distributions between what were used as dimensions versus variables in the generation of a data set, and, when there is no difference between the distributions, there is no logical way of distinguishing which types were used as dimensions and which were used as variables in the generation of that data set. The more a type is usable as a dimension in a data set, the more the unique values of the dimension in the data set are in one-to-one correspondence with a contiguous range of the values of the dimension's definition in meta data, and, the more the number of instances of each dimension value in the table is a constant. When there are multiple types used as dimensions, this creates the Cartesian product that was introduced in Chapter 4 and is used throughout the book.

An easy way to see within the context of a single query result set, whether a type is more naturally used as a dimension or as a variable is to inspect a histogram of the type's values as found in the data set. If the histogram for a type, like the one for time in Figure E.6, shows a constant height for frequency, the type is being used in that data set as a dimension. This is shown in Figure E.8. If the histogram for a type, like sales in Figure E.6, shows a nonconstant, or even better, an interesting distribution, the type is being used as a variable. This is shown in Figure E.9.

To drive home the point that dimensions can be used as either locators or as contents, let's look at some nontypical data sets that, nevertheless, stem from the same

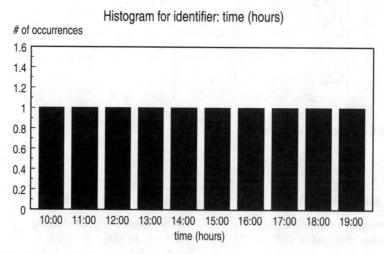

Figure E.8   A histogram for time as a dimension.

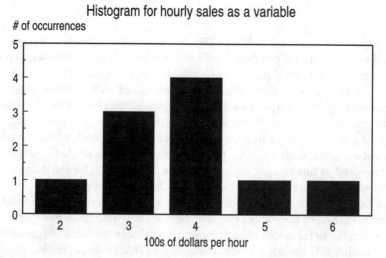

Figure E.9   A histogram for sales as a variable.

sales and time meta data that you saw in Figure E.7. The first one will show sales as a dimension with time as a variable. The second will show time as both a dimension and as a variable. A histogram will be shown for each type.

Imagine a sales-based fundraising effort whose goal is to raise $10,000. And, for the first $1,000, the time that each increment of $100 was raised was recorded so as to indicate the rate of progress and what times were more effective for fundraising than others. A table with this information is presented in Figure E.10. The sales column represents $100 intervals (of fundraising sales); the time column represents the time when the sales amount was achieved. The elapsed time column represents the amount of time elapsed since the last $100 increment.

Notice how the sales histogram (see Figure E.11) is the one with the constant frequency while the histogram for time (see Figure E.12) is the one whose frequency follows a more typical distribution.

Finally, let's look at an example where time, in the same sense of clock-measured time, is used as both a dimension and a variable in the same table. Consider the table in Figure E.13. The first time column represents the time on earth taken at fixed intervals. It is used as a basis for the dimension. The second time column represents the time taken on a spaceship as it is leaving the earth. Imagine that the speed of the spacecraft is precisely known so that the distance of the spacecraft from the earth can be calculated from the time it has been gone, and that the earth sends a signal to the craft at fixed intervals, as measured by the earth. The spacecraft records the time it received each signal and (after correcting for its distance from the earth and other factors) records its local time for each signal reception. Assuming we are close to possessing warp technology (that is, the ability to travel at or near the speed of light), the purpose of the recording is to test whether, and if so by how much, time slows down as the

Sales ($100s)	Time	Elapsed Time
0	9:00	0
1	9:30	30
2	10:00	30
3	10:15	15
4	10:30	15
5	11:30	60
6	12:30	60
7	1:00	30
8	1:30	30
9	1:45	15
10	2:15	30

Figure E.10   Table of time by sales.

Histogram of cumulative sales ($100s) as an identifier

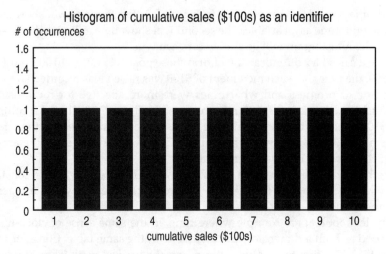

Figure E.11   Histogram for sales as a dimension.

Histogram of elapsed time in minutes as a variable

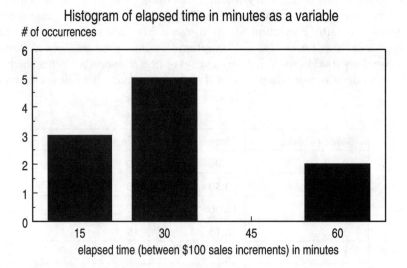

Figure E.12   Histogram for time as a variable.

spacecraft approaches the speed of light. The third and fourth columns represent elapsed time on the earth and on the spaceship, respectively. Entirely derived from columns one and two, the elapsed time columns are what actually get graphed.

Notice how the earth time column has a dimension-like appearance. This is shown in its constant frequency histogram in Figure E.14. Meanwhile, the same time type, albeit in a different use as spacecraft time, shows a variable-like character. Time seems

Earth time	Space time	Elapsed time (earth)	Elapsed time (space)
10:00	10:00	N/A	N/A
10:10	10:10	10	10
10:20	10:20	10	10
10:30	10:30	10	10
10:40	10:38	10	8
10:50	10:46	10	8
11:00	10:52	10	6
11:10	10:54	10	2
11:20	10:56	10	2
11:30	10:56	10	0

Figure E.13   Table of spacecraft time by earth time.

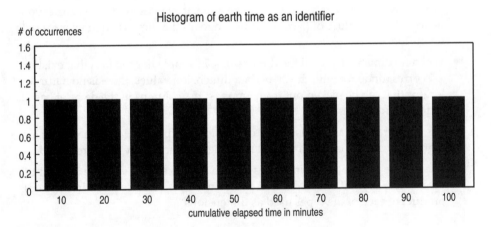

Figure E.14   Histogram of earth time as dimension.

to be slowing down with a limiting point at 10:56. This is shown in the histogram in Figure E.15.

From the above examples you can see five important things:

- The distinction between locators and contents (or dimensions and variables) in a data set represents different uses of a meta data-based dimension and is a

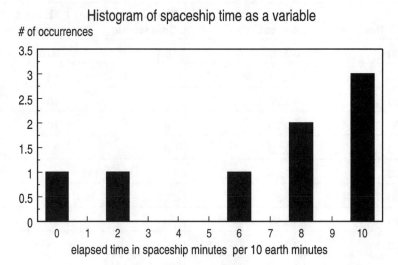

Figure E.15   Histogram of spacecraft time as a variable.

reflection of the original data-generating event. A type that is used as a locator in one data-generating event may be used as a variable in another.

■ When a type is used as a dimension in a table, its values exist in 1-1 correspondence with the values of (a contiguous range of) the dimension in its meta data definition.

■ When no dimension, or all the dimensions, in a table have values that exist in 1-1 correspondence with the meta data dimension values, there is no natural locator that can be picked out from amongst the columns in the data set based purely on its values.

■ The histogram for a type used as a dimension is typically flat, whereas the histogram for a type used as a variable may be (and hopefully is) more varied.

■ The number of applicable instances of each type used as a variable is equal to the number of locations as defined by the number of intersections in the cross product of each of the types used as dimensions.

Summary

In this informally structured appendix, you saw that MD models are collections of locators (or dimensions) and contents (or variables) and that dimensions and variables represent different uses of types. We tried several different ways to get around thinking in terms of variables and dimensions, but could not. Even when we thought we had gotten rid of variables, they surfaced under the guise of some kind of implicit variable. You also saw an objective basis for distinguishing between natural locators and natural contents with the context of a query result set.

Toward a Theoretically Grounded Model for OLAP and Its Connection to the Relational Model and Canonical Logic

Although a detailed critique of the limits of the relational model and canonical logic would require another book, since this book makes use of the Located Content (LC) model as a theoretically grounded candidate standard model for OLAP, I thought it would be useful here in this appendix to outline some of the challenges of articulating any OLAP data model, how any candidate standard OLAP model ought to relate to the relational model, and how any candidate model's underlying logic ought to relate to canonical logic.

Products, Data Models, and Foundations

A *data model* consists of structuring and operational definitions (frequently called a data definition and manipulation language) that apply to all the data that could ever be described or manipulated by software adhering to the model. Data models benefit the community of users, product developers, and researchers by providing a common language of expression independent of any particular tool and in terms of which any tool may be easily understood. In addition, for researchers especially, the language gets reified, thus becoming a thing to be thought about independently of any particular product or problem. A data model is like a map you can reason with distinctly from the terrain it depicts. This is the essence of abstract data-model-based research. When the data model integrates elements from logic, it provides a basis for the design of deductive databases where, given any database state, some other set of states may be logically deduced.

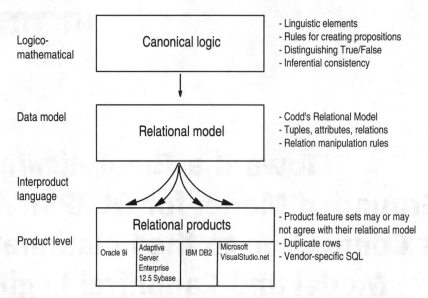

Figure F.1 The relationship between products, data models, and foundations.

Let's contextualize the concept of a data model by considering the spectrum of levels relevant to data models. Figure F.1 is an illustration of that spectrum. There is a products level, which refers to all the software products available in the marketplace that you can use; a common product language level, which refers to any industry-standard API specification; a data model level, which refers to things like the relational model; and, finally, a logico-mathematical level, which refers to things like matrix algebra and predicate calculus. When you consider this spectrum from a broad perspective, it becomes clear that a data model is sandwiched between individual products and standard application programming interfaces (APIs) on one end, and math and logic on the other.

For example, relational database products, such as those produced by Oracle, IBM, Microsoft, and Sybase, can be interacted with through industry standard SQL. Furthermore, they are all grounded in a common logical data model—the relational model of data. The relational model was first introduced by E. F. Codd in his seminal 1970 paper "A Relational Model of Data for Large Shared Databanks."[1] It introduced a set of primitive data structures including domains, relations, tuples, and attributes. It also introduced a set of primitive operations including joins, products, restrictions, and projections. These primitive structures and operations are grounded on the primitive structures and operations of canonical logic (and the theory of relations) including functions, arguments, and connectives. It is interesting to note that the relational model was developed and debated before any products were created that claimed to be relational.

Logic and the Relational Model

Logic, of any provenance, is concerned with information elements that are the smallest bearers of meaning. In the same way that all molecules and compounds are composed of physical elements, all data sets and publicly exchanged thought are composed of information elements. Although logic offers a theory of how any one information element can be true or false, and how arbitrary groups of information elements may connect and be operated on in a truth-state consistent manner, the relational model focuses on a particular group of information elements called relations, and how relations may be operated on in such a way that the output of any relational operation performed on a relation is always another relation. This is crucial to the relational model, because the benefits of the model derive from the benefits of representing data in terms of relations.

Chief among the benefits is the preservation of truth-states or consistency across update operations. In other words, no edit operation to a relational table should ever unintentionally add, remove, or unintentionally change the value of any existent information. Because relations are groups of information elements, the laws of logic must apply to them.

Canonical logic[2] is the name for that body of primitives that is accepted by a majority of practicing logicians and analytical philosophers. Most current logical procedures (with the exception of those going back to Aristotle) can be traced to the turn-of-the-century symbolic innovations of Gottlob Frege's *Begriffsschrift*[3] and the *Principia Mathematica*[4] by Bertrand Russell and Alfred North Whitehead. The relational model is based, in large part, on canonical logic.

Where Do OLAP Models Branch from?

Consider the following questions. Is there a multidimensional model of data separate from that of the relational model? If there is not, then how do multidimensional structures and operations follow from relational primitives? If there is, what is it, and how does it relate to canonical logic? Lastly, can canonical logic support a multidimensional model, or are new foundations required?

Chronologically speaking, multidimensional products were developed in the absence of any standard data model. There was, of course, geometry, which had become multidimensional in the early 1800s, and the matrix algebra that appeared later. These probably were a part of the awareness of individuals who created OLAP products.

Ex post facto, you should at least be able to construct a standard data model of what all these products have in common. Within that collection of common structures and operations, you can distinguish basic or primitive features from ones that are constructed. This would enable researchers, developers, and users to speak a common language and think about issues independently of particular products. As you could see from my critique of implicit models in Chapter 4, the task is not as simple as it might sound because different products differ substantially over fundamental issues. Examples would be whether all dimensions are equivalent or whether variables should be treated differently and whether multiple levels are a part of the same dimension or whether they each belong in a separate dimension.

As stated in Chapter 1, the core logical requirements of any multidimensional model need to include:

- Rich dimensional structuring with hierarchical referencing
- Efficient specification of dimensions and calculations

In Chapter 4, I added the requirement of symmetry. Finally, subsumed within those requirements (though these aren't discussed until Chapter 6) are the additional requirements of providing:

- Procedures for handling logical sparsity
- The capability for data to flow in any direction within the model

As you saw in Chapter 2, SQL databases (even with the SQL/OLAP extensions to SQL 99) have a hard time meeting the first two requirements. As you'll learn, the reason has less to do with the relational model than with the canonical logic upon which it is (at least partially) based.

Multidimensional Features Are Not Directly Supported by the Relational Model

The relational model focuses on structural operations more than data operations (the basic operations of relational algebra, such as joins, Cartesian products, projections, and restrictions, are all structural operations), and on base data more than derived data. The mathematical functions used to define the values of one attribute of a relation in terms of the values of another attribute of the same relation attach to columns. Functions in the relational model apply most naturally in a relation- and column-specific sense.

Oddly enough, the main differences between the relational model and a multidimensional model have nothing to do with the multiple dimensions. From the moment you have multiple columns in a relation, the relation is multidimensional. As you saw in Chapter 2, the key differences are that the multidimensional model focuses on hierarchical relationships, and that it focuses on efficiently defining data derivations by attaching formulas to dimension members. Let's look at these differences more closely.

As was described in Chapter 2, for example, the relational algebra does not efficiently define intradimensional comparisons because they are generally performed between rows within a column. It is far more suited to defining interattribute calculations that generally involve intercolumn comparisons. SQL is so weak on this point that in order to perform interrow calculations in SQL, people frequently transform, in a roundabout fashion, the interrow problem into an intercolumn problem, and then solve the intercolumn problem.

Thus, as illustrated in Figure F.2, core features of multidimensional products are not directly supported by the relational model. Does this mean that any multidimensional model, such as the LC model, is irreconcilable with the relational model, or is there some way both models can be united? Think about it.

Multidimensional Features Are Not Directly Supported by Canonical Logic[5]

The question remains, "Are core multidimensional features supported by canonical logic?" If they are, then, to the degree that the relational model is as complete as the canonical logic, multidimensional features should be derivable from the relational model. If they are not, then some other logic or some extensions to canonical logic are

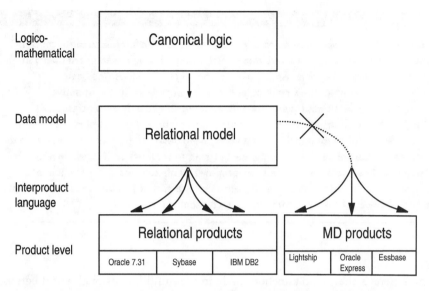

Figure F.2   The relational model does not adequately support multidimensional features.

needed to ground multidimensional features. If some extensions are made to canonical logic, then would it be possible to unify a multidimensional (MD) and relational model under a more comprehensive logic?

The biggest problem that canonical logic has trying to support uniquely multidimensional features, as described later, is its lack of hierarchical dimensions, its lack of symmetry, and its lack of a theory of meaning capable of being used as a procedure for parsing missing and inapplicable data. The latter creates problems for the relational model (where debate is still ongoing as to how best to process invalid data) as much as for OLAP where sparsity, as shown in Chapter 6, is a significant issue.

NOTE   In the discussion that follows, set theory is treated synonymously with (or as extensionally equivalent to) logic.

Hierarchies

On the one hand, it could be argued that level, hierarchy, or resolution is the principle-ordering feature of set theory, characterizing as it does the primitive relationship between element and set. On the other hand, multiple iterations of a many-to-one relationship do not generate a resolutional order. Thus, for example, set theory has no way to distinguish between a 1-to-6 hierarchical relationship, such as a state and its political subunits, and a 1-to-6 relationship that defined an object, such as a table and six sibling-like neighbors such as chairs. It is precisely the primitive nature of the set-membership function that obstructs the construction of a resolutional axis for relating elements, sets, and sets of sets. In addition, the set-membership relation isn't transitive: to be a member of a set is not, by virtue of that relation, to be a member of a set of that set.

MEREOLOGY

Mereology is the only school of axiomatic set theory that even addresses these concerns. Specifically, mereology treats of part-whole relations, modifying the standard theory in such a way as to capture some aspects of resolutional relationships. The basic modifications are simple: The singleton (unit class) is postulated as the primitive element; the parts of a class (or set) are defined to be all and only its subclasses. Classically, because transitivity was not an automatic feature of the set-element relation, part-hole relations (where transitivity is a given) were detached from and subordinated to the broader context of set-membership. David Lewis, in his *Parts of Classes*,[6] inverts this and treats part-hole relations as the more primitive. In his calculus, x is a member of a class y only when x is a member of a singleton that is a part of y. Moreover, we can adapt standard iterative set theory to formally characterize this relationship.

What is clear is that the distinction made in the multidimensional world between ancestral relationships of parent and child versus sibling relationships is not made in canonical logic.

Handling Sparsity: Theory of Meaning

Canonical logic also has a problem defining what constitutes an information element or unit of meaning. Typically speaking, valid information elements are defined according to some syntactic conditions wherein only certain (or well-formed) formulas are considered valid. All, and only, valid formulas possess a truth value that, in the classical two-valued case, may be either true or false. The problem is that there are many seemingly valid syntactic expressions that do not appear to possess any meaning, or that appear to be both true and false. Logicians call the latter expressions paradoxes. The liar paradox, which many readers may have seen in college, is one such example. A modern version of it is "This sentence is false." If the sentence is true, then it is false; but if it is false, then it is true.

The lack of an adequate theory of meaning is a problem for canonical logic that appears in all applications, not just OLAP. In the OLAP world, as shown in Chapter 6, for example, a hypercube typically defines many empty cells (it is important to know which cells are empty and meaningless, and which cells are empty and missing). In the relational world, it is clear that canonical logic has nothing to say about handling invalid propositions. This is why, as described in Chapter 6, the debate continues in the relational world between advocates of two-, three-, four-, and many-valued logics. There is no canonical way to decide the issues. So canonical logic, with its inability to define levels or account adequately for meaning, does not provide a comprehensive foundation for multidimensional models.

Symmetry

Finally, canonical logic does not support symmetry between what it calls functions (contents) and arguments (locators). The distinction between functions and arguments

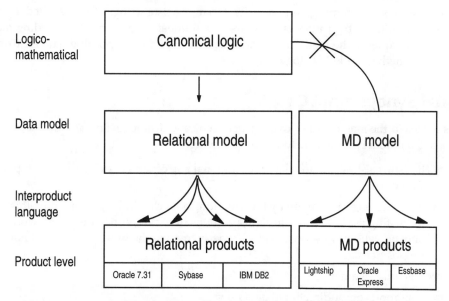

Figure F.3 Canonical logic does not support a multidimensional model.

is primitive; there is no common substrate. In the predicate calculus, the attempt to switch roles requires using what's called second order predicate calculus.

A Tractarian Approach

The term tractarian refers to any of several approaches to language and logic based on the *Tractatus Logico-Philosophicus*[7] by the Austrian philosopher Ludwig Wittgenstein (incidentally number eight in *Time* magazine's list of the greatest minds of the twentieth century for those readers who are not familiar with the name).[8] Wittgenstein wrote the work in the early part of the century, shortly after his studies and collaboration with Bertrand Russell at Cambridge. The final goal of his book was to delineate clearly what can be expressed by means of propositions, these being the proper subject matter for logical treatment. Along the way, it laid the groundwork for distinguishing propositions from nonpropositions, by means of usage- or functionally-based criteria. Perhaps because of the difficulty of the work, few of his innovations were incorporated within the main body of canonical logic. Although it goes beyond the scope of this book to dive into and do serious battle for his ideas, (interested readers are encouraged to read the bibliography's papers on the topic by this author and colleagues), I felt the need to at least minimally describe an approach to logic possessing the requisite properties for supporting multidimensional functionality (as well as relational functionality) and for resolving the problems that plague canonical logic.

LC logic is the name given to a Tractarian-consistent logic that resulted from research conducted over the past 20 years by a number of individuals, including me. Thus, in Chapter 6, the method for handling missing and inapplicable data is attributed to something called LC logic.

Brief Synopsis of LC logic

As relates to the major area of overlap between canonical logic and any multidimensional data model LC logic includes the following:

- It distinguishes positional and resolutional adjacencies in dimension (or type) structures.
- It handles logical sparsity by incorporating a mechanically grounded method for distinguishing meaningful propositions from nonpropositions, and works only on valid propositions while properly treating the two basic types of nonpropositions.
- It is fully symmetrical.
- It supports omni-directional data flows.

LC Type Structures

The LC model's underlying logic, LC logic, articulates a principle for ordering, linking, or relating propositions (or N-tuples with an LC structure) that translates into the MD world as a primitive topology for dimensions (described in Chapter 5). This principle is grounded in the primitive concept of adjacency. There are two primitive types of adjacency: instance or position such as between two cities or persons or between two measurements made in meters; and metric or resolution such as between cities and a state or measurements made in meters with measurements made in angstroms.

THE RELEVANCE OF RESOLUTION OR SCALE TO LOGIC

Traditionally, canonical logic has ignored these distinctions, since it claims to treat only the combinatorial connections between propositions (and, or, not, and so forth), irrespective of their meaning. And surely concerns about adjacency must belong to their semantics, or meaning. However, the logical treatment of two propositions p and q cannot be the same when the meaning of q is part of the meaning of p, as when the two are inferentially independent. This is more evident in the case of predicate logic, which deals specifically with the cardinality relationships between sets and members. According to the LC way of thinking, to say that something is a part of something else (in the resolutional sense of part) is to express a tautology. Similarly, the relationship between an operation and its results (as used, positionally speaking, to express a series of integers) is also tautologous. And tautologies are precisely the domain of logic. Ignoring the relevance of adjacency means the logician must abstain from specifying any criteria for well-formedness (that is, the use of those p's and q's in real-world situations).

Meaning and Sparsity

Traditionally, the term proposition has been used to indicate the meaning of a sentence, following on the observation that two or more sentences may mean the same thing, or (though less often recognized) that the same sentence can have two or more meanings. However, the claim that a consistent logic and a viable theory of representation somehow follow from a theory of propositions is not widely acknowledged.

Canonical logic treats sentences, propositional tokens or signs, well-formed formulae, character strings, and propositions indiscriminately (according to various definitions of well-formedness). Historically, the sentence/proposition distinction has only been invoked in the evident cases where a sentence does not uniquely specify a proposition, or an apparently well-formed sign doesn't yield a proposition at all. One reason is that logicians are inclined to believe meaningfulness can be ascertained from the sign itself—or else by what criteria would we call a system formal? A second reason is that the notion of proposition has never been well-defined.

Aristotle characterized logic within the context of an affirming/denying game (the dialectic in its original sense) and defined propositions as the primitive units of this game. He further diagnosed a certain compositeness of type as their defining character, distinguishing an assertion from what was making the assertion. Yet since Aristotle equated these types with the grammatical distinctions of predicate and subject respectively, he thereby sanctioned the subsequent focus on indicative sentences.

Logicians ever since have been devising ways of preserving that focus. Bertrand Russell, who early on recognized that grammatical form does not always indicate logical form, is a case in point. His theory of descriptions was an attempt to uncover the hidden logical form of sentences whose grammatical subject no longer exists, and so maintain their place in the truth-functional calculus—otherwise, well-formed but meaningless (that is, non-truth-functional) sentences might infect the calculus as a whole. One of the insights behind Wittgenstein's *Tractatus* that is leveraged in LC logic is that well-formedness on the page—however it is defined—is not a strong enough condition to guarantee meaningfulness.

The self-referentially interpreted "This sentence is false" (which if true is, as it claims, false; but if false, is thereby true) is a case in point. It is on all accounts well-formed, but if allowed into the calculus, it would undermine the complementarity or mutual exclusivity requirement of truth and falsity. Both LC and canonical logic, then, begin with the insight that certain well-formed sentences do not take a truth value. LC, however, reasons about these sentences without having to reason with them; that is, without bringing them into the calculus. Because sentences are themselves located contents (as perceptible facts: character strings, tokens, and so forth), it is possible to mechanically parse their representational forms from the outside. One distinguishes the genuine from the putative propositions by attempting to make the terms perform their prototype functions of location and content specification.

Within a two-valued propositional calculus, then, the only presupposition is that propositions alone are treated; and it is expressed in the following manner: Propositions occur in other propositions only as the arguments of truth-functions. P is false is identical to the truth-function $\bar{p}$ (or *not p*). So, even in the case of "This very proposition is false," however strongly the phrase "This very opposition" insists that it is a proposition, it fails the LC compositeness query. Nor can one retreat to the claim that the phrase names a proposition, namely this very proposition is false, because this string of tokens has to submit to the same query—what proposition? Neither this very proposition nor the entire "This very proposition" is false are (on the standard reading of these terms) possible values of p in that p is false (that is, neither can be its own truth-argument in the logical formula $\bar{p}$).

In LC logic, then, meaninglessness never infects a logical formula, since it never enters the calculus. Despite appearances, the expression, "If the square root of 2 is blue, then Bill is in the bar," is not an instance of if p then q. However, it is not the logical formula that is called into question (as if its applicability were no longer global), but the substitution of a nonproposition for the propositional variable p. And if an element of a proposed molecular compound fails the test, the element may be eliminated, generally without having to delete the entire expression. Thus, LC logic takes a firm stand on the issue of invalid propositions and can serve as a useful support for the OLAP (and relational) requirements of logical sparsity handling (as it does in Chapter 6).

Symmetry

In contrast to the referential approach in canonical logic, where both the grammatical Aristotelian and logical Russellian subjects and predicates are distinguished referentially (that is, by reference to individual substances and universals, for the former, and to individuals of acquaintance and sense-data-properties for the latter), LC logic is based on a Tractarian-style functional distinction of types. To this end, it distinguishes two primary or prototype functions necessary and sufficient for determining a proposition: location specification and content specification.[9]

> **NOTE** The terminology is somewhat reversed in logical parlance, where the term "variable" is usually reserved for the locator (the *x* of a propositional function *f(x)*). In a logic, however, both prototype functions (content and location) are expressed by types or variables (the *f* and *x* respectively of quantified expressions).

Data Flows

The coexistent position and resolution adjacency structuring of LC dimensions (or types) relativizes all statement references, and naturally supports an information model (supported by many but by no means all OLAP products on the market) where data flows from anywhere to anywhere. Allocations, inferences, leads and lags are as natural as aggregations. In contrast, canonical logic, as evidenced by Russell's empiricism, his logical atomism, and his Theory of Descriptions (a decompositional approach to transforming ordinary language into collections of quantified logical statements and assertions of primitive sense data), tacitly assumes that data enters at some base level and then propagates upward.

Summary

In this appendix, you've seen that the core features of any multidimensional model are not cleanly supported by either the relational model or the canonical logic upon which the relational model is at least partially based. You've also seen how a combination of a Tractarian approach to logic combined with the primitive notion of positional and resolutional adjacencies is sufficient (and is used in this book) to ground core multidimensional features.

Returning to the question of rapprochement between a multidimensional model and a relational model, in my opinion, all core features of any multidimensional model, including the LC model, can be cleanly integrated with the relational model. The point of integration is the relational notion of domains or what in the LC model I called a type. Types are a method of domain structuring. (It's how we positioned our first product when talking to relational vendors in the early 1990s.) The relational model has historically been mute on the internal structure of a domain beyond simply calling it a pool of potential values (can the pool be hierarchical, can it have any derived values, other domain references ?). I believe that if the core features of a type-based multidimensional model were incorporated into the relational model's notion of domain, and products were built that supported that model, we would then have a fully integrated or unified MD/relational database product. And such a product and its underlying model would in turn be grounded in a Tractarian rather than canonical approach to logic.

Codd's 18 Features

Although multidimensional concepts have been applied to computing for over 30 years (the APL language used multidimensional arrays in 1964), the term OLAP first arose in September 1993 when Codd, Codd, and Salley wrote a white paper entitled "Providing OLAP (On-Line Analytical Processing) to User-Analysts: An IT Mandate."[1]

Due to Dr. Codd's renown as the founder of the relational data model, the white paper generated a lot of attention. However, the attention was not unanimously positive. There were several problems with the paper.

Originally published in *Computerworld*[2] as if it were the product of unbiased research, the paper's credibility was severely damaged when it was discovered that it had been funded by one particular company, Arbor Software, and, if taken at face value, purported to show that only Arbor's product met a significant percentage of Codd's 12 Rules.[3] *Computerworld* later wrote a retraction stating that it was a mistake to have published the article as if it were unbiased research.[4]

The paper attempted to leverage Codd's original definition of the relational model that began with a list of 12 rules (later expanded to more than 300). One of the central tenets of the relational model was the need to separate logical issues, such as the relational schema of a model, from issues of physical implementation, such as how the various relations should be stored and accessed on a computer. The relational model was a logical model.

A cube considered as a logical structuring of data is the same regardless of whether it is instantiated in relational tables on disk using a Star schema, or whether it resides in a server as a RAM cube, or whether it sits on a client tool, or whether it is partitioned between several physical devices.

Codd's white paper, however, clearly confused logical issues with physical issues. One of the original 12 rules, for example, states that a product needs to have physical facilities for handling sparse matrices. (There is nothing wrong with taking a stand on physical issues, but physical issues must be distinguished from logical issues. If you're going to mention physical issues, you need to be systematic about it. You need efficient array processing and data access as much as you need efficient handling of sparsity.)

The 12 rules for OLAP, as originally published, followed 10 pages of background information. In one crucial area, multidimensional aggregation, the background pages distinguished between variable and nonvariable dimensions. (Actually, nonvariable dimensions were called parameters.) It is certainly reasonable to suppose that the 12 rules were intended to represent the crystallization into rule form of a more prosaic description of the same issues. Yet in the body of the 12 rules, rule number 6 for example, stated that all dimensions were equivalent in both structure and operational capabilities.

The advocacy of generic dimensionality would seem to contradict the background material that preceded it. It clearly did not follow from the work Dr. Codd performed in the late 1970s on issues of aggregation. In 1978, for example, Dr. Codd published a paper entitled "Extending the Database Relational Model to Capture More Meaning."[5] This paper attempted to define a minimal set of constructs required to generate all types of semantic abstractions. At no point did the paper even attempt to reduce the set to a single, generic dimension.

Another problem with the paper, if read as an academic work, which is how the paper presented itself (though that is no longer how it is treated), is Codd's definition of a dimension. On page 11 of the original 1993 paper, Codd defines a dimension in the following way: "The highest level in a data consolidation path is referred to as that data's dimension." This would imply that each consolidation path in a multipath hierarchy is a separate dimension because there is a top level for each consolidation path. If a given set of leaf nodes, say stores, connects to three different consolidation paths, cities, store-types, and store-sizes, do stores belong to three dimensions, or do the three consolidated dimensions share the same base level, in which case the dimension does not include the leaf nodes? At the very least, Codd's notion of a dimension is not clearly defined.

Reservations notwithstanding, Codd's efforts certainly brought a substantial amount of mass attention to multidimensional problems and tools, and assigned the easily pronounceable buzzword, OLAP, to the ensemble. In any event, the 12 original rules, later reclassified as features, were expanded to 18 in May 1995 (although you had to pay to be exposed to them) and they deserve to be mentioned, if only for their historical interest. What follows is a brief discussion of Codd's original 12 rules. They are shown loosely dumped (by me) into the categories basic, reporting, and dimensional. The feature numbers correspond to the way they were numbered in the orignal white paper.

Basic Features

Feature 10: Intuitive Data Manipulation

Referring to consolidation path reorganization, drilling down and across, and so on, Codd advocated direct action on the cells of a model as the preferred method of intuitive data manipulation. Furthermore, cell-based action is fine for working with high data but not always optimal for working with meta data—the latter being more often worked on via outline editors. People do not all share the same concept of intuitive. Tools should allow for a variety of interaction methods, from mouse gestures to dialogue boxes and command lines.

Feature 3: Accessibility

According to Codd, the OLAP tool should present a single, logical view of enterprise data originating from a variety of sources. The source of the data in the OLAP model should be transparent to the user. I agree with this, but I would add that end users may also be a source of data.

Feature 5: Client/Server Architecture

Codd states that an OLAP product should be capable of running on the server in a client/server architecture and that client tools should be able to hook up to the server with a minimal amount of effort. For OLAP servers, the latter requirement makes sense, though it begs the question of interoperability standards. (If the OLAP API gets adopted, the latter requirement, at least for browsing, should be easier to fulfill.)

Feature 2: Transparency

Codd states that an OLAP product should act as a transparent support to the end-user's customary front-end tool. While I agree with the goal of minimizing the learning curve for new users of an OLAP product, and while it is admirable to leverage as much as possible from existing client tool investments, literally speaking, transparency is a myth. The way an OLAP server hooks up to a client tool such as a spreadsheet is via an add-in menu box offering function selections such as drill down, dimension member selection, cascade, and pivot, which are meaningless concepts within the spreadsheet paradigm.

Feature 8: Multi-User Support

According to Codd, OLAP tools should support concurrent read/write operations, integrity, and security. I agree with this view.

Reporting Features

Feature 11: Flexible Reporting

Codd seems to be advocating the ability to display a cube's dimensions mapped to any combination of rows, columns, and pages. However, Codd treats rows, columns, and pages equally, which is not possible. While Codd states that any subset of the members of a dimension should be able to be mapped to any row, column, or page, as shown in Chapter 3, it is possible only to display a single member at a time in the page dimension. To do otherwise would be to convert the page into a row or column.

Feature 4: Consistent Reporting Performance

Codd suggests that reporting performance should remain constant as the number of dimensions or size of the database increases. However, there are limits to reporting performance unless the data is all precomputed and stored in RAM. Assuming the data is disk based (a rational assumption if the question is how to maintain consistent reporting as the size of the database increases), all data is clustered in some way on disk. Thus, there will always be some queries that necessitate more disk accesses than others. Also, absolute speed is more important than relative change in speed.

Feature 7: Dynamic Sparse Matrix Handling

I agree with Codd that, in an ideal situation, the physical organization of the data should reflect real data characteristics. And as the data characteristics change over time, so too should the data's physical organization.

Dimensional Features

Feature 1: Multidimensional Conceptual View

Codd states that the user's view of the enterprise is multidimensional in nature and thus the user-analyst's conceptual view of OLAP models should also be multidimensional in nature. In an informal way, this is certainly true. It is fine as a loose requirement, but it assumes that the term dimension has been defined.

Feature 6: Generic Dimensionality

Codd states that each dimension must be equivalent in both its structure and operational capabilities and that additional operations may be granted to selected dimensions. Beyond the fact that the definition is internally inconsistent (once additional operations have been granted to certain dimensions they are arguably no longer equivalent), I have voiced elsewhere my disagreement with this feature.[6]

Feature 12: Unlimited Dimensions and Aggregation Levels

I consider this to be a pretty vacuous feature. Aside from the fact that anything implemented on a finite computer is ipso facto limited (the internal machine representation of the dimensional meta data will always place some finite limit on the number of dimension, levels, and/or cells), the limits of most OLAP servers far exceed most user's practical needs.

Feature 9: Unrestricted Cross-Dimensional Operations

I agree with Codd where he states that OLAP tools' DML "must allow calculation and data manipulation across any number of data dimensions and must not restrict or inhibit any relationship between data cells regardless of the number of common data attributes each cell contains." As a cautionary note, in a world of cross-dimensional calculations, it is very easy to define member-specific formulas that, when combined at a cell, produce a meaningless cell formula. Beyond the simple summations and ratios, it is also easy to imagine dimension-specific formulas for which there is no correct precedence ordering when the formulas are combined across dimensions.

Notes

Chapter 1

1. The term OLAP originated in more of a marketing than a technical context. It was coined by Arbor Corporation in 1993. By using Ted Codd's name (Codd was the creator of the Relational Database Model) and having him coin 12 so-called rules that bore a remarkable resemblance to Arbor's feature set at the time, they hoped to give OLAP legitimacy. By using an otherwise meaningless though pronounceable acronym, they hoped to make it sound less mathematical than the term "multidimensional database."

As a result, the term OLAP lacks the definitional rigor of such neighboring terms as "the relational data model." I debated for a while whether to use the term OLAP in this book. After all, the fundamental technology behind OLAP is multidimensional. Yet there is an essential activity or process that corporations around the world perform every day that could be partially referred to by the term OLAP. Other parts of that process could be referred to by the terms *data mining, decision analysis, data visualization,* or even *data transformation.* And that activity, which consists of analyzing business operations with an eye towards making timely and accurate analysis-based decisions, has no official name. It's as if you wanted to talk to people about the benefits of a good mattress in a language that had no word for sleeping.

For this reason, I take the time to define analysis-based, decision-oriented information processing, or ABDOP, as the natural, larger, and more general category of processing within which OLAP refers to a particular component. By cleanly defining OLAP within the scope of a well-grounded category, OLAP becomes well grounded and OLAP, like transaction processing, deserves to be a permanent part of our computing environment.

2. The first public debate was between Jim Dorian, then CEO of Arbor, and Michael Saylor, then CEO of Microstrategy, during a DCI Datawarehouse conference in New York City in 1995.

3. DCI Data Warehouse Conference in San Jose, April 1997.

4. Thomsen, August 1997.

5. The rapid ascension of purpose-defining pseudo-technical buzzwords has obscured some of the real technical advances that have taken place over the past 10 years. To understand just how extreme the technology industry is compared to others, consider the following analogy.

Automotive technology, from engine design to fuel, braking, and suspension systems, has improved dramatically over the last 100 years. Yet for all the changes that have occurred (including many specialized motor vehicles such as jeeps, trucks, and sports cars), the root purpose—driving—has remained constant. We were driving in 1901 and we are still driving in 2002.

Imagine a parallel universe where no sooner did the automotive industry convince you of the need to drive (and you invested in driving tools, a.k.a. cars) than it convinced you of the need for independent locomotion (and sold you independent locomotors—which bore a curious resemblance to cars). Then, no sooner did you adopt independent locomotion technology than the industry convinced you that what you really needed was autonomous spatial translation and proceeded to sell you autonomous spatial translators (which also bore a curious resemblance to cars). Adopting new technologies would be very confusing in such an alternate universe because useful innovations (such as automatic transmissions, power steering, and anti-lock brakes) would be lost in a sea of marketing jargon.

Unfortunately, business-computing software seems to operate under this parallel universe principle. The terms business intelligence, data warehousing, and decision support all refer to the same purpose.

This author has at various times been involved in industry discussions trying to decide whether to define OLAP, data mining, and other analytical technologies as complementary to data warehousing or as a part of data warehousing. In early drafts of this second edition, I debated whether to simply use the terms data warehousing or decision support or even business intelligence instead of ABDOP. In the end I decided to stay with ABDOP, not in an attempt to turn it into a popular acronym, but because of its probable lack of popularity (I only use it as a starting point for defining OLAP); its meaning is likely to remain constant over the life of this book, whereas the public meaning of the terms data warehousing, decision support, and business intelligence are likely to continue changing.

6. www.informs.org

7. www.kdnuggets.com

8. Han, 2001.

Chapter 2

1. There were also a number of forward-looking desktop products during this time. Javelin, eventually bought by IRI, had the concept of time series and understood how to translate variables between different time periodicities. And TM/1 (for Table Manager 1) was the first multidimensional desktop spreadsheet, though at the time it called itself a relational spreadsheet.

2. Codd, February 1974.

3. Stemple, et al., 1988.

4. Shipman, March 1981.

5. Smith, J.M, and Smith, D.C.P., 1977.

6. Codd, 1978.

7. Celko, 1995; Date and Darwin, 1994.

8. Technically, it is possible through the use of many lookup tables and macros to drive the whole process. However, the resulting model is fragile and difficult to define and maintain. I know this from experience. My former company created such macro-driven models for all the popular spreadsheets to show just how difficult the process was.

9. Kimball, January 1996.

10. Red Brick Software's Red Brick Warehouse implements a proprietary variant of SQL called RISQL that explicitly supports the computation of cumulative sums and the selection of rows based on ranking (top- or bottom-N) and quartile criteria. Chris Date, in a series of articles published in *Database Programming and Design*, explores the area of "quota queries" (queries based on ranking criteria) on how SQL might be extended to support them.

11. Gray, et al., 1995.

12. "Final Proposed Draft . . ." SQL, November 1999; Zemke, et al., May 5, 1999.

Chapter 3

1. Abbott, 1983.

2. *Tractatus Logico-Philosophicus*, 2.161.

3. This term was first mentioned in *The OLAP Report* published in 1995. See Pendse and Creeth, 1995, pp. 52–64.

Chapter 4

1. The word dimension is a rich and, for that reason, semantically loaded term. During most of its 2500-year history, it was used predominantly by mathematicians and carried a largely geophysical or three-dimensional meaning. With the advent of abstract geometries and algebras over the last few centuries, that meaning has expanded into spaces that are more-than-three- or multi-dimensional.

It wasn't until the early 19th century that mathematicians such as Mobius, Cauchy, and Clifford began theorizing about abstract geometrical spaces independent of the three-dimensional limitations of physical space (See Smith 1959).

Today's practical discussions of how dimensions and variables (as a generalization of the concept of measure) should be treated in a multi-dimensional system have their roots going back over two millennia. The term dimension traces back through the old French of the time of Descartes to the Latin *dimetiri* meaning a way of measuring (though many dictionaries translate *dimetiri* simply as "to measure"), which in turn traces back to the Greek. The Greeks had two very different terms for dimension and measure. To the Greeks, these were two different concepts. The concept of measure was a practical concept, and the Romans, being a practical people, easily adopted the concept. But the concept of dimension was another story. The Greeks wondered a great deal about the world. They espoused myriad ontologies. The Romans, in contrast, were not known for their philosophical enterprises. I imagine the Greek word for dimension may have confused them. For the Romans, there was nothing to think about. So to the translators of the time, the Greek word for dimension must only have had meaning in the concrete sense of measuring.

Thus the Latin term for the Greek concept of dimension became wed to the concept of measurement. In fact, for the next 2000 years, with the exception of geometers who maintained a distinction between the meaning of dimension and the meaning of measure, the term dimension became synonymous with the concepts of measurement and number. The dimension of an object referred its size, as it does today when we talk about the dimension or magnitude of a problem.

2. I use the term *issue-specific approaches to OLAP modeling* instead of *model* because the term model implies that you are treating the whole of what needs to be dealt with for OLAP, whereas the former term makes it clear that we are looking at how products work on an issue-by-issue or approach-by-approach basis.

3. Some authors have tried to formulize the distinction between data and meta data by defining a model that connects or maps sets of dimensional intersections in the meta data to sets of elements in the data. In this way, by defining two types of structures—data and meta data—the data becomes part of the overall system. Of course, it then becomes necessary to add all the same conceptual machinery required by the explicit dimension measure approach to provide for queries about the meta data constrained by the data. If the distinction between data and meta data is maintained, but the role switching machinery is not in place, then closure is violated whenever a query is posed about the meta data because the result of a query, a set of meta data, is not a part of the data.

4. The term "functional" refers to any of several approaches to language, math, and logic based on the *Tractatus Logico-Philosophicus* by the Austrian philosopher Ludwig Wittgenstein (incidentally number eight in *Time* magazine's list of the greatest minds of the twentieth century, for those readers who are not familiar with the name, and ahead of Russell, who was a major contributor to what is now considered canonical math and logic). Wittgenstein wrote the work in the early part of the twentieth century, shortly after his studies and collaboration with Bertrand Russell at Cambridge. The major goal of his book was to delineate what can be expressed by means of propositions, these being the proper subject matter for logical treatment. Along the way, it laid a groundwork for distinguishing propositions from nonpropositions, by means of

usage or functionally based criteria. Perhaps because of the difficulty of the work, few of his innovations were incorporated within the main body of canonical logic, though he is remembered as having been the inventor of the truth tables.

5. Although beyond the scope of this book, mathematically speaking, types are rich enough to represent expressions in linear algebra, topology, differential geometry, graph theory, sets, and tensor manifolds. Media-wise, anything can be a type, from numbers or text to audio signals or arbitrary bit patterns. In addition, types can behave like object classes and are capable of inheritance, encapsulation, polymorphism, and messaging.

Chapter 5

1. One could argue that the list of valid instances could be internal to the dimension, and thus that verification need not be external. However, this misses the fundamental point that regardless of whether the list of valid instances exists "within some region defined as being a part of or internal to the dimension" or whether the list of valid instances exists in a clearly external source table or user's manual entry, the point is that the list of valid instances is just that—a list.

This contrasts with the internal or generative rule-based definition of the cardinal series. (One can always define rules that behave like list matchers in the sense that the rule is defined by a list of valid instances.) To be an integer is not to be any particular token. No domain defined on the integers needs to pre-store all integer values. Rather the integers are defined by a generative or process-oriented rule capable of constructing any particular integer.

2. Except in the case of high-cardinality dimensions where large numbers of instances need to directly connect to a parent instance such as a listing of the individual customers that connect to a city and where the tool has a limit on the number of child-to-parent connections, thus forcing the user to insert dummy intermediate parent instances.

3. As this section progresses from nominal through ordinal to cardinal series, the astute reader may feel that I am overloading the = sign, having it behave as an identity operator for nominal series and a position-testing operator for ordinal and cardinal series. After all, does it really make sense to talk about two nominal instances being equal, as in the instance "sports car" of the type vehicle being equal to the instance "sports car" of another type vehicle in the same way that two cardinal instances may be said to be equal, as in the instance 5 of the type integer being equal to the sum of the instances 2 and 3 of the type integer?

My answer here is yes, it does make sense to use the = sign or equality operator in both cases. There are critical distinctions to be made, such as between translation-based equality testing, essentially list-based comparisons, where an instance is validated as belonging in a type because it matched some instance in that type, and between transformation-based equality testing where some set of operations is performed on the instances of one type, say $1 + 1 + 1 + 1$, to test whether the expression is equal to 4. Furthermore, one can use different methods of equality testing at different times for the same expression. For example, the expression $2 + 3 = 5$ can be tested by comparing the symbol 5 with a symbol stored in an answer table, in which case, at that moment, the equality testing for the expression only relied on a translation-based method of equality testing as found in any nominal series. The same expression $2 + 3 = 5$ can also be tested by carrying out an operation, such as a decrement by 1, on each of the two sides and then testing the equality of the number of times the decrement operator could successfully decrement each of the two sides.

4. We have chosen to use the terms *type* and *instance* because they are typically used for similar purposes in computer science and because they are less burdened with ongoing meaning than other terms. In addition, we introduce the term metric, and while recognizing that it represents a generalized notion of its typical mathematical usage, it is nonetheless the term that comes closest to representing the quantitative relationships embedded in hierarchical type structures.

5. The definition of a type in terms of instance-metric pairs is a logical definition that is independent of how the type is physically organized or represented to a user. The closest analogy is a domain in the relational sense, rather than an object, class, or template from an object-oriented (OO) point perspective. (In fact, types are domains in their relational sense of the term.) That said, although one could use OO terms to describe types and their instance-metric pairs, since there are already fixed definitions for OO terms, since object-oriented constructs rely on mathematics and logic and since OLAP applications are inference- and calculation-oriented, I thought it more useful to define types and hierarchies on a mathematical and logical rather than computer science foundation.

6. It is also possible to define mixed hierarchies with fully connected levels, where the hierarchical distance between the instances of the two levels is greater than one. Although I can imagine examples of such mixed hierarchies, I have not found any clients who demanded them for their applications, and their definition can seem a bit theoretical, so I choose to leave their discussion out of this book.

Chapter 6

1. See Appendix G.

2. For example, in a logical system with three values True, False, and Unknown, there is no good way to say "not" to all three values. In most systems offered, Not(True) will be defined as False, Not(False) will be defined as True, and Not(Unknown) will be defined as Unknown. Unfortunately, that means that sometimes Not(x) does not equal (x), and sometimes Not(x) does equal x! In other systems where Not(Unknown) is defined as False, the Not(Not(x)) will sometimes equal x and sometimes not. All of a sudden, logic is not something that can be consistently applied. (See S. Shavel and E. Thomsen, "On Three Valued Logics," from a paper presented at the sixteenth Wittgenstein International Symposium on Cognitive Science.)

3. See Codd, December 1986; and McGoveran, October 1993.

4. Codd, 1991, p. 182.

5. Shavel and Thomsen, 1993.

6. the series of articles by David McGoveran in *Database Programming and Design* 1993; January 1994; February 1994; March 1994).

7. The need to formally distinguish between missing and meaningless data was shown in the paper "On Three Valued Logics." Stated briefly, if two truth values (true and false) are employed, then missing data may be thought of as either true or false, while meaningless data may be thought of as neither true nor false.

8. That approach was described in "On Three Valued Logic," cited previously. As a consultant, I developed a prototype system for performing these substitutions for a large institutional client.

9. That is, regardless of which method is employed by a particular product, under the hood the same referencing needs to occur, and the pitfalls that you, the analyst, might fall into are the same. And once you take steps to avoid any referencing pitfalls, such as defining your application ranges, the distinctions between the different product-based approaches begin to wither away.

10. Kimball (1997).

Chapter 7

1. Thanks to Rick Crandall for pointing out this example.

2. Cross-source selections are also known as links and are treated more carefully in Chapter 8.

Chapter 8

1. Strictly speaking, it is possible to define a table that would take only one kind of data link to extract the data into the cube, but you would never see such a table in real-world use.

Chapter 9

1. Tufte (1983), p. 9.

2. The one pseudoqualification is that of base numbers. I say pseudo because it is not a question of location. The sequence of digits 1011 means something very different in base 2 than in base 10. Nonetheless, given a base number for a string of digits, their meaning is entirely location independent.

3. See, for example, the discussion on misleading graph types in Tufte (1983), pp. 69–72.

Chapter 10

1. Stonebraker (1993).

2. Harinarayan, et al. (1996).

3. See Orenstein (1986) for more information on Z-ordering.

4. See, for example, Faloutsos and Roseman (1989) for more information on Hilbert numbering.

5. The typical product assumption is that sampling-based errors are evenly distributed across all dimensional combinations. This assumption, unfortunately, is unwarranted. What is far more likely is that the standard deviation for some measure varies across dimensions, such as products and/or regions and/or times. Furthermore, it is likely that the standard deviations cannot be calculated on a unidimensional basis because there are interdimensional dependencies. In other words, one couldn't simply calculate the standard deviation for sales by summing the standard deviations for regions, times, and products.

Thus, a correct approach would need in some fashion to estimate the covariances between dimensions. Of course, such covariances could not be effectively calculated at too low a level as there would be too many. So the challenge becomes one of efficiently calculating as many covariances as possible.

Given the need to estimate covariances, it is reasonable to try to identify the circumstances under which sampling is a more efficient route to sufficiently accurate answers than that of creating aggregate tables. In my opinion (and this would need further confirmation), correct sampling will bring the biggest bang for the buck the larger the source data table and the more queries are looking for aggregate values. This is because aggregate tables need to visit every source row and because low-level covariance matrices are prohibitively expensive.

So assuming that sampling will work best on aggregate queries of larger data sets, the challenge is to efficiently sample the source data table and correctly compute the sample statistics, including some measure of dispersion. I suspect that what would be required is some form of stratified sampling (sampling that forces the inclusion of a sufficient quantity of every dimensional category of observation), combined with re-sampling for the determination of sample variance, and some incremental heuristic (which itself will involve resampling) for determining when enough samples of any particular dimensional category have been obtained per some previously defined variance threshold.

Sampling efficiency will improve over time as the system learns, perhaps through clustering, which dimensional combinations are most efficient for the purposes of computing covariances. (In other words, where one might start with 50 members of a product dimension, 12 members of a time dimension, and 25 members of a region dimension, thus yielding 1,500 covariances to calculate, subsequent analysis may reveal that it is only necessary to track 50.)

6. Harinarayan, et al. (1996).

7. Simon, Herbert, "Managing in an Information-Rich World."

Chapter 11

e difference between logical and physical models is crucial and worth explor-
r. Logical models deal with structural and semantic relationships indepen-
ow or where those relationships are stored and accessed. Logical design

strives for the preservation of truth under all valid changes to the data and model. Physical models deal with the logistics of how and where data is stored, calculated, and accessed. Good physical design results in fast access and calculations stored with a minimum amount of space.

As George Tilllman wrote in his book *A Practical Guide To Logical Data Modeling* (1993), "The major purpose of logical data modeling is to communicate the end-users' view of the organization's data to those who will design the system. . . . The logical data model should not be tied to a particular architecture, technology, or product. Logical design breaks down a problem into its lowest logical components so that physical designers can build it back up into a physical interpretation of the logical problem."

2. This assumes you are trying to solve a problem. During the past several years, I have seen a number of organizations embark on exploratory OLAP applications, after having already built a relational data warehouse because they wanted to see what things looked like. Sometimes those things were end-user reports; sometimes they were aggregations or other calculations. In these situations, model design was mostly dictated by the source warehouse schema, typically some star variant. Model implementation consisted of linking to dimension tables followed by defining a few variables and then loading them by linking to the fact tables.

3. A logical model in the OLAP world is quite different from a logical model in a classic database setting relational world. In the relational world, logical data models do not model derived data. As you've seen throughout this book, one of the main problems for SQL, as the commercial implementation of a relational DDL/DML, is its inefficiency for specifying many types of derivations (especially complex multilevel aggregations and allocations) that need to be performed on a regular basis. In this sense, one of the chief missions for a multidimensional information system is to provide an environment for the clean specification of complex derivations. Any logical model of a multidimensional information system has to model the derivations as much as the raw inputs.

4. These types of tables and their links to a cube were defined in Chapter 8.

5. Kimball (1996) pp. 101-106.

6. The astute reader may be wondering how a single dimension can support multiple hierarchies without violating the rules for well-formed hierarchies defined in Chapter 5. How, for example, can a level based on product color, when used as a grouping principle for a product dimension, be quantitatively comparable with a level based on product name? When a seemingly single dimension supports multiple seemingly quantitatively noncomparable hierarchies, it is hiding the fact that there is always some additional table such as an attribute table that is the source of the data values used for the alternate groupings. For example, a product dimension may be associated with an attribute table composed of color and size. If the color attribute is used to create an alternate hierarchy or grouping, there is an implicit joining of the color attributes with the product dimension members at the leaf level so that each product could be thought of as a nominally ordered instance of a product color. If the color attribute values didn't attach to the leaf level of the product dimension, there would be no way to aggregate the product members into color groups. Thus, strictly speaking, each distinct association of leaf-level product members with attribute values represents a distinct type.

Chapter 13

1. In reality, were FCI to be that affected by daily fluctuations in exchange rates, the company would probably hedge its currency risk by acquiring longer-term exchange rate contracts. Also, although currency exchange impacts every facet of FCI's business and would normally be treated as a general process alongside other management functions, for these chapters I have only treated currency exchange within the context of purchasing.

Chapter 15

1. Note that the package type distinction is treated as a distinction within the Food-cake dimension for the calculation exercise in Chapter 17 in order to keep the formulas from getting overly complicated.

2. Variance is a measure of dispersion about the mean. It is typically calculated by taking the square root of the sum of the squares of the differences between each value, in this case total_revenue, and the mean value. The squaring of the differences, in this case dollars, accounts for the variance units to be in $2 . Standard deviation is based on variance.

3. This section on value states began as an article I wrote for *Intelligent Enterprise* magazine, December 5, 2001.

4. In "Symmetry Lost," *Intelligent Enterprise,* March 30, 1999, I wrote about the need for treating so-called dimensions and measures or variables as distinct use cases of the same underlying structure; there was no inherent difference between dimensions and measures.

Chapter 16

1. Although from an accounting perspective there are many tricks that a corporation can use to artificially manipulate reported earnings, and although as a result there are many alternative measures of value being proposed, the purpose of these application chapters is to teach you how to create an activity-based management style application that spans several business processes. So, rather than espouse any particular formula for calculating net value, I choose to work with the most widely used (if sometimes abused) measure of net value—earnings.

2. Although we are only looking for two tuples, namely the Qty sold of batch 123 in Cambridge and the Qty sold of batch 101 in Allston, as phrased, Qty sold will be returned for both batches for both Cambridge and Allston. Since batch 101 is not applicable to Cambridge and batch 123 is not applicable to Allston, the not applicable ᵧs will drop out of any aggregation, and ideally any view. The query was phrased ᵧs because A) it is a simpler query that way and B) it allowed for this opportu-ᵧak about the distinction between querying for specific tuples versus query-ᵧular array.

Chapter 18

1. Date (1995) p. 57, 77.

Chapter 19

1. I use the term "product language" because there are many aspects to a product that can be evaluated, from its method of storing and accessing data, to its security, to its robustness, that are not covered by the product's language. Even though the LC model is just that—a model for which no product implementation exists—it is fair and instructive to compare LC language expressions with those of the various product languages.

2. For all these examples, I used the term *could* instead of *would* because there are many different ways within each product that the same formula could be expressed, depending on how the dimensions were defined, how the variables were defined, how any cubes might have been defined, where the formula logic occurs and even what the previous formulas may have been.

3. The vendors who publicly ran the APB-1 benchmark used every trick at their disposal to speed up the performance of their respective products, so the code snippets included in this chapter are not exactly what you might do as an application developer were you to use one of the products. However, the snippets are close enough to what you would probably do and illustrative enough of how the product languages are designed that I felt it pedagogically beneficial to include them.

Chapter 20

1. For a more complete treatment of the DEER cycle, please see the series in *Intelligent Enterprise Magazine* (Thomsen, June 13, 2001; June 29, 2001; August 31, 2001).

2. Thomsen (October 1998).

3. Hegel, in *Phenomenology of Spirit* (1977), may have been the first to write about the fact that at any level of discourse or personal reflection whatever is being discussed or deliberated is always relative to a background where some things are held as certain. But that what is held as certain at one level of discourse may be questioned (using again something else as certain) at another.

4. By the term knowledge, I also mean as differentiated from skills, where skills are learned sensory-motor patterns far too numerous to ever be spoken by a person in real time.

5. Statisticians, as first mentioned in Chapter 4, frequently use the term variable as a synonym (albeit internally unstructured) for what, in this book, has been called a type. They speak of dependent and independent variables whereas we would speak of dependent (or those types appearing on the left-hand side of an equation) and independent types (or those types appearing on the right-hand side of an equation). The term case means something analogous to record number.

6. Grossman, et al. (2000).

7. Kamber, et al. (August 1997).

8. Material for the first part of this section is from Thomsen (Oct. and Nov. 1997).

9. For a clear explanation of affinity analysis, see Berry and Linoff (1997).

10. The fact that centroids no longer move does not necessarily mean that you have found a set of globally ideal clusters. It is possible that you have found a set of clusters that are only locally ideal. The problem of finding local instead of global minima is common to many algorithms, including most neural net algorithms. There are ways to minimize the chances of this happening, such as by using stochastic searches, but success is not absolutely guaranteed unless you are willing to expend a lot of computing horsepower. For more information, see Masters (1995).

11. Hotelling (1931).

Appendix E

1. Even in a business sense, the term perspective has a subtly complex meaning. What exactly does it mean to say that we need to examine our business from a customer perspective? It means that we need to look at all noncustomer aspects of the business, such as all types of sales of all types of products at all different times in terms of how any of that varies as one looks at different groups of customers. For example, how have sales evolved over the last 12 months to persons under 30 versus persons over 30. In addition, and instead of being arbitrarily grouped, the members of dimensions may be ordered. There may, for example, be an income ordering placed on customers. One could then define how sales varies as a function of changes in customer for customers ordered by personal income.

2. See, for example: Minsky, Marvin (1975); Lenat and Guha (1990); Cohen (1982).

3. The goal of most, if not all, data modeling efforts over the years has been to mimic real-world structure. Of course, as Kant pointed out, mimicking real-world structure amounts to mimicking human perception. (Kant, 1986). Locators and contents (or dimensions and variables) are a crucial component of any modeling effort because they stem from the way we structure thoughts (hence the connection to logic). The major reason MD systems appear intuitive is because they do their business the way we do ours.

4. Kimball (1996).

5. Codd (1991).

6. Ibid. p. 176.

Appendix F

1. Codd (February 1970).

2. More precisely, by "canonical" I mean "standard," nondeviant, predicate logic (Principia-like) and axiomatic set theory (Zermelo-Fraenkel-like) with intended reference to W. V. Quine's "canonical notation" for refining scientific discourse. In the context of this (rather skeletal) overview, I refer to predicate logic and set theory

interchangeably (such that Fx can be expressed as $x \in F$ and vice versa). Also, I use "set" and "class" interchangeably. Set is usually given as a restricted version of class, but the reasons for these restrictions are precisely the ones addressed in LC logic as found in Shavel and Thomsen (1990).

3. Begriffsschrift, a formula language, modeled upon that of arithmetic, for pure thought. See Gottlob (1879).

4. Whitehead and Russell (1910).

5. Steve Shavel was the principal author of this last section.

6. Lewis (1991).

7. Wittgenstein (1961).

8. "The 20th Century's Greatest Minds." March 29, 1999. *Time.*

9. For a detailed treatment of these functions, please see Shavel and Thomsen (1990).

Appendix G

1. www.essbase.com/whitepaper/olap/olap.pdf

2. "He's Back," *ComputerWorld,* September 1993.

3. *On-Line Analytical Processing: An IT Mandate,* distributed by Arbor Software, p 18.

4. Editorial page, *ComputerWorld,* October 1993.

5. Codd (1978).

6. "Letter to the Editor." *DBMS.*

Bibliography

Abbott, Edwin. 1983. *Flatland*, New York: HarperCollins.

Agarwal, Rakesh, Ashish Gupta, and Sunita Sarawagi. April 7–11, 1997. "Modeling Multidimensional Databases." *Proceedings of the Thirteenth International Conference on Data Engineering*. Birmingham, U.K.

Agarwal, Sameet, Rakesh Agarwal, Prasad M. Deshpande, Ashish Gupta, Jeffrey F. Naughton, Raghu Ramakrishnan, and Sunita Sarawagi. 1996. "On the Computation of Multidimensional Aggregates." *Proceedings of the 22nd VLDB Conference*. Mumbai (Bombay), India.

Arbor Software. *On-Line Analytical Processing: An IT Mandate*.

Bentley, Jon L. 1979. "Multidimensional Binary Search Trees in Database Applications." IEEE.

Berebson, Mark L., and Daniel M. Levine. 1979. *Basic Business Statistics: Concepts and Applications*. Englewood Cliffs, NJ: Prentice-Hall, Inc.

Bernstein, Philip A. "Repositories and Object Oriented Databases." Redmond, WA: Microsoft Corp.

Berry, M., and G. Linoff. 1997. *Data Mining Techniques*. John Wiley & Sons.

Boulton, Richard E.S., Barry D. Libert, and Steve M. Samek. 2000. *Cracking the Value Code: How Successful Businesses Are Creating Wealth in the New Economy*. New York: HarperCollins.

Brown, Judith R., Rae Earnshaw, Mikael Jern, and John Vince. 1995. *Visualization: Using Computer Graphics to Explore Data and Present Information*. New York: John Wiley & Sons.

Burn, R.P. 1985. *Groups: A Path to Geometry*. Cambridge University Press.

Celko, Joe. 1995. *Instant SQL Programming*. Chicago: Wrox Press Ltd.

Cleveland, William S. 1994. *The Elements of Graphing Data*. Summit, NJ: Hobart Press.

Codd, E. F. February 1974. "A Relational Model of Data for Large Shared Data Banks." *Communications of the ACM*.

———. 1978. "Extending the Database Relational Model to Capture More Meaning." Association for Computing Machinery.

———. December 1986. "Missing Information (Applicable and Inapplicable) in Relational Databases." *Association for Computing Machinery, SIGMOD Record* 15:4, pp. 53–78.

———. 1991. *The Relational Model for Database Management: Version 2*, Reading, MA: Addison-Wesley Publishing Company, Inc.

Cohen, Paul, Edward Feigenbaum, and Avron Barr. 1982. *The Handbook of Artificial Intelligence, Volume 1*. William Kaufmann Heuristech Press.

Cunto, Walter, Gustavo Lau, and Philippe Hlajolet. "Analysis of KDT-trees: KDT-trees Improved by Local Reorganizations."

Dahl, Veronica. 1979. "Quantification in a Three-Valued Logic for Natural Language Question-Answering Systems." International Joint Conference on Artificial Intelligence, Tokyo.

———. 1980. "A Three-Valued Logic for Natural Language Computer Applications." *Proceedings of the 10th International Symposium on Multiple-Valued Logic*.

Date, C. J. 1994. "View Updating and Database Design or, Two for the Price of One."

———. 1995. *An Introduction to Database Systems*, 6th ed. Reading, MA: Addison-Wesley.

Date, C. J., and Hugh Darwin. 1994. *A Guide to the SQL Standard*. 3rd ed. Reading, MA: Addison Wesley.

Dragoo, Bob. 1995. *Real-Time Profit Management: Making Your Bottom Line a Sure Thing*. New York: John Wiley & Sons.

Eccles, Robert G., Robert H. Herz, E. Mary Keegan, and David M.H. Phillips. 2001. *The Value Reporting Revolution*. New York: John Wiley & Sons.

Eckerson, Wayne W. 1996. "Approaches to OLAP: Making Sense of the Religious Wars Surrounding OLAP Implementations." *Open Information Systems* 11:2.

Eckerson, Wayne W. April 1999. "Criteria for Evaluating Business Intelligence Tools." *TDWI*.

Editors. 1995. *Proceedings of the 21st International Conference on Very Large Data Bases*. San Francisco: Morgan Kaufmann.

Errman, Lee D., and Victor R. Lesser. 1975. "A Multi-level Organization for Problem Solving Using Many, Diverse, Cooperative Sources of Knowledge." Computer Science Department, Carnegie-Mellon University.

Faloutsos, Christos, and Shari Roseman. 1989. "Fractals for Secondary Key Retrieval." University of Maryland, College Park.

Frank, Maurice. July 1994. "A Drill Down Analysis on MDDBs." *DBMS*.

Freeston, Michael. 1987. "The BANG File: A New Kind of Grid File." Munchen, West Germany: European Computer-Industry Research Center (ECRC).

Gottlob, Frege. 1879. Reprinted in *A Source Book in Mathematical Logic*. 1879–1931, edited by Jean van Heijenoort (1967) by the President and Fellows of Harvard College. Cambridge, MA: Harvard University Press.

Gray, Jim, Adam Bosworth, Andrew Layman, and Hamid Pirahesh. October 4, 1995. "Data Cube: A Relational Aggregation Operator Generalizing Group-By, Cross-Tab, and Sub-Totals." Technical Report. Microsoft Research, Advanced Technology Division, Microsoft Corporation.

Gries, David, and Narain Gehani. 1977. "Some Idea on Data Types in High-Level Languages." Association for Computing Machinery.

Grossman, David A., and Ophir Frieder. 1998. *Information Retrieval: Algorithms and Heuristics.* Kluwer Academic Publishers.

Grossman, David, M. Catherine McCabe, Jin Ho Lee, Abdur Chowdhury, and Ophir Frieder. 2000. "On the Design and Evaluation of a Multi-dimensional Approach to Information Retrieval." Illinois Institute of Technology.

Gupta, Ashish, Venky Harinarayan, and Dallan Quass. 1995. "Aggregate-Query Processing in Data Warehousing Environments." IBM Almaden Research Center, Stanford University.

Guttag, John. 1977. "Abstract Data Types and the Development of Data Structures." Association for Computing Machinery.

Han, Jiawei. March 1998. "Towards On-Line Analytical Mining in Large Databases." *Sigmod Record*, 27:1. Intelligent Database Systems Research Laboratory, School of Computing Science, Simon Fraser University.

Han, Jiawei, Yandong Cat, and Nick Cercone. February 1993. "Data-Driven Discovery of Quantitative Rules in Relational Databases." *IEEE Transactions on Knowledge and Data Engineering*, Volume 5.

Han, Jiawei, and Yongjian Fu. 1995. "Discovery of Multiple-Level Association Rules from Large Databases." School of Computing Science, Simon Fraser University.

Han, Jiawei, and Micheline Kamber. 2001. *Data Mining: Concepts and Techniques.* San Francisco, CA: Morgan Kaufmann Publishers.

Han, Jiawei, Micheline Kamber, and Jenny Chiang. February 1997. "Mining Multi-Dimensional Association Rules Using Data Cubes." Database Systems Research Laboratory, School of Computing Science, Simon Fraser University.

Harinarayan, Venky, Anand Rajaraman, and Jeffrey D. Ullman. 1996. "Implementing Data Cubes Efficiently." Stanford University.

Heath, Thomas, ed. 1956. *The Thirteen Books of Euclid's Elements.* New York: Dover Publications.

Hegel, Georg W.F. 1977. *Phenomenology of Spirit.* Oxford University Press.

"He's Back." September 1993. *ComputerWorld.*

Hotelling, H. 1931. "The Generalization of the Student's Ratio." *Annals of Mathematical Statistics.* Volume II: 360–378.

Inmon, W. H. 1992. *Building the Data Warehouse.* New York: John Wiley & Sons.

Johnson, Theodore, and Dennis Shasha. 1996. "Hierarchically Split Cube Forests for Decision Support: Description and Tune Design." Working Paper. http://citeseer.nj.nec.com/johnson96hierarchically.html.

Kamber, Micheline, Jiawei Han, and Jenny Y. Chiang. August 1997. "Metarule-Guided Mining of Multi-Dimensional Association Rules Using Data Cubes." *Proceedings of the 3rd International Conference on Knowledge Discovery and Data Mining.* Newport Beach, CA: In press.

Kant, Immanuel. 1986. *Philosophical Writings.* Edited by Ernst Behler. The Continuum Publishing Company. Originally published in the preface to the Second Edition of *Critique of Pure Reason.*

Kaplan, Robert S., and David P. Norton. 1996. *The Balanced Scorecard*. Boston, MA: Harvard Business School Press.

Keller, Peter R., and Mary M. Keller. 1992. *Visual Cues: Practical Data Visualization*. Los Alamitos, CA: IEEE Computer Society Press.

Kimball, Ralph. September 1995. "The Database Market Splits." *DBMS* 8:10.

———. December 1995. "Data Warehouse Insurance." *DBMS*. 8:13.

———. January 1996. "The Problem with Comparisons." *DBMS*. 9:1.

———. January 1996. "A Freshman in Business Needs a Ph.D. in SQL." *DBMS*. 9:1.

———. February 1996. "SQL Roadblocks and Pitfalls." *DBMS*. 9:2.

———. 1996. *The Data Warehouse Toolkit*. New York: John Wiley & Sons.

Lauwerier, Hans. 1991. *Fractals: Endlessly Repeated Geometry Figures*. Princeton, NJ: Princeton University Press.

Ledgard, Henry F., and Robert W Taylor. 1977. "Selected Papers from the Conference on Data: Abstraction, Definition, and Structure." Association for Computing Machinery.

Lehner, Wolfgang. 1998. "Modeling Large Scale OLAP Scenarios." University of Erlangen-Nuremberg, Dept. of Database Systems. Erlangen, Germany.

Lenat, Douglas B., and R.V. Guha. 1990. *Building Large Knowledge-based Systems*. Reading, MA: Addison-Wesley.

Lewis, David K. 1991. *Parts of Classes*. Oxford University Press.

Manning, Henry P. 1919. *The Fourth Dimension Simply Explained*. New York: Munn & Company Inc.

Mansfield, Edwin. 1983. *Statistics for Business and Economics*, 2nd ed. New York: W. W. Norton & Company.

Martin, Daniel. 1985. *Advanced Database Techniques*. Cambridge, MA: The MIT Press.

Masters, T. 1995. *Advanced Algorithms for Neural Networks*. New York: John Wiley & Sons.

McGoveran, David. October 1993. "Much Ado About Nothing." *Database Programming and Design*. 6:10 (46–53).

———. December 1993. "Nothing from Nothing (Or, What's Logic Got to Do With It?)." *Database Programming and Design*. 6:1 (32–41).

———. January 1994. "Classical Logic: Nothing Compares 2U." *Database Programming and Design*. 7:1 (54–61).

———. February 1994. "Nothing from Nothing: Can't Lose What You Never Had." *Database Programming and Design*. 7:2 (42–48).

———. March 1994. "Nothing from Nothing: It's in the Way That You Use It." *Database Programming and Design*. 7:3 (54–63).

McTaggert, James M., Peter W. Kontes, and Michael C. Mankins. 1994. *The Value Imperative*. New York: The Free Press.

Mendenall, W., L. Ott, and R. F. Larson. 1983. *Statistics: A Tool for the Social Sciences*, 3rd ed. Boston: Duxbury Press.

Minsky, Marvin. 1975. "A Framework for Representing Knowledge." In P.H. Winston, ed. *The Psychology of Computer Vision* (211–277). New York: McGraw Hill.

Nielson, Gregory M., Hans Hagen, and Heinrich Muller. 1997. *Scientific Visualization: Overviews, Methodologies, Techniques*. IEEE, Inc.

Orenstein, Jack A. 1986. "Spatial Query Processing in an Object-Oriented Database System." Computer Corporation of America.

Osborn, Sylvia L., and T. E. Heaven. 1986. "The Design of a Relational Database System with Abstract Data Types for Domains." London, Ontario: The University of Western Ontario.

Pendse, Nigel, and Richard Creeth. 1995. *The OLAP Report Succeeding with Online Analytical Processing*. Norwalk, CT: Business Intelligence Inc.

Pindyck, Robert S., and Daniel L. Rubinfeld. 1981. *Econometric Models and Economic Forecasts*. New York: McGraw-Hill.

Raab, Francois. 1995. "TPC Benchmark™ D (Decision Support) Working Draft 9.0."

Raden, Neil. October 30, 1995. "Data, Data Everywhere." *Information Week*.

Reiner, David. February 1998. "Sold on Database Marketing." *DBMS and Data Programming and Design*.

Rich, Charles. 1982. "Knowledge Representation Languages and Predicate Calculus: How to Have Your Cake and Eat It Too." The Artificial Intelligence Laboratory, MIT.

Richards, E.G. 1998. *Mapping Time: The Calendar and it's History*. New York: Oxford University Press, Inc.

Robert, Paul. 1967. *Petit Robert: Dictionaire alphabetique et analogique de la langue Francaise*. Paris: Societe du Nouveau Littre.

Saracco, Cynthia Maro. 1998. *Universal Database Management: A Guide to Object/Relational Technology*. San Francisco, CA: Morgan Kaufmann Publishers.

Sarawagi, Sunita, and Michael Stonebraker. 1994. "Efficient Organization of Large Multidimensional Arrays." Computer Science Division, University of California at Berkeley.

Shavel, Steve, and Erik C. Thomsen. 1990. "A Tractarian Approach to Information Modeling." *Proceedings of the 14th International Wittgenstein Symposium on the Foundations of Logic*. Vienna: Verlag Holder-Pichler-Tempsky.

———. 1993. "On Three-Valued Logic." Power Thinking Tools, Theoretical Background.

———. 1994. "A Functional Basis for Tractarian Number Theory." Northampton, MA: Power Thinking Tools, Inc., Power Thinking Tools: Academic Background.

Shipman, David. March 1981. "The Functional Data Model and the Data Language DAPLEX." *ACM Transactions on Database Systems,* 6: 140–173.

Simon, Herbert. 1997. "Managing in an Information-Rich World" in *Models of Bounded Rationality, Volume 3*. Boston: MIT Press.

Smith, David Eugene, ed. 1959. *A Source Book in Mathematics*. New York: Dover Publications.

Smith, Henry C. 1985. "Database Design: Composing Fully Normalized Tables from a Rigorous Dependency Diagram." Association for Computing Machinery.

Smith, John Miles, and Diane C. P. Smith. 1977. "Database Abstractions: Aggregation and Generalization." Association for Computing Machinery.

Sokal, Robert R., and F. James Roglf. 1995. *Biometry: The Principles and Practice of Statistics in Biological Research*, 3rd ed. New York: W. H. Freeman and Company.

Stamen, Jeffrey P. October 1993. "Structuring Database for Analysis." *IEEE Spectrum*, 30:10.

Stemple, David, Adolfo Socorro, and Tim Sheard. 1988. "Formalizing Objects Using ADABPTL." *Advances in Object-Oriented Database Systems*, 2nd International Workshop.

Stigler, Stephen M. 1986. *The History of Statistics: The Measurement of Uncertainty before 1900*. Cambridge, MA: The Belknap Press of Harvard University Press.

Stonebraker, Michael, ed. 1993. *Readings in Database Systems*. San Francisco: Morgan Kaufmann.

Sullivan, Dan. 2001. *Document Warehousing and Text Mining*, New York: John Wiley & Sons.

Thomsen, Erik C. 1992. "Synthesizing Knowledge from Large Data Sets: The Need for Flexible Aggregation." Power Thinking Tools, IT Europe. London, England.

———. August 1997. "Beyond the MOLAP/ROLAP Wars." *Database Programming and Design*. 78–79.

———. October 1997. "I Shop Therefore I am." *Database Programming and Design*.

———. November 1997. "Is Anybody Out There." *Database Programming and Design*.

———. October 1998. "Decision Alchemy." *Intelligent Enterprise Magazine*.

———. November 1998. "Defining a Functional Approach to DSS." *Intelligent Enterprise Magazine*.

———. March 30, 1999. "Symmetry Lost." *Intelligent Enterprise Magazine*.

———. June 13, 2001. "Information Impact: Business Analytics Revealed." *Intelligent Enterprise Magazine*.

———. June 29, 2001. "Information Impact: Business Analytics Revealed, Part 2." *Intelligent Enterprise Magazine*.

———. August 31, 2001. "Information Impact: Business Analytics Revealed, Part 3." *Intelligent Enterprise Magazine*.

———. December 5, 2001. "Never the Same." *Intelligent Enterprise Magazine*.

Thomsen, Erik C., and Steve Shavel. 1993. "A Tractarian Basis for Number Theory." *Proceedings of the 15th International Wittgenstein Symposium on the Philosophy of Mathematics*. Power Thinking Tools. Vienna: Verlag Holder-Pichler-Tempsky.

Tillman, George. 1993. *A Practical Guide to Logical Data Modeling*. New York: McGraw-Hill.

Tufte, Edward R. 1983. *The Visual Display of Quantitative Information*. Cheshire, CN: Graphic Press.

"The 20th Century's Greatest Minds." March 29, 1999. *Time*.

Van de Geer, John P. 1971. *Introduction to Multivariate Analysis for the Social Sciences*. W.H. Freeman & Co.

Whitehead, A.N., and Bertrand Russell. 1910. *Principia Mathematica*. Cambridge University Press.

Wilkinson, Leland. 1999. *Statistics and Computing: The Grammar of Graphics*. Springer-Verlag New York Inc.

Wittgenstein, Ludwig. 1921. *Tractatus Logico-Philosophicus*. English edition, 1961. London: Routledge & Kegan Paul.

Zelazny, Gene. 1985. *Say It with Charts: The Executive's Guide to Successful Presentations*. Homewood, IL: Business One Irwin.

Zemke, Fred, Krishna Kulkarni, Andy Witkowski, and Bob Lyle. May 5, 1999. "Introduction to OLAP Functions."

Online Papers

"Final Proposed Draft Amendment-Database Language SQL-Amendment 1: On-Line Analytical Processing (SQL/OLAP)." November 1999. http://www.array.nl/DBM/art99/sql_olap.pdf

http://www.cse.iitb.ernet.in:8000/proxy/db/~dbms/Data/Papers-Other/SQL1999/OLAP-99-154r2.pdf

http://www.dwinfocenter.org/standard.html

Index